Social History of Africa Series

WHITE FARMS
BLACK LABOR

Social History of Africa Series
Series Editors: Allen Isaacman and Jean Hay

WHITE FARMS
BLACK LABOR

The State and
Agrarian Change in
Southern Africa, 1910–50

Edited by

Alan H. Jeeves
and
Jonathan Crush

HEINEMANN
Portsmouth, NH

UNIVERSITY OF NATAL PRESS
Pietermaritzburg

JAMES CURREY
Oxford

Heinemann
A division of Reed Elsevier Inc.
361 Hanover Street
Portsmouth, NH 03801–3912

James Currey Ltd
73 Botley Road
Oxford OX2 0BS

University of Natal Press
Private Bag X01, Scottsville 3209
Pietermaritzburg, South Africa

ISBN 0–435–08991–9 (Heinemann cloth)
ISBN 0–435–08993–5 (Heinemann paper)
ISBN 0–85255–674–8 (James Currey cloth)
ISBN 0–85255–624–1 (James Currey paper)
ISBN 0–86980–933–4 (University of Natal Press cloth)
ISBN 0–86980–935–0 (University of Natal Press paper)

First published 1997.

Library of Congress Cataloging-in-Publication Data
On file at the Library of Congress

British Library Cataloguing in Publication Data
White farms, black labour: the state and agrarian change
   in Southern Africa, 1910–50. – (Social history of Africa)
   1. Blacks – Africa, Southern – Social conditions
   2. Agricultural laborers – Africa, Southern – Social
   conditions 3. Land reform – Africa, Southern – History
   4. Africa, Southern – Race relations
   I. Jeeves, Alan II. Crush, Jonathan (Jonathan Scott), 1953–
   333.3'1'08996'068

Cartography by Cartographic Unit, Queen's University, Kingston.
Cover design by Jenny Greenleaf.
Text design by G&H Soho Ltd.
Printed in the Republic of South Africa.
97 98 99 00 01 9 8 7 6 5 4 3 2 1

CONTENTS

NOTES ON CONTRIBUTORS

William Beinart is Professor of History at the University of Bristol, U.K. His recent publications include *Twentieth Century South Africa*. Oxford University Press, and *Environment and History: the Taming of Nature in the USA and South Africa*. Routledge with Peter Coates. He is currently researching on environmental history in South Africa and on land reform.

Richard Bouch is a historian who has lectured in the Department of History, Rhodes University, Grahamstown.

Shirley Brooks is a historical geographer who lectures on rural development at the University of Durban-Westville and is completing a PhD at Queen's University, Kingston. She is researching on environmental issues in KwaZulu-Natal. Her publications include, "The Environment in History: New Themes for South African Geography," in *Geography in a Changing South Africa: Progress and Prospects*, eds., C. Rogerson and J. McCarthy. Oxford University Press.

Wiseman Chijere Chirwa is senior lecturer in History at Chancellor College, University of Malawi. He is a graduate of the University of Malawi and has a PhD from Queen's University, Kingston. His publications include articles in *The International Journal of African Historical Studies*, *The Journal of Southern African Studies* and other journals.

Jonathan Crush is Professor of Geography at Queen's University, Kingston. His publications include *The Struggle for Swazi Labour, 1890–1920*. McGill-Queen's Press, and the co-authored book *South Africa's Labor Empire*. Westview Press. He has also co-edited *Liquor and Labor in Southern Africa*. Ohio University Press with University of Natal Press.

David Duncan is a graduate of Aberdeen University (Scotland) and has MA and PhD degrees from Queen's University, Kingston. He is the author of *The Mills of God: The State and African Labour in South Africa, 1918–1948*. Witwatersrand University Press. A former Visiting Research Fellow at the University of the Witwatersrand, he is currently Secretary to the Scottish Consultative Council on the Curriculum.

Alan Jeeves is a historian at Queen's University, Kingston. His research focuses on labor in southern Africa's mining and farming industries.

David Lincoln lectures in the Department of Sociology at the University of Cape Town. Another of his publications on agrarian labor in southern Africa, which complements his chapter in this book, is "Settlement and Servitude in Zululand 1918–1948," *International Journal of African Historical Studies* 28(1995).

Charles Mather is a lecturer in the Department of Geography, University of the Witwatersrand. His research interests focus on rural transformation, contemporary agricultural restructuring and sustainable agriculture in South Africa.

Robert Morrell has lectured History at the Universities of Transkei, Durban-Westville and Natal. He is presently a senior lecturer in the Department of Education at the University of Natal, Durban. His research interests include agrarian history and historical constructions of masculinity. He is editor of *White but Poor*. Pretoria UNISA.

Martin J. Murray is the author of *The Development of Capitalism in Colonial Indochina 1890–1920*. University of California Press; *South Africa: Time of Agony, Time of Destiny* Verso; and *The Revolution Deferred: The Painful Birth of Post-Apartheid South Africa* Verso. He is currently engaged in research on agrarian relations in the South African countryside and questions of methodologies.

Steven C. Rubert has a PhD from the University of California (Los Angeles) and is an assistant professor of African History at Oregon State University, Corvallis. He is author of the forthcoming "Black Workers, White Farmers . . . in Colonial Zimbabwe 1900–1945" and principal co-author of the 3rd edition of the *Historical Dictionary of Zimbabwe*.

Stefan Schirmer is an Economic History lecturer at the University of the Witwatersrand. He completed a PhD in 1995 on African struggles in South Africa's so-called white farming districts. He is working on rural development in South Africa during the nineteenth and twentieth centuries.

Charles van Onselen is Director of the Institute for Advanced Social Research at the University of the Witwatersrand. The latest of his many publications on southern African rural and urban social history is *The Seed is Mine: The Life of Kas Maine, a South African Sharecropper, 1894–1985*. David Philip.

FIGURES

TABLES

ILLUSTRATIONS

PREFACE

In 1988, the editors set up an interdisciplinary research and graduate training program in southern African labor studies at Queen's University, Kingston. Since its inception, the program has been generously funded by the Social Sciences and Humanities Research Council of Canada (SSHRCC). In 1992 with additional support from the SSHRCC and Canada's International Development Research Centre (IDRC), we organized a workshop at Queen's University that brought together an international group of historians and social scientists in an effort to combine historical and contemporary perspectives on agrarian change in southern Africa. The first product of that workshop was a special issue of the *Canadian Journal of African Studies* on "Transitions in the South African Countryside," published in 1993. This book is the second. We are grateful to the participants in the workshop for making their papers available to us and for their patience during the book's long gestation period. We wish particularly to acknowledge our indebtedness to the SSHRCC and the IDRC for their continued support of southern African research in Canada during a period of shrinking budgets.

We have benefited greatly from working with the talented group of graduate students who gathered at Queen's over the past decade, including Yvette Abrahams, Craig Atkinson, Cecile Badenhorst, Julie Baker, Shirley Brooks, Wiseman Chirwa, Tim Clynick, Camilla Cockerton, David Duncan, Dominic Fortescue, Kalina Grewal, Susanne Klausen, Jeremy Martens, Charlie Mather, Simone McCallum, James Meier, Miranda Miles, the late Lewis Mtonga, John Nauright, Mary Ntabeni, Sally Peberdy, Markus Reichardt, Chris Soutter, Philip Steenkamp, Doug Stewart and Louisa Teixeira.

Our colleagues in the Canadian Research Consortium on Southern Africa (CRCSA) have done much to make CRCSA a most stimulating and congenial research environment. Among the African Studies group at Queen's, we are especially indebted to Rosemary Jolly and Bob Shenton.

Throughout the research phase, we had valuable assistance from librarians and archivists in both South Africa and Canada. In the Stauffer Library at Queen's, Dianne Cook has been particularly helpful as we worked to build the southern African collection. We have had great benefit from the excellent collection in the Government Publications Library at the University of the Witwatersrand, Johannesburg. At the State Archives in Pretoria, Letitia Coetzee, the Chief of the Central Archives Depot, and her staff have provided much valuable advice on the use of the collections both to us and to our students. Petria Engelbrecht, an independent researcher, assisted with the research at various repositories in South Africa.

We wish to thank those who have helped to see the book through the production phase. At the University of Natal Press (UNP), the Publisher, Margery Moberly, was encouraging when we first discussed the project with her, long before there was a manuscript to consider, and she has been supportive throughout. Our editor at UNP, Jenny Edley, worked hard to move the book through the press with speed, efficiency and unfailing good humor. Allen Isaacman encouraged us to submit the manuscript for consideration in Heinemann's Social History of Africa series; the co-editor of the series, Jean Hay, helped to remove obstacles that slowed the book's production.

Finally, our grateful thanks go to Mary Bentley and Linda Crush for their help at the editorial stage and their more general support.

Jonathan Crush and Alan Jeeves
October 1996

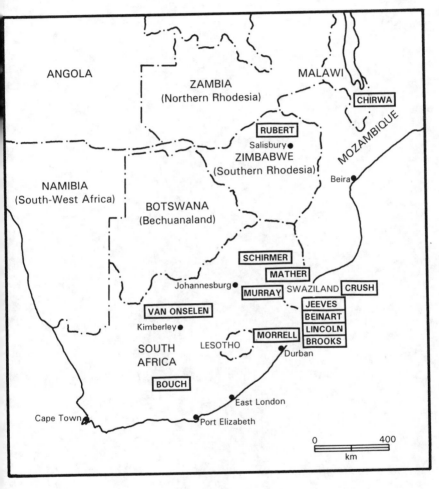

Southern Africa, Chapter Locations

1

Introduction

ALAN H. JEEVES AND JONATHAN CRUSH

The years between 1910 and 1950 brought major social and economic changes to the white farming districts of southern Africa. Although the pace was variable and the distribution uneven across the subcontinent, these developments in combination amounted to an agricultural revolution. In most modern societies industrialization originated in agricultural transformation that freed both labor and capital for employment in commerce and industry.[1] The productivity and wealth created in farming made possible broader economic expansion and diversification. Southern Africa's mining-led industrialization was very different. Farming always lagged behind the other sectors. Ecological and economic conditions retarded agriculture for generations. With important exceptions, white farmers were slow to innovate, and slow to develop the vast estates handed to them during earlier phases of colonial conquest and dispossession.[2] When transformation came, as it did during the years covered by this volume, commercial farming relied heavily on state support for the human and material resources that eventually secured its prosperity and modern development. Contrary to the experience of many other developing economies, commercial agriculture in southern Africa became more rather than less important compared with other sectors.

Although the pace quickened in the inter-war period, the emergence of modern, commercial agriculture in the region was prolonged. As Sir Keith Hancock pointed out many years ago, its small beginnings go back to the wheat and wine farms of the Western Cape in the eighteenth century, South Africa's first frontier of agrarian development.[3] They continued with the nineteenth-century settlement of the Eastern Cape and Natal and the experimental farms established by Cecil Rhodes and others at the Cape.[4] Agricultural development on the South African highveld, it has recently been shown, occurred in the period immediately after the South African War when white landowners, both English and Afrikaner, consolidated their monopoly control over land and other rural resources and used their political power to mobilize and discipline a black labor force.[5]

While agreeing that the modern transformation of white agriculture began then, the argument here is that only in the inter-war period were the foundations for its prosperity within South Africa firmly established. The forces leading to that result were political more than economic, and there was nothing pre-ordained about them. The state, rather than the market, defined the parameters of agrarian change in South Africa. No ineluctable element in modern capitalism drove the economy toward the sort of agricultural system that emerged under white hegemony.[6] It required the instruments of state power created by Milner after the South African War and the modern bureaucratic institutions and norms with which it was equipped.[7] Operating as much in pursuit of ethnic as economic interests, this new state acted "to support and sustain a far-reaching process of indigenous class formation and social restructuring."[8] The dependence of white farming on state support began early and grew in intensity; it was no mere passing phase, over once the transition to large-scale commercial operations had been secured. There is a consensus in the literature that without this constant nurturing, the South African agricultural sector could never have achieved the spectacular growth in output which by 1945 had overtaken in value that of the gold-mines.[9]

Paradoxically, an alternative source of low-priced farm products had begun to develop in the first years of South African industrialization. African peasant agriculture in many parts of the region experienced an early period of growth, prosperity and even modernization.[10] Systematically disadvantaged by state policy, it generally failed to survive as a source of cheap food in competition with white farming. The increasing poverty of most African farmers was not simply the product of racially motivated government neglect; it also stemmed from deliberate policies to restrict their access to land, to handicap their farming and to promote the extrusion of their labor for the benefit of white-owned rural and urban enterprise.[11]

Advantaging white agriculture, therefore, not only removed a source of competition in the peasantry but also left those same peasants, as they became increasingly impoverished, with only their labor to sell. The effects of the policies that, in combination, benefited white farmers included distortion of the development of the regional economy, diversion of resources from other sectors which might have used them more productively, and depression of farm wages.[12] The fate of African pastoralists and cultivators in the region has generated a thriving literature and is therefore not specifically addressed in this volume. By contrast, the history of commercial farming is only beginning to be written.

The twentieth-century transformation of the South African countryside exacted a heavy cost that went far beyond the matter of state financial support (itself not trivial). Environmentally destructive modern farming methods, in southern Africa as elsewhere, did great damage.[13] State subsidies and price supports encouraged expansion and the cultivation of marginal lands better used for pastoralism or left uncultivated.[14] Socially, the cost was measured in the hardship and poverty that agricultural policy brought to poor white rural dwellers, to the African tenants, sharecroppers and wage laborers who produced the food and to the black consumers who bought much of it. Although designed to keep whites on the land, state agricultural policy mostly favored the larger, modernizing farmers and had the ironic effect of accelerating the urbanization of the white poor.[15] Black labor in farming was used as wastefully and inefficiently as the other factors of production. Cruelty and exploitation blighted the lives of most farm workers.

The first half of the twentieth century saw impressive gains in production and productivity across a whole range of agricultural sectors and commodities. At the same time, white farming became increasingly differentiated as distinctions of wealth and status among farmers grew deeper. Initially confined to the rich farmlands of the Western Cape, large-scale commercial farming spread, from the middle of the nineteenth century, to the sheep farms of the Cape interior and the southern Orange Free State. By the 1890s, cattle ranching and the production of maize and wheat on the Transvaal, Orange Free State and Rhodesian highveld had begun to take on the character of substantial agribusiness. Plantation agriculture originated with the sugar estates of Natal in the 1840s and expanded into Zululand after about 1905. Sugar production only became an important South African industry in the twentieth century. Citrus and other plantations developed in the eastern Transvaal lowveld in the decades after the South African War. Production and labor systems also diverged, with the more commercially oriented, progressive and prosperous planters turning gradually away from semi-feudal labor tenancy and sharecropping arrangements in favor of the use of migrant labor to meet seasonal peaks in demand and settled wage labor to draw experienced workers into permanent employment.[16]

In general, the pace of change quickened between 1910 and 1930 and surged in the twenty years after about 1935 (figure 1.1). However, agricultural transformation occurred very unevenly across the subcontinent. Over wide areas, white farmers remained wedded to primitive methods and content with levels of output that provided barely more than subsistence. Even in the most developed parts of the southern African countryside, the emergence of modern agribusiness took decades to accomplish. Differences of wealth, background and status among farmers gradually grew larger but did not prevent considerable political solidarity among them as they struggled against the competition for labor from the mining and industrial sectors.[17]

During the early years of the century, labor tenancy, in which black families traded farm work for access to white land for grazing and crops, was the dominant form of farm labor mobilization and control throughout much of the region. By the 1930s, however, migratory wage labor had become an important source of farm labor as well as the central labor institution of the South African and, increasingly, the entire regional economy.[18] Over the period covered by this volume, farming, like mining, also became more dependent on wage workers, many of whom were migrants. Farmers thus became major competitors both for domestic migrant workers and for the thousands who streamed southwards across colonial boundaries in search of work.[19]

Migrant labor on the farms was, however, neither an inevitable move beyond tenancy and sharecropping, nor an intermediate step on the road to a proletarian, settled labor force.[20] In certain agricultural sectors, and in certain areas, migrancy displaced earlier forms of labor mobilization at a very early stage. Farm work was rarely, if ever, the preferred option either for migrants from within South Africa or for those who crossed into the country from the north. The result was that many farmers — unable or unwilling to pay the wages that would have secured a stable labor force — continued to use primitive forms of labor mobilization and to press governments for ever more Draconian controls. As this volume attests, within a single district (and even on a single farm) multiple labor forms often co-existed.

The essays in this collection also suggest that the transformation of the labor system on white farms was slow and halting, as a consequence of uncertain political

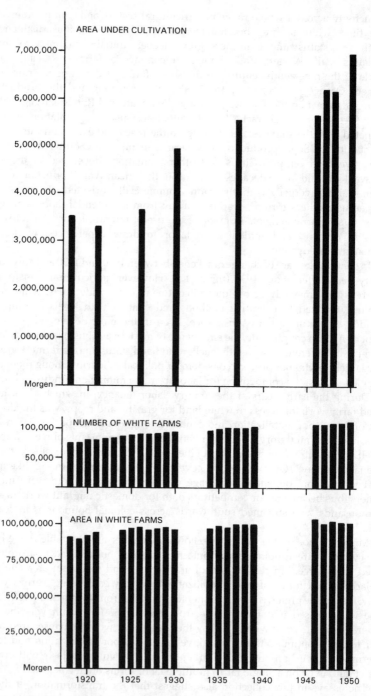

Figure 1.1 South African Agricultural Expansion, 1920–1950

and economic circumstances and of local struggles over the conditions, timing and rewards of farm production. The collection focuses primarily on the changes in farm-labor systems after 1910. Most of the chapters are case studies, centered on particular farming districts and sectors. Together, they aim to present something of the variety of the farm-labor experience and to illustrate how local circumstances and broader processes combined to create distinctive patterns of change. As presented here, the picture is neither comprehensive nor complete. Surprisingly little research, for example, has yet been done on the Cape and Orange Free State during the inter-war period.[21] Despite the gaps, the collection aims beyond the purely local to address important general issues in the social and political history of southern African agriculture.

Having described the political and economic contours of South Africa's agricultural revolution, and its regional impact, this chapter turns to the central themes that run through the individual case studies. While the political economy of agriculture provides the broad framework for interpreting these important changes, the collection is also interested in how that revolution was experienced at the local level. During the period under consideration, new modes of mobilizing, organizing, utilizing and disciplining labor emerged and spread throughout the region. The general, though uneven, replacement of tenancy by wage work was hastened by urbanization and the simultaneous expansion of the industrial and mining sectors which stripped many districts of their formerly tied agricultural labor. The farms, like the mines before them, turned to other forms of tied labor (such as prison labor) and also to long-distance contractual migrancy. As the essays in this volume demonstrate, the emergence of low-wage migrant-based labor systems brought great wealth to an elite class of capitalizing white farmers and great hardship and misery to the field workers on whose labor agricultural transformation depended.

State Regulation and Agricultural Production

The total value of agricultural output on white farms in South Africa increased from £29 million in 1911/12 to nearly £200 million in 1948 and more than £385 million in 1959/60, while wage employment figures (excluding labor tenants) rose from about 500,000 in 1918 to nearly a million in 1957.[22] South Africa changed its status from that of a substantial importer of food at the time of Union, to that of an expanding exporter. Following World War I, agricultural exports constituted between 20 and 33 per cent of total exports annually.[23] Export growth was interrupted in the Great Depression (confined in South Africa to the years 1929–32) but grew especially strongly thereafter (figure 1.2).[24] None of this could have been achieved without state regulation of production, and export markets which expanded rapidly from 1924 and became comprehensive during and after the depression. As a result of controls on imports and price supports, dairy production grew strongly during the depression. Always an importer of dairy products before 1930, South Africa had become a significant exporter by 1932. In response to the same kinds of regulation and support, wheat farmers greatly extended acreages under cultivation. Their increased production, exports and resulting prosperity were subsidized by consumers, who paid local prices well in excess of world prices.[25]

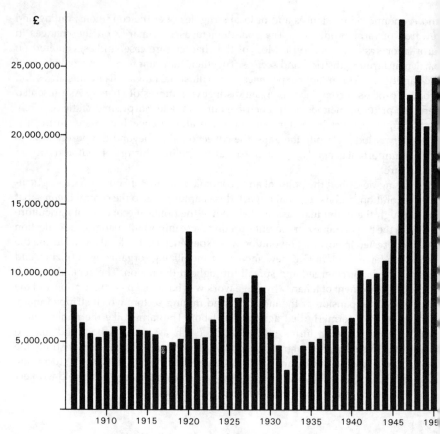

Figure 1.2 South African Agricultural Exports, 1905–1950

The spectacular growth of plantation and estate agriculture in South Africa is well illustrated by the experience of the Natal and Zululand sugar industries.[26] Sugar production rose from 82,000 tons in 1910/11 to 522,732 tons in 1938/39, an increase partly achieved through protection of the domestic market (figure 1.3). Sugar imports shrank in the same period from 32,321 tons to fewer than 2,000. Acreages under cane on European farms grew from about 200,000 in 1924 to more than 350,000 in 1938 and the tonnage of cane crushed from slightly over 2 million in 1926/27 to more than 4.5 million in 1938/39. Maize, pastoral and fruit production also expanded, although unevenly in this period (figures 1.4, 1.5). By 1939, maize exports had increased to sixteen times the level of ten years before.[27]

Increased output, prices and profits characterized the period after 1932, although the recovery from the depression was slow and variable at first. State assistance, which went disproportionately to the most commercial parts of the white farming sector,

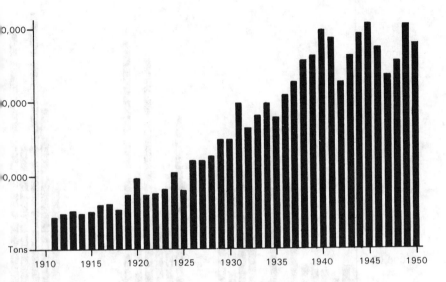

Figure 1.3 South African Sugar Production, 1910–1950

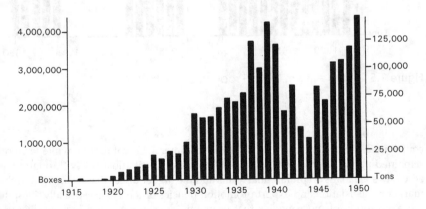

Figure 1.4 South African Citrus Fruit Exports, 1920–1950

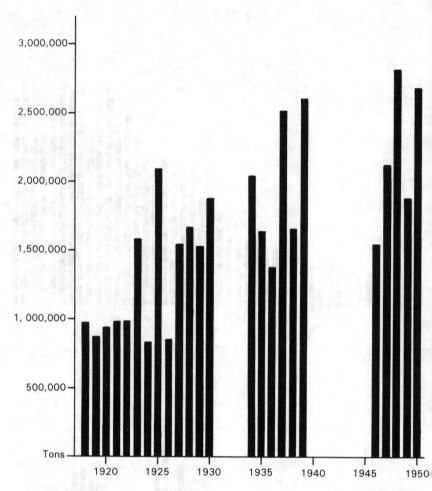

Figure 1.5 South African Maize Production, 1918–1950

contributed greatly to these trends. Yet the commercial revolution in white farming remained partial. Many small, inefficient producers kept afloat solely through their access to state loans on preferential terms and the higher prices that resulted from the marketing legislation and export promotion policies of the 1930s especially. Despite the assumption of most models that economic development and industrialization require increased agricultural productivity and the release of labor to other sectors, white farming responded only gradually in the predicted direction. While capital investment in agriculture grew rapidly, especially after 1932, the growth of investment per unit of labor was much less impressive. Many farmers were slow to mechanize and slow to adopt modern, labor-saving techniques until the 1950s.[28]

The crucial role of the state in the transformation of white agriculture in South Africa was already evident to the the historian C.W. de Kiewiet, writing at the beginning of the 1940s, and prompted his famous aphorism that the country "was armed from the two capitals."[29] Contrary to certain more recent accounts, systematic state support of white farmers did not originate under the Pact government when it came to power in 1924, but began much earlier.[30] It is true that government control over the production and marketing of farm products grew very rapidly in the fifteen years after General J.B.M. Hertzog became Prime Minister. However, much that his government did had important precedents in the labor, tariff, agricultural credit and support policies of the Botha and Smuts governments from the early years of Union. The establishment of the Land Bank in 1912 and of state support, through the Bank, for the cooperative movement in agriculture, disastrous though the experience of many of the cooperatives initially was, established an interventionist approach to farming that the Pact and later governments developed further.[31]

Much of the initiative to improve breeding stock, to raise crop yields and to deal with the diseases of both livestock and agricultural plants came from the state, not private farmers. Railway tariffs subsidized the transport of agricultural products, especially exports, while levying higher rates on the imported goods, raw material and migrant labor needed particularly by the mines.[32] Through preferential railway rates, maize production in the interior was stimulated in order to provide loads for trains which otherwise would have returned empty from the Witwatersrand to the ports. The rates were kept so low as to achieve "the near elimination of transport costs from maize marketing."[33] Other support measures included produce marketing legislation, tariff protection, export subsidies, generous loans and other government-financed credit schemes.

For decades, direct state grants and loans to farmers subsidized fencing, irrigation schemes and other improvements by, according to some estimates, as much as £112 million in the period 1910–36 alone.[34] Official policy kept agricultural prices artificially high and at the same time ensured that the advantage was distributed in a racially discriminatory way. White farming also benefited from a tax regime that channeled revenue from the mining sector and from consumers into agriculture. The state taxed farm products to pay for expensive marketing arrangements, and through domestic price support passed the cost on to consumers. High food prices not only disadvantaged consumers, especially urban African consumers, but also meant added costs for the gold-mining industry, the country's largest purchaser of food to feed its black labor force.[35]

A review of South African legislation related to farming, published in 1933, identified about eighty acts passed since 1910 that supported the farming sector.[36] The author of the survey found no clear pattern but rather a "hotch-potch" of legislative measures, some with major implications, others very minor; some general in their applicability, others narrowly specific. He divided them into six major groups: (1) legislation to encourage settlement on the land and to improve farming, including farm finance; (2) relief measures designed to protect farmers and farm incomes; (3) regulations concerning the quality and grading of farm products; (4) enactments relating to producer organization; (5) measures to promote agricultural marketing; and (6) emergency legislation.

During the 1920s, the pace of government regulatory measures quickened, and the state began to intervene directly in agricultural markets. The operation of the Land

Bank was overhauled and made more effective. Regulations relating to the quality and grading of farm products were similarly improved. The Drought Relief Act was reformed and its benefits extended to white victims of floods. In 1924, Parliament approved a proposal to write off large loans which had been extended to maize farmers during the post-war depression and price collapse. In the much more serious crisis of the early 1930s, when severe drought compounded the impact of the depression in threatening the livelihood of thousands of white farmers, the Hertzog government put through Parliament a scheme to distribute £5 million in farm relief. Controls over farm output also accelerated at this time, for instance through the provision of export bounties first introduced for beef in 1923 and extended widely in 1930 and 1931. Between 1931 and 1933 administrative regulation of farm production was broadened to include sugar, maize, dairy products, wheat, flour, tobacco and wine and spirits. At the same time, tariffs were steadily increased and anti-dumping duties imposed. In company with most other agricultural producers, South Africa raised its import duties to prohibitive levels, but the benefits to farmers were limited by the small domestic market. The negative effects of the decline in Union exports of farm products exceeded for the most part any benefit to farmers in the domestic market from the greatly increased tariffs (figure 1.2).[37]

As the depression in the agricultural sector deepened, compounded by the worst drought of the century, and leading to widespread and very severe distress in the *platteland* (countryside), there were intensified demands in Parliament for stronger action to maintain prices, to restore farm incomes, to deal with surpluses and to provide "orderly marketing."[38] In the wool industry, growers' local and regional associations grew rapidly, as they pressed for measures to increase their control over marketing arrangements and to encourage quality improvements.[39] Pressure for change also came from within the Department of Agriculture and Forestry.[40] Earlier marketing legislation had mostly been passed as piecemeal responses to crises in particular sectors. The political power of farmers and their declining incomes were compelling arguments for more interventionist and comprehensive measures. The department wanted to put white farming on an entirely new basis and to use the power of the state to rescue commercial agriculture and to ensure its future prosperity.

From the mid-1930s, the South African economy was in the midst of a major upswing fueled by a huge expansion of gold-mining. With only a small domestic market and with high levels of protection in export markets, South African farming was slow to benefit from the general expansion which set in following the surge in the gold price after South Africa devalued its currency at the end of 1932. Soaring government revenues provided a congenial environment in which to contemplate the overhaul of agricultural support policies.[41] Although the moment was politically opportune, officials hesitated at first to accept central regulation of agricultural marketing and prices.[42] Perception of the need to innovate grew slowly among politicians and bureaucrats made circumspect by entrenched economic orthodoxies and years of depression, debt and currency crises.

By 1936, however, policy had shifted decisively toward compulsory marketing arrangements, one-channel sales, and price controls, all of which had been considered and rejected only three years before. To stimulate production for export was a particularly important objective. Dr P. R. Viljoen, the Secretary of Agriculture and key architect of the most comprehensive marketing legislation devised in South Africa that point, told the Select Committee on the Marketing Bill in 1936 that "we are an agricultural country with enormous possibilities of development and further increase of production, and if we are at this stage to say that we must curtail our production to our own requirements, then I see very little hope for agriculture for the next few decades."[43] A first effort to legislate comprehensively failed in 1936 after a threatened backbenchers' revolt. The Marketing Bill was withdrawn and reintroduced a year later. In the meantime, department officials toured Europe to investigate trends in marketing legislation there.[44] They brought back from the Netherlands the idea of a national marketing council that became a prominent feature of the 1937 act.

Under the Marketing Act (No. 26 of 1937), the council had broad powers to regulate production and prices for both internal consumption and export and to restrict or prohibit imports, subject only to the overriding authority of the minister. The council could recommend taxes on agricultural commodities and use the proceeds to fund its activities. Intended as enabling legislation, the act provided for additional regulatory boards to control the production and pricing of particular commodities and structured the boards to ensure the dominance of producers. Separate producers' and consumers' committees were also created to advise the council. Rejecting both "the ideal of a perfect competitive system" (unattainable) and "complete centralised planning" (undesirable), Viljoen aimed in the 1937 act for a flexible blend of competition and planning" to stabilize markets and ensure agricultural expansion and prosperity under the benign supervision of his department.[45]

In keeping with government priorities and the balance of political power, the consumers' committee was kept weak and confined to an advisory role. Despite rhetoric from officials stressing the desirability of balance between consumers' and producers' interests, few could have been misled or have failed to see the reality that shone through in the legislation.[46] Consumers, with one exception, were too unorganized to challenge the entrenched hegemony of agricultural interests. The exception, of course, was the country's principal consumer of food, the gold-mining industry. The mines complained vehemently that the proposed act would give "almost unrestricted control" to the producers; the Chamber of Mines in its statement to the Select Committee on the Marketing Bill in 1936 warned that the legislation was "unsound" for the country, detrimental to the interests of consumers and, less plausibly, contrary to the long-term interest of the producers themselves.[47] A delegation representing municipal and local authorities testified strongly in opposition to the act.[48] Academic economists also came out in full cry against it. One group complained about "the compulsory rationing of food supplies in South Africa in time of peace, in favour of the vested interests of those who own a particular form of property."[49] Another called the marketing schemes of the period a "highly regressive form of indirect taxation," bearing most heavily on those least able to pay.[50] These protests all received short shrift from the authorities.[51]

The Marketing Council, like the marketing boards established under it, became a much more political body than the government had initially envisaged. The only surprising element in this outcome was the bureaucrats ever imagining that such an important regulatory authority with plenary powers over the basic profitability of agriculture could be kept free from political control and out of the hands of farmers. Nevertheless, Viljoen and his aide, S. J. de Swardt, convinced their political masters that the Western world was entering a new era of regulation in the handling of agricultural production and prices, that free trade was gone forever and that the law of supply and demand had no place in the regulation of agricultural markets.[52] The Minister of Agriculture and Forestry, in a speech to the South African Agricultural Union (SAAU) described the act as the "Magna Charta" of farmers, adding that he was sure farmers would "never abuse" the "great responsibilities" that the act conferred on them.[53] Although the minister spoke sanctimoniously about responsibilities and trust the Marketing Act was really about power and wealth. While rescuing marginal producers, its provisions delivered the greatest benefits to the most commercially oriented farmers and acted directly to stimulate mechanization, the emergence of larger farming units and capital-intensive farming.

There were many whose interests were not served by the sweeping extension of state control over agriculture, by the imposition of comprehensive regulatory power in the hands of producer-dominated boards and by the consequent higher prices. As usual, Africans were the principal losers from these new arrangements. Peasant producers secured no assistance. Mostly denied access to the marketing boards, they were excluded from the other benefits, particularly subsidized agricultural credit which the state made available to its white rural constituents. Despite the earlier introduction of subsidies for brown sugar, maize meal, bread and other staples (measures intended to stimulate local demand for the further benefit of producers) black urban consumers were also penalized.[54] Growing deprivation and hunger particularly among children, were among the costs to which the new marketing arrangements contributed. Although few black voices were heard in public protest against the bill, its effects on them were ubiquitous and profound. In one of the cruel ironies typical of South Africa in this century, widespread malnutrition was principal social effect of a measure designed to promote the production of food.[55]

The increasing extension of the South African government's regulation and control over agricultural markets and pricing had wider regional influences and effects. White farmers in the colonies neighboring South Africa became, in a very direct sense, the victims of South African success. Farmers in Nyasaland, Northern Rhodesia, Bechuanaland and Swaziland were severely disadvantaged by the South African government's lavish patronage of white agriculture.[56] Hard as they tried impecunious colonial governments failed to match the level and intensity of support offered by the South African state to its own farmers. Neighboring producers found their access to South African markets restricted or denied. In addition, farmers on distant white frontiers could not compete with South African employers for the labor which moved steadily south toward higher-paying jobs.[57] Handicapped by the distance from markets, by political weakness, and by lack of capital, white farmers in the wider region struggled, often unsuccessfully, to maintain themselves.[58] Peasant producers were doubly hampered by discriminatory South African policies and by government support for white farmers in their own countries. Yet they had superior knowledge of local conditions, typically produced at lower cost and, given half chance, did well.

After South Africa, Southern Rhodesia had the most developed commercial farming sector in the region.[59] Even more than the South Africans and partly because of them, its farmers remained, as a group, economically weak and vulnerable throughout the inter-war period. The case of the tobacco industry is instructive. The introduction of an imperial preference after World War I, higher prices and the arrival of a small but significant number of new settlers led to rapid

xpansion of production, from about 1.2 million pounds in 1918/19 to 5.3 million in
925/26, and in a surge to about 24.5 million in 1927/28. Yields per acre improved
nd prices rose sharply until 1925/26. Following a severe price collapse in the next
vo years, many producers were left with large debts and their entire crop
nmarketable. They had flooded the South African market, and the low quality of
tuch of their crop made it unsaleable in Britain. The history of tobacco production
uring the first wave of expansion in the decade before 1914 repeated itself.
ankruptcy overtook most of the producers. In all, 75 per cent of them failed to
urvive the 1928 crisis. Southern Rhodesian tobacco farmers went under before the
reat Depression. Maize, cattle and other producers soon joined them, as markets
nd prices collapsed world-wide after 1929. Maize was rescued by state intervention;
attle production never recovered.

Only in the period during and after World War II did white agriculture in
outhern Rhodesia enter into a period of sustained growth. As in the case of South
frica, recent research is revealing a more nuanced picture of the white farming
ector. It appears that the most efficient producers in the tobacco, maize and coffee
idustries of Kenya and Southern Rhodesia were competitive in world terms and not
enerally less efficient than their main rivals elsewhere.[61] They were the minority,
owever. The experience of these colonies mirrored South Africa's. The political
ower of the farming sector as a whole tended to bring the government behind the
veakest, most vulnerable producers, ensuring the survival of many who could not
iaintain themselves without government subsidies. Yet politics set limits to this
end. Early in the period of white settlement, small farmers battled with the large
oncession holders for state policies favorable to their interest. Later, the struggles
ccurred rather between different agricultural sectors and between producers and
onsumers. Indeed the growing strength of the African majority, in Nyasaland and
ven Southern Rhodesia (but not South Africa) after World War II, set some
onstraints on governments' willingness to antagonize black peasants and consumers
y subsidizing estate agriculture at their expense.

The Great Depression devastated white agriculture throughout the region and
ed, north as well as south of the Limpopo, to greater government regulation of the
gricultural sector.[62] When Pretoria enacted the Dairy Industry Control Act, Rhodesia
oon followed with regulations of its own, so closely were the two industries bound
ogether. After South Africa established a quota for the entry of duty-free Rhodesian
obacco, Salisbury had to set up a tobacco marketing board to allocate the quota
mong growers. A Maize Control Act and a Cattle Levy Act also came into force in
hodesia in this period. The revised Maize Control Act of 1934 put the government
quarely behind the smaller white producers, favoring them against both African
easants and the large-scale commercial farmers. For tobacco, the Reserve Pool Act,
lso passed in 1934, and the Market Stabilisation Act, introduced two years later,
ghtened the government's authority over producers. The latter act provided for
ompulsory selling through a marketing board and licensed auction floors and
uyers. The board advised the government on producer quotas for sales in protected
iarkets. By 1937, the state had extended its control over most items of agricultural
roduction in the commercial sector, excluding only poultry and eggs.

In Rhodesia, as in South Africa, extensive direct government assistance to the
vhite farming industry became essential. Between 1928 and 1933, the state spent over
1.5 million on bounties, subsidies, agricultural services and direct rescue of

producers. Most of this money went into the tobacco industry following the disastrou collapse of its markets in 1928. Following South African precedents, the governmer paid export bounties on some agricultural commodities, including beef and maize There were many other measures of subsidy and support besides, although the result were mixed. Having shed hundreds of uneconomic small growers in the boom an bust of the late 1920s, the tobacco industry resumed expansion, particularly on the basis of the competitive advantage derived from imperial preference in Britis markets.

Following the collapse in 1928, the output of tobacco rose again after 1930 b 400 per cent to about £20 million pounds annually. While the recovery of the maiz industry was less spectacular, its producers did achieve a measure of stability as result of the revised Control Act of 1934. The cattle ranchers did not fare nearly a well.[63] Many of the larger producers went out of business in the 1930s, and the sma ranchers remained heavily dependent on state subsidies. In the maize industry mos of the producers were smallholders who worked inefficiently and secured yields tha were well below average. By contrast, the larger firms, some of them foreign owned tended to be productive, efficient, high-yielding operations.[64]

The crucial role of the state in propping up white farming in the settler economie may be further illustrated by examining the experience of colonial Malawi.[65] Here white settlers were fewer, much weaker politically and consequently less able t extract concessions from the colonial government. During the inter-war period Nyasaland's small white farming community tried to develop tobacco, cotton and te estates. Few of them did very well.[66] White farming in Nyasaland was, with few exceptions, a story of defeat and disaster.[67] Most of the farmers who dropped th production of cotton to try to take advantage of the tobacco boom in the mid-1920 were wiped out in the collapse of 1928. To those who survived on the land, the depression dealt the same savage blows as it did to farmers elsewhere. Precarious a the best of times, the whole white farming community was adversely affected by high railway rates, insecurity of tenure and lack of access to fresh capital. There was no land bank in Nyasaland to supply settlers with funds at preferential rates on the model tha sustained their counterparts in Southern Rhodesia and South Africa. Few of them could survive after the depression brought the collapse of agricultural prices.

For the colony's white farmers, in contrast to their counterparts further south political remedies tended to founder on their small numbers. Preoccupied with shortfalls in revenue, the local state lacked the means to bail out a group of farmer that was marginal and perpetually in difficulty. Awkward, blundering and weak, the Nyasaland government was "incapable of offering the sustained support to settle interests that was provided in Southern Rhodesia, yet often obstructive and threatening in its attitude to independent peasants."[68] Nevertheless, by the end o the 1930s, the black peasant grower of tobacco and cotton, rather than the white farmer of small means, was emerging as the dominant element in Nyasaland's agriculture.

Only tea production initially resisted the trend; its local development resulted from the international tea agreement of 1933.[69] British companies, rather than loca settlers, dominated the industry. They were well endowed with capital and well connected in London. With output restricted by agreement among the world' principal producers, prices rose, and even a low-quality grower such as Nyasaland go some benefit and a degree of prosperity. From less than £2 million in 1930, tea export from the colony grew to over £11 million in 1939 and to nearly £13 million ten year

ter. Tea production was one of the few economic activities in the colony that were
profitable for whites. Growth was slow, however, and the planters were chronically
unable to improve quality and to solve their labor-supply problems. Changed
imperial policies in 1948 and 1950 exposed the local industry to world-wide
competition, and the planters were powerless to prevent it.

In Nyasaland where the settler presence was weak, peasant producers survived
and, from the 1920s, began to thrive. They did so on the basis not of food but of export
crops, tobacco and cotton particularly — and only after the state finally abandoned
inefficient and incompetent white farmers. The policies followed by the British
administration in Swaziland were, in their support of the white farming minority,
much closer to those of South Africa than those of colonial Nyasaland.[70] The same
large-scale land alienations had occurred early in the colonial period, and the same use
was made of state power to advantage white at the expense of black farming. In
southern Rhodesia, African maize producers got some protection from the fact that
many white farmers relied on them for the food they needed for their workers and
stock. Even in Southern Rhodesia, however, the number of Shona peasants forced to
seek wage labor rose sharply in the 1930s.

In the case of Swaziland, neither white farmers nor Swazi peasants could
penetrate the neighboring South African beef and tobacco markets to any significant
degree in the 1920s and 1930s. Large tracts of potentially productive land remained
locked up under the control of absentee landlords, one of the many adverse
consequences of the British colonial land partition of 1907.[71] In the late 1920s and early
1930s, international cotton markets were opened to local producers but prices were
always volatile and, especially where settler numbers were small, colonial governments provided limited relief. Facing ecological conditions and economic circumstances nearly as adverse as those that defeated the settlers further north, the
Swaziland settler community occupied the land just as unproductively. Yet they
continued to receive for many years the near-unqualified support of the local
administration, long after the Nyasaland government had abandoned its settler class.
Swaziland's agricultural revolution was to come somewhat later, in the 1950s and
1960s, when large British and South African agribusiness firms transformed the
countryside, putting vast areas of land under forest, sugar and citrus.

The State, the Farmer and the Labor Market

White southern African farmers not only demanded state aid to regulate production,
prices and markets, these same sheltered, subsidized, and protected agriculturalists
insisted also that governments provide them with labor at sub-market rates. For
many, the ability to operate profitably depended on cheap labor; for the least efficient,
their survival required it. After 1936, the expansion guaranteed by the Marketing Act
ensured that South African farmers would need more not less of it. While marketing
regulations, agricultural credit and export bounties were some of the more visible
forms that state aid took, the measures to protect and regulate farmers' labor supply
were at least as important.

Within a year of the achievement of Union, the new South African government
began to entrench the migrant labor system by means of regulations under the Native

Labour Regulation Act (No. 15 of 1911). One of the central purposes of this act was t
divide available black labor between the mines and the farms. By banning non-farr
labor recruiters from most of the white farming areas, the state tried to protect th
white farmers' large work-force.[72] Other provisions of the 1911 act applied in Labou
Districts and was principally intended to regulate recruiting and working conditior
in the mining industry. Except in the sugar mills (from 1937), the act did not apply t
farmers, who also received special concessions from the Native Affairs Departmer
(NAD) to facilitate the recruitment of farm labor. Recruiters when employed directl
by farmers (those who were not private labor contractors) did not require license
could recruit workers under eighteen and in general faced much less scrutiny tha
recruiters for other employers.[73] Together these special concessions and arrangement
failed to ease the political pressures on the NAD from farmers who sought its direc
involvement in the supply and management of farm labor.

The NAD always doubted that state control could provide a simple answer t
farmers' problems with their labor supply. From early in the Union period, th
department argued that the market, not the government, would eventually determin
whether farmers would secure sufficient labor. Africans had a right to sell their labc
in the best market. The efficient operation of the economy and full development of th
work-force required recognition of market conditions. If farmers were uncompetitiv
in terms of wages and working conditions in those markets, as they were, they coul
expect eventually to lose their labor to other industries, and the department would b
unable to prevent it. A labor policy built on coercion alone could not succeed, if onl
because the state lacked the coercive power to achieve what farmers expected.[74]

NAD bureaucrats were willing to accept the large government-imposed burde
of disciplining workers and preventing desertions, but wanted to balance that wit
effective regulation of working conditions.[75] They saw themselves as the monitors c
minimum standards for recruitment, sanitation, food and working conditions i
farming. Workers would be controlled, their strikes prevented and labor contrac
enforced, but they could not have their mobility constrained to the degree that man
farmers wanted. In this way, officials proposed to make the agricultural secto
competitive for labor with other industries. The NAD had to respond to multipl
political constituencies. Capitulation to farmers' interests alone, on the model of th
Marketing Act, was not an option. While that act effectively turned the control c
agricultural production and pricing over to the farmers themselves, Native Affair
could not do the same for labor policy. NAD officials had to be mindful of the interest
of both farmers and other employers and that meant opening the farm-labor market t
competition.

Other departments of state perceived no such need for balance. That c
Agriculture and Forestry tended to side with farmers and against the NAD wheneve
the issue of wages and working conditions on farms arose.[76] Secretaries of Agricultur
opposed the extension of Act 15 and rejected proposals coming from the NAD to sen
in inspectors to monitor conditions on farms. The Department of Justice stood fc
rigorous enforcement of the pass laws and of a rigid labor discipline in the rural area
to keep, in particular, African juveniles in farm-labor service.[77] The Justice Departmer
and not the NAD sponsored and carried through parliament the important Nativ
Service Contract Bill in 1932, which most fully embodied white farmers' consisten
view that ever-tighter measures of authoritarian control would "solve" their labc
problems.[78] Eliminating squatting and controlling labor tenancy had been high on th

rmers' agenda for a generation and were written into the 1932 bill. Governments of ιe period shrank, however, from the chaos which would ensue if tens of thousands of frican squatters were summarily evicted. There was no room for them in the reserves ιd controls were insufficient to keep them out of the towns. The powers that the act ϸnferred to disallow African tenancies on white farms were held in abeyance. For the ιme reasons, the anti-squatting provisions of the 1936 Native Trust and Land Act ϸmained unproclaimed, except briefly in Lydenburg, into the 1950s.[79]

Insistent political pressures from farmers, through their parliamentary represen-ιtives and their regional and national associations, drove the state in a direction ϸpposite to that advocated by successive secretaries of Native Affairs and led to ϸlicies that in their control of African workers were, if anything, more interventionist ιan those devised to control the production, sale and price of agricultural products. ϸnly gradually did the more substantial commercial farmers and the SAAU, which ϸoke for them, come to acknowledge the essential truth of the farm labor ιarket — that the amount of labor available to farmers was, by the 1930s if not before, ιarying inversely with the extent of coercion applied to it. Bad wages, conditions and ϸeatment, which were the norm, especially in the poorest farming areas, but prevalent ϸso on some of the most prosperous estates, damned the whole farming sector in the ϸyes of the labor force.

By the early 1920s, the NAD had decided to try to bring the large farm employers, ϸarticularly the Natal plantations, under the general provisions of the Native Labour ϸegulation Act of 1911, to regulate recruitment, living conditions and food, and to ϸend in inspectors with powers of enforcement. By 1920, the 1911 act had largely ϸhieved the department's objectives in the mining industry.[80] Department officials ϸelieved that regulation of farm labor, along the same lines as in mining, but with less ϸnerous and expensive standards, would lead to improvements in wages, working ϸnd living conditions which would be in the long-run interest of farmers themselves; ϸr without such improvements they would entirely lose the labor that was already ϸaking away.

This, at least, was the case that the NAD made to successive ministers and to the ϸood of farmer supplicants demanding ever more stringent state coercion of their ϸorkers. In truth, the argument had little effect. While inspectors were appointed in ϸatal and the Transvaal, they were left without regulatory powers, and the act was not ϸpplied (except eventually to the sugar mills) throughout this period. The NAD and its ϸabour Bureau, as well as groups such as the Transkeian General Council (the Bunga) ϸnd the Pondoland Council, made no headway in securing the extension of Act 15 to ϸny part of the agricultural industry in the 1920s. Political opposition from farmers ϸas too strong, and ministers of Native Affairs repeatedly refused to act in the face of ϸ. By the 1930s, the political pressure on the state to "solve" the problems of the ϸarmers' labor supply had intensified greatly. Additional coercive legislation and ϸighter regulation of the movement of Africans failed to provide a remedy and did ϸothing to abate the flood of farmers' complaints. Despite NAD insistence that ϸontrols on labor mobility offered no long-term solution, its civil servants found ϸhemselves forced, by piecemeal administrative action, to allocate labor among ϸompeting employers.[81]

One key tactic of farmers and their political allies mirrored a sleight-of-hand ϸtrategy earlier conceived by the mining industry.[82] By defining the needs of the ϸndustry as a whole in accordance with those of its weakest producers, large

commercial farmers used the precarious economic position of the smallest farmers to
provide justification for below-subsistence wage rates and their refusal to provide
housing and working conditions which met even minimal standards of health
sanitation and safety.[83] Claiming chronic poverty and pointing to the smaller
producers, the large farmers said they could not pay more and attract local labor. They
demanded exemption from regulation and turned to recruitment of cheap labor at a
distance. Echoing the mine owners, they said they could not afford proper hospitals
accommodation or food. Rates of illness and death, particularly from infectious
disease, were very high. As in the mining industry earlier, these arguments about
marginal profitability were used to delay or prevent government control efforts.

Throughout the 1930s, official reports repeatedly called for effective regulations to
govern recruiting and labor conditions in the farming industry.[84] Ever mindful of the
political power of the farmers and the planter lobby, however, the government
ignored these recommendations. The farming lobby ensured that the farm-labor
recruiting system remained minimally regulated and riddled with abuse. In arguing
for improvements in farm wages and conditions, officials came up against the
completely unreceptive farmer MPs who used their parliamentary positions to call
incessantly for even more regulations to immobilize black labor at low wages on their
estates.[85]

The appointment of the Native Farm Labour Committee in 1937 was the climax of
more than a decade of increasing concern about the growing shortage of labor. The
product of two years of investigation, its report represented the most comprehensive
effort of the South African government up to that date to investigate the reasons for
farm labor shortages.[86] The committee concluded that the root of farmers' difficulties
lay in the development of a country-wide labor market in which farmers, with their
low wages, insistence on lengthy periods of unpaid labor, and poor conditions of
service, were distinctly uncompetitive. Faithfully echoing arguments repeatedly
made by the NAD (the committee chair, Major J.F. Herbst, was a former secretary of
the department), the committee urged that it was in the interest of the economy, the
country and even farmers themselves that Africans have the freedom to sell their labor
in the best market. It implied that existing controls on labor mobility could only be
justified as a transition device, and that eventually farming, like other industries,
would have no choice but to become competitive in the wages and working conditions
it offered.

The committee also failed to endorse the widespread view among farmers that a
solution could be found in farm-labor recruiting outside South Africa. Rejecting
large-scale recruiting of migrants either foreign or local as the solution, the committee
called for the thoroughgoing proletarianization of the farm-labor force: "The only real
remedy is the creation and organization of a corps of Union workers, efficient,
contented and willing to make farm work a permanent occupation."[87] The recommendations of the Farm Labour Committee, dutifully following as they did the views of
the NAD, also received short shrift. The bureaucracy and the various departments of
state remained divided on many of the key issues. While some of the more progressive
elements in the SAAU recognized the sense in these recommendations, *platteland*
members of parliament and their constituents stood resolutely against anything
progressive in the field of labor relations that might add to farmers' costs or diminish
their untrammeled control of the workers.

The report of the Native Farm Labour Committee represented another, nsuccessful, effort to convince farmers that reform of their labor practices, provision f better working conditions and higher wages rather than more coercive labor gislation would alone ease their labor "shortages." Although the NAD's reform fforts repeatedly failed, protracted negotiations between its officials, the mining ompanies and farmers' associations had produced an uneasy compromise by the end f the decade concerning labor from the tropical, northern parts of the subcontinent. he mines received (by 1934) what they had long sought, renewed access for their cruiters to the labor of the tropical regions.[88] Farmers extracted still more oncessions to improve their ability to recruit and employ clandestine workers who ltered into the country as well as regulations to keep those workers out of the cities nd in motion toward the farms.

As agricultural production expanded and labor shortages grew during World Var II, the SAAU, which represented mainly the larger commercial farmers, began to onsider radical alternatives to protect the farm-labor supply. Farmers' demands for tate remedies intensified and reached crisis proportions in 1942–44, when the overnment temporarily relaxed the pass laws.[89] Their agenda had not changed and ncluded implementation of Chapter four of the 1936 act to clear squatters from hite-owned areas, permission to recruit in Mozambique and the tropical areas, more rotection from mine recruiters, and permission to employ children even without the ermission of parents. One of the SAAU's proposals, extensively discussed within the overnment, was to divide the South African labor force permanently between the rban and the rural areas.[90] Farmers had always opposed any step that would ecognize and accommodate the increasing numbers of Africans who had settled in he cities. They wanted them deported to farms.

Under the SAAU's new thinking, industrial workers would cease to be migrant; hey would live permanently in the cities with their families. The SAAU wanted armers to develop a complementary labor system with a core of permanent farm vorkers, supplemented on a seasonal basis by migrants. Reviewing the proposal in a ong memorandum to the Prime Minister about a year later, the Minister, Major Piet an der Byl, noted that recognition of African labor as a permanent feature of urban fe coincided with the long-term aims of the NAD and was advocated by the Natives Representative Council.[91] He might have added that it also faced facts. The ermanently urbanized black population had been growing strongly despite legisla-ion to restrict access to the cities and to segregate families who managed to establish ermanent residence in town.

Van der Byl's report indicates that, in the hands of the NAD, the SAAU's proposal ad developed into a comprehensive effort to address the competing labor needs of nining, farming and manufacturing. Mining would continue to find its labor through he migratory system. At the supply end, the system would be stabilized by investing n agricultural rehabilitation in the reserves, helping a minority of the inhabitants to naintain their subsistence farms, and housing the majority in rural villages from vhich the men would go out as mine migrants to support their households. Both arming and manufacturing would find their labor in a stabilized working class, part f it settled in the cities and the remainder living in family housing on the farms.

The SAAU's support for recognition of a permanent black labor force in the cities emained anathema to many whites. It was in the end rejected by the Smuts overnment. Smuts and his ministers shrank from acknowledging that an African vorking class was a permanent feature of South African industrial life and should be recognized and accommodated.[92] After some equivocation during the early war year when it briefly seemed that the government might contemplate striking out in a new more liberal direction, the old policies were reasserted. By 1945, the state ha hardened its stand considerably. The amendments, that year, to the urban area legislation drastically tightened the restrictions on Africans living permanently i towns. With the state's still limited powers of bureaucratic and police control, this lou legislative gunshot yielded little initially in the way of an effective enforcement bulle Labor demands in the urban areas and the pressure of growing deprivation an poverty among blacks in the reserves and white farming areas were more than a matc for the controls. Black families continued to flock to the cities, which meant tha farmers were becoming even more dependent on clandestine migrants entering th country from Mozambique and the north.

Once again in 1946–48, the South African government found itself attempting t bring order among the contending groups that had an interest in "tropical" labor. I several meetings with northern Transvaal employers and (separately) with th Central African governments, the NAD proposed to revive its lottery scheme of th late 1920s to allocate illegal migrants to farmers. Briefly introduced in 1947–48, th scheme failed completely. The workers simply evaded the government depot crossing the Limpopo above or below the border points using the many secret foc paths, a close knowledge of which was part of the lore of the long-distance migran Once again the workers and the recruiters who lived on them quickly defeated th government's regulatory plans.[93]

The farmers had to wait until the advent of the National Party government i 1948 for the Draconian measures required to deliver the labor they had bee demanding for so long. In 1954 the anti-squatting provisions of the Native Trust an Land Act of 1936 were finally proclaimed and summarily enforced, in theory makin a large new pool of workers available for agricultural employment.[94] Rigorou application of the pass laws tied farm labor more tightly to the land and streng thened the segmentation of the agricultural labor supply from that of the othe economic sectors. This failed, however, to stem the steady leakage of resident farn labor to the towns. The farmers responded by substituting migrant labor on a stil larger scale. Access to clandestine migrants thus became even more important. I addition, a new source became available. Stricter enforcement of influx contro regulations produced a swelling harvest of statutory offenders whom the state mad available to farmers as cheap convict labor. Unlike the Smuts government, it successor had no qualms about supplying such labor in quantity to individual farn employers. The new labor which the state put in place from the early 1950s wer designed to make "surplus labour" in the reserves available to farmers. The intentio of these measures was, first, to raise the fences around the labor pool resident in th farming areas and, second, to give the farmers renewed access to some of the labo from the reserves.[95]

Labor Systems in the Farming Economy

Before 1910, most white farmers in the region met their labor needs in very rudimentary ways. Lacking capital and cash, they let out land to African squatter for a rent in cash or kind (farming Africans rather than the land, officials said) o

sed labor tenants rather than settled wage labor or migrant workers.[96] The spread of
abor tenancies in the Transvaal and Natal was itself partly the product of the Natives
and Act of 1913 with its anti-squatting provisions.[97] Although not enforced initially,
xcept in the Free State, the act affected farmers' behavior and that of their tenants. The
tate's opposition to cash-and-kind tenancies for Africans on white-owned land, while
ar from completely successful, had led growing numbers of landlords to turn their
quatters into labor tenants on threat of eviction.

Subject to variations in detail over different parts of southern and South Africa,
abor tenancy arrangements shared certain basic features. Tenant families worked as
npaid or low-paid farm hands for three, six or nine months of the year. Typically, the
ontract included the labor of the male tenants' dependents, wife or wives, and minor
hildren. Indeed, in the most common arrangement, the household head himself did
ot work for the white farmer but delivered the labor of his male children. In return,
enants received access to grazing and sometimes arable land. When not engaged on
he farms, labor tenants and their male children migrated to better-paid work
lsewhere. Wives and female children helped on the land at harvest time or served as
lomestics in the white households. At a stage when many farmers remained only
veakly committed to the market, labor tenancy arrangements therefore represented a
uccessful effort to capture, at minimal cost, a share of the productive potential of the
African family. Lacking cash, they traded the use of land for labor.

At least for the years before 1930, the character and role of rent and labor tenancy
as been a recurrent theme in the region's agrarian historiography. So too has the story
f sharecropping. This volume provides additional district-level case studies of the
ocal complexities of on-farm relations between landlords, tenants and share-
roppers.[98] By adopting a regional rather than an exclusively South African purview, it
lso raises questions about the fate of tenancy and sharecropping on the geographical
nargins of white farming.[99]

Despite its advantages to the least commercial white farmers, labor tenancy as a
ystem was visibly failing within South Africa by the 1930s. The primary reason for its
hreatened collapse was the flight of growing numbers of women and young males to
etter-paid employment in the cities, a phenomenon which reflected the development
f the South African labor market and the growing struggles of the rural labor force
gainst oppressive conditions.[100] They had supplied much of the farm labor, and their
light was a disaster for farmers, particularly the poorest among them. The pull of
outh African cities was felt throughout the region,[101] throwing labor tenancy into
risis in areas such as Swaziland, Bechuanaland and Southern Rhodesia as well. In
olonial Malawi, a rather different dynamic developed. As sharecropping went into
lecline in many parts of the South African countryside, it surged in importance in the
obacco and cotton belt to the north as white farmers capitulated to ecological and
conomic imperatives.[102]

Labor tenancy was fundamentally unsuitable in the intensive, highly commercial
state agriculture that began to develop in many parts of South Africa in the decades
fter Union. Plantation owners increasingly found labor tenancy inefficient and
nsatisfactory and turned to other forms of labor mobilization.[103] Furthermore, they
egan to put pressure on the state to act against those less advanced farmers who
ontinued to depend on squatters or labor tenants. Limiting the number of labor
enants and the abolition of squatting would, large farmers believed, release labor for
states that would use them more productively. Some of them wanted to proletarian-
ze their labor force and work their farms with a core of resident wage laborers.

Yet to speak of a single transformation from tenancy through sharecropping ⁞ wage labor is misplaced. Sharecropping, ubiquitous in the northern Orange Free Sta⁞ and southern and western Transvaal maize belt, was virtually absent in much of th⁞ east and far west of the latter province as well as in neighboring Swaziland. I Lydenburg, following a decade of fierce struggle between landlords and tenants, labc tenancy persisted as an "uneasy compromise" into the 1940s. One of the consequence was the mass defection of farmers to the National Party in the run-up to the aparthei election of 1948.[104] In the nearby lowveld of the eastern Transvaal and in norther Natal, despite the emergence of large-scale irrigated plantation agriculture, tenanc and wage work persisted side by side and even on the same farm.[105]

For most commercial farmers, whose labor needs were growing rapidly in th decades after Union, migrant labor became the principal solution to their chronic labo shortages. Before the 1920s, therefore, commercial estate owners began to invest in th organized recruitment of migrants. The Bethal potato farms and the Zululand suga estates, both explored in some depth in this volume, represent the most highl developed example of long-distance recruiting of agricultural labor.[106] Althoug farmers were never able to combine in a single organization for this purpose, as th gold-mines had, they did form loose recruiting associations or used the privat companies which had emerged initially to supply labor for the mines.[107] With th completion of the gold-mines' recruiting monopsony (an employers' monopoly) b 1919, most of the private labor contractors were ejected from the mine labor systen and turned to supplying the farms.[108] They delivered workers who served for varing periods, usually six months, living while on the farms as "bachelor" workers ir barracks or compounds. Many of them were children subject to exploitation by thei employers and to sexual and physical abuse by older workers.

Farmers resorted to migrants when their labor needs were most intense, as durin the harvest and when local labor was unavailable at the low wages offered. The recruited in the South African reserves, taking mainly workers too young, too aged o too infirm for other better-paid employment. They also recruited foreign migrants from ever more distant areas where wages were much lower than in South Africa Estate owners believed that workers from a distance were more reliable and less expensive than locals. They were also far more vulnerable to exploitation and abuse Most white farming districts were uncompetitive for labor even compared with other low-wage employers. Wages were poor or wanting, hours long and the work hard Increasingly, white farms could expect only the labor remaining when all other employers had been served.

In the 1930s, experienced South African workers maneuvered with increasing success to avoid the low wages and bad conditions that prevailed on most mines and farms. The gold-mines responded by seeking their labor in more remote regions where competition was less and the workers without attractive alternative employ ment.[109] In farming, the supply of South African workers dwindled. A small minority of commercial and progressive farmers began to shift their labor systems toward the use of settled wage labor or, like the mines, intensified their use of long-distance migrants, many of them from outside the country. Less commercial farmers were left with labor tenants, with the aged, the infirm, older women and the very young. In general, reliance on the most vulnerable workers in these categories became greatest when production was increasing and labor shortages were most extreme.

Throughout the period covered in this volume, South Africa received a

ontinuous, steadily expanding influx of labor from the wider region, a flow that grew
specially quickly in the 1930s and 1940s. The most striking feature of intercolonial
abor relations in the inter-war period was not the penetration of the gold-mines'
ecruiting organization, WNLA, but the development of long-distance competition for
abor between white farmers from throughout the region in an increasingly
ubcontinental labor market.[110] Many migrants simply came unsupervised across the
rontiers, easily evading control posts and occasional police patrols, and giving border
armers an important supplement to their labor supply.

Commercial farmers in other areas also relied on migrants. These workers had
nade their own way to South Africa and were recruited by labor agents either inside
he border or (illegally) across it.[111] After the 1913 ban on the employment of tropical
abor on gold-mines, foreign workers were diverted through clandestine channels and
nto other employment. Northern and eastern Transvaal farmers, the Natal collieries
nd Zululand planters were the main beneficiaries. Between 1925 and 1929, the influx
ncreased greatly because the government of J.B.M. Hertzog had loosened the pass
equirements for foreign workers going to the Natal sugar fields. The South African
NAD implemented a lottery scheme in 1926 to distribute foreign workers crossing into
outh Africa to farmers, using its offices at Messina and Louis Trichardt. As migrants
ecame more adept at avoiding the agents of the state, the lottery system was
bandoned.[112] The inward flow continued at an accelerating rate. Migrants heading for
he Rand duped the farm recruiters and their employers, accepting contracts and
ransport to the rich farming districts of the eastern Transvaal and then deserting at the
irst opportunity. Plantations in the eastern Transvaal lowveld and Zululand also
lepended on clandestine migrants coming across the border from Mozambique.[113]
`he availability of foreign labor meant that even though competition from other
mployers intensified in the 1930s, commercial farmers were still able to avoid raising
vages or providing better working conditions. Without subcontinental migration, the
levelopment of South Africa's large agricultural industries would have occurred
nuch more slowly, or perhaps not at all. Even when mine recruiting in tropical areas
vas restored after 1933, clandestine immigration continued strongly.

For workers from the populous British and Portuguese colonies lying to the
north, who were lured by the higher wages of South Africa, the main transit route ran
ılong the Rhodesian borders. The eastern frontier, with Portuguese East Africa, was
ın inhospitable, but well-traveled wilderness that neither government administered
ır policed effectively. Thieves and labor touts lurked there and recruited or captured
nany migrants for South African and Rhodesian employers before they crossed the
ıorder.[114] Migrants also outflanked Southern Rhodesia on the west and traveled the
ength of Bechuanaland to reach South Africa. Southern Rhodesian officials referred to
he stream of labor as "the leak in the bucket," but were powerless to stop it. The
unners and labor agents working for South African recruiting companies competed
rantically with each other and ranged far into Southern Rhodesia and Mozambique to
ntercept the southward moving migrants before their rivals reached them. Their
nethods were crude but effective. The lawlessness that characterized labor recruit-
nent in the border regions lasted for decades.

Even the recruiters themselves acknowledged that they were "at war" with each
ther. Early in the century, one official described the situation as nothing less than a
<ind of slave trade. In 1947, the Director of Native Labour called it "a selling and
ıuying of human bodies."[115] Recruiters also crossed into Bechuanaland with impunity

to pick up local youths and long-distance migrants whose labor was particularl
sought after on western Transvaal mines and farms.[116] Farmers drove their truck
across the unmarked border for the same purpose. The hardship endured by th
migrants was extreme. The journey from as far away as northern Nyasaland c
southern Angola was often completed entirely on foot and could involve distances i
excess of three thousand kilometers. Workers who traveled in this way usually arrive
starving and in rags. Some did not arrive at all, having been captured along the way b
labor touts working for Southern Rhodesian employers, attacked by lions, c
murdered by the thieves that operated in the border regions. Despite the hazards c
the journey and the barriers put in their way, migrants continued to pour across Sout
Africa's borders, much to the chagrin of mine and farm employers, and thei
governments, in the areas that supplied the labor.

Marginal farmers outside South Africa, chronically short of labor, resorted to th
same desperate measures as their South African competitors. Control of the large flov
of labor toward South Africa became a major political issue within the region in th
1930s. Seeing "their" labor draining away to the south, farmers to the north and eas
sought the help of governments to keep it at home. Like South African farmers, the
demanded police measures, pass laws and other constraints on worker freedom, bu
met with variable success.

From the turn of the century, Nyasaland became a labor reservoir, first fo
Southern Rhodesia and soon also for South Africa. Settler groups opposed the exodu
of large numbers of "Nyasas" to the areas with higher wages further south, but wer
unable to do much to limit the emigration. As did all of the colonies of the regior
Nyasaland lacked the police power and administrative capacity to control its border:
Although the colonial state came to accept the need to control clandestine emigratior
it was without the means to do so.[117] Instead, desperate farmers established their ow
local migrant labor system, encouraging impoverished Mozambican peasants to wor
on their estates.[118]

In Southern Rhodesia, the colonial government worked adroitly to restrict th
operations of WNLA in the region.[119] However, it was unable to control the migratio
of workers from and through its territory. The Rhodesians and the Portuguese bot
complained bitterly about the loss of labor: the first because they wanted the labor fo
their own mines and farms; the second because illegal emigrants rarely paid fees an
taxes. After failing to get the agreement of South Africa to joint control of interstat
migration and restrictions on the drain of labor south, the Rhodesian governmer
proposed in the late 1930s to close its entire border along the Limpopo and ban th
passage of Africans through it, except those using authorized transportation. Thi
measure did not pass Parliament. The Rhodesian government lacked the power t
enforce such a prohibition in any case, and may have conceived it mainly as
negotiating instrument to try to force the South Africans to agree to restriction:
Nevertheless, the Rhodesian government worked single-mindedly throughout th
inter-war period and after to protect the labor supply of its mining and farmin
constituents.[120]

The white settlers of Mozambique were similarly determined that the Portugues
colonial government should safeguard their labor supply and restrict its leakage int
South Africa. They aimed to curtail organized migration to the mines and stop
clandestine migrants leaving the country. Plans for the expansion of estate productio
in the 1920s demanded that sufficient labor remain in Mozambique.[121] In 1927–28, the

ecured a total ban on clandestine immigration to South Africa from Mozambique and requirement that South Africa repatriate the thousands of illegal Mozambican nigrants in its territory. This measure, unenforceable in practice but nevertheless rksome to South African farm employers, was withdrawn in 1934 as a result of a evised agreement with the Portuguese. The effects of the depression and the fall in evenue as a result of the reduced flow of workers to the gold-mines forced the Mozambican state to agree to regularize the employment of their clandestine workers n condition that those workers pay the required fees to Portuguese officials stationed n South Africa for the purpose.[122] Yet, though temporary, the ban did illustrate very vell the political power of the Mozambican agricultural sector.

On the Farms

'or many of the migrants who ended up on farms, the hardship of the journey was only the beginning. Like their mine counterparts, they were the object of intense urveillance and relentless discipline. Most accounts of working and living conditions on southern Africa's mines and farms stress the pervasiveness of racial violence and brutality.[123] The *exposés* of earlier generations of journalists, academics and researchers kept alive the reputation of the white farm as a place of unrelenting ruelty.[124] Cultures of white authority and coercion on the farm were replicated in the egion's all-male private schools. The authoritarian and masculine ethos of the schools vas carried back to the farms, as brutalized schoolboys became brutal farmers in urn.[125] The eastern Transvaal district of Bethal, site of scandal after scandal, came to tand for everything bad associated with farm labor. Grounded in the suffering of housands of workers, the evils of Bethal entrenched themselves in popular onsciousness and the official mind. A number of the chapters in this collection lemonstrate, however, that Bethal was just one, admittedly extreme, example of the violence that plagued the white countryside.

In the mistreatment of workers, Natal sugar planters and cotton and wattle growers and Transvaal citrus producers were not far behind their Bethal counterparts. On these modernizing estates, labor relations remained primitive. Workers were housed in cold, filthy compounds modeled on those of the mines. At night they were ocked in so that they could not escape. Sometimes their clothing was confiscated for he same reason and they labored in mealie sacks, often from dawn to dusk. Some armers demanded longer hours than these and forced the workers to begin work before first light, to continue after sunset and to turn out on Sundays. Laborers found heir meager wages frequently withheld; if paid at all, the wages were often reduced to cover the cost of pass fees, transportation and even recruiting expenses. The food provided on most farms was inadequate. Poor in quality, meals lacked the essential equirements of a balanced diet; often the workers received only mealie meal. Without resh vegetables, protein and fat, the typical farm diet could not sustain the health and vitality of workers expected to carry out hard manual labor.

Because workers were frequently underfed and weak on arrival, they were especially vulnerable to the bad conditions they encountered on the farms. Although proper statistics were not kept, death rates on farms were undoubtedly high and life expectancy low. Since farm work was the least attractive of all employment in the economy, the operation of labor markets tended to ensure that it was mainly those workers who were too sick, malnourished or incapacitated to find work elsewher who ended up on farms. The sugar estates in Natal and Zululand took both foreig labor from southern Mozambique and workers from the Transkei, Pondoland an Basutoland. Most of the workers were those who could not get employment on th mines, often for health reasons. Throughout the inter-war period, a steady stream c seriously ill, disabled and dying workers moved daily to the south, returning alon the roads and lines of rail from the Natal and Zululand plantations to the supply area in Pondoland, Basutoland and the Eastern Cape. They passed an equally persister and large stream of new victims moving north.[126] Not confined to the period covere by this volume, abuses continued for decades.

Large numbers of workers would be suffering from diet-deficiency and othe chronic diseases at recruitment. Tuberculosis, bilharzia, sexually transmitted disease and malaria were pervasive throughout the rural areas of southern Africa and wer mostly untreated. Of all the inadequacies of farm conditions, the lack of prope medical facilities was one of the most serious. The Zululand planters, in particula remained reluctant to confront the malaria problem.[127] Like their counterparts furthe south, they often failed to provide basic medical treatment. Even when employers di provide hospitals, they and their overseers tended to be slow in getting their worker to needed medical attention. The assistant medical officer in Durban complained tha the planters tended to use their hospitals as morgues; he found that workers who wer finally sent for treatment arrived too late and were frequently beyond help.[128] Ofter the plantations avoided medical treatment for their workers entirely; they simpl ejected from the estates workers who became too ill to work and left them to mak their own way to their homes. Compliant medical staff connived in this strategy b certifying as "fit to travel" workers who were obviously not.

What recourse was open to workers when they encountered these kinds c conditions and abuses? Formal organization was virtually impossible given th dispersed nature of the agricultural work-force, the urban emphasis of mos contemporary union organizers and political parties, and the unrelenting hostility c employers and the state. Clandestine workers were also reluctant to identif themselves to the authorities through participation in organized protest. Despit these formidable obstacles, farm unions did arise and briefly flourish at certain time in certain parts of the country, most notably the Industrial and Commercial Workers Union (ICU).[129] Far more common were individualized, hidden forms of protest suc as crop theft, arson, machine wrecking, dissembling, go-slows and the like.[130]

The new historiography of mine labor — with its emphasis on experience agency, culture and resistance — has shown that in concert with managers an owners, workers did forge paternalistic moral economies that often blunted th worst excesses of coercion and violence.[131] The applicability of this model to th farming sector, at least for the period covered by this volume, is far less certair On-farm relations (particularly in the sharecropping belt where tenant household had some bargaining power) were certainly ameliorated by paternalism.[132] Short term migrant workers, who had few opportunities to develop longer-term relation ships with farmers, could expect no such tempering. And yet, even these mos vulnerable of workers were never helpless against fraudulent recruiters, bruta employers and bad working and living conditions. Migrants arriving at the borde from the north were well informed of conditions in South Africa. Recruiters workin or unpopular employers or those who misled recruits about wages or conditions ound themselves boycotted.

The most effective weapon at the workers' disposal, however, was undoubtedly lesertion. Throughout the whole period covered by this book, desertion from farms vas rampant. Migrants absconded even from farmers and estates who paid them egularly and treated them reasonably. They did so because they viewed the farms imply as staging points where they could accumulate sufficient funds to get to the igher wages and better conditions available in the towns. Most desertions were by ndividuals or small groups which had been recruited together. Not infrequently, owever, whole gangs walked off the job, usually in desperate protest against some articularly egregious situation. While mass walkouts always attracted the attention f the authorities and could lead to some redress, they usually also ended with the vorkers' involuntary return to the estate from which they had fled. The severity of armers' efforts to immobilize their workers on the estates by confiscating their lothing, locking them into compounds, chaining them up and supervising them with rmed guards testify to the effectiveness of the desertion weapon. The prison-like onditions on many estates notwithstanding, desertion continued little diminished. Despite this widespread flight, most of the farmers refused to recognize the message hat cried out from this behavior and to carry out even the minimum improvements hat might have enabled them to retain a labor force.

Conclusion

During the forty years between 1910 and 1950, white farmers in South Africa and its principal neighbors were very successful in securing legislation to subsidize their production, to support domestic prices and to shelter them from foreign competition. Both the marketing and the credit policies of the Union and Southern Rhodesian governments operated to protect whites from competition from African producers and to support some of the least efficient white farmers. Through the Marketing Act and the establishment of control boards to regulate the production and sale of particular products, the Union Parliament, under the influence of officials in the Department of Agriculture and Forestry, brushed aside the opposition of academic economists, subordinated the interests of the poor and consumers (while claiming to protect them) and eliminated the market as the primary regulator of agricultural production and prices.

A strong element of state planning and producer self-regulation would, according to these officials, bring order to the production and prices of food and restore white farmers to prosperity and independence. White farmers in Southern Rhodesia may have had an "instinctive" preference for free-market theory and proclaimed it obsessively, but many of them would not have survived without the state support lavished on them in the 1930s. In both countries, the regulatory framework established in the inter-war decades provided the basis for white farmers' prosperity and political dominance that grew in those years and later.

The official record reveals the extraordinary extent of state support of white farming over the whole period covered by this volume. Those policies, however, had contradictory and paradoxical effects. On the one hand, marketing, credit, price-support and other measures were instrumental in the emergence of the large-scale

commercial farming that transformed South African agriculture particularly on th
highveld maize belt and in the subtropical areas. Similarly, the labor policies of th
period protected farmers' access to a servile labor force and made it available a
sub-economic rates. On the other hand, these policies impeded the development of
farming sector appropriate to the country's demography and environment. Th
artificially high farm prices, low costs and protection from imports that resulted fror
marketing, credit and tariff legislation encouraged white farmers to use land fc
agricultural purposes that was better suited, because of the semi-arid condition c
most of the country, to pastoralism. The exclusion of black peasant farmers from ani
benefits from the various subsidies that the state doled out to whites eliminated
source of cheap food that had been important during the first stages of industrializa
tion. The labor policies of the period shored up the labor tenant system, which wa
already recognized as an anachronism by 1932.

Any agricultural revolution has victims as well as victors and southern Africa wa
no exception. Agricultural policies kept migrants in miserable, low-wage employmer
when they could have been much more productively employed elsewhere, both t
their benefit and to that of the economy. Amongst the ranks of South Africa's poc
whites were many former landowners who had failed to make the grade. Withi
virtually every district, even the most prosperous, some farmers inevitably strugglec
In the rich farming districts of the eastern Transvaal, for example, the white farmin
community was always deeply divided between struggling small plotholders an
mortgaged farmers, and the wealthy landowners who could afford to farm on a ver
large scale. In ecologically marginal districts the risks and disasters were intens
These districts were a particular focus of many of the region's white settlemer
schemes where unscrupulous land speculators looked forward to unloading tracts c
unfarmable land on the unsuspecting settler.[133]

Measured in terms of overall output, the range and variety of the crops producec
and increasingly their quality, the development of white agriculture was remarkabl
However, the costs imposed on the society were at least as great, both in th
deprivation that spread among Africans as a consequence of the bounty that stat
policy conferred upon the white farmers and in the distorted development of th
economy that such massive support of white agriculture produced.

2

Farm Labor and the South African State, 1924–1948

David Duncan

In her book *Working for Boroko* Marian Lacey argued that the forms of regulation and coercion developed in South Africa from 1924 to 1948 represented a coherent effort to ensure that farmers had adequate supplies of — and control over — farm labor. "The long battle between mines and farms since the 1890s was at an end," she wrote: Hertzog's intervention had given rural labour supplies to the farmers."[1] The more closely one inspects the internal workings of the state in the 1920s and 1930s, the harder it is to sustain the idea of a "grand plan" aimed at assisting farmers to the detriment of their workers. In broad terms, the state sought to stabilize a pool of farm workers by promoting wage labor and controlling the drift to the towns. Throughout this period, the state's approach to farm labor was uncertain and contradictory. On the one hand, there was a move to extend existing mechanisms of control, though elements within the state opposed this. On the other, the years 1925–37 saw the development of administrative and territorial segregation; and yet these laws were not designed to have a direct impact on labor in commercial agriculture. The contradictions can be partly explained by a closer examination of the state.

Just as change in the countryside was slow-moving and fraught with contradictions, so the development of state policy was anomalous and uneven. In part, this inconsistency was due to changes in government: elements in the National Party, which took power in 1924, regarded themselves as the representatives of white farmers, and were anxious to appear to be doing more for that constituency than had their predecessors. The lack of consistency also owed much to competition between different sectors in the economy: mine owners, industrialists and farmers found themselves competing for cheap labor, and tried to influence the state to serve their own ends. A third reason, highlighted here, was related to the internal dynamics of various branches of the state: in particular, the Departments of Agriculture, Justice and Native Affairs (NAD). Their differing positions on farm labor arose to some extent from their respective roles — the Agriculture Department representing white farmer the Justice Department wielding the more overtly repressive arm of the state, and th NAD charged with protecting the interests of the African population. Several othe factors — such as the role played by individual ministers and administrators, th pressure from white farmers on the Justice Department, and the NAD's regulation recruiting for the gold-mines — also merit careful examination.

It is not intended to give an overview of white agriculture here; suffice it to sa that even though the state increased assistance to white farmers by means of cred extension, marketing schemes and technical expertise through the 1920s and 1930s most farmers remained small-time, underfunded and heavily dependent on blac labor tenants. These labor tenants were supplemented by significant numbers of sharecroppers and rent-paying tenants who continued to farm "white" lanc especially on farms owned by less "progressive" farmers or by absentee landowner and land companies.[2] It should be stressed that white farmers were far from united i their attitudes to labor. By 1924, a minority of large-scale farmers were alread maximizing their profits from the land and moving towards full-time wage labor. Th larger farmers, who controlled the provincial and national agricultural unions, wer more willing to accept progressive state initiatives against sharecroppers and tenanc agreements. However, even they sought state intervention to provide them witl workers. The root of the problem, as white farmers saw it, was that young Africar farm workers were drifting to the towns in ever-increasing numbers, thus depriving farmers of their most productive labor. In the past, they had been able to keep African on the farms by granting land, grazing rights and a paltry wage in cash or kind t families of squatters in return for labor. The growth of secondary industry, especiall during World War I and again after South Africa came off the gold standard ii December 1932, made this recruitment more difficult. Across the country, farmer responded by bonding together in local, regional and provincial associations anc bombarding the government with requests for assistance. Among these requests wa: one for the right to preferential access to migrant Africans from neighboring colonies.

In the 1920s, senior bureaucrats in the Department of Agriculture approached the problem from the standpoint of the overall production costs of the white farmers Helen Bradford, in her work on the Industrial and Commercial Workers' Union (ICU) suggests that the department's English orientation and promotion of modernized commercial farming left it out of touch with small, Afrikaans-speaking farmers.[3] Yet throughout the period 1924–48, Agriculture officials argued that the state shoulc guarantee farmers adequate supplies of labor, an argument that suited the majority of small-time, under-capitalized farmers who sought labor through coercion anc control. Officers in the Department of Agriculture embraced the white farmers' clair that they could not stem the seepage of labor from rural areas on their own. This view was shared by the Minister of Agriculture from 1924 to 1935, General J. Kemp.

In the Department of Justice, policy in the later 1920s and early 1930s was dictatec more by the ministers than by their senior civil servants, for whom farm labor was no a central concern. Ministers Tielman Roos (1924–29) and Oswald Pirow (1929–33 both contributed to the extensive range of powers that could be used to control African farm workers. They steered through Parliament the Masters and Servants (Transvaa and Natal) Amendment Act of 1926 and the Native Service Contract Act of 1932. The Draconian nature of the latter law produced a storm of protest, not least from the

NAD. African organizations and newspapers joined with liberals in the Joint Councils, the South African Institute of Race Relations (SAIRR), several churches, and the left wing of the South African Party, in arguing that the NAD and not the Department of Justice, should be responsible for the matters covered by the bill.

In 1929, the NAD was removed from the Prime Minister's portfolio and given its own Cabinet Minister in the person of E. G. Jansen (1929–33). Jansen did not exert any great influence on his department's policies; the opinions of its chief bureaucrats continued to prevail. At the local level, Native Commissioners faced more immediate pressure from irate farmers who demanded action against absconding laborers. At least some district officers identified with the farmers' plight. However, at head-quarters in Pretoria, senior officials generally rejected a policy of further state intervention to provide farmers with labor. The farmers themselves, they argued, should attract workers through better remuneration and enhanced living and working conditions. The NAD's position was based on both practical and moral considerations. First, there was the belief that farmers would never have sufficient labor unless they raised cash wages and improved amenities. At the same time, many officials found the maltreatment of farm laborers by their employers morally offensive. Even hedged round as it was by mutual back-slapping and heavy paternalist rhetoric, a measure of genuine outrage at the appalling conditions of service on many farms was significant in the evolution of farm labor policy.

This theme is illustrated in the following section, which deals with the debate between the NAD and the Department of Agriculture over farm labor conditions and related topics. The subsequent section examines relations between the Justice Department and the NAD in the late 1920s and early 1930s. By 1935, Justice had given up trying to regulate farm labor, and the NAD's policies had gained wider acceptability within the state. The government underlined this development by appointing the former Secretary for Native Affairs (SNA), J.F. Herbst (1923–34), to head a committee to investigate the farm labor shortage in 1937. With the onset of World War II in 1939, the state made some effort to act concertedly to aid white agriculture, exhorting blacks to remain on the farms, supplying farmers with prisoner-of-war labor, and experimenting with state-run labor gangs. The causes, nature and extent of this apparent unity within the state are considered in the fourth section. The final section focuses on policy regarding foreign workers, and the various attempts made to alleviate farm labor shortages by enlisting hapless migrants from the north.

The NAD and the Department of Agriculture

In the period from 1924 to the late 1930s, senior administrators in the Agriculture and Native Affairs Departments clashed regularly on questions of policy relating to African farm workers. Put crudely, Agriculture officials placed the onus of providing farmers with labor on the state, and accused African laborers of sloth, ignorance and greed; the NAD blamed white farmers for frightening labor off with bad conditions and low wages.

One obvious point of conflict was the Department of Agriculture's Veterinary Laboratory at Onderstepoort, near Pretoria, where 180 Africans were employed on research-oriented agricultural work.[4] Protests from the ICU in 1928 caused an

investigation to be held by the local Additional Native Commissioner, who found
range of inadequacies in the laboratory's care of its workers.[5] Herbst was incensed b
this report. If the state could not set suitable standards, he argued, how could th
Native Affairs and Public Health Departments persuade farmers to change the
treatment of African employees? On the basis of the NAD's role as trustee, th
department's officers claimed they were obliged to "urge that conformity on the pa
of State Departments with more modern ideas regarding the treatment of labour is a
the present day eminently desirable."[6]

The Department of Agriculture approached the problem from a completel
different angle. With Kemp's support, its officials argued that Onderstepoort alread
paid its workers more than neighboring farmers, who blamed it for the local labo
shortage. They implied that any further increases would be deeply resented b
farmers, and that the department was not prepared to cloud its relationship with then
for the sake of a few laborers.[7] The department's contempt for African workers cam
out in some of their other arguments: the laborers would not know what to do with th
fresh vegetables the Native Commissioner had advised; and the whole point o
employing blacks was to keep costs down — if a wage increase was introduced, i
would be as well to sack the entire staff and take on whites.[8]

The controversy over Onderstepoort passed into history along with the disin
tegration of the ICU's rural protest, but farm labor remained on the agenda of th
Native Affairs and Agriculture Departments. Three major reports addressed the issue
each time considering how to provide farmers with adequate supplies of labor, give
the general shortage and the impecuniosity of many farmers. The first two — the 193(
Labour Resources Committee and the 1932 Native Economic Commission —
produced few solutions. The 1930 committee gently supported the amelioration o
working conditions, but accepted squatting as a necessary part of the existing eco
nomic system. The Native Economic Commission paid heed to farmers' evidence tha
labor tenants were well fed, treated and remunerated, but recommended experiment
with written contracts and cash wages. It was not until the 1939 report of the Farn
Labour Committee, a body led by the former SNA but manned by prominent and suc
cessful farmers, that a blueprint for state policy towards farm labor was drawn up.

In the meantime, the NAD and the Department of Agriculture continued to pul
in different directions. Although often critical of farmers' labor practices, the NAD
sympathized with their difficulties. In 1928, the SNA went so far as to outline a scheme
for recruiting black South Africans for the farms.[9] Thereafter, the departmen
encouraged Native Commissioners and Magistrates to put prospective employer
and farm laborers in touch on an informal basis.[10] Periodic attempts were also made to
tighten up on travel passes and urban service contracts, and to prevent labor tenant
overstaying their leave in the towns.

In general, however, the NAD had grave reservations about introducing furthe
coercive measures against blacks for the sake of white farmers. There were severa
reasons. In the case of blacks who moved from white farms to the reserves, the NAD
regarded restrictions as contrary to the segregation policy expounded by
J.B.M. Hertzog's government in the mid-1920s. Hertzog's goal was to extend
territorial segregation. Only Africans who were economically necessary as employee
would remain in white areas, while the rest would eventually be accommodated in
enlarged reserve areas. The department was prepared to discourage laborers from
leaving for the reserves, but Native Commissioners would not refuse passes.[11]

On another tack, the NAD insisted on the right of Africans to sell their labor in the nearest market. The NAD's position on passes was always equivocal; the usual line was that Africans' irresponsibility and lack of stability made passes necessary, and that passes helped to stem an influx of so-called "raw natives" into the towns. But Native Affairs officials were aware that enforcing the pass laws outside the Cape tarnished their reputation as the protector of Africans. Some officials also considered passes unnecessary, since the Urban Areas Act of 1923 allowed municipalities to control their own African populations. In any case, the mass of unemployed, idle, urban Africans, which many farmers believed was behind their labor problems, simply did not exist for most of this period.[12]

Rather than forcing Africans back to the rural areas, the NAD sought to help farmers keep workers by ameliorating conditions. NAD officials argued (for the most part, ineffectually) that farmers had to provide cash wages, proper housing, schools, medical care and a balanced diet.[13] The department viewed the labor tenant system as disastrously wasteful of land and labor. On occasion, the NAD made a direct attempt to change things. In 1928, the SNA proposed the introduction of Inspectors of Farms, similar to those active in proclaimed labor areas under the Native Labour Regulation Act of 1911. The SNA hoped farmers would accept inspectors as a means of combating the current wave of ICU activity, but the Department of Agriculture rejected the idea.[14] In the late 1930s, the NAD duly turned to the Department of Public Health to deal with a shocking wave of maltreatment in the eastern Transvaal district of Bethal.[15] On the whole, however, Native Affairs officials lacked the resources and power to enforce changes in farm labor conditions. It would have required a major government initiative to extend the NAD's ambit beyond labor in mining and industry. Hertzog's government balked at alienating an important constituency by expanding the regulation of African labor in this way. In the meantime, the SNA ordered local officers to use their influence to improve conditions; it was up to the farmers to decide whether to comply or not.[16]

The Department of Agriculture took a more direct approach to solving the farm labor problem. Unlike the NAD, Agriculture officials adopted a lenient attitude towards the labor tenant system.[17] They conceded that it was to the advantage of the farmer to pay cash, but argued that it was impossible for him to keep his labor without providing land and grazing. For years, the Secretary for Agriculture pleaded with other departments to help alleviate the white farmers' position. A stream of letters was dispatched to persuade those responsible for provincial and national roads, and the South African Railways and Harbours authorities, not to strip the agricultural sector of its labor.[18] The activities of these departments were a perennial cause for complaint from farmers; as one platteland MP pointed out in 1937, laborers could earn up to two shillings a day in cash on the roads, while most farmers paid much less.[19] Yet the department rejected any suggestion that the state should enforce uniform standards on the farms. In the later 1930s, its officials appear to have been less active on the issue, passing correspondence to the NAD and quoting the SNA in replying to farmers' associations.[20] After the initial failure to implement direct state assistance for farmers, Agriculture officials preferred to eschew responsibility for farm labor. Instead, they concentrated on other forms of state aid, such as subsidies, protection and price stabilization.

However, when the Herbst Committee met in 1937–39, S.J. de Swardt, an official in the Department of Agriculture and Forestry and an adviser to the Secretary of

Agriculture, P. R. Viljoen, provided a clear statement on labor policy for his department. He emphasized the practical steps the state could take to help farmers.[2] He stressed that farmers could not afford to raise cash wages within their present cost restraints. This attitude was very much in line with that of the provincial agricultural unions, who would also have endorsed his condemnation of those who "preached" to farmers, and agreed with his argument that the remuneration received by farm laborers was as good as that obtaining in the towns. De Swardt advocated propaganda work among farm laborers to emphasize the value of a wage in kind and the importance of sharing a cash wage among a whole family. Significantly, he favored measures that would be carried out by the NAD, rather than the Department of Agriculture. In this way, he reaffirmed certain aspects of his department's old policy of direct state action to improve the lot of white farmers.

The Herbst Report of 1939 reflected the NAD's attitude towards farm labor more than other reports of the period.[22] Herbst's main proposal was that Chapter four of the Native Trust and Land Act of 1936, aimed at eradicating rent tenancy and regulating the number of labor tenants on each farm, be implemented. In contrast to De Swardt's recommendations, however, the weight of the report was behind steps that farmers and municipalities could take at the local level. Contrary to the view of many farmers, the report denied that there were hordes of unemployed, urban Africans who could be compelled to move to the rural areas.[23] Further coercive controls of Africans on the farms by the NAD were pointless, and the time was not ripe for written contracts for all. Farmers must improve conditions and bring an end to labor tenancy; and the towns must strictly enforce the Urban Areas Act against the influx of casual black workers. The farmers must establish their own labor organizations, while the role of Magistrates and Native Commissioners should be restricted to giving farmers advice on new Local Advisory Boards. Shortly after the report was published, the outbreak of World War II disrupted the government's careful evaluation of the Herbst Report. After September 1939, the report was not forgotten, but the chances of realizing its more far-reaching proposals — in favor of improved conditions and against squatting — were at once diminished.

The Native Service Contract Act and the Ascendancy of the NAD

The first piece of legislation that directly affected farm labor was the Masters and Servants (Transvaal and Natal) Amendment Act of 1926. Marian Lacey presented this act as an important departure, but her account contains several factual inaccuracies.[24] For example, Lacey stated that the act gave Transvaal farmers the right to bind laborers for six months instead of the traditional three, and "extended whipping to labour tenants." Neither of these clauses featured in the act. The chief purpose of the amendment, according to Lacey, was to bolster labor tenancy — "the pillar of the Nationalists' farm labour policy" — until Hertzog's Native Land Amendment Bill could entrench it in a more comprehensive manner.[25]

Helen Bradford refuted the view that the Pact government immediately responded to the farmers' cries for help. As she pointed out, the 1926 act was nothing more than an attempt to patch up holes in the Masters and Servants laws created by a series of Supreme Court decisions in the early 1920s.[26] In the nineteenth century, Masters and Servants laws in all four future provinces had made breaches of contract etween employers and employees criminal offences. The Rissik Act of 1909 was ntended to remove all doubt as to whether squatters should come under these laws.[27] his legislation was overturned in the 1921 case of *Maynard versus Chasana*, in which it vas ruled that squatting agreements created different relationships from those escribed in Masters and Servants laws.[28] Employers continued to protest that many bor tenants who left to work off the farm did not return to complete their period of ervice. The difficulty extended beyond the heads of families who entered into ontracts: their dependents, who were usually party to the agreements, often bsconded to earn money for themselves.

Faced with widespread protests from farmers, the Smuts government drew up a Jative Registration and Protection Bill (1923), but the draft became tied up at the select ommittee stage.[29] The issue was later taken up by the Nationalist Minister of Justice, ielman Roos.[30] Roos earnestly desired to help farmers with repressive legislation, but he 1926 act did not meet the more extreme (and legally unenforceable) demands of the rovincial agricultural unions — that the farmer's word should be enough to secure he arrest of a laborer, and that chairmen of farmers' associations should be allowed to ry labor tenants.[31]

The act of 1926 covered both the Transvaal and Natal, and brought oral and vritten contracts between farmers and labor tenants under the Masters and Servants aws. The act did not require such contracts to stipulate when service should begin. he legislation merely restored the position to what it had been before 1921, and was herefore acceptable to the NAD. Departmental officials generally disliked the Jasters and Servants laws, but felt they were still necessary, given prevailing ircumstances in the countryside. The fact that the Department of Justice had ntroduced the bill helped to shield the NAD from criticism by Africans and liberal vhite sympathizers. The SNA thanked the Secretary for Justice, W. E. Bok, for taking n this "thorny subject," and politely spurned Bok's attempt to hand responsibility for he bill to the NAD.[32]

The harmony within the state did not last for long. Ceaseless complaints from armers over the difficulties of securing and controlling farm workers soon caused Roos to hatch a new amending bill. This emerged fully fledged as the Native Service Contract Act of 1932.[33] The Joint Councils, Churches and the remnants of the ICU in the Drange Free State strongly opposed the bill. Lacey insisted that the main opposition ame from mining magnates represented in Parliament by the South African Party.[34] Yet, as she herself admitted, the parliamentary opposition did not attack the bill on the grounds that the mines' labor supply would be adversely affected. They complained, ather, that the bill would not work — the state could not compel Africans currently quatting on company-owned farms to distribute themselves evenly round other arms.[35] In addition, it would provoke widespread opposition among Africans. Thirdly, as J. H. Hofmeyr pointed out, the bill would be seen overseas as a forced labor measure.[36] All these arguments were valid, and provided cogent reasons for the South African Party to oppose the bill. The mines did not send a delegation to the select ommittee on the bill, nor is there any evidence that they would have agreed with Lacey that the bill marked the end of the "long battle between mines and farms."[37]

The Native Service Contract Bill was formulated and implemented by the Department of Justice under the guidance of Roos's successor, Oswald Pirow. Pirow had campaigned for more stringent controls over farm laborers while still on the back benches.[38] As Minister of Justice, he had the full support of the departmental Secretary,

Hans van Rensburg, who later gained notoriety as the head of the pro-Nazi Ossewabrandwag.[39] Between them, they produced a bill of unsurpassed repression which caused a huge stir both inside and outside the bureaucracy. The chief clause strengthened the power of African parents to enter into binding contracts on behalf of their children; allowed the farmer to evict the whole family if one member failed to render service; prevented labor tenants from acquiring "seek-work" passes for the towns without the farmer's written permission; gave the government the power to tax owners of land worked by sharecropping or rent-paying tenants; and introduced whipping for contraventions of the Masters and Servants laws. The Cape Province was excluded from the act, while the Free State was only affected by a few minor clauses.[40]

In Parliament, the Minister of Native Affairs, E.G. Jansen, kept a low profile during the debates on the act. His caution was partly a result of his own conservative leanings (he reappeared in the same office in D.F. Malan's first Cabinet). It was also due to his structural position as head of the NAD. The African press and the Conference summoned (as representative of informed black opinion) under the Native Administration Act of 1927 to discuss the bill, harangued him for failing to fulfill his duties as "Father of the Natives," and condemned the "whipping clause" (section 11) as barbaric and medieval.[41] R.R. Dhlomo referred in horror to Jansen's defense that "Cuts could only be inflicted by order of a Magistrate." Papers such as *Umteteli wa Bantu* reported widespread opposition to the bill from predominantly white Churches and liberal organizations.[42] The Johannesburg Joint Council warned that it would have "a disquieting and unsettling effect . . . on the native mind."[43]

Senior NAD officials were deeply disconcerted by this barrage of protest, and refused to follow their Minister in defending the legislation. The main concern for the NAD was that its officers would be left to enforce the bill's provisions.[44] It was all very well for Pirow to take the credit from farmers; but it was the NAD that faced the anger of urban employers and Africans whom the new regulations affected. The NAD's reputation as the organization that "held the balance between white and black" took a severe hammering on account of this bill, and members of the department felt the blows keenly.[45]

Equally irritating for NAD officials was the fact that the Native Service Contract Act was a nightmare to administer. The central difficulty concerned the coordination of the many different forms of pass that by then existed. The 1932 act sought to combine all these into one official document; but its effect was to create yet another piece of paper to be produced on demand. If a juvenile appeared at the Native Commissioner's office without permission to seek work, he now had to be sent home to obtain it. Employers were prevented from paying their workers' taxes all at once, because the new law required a man's fingerprints to be taken prior to the issue of a new tax receipt. And the old tax receipt could no longer be used as an identification document, since the act insisted on the issue of a new one.[46]

Within months, farmers' organizations were again complaining that the law failed to ensure the return of labor tenants for their contracted period of service.[47] The NAD was divided internally as to how far the department could be expected to assist farmers who had not drawn up written labor contracts. The Director of Native Labour (DNL) argued that his overworked staff should not be responsible for contacting urban employers when the leave period of tenants was about to end. Such a move would, in any event, have had little effect as Africans could simply report passless and vith new particulars, or move from one district to another. A lucrative trade in forged armers' "leave-notes" developed, which the pass office found it difficult to do nything about.[48] Other problems rendered the act less and less workable: for xample, it was discovered that foreign migrants could not be bound by its provisions, ince they were not required to carry the specified form of identification. More lamaging still, the case of *Rex versus Mnyeza* brought back the old problem that ontracts had to state a precise time when the labor tenant should commence work.[49] Yet another act would be necessary to allow farmers more latitude.

In 1934, the Department of Justice, now with the steadying hand of General Smuts t the helm, quietly passed the administration of the Native Service Contract Act to the NAD.[50] By coincidence, the same year saw the transfer of D. L. Smit, formerly Under-Secretary in the Justice Department, to the job of Secretary for Native Affairs 1934–45). In the past, Smit had deflected the NAD's complaints by countering that hey, and not Justice, were in charge of "Native Administration;" now, by contrast, he mmersed himself in the attitudes of his new department, rejecting a scheme to tighten up the act with the comment, "We have gone as far as we can in the way of assisting armers."[51]

The NAD did make periodic attempts to appease farmers, by ordering closer iaison between town and country offices on the movements of labor tenants.[52] At no point, however, did the NAD agree to the farmers' request to contact urban employers when labor tenants were due to return to the farms. Such a policy would have required the cooperation of urban employers, which was often not forthcoming. Equally problematic was the fact that the urban officer's writ extended only to the town limits, a situation that allowed workers expelled from the town to find clandestine employment in peri-urban areas. In general, the difficulties encountered over the Native Service Contract Act appear to have convinced NAD officials that additional coercive measures were pointless.[53] Like their colleagues in the Department of Agriculture, Justice officials no longer questioned the NAD stance. Protests from farmers' organizations were referred to the SNA, and the Justice Department was not represented on the Herbst Committee.

Lacey has suggested that the segregation legislation passed between 1935 and 1937 was an integral part of the state's attempts to assist farmers.[54] This begs the question of why a department committed to improving conditions for farm laborers, was none the less prepared to support these laws. There are two answers to this. The first involves the NAD's perception of what Hertzog's government was trying to do. In Smit's eyes, the state was moving towards "the adoption of a policy of modified segregation and trusteeship, under which, while the native would be allowed to play his role in the development of and to obtain employment in the industries of the country, there would be residential and political separation between and parallel development of the two races."[55] In other words, Smit regarded these acts as providing for separate administration, coupled with distinct residential areas for Africans, and not as a scheme to guarantee cheap, coerced labor for various sectors of the economy.

The second point concerns the actual content of the bills. In most cases, it is hard to see how the new legislation could have assisted in solving the farm labor "problem." Lacey argued that the Native Taxation and Development Act of 1925 pushed Africans in rural areas into working for white farmers. Yet the act did away with the old farmer's certificate in the Transvaal, by which labor tenants were taxed at a lower rate

so long as they worked for a farmer for ninety days. Farmers complained bitterl
about the ending of this device.[56] Moreover, the whole question of desertions aros
partly because farmers did not give high enough wages to allow agricultural labore
to pay their taxes. The 1925 act did not drive rural-based Africans to work for farmer
it forced them to abandon their homes and look for work in the towns.

Likewise, the Urban Areas Amendment Act of 1930 and the Native Law
Amendment Act of 1937 would surely not have increased the municipalities' right
over the ingress and egress of location residents if its real aim had been to help farmer
keep their labor. Urban authorities felt no duty to help farmers — they used the new
laws to serve their own local requirements, as and when they saw fit.[57] Th
government thus raised the barriers between separate pools of mining, industrial an
agricultural labor; however, it continued to permit the flow of labor between th
different sectors in line with the changing needs of the South African economy.

The only other piece of legislation that might have had a significant impact on th
rural labor market was the 1936 Native Trust and Land Act. Here again, the act pulle
in different directions. Anti-sharecropping clauses established incremental fines fo
landowners with "unemployed" squatters. The act strengthened the state's long
running opposition to sharecropping, though in the short term it was no mor
effective in curtailing it than the 1913 act had been. The legislation also lengthened th
period of service for labor tenants in the Transvaal to six months (in that an employe
could be registered as a labor tenant only if he contracted for 180 days) and create
mechanisms for a more even distribution of labor tenants. These provisions wer
intended to prevent the supply being monopolized. Only the six-months' clause stoo
to benefit farmers generally; the others would merely have helped one group o
farmers over another. With the exception of a brief effort in the eastern Transvaa
district of Lydenburg, the relevant chapter of the act was not implemented until afte
World War II, partly because of the lack of unanimity among farmers.[58]

Clearly, there were good reasons why NAD officials were able to applaud
Hertzog's segregation laws, while remaining opposed to further coercive measure
against farm laborers. The very fact that the government felt the need for a Farm
Labour Committee in 1937, would suggest that it had not created a successfu
"coercive labour system" over the previous twelve years. On the contrary, the late
1930s saw the ascendancy of a less repressive, more constructive policy towards farm
workers, which had its roots within the Native Affairs bureaucracy.

Farm Labor After 1939

The dissension that existed between Justice, Agriculture and Native Affairs was les
marked from the late 1930s. During the war, there was even more incentive to pul
together on the farm labor question. The state came under increasing pressure from
white farmers to ensure an adequate labor supply. This pressure was brought into th
political arena by the many MPs who represented rural constituencies, some of whom
had personal experience of labor shortages.[59] The farmers' problems were exacerbated
by the rapid expansion of war-related economic activity, which further stimulated th
flow of labor away from the countryside. Although a fair proportion of this outflow
was temporary, successive government commissions recognized a growing perma
nent, urban, African constituency that had irrevocably cut ties with the rural areas.

According to O'Meara, the Van Eck Commission of 1941 set the pace for a policy favoring the labor requirements of secondary industry and mining, by encouraging Africans to leave their homes in the rural areas.[60] This policy was in keeping with the state's long-term aim of promoting more efficient farming based on mechanization and scientific methods, rather than on cheap labor. But the commission's recommendations were not intended to deprive farmers of the labor they needed under wartime conditions. On the contrary, the Van Eck Report assumed that the transfer of population would take place only after the reform of agriculture. There was a further assumption that most of the manpower absorbed by industry would come from the reserves, and not from white-owned farms.

At the interdepartmental level, officials made a more determined effort to ensure an adequate supply of farm labor. In 1942, the Food Controller instigated a committee comprising his own representative and representatives from the Native Affairs, Agriculture, Justice and Defence departments to report on ways of remedying the situation. The committee came up with three recommendations, all of which involved further action by the state. The first — the appointment of a Controller of Unskilled Labour to coordinate a "fairer" distribution of labor — was never taken up, largely because of the DNL's strenuous opposition to further coercive measures. The other two — the extension of schemes to send Italian prisoners of war to work in the fields and to prevent the indiscriminate enlistment of farmers — were accepted by the government.[61]

Although the NAD was in no way shielded from the pressure from white farmers, in most areas the department chose means other than brute force to improve the farm labor situation. This policy was the result of several factors: the belief that influx controls would not be effective; the clamor of industrial and mining employers for more labor; the realization that coercion would lead to unrest; the threat of opposition to repressive measures; and the feeling that restrictions without adequate official protection were morally indefensible. Part of the NAD's strategy involved crude propaganda to dissuade Africans from seeking higher wages away from the farms. More importantly, the NAD sought to improve matters by speaking to farmers' associations. The high point of this initiative came in 1944, when Piet van der Byl, Minister of Native Affairs from 1943 to 1948, met the Transvaal Agricultural Union (TAU) and the South African Agricultural Unions (SAAU) in quick succession.[62] At both meetings, Van der Byl, whose policies were heavily influenced by his liberally inclined SNA, D.L. Smit, pushed the line that the state could not intervene in one industry while there was a shortage of labor in all sectors.[63] He also repeated the argument that Africans had to be allowed to take up employment with the highest bidder. He and the SNA rejected, one by one, the more radical proposals of the local farmers' associations. The NAD could not clear surplus labor from the urban areas without providing alternative accommodation under the 1936 Trust and Land Act. The only surplus labor available in the towns was of the criminal type, which would be useless on the farms. Africans in urban areas already had to carry up to five passes at once, and the introduction of another identification document would be seen as retrogressive. And the department could not oblige farm laborers to work the whole year, because farmers were divided over whether or not they favored a purely cash wage system.

The sort of government intervention the Minister was prepared to applaud was that which was more welfare orientated. The Secretary for Social Welfare,

G.A.C. Kuschke, expressed his department's support, in a general way, for better housing and improved medical and school facilities. Smit emphasized that the NAD could make money available for farm schools for African children, in which the education would have an agricultural bias. The Minister proposed inspections of farms by NAD officers, if and when the local farmers' associations felt ready for them. In an internal memorandum, the SNA also supported sub-economic housing loans for farmers on the same basis as those granted to municipalities. All these points involved the extension of state assistance to the farming sector, but in a fashion more in keeping with the Herbst Report of 1939.

Following the 1944 meetings, the NAD faced increased pressure for greater intervention on behalf of white farmers. At the Minister of Native Affairs' request, the SAAU formed a Special Farm Labour Committee that subsequently met NAD officials for more intimate colloquies.[64] The committee made several recommendations, chief among which was the division of the African population into more rigid rural and urban groups. It also called for a harsher application of influx controls, government regulation of company farms, an end to the squatter system, standardized identification documents, farm labor apprenticeships, and the regulation of youths leaving the farms to find work elsewhere. The SAAU was clearly in favor of wage labor, but was unwilling to dispense with repressive controls over farm laborers and their families. The recommendations underlined the extent to which farmers believed existing controls under Masters and Servants laws, urban areas legislation and the Native Service Contract Act were not functioning.

The state's response to this pressure revealed its ambivalent attitude to white farmers. The NAD made a great show of tackling the committee's recommendations and keeping the SAAU informed about its progress.[65] Smit and Van der Byl were also attracted to the idea of varying Hertzog's segregation policy of 1936–37, by recognizing the African's right to live in the towns, while proletarianizing the core of labor on the farms as a permanent class of wage workers. With the Prime Minister's permission, Van der Byl outlined the scheme in the House of Assembly, and met with no opposition.[66] Yet, the government did not make any major interventions in farm labor, for both political and administrative reasons. Although the government was anxious to be seen helping farmers, Smuts was sensitive to divisions within the farming community. The SAAU committee members—G.J. Rossouw, T. Wassenaar, H.C. Steyn, J.H. Botha and D.T. du P. Viljoen—represented progressive farmers who organized their agricultural operations on sound business principles, and were committed to full-time wage labor. They were, as Smuts told Smit and Van der Byl "men like ourselves."[67] Meanwhile, there were still large numbers of smaller, less successful farmers who depended on labor tenants, and who would strongly oppose the abolition of squatting. Smuts was not prepared to arouse that opposition; instead he drafted a statement that the government would proceed "tentatively and provisionally" on the lines suggested. Van der Byl later proposed the long-term policy of dividing the population between rural and urban areas, and encouraging the employment of full-time agricultural labor.

For the senior NAD officers, Smit, C.P. Alport (DNL) and F. Rodseth (at that time Chief Native Commissioner for the Northern Areas, and later Under-Secretary), there were other problems with the SAAU's recommendations. Most importantly, squatting could not be abolished unless the Native Trust found land for those removed from the farms. Investigations showed that there were few surplus Africans in the urban reas who would be suitable for farm work. Officials also repeated their argument that ew identification documents would cause "great resentment" if applied only to fricans, as the SAAU envisaged.[68] As far as moving labor off company farms and nsuring a more equal distribution was concerned, the farmers should tackle these roblems by themselves, through their local associations. There was no point in the NAD inviting criticism from business interests by becoming involved.

Two schemes begun in the mid- to later 1940s did at least show that the overnment was, as Smit said, "anxious to help farmers." The first was the brainchild f one P. J. de Beer, a staff member at the Native Commissioner's office, Johannesurg. In 1947, he came up with a plan to offer petty pass law offenders work on white arms, instead of going to jail.[69] The DNL, by that time J. M. Brink, was not overly oncerned about the illegality of the venture. By 1950, the Department of Justice had lecided that persons, once arrested for pass offenses, had to stand trial. In practical erms, the venture was open to much abuse, and eventually De Beer was transferred to ther work. In the meantime, the Native Commissioner's office had provided a total of 722 laborers to farms in the eastern Transvaal by the end of 1948.[70]

The third NAD initiative was less appealing to farmers — the appointment of an nspector of Farm Labourers (IFL) under the DNL. This was in line with the NAD's raditional goal of improving living and working conditions, and so enticing Africans nto farm labor. The appointment arose out of the scandal that erupted in the Bethal listrict. In 1947, the Rev. Michael Scott exposed the appalling conditions under which Africans, many of them captured by labor recruiters as they crossed the border into South Africa, lived and worked in that area.[71] It was normal to work laborers in gangs rom before sunrise to sunset, to lock them up at night to prevent desertions to the nearby Rand, and to house them all together in ramshackle, flea-ridden compounds. As a further precaution, some farmers removed the new recruits' clothing and distributed sacking in its place. They provided only a minimum of food, beatings were common, and wages (as little as ten shillings a month) were retained until the end of a contract.[72]

The NAD had been aware of conditions in Bethal since at least the 1930s, but made no coherent attempt to change the situation until the outcry in 1947. Several farmers were taken to court.[73] Thereafter, J. J. Smit, IFL, produced report after report on conditions in the eastern Transvaal, describing what needed to be done on each farm to bring them up to a minimum standard. The NAD and the Public Health Department then tried to persuade the farmers to provide adequate housing, cooking facilities, sanitation, diet and clothing and to use proper contracts. Their efforts were partly frustrated by the lack of personnel (only one IFL was appointed) and by the intransigence of farmers, who often argued that their lease would soon be up, or that they could not afford the necessary improvements. The introduction of an IFL was clearly an irritant to the farmers, but it cannot have had much impact on the overall plight of farm laborers, given that he lacked the legal power to force changes. As F. Mears, D. L. Smit's successor, admitted in 1948, the NAD had a long way to go; in the absence of compulsion, it was near-impossible to persuade laborers to work on farms under contract.[74]

The State and the Migrant Labor Option

As we have seen, officials of the NAD showed a preference for stabilized wage labor on South African farms, and looked to progressive, well-capitalized farmers to lead the way. However, up and down the country, farmers were reluctant to accept the logic of the NAD's arguments. Far from shouldering the responsibilities of a permanent, full-time labor force, many farmers sought an answer to their labor shortages in temporary, migrant labor. On the highveld and lowveld of the eastern Transvaal, and the sugar plantations of Zululand, the bulk of this labor came from territories across the Limpopo River. The NAD termed these workers clandestine immigrants, to distinguish them from the "legal" migrants brought into the Union by the gold-mines' recruiters.

The overriding reason for hiring "clandestines" was their relative cheapness compared with locally available black labor. This, coupled with the fact that clandestine immigrants were, for a multiplicity of reasons, more readily exploitable than local labor, increased their potential value to white farmers.[75] There were other advantages too: the seasonal nature of agriculture made it undesirable to pay for full-time wage labor, while the combined vagaries of the market and the weather discouraged farmers from making long-term investments in their workers.

A strong preference for migrant labor emerged in areas where farming could be profitably conducted through a labor-intensive production process — such as the sugar plantations of Zululand, and the maize and potato farms of the Bethal district of the Transvaal.[76] In these areas, too, farmers were operating on a sufficiently large scale to make it worth their while to emulate the labor practices of the gold-mines. Certain farmers took the regimentation of working and living spaces to new levels of brutality. Moreover, migrant labor was especially attractive in districts such as Bethal because of the relatively high value of land; South African landowners were reluctant to squander fields on squatter or labor tenants when every acre could be converted into profit. The final factor that made migrant labor attractive was its accessibility. The steady stream of immigrants from the Rhodesias, Nyasaland and Mozambique was too great a temptation to resist for labor-hungry farmers in Zululand and the eastern Transvaal.

Drawing on research on Bethal, Helen Bradford argued that the representative of the capitalist state — in this case, officials of the NAD — willingly fell in with the farmers' predilections.[77] She went further, stating that the department deliberately favored the needs of big capitalists in the agriculture business, and that such favoritism successfully countered the labor shortages experienced by the big farmers, at least from the late 1930s. This situation, she argued, did not alter greatly until after 1948, when small-time, predominantly Afrikaner farmers became politically more significant.

A wider review of the evidence does not reveal the degree of commitment by the state to the supply of foreign migrant labor that Bradford suggested. Indeed, in this, as in other areas of farm labor policy, the state's response was characterized by hesitation, internal division and lack of coherence, rather than by single-minded clarity of purpose. As William Beinart has shown for Transkeian migrants to the Natal sugar fields, NAD and other officials disagreed over the extent to which they should service the needs of sugar planters, and over the possible benefits of regulating the sugar industry's labor process.[78] Recent research on the eastern Transvaal has revealed similar reluctance on the part of state officials to accept a cheap migrant labor onomy on the farms, and the repeated failure of such schemes as were developed.[79] ost importantly, this work showed that, as with migrants from Pondoland, the state ould not permit the recruitment of migrants for the farms to interfere with the pply of labor to the gold-mines. Farmers were restricted to supplies of youths, old ople and medical rejects who were deemed not strong enough to work under- ound.[80]

This is not to say that white farmers in the eastern Transvaal and Zululand did not crease their reliance on foreign migrant labor during this period, or to deny that the ate occasionally assisted in this trafficking. The Pact government's initial opposition foreign migrant labor gave way in the face of protests, and from 1925 to 1928, the AD was permitted to run a depot at Louis Trichardt for the distribution of andestine immigrants.[81] However, from the farmers' perspective, the depot was a peless failure, partly because of the high capitation fees it charged. Moreover, the mpulsory attestation of migrants, before NAD officials at Louis Trichardt and ietersburg, gave them a chance to escape from labor recruiters, and to acquire ermits for municipal service, road construction work and other employment in the wns.

In later years, the NAD did try to keep Africans out of the towns, but these efforts ere only sporadically effective. More useful for the farmers was the 1934 agreement etween the government of Portuguese East Africa and the Union to allow limited cruitment of clandestine Mozambican labor for farms in the Transvaal and luland.[82] Subsequently, in 1937–38, the NAD lifted the ban on recruiting by farmers the twenty-mile zone along the border, allowing groups of farmers to create their wn agencies to recruit migrants.[83]

Bradford recorded a fourfold increase in the numbers of foreign migrant farm borers in the Bethal district from 1937 to 1947.[84] For the most part, however, the state layed little part in regulating the flow. The poverty of the colonies to the north made inevitable that Africans would seek work, across the long, unguarded border, in the elatively wealthy and growing economy of South Africa. Migrants were naturally ttracted to the better wages and less difficult work on offer in the towns, and many ere bound to find temporary employment as they traveled through the rural areas. the process, thousands of migrants found themselves tricked or trapped by cruiters into long, arduous contracts at very low wages; their response, exercised peatedly throughout the period, was to desert the farms and seek more lucrative mployment elsewhere. The NAD's impact in this cycle was chiefly a negative one, in at it failed to intervene to protect foreign farm workers from exploitation.

The NAD's direct action in this area after 1937 was no more successful than it had een before that date. In 1942, the NAD failed to persuade the Portuguese Curator to llow medical rejects from the Zoekmekaar mines' recruiting depot to be deployed on he farms.[85] Three years later, the SNA contemplated, but ultimately declined, ntervention in the closure of the district of Eshowe to gold-mines' recruiting for the ake of improving the farm labor situation.[86] On a larger scale, Smuts's 1945 eactivation of depots for attesting and hiring out immigrants to farmers failed, as the epots could not compete with the more ruthless independent recruiters.[87] The scale nd nature of state interventions had not altered greatly since the late 1910s, while for he farmers the solution continued to lie in private recruiting by unscrupulous gents.

Overall, state policy toward migrant labor in this period might best l characterized as an *ad hoc* reaction to economic changes and to the varying successes (political lobby groups, including the TAU, the SAAU, and the Zululand planters. / A.H. Jeeves has argued, after 1937, the state possessed increased powers to contr Africans and segment the labor market, but it was reluctant to use these powers reinforce white agriculture's partial dependence on foreign migrant labor.[88] Tl NAD's preference for a system of wage labor, properly regulated by its own officer was surely at work here. Also significant were the physical limits of state power in th period of rapid change, for while the state could create barriers between differe sectors, the barriers themselves were becoming increasingly porous as enormou political and economic pressures pulled the edifice of a balanced "native" administr tion apart.

Conclusion

There are two extremes in the secondary literature on the regulation of farm labo First, Mike Morris argued as long ago as 1977 that the state favored mining an industrial interests over farmers, who duly shifted support to the National Party i 1948.[89] The second interpretation, put in different forms by Marian Lacey and Hele Bradford, is that the state did indeed provide for white farmers' labor needs (or at lea for those of big farmers), by assisting in the development of coercive, highl exploitative labor practices. Both arguments contain elements of the truth; the SAA was clearly dissatisfied with the lack of government intervention on its membe behalf, while the NAD made some efforts to help farmers in certain parts of tl country. However, the state's policies towards farm labor have to be analyse chronologically and in terms of divisions within the state. In this context, the idea (the state as a unit favoring one or other capitalist sector, is inadequate as a explanation of shifts in policy. At the same time, one has to weigh the extent of sta initiatives and the degree to which they were implemented, before judging tl government to have been firmly on the side of big agricultural capital.

The regulation of farm labor after 1939, no less than in previous years, was complex process. On the one hand, there was more or less constant pressure fror farmers for state assistance, with governments, especially after 1924, at least makin an appearance of attempting to alleviate the farm labor shortage. This politic, pressure was particularly important in the later 1920s and early 1930s, and agai during and after World War II. In the latter period, however, the Smuts governmei was much more cautious than had been Kemp and Pirow, whose hands-on approac to solving the farm labor shortage had provoked considerable opposition, withou really helping farmers.

In assessing state policies, one has to consider the debate on farm labor at tl administrative level. In the departments of Agriculture and Justice, the initiative cam both from the ministers and from the bureaucrats who advised them. They generall favored direct state intervention, usually of a repressive nature, and advocated extr duties for the NAD. In that department, the officials themselves were responsible fc devising an alternative policy, based on extending the system of regulations alread existing for mines and industry. They supported the complete proletarianization (farm labor, but realized this was impossible unless the Native Trust could provid land for surplus squatters.

The Herbst Committee Report of 1939 reflected the ascendancy of the NAD's policy, with both Agriculture and Justice allowing Native Affairs to take the lead in dealing with the farm labor "problem." In the 1940s, the war and political pressure from the farmers' lobby prevented any major changes in policy. Instead, the various departments were compelled to pool their resources to help farmers locate labor through various schemes. These initiatives did not go nearly as far as the SAAU wished in terms of coercing Africans. Smuts was cautious about any rapid or radical change in policy, partly because of divisions within the farming community; the NAD still felt that farmers themselves could do more to improve the situation, and were wary of African opposition and resentment. The department's position helped to limit the application of repressive controls in the countryside, even when legislation providing for such measures already existed. The period ended with the SAAU still pressing the government to assist in augmenting their labor supply.

3

Land, Legislation and Labor Tenants: Resistance in Lydenburg, 1938

Stefan Schirmer

In 1936 Chapter four of the Native Trust and Land Act represented the latest in a long series of efforts to regulate labor tenancy and to abolish cash-and-kind tenancies on white farms. It was part of the state's response to white farmers' demands for more control over labor tenants. During the United Party's period in power, the Chapter was applied only once, in the Transvaal district of Lydenburg during 1938 (figure 3.1). It was suspended early in the following year after widespread conflict broke out in the district. As an example of the United Party's failure to assist undercapitalized white farmers, the Lydenburg experiment has been described a number of times.[1] However, these accounts did not assess the role of the black resistance that was the central cause of the failure of Chapter four in Lydenburg. This paper focuses on that resistance and argues that the African reaction to Chapter four emerged out of a pre-existing process of struggle between African tenants and white farmers. It is true that the immediate outbreak of resistance in 1938 was precipitated by the activities of two white paternalists and sustained by a group of African landowners, but their activities cannot adequately explain its extent and level of determination. The conflict of 1938 should be seen as part of a continuous regional process. Throughout the 1930s, African families had been defending their independence against white farmers' growing labor demands. They did not have to be told that the 1936 legislation imposed a longer period of labor service and undermined their ability to negotiate terms of employment. The opposition to Chapter four, therefore, was part of a long-standing

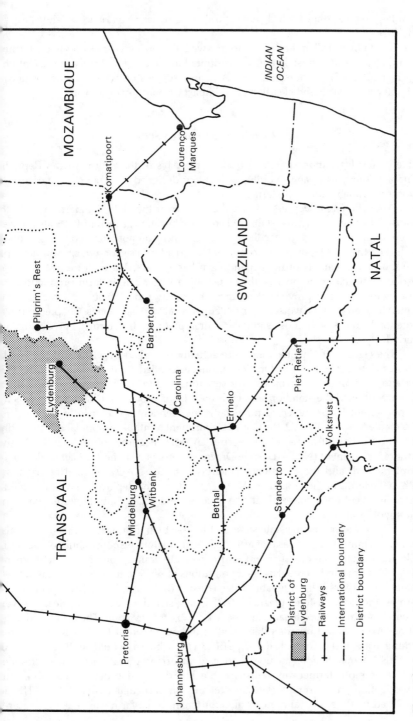

Figure 3.1 Lydenburg District and the Eastern Transvaal

family-based resistance, which was central to the African experience of white farms
the 1930s.[2]

The failure of Chapter four led to renewed tension between poorer white farme
and the state and almost certainly contributed to the election victory of the Nation
Party in 1948. Thus the small-scale African struggles on which the opposition
Chapter four was based clearly had an impact on South African history.

Chapter Four and the State

Like earlier legislation stretching back to the days of the South African Republi
Chapter four was a labor-mobilizing strategy designed to make more agricultur
workers available for white farmers.

After the Great Depression and the crisis over the Gold Standard in 1932, th
South African economy first stabilized and then began to grow rapidly. State policie
more than ever, tried to facilitate internal and autonomous economic growt
including the development of a commercial agricultural sector, which would supp
the food requirements of the expanding urban centers. Through the regulation
agricultural marketing boards, the state took a larger role in farm production an
pricing in order to improve farmers' income security and profitability. Other contro
aimed to overcome the worsening problem of rural labor shortages. Chapter four wa
potentially the state's most significant attempt to control farm labor during th
period.

The clauses of Chapter four were actually reworked provisions of the Nativ
Service Contract Act, enacted in 1932 but never applied. After the failure of the 193
act and a lull in farmer protests over squatting and tenancy arrangements, farme
again petitioned the state for help with their labor problems. Chapter four was th
response, but it also reflected politicians' independent acceptance of the need fc
direct intervention. In 1932, the Justice Department's enthusiasm for labor-mobilizin
action on behalf of farmers had overridden resistance from officials of the Nativ
Affairs Department (NAD). Despite Draconian provisions, the 1932 act could not b
implemented, and the experience gave point to the NAD's original reservation
While the terms of the 1936 Land Act suggested that the department now accepted
more interventionist approach, it also gave NAD officials control over the pace an
timing of its application.[3]

Chapter four was the state's attempt to assist labor-hungry farmers, but it als
contained important clauses that affirmed the regulatory responsibilities of the NAI
Like the 1932 legislation, Chapter four proposed to limit the number of labor tenan
on white farms and to regulate their conditions of service. It required magistrates t
maintain registers of labor tenants in each district (S.27.1) and levied a six pence fee o
farmers for each registered tenant (S.27.2). Unregistered Africans on white farms we
deemed not to be labor tenants and because subject to eviction. The act provided fc
labor tenant control boards established at the discretion of the Minister of Nativ
Affairs in any district outside the Cape (S.28.1). The boards would be chaired by NA
officials, but membership included two resident farmers on each of them. If petitione
by six or more farmers in a district, the boards could order a reduction, afte
investigation, in the number of labor tenants on particular farms (S.29.1). The a
provided that the normal number of labor tenants on a farm was five and require

cences for each tenant above this number. The act defined a standard period of
unpaid service to be provided by the tenants (S.30.1). The intention here was to
respond to the widespread belief among farmers that large numbers of Africans were
sheltering idly as labor tenants on some farms and could be made available to other
farmers needing labor. Under other provisions of Chapter four, even harsher
measures could be applied to restrict the number of black, rent-paying tenants
(squatters) on white farms. The act required white landowners to pay an annual tax for
each rent-paying tenant that would increase each year, until it reached £5 pounds per
head after ten years. Together these stipulations had the potential to cause widespread
evictions of labor tenants and squatters and to lead to mass migration and
disruption.

For these reasons, the act provided for the application of Chapter four by
proclamation in individual districts, so that the NAD could manage its implementation so as to minimize disruptive effects. The Minister told Parliament that steps to
control labor tenant numbers, and to eliminate squatting, would proceed "gradually"
and that the process would "take a long time."[4] Section 38 imposed on the government,
through the NAD, "the duty . . . to make such provision as may be necessary and
adequate in the opinion of the Minister for accommodating . . . any native displaced . . . by reason of the operation of the provisions of this Chapter . . ." In keeping
with the logic of segregation, this section ensured that the victims of Chapter four
would still have land on which to "develop." Officials worried, too, that without
alternative land arrangements, evicted tenants would end up in the cities, a concern
that was further addressed in amendments to the urban areas legislation embodied in
the Native Laws Amendment Act of 1937. Indeed, one of the motives for the 1936
legislation was that the intended further tightening of urban segregation required
it.[5]

Despite provision for gradual implementation at a pace determined by cautious
officials in the NAD, the Chapter was designed to bring about dramatic changes.
When the Land Act was debated in Parliament, the government agreed that
implementation of its most disruptive provisions would not occur until additional
land had been acquired by the South African Native Trust, modeled on the Natal
Native Trust and established in terms of the act. This undertaking reflected the NAD's
understanding that Africans displaced from white farms by the operation of Chapter
four could not be accommodated in the already-crowded existing reserves. While the
Prime Minister promised Parliament to provide £10 million for land purchase over the
following five years, nothing had been done by the time the outbreak of war
precipitated the fall of his government.[6]

Some farmers' representatives had already expressed their impatience during the
debate on the bill, and by 1938 delegates from Pietersburg, Louis Trichardt and
Lydenburg were demanding that the Chapter be immediately applied in their
districts. The NAD ruled out the first two districts because they housed thousands of
squatters who could not be accommodated in the surrounding reserves.[7] Lydenburg
had fewer squatters and applied "immense pressure" on the Department.[8] The
pressure came primarily from Elias de Souza, Lydenburg's vociferous Member of
Parliament, and other farmer representatives. During the debate on the bill, De Souza
had complained that the amount of new land to be acquired for Africans was
"unreasonably large." He was unhappy that white landowners in the Transvaal
would have to give up twice as much land as those in all the other provinces combined

and urged the Minister to proceed very slowly with land purchases. He had whi
bywoners in his district and wondered if the government proposed to treat them
generously as it planned to treat "natives"?

Farmers needed labor, De Souza insisted, and it was "foolish" to pay attention
"negrophilists." He expressed the opinion that ". . . even to-day there is too muc
land for the natives"; and objected to land purchases that would drive more whites o
the land to make room for blacks. De Souza thought that ten years was much too lor
to wait for effective action against squatting and urged immediate implementation
the 1932 act.[9] In 1938, he again demanded urgent action, notwithstanding th
obligation under Section 38 to provide alternative land. Although there were tw
rent-tenant farms in Lydenburg — with 264 squatters — and two African-owne
farms, they did not become an issue in 1938. The squatter tax was never implemente
and the African-owned farms were exempted from the Chapter.[10] Thus Chapter fou
as applied in Lydenburg, was directed to the transformation of labor tenancy. This, i
turn, has to be understood in the context of the district's economic development.

White Farming in Lydenburg

Lydenburg was not highly capitalized in 1938. In 1937 the manager of the cooperativ
had sold the first tractor, and by 1939 there were only 46 tractors in the district.[11] Ever
farmer offered labor tenant contracts.[12] Additional seasonal employees from Sekhul
huneland were rare, as was any form of cash wage or bonus. Farmers in the Waterfall
Steelpoort and Ohrigstad valleys irrigated some of their fields with canals and floo
methods (figure 3.2). On these irrigated fields they double cropped, planting maize i
summer and wheat in winter, while on the dry lands they grew only maize in summe
Farmers in the higher central parts of the district farmed with maize and wool shee
Many of the sheep farmers owned or hired additional farms in the eastern lowvel
parts for winter grazing. In the southern part of the district, towards the town c
Dullstroom, most farmers grew maize on dry-land plots.

Despite the "backwardness" of the district, production improved steadily afte
1933. Post-depression agricultural prices generated substantial increases in wheat an
wool production.[13] Maize also improved, though cattle remained "of an inferio
type."[14] The expansion was, however, uneven and it is probable that only a few of th
larger farmers experienced significant growth. One was R.J. Schurink who, on hi
death in 1942, was described by the *Lydenburg News* as the ideal farmer: "Through th
planting of trees, the building of dams, bridges, the erection of sheep kraals, sheds an
the application of mixed farming, he converted the original farm into a pleasure resor
of scientific farming."[15]

The majority of Lydenburg farmers experienced only small production increase
and some stagnated. In 1933, the Standard Bank Inspector condemned the farminj
practises of the majority: "It is to be regretted that [this area] is peopled with a mos
retrogressive type of farmer of poor ability, following primitive methods, and whos
business integrity generally leaves much to be desired."[16] In 1938 the picture ha
changed only slightly: "Little, if any, headway is being made by the farminj
community, which, incidentally, is heavily bonded . . . A few of the progressiv
farmers are now concentrating on improving their cattle herds."[17] The picture tha
emerges from this, and other, evidence is of a stratified community with a minority o

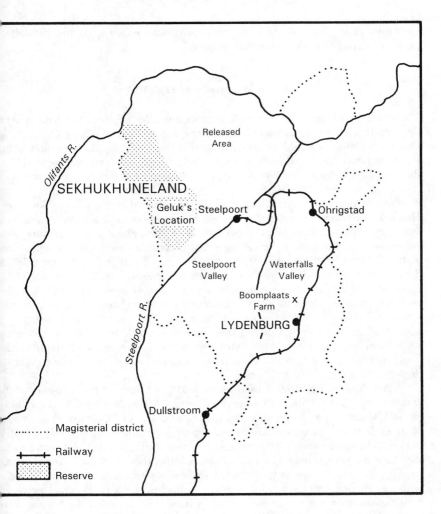

Figure 3.2 Lydenburg District

rge, progressive farmers at the top and a majority of small, struggling farmers
elow.

The conservatism of most of the farmers might have played a role in the absence
f development, but the shortage of capital was probably more important. Farming
nterprises were risky ventures subject to economic fluctuations and the vagaries of
ature. As a result farmers hesitated to reinvest their small surpluses. Many of the
progressive" farmers who did invest had access to other sources of capital. They were
overnment officials, teachers, lawyers, mill owners, cooperative managers or

store owners and could afford to be progressive because they could always fall bac
on their salaries and other sources of income.[18]

Labor in Lydenburg, 1930–1937

The evidence collected by the Native Economic Commission (NEC) of 1930–3
suggests that labor tenancy was particularly exploitative in Lydenburg. One witnes
Onasimus Phokanoka, told the commission that "the 1908 law said three months b
today the whole family works from January to January."[19] He was referring to a law o
the Transvaal Colony, a revision of the South African Republic's original rural labo
regulating measure, the *Plekkers' Wet*, which was the source of the idea that th
number of labor tenants on each farm should be restricted to five. Elias de Souza an
Hendrik Neethling, two successful farmers and leaders of local farmers' unions, sai
that they expected their labor tenants to work throughout the year. Interview
conducted by the author, however, indicate considerable variation within th
district.[20] Many labor tenants worked their own fields within the time regarded a
devoted to "labour on the farms" and met their cash needs by selling crops to the loca
cooperative. The practice of hiring labor tenants for three months in a year was als
widespread.[21] Elsewhere, absentee landowners still offered conditions that allowe
Africans considerable discretion (mostly three months' labor and very little superv
sion). Sheep farmers only expected labor tenants to work during the season whe
sheep were moved to one of the two farms. Some farmers owned "labour farms
populated entirely by Africans. These tenants usually worked their three months o
the white farmer's residential farm.[22]

Many Lydenburg farmers tried to demand labor from all the members of th
tenant family. In 1932, the Native Service Contract Act made it legal for a farmer t
bind children (male or female) over the age of ten to labor tenant contract
Meanwhile, more and more children were deserting the farms. As De Souza explaine
in 1932: "The young workers go away and they never come back. Five left my farm an
they have not yet returned. We do not know whether they are dead."[23] The evidenc
from Lydenburg to the NEC contained expressions of similar concerns. Africa
witnesses thought that the youths were leaving because white farmers had increase
their demands on tenant families. White witnesses claimed that the youths wer
attracted by the bright lights of the city.[24] De Souza proposed to solve the problem b
placing the youngsters in strictly supervised employment. By 1937, more youths tha
ever were leaving.[25] In response, farmers turned increasingly to women's labo
though this was still limited in 1938.[26] One report stated that women's labor was onl
used during the busiest times.[27] Interviews reveal that in the 1930s most Africa
women on the farm were still domestic workers.[28]

In the late 1930s, Lydenburg farmers once again complained of a shortage c
labor. Expanded production intensified the demand for labor even as escalatin
migration depleted the supply. Farmers who raised the workload of labor tenar
families only added impetus to the exodus from the farms.[29] A rise in the number o
farms also boosted demand. In 1929, the Agricultural Census reported 651 farmers i
the district. This figure had grown to 742 by 1935 and to 765 in 1936.[30] Apart from th
fact that more farmers were demanding labor, many of them had less land to offer, a
development that further reduced the attractiveness of labor tenancy for Africa
families.

The shortage of labor in Lydenburg affected all the white farmers, whether they ere expanding production or not. The bargaining position of labor tenants nproved. Many moved to the larger farmers, who offered more land.[31] Furthermore, rmers with available capital often paid the taxes of their tenants.[32] Poorer farmers st their labor, while richer farmers were forced to offer improved conditions to :tract it.

The farmers of Lydenburg asked for Chapter four to be implemented because ley thought it would help to solve the problem of labor shortages. Many hoped that a bor tenant control board would regulate laborers and farmers alike. As J.J. Smit put , "Farmers . . . steal labour from each other because they need the labour and do verything they can to get their hands on it."[33] Most farmers realized that a labor nant's ability to oppose unacceptable conditions by moving between farms was cilitated by farmers who overlooked the pass laws in order to get sufficient labor. urthermore, a number of farmers kept labor in excess of their needs.[34] The farmers emanding Chapter four hoped that, with state help, they could bring about a more ntrolled system in which labor would be evenly distributed and the ability of fricans to resist their demands would be seriously undermined.[35] Standardized ngths for contracts would ensure that labor tenants would not gravitate towards rms offering shorter periods.[36]

The farmers of Lydenburg also supported Chapter four because they believed lat all labor tenant contracts would in future have to be six months long (instead of le previous three months) in order to be legal. They had, however, misread the new w that required a minimum four-month labor period. The guidelines to the labor nant control boards assumed an average six-month labor period, and the farmers ad mistakenly thought that these guidelines applied to all legal labor tenant ontracts. Farmers also overestimated the powers of the board.[37] Many were under the npression that the local board could supply them directly with labor tenants. In fact le board was only supposed to ensure that farmers did not keep excessive numbers f labor tenants on their farms.[38]

De Souza and the Lydenburg North Farmers' Union felt strongly about an bligatory six-month period. When they found out the truth, they demanded that the JAD withdraw Chapter four unless the labor period was changed. Other farmers elieved that Africans would not submit to the longer contracts and opposed a linimum six-month period.[39] They were unable to make themselves heard above)e Souza's representations, and in early 1938 the NAD decided to change the required eriod to 180 days.[40]

Opposition to Chapter Four

loth the state and numerous white farmers were concerned about an African reaction o Chapter four. Farmers feared "serious disturbances" and worried that Chapter four vould drive labor tenants out of Lydenburg.[41] Most farmers were none the less opeful that Africans would be too attached to the district to move to other areas.[42] lelieving that large numbers of surplus labor tenants were harbored on some farms in he district, advocates of tighter regulation assured the NAD that "not many labourers vould be displaced by the Chapter."[43]

Contrary to these expectations, however, the proclamation of Chapter four produced determined African opposition that threatened both white farmers and tl state.[44] In Lydenburg, nearly all the labor tenants refused to be registered under tl Chapter. They thus risked becoming "illegal residents" on the white farms ar suffering automatic eviction under the new law. Many labor tenants did not wait f(their eviction notices and instead looked for land outside Lydenburg. In the year th Chapter four was proclaimed, the Native Commissioner (NC) reported that 2; Africans had left the district to find residences elsewhere. Others — some ten twelve per day — applied for land from the government.[45] The NC also estimated th nearly a hundred people had left the district without acquiring passes from him. F managed to monitor the exact movements of many of the families — eleven moved (farming districts similar to Lydenburg; nearly a hundred moved to areas containir mainly company farms and reserves, including Pilgrim's Rest, Pokwani and Sekhu huneland; three moved to Johannesburg and one to Pretoria.[46]

Despite the pass laws, it was relatively easy for the people who fled Lydenburg (find white landlords who would accommodate them. There were many farmei prepared to accept Africans without proper documentation, and the NAD found virtually impossible to track them down. The persistence of rent tenancy in distric like Pilgrim's Rest also proved attractive to migrating tenants. Although NCs i neighboring districts frequently referred to over-crowding in the reserves in the 1930 the pressure was not nearly as severe as it later became. Evidently, there was still roor for displaced tenants fleeing from Lydenburg.

Labor tenants saw Chapter four as an attempt to restrict their freedom an independence. In the opinion of Samson Mnisi, an African who lived on a farm i Lydenburg at the time, people left the district because "they want places where the are free."[47] Many said that Chapter four was tantamount to slavery, an idea whic originated from the provision that all labor tenants had to register at the NC's offic(Tenants believed that registration would force them to work from sunrise to sunsc and forever bind them to the farmer who paid the registration fee. Some even claime(that farmers were actually buying their labor tenants for the six pence registration fe(Rumors also circulated that the cattle of labor tenants would become the property c white farmers.

African residents of Lydenburg had long memories. After the South African Wai the Milner administration had disarmed Africans, confiscated cattle and activel supported reoccupation of abandoned land by Boers.[48] Africans experienced thi process as a direct form of land alienation. For example, Micha Dinkwanyane, wh(remained in Lydenburg and played a role in the resistance of 1938, had to abandon hi claim to the entire Waterfalls Valley of Lydenburg, which he had occupied during th war. He and his followers were forced to take up rent tenancy on the Berlin Missio Society farm outside the town. Chapter four, coming on top of pass laws restrictin; freedom of movement, rekindled memories of earlier state depredations. The direc involvement of the NC in the registration process only enhanced this impression.

In Lydenburg local opposition to Chapter four focused on registration and th six-month period. In the words of Sekwatane Mosehla, "the six month thing was a ba(thing and I think it was a good decision to leave that farm because we didn't lik(that."[49] Similarly Sekwati Hlatswayo, a labor tenant on the farm of Elias de Souza' elder brother, Louis, explained, "the only thing we disagreed with was de Souza's son he introduced some laws that they said we should work for six months — it used to b(for three months — and that angered us and we said we can't work for that si;

months."[50] Sekwati Hlatswayo had in fact been expected to work throughout the year on Louis de Souza's farm. He nevertheless opposed any change to the minimum required by law.

This attitude puzzled a number of the people involved in the events of 1938. The NC for Lydenburg, W.B. Biddulph, reported that "in many cases natives who tendered seven to nine months labour refuse to be bound for 180 days per annum and object to registration."[51] Biddulph concluded that "the natives are organized to oppose the application. Their organization is powerful as they accept from their leaders that the application is strongly against their interests . . . They do not question [their leaders] in any way."[52] The Chief Native Commissioner was less sure but noted that "the unanimity of [the opposition] is remarkable and makes one wonder whether this opposition is not to some extent organized."[53] Farmers needed no convincing that "communist agitators" were responsible.[54]

Despite earlier and subsequent involvement in the area, none of the major black political movements of the time — including the Communist Party, the ANC, the Industrial and Commercial Workers' Union and the Transvaal African Congress — linked up to this particular grassroots struggle.[55] The ANC received a direct request to "look into the trouble in Lydenburg" but merely gave the feeble assurance that it would "review the Land Act" at a later stage.[56] Communist Party members were certainly aware of the implications of Chapter four, but their calls for action were directed at the central state and came too late to affect the situation in Lydenburg.[57] Sympathetic whites, by contrast, including the Native Commissioner of Lydenburg, did play a role in organizing the resistance to Chapter four.

Organization and Resistance

W.B. Biddulph, Magistrate and NC Lydenburg, was influenced by the NAD tradition of paternalist and personalized administration, so strongly advocated by the recently retired Major D.R. Hunt, NC of the neighboring Sekhukhuneland district.[58] Biddulph dealt with the emerging trouble around Chapter four by holding personal meetings with the disgruntled labor tenants. He hoped to clarify the NAD's position and dispel the rumors about the effects of the Chapter. All that Biddulph succeeded in doing was to provide the widely dispersed labor tenants with a forum where they could come together to declare their opposition and solidarity. Biddulph held meetings with about twelve hundred labor tenants and came across unanimous and deeply felt opposition: The natives were infuriated and showed and expressed their anger very loudly."[59]

White farmers claimed that Biddulph's methods were contributing to the resistance movement. Chris Bauling, a local missionary and farmer, thought that "the Native Commissioner was quite wrong in holding meetings and making . . . explanations."[60] Another farmer called for a return to earlier conditions, when NCs were local farmers rather than professional bureaucrats. "A local man," he claimed, "would know how to handle the natives properly."[61]

Although sensitive to the problems confronted by the labor tenants, the NC was ultimately more sympathetic to the interests of the whites.[62] NAD officials were fully accepted as part of the white community of Lydenburg.[63] Biddulph sat on the governing body of the white high school and the board of the white hospital.[64] He and his wife would leave many white friends behind when they departed from

Lydenburg in 1939.[65] Biddulph attempted to stem the flow of laborers out of th
district by trying to persuade Africans who came to his office to accept the new labc
conditions and by refusing to give Africans passes that would enable them to leav
legally.[66] As Africans became aware of his divided loyalties, he was soon shut out an
regarded as a dangerous enemy.[67]

In contrast to the NC, Senator J.D. Rheinallt Jones, head of the South Africa
Institute of Race Relations, was able to establish a longer-lasting alliance with th
African residents of Lydenburg. He had first established links with the district in 193;
when he was elected the "native representative" for the Transvaal and Orange Fre
State under the Representation of Natives Act (Act 12 of 1936). The election campaig
had produced an electoral committee in Lydenburg and its members naturally turne
to their representative for help in 1938. Rheinallt Jones responded by holding meeting
in Lydenburg with those opposed to Chapter four. He also began to petition the stat
on behalf of the labor tenants.

Rheinallt Jones's decision to join the fight against Chapter four was not mad
merely to keep the support of his constituents. He was deeply opposed to the Chapte
himself, seeing it as an attempt by the state to prop up labor tenancy, which he an
other liberals regarded as a form of slavery imposed by Afrikaner farmers on haples
African victims.[68] They wanted labor tenancy replaced by wage labor. This solutio
was unacceptable to labor tenants, however, because it thwarted their most importar
aspiration: access to land and cattle.[69] At this time, Rheinallt Jones supported th
general thrust of segregation and saw the 1936 Land Act as a broadly positive step.
He was opposed only to Chapter four and advised labor tenants to contest it usin
non-violent means. Rheinallt Jones saw tenant protest in Lydenburg as a tool to forc
NAD officials to reconsider Chapter four. He believed, with good reason, that man
NAD officials also opposed Chapter four[71] and thought that the NAD would have t
repeal it when faced with labor tenants' mass refusal to cooperate.

The problems faced by the NAD were compounded by Section 38, which oblige
the department, subject to the discretion of the Minister of Native Affairs, to find lan
for any person displaced by Chapter four. The NAD tried to interpret the sectio
narrowly in a way that would exclude the labor tenants of Lydenburg from i
provisions, and the NC tried to persuade labor tenants that as land was not availabl
they could not expect to be accommodated. Rheinallt Jones challenged the NAD'
interpretation and informed the labor tenants of the NAD's obligation to provide fc
them elsewhere.

Rheinallt Jones thus played the role of intermediary between the world of th
largely illiterate labor tenants and the domain of white officials and their legislation. I
1930, labor tenants had complained that "our trouble with the white man is that we d
not know their rules."[72] They realized that white farmers' knowledge of the law
enabled them to interpret and enforce these laws in any way they liked, while Africar
remained ignorant of their limited rights.[73] Labor tenants asked for a "white man" t
explain the laws as they were passed. Rheinallt Jones was this white man. Although h
tried to limit the opposition that broke out in 1938, his badgering of the NAD and hi
emphasis on the state's obligations imposed by Section 38 made an importar
contribution to the eventual repeal of Chapter four.

Members of the electoral committee, established in Lydenburg in 1937, automa
tically became intermediaries between the labor tenants and Rheinallt Jones. One c
the members of this committee was a labor tenant called Samson Mnisi. He went fror

rm to farm, trying to persuade the white farmers to agree to the old minimum period
f ninety days. Some farmers acceded to this request but others were convinced that
Mnisi was an agitator and threatened to take action against him if he continued to
cause trouble.[74] Reacting to these threats in a letter to Rheinallt Jones, Mnisi explained
hat it was a spontaneous mood of dissatisfaction rather than any extensive
rganizational activity that was causing the widespread defiance.[75]

The most active member of the committee was Nathan Modipa. He belonged to a
family that had been instrumental in 1906 in buying the Boomplaats farm, just outside
the town of Lydenburg. Modipa was not a labor tenant, nor was he directly affected by
chapter four because Boomplaats was excluded from the 1938 proclamation.
Nevertheless, he articulated tenant grievances that year just as he had done to the
Native Farm Labour Committee in 1937. Modipa and James Morena drew up a list of
demands in 1938 for better treatment and higher wages for Africans on white farms.
They also requested free education, the abolition of pass laws and a change in poll tax
regulations.

Modipa's concern with the plight of labor tenants reflects the numerous links that
the landowners on Boomplaats had with other Africans in Lydenburg. A number of
the people who owned and farmed land there would undertake temporary work on
the surrounding white farms in order to earn extra money.[76] They were thus directly
concerned with the conditions obtaining on these farms. Furthermore, many of the
original buyers had been labor tenants before they acquired Boomplaats, and since at
least the early 1920s numerous labor tenants had left the white farms and moved to
Boomplaats. The latter group paid rent to Chief Dinkwanyane, which meant that
dissatisfied labor tenants were a potential source of income for the Chief. In 1938 the
residents of Boomplaats offered pieces of land at a price of £2 10s. per annum to a
number of protesting labor tenants and thus brought Boomplaats even closer to the
conflict on the white farms.[77] However, the most important factor that caused African
landowners to align themselves with labor tenants was their long-standing conflict
with white farmers who objected to African landownership in the district. The
Boomplaats residents saw the Land Act of 1936 as a renewed threat to their land
rights.[78] When Elias de Souza called on the state to remove the African-owned farms in
Lydenburg in 1938, his demand only strengthened the perception that labor tenants
and African landowners were fighting a common enemy.

In October the NAD tried to defuse the situation in Lydenburg by offering a
compromise. The department suggested that the six-month period be cut back to four
months. At meetings with Rheinallt Jones to discuss this proposal, Africans in
Lydenburg unanimously rejected the compromise. They were not prepared to settle
for any obligatory labor period in excess of three months. At about the same time the
committee on Boomplaats embarked on its most ambitious organizational activity.
Aware that the NAD was obliged to provide land to all the unregistered labor tenants,
the committee members took the initiative. A meeting was held on Boomplaats at
which a return to the three-month labor period was demanded. If this demand was
not met, the labor tenants would move *en masse* off the farms onto the Trust Land to
which they were entitled. The committee also insisted that the NAD provide loans to
assist people participating in this voluntary resettlement scheme. Realizing the
impossibility of meeting these demands, the NAD approached the white farmers of
Lydenburg with a view to ending the conflict caused by Chapter four.[79]

White farmers had largely adopted a wait-and-see attitude to the labor tenant agitation. By mid-1938 some farmers had apparently become dissatisfied with th effects of applying the Chapter, while others felt "that it is too early to express a opinion" and were "under the impression that the native will gradually accept th position."[80] The Lydenburg North Farmers' Union requested a postponement of th registration deadline, explaining that its members needed about five or six months persuade the labor tenants that the effects of Chapter four were not as bad as the leaders were claiming. The registration deadline was postponed, but by October th refusal to comply with Chapter four was as determined as ever.[81]

Explaining Unorganized Resistance

The organizational activities carried out, and stimulated by, the NC and Rheinal Jones were not sufficient to explain the determined opposition of Lydenburg Africans. In order to fully understand this resistance, it is necessary to locate it with the historical struggle between individual white farmers and labor tenant familie Labor tenants felt that they needed time in order to tend their own fields. Some als wanted nine months during which they might be free to migrate to earn extra mone As Samson Mnisi explained, "Three months is preferable because it gives one mo time to work for oneself."[82] Nathan Modipa gave more details:

> There is no one to keep the hut in order because everybody works, sometimes the man works from January to January. Thus they can not plough the land properly. Some kaffers [sic] must sell the food that they get to pay their tax because they do not get enough time to earn money for this purpose.[83]

Labor tenants who already worked longer than three months had good reason oppose the institutionalization of the six-month period.

The six-month provision threatened to destroy the chance of getting a thre month contract in the future and also undermined the tenant's bargaining positio Under the three-month contract, farmers were only able to acquire year-round lab by establishing themselves as reasonable and flexible employers, allowing a larg number of families onto their farms and paying the taxes of their employees. Th establishment of uniform conditions would mean that farmers would no longer hav to make such concessions.

The concern with free time was linked to the conflict between white farmers an tenants over the control of family labor. The head of a tenant family could keep himse entirely free of obligations to a white farmer if he could control the labor of h grown-up sons. However, many of the families on the farms, according to people th author interviewed, consisted of a husband, usually one wife and their dependen unmarried children. In these cases the head worked for the farmer and relied on h family to maintain the household, the agricultural plots and the cattle. But this practic was increasingly being threatened by the labor demands made by farmers. Desertio from the farms was a solution for the youths, but only exacerbated the problems of th head of the family. Thus the representatives of the labor tenants in Lydenbur complained about children being forced to do farm work.[84]

Although Chapter four was silent on the obligations of women and children, any farmers used the proclamation as a basis to demand labor from the whole mily.[85] They were inspired to take the initiative by the mere fact that state legislation ad been passed to back up certain of their demands on labor tenants. One example as the case of a white farmer named Jacobsz. He was a particularly poor farmer who nployed only one labor tenant family. After the proclamation of the Chapter he agerly went to register the tenant, without obtaining the latter's permission. He then sed the registration to demand labor from the tenant's wife who objected and was ssaulted by Jacobsz's wife. The family refused to submit and asserted that the registration was invalid because it had been undertaken without their consent. They ecided to move from the farm, leaving Jacobsz and his wife to tend it themselves.[86]

Hosia Phala spoke with pride about his own father's independence from "the p-called whites":

> [Our parents] can carry out everything themselves, they can manage themselves . . . [My father] would only go [to work for a contract] when it is necessary when he feels that he can maybe buy something that he needs . . . Three months is enough, or maybe six months. He would come home and do his own ploughing with us, his children.[87]

abor tenants were motivated by ideas like these to fight for the right to some adependence and self-sufficiency within their contracts with white farmers. The titude they desired was, however, being threatened and gradually undermined on any farms in Lydenburg. The conflict that resulted was usually scattered across dividual farms.

Chapter four crystallized opposition to a process of increased demands on labor at had gradually emerged. The six-month labor period was to be permanently tablished and the state would, by means of the registrations, monitor and enforce the new uniform labor system. Africans in Lydenburg found themselves with a pmmon grievance that was easy to identify. They responded with a determination ot to accept this change in their status, even if it meant leaving the area where many, ke their parents before them, had lived all their lives. In the words of Rheinallt Jones, the labor tenants responded to state legislation in 1938 with "a resounding No!"[88]

The opposition to Chapter four was mainly led by the male heads of families. The position of women was more ambiguous. Women were unlikely to defend, with the ame amount of enthusiasm, a system that to a large extent depended on their abservience and labor. Nevertheless, as is illustrated by the case of the wife of the abor tenant on Jacobsz's farm, women were also opposed to farmers' demands for neir labor. Interviews conducted with a number of women who lived on the farms in ydenburg reveal that their strongest objections were to the farmers' interference in neir lives. For example, Emily Mkhonto explained that she was opposed to white armers' control because it did not give her enough free time and interfered in the elationship that she had with her children.[89] In the context of a conflict that took place argely along racial lines, many women supported their husbands' determination to eep the family away from white control. Lydenburg's tenants had long defended free me and were hostile to any move to extract extended periods of work from the whole enant family.[90]

The Withdrawal of Chapter Four

A number of farmers gave in to the resistance fairly early and reduced the period compulsory service on their farms.[91] However, leaders such as De Souza were n ready to give up their attempt to convert labor tenancy into a more controlled ar exploitative relationship. The NAD's proposal either to withdraw the proclamation Lydenburg or to reduce the compulsory labor period to four months was rejected. Th farmers' representatives explained that both suggestions meant admitting defe which would create "an impossible situation between the farmers and the natives.'

Soon after, the continuing exodus of Africans out of Lydenburg prompted a ma meeting of white farmers.[93] They tried to salvage the situation by demanding th Chapter four be proclaimed throughout the Transvaal. The NAD refused to consid this option. Eventually the meeting decided that, "in order to give the natives time adjust themselves," farmers would ask the Department of Justice not to prosecu offenders for several months.[94]

In fact, the provisions of the Chapter remained unenforced until early 1940 whe the proclamation was finally withdrawn. The state temporarily retreated from th experiment in direct involvement in the "white rural areas." The organization that ha coalesced around Chapter four faded away, but the conflict between individual labc tenants and white farmers continued. While the labor tenant system persisted as a uneasy compromise, white farmers still had the upper hand and the terms (occupancy became increasingly disadvantageous for tenants.[95] Nevertheless, b defeating Chapter four the labor tenants of Lydenburg had ensured, at least for while, that their aspirations and demands would continue to influence the shape (farm labor relations in Lydenburg.

Conclusion

The resistance to Chapter four in Lydenburg was an important moment in continuum of low-level conflict between white farmers and black tenants. Lyder burg's Africans achieved a local victory in 1938, and their success had importar consequences for the rest of South Africa. Despite endorsement of Chapter four, th NAD had remained ambivalent about assisting undercapitalized farmers who coul not compete for labor in the market. After the failure of the effort to proclaim it i Lydenburg, the department's hesitancy hardened into a refusal to make further use c Chapter four on behalf of farmers. Until the 1950s, all later demands for the Chapte were rejected with reference to the "disaster" in Lydenburg.

The failure of labor control in Lydenburg also had political ramifications. probably reinforced the trend toward far-right political options in the district. Apar from the formation of a local fascist movement called the Suid Afrikaanse Volksbe weging, and growing support for the Ossewabrandwag, the Lydenburg Member c Parliament, Nic Schoeman, and Elias de Souza, joined the Nuwe Orde of Oswal Pirow.[96] As members of this movement, they advocated regional development policie that would have necessitated massive state intervention. The local appeal of fascism i the 1930s and early 1940s played a central role in the eventual victory of the Nationa Party in Lydenburg in 1948.[97] Resistance in Lydenburg allowed labor tenants t maintain the *status quo*, and to keep the conflict on the farms away from the direc attention of the state. In the long run, however, it had the unintended consequence c encouraging the swing by white farmers to the National Party in 1948.

4

Wage Workers and Labor Tenants in Barberton, 1920–1950

Charles Mather

the mid-1940s the South African Institute of Race Relations published an important emorandum on farm labor in the Transvaal, prepared by Edith Rheinallt Jones.[1] The aper was based on extensive fieldwork and revealed a striking variety of labor onditions on white farms in the province.[2] To bring some order to this great diversity, heinallt Jones divided farm workers into two broad categories — labor tenants and age laborers. While conditions varied significantly within each group, labor tenants ere usually obliged to provide the landowner with the unpaid labor of one or more embers of the household for a period that ranged from 90 to 180 days. In return, the ousehold was permitted to use land for maize and other crops and run cattle on the rm. Cash workers, in contrast, were paid for their labor. "Family privileges," cluding arable and grazing land, were generally restricted or absent. While some orkers were resident and also paid in cash, most wage laborers migrated from the eserves or neighboring countries. Of the two systems, Rheinallt Jones concluded that bor tenancy was dominant in the 1920s and 1930s: "The basis of farm labour roughout the Transvaal is the labour tenant system."[3]

Recent research has confirmed not only that labor tenancy was the most pervasive ocial relation on the land in the Transvaal during the 1920s and 1930s, but also that it as the "terrain over which agrarian class conflict was fought."[4] For white farmers ith little or no cash, the unpaid labor of African tenants was a crucial resource.[5] lembers of the household could be forced into the fields when farmers were enerally unable to attract or pay for non-resident labor. Under the constant threat of viction, African men, women and children had no choice but to work in the fields, specially during the planting and harvesting seasons.

Although unpaid labor was the norm in the Transvaal, with rising land prices ar
more generalized agricultural prosperity from the 1920s, a numerically small b
important sector of white agriculture was turning to wage labor. These landowne
viewed labor tenancy as anachronistic; it tied labor on the farms and exacerbated lab
shortages in agriculture.[6] Moreover, since labor tenants were given access
increasingly expensive arable and grazing land, it was also an extremely uneconı
mical way of farming.[7] These highly capitalized farmers pressed for the abolition
labor tenancy to alleviate labor shortages and urged the state to proclaim legislatiı
that would redistribute labor in the countryside. Many of these landlords wh
"preferred" to pay wages were large "cheque book" farmers and "progressivı
agriculturalists.[8] Labor tenancy was also being eroded from below as househol
heads found that they could no longer bind their children's labor to the whi
farmer.

The emergence of wage labor on white-owned farms during the 1920s wa
restricted to several distinct regions in the Transvaal. The most notorious of these wa
undoubtedly the area around Bethal, where workers were locked in compound
forced to labor twelve or more hours a day, and constantly harassed and brutalized b
repressive *baasboys*. Many of these farmers introduced the ticket system, which was ı
vogue on the mines, to remunerate farm workers. Indeed, conditions on the Bethe
farms were modeled on those on the mines.[9] Wage labor, compounds and recruitin
systems also emerged in the eastern Transvaal lowveld during the 1920s.[10] Thus whe
Africans on white-owned land in the northern Transvaal were struggling over th
length of periods of unpaid labor and access to livestock and arable land, farm worker
in the eastern Transvaal lowveld were demanding overtime pay and higher piec
rates.[11]

There is a tendency in the literature to juxtapose labor tenancy and wage labor
In examining the eastern Transvaal highveld, for example, Robert Morrell noted tha
"intensive, large scale Bethal farmers' desire for full time wage labour diverged fror
the needs of medium to small scale farmers for labour tenants."[12] In other words
farmers who relied on labor tenants were smaller and "backward," while highl
capitalized and "progressive" farmers pressed for wage labor. However, evidenc
from the Barberton district of the Transvaal lowveld suggests that unfree labor wa
not the sole preserve of "backward" and undercapitalized farmers and confirms tha
the move to wage labor was geographically and temporally uneven even within on
district.[13] In practice, white landowners relied on a wide variety of forms of labor
regardless of their stated preferences; small and uncertain markets, periodi
droughts and constant debt ensured that even large landowners were not averse tı
using the unpaid labor of African tenants. African resistance also played a role in th
persistence of labor tenancy in some regions. Tenancy allowed African household
to retain access to arable and grazing land, and in exchange many submitted to thı
white farmers' demands for unpaid labor.[14] Faced with severe labor shortages
farmers who "preferred" to pay wages were compelled to retain some labor tenant:
and permit access to arable and grazing land. In the Barberton district there were ı
multiplicity of labor forms at any one time, or on any one farm through time. Unpaiı
labor, labor tenancy, compounds and the ticket system were not always mutuall
exclusive.[15]

This chapter is about the emergence of wage labor in the Barberton district (figurı
4.1). The first section explores the conditions leading to wage labor on white

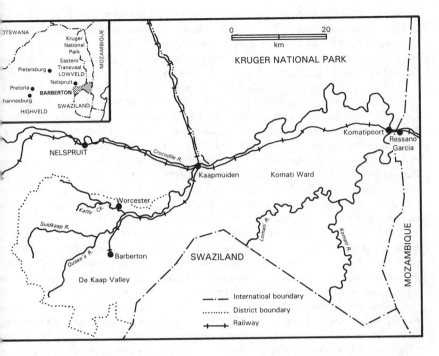

igure 4.1 Barberton District

wned land as well as the reasons for the continued persistence of unfree forms of ibor. Evidence from this region suggests that the contract arrived at between white irmers and African tenants cannot be deduced from the "backwardness" or progressiveness" of white farmers. The second section of the chapter refines the icture of wage labor and life on the district's farms through oral testimonies.

Wage Labor and Labor Tenancy, 1920–1950

\s early as 1914 the Sub-Native Commissioner in Barberton reported that while most irmers demanded at least three months' free labor, there were several "successful irmers" in the district who paid wages. Nevertheless, even these successful farmers ·nly provided a salary after three months' unpaid work.[16] By the late 1920s, conditions n many white farms had been transformed. The cultivation of labor-intensive crops uch as cotton, citrus and tobacco from the early 1920s had wrought significant hanges in the physical and social landscape, especially along the fertile river valleys n the region. On these farms, African tenants were not labor tenants in the "true ·ense." The Barberton magistrate described them instead as ". . . ordinary monthly ervants [who] get more or less the same wage as the outside natives."[17] Oral evidence lso suggests that wage labor was far more common in the region from the 1920s.[18] The

primary reason for the relatively early emergence of wage labor was that tobacco ar
cotton farmers with relatively small farms could not afford to have labor tenants wh
demanded land for livestock and food crops. Africans resident on these farms we
only permitted to cultivate "small gardens" around their houses or in sma
"out-of-the-way" places, presumably on barren ground.[19]

There is evidence that by the late 1930s wage labor was becoming entrenche
especially on intensive arable farms in the lowveld. According to one group
farmers, "The general trend has been to organise and industrialise farms."[20] Mo
farmers employed resident workers on twelve-month contracts and paid wages: "Th
major farming industries," they reported, "rely on the cash labourer."[21] In the vicini
of White River, where agricultural conditions were similar to those that prevailed
Barberton, labor tenants were also in the minority and most farmers depended o
contract labor from the reserves.[22] On land closer to Barberton, the labor needs
farmers were incompatible with a system of labor tenancy. According to on
Barberton farmer, he "would have to fill his farm with natives to have a sufficie
supply of labour and the land is too expensive to give it to the natives."[23] Since mo
than half of the farms in the lowveld were under a thousand morgen, many farme
could not afford to allocate large tracts of land to their African tenants (table 4.1). Eve
the definition of labor tenant appeared to be changing: one skilled labor tenant worke
for wages and was not permitted to plow land or run livestock.[24]

When the question of implementing Chapter four of the Native Trust and Lar
Act (1936) was raised in the late 1930s, the Barberton committee found that there w
no need to implement the clause that taxed labor tenants. According to the repor
"The 90 days free labour method is disappearing and has already been abandoned b
all of the progressive farmers who have adopted the practice of paying full wage
throughout the year to natives resident on their farms."[25] Tenure on the land for thes
permanent skilled workers was a "gift."

In the early 1940s, when the Native Affairs Department was searching for ways t
solve the general farm labor shortage, it identified the persistence of labor tenancy as
major problem in the Transvaal. But as the Secretary for Native Affairs remarked in
letter to the Low Veld Farmers' Association, since labor tenancy was not "in vogue" i
the lowveld, it was unlikely that measures to restrict tenancy would solve the labo
shortage there.[26] By the late 1950s, when the state clamped down on farmers with labo
tenants, the committee in Barberton commented that registering labor tenants woul
involve no hardship for local farmers.[27] Indeed, although there were still a hundre
and fifty labor tenants on twenty-six farms in the region, one of the members of th
labor tenant control board remarked that he was kept far more busy on th
cooperative and irrigation boards.[28]

From a relatively early date, therefore, farming in the lowveld was characterize
by wage labor, incentive and piece-work schemes and compounds. During th
harvesting season, owners of cotton, tobacco and citrus plantations relied on me
women and children from the reserves, crown farms, or Swaziland and Mozambiqu
A few farmers in the Barberton valley constructed "women's compounds" and se
them apart from the rest of the workers' houses on the farm.[29] In one instance
women's compound was deliberately constructed between the landlord's own hous
and the rest of his tenants' houses to ensure that the women were not disturbed b
other farm workers. Men who visited the women's compound were severe
punished: according to one farmer, the only time he had lashed an employee wa

Table 4.1   Classification of Farm Size, Barberton District, 1937

Farm size (morgen)	Number of farms
Under 5	4
5–20	15
21–100	74
101–500	140
501–1 000	88
1 001–2 000	89
2 001–3 000	29
3 001–5 000	34
5 001–10 000	3
10 001 and over	2

Source: CAD, K365, Native Farm Labour Committee (Chair: Major J.F. Herbst), 1937. Evidence supplied by Sub-Native Commissioner, Barberton.

when he discovered one in the women's compound.[30] By reproducing patriarchal relations on their farms, landowners hoped to attract women who, under normal circumstances, would not be permitted to leave the household and work for wages.[31]

Wage-incentive systems were also widespread on cotton, tobacco, citrus and vegetable farms from the early 1920s. The Empire Cotton Corporation and the Barberton Cotton Research Station encouraged the spread of piece-work and bonus schemes on cotton and tobacco farms. During the 1920s cotton boom there was an accepted rate of three pence per ten pounds of cotton picked.[32] Farmers also publicly shared their experiences and experiments with incentive schemes. According to one landowner, the only way to harvest cotton was on a contract basis. He suggested that when workers demanded higher wages, farmers should respond by demanding that they pick more cotton. To improve the productivity of the workers, he recommended that cotton farmers identify and encourage emulation of the best picker and highest wage earner. This technique, he claimed, had doubled the average amount of cotton collected from forty pounds to eighty pounds per worker. As a further incentive, farmers gave small daily bonuses to laborers who exceeded their usual capacity. Control and surveillance were integral components of such schemes. Workers who failed to earn bonuses were usually taken off the harvesting teams and placed elsewhere on the farm. And since cleanliness was important to the overall quality of the cotton, workers who delivered soiled cotton seed lost their bonuses.

Farmers paid most resident wage laborers according to the ticket system. Each ticket consisted of thirty shifts or working days and during the 1920s and 1930s was worth from fifteen to thirty shillings for adult men. Women, juveniles and children were usually paid much less.[33] While the tickets were known as monthly tickets, in practice they took far longer to complete. The ticket system was often associated with a task or *gwazo*. At the beginning of every day the workers would be assigned a specific task; if it was completed before the end of the day the workers could leave early. However, the size of the task was a source of frequent conflict, particularly when it could not be completed in a single day and had to be carried over to the next.[34]

There are several reasons why labor tenancy did not become as entrenched in th Barberton district as it did in other regions of the Transvaal. For one thing, landowner with smaller farms lacked the land to provide African tenants with grazing and arab plots. According to one estimate, white farmers required at least four times as muc land as they actually cultivated to maintain their working oxen. Additional livestoc required further land. On vegetable farms that were as small as forty acres, lan shortage was a major constraint on tenancy.[35] Because of their large and seasonall specific labor needs cotton and tobacco farmers relied on recruited or voluntary wag labor. Since most of the crops grown in the area were perishable, quick reaping wa crucial. In the case of cotton, for example, if bolls were not harvested when the opened, they fell on the ground. Soiled cotton was either not fit for sale or fetched a fa lower price on the international market.[36] Citrus farmers needed labor for harvesting combating diseases and preventing further infestations. In the 1930s the labo shortage on one estate was such that the spread of coddling moth through orange tree could not be prevented.[37]

It was generally more expensive for farmers to allocate land to tenants, fo cultivation and livestock, than to pay women and children extremely low wages fo harvesting cotton, tobacco and vegetables. African resistance and the structure c landownership in the region also discouraged labor tenancy. When farmers de manded more labor from African tenants and their families, many moved off ont crown farms, Trust land or absentee-owned farms rather than face new, more onerou conditions. Farmers found too that unpaid labor was generally more difficult t control.[38]

Although labor tenancy was always less widespread in Barberton than ii neighboring districts, it never died out completely. As late as the 1950s, the loca Commissioner in nearby Bushbuckridge was still registering thousands of labo tenants every year. In other districts, notably Lydenburg and Belfast, the majority o Africans resident on farms were labor tenants.[39] Wage work had become the norm ii Barberton by the 1920s and 1930s particularly on the intensive cotton, tobacco anc citrus farms along the rivers. The introduction of wages and piece-work systems wa: slower, however, on some farms than others.[40] Farmers testifying before the Nativ Economic Commission and the Farm Labour Committee in the 1930s tended to stres the importance of wage labor in the district. But other witnesses highlighted th persistence of tenancy. One argued that the three-months' unpaid labor system wa still operational in the district.[41] A member of the local Native Location Advisor Board felt that the "rule" was ninety days' free labor.[42] One African witness said that h "didn't know of any instance where money is paid."[43] While this statement perhap reflected his knowledge only of local conditions, several African tenants indicated tha their contract on a white farm included a period of unpaid labor that ranged fron thirty to ninety days. One even noted that "in some cases the squatter is expected to d three months free and his wife is expected to do the same."[44]

Oral testimony collected for this study in 1990–91 confirms that mahala (free labor was still demanded in the 1930s.[45] A white landowner who started farming ther recalled that he required three months from at least three members of each househol on the farm. Once this period was over, the tenants could work for wages on the farn or, more commonly, seek employment on one of the local mines or in town.[4 Landowners on less intensive farms, far from permanent sources of water, continue to allow African tenants to run livestock and cultivate arable land. Many of thes

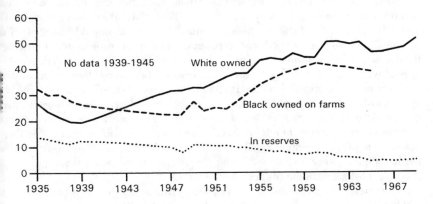

gure 4.2   Cattle in Barberton District, 1935–1969

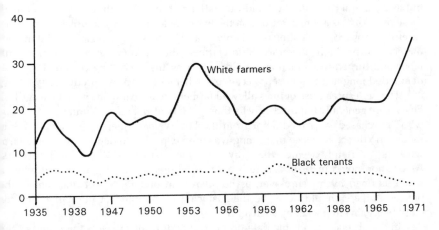

igure 4.3   Maize Production on White Farms, Barberton, 1935–1971

wners were absentees who lived on the highveld and used the land only for winter
razing. New settlers with little cash were also less likely to pay tenants for their labor.
'ven in the 1950s, when farmers occupied the area previously controlled by the
Jgomane, most new settlers demanded free labor in return for running livestock and
heep.[47] Non-resident labor could also be harnessed (illegally) by renting a crown farm
rom the Department of Lands and demanding a period of unpaid labor from the
:nants of the farm. If the land was heavily occupied, the small rent due to the state was
nore than recovered.[48]

The statistical evidence suggests that African cattle holding and maize product tion on white-owned farms were extremely resilient, albeit at low levels (figures 4. and 4.3). Even in the 1950s, owners continued to demand unpaid labor, often i combination with wage work. Some were amongst the most "progressive" farmers i the district. The huge farming company H. L. Hall and Sons, for example, demande unpaid work from its resident laborers. The organization owned large tracts of lan throughout the region and continued to take up to three tickets (ninety days) free fror all "boys of working age" (thirteen years and up). On its other landholdings the firr demanded only one ticket or thirty days' free labor from the tenants, but fou additional tickets at current rates of pay. Tenants could continue working after thes tickets were filled, but only for Halls. Residents could run livestock but were charge five to six shillings per animal for dipping. One tenant "with wives" paid as much as £ every year for maintaining his herd on the farm.[49]

Commercial farmers were dogged by wildly fluctuating prices for their product and many continued to draw on unpaid labor to limit cash payments to a minimum During the 1920s and 1930s forms of unfree labor co-existed with wage labo piece-work and tasks schemes and the restrictive compounds. As L. J. Hall warne "You might get a line, say of tomatoes, with which you may have a very good month but as a general rule I doubt it and I think I am absolutely right in saying that in a these prices one is apt to come out on the wrong side of the ledger, unless one is ver careful."[50] Tobacco and cotton could only "stand" wages as "high" as one shilling pe day. Not surprisingly, therefore, cotton farmers shunned more expensive male adu labor and turned to women and children during the harvesting period. They als demanded long tasks and used piece-work schemes to improve productivity.

The widespread use of fines allowed farmers to make inroads into the wage bill Fines were generally imposed only by those who paid wages to voluntary workers o who "purchased" recruited labor from the Low Veld Farmers' Association. Whil there is no direct evidence that fining was used explicitly to depress wages, to farm workers it certainly seemed that way. As a member of the White River Farmers Association noted in 1928: "There is a danger, unrecognised by most, that when a native is fined by his employer, as he often is in preference to being sent to the police . . . there should never be the suspicion in the mind of the native that his employer gains in pocket by such a fine."[51]

In the absence of reliable data on fines, it is difficult to assess the extent of the savings to farmers. Nevertheless, a £1 fine in the 1920s and 1930s was more than mos farm laborers earned for thirty days' work. When wage bills were comparatively high and it was easy to end up on the "wrong side of the ledger," small savings could be crucial. Since local markets for vegetables were fickle, and prices on the world marke for cotton and citrus unstable, wages were the only cost over which farmers coulc exert some control.[52] Extracting "free" labor from workers who contravened any on of the hundreds of formal and informal rules of the farm was undoubtedly crucial ir controlling costs.

The system was modeled on the magistrate's courts that sentenced "criminals" to pay a fine or to submit to a period of forced labor. During the 1920s, the Barbertor court fined thieves £1 or one month's hard labor; for drinking, the sanction was £1 (seven days) or £2 (fourteen days) and for scratching a farmer's face, £1 or three weeks' hard labor.[53] The more serious the offense, the higher the fine or sentence: for growing cannabis, the fine was £4 or six weeks in jail with hard labor.[54] Farmers

Table 4.2   Offenses and Fines on the Estates of H. L. Hall and Sons, 1930

Offense	Fine	
	£	s.
Late for work	0	1
Allowing a mule to hit a paw-paw tree	0	5
Damaging a tree	0	5
Leaving a gate open	0	5
Allowing a donkey to stray	0	10
Taking waste oranges	0	10
Plowing too near a lemon tree	0	10
Breaking a window	1	00

Source: Barberton Herald, 25 August 1930.

attributed the need for their own system of fines to the small number of police in the district and the inaccessibility of the magistrate's court in Barberton.

In August 1930, the Draconian use of fines on labor-intensive farms was publicly laid bare. L. J. Hall, one of the largest farmers in the district, a prominent member of the Low Veld Farmers' Association, and the director of its recruiting arm, was charged with sixty-three counts of extortion and five of assault.[55] A number of Africans working for Halls came forward and pressed charges. The nature of the offenses and the size of the fines are remarkable — considering that most of these workers would be earning not more than twenty-five shillings per month. Minor misdemeanors such as plowing too near a lemon tree, allowing donkeys to stray and taking oranges without permission all resulted in illegal ten shilling fines (table 4.2).[56] Oral testimony from farm workers confirmed the pervasiveness of the system, and stressed how a relatively small infraction could result in a large fine.[57]

At the trial, Hall's defense attorney called a number of other farmers as witnesses. They explained that, in the lowveld, fines were part of the natural order, the president of the Low Veld Farmers' Association noting that it was the "universal [practice] in that part of the country for farmers to inflict fines."[58] He himself regularly used the system to "maintain discipline." In his own defense Hall explained that the fines were used for "native welfare" on the estate to provide film shows and other recreational activity. In summing up, the judge requested the jurors not to allow their deliberations to be clouded by the fact that the system was the norm in the region. In spite of the damning evidence, they found Hall not guilty by a seven to two margin.

Fines and other arbitrary deductions probably played an important role in encouraging desertion and other forms of resistance on white farms, particularly amongst workers recruited by the Native Labour Board of the Low Veld Farmers' Association.[59] When these deductions were added to fines, farmers could extract as much as one ticket *mahala*. Desertion was a serious problem for farmers with seasonal demands for labor. Because farm workers often deserted in groups, the impact on production could be very disruptive. Landowners who recruited through the Low Veld Farmer's Association were particularly concerned with desertion since they lost not only valuable labor, but also unrecoverable capitation fees. In 1937, one large farming company lost almost £450 on recruiting fees through workers deserting soon after arrival on the farm.[60]

The inability of farmers to control desertion was yet another reason why son
farmers who relied chiefly on wage labor retained labor tenants on their land. Whi
wage laborers and recruited workers were usually more vulnerable to charges und
the Masters and Servants acts, their mobility was always greater than that of labc
tenants. Single migrant farm workers could break their contracts and leave the farm k
simply deserting. In 1936, the magistrate in Barberton found that the thirty-da
contracts, under which most recruited and voluntary workers labored, did not fa
under the provisions of the Masters and Servants legislation. Their ability to escap
prosecution for desertion immediately increased. By contrast labor tenants, with
permanent dwelling and other assets, including livestock, on the farm, were mor
circumscribed in their movements, especially from the mid-1930s as white settlemer
in the region increased and overcrowding in the reserves worsened. Many farmer
who usually paid wages retained a core of labor tenants who were particular!
vulnerable to the threat of eviction.

Market Intelligence

The importance of wage labor, compounds, piece-work and incentive schemes i
Barberton in imposing discipline and extracting work from African laborers repre
sents only one side of the story. Oral testimonies indicate that migrant laborers had
highly sophisticated system of market intelligence informing them of the condition
on white-owned farms. The key was a system of nomenclature for white farmers
Some names evoked a hard, though not necessarily brutal, working environmen
Mazibambela was so named because he continually urged his employees to "keep it up
(*zibambela ndoda*) when they were at work in the fields. *Ngoma* (song, hymn
encouraged his employees to sing because "if you weren't singing, then it meant you
weren't working."[61] And on *Mdisiphansi*'s ("don't sit on your ass"), there were few
opportunities for taking a rest. Other names were more menacing, evoking images o
violence and oppressive working conditions. *Mashaibongolo* ("killer of donkeys") wa
a harsh and violent man who patrolled his land and farm compound at night with a
gun and a pack of large vicious dogs. *Dabulasigogo* ("the man who beat the skin of
you") and *Mashaiasbagele* ("fist beater") were clearly farmers to avoid.[62] In most cases
knowledge of the working and living environment on such farms, as well as the name
of the farmers, was hearsay and was often recounted with conditional clauses:

> There is another one there at Malelane . . . . We used to call him *Mpondo*.
> That one, if you have done anything wrong, his boss boy brings a sack of
> mealie meal and puts it in front of you and orders you to lie on it. And after
> you lie on that bag the boss boy comes with a shambok and he beats you.[63]

The informant who told this tale of brutal violence had not witnessed these events, no
had he worked on the farm. Nevertheless, he could with certainty and authority
describe what could happen *if* you stole vegetables, or *if* you did not wake up on time
for work, or *if* you arrived to work on a Monday with a hangover. Farms like these
were to be avoided at all costs: violence was endemic, wages low or non-existent and
rations meager.

Although nicknaming was an important part of the rural information network
the names were not always an obvious sign of conditions on the farm. Several

interviewees had worked on a farm owned by Tonetti (*Mtarian*, "Italian"). His name provided no clue about working conditions on the farm. Nor did *Mangculweni*'s (hip). Nonetheless, they were well aware that conditions on *Mtarian*'s farm and other plantations were better than on smaller operations. On the larger farms, migrant workers were assured of cash wages, rations, additional food in the form of vegetables and fruit that were below market standard, and reasonable living and working conditions. These were factory farms and agribusinesses where there were relatively rigid rules for employment, wages, overtime, and rations. One farm even had a procedure for complaints. This was an important consideration for Judas Nkuna, who preferred these farms because "there were people who dealt with your problems, so on those farms you just went to the office and demand what you want."[64]

Former workers on some of the commercial farms said that they were hired through a "join," a term usually reserved for mine contracts. The resignation procedure was also more structured: when Nkuna left *Mtarian*'s farm, for example, he gave the farmer notice and departed without trouble after the period of notice was over. Task and incentive systems were the norm on these farms, making personal supervision and control less important than on farms where the working day was defined by the number of daylight hours. Moreover, there were usually large labor forces on plantations, ensuring a certain degree of anonymity not present on smaller farms. And while violence and unfair labor practices were certainly not absent from factory farms, these operations stood in contrast to those where working conditions were rarely standardized and personal control was the order of the day:

> I can say that it was better at Mataffin and at Tonetti because there were people who were dealing with the stuff [problems]. But when you found someone with his own farm, you didn't even ask the farmer because now he is here and he is with you, now he fights with you and now he is off.[65]

Without a formal contract of any kind, it was also more difficult for farm workers to leave these farms of their own free will. On smaller owner-occupied farms, desertion usually superseded the structured process of giving notice.

White farmers were certainly not oblivious to the existence of rural information networks and tried to turn them to their own advantage. In the Barberton district, they came to depend on them during the harvesting season when their labor needs were greatest. "Putting the word out" that labor was required was a common way of filling labor shortages. Those farmers with a "good reputation" in the reserves would usually be certain of a full complement of labor within a week. As one farmer noted, "There again, when your credibility amongst the people in the homelands was good then you had no problem with labour."[66] However, market intelligence was highly effective and could also work against farmers, even those with "credibility." One farmer in the Komati Ward recalled a situation during the 1950s where his labor "dried up" even though he considered himself to be a fair employer.[67] He was producing cucumbers and squashes at the time, a highly labor-intensive crop especially during the harvesting period, and drew most of his seasonal labor from the nearby Trust area. In this particular year, just when he was drawing a full complement of migrants from the reserve, his work-force moved, as he described it, *en masse* to the farm of his neighbor, who, as an incentive, was allowing his workers to consume all the produce not suitable for sale. For the workers this was an important source of food, or of cash through selling in the reserves. Since the cucumber farmer did not provide what is known

colloquially as "cheap line," the workers chose his neighbor. To secure enough lab
for the harvest, he was forced to provide a "cheap line" of his own.

In the countryside around Barberton, information about conditions on particul
farms was based on place, community and familial ties. When Judas Nkuna le
Tonetti's farm, he did so knowing full well that he would find a better-paying je
elsewhere: "Because you will hear some other people say that on that farm they a
earning this much and then you will go to that farm and work there."[68] Since mai
men and women worked for wages only during the harvesting season, the rur
networks were continually refreshed by their experiences on particular farms. Tl
new information shaped their strategies for the following year.

These rural networks bear a striking resemblance to the "market intelligence
system of Rhodesian mine workers reconstructed by Van Onselen from archiv
evidence.[69] Oral testimonies collected in the Barberton district suggest that migra
farm workers also relied on a similarly sophisticated system of market intelligenc
The rural networks provided information on farms where cash was forthcomin
conditions were relatively better, and "cheap line" was available. In the 1930s ar
1940s Africans sought employment with what were considered at the time "progre
sive" fruit, tobacco, cotton, and vegetable farmers. These farmers relied mainly c
wage labor and a highly structured work regime that included either a ticket system
a task (gwazo) and piece-work scheme. However, it would be wrong to exaggera
conditions on these farms or the infallibility of the market intelligence systems. Mai
farmers, while relatively "progressive" in outlook themselves, relied on white fari
managers who were not averse to using physical punishment to discipline worker
Indeed, on some of the large farms, punishment was administered solely by manage
and foremen: "You know those white employees we used to call them malala pipe [r
place to live], and it was those who used to beat us. It is because they were also hungi
[poor], that is why they used to beat us."[70] Even though they were "also hungry," the
was no love lost between them: "They kicked you very hard, and when you aske
them why they said they didn't talk to kaffirs."[71] In some situations market intelligenc
was of little use. When a farmer new to the district purchased a tract of land, worke
could find themselves temporarily locked into an undesirable contract with
particularly brutal farmer.

Another issue that loomed large in the testimonies collected from ex-fari
workers and tenants was the constraints on protest when on a white farm. Hele
Bradford cited one informant who, when questioned about resistance on white farm
responded by demanding, "How can you 'strike' when you are in a white man
house, 'strike' in a white man's house . . . you can't do that."[72] This suggests that thei
is something distinctive about the space of white farms. Aninka Claasens ha
suggested that the brutal violence committed against farm workers persists becaus
white farmers consider their actions on their own land above the law, and Coli
Bundy has argued that this "power over space" is based on legalized private propert
rights for land.[73] In a very different context, James Scott suggested that certain sites ai
power-laden, in that dominant classes and individuals may wield power moi
effectively in particular locations.[74] In other words, power is often structured by
situational logic.

White farms were clearly spatially constituted in ways that affected the action c
African workers on the land. Many interviews revolved around a discussion of th
relative "freedom" of resident and migrant farm workers. Without exceptio

formants argued that migrants from the reserves had more freedom than resident
rm workers. When James Sambo was asked about cash wages he responded by
mparing his situation with that of resident farm workers: "The one who is forced to
ork is the one who stays on the farm, otherwise you are not forced to work."[75]
ment Ngomane, who labored on white farms all his life, linked violence on white
rms and the ever-present sjambok to landownership in a systematic way: "[They
at us] because they had already bought the land and they said there that your land
as already their land."[76] Another informant, Elias Mkizi noted that on farms where
e conditions were particularly brutal, it was advisable to act submissively:
Vhenever you are there on the farm what you must do is keep quiet, even if there is a
oblem between him [the farmer] and you, you must take it as if you know nothing,
d then be thankful when you go to sleep."[77] According to Ngomane, the demise of
olence on white farms was tied to the rise of migrant labor. Migrants, as temporary
sidents of the farm, were less subject to this power.

The farmer's control over the space of the farm was never absolute, and there are
umerous examples of both open and hidden resistance to his power, usually
volving damage to property, livestock and crops.[78] These everyday forms of
sistance are articulated in the rural legends Africans tell each other. One such legend
, in typical fashion, an account heard from a "friend of a friend," in which the main
naracter remains nameless. The narrative begins with a young African male taking a
ort-cut through a white-owned farm. On his journey, he stops and defecates. As
on as he is finished, however, the farmer arrives on horse-back toting a large gun.
he image conjured up here is a classic one: a large horse bearing an equally large
rmer dressed in khaki clothing, wearing a brown hat adorned with a strip of leopard
kin, and at his side a menacing rifle. When the farmer arrives he shouts angrily, "Hey
affir, what do you think you are doing on my land?" The African responds by placing
is hat over the deposit on the ground and replies meekly, "Sorry baas, I have a guinea
wl under my hat here and I am hungry and I want to eat it." When the story is told,
e narrator assumes a position of total submission, not meeting the white farmer's
yes and bowing in servility. Upon hearing that the trespasser has captured a fowl on
is land, the farmer states that anything caught on his land belongs uncategorically to
im. The would-be poacher agrees, apologizes profusely for his actions and hurries off
ne farm. In the meantime the farmer climbs off his horse and moves slowly and
uietly to the hat that is ostensibly covering the trapped guinea fowl. When he is
vithin a short distance of the hat he kneels down and very slowly lifts the hat, and then
vith a quick movement thrusts his hand under the hat to capture the bird.

The individual described in this rural tale corresponds closely to the "trickster"
igure in other cultures. Tricksters are by definition less powerful than their enemies,
ut nevertheless win all confrontations through wit and cunning. Deception is
ometimes achieved by relying on the aggressor's unsavory characteristics that might
nclude avarice, filth, and stupidity. The trickster might also act mute, stupid or
lumsy to delude the more powerful aggressor. In the Barberton version, the trickster
cts submissively, but at the same time uses his cunning and the farmer's greed to
leceive his antagonist. Moreover, the trespasser escapes, having lost only his hat, and
vith the satisfaction of knowing what the farmer did in his absence.

Stories involving tricksters have played an important role for the oppressed
lsewhere, in providing a figure with which to identify, a figure that overcomes the
dds to defeat the enemy.[79] Although a legend, the tale remains an important form

of veiled resistance to the farmer's power over space.[80] By defecating on the farmer land the trickster not only defies, but also defiles this power over space. The your man hands the farmer the greatest possible insult and then escapes scot-free.

Conclusion

By the mid-1950s, officials in the Native Affairs Department did not view labe tenancy in the Barberton district as a serious problem. Of the approximately fiv thousand Africans resident on white-owned farms, seven hundred fell under tl category of labor tenants.[81] By the end of the decade, this figure had dropped to only hundred and fifty. Most of these labor tenants lived on farms owned by highve landlords. These landowners used their lowveld "labour farms" to supplement the work-force on the highveld. Labor tenants were also still found on cattle farms owne and occupied by whites. Much of the land where tenancy persisted was too far fro permanent sources of water to allow irrigation.

The Barberton district was clearly one area where wage labor emerged relative early, and was soon entrenched, on productive cotton, vegetable, tobacco and fru farms along the river valleys with access to water for irrigation. Work on these farn was associated with compounds, sophisticated payments systems and close surve lance: the classic factory farm. In the context of droughts and the vicissitudes of tl international market, however, these "progressive" farmers were not averse to rentir land or purchasing farms to extract unpaid labor from African tenants. They also use a system of fines, which meant that "wage" workers spent periods of time working fe nothing. These practices, together with the existence of unproductive farms in tl region where labor tenancy was more common, ensured that the emergence of wag labor and the disappearance of unfree forms of labor was uneven.

In 1954 the Native Trust and Land Act was amended to facilitate the transform tion of labor tenants into wage laborers. From the beginning of 1957 all African labe tenants on white-owned land had to be registered. After this date, all tenants we required to provide at least 122 days' labor every year. To monitor conditions c white-owned land, the state established labor tenant control boards in each distric The boards consisted of three local farmers and one member of the Native Affai Department. One of the obstacles to the implementation of the initial act — the claus that obliged the state to provide additional land to those evicted from white-owne farms — was dropped in the amending legislation. The Native Affairs Departme was aware that the new law would have the greatest impact in the northern Transva and parts of Natal where labor tenancy was still firmly entrenched. In the rest of tl country the impact of agrarian transformation had already taken its toll on labe tenancy.

5

Factories in the Fields: Capitalist Farming in the Bethal District, c.1910–1950

MARTIN J. MURRAY[1]

[Be]thal is a place with a reputation. The early Dutch-speaking settlers were so gratified [to] have found such a lovely place that they borrowed a name from the Book of Genesis; [it] means "abode of God." They thought that it would give the area distinction as a holy [pl]ace, like the original spot where Jacob rested and dreamed that a ladder stretched [fr]om earth to heaven, and where he felt himself to be in the presence of God.[2] Yet the [re]putation that Bethal acquired owed little to sacred ideals and a great deal more to the [pr]ofane realities of profit-making. With the growth and development of commercial [ag]riculture in the early twentieth century, the district became one of the most [pr]oductive farming regions in South Africa. Its wealthy farmers — with their huge [es]tates and great success in growing staple crops for distant markets — became the [en]vy of the "little men" who struggled to stay afloat under crushing debt, high prices, [an]d low returns. These large-scale Bethal farmers were often portrayed in ruling-class [ci]rcles as the standard-bearers of economic advance in agriculture.[3] Yet this image of ["p]rogressive" farming contrasts sharply with the historical memory of those who bore [th]e brunt of decades of cost-cutting and profit-maximizing measures. In their [re]lentless pursuit of profit, the farmers of the district subjected their African laborers [to] such abusive treatment that it was not long before the name *Bethal* became [sy]nonymous with callous brutality, ill-treatment, and violent death. In the minds of [A]fricans, working on the white-owned farms there was akin to slavery and was to be [av]oided at all costs.

Bethal is a small *platteland* town situated in the heartland of the fertile farmi
zone of the eastern Transvaal highveld, about half-way between Johannesburg ar
the Swaziland border. It is located on the eastern portion of a large region commor
known as the maize triangle, with its apices at Ladybrand in the south, Ermelo in t
north-east and Lichtenburg in the north-west. Classified as intensive arable, or an ar
suitable for staple crop production,[4] the Bethal district by the 1940s accounted f
around 60 per cent of the total maize output of the Union.[5]

The district is set apart by its special blend of highly favorable ecologic
characteristics. The most important climatic determinant of crop yields is rainfa
Throughout South Africa, an annual isohyet of 20 inches is generally consider
sufficient to grow maize. On the highveld, the highest yields per morgen have be
found near the 30-inch isohyet, in the Bethal-Standerton area, where the annu
rainfall during the crucial growing months of December, January, and February
more or less evenly distributed. Only in the midlands of southern Natal, with a
annual rainfall of between 30 and 40 inches, have these yields regularly be
exceeded. The loamy, doleritic soils of the highveld maize belt make the regi
exceptionally fertile and, with the favorable rainfall, help account for the hi
productivity of the Bethal-Standerton-Ermelo area.[6]

These natural endowments laid the foundation upon which the landownir
classes reshaped the physical landscape in their headlong drive to produce cash cro
for the market. In order to account for the predicament of farm workers in the Beth
district, it is necessary to explain the historical processes of capitalist developme
there and to place these processes within a broader comparative framework.[7] The
were three characteristics that set the development of commercial agriculture in t
Bethal district apart from the general pattern of agrarian transformation in the easte
Transvaal highveld. First, the leading capitalized farmers there organized agricultur
production on large-scale, landed estates and employed semi-permanent workers (
long-term contracts. By imposing a social dimension — stretching out work over tl
course of the entire year — upon the natural rhythms of agricultural production, the
enterprising farmers were able to fashion what were, in actuality, "factories in tl
fields." Unlike undercapitalized farmers who struggled to "tame" labor-tena
households, the large-scale farmers of the eastern Transvaal maize belt tried to mal
the most of their labor resources by hiring wage-laborers on a full-time basis ar
putting them to work in a highly disciplined and productive fashion.[8]

Second, because of persistent labor shortages throughout the eastern Transva
highveld, large-scale farmers of the Bethal district depended in the main upon migra
workers to supplement the small labor force permanently settled on their propertie
They regularly appealed to the state for assistance in recruiting labor fro
neighboring territories, particularly Southern Rhodesia, Portuguese East Africa, ar
Nyasaland. But they also took matters into their own hands, creating their ow
recruiting agencies and sometimes relying upon illicit labor traffickers. During tl
early years of expansive growth up to about 1940, Bethal farmers illegally recruit
umfaans, or child labor, and later they tapped into the prisons.[9]

Third, and finally, the large-scale landowners in the Bethal area modeled the
farming operations on the Johannesburg mines. As a general rule, they recruit
young men in the prime of life who were housed in barracks-like compounds, whi
were guarded around the clock. They depended upon piece-work to speed up ar
stretch out the working-day, and they introduced the "ticket system" as the princip

ans of payment. They relied upon African intermediaries to supervise their
orkers. In addition, they used harsh treatment, including physical abuse, to instill
ar and compel compliance.[10]

The Despotic Labor Regime on the Bethal Farms

e basic elements of agrarian relations in the eastern Transvaal maize belt evolved
er several decades, but were firmly in place by the mid-1930s. At the top of the
erarchy was a small minority of wealthy, large-scale landowners. They set the
onomic and political tone for the whole region because they contributed dispropor-
nately to overall output, had much higher yields per morgen, raised a wider variety
crops for sale on distant markets and employed most of the imported labor. Their
ealth and local prominence gave them influence with the highest levels of
vernment. At the bottom of the hierarchy were the majority of poor farmers:
ckward, producing low yields and saddled with high indebtedness. Between these
oups, a class of middling landowners were without the wealth and influence of the
te but less burdened than their poorer fellows. Most white farmers in the Bethal,
uthern Middelburg, Witbank, and Ermelo districts did not employ recruited labor
a regular basis, but instead depended upon labor tenants who resided with their
nilies in huts scattered about their farms and provided seasonal labor when called
on to do so.
    The steady expansion of commercial agriculture in the Bethal district was
companied by a substantial increase in the size of the permanent African population
om 18 000 in 1921 to 39 000 in 1946. This increase was largely the result of the influx
extra-Union Africans from Southern Rhodesia and Nyasaland, who had initially
me to work on the farms but who stayed on at the expiry of their contracts, filling up
ches in the local labor market.[11] By the 1940s, just over a hundred of the largest maize
rmers in the eastern Transvaal maize belt employed "foreign" workers who were
used in closed compounds.[12]
    The first step towards incorporating African work-seekers into the alien world of
e large estates began well before they set foot in the maize belt. The great majority of
igrants who came to the white-owned farms worked under six- or twelve-month
ntracts. Upon recruitment the recruiters brought them before a magistrate or other
testing officer," who verified that they had agreed to work and understood the
rms of employment. The formal appearance before an official gave the stamp of
nsent and legitimacy to a highly unequal relationship that invited fraud and
ception. Scattered evidence from the archival and other records suggests that
fricans understood little of the procedures conducted in their name, had scant
fluence over where they contracted to work, and were frequently surprised to find
emselves on white-owned farms when they expected to be elsewhere.[13] One
rticular episode, involving twenty-five Africans transported against their will from
mberley to Bethal in March 1921, illustrates the unscrupulousness of some labor
ents. Recruiters operating out of Kimberley, and employed by the Johannesburg-
ised labor agency Theron and Company, had "signed on" this group for a short stint
farm labor. After arriving unexpectedly in Bethal, these men refused to work,
aiming that they had been promised employment in the Yokeskei River area.
onsequently, they were brought to court and charged with failure to honor their

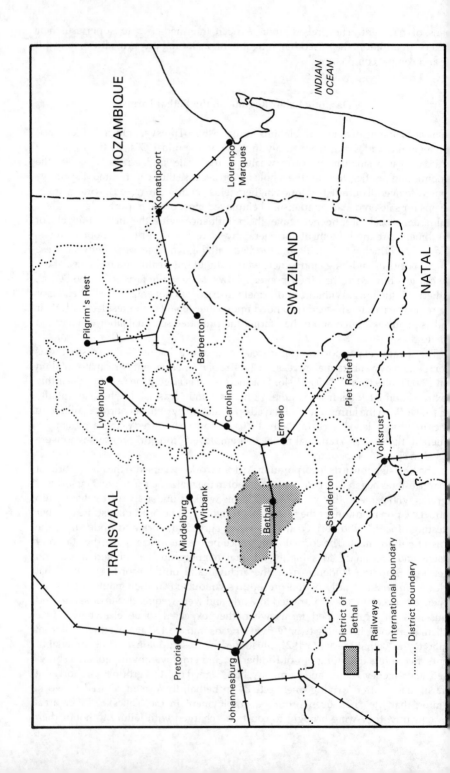

ntractual obligations.[14] The labor contract imposed a new legal identity on the
cruits. Binding them to a fixed term of employment under specified conditions, the
ntract subjected them to penal sanctions, including imprisonment and deportation.
n their part, farmers called for stiff penalties for breach of contract and demanded
ate assistance in tracking down deserters.[15]

The built environment on the large estates mirrored the relations of power
tablished there. Divided into two socio-cultural worlds, the estates kept master from
rvant, European from "native" and propertied from non-propertied. The spacious
ring quarters provided for the owner or manager and his family contrasted with the
ab, prison-like quarters where the workers were housed well away from and
ually out of sight of the center of the estate. The biggest farmers took the Rand mines
r their model and housed their workers in barracks-like compounds. Details of these
rangements are readily available in the reports of the farm inspectors sent out by
rious state bureaucracies prodded to action by alarming reports of ill-treatment on
e Bethal estates. The inspectors routinely reported that compounds were sur-
unded by high walls or barbed wire.[16] With their barred windows and locked gates,
any compounds were watched around the clock by armed sentries to prevent
sertion.[17]

The "natives" usually slept on dirt floors with only straw mats or sacks to shield
em against the cold in winter. Most compounds did not provide proper lighting and
ntilation and were without toilet facilities.[18] They were "verminous, filled with flies
d indescribably filthy." Extreme overcrowding was commonplace, and farmers
equently housed the spillover from the compounds in sheds and backyard hovels
spersed around their properties.[19] By the mid-1940s, the larger estate owners were
nstructing brick and cement compounds with proper ventilation, latrines and
aces for washing and bathing. While less dilapidated than the structures they
placed, they were, in the words of the Secretary for Public Health in 1947, "nothing
se but formidable prisons."[20]

One of the most striking features of the labor system on the large maize-belt
tates was the rigid regimentation of the working day. Farm work was backbreaking
bor that, depending upon the time of the year, went on from 5.00 a.m. till after
00 p.m.[21] In contrast with the laxer methods of agricultural production on the small
rms, the Bethal farmers used Taylorist methods to accelerate the pace of work.
orkers were organized into gangs and had their tasks fragmented, simplified and
id according to piece-work to prevent loafing. The young, the old, and even the sick,
d to keep pace with the others. Foremen withheld the pay of those who failed to
mplete their quota. One of the most successful farmers, Esrael Lazarus, explained
at "part of the secret" of operating large-scale farming enterprises involved the
ficient and judicious use of labor-time. "If a kaffir would remain in employment on
e Lazarus Estates," he contended, "he must work to time; he must promptly and
nartly obey orders and execute tasks. All his working hours belong to the employer,
ho pays him a money-wage and supplies him with his needs."[22]

Work activities consisted of little more than simple cooperation, with laborers
lying primarily upon hand-held implements. Largely lacking mechanical equip-
ent, farmers used draft animals for the heavy work of plowing, harrowing, and
ulage. A corollary to a labor regime that depended principally upon sweated labor
d primitive tools was the extensive use of force and violence. "Throughout the
urs that the labourers are at work," one inspector reported, "they have to work *hard*

and continuously and are naturally continually being urged on."[23] "Native forem‹ and frequently white overseers on horseback," followed behind the gangs of fi‹ hands, "invariably with whips or some instrument in their hands."

Workers were paid on the ticket system under which the completion of thi separate shifts was counted as a month of contracted labor service.[24] Laborers were ‹ paid for Sundays and for days not worked because of illness or the weather. Pro‹ records were practically non-existent, and workers were cheated at every opportu ity. They frequently complained that their tickets were not marked when work ‹ stopped on account of rain. They also protested bitterly that "if anyone talked in ‹ lands while working, or became ill and could not carry on, or lagged behind wh working or proceeding to work, he was sent back to the compound, got no food dur‹ the day, and his ticket for that day was not marked."[25] Wage rates on the Bethal esta‹ naturally fluctuated over time and by category of worker. By the mid-1930s, wages contract workers ranged from fifteen shillings for youths to thirty shillings for adu‹ per thirty shifts worked, along with food and quarters. Long-service employees w‹ occupied intermediate posts such as *baasboys*, foremen and oxen drivers had spec‹ privileges such as separate married quarters and received wages that sometin‹ reached £2 10s. per month.[26]

Compound managers made every effort to save on standard expenses, partic‹ larly on non-wage costs such as rations, housing and medical care. Farmers forma‹ agreed to provide rations, including separated milk, vegetables, and meat, over ‹ duration of the labor contract. Workers, however, rarely if ever received what th‹ were promised. The principal article of food was mealie meal served thrice da‹ laborers complained that milk was provided only at the evening meal. Workers ‹ their breakfast and midday meals in the fields. "Some natives have little billy cans i‹ which their porridge is placed," the Director of Native Labour explained. In m‹ cases, however, "they are simply given the food in their hands which, of course, th‹ have no opportunities of washing." Some farmers regularly sold carrion to th‹ laborers. In accordance with common practice, the price of the meat purchased w‹ marked on the back of the ticket and deducted from wages due.[27]

The large estates also employed full-time cooks. Food preparation was primiti‹ taking place either over open fires in three-legged pots or in unscreened sheds. Esrael Lazarus's estates, Bombardie, Cologne, and Longsloot, there were br‹ fireplaces with large built-in pots, in corrugated-iron roofed sheds with open sid‹ Yet in all these places, it was noted that "flies are much in evidence and little eff‹ seems to be made to keep them down." At Cologne and Bombardie, the compoun‹ had water spigots; but at Longsloot, laborers fetched water in large drums from considerable distance. In other places, water was obtained from the usual farm sup‹ and washing facilities were located at dams and spruits. Farm laborers, and especia‹ the so-called "tropicals" (foreign workers from north of 22°SL), were particula‹ susceptible to respiratory diseases. Gross overcrowding in the compounds facilita‹ the rapid spread of contagious diseases, and poor or non-existent sanitation ensur‹ constant exposure to infection.[28]

Once absorbed into the labor regime on the estates, farm laborers found‹ extremely difficult to break free. After accepting advances ranging from £1 to £4, ‹ recruits arrived on the farm already in debt. They were expected, moreover, to rep‹ the costs of their rail or lorry transport to the farm. It was thus not unusual for fa‹ workers to toil for three months before receiving any cash, by which time they w‹

sually in debt at the farm store. Farmers automatically deducted the costs of items
urchased from wages due. Hence, almost all workers had virtually nothing to show
or their labors by the time they completed their contracts.[29]

Even at the expiry of their contracts, recruits found it very difficult to leave.
armers resorted to all sorts of tricks to hold them.[30] Generally speaking, farmers
ithheld wage payments to their laborers for at least a month as a deterrent to
esertion. Since the amounts withheld were usually meager, workers would desert
nyway when conditions were bad enough. By the 1940s, Bethal farmers had to recruit
pwards of thirty thousand migrant workers annually in order to meet their
equirements of between fourteen and eighteen thousand workers. Desertion rates
aried from farm to farm and year to year. On balance, perhaps as many as 20 per cent
f the migrant laborers fled the farms before the expiry of their contracts.[31]

"An Epic of the Soil": Esrael Lazarus, the "Mealie King"

y the early twentieth century, town and country in South Africa had come to rely
ntensely on each other, and it was commercial agriculture that provided the principal
onnection between the burgeoning urban markets and their supplying hinterlands.[32]
ertile soil, sufficient rainfall, the long growing season, and relatively flat terrain
ombined with close proximity to the Rand's mines and markets to make Bethal
ttractive for commercial farming. In the decade or so after the South African War
(1899–1902), when agricultural production in the highveld experienced a decisive
take off" under the protective shelter of the Reconstruction administration, a sizeable
umber of English-speaking farmers, including some Lithuanian Jewish immigrants,
cquired farms in the southern Middelburg and Bethal districts. These English-
peakers joined an already established group of landowning Boer notables whose
amilies had expropriated land from the original African inhabitants in the nineteenth
entury.[33] The demand of the gold-mining industry for cheap foodstuffs created a
eady market. The new arrivals concentrated on maize production as their principal
ash crop. By the 1920s, white farmers producing for both local and overseas markets
ad transformed the entire region east of Johannesburg into an intensive maize-
rowing belt.[34]

Esrael Lazarus epitomized the rise and expansion of capitalist farming in the
ethal district. An emigrant from Lithuania at the end of the nineteenth century,[35] he
rrived virtually penniless, initially found work as an assistant store-clerk and, within
few years, opened his own small trading store. By the turn of the century, he was well
laced to turn to farming and to take advantage of certain opportunities that arose
ollowing the South African War. During the post-war Reconstruction period after
902, the British administration, headed by Lord Milner, aggressively pursued twin
conomic and political goals. On the economic side, Milner sought to resuscitate
ommercial agriculture, which had been virtually destroyed during the war. Toward
his end, his administration created the Transvaal Land Board and the Land Bank as a
neans of facilitating land settlement, putting a brake on spiraling land prices, and
roviding easy credit for farmers willing to offer their land as collateral. On the
olitical side, the administration aimed to break the back of a lingering spirit of Boer
ebelliousness by sprinkling the countryside with English-speaking yeoman
armers.[36]

Even the best-laid plans sometimes go awry. With the onset of the agricultur depression of 1907–11, many financially hard-pressed farmers were forced off t land by high costs and low profits. As a result, large numbers of farms chang hands.[37] Lazarus reached the conclusion "that maize growing could be made mo profitable than maize selling." Along with a number of other Lithuanian immigran who had made substantial profits in urban-based commerce, and with outsi financial backing, he purchased prime farm land in the eastern Transvaal maize be Access to credit was crucial to the success of commercial farming. Aspiring farme with capital were able to obtain large and already improved farms, which served collateral for much-needed credit. By contrast, other white landowners with limit capital or little land found themselves in a desperate situation.[38]

By 1911, Lazarus had begun farming on a "prodigious scale."[39] He used prof from his expanding network of trading stores, along with revenues derived from lar sales and milling activities, to finance more land purchases. In 1916, he bought tw farms, Cologne and Bombardie, from Transvaal Consolidated Lands, Ltd. The properties, located south of Oogies and north of Kinross, were ordinary farms wi land of not more than average quality and average yields.[40] Yet by the mid-192(Lazarus had made them the Transvaal's maize-producing showpieces. "A plant le than eight or nine feet high was a rarity and many were twelve or thirteen feet enthused a visitor. "So immense were the fields that from some points of view a visit could have imagined that he was on a planet clothed with growing maize. Equally striking as the magnificent uniformity of the crop was the cleanliness of the soil (which it grew. Weeds have a very thin time on the Cologne and Bombard Estates."[41]

By 1924, Lazarus could boast that he was the "largest maize farmer in t world."[42] The Bombardie and Cologne Estates alone produced more than a hundr thousand bags of mealies from the estimated six to nine thousand morgen und cultivation, and produced an annual harvest of seventy to eighty thousand bags potatoes from four hundred morgen. In 1928, the average yield of maize surpass(thirty bags per morgen, and in some parts exceeded forty to fifty bags.[43] In 1924–30, t average yield for the Bethal district was 9.24 bags per morgen and for the "mai triangle" as a whole 6.35 bags per morgen.[44] Lazarus used about twelve hundred to of fertilizer a year and maintained over two thousand oxen.[45] On his Longsloot Estat near Kinross, a few miles south-east of the Bombardie and Cologne Estates, Lazar placed an estimated eighteen hundred morgen under cultivation, of which near fifteen hundred were devoted to maize. In 1928, this farm yielded an estimated forty forty-five thousand bags of maize. He also branched out into other crops, producii such staples as oats, turnips, beans, and rye. In particular, he devoted about thr(hundred morgen to teff, a common feed crop for livestock. He also specialized raising pure-bred Afrikander cattle, show horses, and prize-winning sheep.[46]

Yet mealies remained the mainstay of his operations. "The best sort of farming f any settler to start with on the high veld of the Eastern Transvaal is the mealie," l insisted. "If any young man takes up the mealie seriously he can learn a very gre deal, and at the same time acquire practical experience which will enable him to { forward into mixed farming later on."[47] According to agronomists, the clue to the hi; productivity on the Lazarus farms was the careful attention to tillage. "The cle: field," it was said, "the weedless field with the solid mulch of a fine tilth, with brok(earth extending well below the surface, conserves moisture." This method of intensi

ltivation contributed more than any other factor to good crops during the "lean
ars" of drought. According to Lazarus, the fundamental axiom for successful
rming could be summarized in a single sentence: "What you take out of the soil you
ust put back again."[48] Altogether he used between two and three thousand tons of
rtilizers annually on his farms. In addition to two white farm managers to oversee
s farming empire, he also employed around forty white overseers, foremen, and
indymen — "and the number is trebled when their families are counted." At the
ottom of the hierarchy, he engaged anywhere from six hundred to seven hundred
id fifty Africans for unskilled, manual labor on the farms.[49]

Lazarus was only one of a sizeable group of *parvenu* capitalist farmers who
erated in the maize belt of the eastern Transvaal highveld. Another was Andries
eytenbach, a friend and neighbor of Lazarus, whose example provides a helpful
impse into how these farmers took advantage of market opportunities to become
odestly wealthy men in a notoriously fickle business. Breytenbach and his sons
vned a portion of the original farm of Longsloot, the remainder of which had been
irchased by Lazarus. Starting with one hundred and sixty-one morgen, Breytenbach
ok a leasehold on about three hundred morgen and launched himself into the
clusive cultivation of mealies. By the mid-1920s, he annually produced from forty to
ty thousand bags of mealies. In 1928, he owned freehold title to over five hundred
orgen and had diversified into mixed farming as well as sheep-rearing.

Breytenbach's eldest son also started in mealie farming with one hundred
orgen. He gradually expanded his operations, and by 1928 he owned four hundred
id thirty-three morgen of freehold lands. Another son, recently graduated from
hool, received eight morgen of land from his father, along with "a few oxen and a
ccanin." He reaped 208 bags of mealies (or an average of 26 bags per morgen) during
e 1927 season. In 1928, he produced about 250 bags from the same land. With a
ortion of his earnings, he purchased from his father an additional forty morgen of
eehold.[50]

To contemporaries, agrarian entrepreneurs like Esrael Lazarus seemed the
chetypal self-made men, who symbolized the great strides made by progressive
rming in the South African countryside. "The story of Mr. Lazarus's work is an epic
the soil," one correspondent exclaimed.[51] Lazarus embodied the spirit of capitalism
it was understood in South African ruling-class circles. Faced with the growing
poverishment of poor whites in the countryside, captains of industry, civic leaders,
id state officials alike sought after "success stories" to inspire struggling white
rmers. Lazarus was not averse to self-promotion and joined in cultivating an image
himself as a man of humble origins who exemplified the virtues of perseverance,
ligence, and thrift. Responding to allegations that staple farming offered a "doubtful
id at best very risky return," Lazarus proclaimed that "[successful farming] has
irely been demonstrated by neighbours and myself, practically all of whom started
ith nothing, and to-day own thousands of acres of profit-earning land due to mealies
id other crops under high production." He proudly pointed to the success of the
eytenbach sons, declaring that "this shows how a youngster can get ahead by
tilizing the mealie to start farming."[52]

The so-called "millionaire" farmers like Esrael Lazarus were not without their
etractors. In coming to the defense of "pauper farmers" like himself, G. E. Haupt, for
cample, complained that "this sort of farming cannot be successfully indulged in on a
nall scale and by small men, and is, therefore, just the last form of farming that a

settler with small or no capital should follow." The production of staple crops requir
substantial cash reserves or access to credit, was extraordinarily expensive, a
necessarily involved great risks.[53]

Labor Shortages in the Bethal District

As a general rule, chronic labor shortages and lack of capital were the princip
barriers to the growth and development of commercial agriculture in the easte
Transvaal highveld during the early decades of the twentieth century. For farme
securing reliable workers was a constant source of tension and irritation. The stea
expansion of cash-crop production generated a demand for labor that far exceeded t
capacity of the local resident work-force. Capitalizing farmers quickly absorbed wh
local supplies were available at the wages they were willing to pay, driving the mark
price upwards and causing considerable ill-feeling amongst those who were l
empty-handed.[54] What complicated matters was that farmers in the maize belt we
located far from concentrated pockets of African settlement.[55] The entire easte
Transvaal highveld was "practically without Reserves."[56] Capitalizing farme
nevertheless stood steadfastly against the creation of a reserve in the district becau
this would permit African owner-occupiers to acquire choice lands in the settl
highveld. As one irate Bethal farmer contended, "It would be an impossible position
have native farmers in amongst the Europeans. There is no room for a native area
the district."[57]

Until the 1940s, agriculture remained primarily a labor-intensive activity, ar
expanded production was mainly achieved through the simple expedient of enlargir
the absolute size of the labor force. As the commercializing impulse gathere
momentum, labor shortages became more pronounced. Those farmers who wished I
increase production of staple crops were intent on bringing as much acreage und
cultivation as possible. They were understandably hesitant to accommodate lab
tenants because agreements of this sort meant setting aside some of their land f
resident African labor tenants and their families.[58] Farmers turned to recruitin
agencies for assistance, and these companies, with their well-organized network
tapped into the slums that had sprung up around Johannesburg.

From the start, the fortunes of the large-scale maize farmers of the Bethal an
Middelburg districts turned on the regular supply of hired labor. In putting the
operations on to an efficient and profitable footing, progressive farmers quick
exhausted local labor supplies. Farmers also formed their own recruiting organiz
tions, and these private associations were exempted from the licensing and oth
requirements of the Native Labour Regulation Act (NLRA) of 1911. In 1912, Esra
Lazarus and other enterprising Middelburg/Bethal farmers formed the Transva
Farmers' Labour Agency (*Transvaalse Landbouwers Arbeids Maatschappij*) with the ai
of coordinating and streamlining their efforts. The Middelburg/Bethal farmers ha
hoped to imitate the large-scale mining houses with their formalized and high
successful recruitment practices. Other groups of farmers followed suit, and soo
there were a large number of farmers' recruiting associations operating in th
field.[59]

From the outset, the Farmers' Labour Agency began to bring in thousands c
foreign migrants from the northern Transvaal. Mostly they were male children style

icannins."[60] While the 1911 NLRA banned the employment of *umfaans* (children
ider eighteen years of age), this restriction had been waived for farmers by
iministrative fiat. Labor relations on the great majority of South African farms, most
which still operated through systems of labor tenancy, were inextricably inter-
'ined with the widespread use of child labor.[61] The common abuses associated with
cruiting *picannins* for field work landed a few farmers in court but, except in the
treme cases that came to their notice, government officials rarely interfered.[62] Yet, as
rmers must have learned, child labor provided only a partial solution to shortages,
ice they lacked the physical strength to provide heavy manual labor. Child recruits
ainly supplemented the seasonal work of labor tenants already settled on
hite-owned farms, and assisted adult male Africans dragooned from bushveld
rms in order to "work off their rent."[63] In time, the mining houses discovered that
eir own licensed agents had surreptitiously assisted the Farmers' Labour Agency in
taining labor and, desiring to eliminate unwanted competition, they lobbied
iccessfully to close it down.[64]

Recruitment of "Foreign Natives" for the Bethal Farms

1913, the state, concerned about scandalously high death rates, prohibited not only
e recruitment of so-called "tropical natives" (Africans living north of 22°SL) but also
eir employment on the mines. Barred from recruiting in the north, the mines
rengthened their operations within the country. The result was an intensified
mpetition for low-cost black labor that brought mine owners and large-scale
rmers on to a collision course.[65] The seemingly insatiable demand of the mines for
bor created opportunities that small-scale entrepreneurs were quick to fill. Promi-
nt recruiting agencies, headed by such well-known men as Erskine, Hadley, Kantor,
ieron, and many others, established offices in such places as Messina, Pietersburg,
d Louis Trichardt, which straddled the main labor corridors heading to Johannes-
irg and the gold-fields. Their object was to intercept the workers from the tropical
eas who continued to arrive in large numbers despite the ban on their employment
gold-mines. These licensed agencies did their best to cultivate an image of
gitimacy, but they secretly operated across South Africa's borders in league with
dicensed "freelancers" who transformed "illicit trafficking in natives" into a thriving
iderground business.[66] These notorious "labour pirates" congregated along the
rder in rugged, inhospitable terrain, intercepting gangs of long-distance migrants
ho came into the northern Transvaal by the thousands from Southern Rhodesia,
yasaland, and Portuguese East Africa in search of work on the Rand.[67]

Despite genuine efforts to curb rampant "illegalities," and to enforce the ban on
ine employment of tropical workers, the administration proved to be no match for
cperienced unlicensed recruiters, who openly defied the law.[68] Throughout the
ecade after 1910, illicit recruiting along the border spun out of control. In December
118, a strongly worded government circular issued special instructions to Native
ommissioners explicitly prohibiting licensed agents from recruiting "Rhodesian and
ast Coast natives" for any employment. Even when the Director of Native Labour
id granted permission to farmers to employ such labor, it was only on condition that
bor agents be excluded from the recruiting process. In labor catchment areas such as
ouis Trichardt, scrupulous government officials enforced the ban on tropical

workers against the claims of labor agents and their clandestine associates called tou
In refusing farmers the necessary permits to transport tropical work-seekers
white-owned farms, these low-ranking bureaucrats incurred the wrath of large-sc
employers such as Lazarus.[69]

Farmers' organizations kept up a steady stream of protest to high-ranking sta
officials, complaining bitterly about their labor difficulties and the lack of governme
assistance. The South African Maize Breeders', Growers' and Judges' Association, 1
example, appealed to Prime Minister Jan Smuts in 1920 to remove the ban on t
recruitment of tropical workers for farm work. The association argued that the
restrictions were necessary to protect African laborers "from the dangerous work
underground mining" and that they "should not apply to the healthy occupation
work on the land."[70]

The demand for access to tropical labor reflected the growing desperation
farmers on the eastern Transvaal highveld. It was an open secret that they routine
ignored existing labor statutes. In order to combat the dramatic increase in illeg
recruiting in the 1920s, the state heaped new regulations upon the older, mo
ineffectual ones. The resulting complexities and ambiguities made it an almo
impossible task for officials to determine what was permitted.[71]

The large-scale farmers of the eastern Transvaal highveld took advantage of t
bureaucratic uncertainty to broaden the geographical scope of their recruitme
efforts.[72] The particular methods of Lazarus illustrate the ingenious strategies adopt
by labor-starved farmers to obtain Rhodesian workers. Beginning after 1910, Lazar
employed labor agents operating in the Johannesburg slums and in the northe
Transvaal in search of work-seeking migrants who had crossed the Limpopo and we
heading for Johannesburg on foot. However, this approach produced only haphaza
and inadequate results.[73] With his steadily growing labor needs, Lazarus w
undeterred by bureaucratic obstacles. Bested by the recruiting agencies that suppli
labor illegally to the mines, he turned his attention beyond South Africa's borde
and, in 1919, wrested at least unofficial permission from the Director of Native Labo
to recruit Rhodesian laborers.[74] Lazarus worked in league with recruiting agents wl
transported food by wagon to their camps located near the migrants' establishe
crossing-points in remote areas along the Limpopo. These agents and their "nativ
runners" lured impoverished southward-moving migrants from the Rhodesias ar
Nyasaland with food and cash advances, drawing them into farm employment wi
false promises of good working conditions and high cash wages.[75]

In mid-1920, the Supreme Court of Natal and the Eastern Division of the Suprem
Court of the Cape Province overturned existing regulations restricting labor recru
ment, and authorized employees of white farmers to recruit Rhodesian labor on
they had crossed into South Africa.[76] Almost immediately, Lazarus appointed tw
men to act as his official labor agents. In actuality, these employees masked tl
operations of "the real recruiters carrying on a profitable business" of gatherir
labor.[77] The mealie king depended upon "native runners" to make initial contacts wi
migrants on the Rhodesian side of the border and to bring them to Louis Trichard
where they were handed over to G. E. W. Gould, a labor agent who was employed b
both Lazarus and Erskine. In turn, Gould fed, clothed and sent the recruits by rail
Lazarus at Oogies Station in the Bethal District.[78]

T. E. Liefeldt, the Sub-Native Commissioner stationed at Louis Trichardt, o
jected to this effort to circumvent existing recruitment regulations and, on at least or

:casion, reported violations to the police. To complicate matters, Liefeldt "declined to cognize any claim to the services of Rhodesian natives, by Agents or native unners . . . on behalf of Mr. Lazarus."[79] When Lazarus's agent, Gould, brought the cruits before Liefeldt to have their contracts attested, the Native Commissioner gularly informed them of their options and most took other employment.[80]

In October 1920, Lazarus once again appealed to both the Secretary for Native ffairs, E. R. Garthorne, and the Director of Native Labour "for any assistance ossible to secure further Rhodesian Natives."[81] His persistent requests for a special ispensation eventually succeeded. The Director of Native Labour instructed the ub-Native Commissioner at Louis Trichardt to "recognize the engagement of hodesian Natives by runners working for Mr. Lazarus . . . ," and to "assist as far as ossible to inducing natives to accept farm employment where you are satisfied the onditions are good."[82] Almost immediately, other white farmers also took advantage : this shift in labor policy and their agents and runners increased their activity in the ouis Trichardt area.[83] Ever alert to the possibilities of profit, Lazarus became a upplier of labor to white farmers at Empangeni in Natal, once his recruiters had tisfied the needs of the Bombardie and Cologne Estates.[84]

Soon, however, demand again began to outrun supply. In particular, the rge-scale and highly capitalized immigrant farmers clustered around Kinross were nable to satisfy their own needs through far-flung yet *ad hoc* recruitment efforts. In id-1924, the National and Labour parties allied in the Pact swept the South African arty from office in the general election that signaled a shift of white voters' mpathies toward more formalized segregationist policies. While genuinely sympa- etic to European farmers, the Hertzog-Creswell government was also strongly ommitted to the protection of white wage-earners.[85] In particular, F. H. P. Creswell as ader of the Labour Party had campaigned for years against foreign labor nportation. The publicity he gave in Parliament to the high death rates among opical workers in the mines was a factor in the 1913 ban on their employment. With reswell now prominent in the Cabinet as Minister of Labour, the farmers who were oming to rely on foreign labor had reason to fear the likely policies of the new overnment. A steady stream of influential eastern Transvaal highveld farmers, icluding N. Moss, whom the *Farmer's Weekly* identified as the "the right-hand man" f Esrael Lazarus, trekked to Pretoria to petition for reversal of the widely evaded but :ill irksome ban on tropical labor.[86] However, in September 1924, the new govern- ient announced that the prohibition would remain.

The commercial farmers who used most of this labor were bound to protest. Native labour from Rhodesia and Portuguese Africa is of immense value to us," one armer explained. They worked longer and harder than labor tenants or workers ecruited from within South Africa. Most of the foreign workers contracted for twelve ionths' service and were housed in guarded compounds to maximize control and revent desertion. Recruiting fees were lower than the prevailing rates for South .frican workers and wages were about half.[87] Equally importantly, farmers believed ley were more amenable to discipline and to the drudgery of farm work.[88] 'omplaints against the Pact's policies grew.[89] A number of influential men, including azarus, threatened a "production strike" in order to press their demands.[90] N. Moss varned; "If the Government are not prepared to help us we shall be obliged to ecrease production," and added, "we shall have to give up mealie planting and go in or sheep and other things. In time, South Africa will be driven to importing its iealies."[91]

The government called this rather obvious bluff. Prime Minister Hertzog and D. F. Malan, the Minister of the Interior, responded sympathetically to the crescendo of complaints, but steadfastly refused to adopt the course of action favored by farmers. Creswell insisted that farmers hire white labor,[92] a suggestion that was more than white farmers could bear. Numerous large-scale eastern Transvaal farmers had experimented in earlier years with the employment of white labor and "found it a utter failure." Lazarus himself had abandoned this practice because the poor white were "too lazy to work."[93] "May I point out to the Government," Lazarus warned "that the farmers of South Africa are not going to have the white labour policy of the Labour Party foisted on them. Your poor white labour problem is not a cause, it is an effect. Molly-coddling the native is the cause." He pinpointed the "civilised labour policy" of the Pact regime as an ill-conceived solution to a widely misunderstood problem. Others joined the chorus, placing the blame for labor shortages on the privileged position of the mining industry. "It seems that the Government does not want any other industry in the country than mining," H. Frenkel fumed. "The slightest hint on the part of the 'powers that be' that the mines are short of labour, and the requirements are speedily attended to."[94]

The Segmented Labor Market

The nub of the problem of labor shortages was the inability of hard-pressed white farmers to pay competitive wages. In 1922, the Director of Native Labour reluctantly acknowledged that the "present system of recruiting favour[s] the mines and wealthier and organized employers."[95] Despite the inroads made by capitalizing farmers like Lazarus into the labor reservoirs of Rhodesia, the number of "tropical natives" flowing on to white-owned farms did not approach requirements. Farmer associations, particularly the Transvaal Agricultural Union, increasingly articulated the grievances of agrarian capital, complaining about the preferential treatment that the mines enjoyed with respect to labor recruitment and demanding state intervention to tip the scales in the other direction.[96] In the late 1920s, however, farmers who had applied to the Director of Native Labour to obtain Rhodesian labor at Louis Trichardt were placed on a "waiting list" and were left cooling their heels for more than a year.[97]

While the larger highveld farmers coveted the "tropical natives" of Rhodesia, Transvaal lowveld farmers looked longingly at Portuguese East Africa. High-ranking state officials cautioned white farmers against harboring unrealistic expectations. First, the part of Portuguese East Africa lying north of 22°SL remained closed to recruiting by any industry. Second, an existing agreement with the Portuguese government, the Transvaal-Mozambique Agreement of 1909, gave the mining industry a monopoly over labor recruitment for South African employment in southern Mozambique. Farmers hoped that labor concessions to themselves would emerge as the agreement was renegotiated. Talks continued interminably through the terms of the Smuts and Hertzog governments before the Mozambique Convention was signed in 1928. In the event, the Portuguese government insisted both on confirming the mines' recruiting monopoly and on regulations to prevent non-mining employers from using even the clandestine labor on which border farmers in the eastern Transvaal and northern Zululand had come to rely. The idea that Mozambique would be an "'Eldorado' of labour"[98] for farmers was completely unrealistic.

High-ranking state officials worried about the obstacles to the free circulation of labor-power. "I regard with the greatest distrust," the Director of Native Labour declared, "the continuation of a system which places in the hands of the Chamber of Mines the power of practically starving other industries of labour and regulating the flow of labour to their own industry at will."[99] The nearly inexhaustible appetite of mining capital for the labor-power of able-bodied young men greatly depleted available supplies. Despite statutory prohibitions, many large private recruiting companies continued to supply the Transvaal gold- and coal-mines with "foreign" labor.[100] Other labor contractors specialized in supplying "foreign" labor to white employers located away from the Witwatersrand proper. Only a handful of the many recruiting agencies with their head offices in Johannesburg bothered to branch out into the risky business of supplying farmers with labor.[101]

White farmers accused the Chamber of Mines of monopolizing the most valuable laborers and leaving the "rejects" to be picked over by labor-starved farmers.[102] Moreover, even these workers were costly to obtain. One agricultural expert called labor recruitment for white farms "an old, festering scandal" and complained that it was used "by private 'enterprise' for private profit." Recruiting agencies concentrated in supplying the mines, "with a fitful by-pass to the farmer of boys too old, too young, or too unfit for mine work; under no control, with no visible system, and on fees which are simply a blood-tax screwed out of the farmer's dire necessity."[103] Without exception, farmers failed to address their labor supply problems satisfactorily "for the simple reason that it is impossible for fifty or a hundred farmers in any district to organize themselves into an association and successfully carry out a labour scheme."[104] The Rand mining groups learned through bitter experience the folly of maintaining their own separate labor recruiting organizations. The resulting competition increased costs for all the mine employers. While combination prevailed in the mining industry, as it did after 1919, bringing farmers together to curtail competition remained out of the question. The sugar producers came closest, but their industry-wide recruiter, the Natal Coast Company, could never enforce its monopoly and had collapsed by 1930. Comparatively speaking, the *Farmer's Weekly* explained, while it was quite an "easy matter for five or six heads of the mining industry, all living in Johannesburg, to meet and establish an organization to supply the mines with labour, it is an entirely different matter for thousands of farmers spread out all over the Transvaal and Free State, with the varying conditions and circumstances under which they are farming, to form such an organization."[105]

Most white farmers were fiercely individualistic, and their local associations had difficulty getting them to cooperate. Nevertheless, there were a few success stories. In the early 1920s, the Lydenberg-North District Farmers' Association, for example, had gone to great lengths to "place their native farm labour on a less slipshod basis." The farmers divided "their areas into little circles of perhaps a half a dozen farms, the number of farms in each circle being greater or less according to local conditions." The association appointed a leading farmer in each circle "to look after their common interests," including the all-important matter of ensuring that available labor was evenly distributed."[106] During the 1920s, farmers in the Bethal, Middelburg, and Ermelo districts began to draw labor from the prisons. Although the idea was not new, the Bethal/Ermelo experiment was on a much larger scale than any that had been made before.[107] When the Prisons Department agreed to supply Bethal farmers with large batches of prison labor, they housed "the natives in the same compounds, and

under the same conditions," as those used for accommodating ordinary contra
laborers.[108]

Ad hoc solutions of this sort more or less satisfied local needs, but did not addre
the overall problem. Giving up on the Native Affairs Department (NAD), son
prominent individuals suggested in 1921 that an adjunct branch of the Department
Agriculture be created to coordinate labor recruitment.[109] Opposed to this idea,
were most officials, the Director of Native Labour declared: "There are mai
difficulties in the way of Government undertaking the allocation of labourers
farmers who are not known individually to natives, and some guarantee would hav
to be provided that natives were treated in terms of their contract."[110] Nevertheless,
1925 the NAD opened a special recruiting office at Louis Trichardt with the princip
aim of satisfying the labor demands of eastern Transvaal highveld farmers. This effc
failed within three years, forcing farmers to turn once again to the private recruiter

The illegal methods of the private recruiters put them in constant conflict with tl
NAD. Required to appear before the magistrates to have their contracts attested, mar
of the recruits whom the labor agents had rounded up refused to go to the farms. NA
officials released them from their contracts and permitted them to proceed to Pretor
and Johannesburg where many found employment at much higher wages than tl
farmers paid. Information about higher wages passed by word of mouth through tl
farming districts, and farm laborers deserted their rural employers in search of bett
opportunities in the urban areas. In the early 1930s, the NAD granted speci
permission to the mines to import five thousand workers a year from Nyasaland as ;
experimental measure. Over the next several years, the number of Nyasaland recrui
inched upward to around ten thousand. As the news spread in Nyasaland of tl
availability of mine jobs at higher wages, white farmers once again lost out to tl
Randlords.[111]

The Ambiguities of Conflict and Accommodation

Uprooting Africans from their disparate rural communities and throwing the
together on the Bethal estates did not transform them into a homogeneous proletari
whose shared experience as exploited workers overshadowed and dissolved oth
social bonds. Rather than erasing established social ties, the harsh realities of livir
and working on the Bethal farms appeared to reinforce them, paradoxical as th
might seem. Africans from Rhodesia usually arrived in groups of ten or more ar
refused to be split up. A farmer had to agree to take all of them or none.[112] On the farm
laborers tended to maintain their ethnic affiliations.[113] These minute networks
"cultural reticulation," as Pino Arlacchi called them, prevented any solidarity alor
class lines.[114]

The despotic labor system on most estates ensured workers' dependence ar
insecurity. Farmers played off ethnic groups against each other. They housed the
workers according to "tribal" group and selected *baasboys* from amongst certain ethn
groups to supervise workers from other "tribes." In these ways, they could displa
worker protest into expressions of ethnic rivalry and conflict. Yet class relations we
never entirely absent, never totally submerged by other affiliations such as ethnicit
gender or age, either in the constitution of social identities or in encouraging collecti\
action. It would therefore be wrong to interpret ethnic loyalties as atavistic carryove

without acknowledging their role as survival mechanisms for African migrants working in an alien environment at a considerable distance from home.

The main fault lines dividing the supervisory staff on the large-scale estates were racial, but even here there were gradations in authority, income, and outlook. At the top, white farm managers supervised the whole production process. They occupied, to use Erik Olin Wright's concept, "contradictory class locations."[115] On the one side, successful farm managers often used their experience and savings to vault into landownership, taking the "the poor man's chance" as it was called. On the other side, whites in low-level supervisory jobs marked the downward mobility of poor whites pushed off their land, unable to live independently and forced to work for wages.[116]

Usually, African foremen, or baasboys, directed field labor and possessed supervisory as well as police authority over field hands. "If [the baasboy] hated or disliked you," one African remembered, "he would push you, he would make himself white man. If you fought him, the Baas would thrash you and ask you why you fought his Baasboy." [117] The term baasboy exhibits the inherent ambiguity associated with this particular position in the technical division of labor. Baasboys served as the first line of defense on the farm. They functioned as the "eyes and ears" of the farmer. They were the taskmasters, supervisors, and overseers who ensured the steady flow of profits. Yet in the settler imagination, they remained forever "natives."

Researchers who have studied agrarian relations in South Africa have frequently wondered at the apparent passivity of farm workers despite grinding poverty and daily harassment. It might seem puzzling that farm workers only rarely went on strike or revolted. Grievances accumulated and festered, occasionally spilling over into protest meetings, surging crowds, and rioting, but such protests were unusual.[118] Collective protest of whatever sort invariably invited severe retaliation, and the agrarian underclass seldom had the political or social organization, or the material resources, to make direct confrontation a winning strategy. In the circumstances, farm laborers who served out the terms of their contracts had little alternative but to resign themselves, ostensibly at least, to the iron discipline of their overseers. Yet, though workers perceived themselves to be virtually enslaved on the farms, there is plenty of circumstantial and other evidence suggesting that they were not passive victims. They developed acute feelings of injustice about their situation. In the absence of strikes and independent organization, their struggles to soften the burden of work must be found in the largely hidden, silent and individual acts of resistance to management absolutism. Workers tended to rely on their own devices that included foot dragging, sabotage, and theft, along with other forms of defiance.[119] Although largely spontaneous, these actions were certainly not random. Individualized acts, repeated again and again, forged recognizable patterns of resistance, which kept estate managements off balance.

In the context of persistent labor shortages, desertion was perhaps the most damaging act of resistance. Why contract workers wanted to flee was not difficult to understand. Recruiting practices involving force and deceit often backfired. "It is no use persuading the Natives to go to the farms when they don't want to," one exasperated farmer exclaimed. "Unwilling labour is useless."[120] Those Africans who were tricked into agreeing to long-term contracts or who had been forced against their will to work on the farms often took the first opportunity to run away.[121]

Violence and Social Death

Orlando Patterson suggests that the condition of slavery involves two contradictor principles, marginality and integration. Slavery, he contends, historically entaile "institutionalized marginality," where slaves in society were non-persons who existe in a "liminal state of social death."[122] His understanding of the socio-historic significance of enslavement helps to explain the special place that the Bethal farm occupy in the inglorious history of agrarian evolution and development in the Sout African countryside. Estate workers in the eastern Transvaal highveld were sem permanent aliens. Employers and state officials regarded them as labor units. The most important possession was their laboring capacity, and once it was expended lost they faced expulsion. As outsiders with few legal rights and no social standing contract workers existed in limbo, or at least something akin to a state of suspende animation. In both the press and official government circles, reports surfaced time an again about how unsuspecting Africans had "disappeared," seemingly without trace, from the streets of Johannesburg, from prison, or from elsewhere, only later t be found on the Bethal farms, claiming to have been dragooned into service again their will.[123] Laborers spoke in hushed tones about fellow-workers who had bee beaten to death in the fields, or who perished in the compounds from unknow maladies, only to be buried without an inquest in unmarked graves on the Bethe farms.[124]

In the settler-colonial imagination, "natives" were socially and culturall different from Europeans. They were not thought of as sharing an identical huma nature, a common economic rationality, and a similar psychological outlook with the European superiors. Born of an inferior race, they were best suited for certain types manual labor. The entire system of labor recruitment was informed by this perception By and large, labor recruiters and farmers did not relate to "natives" as free-floatin sellers of labor-power in an unfettered commodities market; rather they saw them "a workers by nature, but workers requiring discipline." Labor contracts did no resemble legal partnerships outlining mutual rights and obligations, but instead wer one-sided economic transactions privileging buyers over sellers, and Europeans ove "natives."[125]

The rituals of rulership on the Bethal estates were intimately connected with th efforts of farmers to assert physical control over their workers. Understanding th ways in which estate managers brutalized workers helps to reveal the molecula underpinnings of agrarian capitalism — or what Michel Foucault has called th "microphysics of power." Physical force was callously applied to discipline the habi and break the spirits of strong-willed workers. "Cheeky natives" were imprisone and chained. The "lazy" and "shiftless" were routinely denied food. Assault floggings, and beatings took place with monotonous regularity.[126] Protected on the estates, owners had virtually absolute power over life and death. Corporal punish ment was the routine instrument of labor discipline. The physical disfigurement an scarring that resulted from beatings and assaults were the stigmata of the oppresse and outward signs of "symbolic death." One shocked labor inspector understood th intimidating power of brute force:

> What struck me particularly on some farms was the cowed appearance of the
> labourers and their demeanour when questioned as to complaints. It was
> obvious that they were afraid to voice any complaints and it was only after I

resorted to the method of examining their bodies that I discovered two cases of gross ill-treatment. In the one case I found a gang of about 60 labourers, 75 percent of whom bore old and fresh marks of beatings — there were fresh weals and old scars all over their bodies, a sight really pitiful to see. According to the natives the beatings had been administered by a native foreman.[127]

he sheer capriciousness that characterized the way corporal punishment was used pread fear amongst the workers. As Alf Ludtke has pointed out, the calculated pplication of physical violence rendered coercion possible. For frightened workers, he omnipresent threat of physical abuse that was applied unpredictably and pisodically engendered a sense of powerlessness, stimulating submission to author-y and compliance with orders.[128]

The exercise of excessive force and violence on the estates was directly linked to he desire on the part of owners to impose new work habits and a new time discipline n raw recruits, particularly *umfaans* and so-called "blanket kaffirs" (unwesternized fricans with little experience of whites), who were more accustomed to the irregular bor rhythms of subsistence agriculture. In the fields, it was a common practice for oth white and African overseers "to use their whips when they consider the occasion arrants it."[129] Workers were routinely treated as unthinking beasts of burden. "We re inspanned like oxen," wrote a group of seven Africans from Northern Rhodesia ho also complained of excessive fatigue and one meal of rationed porridge per day, [our]necks are swollen on account of the yokes we are inspinned [*sic*] to."[130] This nagery of equating the treatment of workers with that of animals appears frequently the archival records. "We are flogged for no reason as cattle," one African mplained. Others protested that "their sleeping accommodation [was] not fit for igs."[131]

Conclusion

he large-scale farmers who specialized in cash-crop production in the eastern ransvaal highveld were painfully aware of just how dependent they were on social nd natural forces beyond their control. They operated in fiercely competitive labor arkets using methods of labor mobilization and recruitment that delivered workers rratically in often insufficient numbers. Difficulties of recruitment did not lead these rmers to recognize the need to improve working conditions and wages. On the ntrary, they used their power to brutalize and dominate their captive labor force. retched living conditions, appalling physical abuse, and the exaction of penal nctions were not aberrations, or a reflection of the moral callousness and cruelty of a andful of white farmers and their overly enthusiastic managers and foremen. stead, these were an integral part of the estate order, central elements in the istorical process through which a large, amorphous, and revolving mass of "foreign" borers were compelled to work against their will on isolated farms in the eastern ransvaal highveld. The profits of the estate owners depended upon squeezing bor-time out of reluctant workers, and it was toward this ultimate end that the avagely harsh labor regime was directed.

6

Eastern Cape Wool Farmers: Production and Control in Cathcart, 1920–1940

Richard Bouch[1]

Cathcart is a district in the "Border" section of the Eastern Cape region of South Africa with an identically named principal town. Originally part of the district of Queens town, which came under colonial rule in 1852 towards the conclusion of the eight Cape frontier war, Cathcart was constituted a separate district in 1879. The are already contained an indigenous Thembu and Xhosa population. A demographi pattern emerged, the principal characteristics of which were extensive white farming settlement, concentration of the African population in rural locations, use o permanent and/or seasonal African labor on the farms and small-scale urbanization o all sections of the population in local market towns.

The district is roughly 1 000 square miles in area. Cathcart town is 100 miles from the harbor city of East London by road and rail. The terrain varies from ope undulating grassveld to rugged and hilly country, with small streams in the valleys Much of it is high-lying, at an average of 3 900 feet above sea level. In normal rainfa seasons, 25 inches per annum may be expected. Perennial rivers include the Zwart Ke Klipplaat and Thomas.

Cathcart and Queenstown are still preponderantly rural districts, with man common economic features. The contemporary Eastern Cape is one of South Africa' least developed regions, although its nineteenth-century mercantile heyday wi nessed extensive capital generation.[2] From the early twentieth century, developmen slackened in comparison with the Witwatersrand and the Western Cape, a tendenc that has continued and intensified.

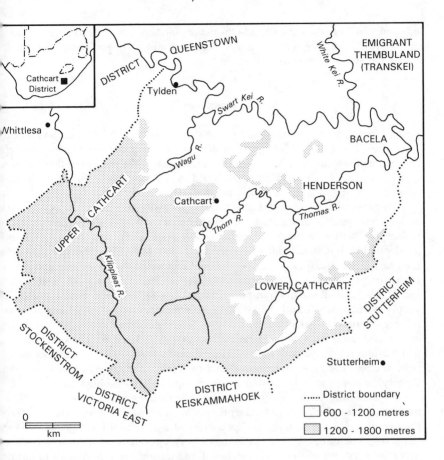

Figure 6.1   Cathcart District, Eastern Cape

Agricultural change within the Eastern Cape has been sharply uneven on several levels. Colossal resource and production imbalance has characterized African and settler farming and there have also been major local variations within the white farming sector in terms of investment patterns, labor employment and bias towards pastoralism or cultivation.[3] The entire region is under-researched, so that anyone working on its rural history operates within a limited historiographical context. For this reason, the analysis that follows ought not to be taken as representative of the whole Eastern Cape. Some conclusions bear application to much of the region, but others are more narrowly applicable to the Border or even to Cathcart exclusively.

Principal questions explored in this chapter include the economics of white farming and the creation and maintenance of socio-political attitudes. Readers may think that labor, the major theme of the book, has been relegated to a subordinate position. But labor — however significant — is only one of a whole set of issues that farmers have to deal with. As this research proceeded two situations became apparent. First, fine details of labor conditions in the brief twenty-year period elude recovery. Second, labor is best investigated in a context which moves beyond

economics to connect with attitude formation, farmers' understanding of authori
and the evolution of agricultural policy. For all these together governed the formatic
and maintenance of the farmers' world.

Background[4]

Sheep farming for wool was firmly established in Albany and districts south of tl
Winterberg by 1850, and bias in favor of it as a dependable source of income w
carried into the future Queenstown and Cathcart districts by the first settlers there. A
expanding capitalist export economy based on Grahamstown and Port Elizabe
offered them access to the London wool market.

Wool growing prospered thanks to high-quality *themeda* grassveld, good rainfa
and the emergence of urban Queenstown as a major wool-buying center. Stratificatic
within the settler farming community developed early and was significant
accelerated by the diamond boom of the later 1860s and 1870s. Many farmers trie
their luck at the diggings and successful ones reinvested their winnings into land c
infrastructural development. Less fortunate or less able men diversified int
small-scale pastoralism and transport-riding. A few became farm tenants and othe
simply left. In the 1870s and 1880s what became the separate district of Cathcart, muc
of it high-lying and cold, was extensively settled. Some of the incoming settlers rente
crown land farms from the state, rather than paying for freehold. These farmers kep
their surplus funds available for direct investment into productive infrastructure an
were amongst the most "progressive" and successful in the region. By the twentiel
century, however, most landholding was on a quitrent ownership basis.

From the 1870s, extensive urbanization at Kimberley and (from the mid-1880s) c
the Witwatersrand encouraged grain production (the area is well suited to wheat) ar
the rise of a dairy industry. The 1880s brought agricultural mechanization as tl
technologies of pumping water, plowing and reaping advanced rapidly. Stratificatic
was reinforced, for in those days state aid and technological assistance to farme
barely existed. While farmers had to mobilize capital and modernize their operatior
on the strength of their own resources, those resources varied. To complicate the issu
farmers did not all agree on how to deal with the central issue of labor. Sheep farmin
continued to have low labor requirements save at shearing time, but even the shee
farms usually had some cultivated lands. Until the late 1870s arable farmers faced
dire shortage of labor caused primarily by the ability of the nearby African rur
locations to support their populations moderately well. From the later 1870s th
subsistence base was seriously undermined, with the consequence that it becam
easier for farmers to engage temporary wage labor or labor tenants. The same perioc
c.1877–85, saw the great majority of established African sharecropper-tenan
expelled from the arable farms as farmers either mechanized or switched to seasons
contract labor. It is worth stressing that these tenants departed *before* the Cape's stri
Location Acts were operative — contrary to current orthodoxy.[5]

By the end of the 1880s, farming and labor relations had settled into the patter
they would keep until the early twentieth century. Cathcart was by then one of tl
premier wool producing areas of the Border. Dairying had become widespread and
beef industry was commencing. Near self-sufficiency had been achieved in meat, mil
and butter.[6] A minority stratum of genuinely well-to-do farmers existed. There wer

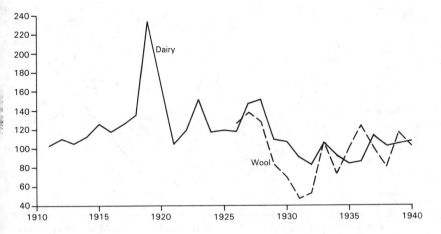

igure 6.2 Wool and Dairy Producer Price Indices, 1910–1940

oughly 290 white-owned farms, almost all of them occupied and worked by their wners, save about six in the remote Bacela rented out to African tenants. (Until the partheid regime dispossessed them, Africans also owned a handful of Bacela farms.)

Requirements for a resident labor force had been reduced by mechanization, xtensive installation of fenced camps and rotational grazing for stock, and also by the roximity of Glen Grey and the Transkei, both of which were sending out substantial umbers of seasonal workers by the turn of the century. Cathcart was comparatively ₊ell-off economically and in terms of labor supply. The contrast between it and (for xample) the poorer districts of Lower Albany, rural East London, Fort Beaufort or ₊omgha in regard to labor is clearly drawn in their differing responses to the stringent ʼrivate Locations Act of 1899: Cathcart farmers were unlikely to require any new ₊rivate locations and "as a body, and individually, [were] strongly opposed to any ₊ative Locations on private property," but a rash of new locations was expected in the ₊ther districts.[7] In 1906 only fifteen private location licenses were issued for Cathcart, ₊ostly to accommodate only one or two laborers each.[8]

During the inter-war years, exceptional demands were made on wool farmers, for ₊e wool price fell sharply at the same time as far-reaching organizational restructur- ₊g (detailed below) took effect. High prices in the early 1920s were only partially ₊ustained. By 1926 the price per pound had fallen by sixpence; a brief rally followed, ₊ut in 1929 the price plummeted. Appalling drought in 1932/33 coincided with record ₊w prices in the final phase of the great world depression. Only in 1936 did the wool ₊rice again come near to the 1926 figure, and thereafter it fell again (figure 6.2). ₊airying, the second major branch of farming in this region, served as a financial ₊ackstop in times of hardship and its scale was largely determined by the wool price ₊ather than by the price of dairy products. Historically, wool had been the staple in this ₊egion and it maintained its status. Farmers tended to assess any other produce with ₊n eye to what it could bring in over and above the wool cheque, without unduly ₊nterfering with sheep farming.

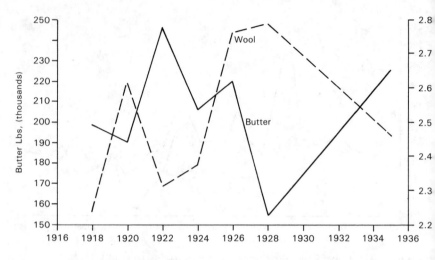

Figure 6.3 Wool and Butter Production, Cathcart District, 1918–1935

Despite fluctuations, the wool price in the early 1920s was sufficiently promisir to induce many farmers to favor sheep farming over dairying. At the beginning of th 1920s a veterinarian noted that the Cathcart farmers "are going in for such extensi' sheep breeding that their farms are practically overstocked."[9] Dairying, subject violent fluctuations in its producer prices, seemed less reliable than the primary stap (figure 6.2). At this time many Eastern Cape farmers invested in additional sheep ar land, only to be badly set back by the wool price collapse during and after th depression. Men who incurred additional debt in this way lacked the diversification their operations which might have tided them over. They were hit doubly har because the price of land was rising fast, resulting in land usually costing considerab more than its real productive value.[10] The majority of Cathcart farmers were n affected by this, as the pattern of landholding was fairly stable. Even so, quitre, payments became increasingly burdensome until a fifty-year campaign to end the succeeded in 1934, a benefit worth between £4 000 and £5 500 per annum to th farmers collectively.[11]

The period under review here included the change of government in 1924 whic led to alterations in state economic priorities. The Nationalist-Labour Pact goverr ment of 1924–33, and the United Party coalition of 1933–39, emphasized industrial ar agricultural development over the mining favored by their 1910–24 predecessor although not with the single-mindedness claimed by some writers in the 1970s Post-1924 governments' patronage of agriculture by no means gratified all Bord farmers, many of whom considered that their affairs were being unjustifiab interfered with. Nor was their sense of dislocation confined to matters on the lan Whereas the English-speaking white community had been politically dominar during the period 1910–24, though in association with wealthier Afrikaner land owners, the Pact victory in 1924 introduced an era of rising Afrikaner dominanc Cathcart was an overwhelmingly English-speaking area with strong loyalties General Smuts and the South African Party. These voters did not relate easily to th political swings which put the South African Party out of power in 1924 and brought ck in 1933 as a coalition partner with most of its erstwhile opponents, the essentials whose economic priorities it now chose to support.

Taken together, all this means that farming at Cathcart in the inter-war years, cluding the issue of labor, has to be interpreted in the light of a deeply formative storical background. On the labor front, little altered in this period because ructures and supply had been determined between *c.*1870 and 1900. But as the astern Cape was the location of significant African protest in this period, and rmers' attitudes towards labor reflected paternalism and illiberality, factors nditioning the whole of the farmers' world require attention.[13]

Wool Growing, 1910–1940

ae wool industry experienced major reorganization after Union (1910). The otorious incident of the imperial wool scheme, in which an effort by the South frican government to secure superior wartime prices, by selling to the British overnment, went awry and left many wool growers with financial losses. It also olitically embarrassed the Smuts government and adversely affected numerous astern Cape and Karoo wool growers. Many, preponderantly the Afrikaans-eaking, transferred their allegiance from the ruling South African Party to the rising oposition star of General Hertzog's National Party.[14] Farmers' demands for organization and protection multiplied with the result that in 1918–20 the overnment instituted a searching enquiry into the wool industry.[15] The outcome was political paradox, but in keeping with the broad trend of policy under the South frican Party government: the state supervised the reorganization of the wool dustry in a manner that left control of it almost entirely in private hands and allowed e government to continue its tendency to favor the mining sector.

Like the majority of farmers elsewhere in settler-dominated regions of the Eastern ape (and several decades ahead of their counterparts in the Orange Free State and ansvaal), Cathcart farmers had participated in farmers' associations since the 1870s. dditional associations continued to be established well into the twentieth century, camples being the Henderson Farmers' Association (HFA) in 1920 and an umbrella ody for the whole region, the Border Farmers' League (BFL), in 1924.[16] Whereas the ssociations handled a wide range of matters at a generalized level, wool farmers had een interested in specific cooperative enterprises since before the world war. Border rmers discussed the subject extensively in 1910, as realization dawned that ombinations of farmers could obtain higher prices by offering larger quantities of uality wool. By that time a majority of Border farmers produced good merino wool hose reception on the London market was marred by long-standing quality roblems with much of the Cape clip. However, although it was necessary to change ae image of Cape wool, the farmers' overriding concern was to protect themselves gainst what they saw, rightly or wrongly, as excessive brokerage charges.[17] This oncern with profitability had much to do with their response to state initiatives later n.

At the time of Union, internal marketing of South African wool was in flux. uring the nineteenth century there had emerged a system of up-front wool urchasing, for cash or barter, by local traders incompetent to assess the quality of ool. By 1900 this had become so entrenched that it survived the development of four ominant wool markets at the seaports of Cape Town, Port Elizabeth, East London

and Durban. Only Durban was a public auction market, where all wool had to b
offered initially at auction. At the other three markets, public auction and priva
treaty ("out-of-hand") selling functioned simultaneously. At East London, the mark
favored by Border farmers because it was readily accessible by rail, not more than ha
the wool was auctioned — a considerably smaller proportion than at Port Elizabeth o
Cape Town.[18] Although by 1910 a large and increasing number of Border woo
growers consigned wool to East London instead of selling to local buyers, the privat
treaty system remained in high favor. This is not surprising in view of its almost entir
prevalence until the later nineteenth century, but may also have reflected the fact tha
good quality wool was most easily and readily sold by private treaty.[19] Queenstow
itself had been one of the biggest private treaty wool markets.

Selling at the central markets was conducted by private brokers who charged 2.
to 3 per cent commission. Farmers believed that brokers operated a ring to infla
brokerage charges — a suspicion which arose in wool growing circles worldwide.
Hence came increasing interest in cooperation: "With a society of which he [th
farmer] was a member, whose policy he could control, and whose profit was returne
to his pocket, a panacea for all these evils, real and imaginary, was offered."[21]

A first attempt in 1910 by Border wool growers to form a regional wool grower
association (WGA) was unfruitful, but circumstances changed after the war. The stat
investigation of 1918–20 recommended that the wool industry should establis
cooperative societies to organize local sales and also establish local WGAs whic
would control quality.[22] Several marketing cooperatives were soon establishe
Boere-Saamwerk Beperk (BSB) in 1918–20, operating in East London, Port Elizabet
and Durban; the Farmers' Co-operative Wool and Produce Union (FCU) in 192
operating at the same three seaports; and the Amalgamated Farmers' Limited. Wit
the establishment of the cooperative marketing bodies and the promulgation of th
1922 cooperatives legislation, WGAs soon multiplied countrywide. In January 193
their national coordinating body, the National Woolgrowers' Association (NWGA
was established.[23]

The creation and instant success of the FCU and BSB, which handled wool at
charge of only 1.5 per cent, renewed Border sentiment against the private brokers. I
1926 the annual congress of WGAs expressed outrage at the attitude of brokers, one o
whom (in Port Elizabeth) openly acted on behalf of buyers as well as sellers. As fo
others, they "made very little attempt to help us, but they occupied a great deal of tim
in an unsavoury debate against the co-operative bodies that handle our wool."[24] Th
principal speaker (himself from the Border) called for voluntary but widely supporte
cooperation:

> Our salvation, our freedom, and our natural rights as primary producers, lie
> in co-operation . . . we make no apology for warning every woolgrower of
> the necessity of being alive to his own interests . . . and not to be satisfied
> until every creditable woolgrower is a loyal supporter of one or other of the
> co-operative bodies.[25]

Attracting rising numbers of shareholders on into the 1930s, the cooperativ
marketing organizations prospered.[26] However, they concentrated their efforts o
marketing wool efficiently and at minimum cost, as well as building up a field staff t
advise farmers about stock selection, classification and packing. They did little eithe
to coordinate sale methods in the coastal markets, or to consolidate market
geographically.[27] Two highly significant consequences sprang from their neglect: first

ı organizational gap was left open for state intervention and, second, Border farmers
·mained confused about the relative merits of auction as against private treaty
·lling.

Although farmers' suspicions of brokers may not always have been well founded,
 detailed investigation in 1929–30 revealed that even at that stage, when the
ɔoperative marketing bodies were well established, buyers' rings operated at
urban, Port Elizabeth and East London. Moreover, the private treaty system largely
iminated competition and thus artificially created conditions resembling a buyers'
ng.[28] Given the tradition of suspicion, Border wool growers would doubtless have
ɔproved the investigators' conclusion:

> The allegations of irregular practices on the wool markets were investigated
> by your committee, and we are convinced that they are founded on facts.
> Evidence was received of brokers discriminating between the wools of
> different clients, and offering the clip of one client cheaply on the condition
> that the buyer pays a higher price for the clip of the favoured party . . .
> Influential farmers are often favoured.[29]

ı this commercial environment the first WGA in the Cathcart district was established
ı October 1930. This Upper Cathcart Wool Growers' Association (UCWGA) was
·ined in 1932 by another local WGA.[30] Both were offshoots of existing farmers'
;sociations.

The initial membership of the UCWGA is unknown, but it had sixty members in
)36.[31] As there were by then at least two other local WGAs, this suggests that over half
ıe farmers in the district supported the movement. From the beginning, the wool
ırmers' most sustained concern was to secure marketing independence: the founding
ıeeting noted that only if all wool farmers formed growers' associations "could we
·cure complete control of our industry."[32] Thus the purposes of the association were
ɔecified as gaining the "absolute confidence" of coastal and inland wool buyers by
roducing the type of wool currently in demand and also by preparing clips in "the
ıost efficient, honest and attractive manner." Moreover, the association would assist
ıembers to classify their clips and flocks and to select suitable rams for breeding
ırposes.[33] Pursuing the goal of control of the wool industry, in 1936 the UCWGA
·ged farmers' associations in and around its district to form additional WGAs.[34] By
)40 recruitment had peaked and the organization reported that "what few remained
·ould never be persuaded to join."[35]

In the UCWGA's determinedly self-interested aims and intentions can be seen a
·nsion which permeated white farming during the inter-war period. Quality
ıprovement was an aim supported by both the state and the cooperative marketing
ɔdies and was in their mutual interest: "progressive" producers knew that the
·putation of Cape wool on the London market had to be radically improved. Their
·fforts paid off, so that in 1931 an observer commented, "South African wool is in high
ıvour, because of its unique manufacturing properties, soft, full handle, and
ıneness."[36] The UCWGA quickly took advantage of the specialized services offered as
ırt of the huge state sponsorship of the farming sector which became effective after
ıe South African War. The Grootfontein Agricultural College at Middelburg (Cape),
ɔened in 1911, was specifically charged with assisting the wool industry. It offered
ɔurses in judging, classing, parasite control, feeding and watering sheep, and wool
ıanufacturing.[37] From 1931 the UCWGA invited wool classifiers from Grootfontein to
ıstruct its members, with the result that by 1936 seven members were qualified

classifiers entitled to use the Springbok Brand (the NWGA's distinctive star
certifying high-quality content and packing) on bales they had examined and fou
satisfactory.[38] This kind of service continued to be used down the years.[39]

Despite the quality improvements, however, severe tension between produce
and buyers persisted and was aggravated by state actions. The state had lost little tir
in entering the wool arena. Even before wool growers created the NWGA in 1931
semi-official supervisory body for the better organization of the wool industry, t
wool council (later wool board), was established in 1929. Act 6 of 1930 prescrib
packing and marketing regulations for all wool sold in South Africa.[40] The wc
council gradually took on an increasing number of functions, so that by 1946 it w
charged with promoting research into the production and marketing of wo
Although ostensibly merely advisory, in reality the wool council represented a maj
augmentation of the institutional and political leverage of the NWGA, for the gre
majority of its members were drawn from the NWGA.[41] Here, in a time of falling wc
prices, lay the root of tensions between the NWGA and certain wool producers in t
1930s. In 1932 the Cathcart WGA expressed deep reservations about relinquishi
marketing to an outside authority, insisting that the wool council's propos
investigating committee should comprise equal numbers of representatives from t
WGAs and the brokers' association.[42]

The Cathcart wool growers soon declared themselves to be only partially in fav
of the measures sanctioned by the developing state-patronized wool superviso
bodies. It is probable that Border farmers were much influenced by the dual selli
system on the East London market — and, equally important, that they were fearful
anything that affected their interests and could not be directly monitored. As they sa
matters, the advantage of the dual system and of the private cooperative marketir
bodies, which were accountable to their members, was that the principle of priva
control remained in place. A seller could stipulate by which method his wool was to I
sold. Although the UCWGA soon discountenanced private treaty sales in favor
auction, in 1936 it opposed efforts at national level to introduce compulsory selling l
public auction.[43] The initiative here came primarily from the wool council, who
thorough investigation at the end of the 1920s convinced its members that the du
system was inherently unsound:

> Private treaty sales and public auction sales should not take place at one and
> the same time on the same market. It is impossible for the buyers in valuing
> the wool, to do justice to it, and they play off the one system against the other,
> so that the competition at the auctions is not as keen as may be desired, with
> the result that it adversely affects prices realized by private treaty sales and
> weakens the position of the seller. *The dual system of marketing is certainly
> highly undesirable* [emphasis in original].[44]

For these reasons the wool council wished to make at least one round of sale by auctic
mandatory before other methods were used.

In preferring auction over private treaty sales, the growers seem to have indicate
awareness of the tendency of the private treaty system to reduce producer prices as
consequence of low prices being paid for the first wool, often poor quality, of each ne
season.[45] However, moves to enforce auction sales raised the specter of buyers havir
full control over the wool price, to the possible detriment of producers.[46]

The UCWGA first signified concern about the direction of reforms within tl
wool industry when it unanimously decided to oppose a decision by the executive

e Cape Province branch of the NWGA to promote control of the sale of wool by eans of legislation. It resolved that it was "not prepared to accept any legislation hat-so-ever that does not entrench the right of the wool organizations to have the solute control of the wool industry, further, we are most definitely opposed to any ctation in the method of the selling of our product."[47] Anxiety reached such a pitch at Border wool growers met in conference at Stutterheim in September 1933. The utterheim conference and Kaffrarian wool growers reached a similar conclusion to at of the UCWGA.[48]

By August 1934 the UCWGA was hopeful that the plan for wool legislation had en successfully rebuffed. That hope was ill-founded. In 1937 an enabling law, the arketing Act (Act 26 of 1937), was promulgated to assist the institution of marketing ntrol boards and a national agricultural marketing strategy. Wool farmers in the astern Cape vigorously opposed attempts to install controls under the act, and also forts by the NWGA to endorse the state's strategy. In March 1938 a mass meeting at athcart overwhelmingly rejected any suggestion that the wool council be granted atutory powers.[49] When it became apparent that the NWGA executive favored the troduction of marketing legislation, the UCWGA asked its representatives on that dy, Messrs Blaine and Malcomess from King William's Town and East London, to sign because it had lost confidence in them.[50] The association formulated a solution for the 1938 NWGA congress restating its total opposition to statutory wers in connection with wool marketing being granted to the wool council, and nsuring the NWGA.[51] Farmers at Bedford reacted similarly, asserting that wool rmers knew better than anyone else how to sell their product.[52]

By mid-1938 apprehension had become strong enough to lead the UCWGA to rite to all WGAs in the grassveld area, inviting them to "to decide on concerted tion to oppose bringing the wool industry under the Marketing Act as contemplated y the executive of NWGA . . . the grassveld representatives on the executive of the WGA maintain that the grassveld area is in favour of a scheme under the Marketing ct and accordingly vote for the scheme. Only by a meeting as suggested can we show em that the majority are against."[53] When the NWGA executive met soon fterwards, the UCWGA reminded Blaine by letter that its members were in complete disagreement with his views."[54] Inasmuch as the UCWGA was confident at its membership comprised the substantial majority of local wool growers, it elieved it had the authority to express a firm standpoint.[55]

Wool farmers' opposition to state regulation of their industry was successful uring the inter-war period, in contrast to the experience of other branches of farming, lmost all of which had been placed under the Marketing Act and control boards by e time of the outbreak of war in 1939. For all that, closer scrutiny reveals that by its ery nature, wool farming was already organized in a manner which corresponded in nportant ways with what the state desired.

Wool being an export item, its selling was already directed toward securing a avorable overseas market — precisely what the state wanted. Collaboration between ool farmers in the interests of better quality and marketing was becoming videspread during the inter-war years because of the rise of the cooperative narketing bodies. Although wool was not marketed under a monopoly scheme, it had een subject to levies since the establishment of the wool council in 1929. Indeed, the vy of one shilling per bale gained the UCWGA's support because the money was sed to finance research and collaboration within the industry. Administration of the

levy was sympathetic: it was suspended between 1932 and 1936 because of th
critically low wool price and drought conditions. In 1936, when increasing interest b
non-British buyers (French, German and Japanese) in South African wool contribute
to better prices, the UCWGA recommended reimposition of the levy.[56] Soo
afterwards, World War II pushed the wool price higher and assured farmers of
market.

During these years the farmers' principal attention was devoted to the issue
explained above. Labor supply was assured. But the economic difficulties of th
inter-war period, and tensions surrounding Border grassveld farmers' relations wit
the state, seem to have combined with a historical predisposition to reinforce
paternalist pattern in labor management that was easily transmuted into intoleranc
reinforced by self-justification.

Just as farmers considered themselves the best judges of how their wool should b
marketed, so they saw themselves as the best judges of what their laborers should b
satisfied with. Self-congratulatory accounts of labor conditions that farmers som
times put forward avoided the issue of how laborers perceived matters (Bord
farmers near King William's Town produced a supreme example of the genre befo
the economic and wage commission in 1925).[57]

It is difficult to reconstruct the details of labor conditions. Helen Bradford claime
that farm workers' wages in the Eastern Cape at this time were "abysmally low," an
named Cathcart as one of the Eastern Cape branches of the Industrial and Commerci
Workers' Union (ICU) "drawing many and sometimes most of their members from th
farms" in the early 1920s, yet there is hardly a reference to the union either i
newspapers or in documentation.[58] Although the ICU had a branch in Cathcart tow
it made minimal impression in the countryside.[59] The ICU did not concern Cathca
farmers very much at all. To what extent its ineffectiveness reflected organization
shortcomings and/or local conditions of labor is impossible to gauge accurately. Th
Native Economic Commission (NEC) of 1932 did not collect details of the conditions
Cathcart farm laborers. The ICU, however, deposed in 1925 that in this region a cas
wage was often supplemented with the use of a small field for cultivation. Accordir
to the ICU evidence, laborers had to erect their own homes. In some, but not al
instances rations (one source suggests maize constituted a large proportion of thes
were supplied over and above the wage.[60] Some farmers appropriated the crear
produced by laborers' cows (where there were any) — a practice also described by
Queenstown witness to the NEC. He justified it with smug paternalism on th
grounds that "there is that principle underlying it to make the Native realize that afte
all the master is looking after his cattle and looking after him and, therefore, he mu
have some say in the matter."[61] The ICU also indicated that laborers resented bein
given carcasses of dead animals in place of a regular meat ration.[62]

In the adjoining district of Queenstown, where conditions frequently approx
mated to those in Cathcart, laborers received between twelve and twenty shillings pe
month and, occasionally, items of clothing. Some had the opportunity of keepin
sheep and cattle.[63] But that was a limited privilege; the more common reality may b
seen in farmers' anxiety that drought would render them incapable of feeding the
workers. At the end of the 1930s, lack of rain caused almost complete failure of th
mealie crop, compelling farmers to buy mealies for "the feeding of Native Farr
Servants and Livestock."[64]

In the later nineteenth century Border farmers had been greatly concerned by th

sue of laborers' beer-drinks — largely social occasions that sometimes had cere-
onial overtones. This anxiety persisted. Fearing drunkenness amongst workers, the
FA resolved to limit the quantity of liquor available at these gatherings. The
agistrate was asked to enforce this suggestion, with the paternalist proviso that the
olice would not interfere as long as the regulation was complied with.[65]

Beer drinking was a social fact that would not go away, however much farmers
ished it would. Workers' education, on the other hand, appeared a near irrelevancy
1d opportunities for it were scant. In 1935 a deputation of African parents from farms
;ked the church minister at Hilton to try to obtain a state teacher for their children,
ome thirty in number. The minister had already attempted to set up a school on one
rm where the owner was sympathetic, but was unable to keep the services of a
acher owing to scanty resources. It transpired that although the Native Affairs
epartment could assist the provincial administrations with money for African
lucation, it was unlikely to be forthcoming in this instance.[66] Over ten years later the
tuation seems barely to have been ameliorated, judging by the experience of a farmer
ho ran a school solely for the children of his staff. By 1947 he was receiving numerous
·quests to have children from surrounding farms attend. His reaction was to ask the
ate to take over the school on a different site a short distance away, for "it would [not]
e wise for me to have dozens of young natives streaming onto and off my farm."[67]

Of course these are all generalizations and we may pause to note the enlightened
·lf-interest of one farmer who allowed his labor-tenants to keep sheep. After the
ipping inspector neglected to order dipping at the correct time he objected, "By
ipping them now the wool will be damaged, causing considerable loss to the owners
f the sheep and indirectly to myself who am still waiting for my rent."[68]

The thinness of the line between controlling laborers and keeping them
utwardly satisfied explains why wages were often discussed in a context of labor
ontrol, as when one farmer said that shearers' rations required examination because
he numerous demands made by shearers was [sic] getting beyond bounds."[69] In 1930
1e matter came before the BFL, which recognized what it called "the futility of trying
y a resolution to bind their brother farmers in matters more or less personal and
rivate," but recommended a maximum wage for sheep-shearers of ten shillings per
undred sheep.[70] The following year, when wool prices were falling, Upper Cathcart
1rmers vetoed a suggestion by their Thomas River colleagues that shearers' wages be
·duced.[71] This was probably a sensible recognition of what was politic. But pressure
ontinued and in 1937, when prices were rising, shearers at Upper Cathcart demanded
fteen to twenty shillings per hundred sheep.[72]

In 1923 and 1924, farmers at Cathcart and Stutterheim had mobilized in protest
;ainst suggestions that the state purchase land for Africans in these districts. The
1ajor race relations legislation of 1936, ending the Cape African franchise in unilateral
art exchange for a land deal, revived old frontier fears. The *Farmer's Chronicle* called
or a high color-blind franchise qualification in order to "assure white supremacy far
ito an indefinite future. This still seems the right way: the only just way."[73] Showing
1e bedrock of fear, farmers mobilized in 1936 to protest against government
roposals to purchase a Cathcart farm for African settlement. Their Member of
arliament, C. M. van Coller, told them that as the Native Trust and Land Act aimed to
stablish territorial segregation, it would be perverse for the state to set up a new
olack spot" amidst an area of white settlement.[74] In October, fifty farmers waited on
1e Native Affairs Commission when it visited Cathcart and stressed that the sheep

farming areas were unsuitable for African farming.[75] The proposal to purchase the land was dropped.

Controlling the Environment

In order to widen the context of the foregoing discussion, this part of the chapter moves onto the terrain of attitude formation and concepts of management and control. In particular, it attempts to broaden the context of labor relations beyond issues of production economics to include attitudes and historical preconditioning.

The Eastern Cape has a lengthy history of black-white tension and conflict over land and resources. Numerous incidents, notably during frontier hostilities, gave settlers an impression that African communities were well-off. Until the end of the eighth frontier war (1850–53), the large-scale cattle-plundering indulged in by semi-disciplined soldiery and some farmers can only have strengthened such perception.[76] After 1853 there were no more major conflicts but the African population physically confined in rural locations or as farm tenants ("squatters"), continued to exhibit the prosperity now associated with the development of an Eastern Cape peasantry. Although prosperity was in truth very unevenly distributed within the rural Cape African community, it was visible and public enough to convince many administrators and members of the settler public that Africans enjoyed adequate means in all but the worst seasons.[77] An exaggerated impression of African access to wealth became entrenched. "Away in the locations" became a complacent, disengaged way of thinking, acceptable because it suggested that there was nothing to worry about — the people would take care of themselves.[78] Similarly, as a large proportion of the African community declined into impoverishment it was easy to reason that this was a normal condition amongst black people.

Their outlook on their subordinate human environment blended with the settlers' other major conditioned perspective, formed as generations of the same families fought in successive frontier conflicts, of a need for authoritative control of the numerically superior indigenous population. Thus a paradigm was created with which to define objects that might require control (whether people or not), as well as the means of control. In this vein William Beinart has shown that the notion of environmental control, in the form of a ruthless assault on sheep-killing jackals, swept the wool-producing areas of the Eastern Cape in the early twentieth century to reach a massive reward-driven climax just after World War I.[79]

Farmers thought in terms of two communities, two economies and two sets of social and moral values. Dualism is still vividly manifested in the Eastern Cape in the close-knit fabric of rural white communities: the vital function of reserved sporting facilities (tennis club, recreation hall, village-green-cum-cricket-ground), and the closed community, in fostering a sense of identity and mutual support is evident when one reads the documents or speaks with members of the community. Weekend sport brings people together in a social circle. Farmers' association meetings may be marked by expressions of condolence to members whose wider families, scattered throughout the district, have suffered bereavement. As in rural England until well into the twentieth century, "Ties of friendship very often bind the rural community, and family ties cement it."[80] Two major transforming technologies of the twentieth century, motor transport and telephones, became common between the world wars and eatly assisted the conduct of business and more frequent contact within the already lf-conscious Border community.

Further exploration of this neglected subject in Eastern Cape social history is not ossible here, but some observations may be made. C. Crais has proposed that even ter the end of major conflicts, "the Eastern Cape remained an ambiguous land" in hich settler dominance never became absolute.[81] Contemporary political cir- imstances support his reasoning. In this there appears to be a significant contrast ith other colonies of Victorian origin, where settlers outnumbered indigenes and a rgely favorable socio-economic environment provided escape from mother-country cial conflict and anxiety about status.

For example, with regard to mid-nineteenth-century New Zealand, M. Fairburn is challenged a whole set of historians' orthodoxies to rehabilitate the essentials of ie Arcadian vision of the colony during that time. He has rebutted later assertions at the society was hierarchical, divided by social class or cohesive at the local level. ttlers understood themselves to be in a tranquil society, feeling that their persons id property were safe. By the turn of the century this background had contributed to owerful agencies of social and political stability."[82] In another compelling revision New Zealand history, J. Belich has demonstrated how Maori successes during the ew Zealand wars so battered Britons' and colonists' preconceptions of their own oral, ethical and cognitive superiority that subsequently a defensive and justifica- ry historiographical orthodoxy gained sway, although growth and good prospects r settler society were not in doubt.[83]

In the vastly more fragile and anxious world of Eastern Cape settler society, efensive perceptions and alliances might be still more readily constructed. The gion notoriously lacked conditions akin to those which made New Zealand seem rcadian. In the twentieth-century national context, too, the Eastern Cape was caught ɔ in the segregationist search for what Saul Dubow described as "a complex political ickage which was first and foremost concerned with ameliorating the threat to white ipremacy" — wherever the threat might come from.[84]

Thus a defensive consciousness fueled a paradigm of management and control in variety of matters from labor to relationships with the state. Cathcart farmers could ɛ quick to challenge authority, apparently on the assumption that the community insciousness and defined socio-political perspectives within their own group should ɛ shared by the authorities as a matter of course. One sees this best at the lower levels local government, where there was a close articulation between electors and ɛcted. Perhaps the most glaring example is the assenting clause spelt out on ɔplication forms for private locations in the early 1900s, "I am quite prepared to carry ıt the wishes of the Divisional Council by prohibiting native gatherings for the ırpose of Beer drinkings."[85]

In 1922 an incident occurred which encapsulated both the tendency for local ıthority to push to the limit its power to control the human environment and the fact at higher authority might neglect to stand up adequately to such behavior — so, of ɔurse, tacitly permitting it to go on. One of the African-owned farms in the Bacela ıanged hands; it remained under African ownership but the new owner, William abizela, found that the farm's private locations license had been canceled, depriving m of rental income and labor. He protested, maintained the location and was ɔosecuted and fined. Then he approached Professor D. D. T. Jabavu of Fort Hare niversity College for assistance and a series of letters ensued.

On being approached by the magistrate, the police commander at Cathca claimed that the divisional council had abolished the location on his recommend tion:

> Serious objections in this District to the renewal of licences of existing Locations have been made by Farmers Associations . . . The policy of the Police is to discourage Locations of this sort — principally owing to recorded facts that such places are used as squatting loafing and Beer drinking resorts of natives who steal Stock etc. . . . considerable supervision by the Police is necessary to suppress the theft of Stock in the neighbourhood and it is thought that no further licences are necessary unless the proposed Private Native Location has European Supervision.[86]

This came to the attention of the Secretary for Native Affairs who, in separate letters (the same day, displayed both concern and unwillingness to intervene decisively. 1 Jabavu he wrote, "The Divisional Council is presumably composed mainly of practic farmers who should be judges of the necessities of the case"; to the magistrate he note that applying the notion of white supervision "to the case of native-owned farms as principle would obviously deprive native farmers of benefits allowed by the law Some days later the secretary wrote again to the effect that an African landown could not be compelled to appoint a white supervisor, and pointed out that th divisional council had arrogated powers that actually belonged to his department taking a decision about the presence of labor tenants on the farm.[87] Caught in th middle of all this, the police commander was embarrassed by his ignorance of th technicalities of the law and by his role as license inspector with responsibility to mal recommendations to the council.[88]

Clearly the farmers valued the goodwill of representatives of the state highly, b it does not follow from this that the authorities necessarily patronized them, or th farmers took especial care to win officials' goodwill. Such close meeting of minds the politico-economic order bestowed on farmers and the divisional council Mabizela's case was not so easily maintained at higher levels of authority. When th HFA asked the magistrate to exercise extreme care in granting stock removal permi to Africans living outside the district and to ensure that landowners provided writte approval for such removals, he annotated the letter, "Awful cheek — under wh authority has this Association been authorized to dictate the Policy of this Office."[89] A the same, it transpired that although there was no statutory requirement for African to carry a stock removal certificate, the magistrate's office routinely did require on and, moreover, the commander of the police stock-theft patrol unit had ordered h men not to issue such permits without the landowner's consent.[90]

In fact relations with the police were ambivalent. Although farmers regarded th police force as a natural ally by definition, the police were not necessarily of like min Few if any matters agitated the farmers more than stock theft, and they frequent demanded stringent police action (invariably against Africans) to stop it. Punishmen meted out by the magistrate's court inclined to great harshness.[91] However, a minori of farmers recognized that thefts were often exaggerated and also that the worst thef were usually perpetrated by white persons. Using letters from his constituents to bac his case, Van Coller reported to parliament in 1934:

> It is not so much the "pot" stealers [i.e. African thieves] to-day who are the serious factor in the problem . . . When you find that a single sheep has been stolen, you can be certain that it is a native stealing for the pot, but when you

find 30, 40 or 50 sheep stolen at a time, you can be almost certain that a European is connected with the theft.[92]

nior policemen grasped the need to treat laborers well and agreed that the agitation er thefts influenced race relations in an undesirable manner. Colonel Fitzpatrick, e Eastern Cape deputy commissioner of police, addressed the Lower Cathcart rmers' Association in almost confrontational terms in 1924, when the ICU was thering strength. Claiming that very many farmers did not keep stock registers and en reported non-existent stock losses, he continued:

> Those of you who have never been out of this country cannot really realise what an asset the native is as a farm servant . . . Compare your wages bill with what has to be paid by farmers in other countries, it is not a tenth of what is paid in Australia. There is a big movement in this country by the native for better conditions on the farms, and I can tell you that if this comes off you farmers will be up against a serious problem. You do not provide a meat ration, but it will have to come to that yet. I have spoken to farmers who told me that they did give a meat ration, but when pressed they admitted that it was only when a beast died. I repeat, that you people who have not been out of this country do not know what an asset the native is to the farmer, and I ask you farmers: do you really play the game?[93]

fficient evidence has been put forward here to permit cross-referencing to the bjects of urban segregation and health, where control was also a core issue. Packard's study of tuberculosis has shown how medical and lay interpretations of ban Africans' vulnerability to the disease in the first third of the twentieth century laced responsibility for the conditions under which Africans lived on the Africans emselves."[94] Such thinking derived from a seriously imperfect comprehension of ay Africans lived in physical conditions that undermined their health; observers aded to overlook the dire economic deprivation that circumscribed their ability to nedy their environment. Religious and civic leaders could be just as blind to the ality.[95]

Likewise, Cathcart farmers' association records indicate, as a prevalent attitude wards Africans, a reluctance to confront the conditioning circumstances of African e. Analysis therefore tended to be superficial. Suggestions for remedies to perceived oblems were correspondingly heavily reliant upon the organizational or coercive sources of the local authority. Again paralleling the tendency widespread in other cles at that time, there was an inclination to believe that African behavior was at root rverse, obstinate and so difficult to comprehend that the application of reason to al with it was largely a waste of time and effort. The farmers were perfectly nscious of problems amongst the black community that threatened to spill over into eir own: thus in 1920 they requested a high-level investigation into the continuing read of venereal disease amongst Africans living in urban and rural locations and farms. But their conception of remedial measures extended no further than a radigm of control and regulation. They demanded effective and stringent medical ion and utterly failed to consider factors such as involuntary overcrowding, or the cturing of social controls amongst the black community by forces largely beyond its ntrol.[96]

The threat of disease, capable of exciting much socio-political alarm amongst tlers, as Bill Swanson has shown in his study of South African urban segregation, ught out the rawest aspects of the rural control syndrome.[97] In 1937 the farmers drew attention to "the alarming spread of tuberculosis in natives and the inefficien manner of treating same," and in 1938 they reiterated their demand for better medic. facilities for Africans, asking that these be enforced.[98] They also urged that person sanitary regulations be enforced for Africans working on farms — a blanket resolutic that would apply also to divisional council laborers carrying out council work c farms.[99] But the most extreme of all these misassociations of other persons with soci affliction occurred in 1938 when Lower Cathcart farmers asked the divisional counc to extend its official mandate of exterminating vermin to include compulsor fumigation of all African huts.[100]

The foregoing discussion of wool farming, insecurity and control reinforces tl point that the farmers' total environment conditioned them to devise or expect ster. determined and authoritative responses to issues. The argument suggests th economic exploitation, however defined, is a dubious bottom-line for analysis of rur relationships in the Eastern Cape because it ignores the dense weave of justificato thinking that gave coherence to settler mythology. Even more seriously, when applie to farmers it ignores the possibility that, like the medical men, they genuinely did n understand the circumstantial forces at work within the African community proximate to them. Indeed the issue goes even beyond that, raising the question whether either or both of the parties to change understood that change can lead to a sorts of unintended consequences — many of them detrimental.

Several years ago Beinart opened discussion about the intricate linkages betwee early to mid-twentieth-century conservationism and a set of ideas and prescriptio that could be applied to settler and peasant agriculture. He noted:

> Interventions assumed a social vacuum, or at least capitalist social relation-
> ships where the land owner had the capacity to reshape land use on the
> whole unit of production. When applied in African occupied areas, such
> schemes were insensitive to rural social relationships, or directly attempted
> to change them.[101]

Echoes of such thinking resound in the present discussion, notably with regard controlling Africans. But it has also been made clear that the Cathcart farmers ha minds of their own. While they had the capacity to alter their methods on outsic advice, their thinking about marketing and labor shows that they preferred to kee affairs under their close supervision. A further demonstration of this domina tendency is found in the subject of parasite-related stock disease which endangere the vital mainstay, sheep farming.

The 1870s–80s had witnessed the first major occurrence of parasites in what w originally excellent grassland throughout the Border region. In 1880 the Cap government appointed a colonial veterinary surgeon. Although the other gover ments within South Africa eventually followed suit, the Onderstepoort Laborator the future center of veterinary science in South Africa, did not come into operatic until 1908.[102] A far worse upsurge in parasitic activity, causing mortality among between 10 and 30 per cent of the lambs, occurred in Cathcart during World War I ar persisted into the 1920s. Virtual panic resulted, exacerbated by the loss of some for thousand sheep and angora goats in the district during the cruel 1921/22 drought. This time, unlike the first, scientific support existed on a significant scale. Furthe more, the magistrate at this time, A. J. van der Byl, was more than usually sympathe towards farmers. He helped to secure visits in 1922 by B.G. Enslin, the chief of tl sheep division in the Department of Agriculture, and a parasitologist from Onders poort, F. Veglia.

Veglia visited infected farms at Henderson and Thomas River in March 1922. Left no doubt of "the determination of farmers of Cathcart district to see the problem of their sheep diseases brought to a solution," he also had to face the commonplace situation that some farmers were better informed and more efficient than others.[104] For example, during the previous year James Field of Field Brothers at Thomas River, a major sheep farming enterprise, had accurately identified nodular worm as the principal cause of the losses and pointed out that regular and frequent anti-worming treatment was the only remedy.[105] But despite Field's personal competence, Veglia discovered that in some instances the efficacious government wireworm remedy was either ignored or misused:

> I heard from farmers of a score of Wire-Worm remedies that they use indiscriminately on their lambs at intervals of 15 days or every week, thus hampering the resistance of the lamb and often leaving the worms undisturbed ... The sole objection of farmers against more extensive application of the Government Wire-Worm Remedy is the high price of the drug.[106]

Perhaps prices were high in 1922, before the Pact era of support for agriculture, yet in 1939 the drug cost a mere nine pence for one hundred doses and Onderstepoort's remedy for nodular worm cost one shilling for the same quantity.[107] Veglia advised farmers to dose with the remedy on a proper basis and also to avoid running flocks on low-lying pastures where larvae multiplied most vigorously. Instead, these lands would be used for green fodder crops — advice which seems not to have been followed because farmers already grew sufficient oats and barley for that purpose. But Veglia also recognized that the large scale of parasitic infection was partly due to factors beyond immediate control:

> The configuration of the Cathcart district (hills and deep valleys with ravines and vleis) and the abundant atmospheric precipitation are responsible for the prevalence of verminous diseases in sheep. The heavy rains of the year 1917 are apparently to be blamed for the unusually severe infection of Wire-worms and Nodular worms noticed in the last few years.[108]

In the wake of Enslin's and Veglia's visits the consternation and excitement died down. One farmers' association thanked magistrate Van der Byl for his assistance and concluded, "assuring you of this Association's hearty cooperation towards the welfare of the community generally."[109] Van der Byl informed Enslin that "since your visit here the sheep farmers are quite quiet and they have left off worrying me about sheep matters."[110] James Field enthused to Van der Byl, "We all feel that our interests and requirements are at all times well represented by you to the Government."[111]

By 1930 the tendency to panic had re-emerged, expressed in deep unhappiness on the part of the BFL at a veterinary research officer's report that the Border's veterinary problems were not so unique that they could not be investigated in existing laboratories in the Transvaal. The farmers demanded a detailed local study and establishment of a local experimental farm or research station.[112] Four years later this was still a strident demand: alleging large-scale Border losses to fever and worms, the BFA asked the Eastern Province Agricultural Union to press for an experimental station in the eastern grassveld.[113] The association prejudged the issue with a comment about "the apparent inability of the available Government remedies to arrest [the worms]."[114] In response, Dr Monnig from Onderstepoort investigated mortality at

Cathcart and reported that heavy rains following the 1933 drought had creat
excellent conditions for worms, particularly lungworms and hookworms. Grass h
grown too rapidly to accumulate adequate nutritive content. Moreover, farmers we
still misusing the government wireworm remedy. Monnig commented,

> It has been found previously in this area that there is a tendency to dose with
> a variety of remedies and mixtures which produce no good results . . . If
> farmers would read more and attempt to apply the recommendations made
> many of the present troubles could have been avoided.[115]

He might as well have saved himself the trouble, for in response some four hundr
farmers gathered at Stutterheim to hear A. F. Lyon, Komgha farmer and ex-creame
chairman, say that the Border "had been left in the position of only being able to get a
from men who knew less about conditions here than the farmers themselves." It w
obliquely suggested that the comparative newness of the parasite problem prov
that farmers knew best: if farmers had managed to rear stock without parasites for fii
years, surely that proved their underlying competence.[116]

Conclusion

Although the inter-war years were a distinctive crisis period in the South Afric
farming sector as a whole, in the case of Cathcart and the Border they require
analysis which takes the relatively time-deep colonial experience there into accou
Extensive farming capitalization and socio-economic control of the indigeno
population occurred alongside extreme violence in many regions of the Eastern Ca
and earlier than in much of the interior. Accustomed to the strong arm of the st
securing its occupation of the land, the Border settler community responded
inter-war vicissitudes and challenges in a manner that presupposed continued st
action on its behalf and at its behest. As crucial players in local politics, the farme
continued to score successes. The Cathcart farmers actually seem to have campaign
successfully for the removal of a magistrate in 1935 on the grounds of his leniency
dealing with Africans accused of various offenses amongst which stock theft featur
largely.

Success and stability were precarious, however. It has been suggested above th
during the inter-war years relations with higher authority became less predictable.
front-line members of the agricultural production system, farmers believed that th
ought to have the privilege of specifying what decisions the state should or should r
implement on their behalf. Such assumptions became increasingly untenab
Agricultural modernization after World War I departed in significant ways fro
development during the nineteenth century, when farmers had still called the tur
From 1918, and gathering pace after 1924, the state determined farmers' priorities

Dr Monnig's vexation ("if farmers would read more and attempt to apply t
recommendations") was countered by stubbornness and closely echoes a reveali
comment made in 1938 by the secretary of one of the farmers' associations: "How ve
ignorant some young and even old farmers were with regard to political and gene
subjects; this could not be the case if farmers regularly read one or two go
newspapers."[117] It may be that insufficient agricultural discourse was being conduct
within the district. Reluctance to receive criticism may also reflect the dilemma
having invested in one or two specialities too long, and then being faced with t

ospect of change at great financial and attitudinal cost. It is important to make the qualification, however, that the Upper Cathcart farmers' increasing acceptance of creameries in the late 1930s, and their interest in soil conservation in the 1950s and '60s, show that the district had not rejected modernization. Parliamentarian M. van Coller once declared himself "an out and out segregationalist," but at the same time indicated awareness that Africans could not be manipulated indefinitely:

> [He said he was] a South African who had inherited prejudices against the native and coloured people, yet . . . if people imagined that the native was a man who got up in the morning, attended to his work, ate his food and then went to sleep, they were greatly mistaken; he was a shrewd thinker, a keen observer and was seriously affected by his contact with the white man.[118]

This consciousness was only faintly echoed by some of his constituents. This account has revealed a paradox of local authoritarianism sheltering under the wing of statutory authority, yet fearful and ambivalent as it realized that the higher authority was largely beyond its power to influence. Coupled with unprecedented difficulties affecting wool and dairying, pressure to adapt and change could provoke parochial attitude or an aggressively independent spirit — for example, when farmers claimed that they knew best how to sell their wool or disregarded specialist veterinary advice. The overall impression that emerges is of a community conditioned to an ethos of prescriptive control over its human and physical environment and with an underlying suspicion of change.

7

Migrant Workers and Epidemic Malaria on the South African Sugar Estates, 1906–1948

ALAN H. JEEVES

During South Africa's early industrial period, the emergence of commercial farmin employing significant concentrations of black workers, developed much faster tha the government's will and capacity to supervise it. On the sugar estates, repeate health scandals and outbreaks of malaria and other diseases cost thousands of live Epidemic malaria on the industry's Zululand frontier arose more from social a economic changes than from environmental conditions; the epidemics had politic not medical origins. After several severe malaria outbreaks, officials in South Afric Department of Public Health (DPH) developed a response that focused on preventi and was on a scale unique in Africa. However, its work suffered from the absence regulatory authority. Even when the state decided to act, as it eventually did, combat malaria, it found itself frequently thwarted by the political power of t farming lobby.

The establishment of sugar estates in coastal, malarial Zululand created larg scale labor demands that led to the introduction of whole new populations to the ar The industry brought to Zululand thousands of workers who were without previo exposure to malaria and created the preconditions for epidemiological disaster. T expansion of commercial farming there was part of a more widespread and rap growth of white agriculture that began to gather speed in the decades after Union 1910.[1] Estate owners needed large amounts of labor. Since the profits of most, like t sugar planters, depended on volatile commercial markets, they demanded it at t west possible price. Unable to mobilize sufficient labor in Zululand itself, the planters turned to the recruitment of long-distance migrant workers.

They quickly became dependent on recruiting companies to supply the labor. The recruiters brought workers from the Eastern Cape, Basutoland and southern Mozambique.[2] The migrants worked on a contract basis for varying periods, living while on the farms as "bachelor" workers in huts or compounds (barracks). As they paid low wages, used coercive labor practices and provided unhealthy living conditions, the planters were unpopular employers. They depended mainly on those without better prospects and too young or old, sick or disabled to go to the mines. The planters invoked politics to offset their competitive weakness in the country's labor markets.

To a much greater extent than the gold-mine controllers, farmers were politically powerful and well represented in Parliament. They defeated or evaded government regulatory measures for decades. Officials found the sugar planters consistently opposed even to implementing malaria prevention and basic sanitation measures, an opposition which put everyone on their estates at risk, including their own families.[3] From the early 1920s, the Department of Native Affairs (NAD) wanted to bring the Natal plantations under the Native Labour Regulation Act.[4] Passed in 1911 (Act 15 of that year), the law applied in Labour Districts, initially mainly the coal- and gold-mines of the Transvaal. Regulations under the act and associated legislation controlled and licensed labor recruiters, required and defined labor contracts, specified minimum standards for food, housing and working conditions and provided for regular inspection by labor inspectors attached to the Native Labour Bureau (NLB), an agency of the NAD.[5]

Officials proposed to apply a modified, less rigorous version of the regulations to the sugar industry.[6] Extending control to include farming required legislation, however. Despite repeated efforts by officials (several draft bills reposed in departmental files), successive ministers simply declined to take the required amendments to the House of Assembly, because they rightly feared the power of farmers' representatives there.[7] In 1921, the NAD introduced legislation to curb the size of wage advances given before recruitment to farm workers (large wage advances encouraged desertion).[8] The amendment, "simple and free from objection as it appears to be," passed Parliament only on the casting vote of the President of the Senate. With this experience in mind, the Minister refused to consider the further measures needed to bring farms fully under the Native Labour Regulation Act. A department official commented that "a fate (a very evil fate) attends all attempts at native legislation, however desirable."[9] On crucial occasions the sugar planters' representative in Parliament from 1920, George Heaton Nicholls, a Zululand estate owner himself, was solely responsible for blocking legislation.[10] Throughout his parliamentary career (he served into the 1940s), Nicholls remained a vehement and effective opponent of regulation. For more than two decades, he was an influential South African Party and later United Party backbencher with the ear of the party leadership.

Despite the opposition of Nicholls, and the power of the sugar lobby, the NAD managed to appoint inspectors on the sugar and other Natal estates (such appointments could be accomplished by administrative action) but left them without adequate regulatory powers. The setting of minimum housing standards for workers was achieved under the Public Health Act, but enforcement remained uneven. Substandard housing resulted partly from farm owners' parsimony, but also from

workers' preference for traditional accommodation.[11] Farm employers remain
largely unregulated until the National Party brought them under the Native Labo
Regulation Act in the 1950s. In 1937, the department did manage to secure t
application of the act to the sugar mills.[12]

The near-complete exemption from regulation helped farm employers in ma
ways. The sugar estates, like other agricultural employers, could legally recruit a
employ underage workers. The Native Labour Regulation Act prohibited licens
labor agents from recruiting those under eighteen. Although difficult to enforce
practice (the births of Africans were not registered which left recruiters and officials
guess at their ages), it did provide some protection from gross abuse. However
farmers and their "*bona fide* servants" could recruit without licenses. The "*bona f*
servants" clause became a loophole which enabled farmers to set up recruiti
organizations, mobilizing workers, including underage workers, for multiple far
employers entirely outside the regulations.

As a result of "administrative relaxation"[13] some years after the act came in
force, even licensed recruiters were permitted to recruit for farm employment tho
between the ages of sixteen and eighteen who had parental permission (loosely a
generously interpreted by officialdom).[14] When the NLB learned that one of tl
magistrates required parents to attend personally to give their consent, it persuade
him to accept a written statement from a chief or headman that the consent had bee
obtained. The bureau knew that recruiters used their African runners (assista
recruiters) to obtain the consent or to claim that they had obtained it.[15] Tl
under-sixteens were not excluded either. Although they could not be formal
recruited, they could be employed as apprentices under long-standing colonial Mast
and Servant regulations.[16] Across southern Africa, an informal division of labor led
the farms getting that part of the migrant labor supply which could not secure mir
employment because of the age, health and gender (the mines did not recruit wome
restrictions which controlled access to it.

By the mid-1920s, this situation was officially recognized. With the agreement
the gold-mines' Native Recruiting Corporation (NRC) and the Director of Nativ
Labour, an official of the NAD, certain Transkei labor agents recruited both for tl
gold-mines and for the sugar estates, until this permission was withdrawn at the er
of 1926.[17] In addition, for a time the NRC permitted some farm recruiters to take "mir
medical rejects" from its camps. The introduction of a stricter medical examination fc
mine recruits in the 1920s, and better screening of those infected with tuberculosis
thought to be at risk, meant higher rejection rates.[18] Many of the workers so rejecte
ended up on the farms. Later, in 1939, the recruiting corporation estimated that 25 p
cent of the Africans arriving at its depots failed the mine medical examination.[19]

Fred Rodseth, an NAD official, told the Native Economic Commission of 1930–3
that, for the recruiters, the sugar plantations were "a very convenient off-loadir
station for all the unfits" and saved the recruiter "losing money on all the derelicts he
collecting . . ."[20] Ill or disabled on arrival in many cases, the workers were high
vulnerable, given the unsanitary conditions and lack of proper medical facilities on tl
plantations. Complaints began concurrently with recruiting for the sugar estates, ar
continued into the 1930s. Improvements were made slowly and grudgingly and on
after repeated health scandals. In a recent article on the Zululand sugar planters' labc
supply, A. de V. Minnaar argued that the lack of medical examination for recruits i
the sugar industry meant that many sick and disabled workers "slipped through

plying that their employment was merely a matter of neglect.[21] On the contrary, eir recruitment and employment became a policy issue, recognized and sanctioned the state.

The diversion of children and the aged, unfit and disabled to the farming industry as viewed by all parties, including the government, as a necessary part of the South rican labor system.[22] For the mines and the government, shuffling unfit and iseased natives" off to the farms eased the labor shortage there and helped to mute rmers' political agitation for even more control of workers and constraints on other ployers in their interest. For the farmers, the labor was better than nothing. though often slow and inefficient and frequently unable to work (most farmers nply thought them lazy), such workers were less able to refuse recruitment, less able desert and less able to protest the poor wages and bad working conditions which ere the norm on most of the Natal and Zululand estates. Workers went to the farms employers of last resort. There was no welfare system beyond the African extended nily, no effective private charity except, on a limited basis, the missions. Whatever e state of their health, however young or old, impoverished people worked or they irved. Officials accepted this reality and accommodated, usually with gaze averted, e employment on the farms of those who were so weak and vulnerable that the work reatened — and often cost them — their lives.

e Growth of the Zululand Sugar Industry and the Emergence of Epidemic Malaria

ie frontier of the Natal sugar industry was coastal, malarial Zululand, where anting began in 1905/6 (figure 7.1). Malaria had long been known in subtropical atal and Zululand. However, the era of large-scale epidemics coincided with the mmercial development of the territory, with the opening of sugar and cotton estates d with the consequent introduction of whole new populations of workers. ommercial farming brought significant concentrations of whites to the Zululand ast for the first time. In 1924–25, a special census of the cane plantations found 606 atal and Zululand white planters farming 212 000 acres.[23] Of this total, 230 Zululand owers had about 70 000 acres under cane. A low-lying, subtropical strip six to fifteen iles wide, extending from the Tugela River in the south to Mtubatuba in northern iluland, the cane belt had a deserved reputation for unhealthy living conditions, rrying a high risk of fever. Many regarded coastal Zululand as "not fit for white ople."[24] It was not very good for black people either and before the advent of the gar industry, population density was low.[25]

However, the climate and soils were well suited to the production of sugar cane, d the demography of the area began to change rapidly with the advance of the white rming frontier. Since the farmers soon found that sufficient labor was unobtainable cally, they began to import it. Local Africans understandably avoided the hard anual labor and low wages involved in cutting and loading cane and disliked orking in fields infested with cane rats and poisonous snakes. The total number of orkers involved grew steadily as the industry expanded. During the period 1910–38 •uth African sugar production increased by more than 500 per cent to 522 732 tons.[26] uch of that increase came from the Zululand estates, which by the mid-1930s nployed fifteen to twenty thousand workers during the cutting season.[27]

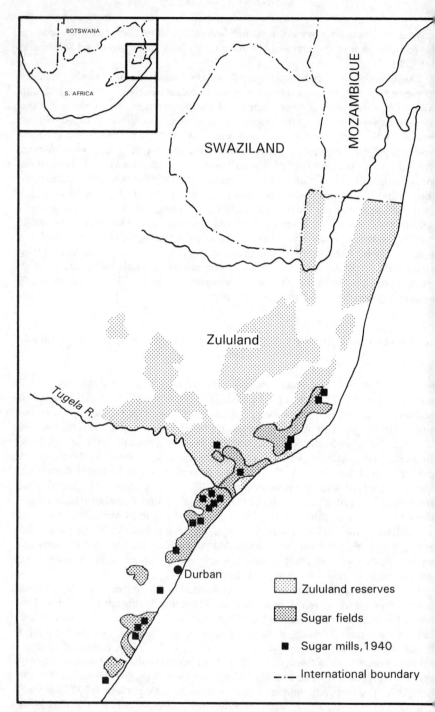

Figure 7.1   Natal Sugar Fields and African Reserves, 1930s

Since most of the workers served short contracts (180 shifts) and fewer of them
ere needed outside the cutting season, the Zululand planters used perhaps
venty-five to thirty thousand laborers annually. Given the poor physical condition
d bad health of many of the workers, more of them had to be recruited to maintain
bour complements. Only about half of the work-force could be obtained locally.
ailway and road development required by the expansion of commercial farming also
ought in large and vulnerable populations of unskilled migrants. For instance, the
nstruction of the Mtubatuba-Pongola railway line in the 1920s introduced several
ousand workers, most of them without previous contact with malaria.[28] Like
anters further south, the Zululand estate owners recruited workers from Pondo-
nd, the Transkei and Basutoland.[29] A more important external source of labor for
ululand was southern Mozambique, and all of these workers had had continuous
posure to malaria from childhood. Thus, many were carriers of the malaria parasite,
asmodium falciparum.[30]

Although malaria appeared every year in Zululand, its incidence tended to be
ariable and confined mostly to the wet summer months (October–May); some years
perienced serious outbreaks, while others were mostly disease free.[31] Because of the
asonal character of malaria in much of the area, the local population in the cane belt
d less tolerance than workers from Mozambique and the two northernmost
ululand districts, Ubombo and Ingwavuma, where malaria was continuously
esent. In explaining the incidence of malaria, the white residents tended to focus on
e environment, rainfall and the presence of mosquitoes.[32] However, the demogra-
ic changes which resulted from the expansion of commercial farming in the malaria
lt were crucial.[33] Labor migration and the introduction of new working populations
both carriers and non-exposed groups into Zululand virtually guaranteed a malaria
isis, not only among the non-exposed workers brought in from outside but also
nong the local population. Heavy rainfall in certain years and the associated
roliferation of mosquitoes were important but could not by themselves have
roduced as serious effects.

Until recently, historians of Zululand and Natal have paid little attention to
alaria. Yet its impact during the epidemics of the 1920s and early 1930s is starkly
sible in the archival record. What Alfred W. Crosby has recently written about the
le of smallpox in the Spanish conquest of the Americas applied also to malaria in
frica:

> Contact between people among whom smallpox was endemic and people
> among whom the disease was unknown would always mean deadly
> epidemics for the latter. Examples of this would be easy to find because
> smallpox was anything but subtle. It moved fast, made people very sick,
> sometimes hideously so, and often killed them. Smallpox was a thug; it
> mugged and murdered and forced its way into the record.[34]

1928–32 malaria swept through the estates and the reserves of Natal and Zululand
ith an intensity never before seen in southern Africa. On a small scale, it reproduced
e kinds of effects associated with the ravages of smallpox among the Amerindian
opulation in the first decades of European expansion. The virulence of the disease
a its epidemic form shocked even those whites whose long residence in Zululand
ad bred familiarity with malaria.[35] Their experience had been that, with the
vailability of quinine, serious consequences could be avoided. Nothing in that

experience prepared them for the thousands of deaths associated with the epidemic
Although the mortality was mainly among Africans, it frightened the previous
complacent settler population and threatened to disrupt completely the commerci
farming economy.

The disease struck with special virulence among the laboring population
brought in from non-malarial areas. Often very young or "mine medical rejects,"
these workers were particularly at risk from infectious disease. With no or litt
previous exposure to malaria, they were especially vulnerable. The epidemiologic
character of malaria intensified the risk to all those exposed to it. Infection by th
parasite did not confer assured future protection. In malarial areas, the disea
produced high infant mortality and an acquired partial tolerance among th
survivors, often wrongly characterized at that time as "immunity." Even that limite
tolerance faded from the infected population once they were removed fro
continuous exposure. Chronic malaria went with chronic anemia and often malnutr
tion, which reduced workers' energy and efficiency and made them vulnerable
other diseases. For this reason, plantation owners preferred to recruit from no
malarial areas. Nevertheless, the malaria-tolerant workers from southern Mozamb
que were a principal component of the estate labor force. Although often witho
obvious symptoms, they provided the essential reservoir of infection which w
transmitted to others through contacts with the mosquito vector.[37] Bringing the
together with workers who were without previous exposure was largely responsib
for the severity of the outbreaks in these years.

Striking down the non-exposed workers on the plantations, epidemic malar
also overwhelmed the acquired defenses of the indigenous inhabitants in the adjace
reserves, those with moderate previous exposure and therefore moderate tolerance
the disease. That the introduction of a non-exposed population into a malaria endem
area increased the danger both for them and for the local population that had son
tolerance for the disease was well known to public health practitioners in South Afri
and abroad: ". . . the introduction of any considerable number of non-immunes w
stimulate a local increase in the virulence of the disease, to a point where the toleran
of the indigenous immunes is insufficient to cope with it."[38] The results were seen
the thousands of victims who succumbed both in the African reserves and on th
estates in 1928–32.

In the epidemic form that Zululand and Natal experienced in the 1920s and 193(
malaria was, therefore, not the result of an original environmental condition but
product of the commercial exploitation of the territory. At the height of the wor
outbreak, a medical missionary at Mahlabatini reported that the Zululand midland
had experienced a serious malaria epidemic for the first time. He estimated that near
three-quarters of the population became ill and that at least one thousand deati
occurred. Malaria carriers arriving from the coast brought the disease into the area, h
believed, and the proliferation of mosquitoes following the late rains in Ap
encouraged its spread.[39] Migrancy and the continuous flow of workers into and out
Zululand distributed the disease throughout Natal and even into the north-easte
Cape and Basutoland, all areas previously largely disease free.[40] Although thousan
died in the malaria epidemics of the 1920s and 1930s, the problem would have be
even worse but for the fact that most of the non-tolerant workers were brought in f
the cutting season which extended from May to December and lay mostly outside th
hot, wet summer period when the risk from malaria was highest.

Public Health, Migrancy and Epidemic Disease

Migrancy as a factor in the explanation of malaria epidemics, and in relation to rural poverty and demographic changes, has featured in recent research on Swaziland.[41] Randall Packard's study found that colonial medical personnel tended to attribute the serious malaria outbreaks of the period exclusively to rainfall patterns and mosquito breeding. They missed the equally important underlying trends in the political economy having to do with labor migration, rural underdevelopment and impoverishment that increased the vulnerability of the colonized.[42] Research on the incidence of disease in colonial Tanganyika also emphasized that medical officials saw the origins of tropical diseases purely in epidemiological terms: the presence of infectious agents in the environment and the lack of immunity in the target populations. The study concluded that they were mostly ignorant of the role of "larger social changes affecting the structure of society."[43]

Evidence from the 1930s and earlier suggests, to the contrary, considerable awareness on the part of some colonial health workers of the role of social and economic changes in the spread of disease in Africa.[44] The medical missionary at remote Mahlabatini, referred to earlier, had no difficulty concluding that the malaria outbreak in his district had demographic rather than environmental causes. He blamed migrancy for the spread of the disease into his district. Even earlier, during the outbreak of epidemic trypanosomiasis (sleeping sickness) in western Kenya at the turn of the century, it was colonial medical experts who made the link between the onset of colonialism and the eruption of epidemic disease. According to new findings, colonial rule was too recent and its initial effects too tenuous for the indigenous people affected to make the connection.[45] Colonial medical officials, however, attributed the outbreak to colonial labor demands and the associated migration. From the early twentieth century, major campaigns to prevent infectious diseases such as smallpox and plague were frequent in colonial Africa. They were usually led by tropical medicine specialists who were schooled in preventive medicine and very aware that the diseases they were combating had erupted in epidemic form often as a result of the population movements and economic changes associated with the onset of colonial rule.[46]

Whatever the state of public-health awareness among officials in Swaziland and Tanganyika, their South African counterparts did show an understanding of the role of demography in the outbreak of epidemic disease, at least with regard to malaria. However, in acting on this understanding, the Department of Public Health (DPH) faced serious obstacles and initially had indifferent success. A small department, the DPH became a separate entity only in 1919 in response to the world-wide influenza epidemic which had killed thousands in South Africa immediately after the war.[47] The Public Health Act of that year brought together and amended existing provincial legislation (enacted before Union). It defined the department's role as largely advisory to provincial and local health authorities and the district surgeons.[48] Under the South Africa Act, the four provincial councils administered public hospitals. The district surgeons were part-time officials, appointed by the Union government to provide care for the poor; by 1937, there were 363 of them.[49] They mainly treated whites but sometimes also served Africans. As a subdepartment in the Department of the Interior, the DPH had a small budget and a tiny staff. From the beginning, the South

African state found it easier to justify funding measures to protect livestock than
maintain public health.[50]

Throughout the African rural areas, state medical services were crippled by a lac
of personnel and lack of money. The missions and traditional practitioners provide
what health care there was.[51] By 1933, there were seven government-aided "nativ
mission hospitals" in Natal and Zululand and eight state hospitals directly under tl
authority of the provincial council. Some of the provincial hospitals took blac
patients in segregated facilities.[52]

The reluctance of the Department's officials to confront epidemic disease amor
Africans was not the result of any failure to see the underlying social and econom
causes. As their policies to combat malaria showed, they understood that dimensic
very well,[53] but applied their knowledge selectively. Even the best-intentione
proposed to combat poverty and malnutrition among Africans only in a very narro
way. In the achievement of even these restricted aims, they were prevented fro
acting on their understanding as effectively as they wanted to by tight budgets, k
prevailing doctrines about the limited responsibility of the state for individual heal
and welfare, by racial prejudice among farmers, politicians and the white electora
generally, and by the refusal of white employers to invest in disease preventio
Officials urged farmers to recruit only fit workers and to pay, feed and house the
decently. They did not propose to attack the root causes of Africans' ill health, whic
lay in pervasive rural poverty in the reserves.

Although officials eventually extended malaria prevention programs to tl
Zululand reserves, they apparently gave little thought to applying preventiv
techniques to most of the other diseases that afflicted Africans in the rural areas:
bilharzia,[54] for instance, to the childhood diseases that killed on a large scale, or
tuberculosis. Black infant mortality, which was very high, went unremarked becau
African deaths were unrecorded. The DPH funded treatment of Africans afflicte
with syphilis but the program was limited.[55] Treatment was in the hands of tl
part-time district surgeons, and there was only one of them for every eighty thousar
Africans. Few of the patients were able or willing to stay the whole course[56] of
difficult treatment regime extending over more than a year (using the drug salvarsa
by injection[57] at a time when antibiotics were still unavailable). As a result, tl
department's program to combat syphilis among Africans failed to reach many of tl
victims, especially rural ones.

Syphilis, tuberculosis and other common diseases of the African rural populatio
although often eventually fatal, were "silent killers." They did their insidious wo
more slowly than was the case with malaria epidemics. While frequently partial
incapacitated, workers afflicted with tuberculosis, venereal disease or bilharzia cou
keep working, at least for a while. In any case, to address these scourges effective
would have required a comprehensive attack on rural poverty that officia
contemplated only for poor whites.[58] A recent study has shown that the discovery
widespread bilharzia infection in the children of Afrikaner poor whites in the northe
and eastern Transvaal influenced the development of the Pact governmen
comprehensive campaign against white poverty after 1924,[59] but the program was n
extended to Africans.

Malaria Prevention in Zululand

espite a slow start and uneven application, the DPH's campaign against malaria in oth the white areas and the "native reserves" of Zululand was unique. In other parts f Africa, mosquito control was limited to the urban areas and to estates with large orking populations, or to the vicinity of major engineering works in malaria endemic eas, such as the Zambezi Bridge project at Kariba.[60] Unusually in an era when edical thinking focused on curative approaches, South African public-health fficials from the beginning emphasized prevention as the preferred means to combat alaria.

South Africa's DPH managed to avoid in its malaria campaign most of the roblems which, some medical historians now argue,[61] western medicine inflicted on frica. In important respects, the country's public-health experts were at the forefront f international thinking concerning malaria prevention and treatment. During the ter-war period, the League of Nations, through its Malaria Commission, helped to rganize an international network of malaria researchers.[62] They read each other's ublished research findings and corresponded regularly.[63] The South African DPH articipated in that network and through it was in regular contact with health officials sewhere in Africa. Knowledgeable about the etiology of malaria, South African fficials also emphasized the role of economic, social and demographic changes in the uption of serious epidemics. They knew that those without previous exposure to alaria were at special risk from it. They recognized the danger of bringing on-exposed workers together with carriers in the same labor force.[64] They stressed e role of migrancy in spreading the disease and increasing vulnerability to it.[65]

The department's ranking official in Durban, Dr G.A. Park Ross, the Senior ssistant Medical Officer, drew attention to the role of poverty and malnutrition in creasing the vulnerability of African workers to malaria and other infectious iseases, laying down the axiom that "the poor are malarious and the malarious are oor."[66] Since so many of the recruits for the sugar estates, railway works and other terprises in Zululand were malnourished and "verging on scurvy," they were nlikely, he recognized, "to put up much of a fight against Malarial Fever."

No sentimental humanitarian, Park Ross, a crusty and blunt-speaking patho-gist, had a long association with Zululand and often expressed views typical of atal settlers.[67] Unlike many contemporaries in the medical profession, however, he d believe that Africans shared a common humanity with whites. As a paternalist, he as offended by the needless deaths that resulted from employers' failure to provide e most basic facilities for sanitation and malaria prevention. His accounts in 1924–25 his inspection tours of the construction works on the South African Railways' tubatuba-Pongola line in Zululand were typical. He made the first trip following ports of heavy loss of life to malaria. The railway contractors had brought in ousands of black workers to build the line. Recruited mostly from the cities, many of em were sick and partly disabled on arrival. Park Ross reported that "the boys are ying like sheep" in the contractors' camps.[68] Use of non-tolerant labor in the malaria ne, he warned, required "meticulous care," and the contractors had ignored the anger.[69]

While recognizing that railway officials were making some effort to treat the alaria victims, he regarded their policy as ". . . the sort of solicitude which allows the atient to die and then sends a wreath."[70] He meant that treatment came too late and

should not have been needed at all had the railway contractors taken proper care
recruit only the physically fit and to take preventive measures against the disease.
one of his letters on the deaths at the camps, Park Ross showed his impatience with th
complacency and lame excuses that he encountered from both employers and th
NAD: "It is our duty to give the lie direct to an absurd and vicious belief amor
uninformed persons, as many employers unfortunately are, that a mortality abov
normal is to be expected in connection with pioneering enterprises, and I trust that th
information I have been given as to the waste of native life may be proved by you
[Native Affairs] department to be unfounded."[71] He knew and his corresponden
knew that the information was accurate.

After his initial reports in 1924, Park Ross had carried out a follow-up inspectio
early in 1925. His concern arose from additional information that death rates remaine
excessive and that the railway contractors' carelessness put their mainly non-tolerar
labor at high risk.[72] He believed that with proper precautions rates of illness from a
causes could be kept below 8 per cent and the number of deaths reduced to th
minimum. Incidence of disease above that level and any significant number of death
"would represent a failure to carry out proper measures." Writing to the Secretary fc
Public Health (SPH) just before leaving for Zululand, Park Ross said that he wa
encouraged that local railway officials in the construction zone now understood th
malaria danger and had asked for a skilled person to supervise their precautior
against mosquitoes. However, the railway headquarters had not responded:

> If [senior railway officials] would get out of their heads the idea that
> anti-malarial work is a welfare matter and therefore not worthy of their
> consideration and try to look at this problem from the point of view of
> [pounds, shillings and pence] they would perhaps come to the enviable
> conclusion that a failure to take precautions against malaria is on a par
> with failure to paint coaches or oil engines. Probably Dr Malan
> [D.F. Malan, Minister of the Interior and Minister of Public Health],
> however, would like to emphasize the welfare side of the question as well.
> Dealing mostly with commercial men, I have given that up and take only the
> money side of it.

Upon further investigation, Park Ross found that the South African Railways an
Harbours had adequate facilities in the construction zone, and took reasonable care c
its workers, and that the incidence of sickness, especially from malaria, was low. O
the other hand, the situation in the private contractors' camps was "not good." H
reported that most of the contractors "turn off" sick workers, ejecting them from th
compounds, "presumably in order to save hospital fees." Park Ross called urgently fc
the implementation of new regulations: "The questions are serious matters involvin
human life and require decision under the Native Labour Regulation Act and th
immediate attention of the Department of Native Affairs." Two months later, in Ma
he reported[73] that the situation on the railway works had worsened and warned that i
the contractors' camps ". . . a condition amounting to exploitation of human li
obtains in places. Some twenty boys have died under conditions which amount t
deliberate neglect."[74]

The NAD inspectors' reports confirmed Park Ross's charges.[75] In Pretori
however, officials seemed little concerned by the deaths in the camps. Not only did th
government fail to act on the recommendation to extend Act 15 to the railwa
construction works, but senior NAD officials played down the seriousness of Par

ss's findings. Forwarding the response of the Chief Native Commissioner (CNC) of
atal, the Secretary of Native Affairs (SNA), J. F. Herbst, wondered what the fuss was
out. The railway administration, he said, was "doing all that can reasonably be
pected" and was, after all, "under no legal obligation in regard to these natives." The
NC had advised that Natal's health regulations could be used against the contractors
f necessary."[76] The Assistant Medical Officer had to battle on two fronts to get the
essage of malaria prevention taken seriously: with uncaring Zululand employers
d with complacent officials in Pretoria and Pietermaritzburg.

From the beginning, Park Ross had argued that the best means of preventing
idemics was to exclude the most vulnerable workers from the malarial parts of
luland: the whole coastal belt and the lowlands of the north-eastern section. He saw
at the introduction of commercial farming to Zululand had created new dangers by
awing in large populations of workers with no or little previous exposure to
alaria. He understood that migrancy spread the disease in widening circles across
e country. As early as 1910, Park Ross warned the Natal colonial government of the
sks involved in bringing non-exposed workers into the malaria endemic areas.[77] By
25, as commercial farming expanded, migrancy increased and the population of
lnerable workers grew larger, the danger had become more immediate.

Following Park Ross's reports early in 1925 on the railway construction camps,
e doctor and C. A. Wheelwright, the CNC, Natal, submitted a more comprehensive
port in October on labor conditions throughout the malaria belt. They pointed out
at the population of non-tolerant migrant workers in Zululand was growing as a
sult not only of railway employment, but also of the extensive estate development
en under way. North of the sugar belt, in the most intensely malarious parts of
luland, farmers had moved in to grow cotton and other crops. No other part of
uth Africa, they stressed, had such a large "native population" working in so
healthy an environment. Safeguarding the labor force from epidemic malaria
quired "the closest consideration of the government," without which "serious
tbreaks" of the disease were unavoidable. Citing evidence from the 1923/24 malaria
ason, they noted that rates of infection on some estates had reached 100 per cent.[78]

The warning went largely unheeded and by 1929 the situation had worsened.
rk Ross condemned the sugar industry's recruiters who continued to draw labor
om the Transkei and Basutoland, much of it "human trash," the workers rejected by
her industries.[79] He blamed the employers who failed to prevent "the wholesale
mping of unfortunates with tuberculosis and other diseases on the coast belt of
atal." He had information that as many as one third of the recruits were unfit for
ork at any point in the contract period. Nevertheless he would permit the
cruitment of "mine medical rejects" provided that they were fed properly to prevent
urvy and to offset the effects of their poor physical condition on arrival. Park Ross
ged that government doctors examine all workers recruited for the fever belt.

Epithets such as "derelict," "human trash," "mine medical reject" and the "dregs
the recruiters' haul" recur in official correspondence. The workers characterized in
ese ways were so sick, incapacitated or disabled as a result of work on the mines or
sewhere that they were unable to function effectively. Officials blamed the recruiters
r sending them to other employers, blamed the employers for employing and
ploiting them, but also seemed to blame the victims themselves. "Human trash"
rried the connotation of "less than human," of people about whom one did not need
worry too much. Officials had written them off, mentally, as already dead. Like Park

Ross, they resented the recruiters for bringing them in and resented the trouble ar
expense that the government was put to.

Park Ross's correspondence reveals that the public expense worried him mo
than the risk to the unfortunate non-tolerant workers whose recruitment l
condemned. At the end of 1930, he warned the SPH:

> That the sugar industry is continuing to recruit human trash for Natal in spite
> of warnings is only too evident. I signed three refunds yesterday for
> [tubercular] foreign Natives (Transkei and Transvaal) for admission to
> Addington Hospital, and there is no saying how much this sort of thing is
> costing Government. I am going to suggest that it is a more costly business
> for us to have to pay for the treatment of these derelicts than actually having
> to do the examination of recruits on entering into the Province and make the
> recruiter pay for repatriations.[80]

The callous, impersonal approach to the medical problems of Africans, characterist
even of well-intentioned medical officers, comes through in the tone of this lette
Earlier, the Director of Native Labour had explained that there was no regulatory bas
to require medical examinations.[81] Some of the large sugar recruiters arranged fc
medicals, but the "great bulk" of the estate labor was not examined, at recruitment o
at any other time.

Following a tour of Zululand earlier in 1930, Park Ross had renewed his warning
against introducing "masses of raw labour" into malaria endemic areas. One yea
before, malaria had appeared south of the Tugela, in Natal proper, mainly among th
non-immune population.[82] As the malaria menace worsened, the Assistant Healt
Officer stressed more urgently that a long-term solution to malaria epidemics require
the exclusion of such workers from the high risk zone.[83] He took the view that the onl
outside workers permitted to enter the malarial areas should be those from souther
Mozambique. Because of restrictions on the entry of clandestine immigrants fror
Mozambique, written into the 1928 Mozambique Convention at the insistence of tl
Portuguese, the ban could not be enacted until 1935, after the restrictions wer
dropped and the intake of clandestine immigrants was "regularized." Informally, tl
government tried with some success to get planters to limit the intake of non-tolerar
workers. It did not solve the problem, however, as the 1935 decision to make the ba
formal indicated.

A more fundamental reform, proposed by public-health officials long before ar
consultation with outside experts, was to change the labor system on the sugar estate
This proposal went well beyond the improvements in housing, nutrition, and medic
facilities that the department viewed as minimum measures for malaria preventio
and protection of the labor force. Park Ross became an early advocate of settled wag
labor on the estates. He stressed that Natal was contending not merely with a medic
problem but with a social pathology which had greatly increased the susceptibility o
the black population to illness and disease. He wanted to attack the problem at i
social and economic roots; for its adverse effects on families, migrancy was bad i
itself, and it was detrimental to workers' health, fitness and efficiency. Migranc
brought together workers without previous exposure to malaria and chron
sufferers; it created the preconditions for epidemics.

Writing in the *South African Sugar Journal* during the malaria outbreaks of th
mid-1920s, he argued that the establishment of a permanent work-force on the estate
with laborers housed there with their families, could entirely eliminate the need fc

cruitment of workers. Single-room houses were as easy to construct and nearly as heap as compound accommodation. He provided a design for a compound which ould house ten single men and be later converted into a two-room, self-contained ouse.[84] Park Ross wanted the planters to invest in their labor force. Properly fed and oused, living with their families, workers would become more efficient. They would e less at risk from malaria and other diseases. His efforts to persuade the planters, owever, failed totally. Even well-intentioned observers had trouble understanding he relationship between epidemic malaria and the expansion of the commercial rming frontier in Zululand. Writing on the malaria epidemics of the early 1930s, dgar Brookes later praised the work of Park Ross but stated categorically that . . . European settlement and industrialization cannot be blamed for malaria."[85] The octor and a few of his colleagues knew better.

Within the malarial areas themselves, the DPH worked to disrupt the transmission of the disease. Although committed to the view that a permanent solution to alaria epidemics in Zululand required the exclusion of non-tolerant workers from he endemic areas, officials believed that, in the meantime, with proper protection gainst mosquitoes and reasonable care, they could prevent epidemics and reduce the umber of individual cases to a minimum. They focused on eliminating mosquitoes nd larvae. During the late nineteenth and into the twentieth century, medical uthorities had debated the relative merits of vector eradication, usually involving rge-scale engineering projects to eliminate breeding sites, on the one hand, and uinine[86] prophylaxis, on the other, as the preferred method of coping with malaria. ome experts favored mosquito elimination exclusively, while others advocated uinine prophylaxis on its own.[87]

Natal's public-health officials were pragmatists and preferred a combined pproach. They believed that eradication of mosquitoes (called "species sanitation") as readily achievable, and that there was no excuse for failure to accomplish it.[88] hey also worked to identify the human carriers of the parasite and supplied quinine the refined, chemically more stable form that was becoming available in the 1920s.[89] t different dosage levels, quinine was effective for the suppression of symptoms both efore the onset of fever (prevention) and later, during bouts of the disease. The side ffects[90] from quinine were not pleasant and could themselves be incapacitating. The heap and powerful synthetic anti-malarial compounds, particularly chloroquine, hich produced fewer of these debilitating side effects, did not become widely vailable until after World War II. Malaria remains incurable, although a vaccine, after ecades of research, began clinical trials in 1994 in Latin America and Tanzania.

From the mid-1920s, public-health officials in Natal worked to enlist broad upport in the white and, after 1929, the black communities for the campaign of alaria prevention. Park Ross thought education an essential part of the program and rote and toured tirelessly in the malarial areas to promote "malaria mindedness." He nderstood, as did few of his contemporaries, that "the successful practice of public ealth requires salesmanship of a high order."[91] The DPH published pamphlets not nly in English and Afrikaans but also in Zulu ". . . to keep our Natives up to date in alarious matters."[92] It offered lectures on malaria control in the reserves and invited issionaries, "native preachers" and evangelists, and "intelligent natives" generally attend them.[93]

Outside endorsement of the department's emphasis on prevention, "species anitation" to eliminate mosquitoes, and public education came in May 1931 with the report of Professor N.H. Swellengrebel of the University of Amsterdam. Th government had brought him to South Africa in 1930 to advise on the malar problem. A member of the League of Nation's Malaria Commission, Swellengreb conferred the authority of a respected international expert on the advice which th DPH had provided to planters for nearly a decade.[94] Like the department, Swellen grebel recommended that the government ban the employment of non-tolerant labc in the malaria endemic parts of Zululand and that the estates receive priority in th employment of workers from southern Mozambique. This convergence of th department's views and those of a prominent foreign expert led to a much expande program of malaria prevention. It also suggests that the idea of primary, preventiv health care as the preferred approach to combating disease is not quite the moder discovery that is sometimes claimed.[95]

In developing anti-malaria programs, officials opposed a centralized, institu tional approach. For the white areas, Park Ross was an advocate of local committees t direct the work. His reasons were partly budgetary: Public Health did not have th funds for a centrally directed program. He also believed, however, that succes required local leadership to support and finance prevention. The idea that effectiv public-health programs must be rooted in and supported by the communities the serve was not widely understood among Park Ross's medical contemporaries.[96] H advocacy of it grew out of his pragmatism. Throughout the malaria belt, he urged loc white communities to establish their own committees. Persuasion was not sufficier and eventually the provincial administration acted in 1932 to require them to be set up It took the most serious malaria epidemic in the history of the province to prompt th step.

In the black reserves, the department's education campaign was slow to start. had begun following the 1929 epidemic. Park Ross found the "native authorities generally "apathetic" in combating the spread of malaria. Devolving responsibility o them, however, he regarded as the most effective way of securing their activ participation. Thus he proposed to establish local health committees in the reserve modeled on those in the white areas, but was blocked by opposition from the NAI and local opinion.[97] The department's eventual concern to extend malaria preventio in the reserves gives rise to the question: Why was the medical campaign against th disease extended to the black rural community at all? Apart from the sporadic effor of the district surgeons and the few mission doctors, there was nothing to stop th common infectious diseases from ravaging the black rural population unimpedec There was no elaborate preventive campaign against them and not much evidence c official action to provide even basic medical care to Africans outside the urban area The principal reason for extending the malaria campaign to the black rural areas wa probably that Natal whites thought that the malaria menace originated in th reserves,[98] although in reality it first developed more on the estates.[99] Partly also th reasons have to do with the different scale of the effects of malaria compared wit other diseases.

Malaria epidemics incapacitated quickly and killed on a large scale. Outbreaks c the disease spread fear in the white community when widely reported in the pres While the role of African carriers in the transmission of many other diseases to white was similar, the epidemic character of malaria outbreaks made the danger seem muc greater and more immediate. Black malaria victims were more visible than the large numbers who died slow deaths from various chronic diseases, particularly tubercu

sis and syphilis, especially when the sufferings of the former were widely reported
the press.[100] In these circumstances, even hardened white racists might eventually
ecome responsive to epidemic malaria among blacks.[101] Moreover, malaria had
:onomic consequences that erupted suddenly and dramatically. The entire labor
rce on an estate might succumb, bringing work to a standstill.

Once under way, the anti-malaria campaign in the reserves faltered as a result of
adequate funding and the inability of rural people to perceive the need for
rophylactic measures.[102] Park Ross said that the department had encountered
inbelievable" difficulties when it moved into the reserve areas and attributed them
"superstition and ignorance."[103] To help overcome the hostility, he began to train
frican para-medical health workers and sent them out, after rudimentary medical
reparation, to educate chiefs and headmen, distribute quinine and provide informa-
on to local people. By 1936, there were seventy of them at work in the province.[104] The
epartment understood that using black staff for this work would be much more
'fective than relying on native commissioners and other white officials, of whom the
lack population remained deeply suspicious.[105] Even so, it was not easy to recruit and
tain such health workers, who were poorly paid. Park Ross noted that the work
ivolved risks for which they were not compensated. They experienced considerable
ostility and were sometimes chased out of the districts which they were supposed to
rve. Some of them had served as NAD veterinary assistants and stock inspectors and
iced the hostility of the local population's opposition to stock-culling and so-called
etterment schemes. The effectiveness of the whole group was threatened by this
iisguided recruitment policy.[106] During the winter season, the department laid them
ff. In 1932, the doctor complained that he had lost several of his best assistants and
iat but for the depression most of them would have left.[107]

Reluctantly, Park Ross called for collaboration with "native herbalists" to combat
ialaria in the reserves. He planned to distribute quinine to them. Though he shared
rith most western-educated doctors at the time a distrust of indigenous medicine
nd, like them, normally avoided anything that would make the traditional
ractitioners more credible to their patients, he concluded that the government should
nsure that they had an effective medicine to distribute. This step might strengthen
ieir hold over the local population but would also, he knew, greatly assist prevention
1 the reserves. In this, as in other aspects of his malaria program, his essential
ragmatism overcame his prejudices.[108]

There were narrow limits, however, to Park Ross's willingness to tolerate Zulu
ultural norms and social practices, as James McCord, a medical missionary in Durban
1 the 1930s, explained in his account of an encounter with the Assistant Health
)fficer. According to McCord, his Zulu patients would not take quinine or any
iedicine in the form of tablets; they got their medicine from "witch doctors" (his term)
lways in liquid form. McCord's account reveals that he, too, had little sympathy with
rhat they both regarded as the ignorance and prejudice of most of the black malaria
atients. McCord, however, was more willing to take it into account and to try to work
round it. To circumvent their aversion to the quinine tablets during the worst of the
ialaria epidemics, McCord prepared quinine in a liquid solution of lurid color and
appalling taste." He sold the preparation on the suspect grounds that Zulu patients
. . . had no faith in either pills or free treatment." Hearing of the doctor's success,
ark Ross called him in, listened to his explanation, but was not impressed. McCord
elieved that most of the Zulu simply discarded the quinine tablets that were
istributed to them.[109]

The two doctors did agree, however, that medicine should be sold, not give away, and that an important goal of scientific medicine should be to root ou "superstition."

In the meantime, they differed on the degree and kind of adjustment each wa prepared to tolerate to accommodate present beliefs. This episode and many othe encountered during the anti-malaria campaigns demonstrate that, as elsewhere i Africa,[110] established belief systems among the black population of Zululand remaine extraordinarily resilient in the face of the challenge from "scientific" medicin Western-trained doctors were too few, too identified with white structures (domination and control, and the efficacy of many of their treatments and medicin too doubtful (if not entirely wanting), for them to prevail in the way that Park Ross ar most of his colleagues expected.

In the reserves, Park Ross initiated the use of insecticide for hut spraying again mosquitoes and oil spraying of breeding sites to destroy the mosquito larvae whereve large human populations were congregated in malarial districts. Initially, th anti-larval work was confined mostly to the white areas. Officials promoted hu spraying in the reserves but wanted (unreasonably, given the poverty there) loc people to pay for the equipment. For his advocacy of hut spraying, Park Ross wa widely condemned (critics thought the program ineffective) but eventually vind cated.[111] At Park Ross's urging, the DPH even experimented with self-closing scree doors for the traditional beehive huts but abandoned the idea after trials as impractic and too expensive.[112] In order to help drain mosquito breeding sites, the departmer advocated tree planting in the Zululand reserves and proposed schemes for bo government planting and planting by local communities.[113]

The African population paid heavily for the delayed introduction of preventiv measures. By the conservative official estimate (black deaths remained unregistered 14 900 Africans died in the malaria epidemics of 1928–32. Figures compiled by th magistrates put the toll much higher.[114] Between November 1931 and June 1932 alon the magistrates in Zululand reported the deaths from malaria of a total of 134 White 21 122 Africans, 859 Indians and 17 persons of mixed race.[115] Within the Department (Public Health, these data were highly controversial.

Commenting on a table recording the magistrates' estimates of malaria death Park Ross told E. N. Thornton, the SPH, that "a table of this kind has only to get into th hands of the Press or members of Parliament to make even more trouble for us than w have already had." The data were "all the more dangerous," he added, because th figures were official. He and an NAD official, Fred Rodseth, had examined th estimates of the magistrates and regarded them as "absolute and unadulterate tripe."[116] The SPH responded that he was satisfied on the evidence available that th number of "native deaths" did not exceed 10 000 in the 1931/32 season.[117] He cited th reports of black para-medical health workers (styled malaria assistants[118]) whic showed that 30 508 people in the reserves had fallen ill from malaria in the previou season. The assistants had recorded 2 620 deaths. Thornton thought that there migh be under-reporting by about 50 per cent. However, the coverage of the assistant estimates was incomplete and Thornton apparently doubled the figure again to get h estimate of 10 000 deaths.

The only certainty to come out of the controversy was that no one knew ho many Africans had succumbed to malaria. Fearing an outcry in Parliament and th press and a demand for central control and funding of the anti-malaria program, Pai Ross and Thornton had an interest in understating the death rate. Even their figure

)wever, revealed a serious situation. Whatever the actual number of deaths, the
alaria epidemics of the period took a heavy toll, the more so because the Zulu
)pulation was already gravely weakened by malnutrition, as a result of falling
come and employment in the depression and the devastating drought of 1931–33.[119]

White planters living near the reserves remained critical of Park Ross's advocacy
local initiative and control even in the black areas. They claimed that the reserves
ere the principal source of malaria infection and wanted the state to take direct
ntrol of eradication measures.[120] They demanded that the DPH undertake the
)raying of breeding sites in the reserves, but officials rejected the proposal.[121] Park
)ss was unrepentant. He told a native commissioner in 1932 at the height of the
alaria epidemic that the planters should "put their own house in order," rather than
y to shift responsibility.[122] When one of the Natal farmers' associations sent in a
solution to the effect that the cost of the malaria committees' work should be borne
/ the Union government, Park Ross told Sir Edward Thornton that contending with
ich views added a little ". . . to the gaiety of health work in Natal."[123] Earlier, he had
escribed rates of infection as infinitely greater in the coastal farming areas than in the
ljacent reserves.[124]

By 1932, the Department of Public Health had developed a comprehensive
)proach to the malaria problem throughout the malarious districts of Natal. For
-evention, Park Ross could call on eight supervisors, one pathologist and four
boratory technicians who were attached to the department. There were six clerical
aff, three "native spotters," and fifteen full-time and thirty part-time malaria
ssistants, as well as twenty "native sprayers" and twenty "native labourers"
nployed on a casual basis.[125] Although a formal ban on the use of non-tolerant labor
mained politically impossible, department policy was to discourage its use on the
lluland estates. In the sugar belt, the local malaria committees had been appointed
1d their duties defined under Natal Provincial Ordinance 11 of 1932. Department
ficials assisted in delimiting the committees' spheres of responsibility and providing
cessary coordination among them. Dr L. Fourie, a deputy to Park Ross, was working
ll time on the malaria problem together with a DPH inspector; a survey of farms was
anned but only a small number could be visited.

Officials had organized meetings with fifty-one farmers' associations and
ranged other meetings to publicize the program against malaria. The department
-ovided training for local health officers and expanded training for the black malaria
sistants. Experienced assistants received a six-day revision course in 1932 and new
ssistants received ten days' training.[126] In line with the emphasis on local initiative
1d control, the Natal Provincial Council paid the salaries of the malaria assistants.
1e NAD supplied quinine and paid the other costs associated with anti-malarial
ork in the reserves.[127] The budget for 1933 was £5 500 from Public Health funds for
atal and the Transvaal, while the provincial governments spent £11 500. The central
)vernment provided additional sums to hire more staff over the following three
:ars.[128]

What was particularly noteworthy about this program was that it combined an
nderstanding of the social and economic basis of disease and disease prevention with
ie best understanding of the etiology of malaria then available. It was a low-
chnology program that was in today's terms friendly to the environment. Park Ross
:lieved in mosquito nets and screens more than he believed in quinine or anti-larval
)raying.[129] Quinine was needed because of human inefficiency and forgetfulness.

Spraying against mosquitoes and their larvae was needed because people forg(
could not afford, or refused to use their nets or failed to take other precautions.

In 1934, Park Ross reported that the department was "within sight of gettir
malaria out of the Native Reserves," except in the intensely malarious northe
districts. His work had met with most success in the populous Tugela valley.[130] Fro
the beginning, the whole approach stressed prevention, exclusion from the endem
area of workers most at risk, wide dissemination of information, local initiative ar
control, basic training for black para-medical health workers and reliance on simp
technologies. Like Park Ross himself, Public Health officials went often into loc
communities to warn people of the dangers and to encourage the use of simp
preventive measures. They enlisted the newspapers to carry their message
prevention and vigilance.[131] The underlying philosophy of the malaria campaig
seems more characteristic of modern approaches to primary health care than of tl
dominant trends in the medical thinking of the 1930s.[132]

As the malaria season was ending in May 1935, the *Natal Witness* carried i
interview with Park Ross.[133] The doctor explained that the anopheles mosquito ha
been present in unprecedented numbers in the previous summer. This could ha\
been expected to produce "one of the most extensive outbreaks of fever in the histo)
of Natal." However, this potential was not realized, a result which he attributed to tl
success of the preventive measures organized by local malaria committees on the coa
and by the government in the reserves. They had educated the black populatio
inspected estates, encouraged extensive spraying against mosquitoes, made quinir
readily available, and worked during the winter to identify carriers and to find foci (
summer breeding. The population had finally become "malaria-minded" with tl
result that the disease, despite ideal environmental conditions for its spread, failed
gain a hold.[134]

Officials did not doubt that the retreat of epidemic malaria from much (
Zululand resulted from both the exclusion of the most vulnerable workers (a form,
ban was imposed from September 1935[135]) and the continued emphasis on preventic
in Zululand itself. Preventive measures remained important partly because enforc
ment of the exclusion was uneven, and the political forces at work made withdrawal (
the ban a possibility. The industry as a whole, according to estimates from the 1930
still relied heavily on Pondo labor.[136] With so many Eastern Cape workers on car
fields in Natal proper, the temptation to renew their employment in Zululan
remained strong whenever shortages loomed.[137]

The pressure did not come only from the Zululand planters. When the ban can
into force, black councilors in the United Territories Transkeian General Council (tl
Bunga) protested the loss of employment for workers from those territories an
opposed their exclusion from Zululand.[138] Its members were caught in a difficult an
contradictory situation. Although the Bunga was well aware of the excessive dea
rates on the Zululand and Natal estates and had for many years registered complain
about the bad working conditions there,[139] the councilors had to be even more worrie
about high unemployment and poverty in the Transkei. Eastern Cape Members (
Parliament joined the chorus of protest. Louis D. Gilson, MP (East Griqualand), wro
to Douglas Smit, the SNA (from 1934), complaining that the clandestine workers fro
southern Mozambique were driving out Cape workers from the Natal north-coa
sugar fields. "Our Natives," he said, are "starving."[140] When combined with pressu
from the planters, the political opposition to the ban on the employment (

n-tolerant workers meant that recruiting for the Zululand estates in the Eastern pe might be restored. Malaria prevention in Zululand, therefore, remained an portant issue.

Originally, the ban on the employment of Transkeian and Pondo workers plied to the whole of subtropical Zululand, north of the Tugela River. However, by e late 1940s officials moved the southern limit of the exclusion zone north to the mhlatuzana River. Although they attributed the absence of malaria in the newly ened section to the success of the preventive measures pioneered by Park ss,[141] prevention had been greatly facilitated by the use of DDT from the end of orld War II.[142] With malaria under control, the planters began to campaign after the ar for complete abolition of the ban on the employment of non-tolerant labor. owever, Park Ross's successor warned in 1949 that "any relaxation of control will evitably lead to severe outbreaks of malaria," even though he agreed that the uation in the malaria endemic zone was "vastly improved." The planters, supported the NAD, kept up the pressure, but he refused to recommend any relaxation of the striction.[143]

Conclusion

recent analysis of the development of western medicine in British colonial Africa ressed the importance of understanding and decoding the changing bio-medical rratives and discourses characteristic of the inter-war decades. These ideologies nerged as practitioners of tropical medicine struggled to make sense of the alien edical environment of Africa, to take intellectual possession of it, and to explain the ofession's successes and failures.[144] Far from being the product of disinterested and jective science, prevailing medical ideas were socially and politically constructed, d reflected, drew from and helped to sustain the structures of power, class and race at colonial rule brought to Africa.

Such an approach can be helpful in assessing the outlook of the Department of blic Health in the inter-war period. Park Ross's attitude emerges from his blications during the anti-malaria campaigns and from the extensive correspon-nce that survives in the records of the Department of Public Health. His perspective as broadly influential in shaping the outlook of the whole department and neither emed to change very much in the years covered by this chapter. Elsewhere in British lonial Africa, public health and preventive medicine apparently went out of fashion the 1930s,[145] but Park Ross, a man in his fifties at the height of the malaria campaigns, mained an unreconstructed believer in sanitation and environmental medicine. though he did not denigrate curative medicine and was fully cognizant of the best atment regimes then available, he remained committed to prevention. In holding to is view, he both reflected and helped to mold the orientation of the Department of blic Health, and this orientation persisted into the 1950s.[146]

The DPH's malaria campaigns of the 1920s and early 1930s were conducted in the dition of the campaigns against plague and other diseases mounted in various parts British colonial Africa from early in the twentieth century.[147] In accordance with the proach elsewhere, the DPH did not try to establish comprehensive health aintenance and disease prevention programs. The work was instead *ad hoc* and ecemeal. Officials targeted specific diseases and tended to focus on those that, like malaria, had the greatest potential to cross the racial divide from black to white or th‹ again like malaria, most threatened to disrupt the functioning of the economy.

Far from relying on the prophylactic potential that quinine still provided, Pa Ross insisted from the beginning that preventing diseases wherever possible w preferable to trying to effect mass treatment once outbreaks had occurred. From h letters, reading between the lines, there seem to be several reasons for his policy. Ma distribution of medicines such as quinine was expensive; the Department of Pub¹ Health had a small budget. Second, it was difficult not only to get the medicine into tl hands of all of those who needed it, but also to get them to take it. Outside the coast strip, where the white population was concentrated, much of Zululand remaine utterly remote and inaccessible. Campaigns of prevention might have been subject the same constraints of distance and remoteness, but Park Ross was countir (unsuccessfully as it turned out) on local community initiative and control even in tl black areas. "Superstitious" Africans rejected his quinine tablets even when they we proffered by the black malaria assistants who were frequently run out of the rur areas. Finally, quinine at the dosage levels used, unlike, for instance, smallpox vaccir carried persistent and debilitating side effects which led recipients to question i efficacy and which interfered with labor productivity on the estates.

In his understanding of the role of the indigenous population in malaria outbreak Park Ross did not emphasize either racial or cultural factors as predisposing African to the disease. Instead, he developed a political-economy explanation that anticipate some recent advocates of such a view.[148] Rejecting the widespread notion that malar epidemics originated in the behavior of a susceptible population in the reserves, ‹ could be explained simply from conditions in the natural environment, as the settle claimed, he emphasized the hazardous structural problems that estate agriculture ha created in Zululand. Migrant labor brought unexposed workers and chronic malar sufferers into dangerous proximity and spread the disease into southern Natal and tl north-eastern Cape, where it had rarely been known before. Although Park Ross d‹ not propose to overturn the existing racial and economic order, he was certain critical of its deficiencies and proposed remedies that would have changed fundamentally. When the planters and their political allies rejected both his propos to abandon migrancy and the more modest step to legislate against the employment non-exposed workers (until 1935), Park Ross put renewed emphasis on straightfo ward, low-technology methods of preventive medicine and handed to local commur ties the responsibility to implement and pay for them.

Of course, the doctor's understanding of the reasons for the persistence of tl epidemics did not confine itself to the structural changes associated with the growth the settler economy, important as he considered them. Migrancy was a significai causative factor and precondition, but not an insuperable barrier to the prevention outbreaks. Thus he recognized that human behavior was central in explaining tl spread of malaria. The tenacity of the disease was the product of two kinds ignorance. First, there was the ignorance of the indigenous population, which I mainly attributed to "superstition" and the baneful effects of "witch doctors." Th he was not excessively judgmental in this view is suggested by his proposal nevertheless, both to work with the herbalists and to enlist local people in the reserv in the anti-malaria work on the model of the malaria committees successfull promoted in the white farming areas. Education and the malaria assistants would, I believed, eventually win over the black population.

The obduracy of the planting community was, he recognized, a tougher nut to ack. Theirs was a willful ignorance born of self-interest. Sunk in superstition, as he ewed it, the black population mainly harmed itself. However, the planters put the hole population of Zululand and Natal at risk. They would neither adopt his ructural remedies, nor accept responsibility for species-sanitation measures until ovincial regulation required the establishment of the malaria committees.

It took ten years for the DPH to make headway against the forces opposing fective malaria prevention in Zululand. Even then, its public-health goals were nited and its successes incomplete. The eventual decline of epidemic malaria should ot obscure the state's overall failure to regulate working and living conditions fectively on Natal estates. Reports on health conditions in the industry in the 1930s owed reasonably satisfactory housing conditions on the large estates, but serious ortcomings in the quality of the diet, the state of hospitals and the treatment of the ck. They described circumstances little changed from the first reports twenty years fore. In 1935, the Bunga repeated its frequent demand for a proper system to ensure e safe return of workers repatriated because of illness. Forwarding the resolution to etoria, the Transkeian Chief Magistrate warned that "very much greater improve- ent" was needed. The next year, he complained again of a "deplorable state of fairs," and officials in Pretoria concluded from these and other reports that the pplication of Act 15 to the sugar industry "would be advantageous in every way."[149]

Occasionally, some of the planters supported the extension of the Native gulation Act to their industry.[150] The main motive for this stemmed from the dditional protection that the act would provide against competition for labor from her employers. For most farmers, however, the intrusive government regulation of ages and working conditions, which also came with the act, outweighed any benefits at might flow from it in facilitating labor mobilization.[151] The result of this omplacent and myopic outlook," according to L. J. Phillips, the author of the NAD's)36 report, was that the sugar planters had to make do with workers who could not cure employment elsewhere. The planters had no one to blame but themselves. If the dustry provided decent conditions and reasonable pay, it could, Phillips thought, old its own" even against the mining industry. Because the planters had remained odurate despite twenty years of efforts to persuade them, legislation was essential. In)36, however, the United Party government was no more willing than its prede- essors to face Parliament on the issue. Draft amendments to the act remained in the AD's files.[152]

There was no medical mystery behind the slow progress of the anti-malaria mpaign in the 1920s and early 1930s. The etiology of the disease was well nderstood by the professionals responsible for treating it. Even before the arrival of e League's expert, Swellengrebel, the Department of Public Health had developed mprehensive plans for malaria control in Zululand.[153] Prevention, public education, cal initiative and exclusion of those workers most at risk were the key elements. The sponsibility for failing to act quickly enough to prevent repeated outbreaks of the isease lay not with the public-health establishment, or even the Native Affairs ureaucracy, but with the politicians who, against the repeated advice of their own fficials, refused to confront the Natal plantocracy.

The expansion of the sugar industry into frontier Zululand both created the alaria epidemics of the period and produced the pressure to deal with them. If alaria had not threatened the planters' labor supply and their production system,

the state would probably not have invested the money and committed the personn
to deal with it that it eventually did. Yet the DPH was not acting merely as the agent
the planters. Officials publicly blamed them for much of the trouble: their reliance o
the migrant system, their callous neglect, and their failure to provide basic medic
care, proper nutrition, or decent living and working conditions. The political power
the planters was such, however, that they successfully defied bureaucratic regulato
efforts into the 1950s.

The sugar industry experienced recurring financial crises in the period 1919–36,
which must have increased its unwillingness to take a longer view of its labor system
Yet resistance even to measures that cost little suggests that these farm employe
needed to make their profits in ways that affirmed their deeply held views about t
racial inferiority of blacks. A refusal to recruit only the medically fit and to provid
healthy living and working conditions was, of course, not unique to the Natal an
Zululand planters. Many other South African industries, including the gold-minin
companies during the first several decades of their existence, treated their worke
similarly. But for the work of Park Ross and a handful of committed officials in th
departments of Public Health and Native Affairs, the expansion of South Africa
commercial farming enterprise would have taken an even higher toll of peopl
health and lives than it did.

8

Plantation Agriculture, Mozambican Workers and Employers' Rivalry in Zululand, 1918–1948

DAVID LINCOLN

bor procurement in Zululand became a fiercely competitive affair during the three cades between 1918 and the ascent of the National Party to state rule. For local nployers in Zululand's infant commercial agriculture sector, and more distant nployers in the Natal sugar industry and the Transvaal gold-fields, the northern end the territory represented a potential source of labor and a convenient thoroughfare r migrant workers from southern Mozambique. In vying for compliant hands to rform some of the most arduous work under some of the harshest conditions on the bcontinent, each of these and the other employers who were embroiled in the ruggle for labor in northern Zululand expected to be individually favored by the ate. The prize in this struggle ranged from Zululand residents, who were the least nenable to sustained submission as agricultural employees, to Mozambican igrants, who had the greatest allure for both the mining companies and agricultural nployers.

Rivalry amongst labor recruiters in Zululand was heightened after World War I y the expansion of labor-intensive estate (or plantation) agriculture north of the hlatuze River. Unpropertied white beneficiaries of the provisions of the Land ttlement Act, most of them returning soldiers, were placed on the land as ate-assisted commercial farmers. Depending on the location of the settlements, ıgar or cotton initially offered the brightest prospects, and there were hopes in some aces for good returns from pastoral and other agricultural production. Since the

cultivation, and especially the harvesting, of both sugar cane and cotton demanded
abundance of labor, these settlements made a significant impact on the way in whi
the regional labor market was formed.

A number of constraints inhibited the flowering of estate agriculture in northe
Zululand before 1948. These included the settlers' indebtedness, the insidio
presence of malaria and nagana, and the vagaries of international commodi
markets. But in terms of security, the settlers were perhaps at their weakest when
came to the procurement of labor. Their participation in the market for labor passe
through three phases between 1918 and 1948. The first was characterized by a conte
between the unorganized employers in Zululand's incipient estate sector and tl
highly organized Natal sugarocracy and Transvaal Chamber of Mines.[1] An inte
mediate phase followed during which the settlers were confronted with the collapse
the local cotton industry, the demise of the sugarocracy's labor recruiting organiz
tion, and the prohibition of the employment of "malaria-intolerant" workers
Zululand. The third phase began in 1937 with the formation of the Farm Labo
Committee by Zululand's cane-growers.

Phase One

As estate agriculture advanced in the post-World War I years, divisions appear
between the various groups of employers who were intent on drawing the men
northern Zululand and southern Mozambique into labor contracts. The Chamber
Mines and the sugar industry were the major adversaries in this employers' strugg
for labor along southern Africa's eastern seaboard. Despite its tentacles stretchir
deep and virtually without hindrance into labor pools throughout the subcontiner
the Chamber of Mines was infuriated by the sugar industry's unregulated recruitme
of Mozambican workers who were then lost to its own recruiters. But employers in tl
sugar industry were hardly a homogeneous group, and Zululand's cane-growers ar
the rest of the employers in the sugar industry were sharply divided over the matter
labor recruitment. The initial source of friction was the activities of the Natal Coa
Labour Recruiting Corporation (NCLRC). The NCLRC functioned along similar lin
to the Chamber of Mines' Native Recruiting Corporation (NRC)/Witwatersrar
Native Labour Association (WNLA). Formed under the auspices of the Natal Sug
Millers' Association, its purpose was to recruit labor on behalf of Natal's millers-cur
planters and several of Natal's larger independent cane-growers. Most of tl
NCLRC's recruits were drawn from Pondoland in the Transkei and, in growir
numbers during the 1920s, from Zululand. Zululand's cane-growers were embitter
by the NCLRC's "poaching" of labor north of the Tugela River, while they we
obliged to scour the Transkei, Basutoland and other regions outside Zululand in the
search for workers.[2]

Those Zulu work-seekers who were not creamed off by the Chamber of Mine
with its superior wages and recruitment infrastructure, were highly valued but wide
criticized by the growers who took them on as cane-cutters. Their shortcoming was
tendency to work in the cane fields only as long as was necessary to earn a desired su
of money. Migrants from further afield were usually considered easier to control ar
contain on the sugar estates than local workers, but even more difficult to procu
against competition from the NRC. Recruiters of migrant sugar workers consequent

id great store by those whom the mines would not accept because they were too
oung or physically unfit to work underground. Zululand's cane-growers, having
ither the financial nor the organizational resources of their competitors in the NRC
d the NCLRC, relied in turn on proportionately larger numbers of women and
ouths to make up their seasonal labor requirements.

Tiered in this fashion, according to the respective employers' standing, the
arket for mine and sugar workers was also graded according to material conditions
the various source areas for manual labor. Compared with Zululand's interior, or
atal's reserves, or the Transkei, the reserves of coastal Zululand generally offered
eir inhabitants far better prospects for production and consumption without
course to continuous employment (see figure 7.1). Zululand's northernmost corner
as especially hospitable and its inhabitants were dislodged by recruiters only under
treme duress.[3] Thus the men of Ingwavuma and Ubombo were commonly
ortrayed by the districts' magistrates as self-sufficient producers and reluctant
iployees; they were pressed onto the labor market in the early 1920s when their
ops were devastated and their lives threatened by drought.[4] While employers were
ot consistently able to recruit workers living in Ingwavuma and Ubombo, these
stricts were traversed by numerous Mozambican workers on their way to
iployment along the South African sugar belt or on the Witwatersrand (see figure
?).

The main conduit into the sugar industry for Mozambican workers was provided
Ndumu Ltd, a trading and recruiting operation in northern Zululand, which
ipears to have had L. E. Rutherfoord as its principal in the early 1920s (while his
other, S. W. Rutherfoord, was striving to make a success of an allotment at the
overnment's Ntambanana settlement). During the next decade and into the 1940s,
dumu Ltd was to grow in influence and in official notoriety, with R.H. Rutherfoord
its managing director. In that period the company had S.W.O.L. Johnson as its
airman and J.K. Johnson as well as Zululand's Member of Parliament, G. Heaton
cholls, on its four-man board of directors.[5] These three co-directors of Rutherfoord's
ere also directors of the Umfolozi Co-operative Sugar Planters, giving Ingwavuma's
ative Affairs Commissioner adequate reason to describe Ndumu Ltd as a firm with
very powerful Directorate."[6]

It was an elaborate system over which R.H. Rutherfoord presided, capable of
obilizing many hundreds of Mozambican citizens as estate workers. In its most
icial period, the system delivered Mozambican workers to their Zululand
iployers as follows: after being taken to one of two border posts by Mozambican
inners," they crossed into Zululand and passed into the hands of one of
itherfoord's three licensed runners, who escorted them to his Othobothini head-
arters; from there they were accompanied to the local police station to obtain their
ward passes before being carried by lorry to the Mkuze station, where they
abarked on the train journey to their prospective employers along the sugar belt.[7]

While Rutherfoord's efforts came to focus primarily on satisfying the needs of
iluland's and especially the Umfolozi Co-operative's cane-growers, many Mozam-
:an migrants were self-motivated or directed by recruiters to take work elsewhere in
iluland or south of the Tugela. The traffic in Mozambican workers was ostensibly
ohibited by the Portuguese and South African governments in the interests of their
ine) labor convention. It nevertheless thrived and was so efficient that the Chamber
Mines developed an obsessive preoccupation during the 1920s with trying to curtail

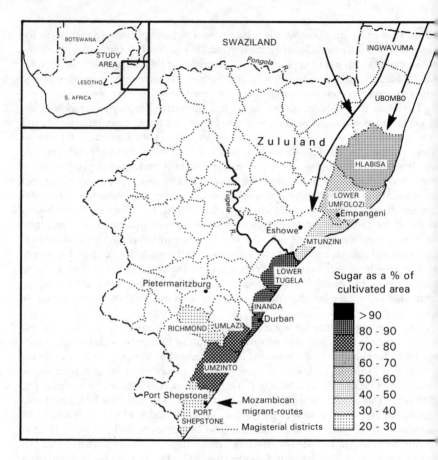

Figure 8.1   Mozambican Migrant Routes to Zululand

it. The Chamber of Mines' W. Gemmill was quick to intervene when he learned
mid-1924 that Mozambicans, assisted by certain Zululand storekeepers and sustaine
by wage advances, were wearing a trail through Maputaland and into Zululan
Initially, Gemmill's complaint and his annoyance that the entire procedure w.
"apparently winked at by the Union Authorities" won him little more from Nata
Native Affairs officials than a lesson on the geography of Maputaland. A few montl
later he resumed his quest to put an end to the labor traffic, this time armed wi
detailed information provided by Dr L. Bostock, WNLA's District Manager
Lourenço Marques. Bostock's intelligence report showed flagrant abuse of bureaucr
tic devices by migrant workers and border officials alike, with a flourishing trade
passes. This must have been something of an embarrassment to J.F. Herbst, tl
Secretary for Native Affairs, for it was inconsistent with the information he ha
previously communicated to Gemmill.

Although Gemmill is not likely to have known of it, Herbst had some oppositic
from one of his subalterns. When it came to dealing with the movements

ozambican workers, Herbst found himself having to challenge the permissive
titude adopted by Natal's Chief Native Commissioner, C.A. Wheelwright, an
titude favoring monitoring rather than policing, and one that was apparently shared
the Johannesburg-based Portuguese Curator, Dr P. de Carvalho.[8] Wheelwright was
idently taken to task by his superiors and in mid-1925 he formally instructed the
agistrates of Zululand that Herbst was unable to "facilitate or countenance" the
migration of Mozambicans into Zululand.[9] This directive did not stop the traffic,
hich continued clandestinely until mid-1928, when Wheelwright informed the
agistrates that Mozambicans could again be admitted into the region for work on
aluland's sugar estates.[10]

State officialdom exhibited an extraordinary level of ambivalence regarding the
mployers' struggle for labor, with individual and departmental initiatives sometimes
enly contradicting others in response to the appeals of different employers' lobbies
the mining and sugar industries. This unevenness became even more apparent
hen other agricultural settlers in Zululand attempted to find a niche in the labor
arket. Cotton-growers formed a significant, albeit considerably smaller, lobby of
mployers bidding in northern Zululand for workers to perform seasonal harvest
ork. It was not a coherent lobby either, its constituents being separated by distance
d infrastructural differences. While the Departments of Lands and of Agriculture
ove to support the cotton-growers as settlers and as farmers, the latter's marginal
sition in the embattled market for labor could not be readily improved by branches
the state which were also expected to ameliorate conditions for the recruitment of
oor by the mines and the sugar industry.

The strongest demand for cotton-pickers came from various growers in the
agudu district, notably R. Rouillard's sprawling Candover Estates. Small growers,
spersed in the Ntambanana, Hluhluwe and Mkuze settlements, accounted for the
mainder of the demand. Although an organization like Candover Estates had the
fluence and administrative capacity to recruit migrant workers from remote areas,
dividual settlers such as those on the Mkuze and Hluhluwe settlements made do
th their own hands, tractors and a few laborers even at the height of the cotton boom
the mid-1920s.[11]

While the majority of the cotton-growers were unorganized and ineffectual
cruiters of labor, the Central Co-operative Cotton Exchange in Durban was
fficiently interested in the supply of cotton lint to appeal to the Prime Minister for
lp. Hertzog reacted in a fashion to gladden the heart of any scholar who holds to an
strumentalist view of the state. From his office, word went out that the Provincial
lministrators of Natal and the Transvaal should attempt to rearrange African
pils' school holidays to coincide with the cotton-picking season. Although the
spective officials seemed compliant enough, Natal's Administrator would not
cind the authority he had accorded the mission schools to set their own semesters.[12]
en if cotton farmers could not quite commandeer school children in the
otle fashion suggested by the Prime Minister, the official green light had been
ven for the use of child labor in the cotton fields of northern Zululand. The state's
ncession to the cotton industry was the latest in a succession of extensions to
e region's labor pool: workers too young or unhealthy for the mines were
nsidered legitimate recruits for migration to the sugar estates, and even younger
ildren were deemed appropriate as pickers when the cotton farmers joined the
ntest for labor.

Phase Two

Labor-intensive estate agriculture in Zululand offered workers lower wages, a poorer housing and other environmental conditions, than they could expect south the Tugela or on the mines.[13] These circumstances undoubtedly contributed more the apparent anarchy of the regional labor market than any other factor. Since or one-quarter to one-third of Zululand's sugar workers were recruited by profession recruiters, most of the ten to twelve thousand workers found their own way to t cane fields as "voluntary" workers. Sugar- and cotton-growers alike adopted furti strategies to recruit or entice workers while keeping public health officials busy tryi to improve conditions on the estates, notably where housing and preventive measur against scurvy and malaria were concerned.

The collapse of the cotton industry in northern Zululand in the late 1920s led the concentration of most of the region's labor-intensive commercial farming in t sugar sector. It was, therefore, workers in the cane fields who bore the brunt of t renewed spate of malaria that ravaged Zululand during the late 1920s and into t early 1930s. The devastating epidemic provided a dramatic context for the publicati in 1931 of the *Swellengrebel Report on Malaria*. N. H. Swellengrebel's recommendatio were decisive in that they precipitated the declaration of Zululand as a zone employment exclusively for malaria-tolerant labor. This meant that the Zulula cane-growers could no longer employ workers from south of the Tugela. It a implied a greater dependence on Mozambican labor.

Other competitors for labor in the region did not face the same restriction Zululand's cane-growers, and the NCLRC for one could now expect to recruit from much larger number of potential workers, in the Transkei and elsewhere south of t Tugela, who were prohibited from taking employment on the mines or in Zulular Moreover, southern Mozambique was seeing a growing exodus, as work-seek went south to compete for jobs with rising numbers of unemployed South Afric victims of the Great Depression. Even if these circumstances produced such a surf of labor as to allow the NCLRC to go into voluntary liquidation in 1931, Zululanc growers still fared poorly in the business of labor procurement.

Three successive legislative developments followed, with the intention bringing the situation under legitimate control and, to some extent, of smoothing t way for the Zululand cane-growers. Firstly, the 1934 revision of the Mozambiq Convention heralded a new dispensation for the Zululand growers; they could no legitimately employ Mozambican workers by paying a registration fee of five shillir per worker, each of whom was obliged to carry an annually renewable pass costing f Secondly, during 1935 the coastal and northern Magisterial Districts of Zululand we declared a Restricted Area, meaning that laborers could only be recruited for wc from within those districts. Thirdly, from mid-1936, the recruitment of Mozambic workers was prohibited within a twenty-mile-wide zone along Ingwavuma's bord with Mozambique.

By mid-1935 the stream of Mozambicans into northern Natal and Zululand h become a flood. Hundreds were arrested and briefly held in police custody befc being released on the instructions of Natal's Chief Native Commissioner.[14] Wheth legitimately or not, others found their way into employment without hindrance, ma with active encouragement. In this respect Rouillard, the former cotton-estate own played a facilitative role, which he evidently regarded as nothing less th blic-spirited beneficence (though it was subsequently to land him in court on minal charges). As he admitted quite candidly, hundreds of Mozambicans, some of :m women, were passing through his large irrigation farm on the Transvaal side of : Pongola River (to which he had moved after the collapse of Candover Estates). is tide had started during the construction of the Pongola irrigation works over the eceding two and a half years, a project that had provided employment for eleven to irteen hundred Mozambican workers until its completion in early 1935. Rouillard nself had about two hundred workers on his books, mostly from Mozambique, and accommodated and fed any additional transient work-seeking compatriots of :irs for four pence a day while arranging employment for them south of the ngola. He would routinely telephone sugar and wattle companies to announce the ailability of this labor and then transport the workers by lorry (for a fee) to ndover, or Melmoth, or even Empangeni, depending on the employers' juests.[15]

This fresh influx of Mozambican labor had a pronounced effect on employment tterns along the sugar belt. Many hundreds of Mozambicans were employed south the Tugela in the sugar mills and cane fields of the Stanger district.[16] The splacement of Transkeian workers by Mozambicans was cause for anxiety among iefs and administrators in the Transkei who foresaw a decline of recruiting in ndoland.[17] By mid-1937 some ten thousand Mozambican workers had arrived in iluland's Restricted Area, but local cane-growers continued to complain about >gal recruiting on behalf of employers outside the area. The time had come for the iluland growers to organize themselves, and the Zululand Farm Labour Committee FLC) was constituted by members of the Zululand Planters' Union. Another of the nfolozi Co-operative's directors, J. A. Erlandson, was appointed as the new body's airman and, not surprisingly, the intrepid Rutherfoord was contracted as the 'LC's recruiting agent.

Phase Three

' combining forces to recruit through a central organization, the growers repre- nted by the ZFLC did not achieve tighter control over the recruitment of ozambican workers. For one thing, the wages in Zululand still trailed the forty to rty-five shillings per thirty working days that field workers were paid south of the igela.[18] For another, the relevant government officials displayed a growing disin- nation to defend the Zululand employers and their inferior employment practices.

The discrepancy between conditions in Zululand and those in the other regions iere workers from northern Zululand and Mozambique took employment, was the ix of the employers' struggle. One after another, African witnesses, testifying in 37 before the Native Farm Labour Committee at Empangeni and Ingwavuma, spoke inadequate wages as the main deterrent to estate work. The cane-growers, on the her hand, repeatedly cited the independence and self-sufficiency of Zululand's rican inhabitants as the root cause of their labor problems, a predicament that, they sisted, would only be aggravated by wage increases.[19] The repellent effect of rticularly poor wages and working conditions no doubt favored the Zululand owers' chief rivals for labor, and as ground was lost in that struggle during the late 30s, rivalry within Zululand's sugar sector itself intensified.

Illegal recruiting by various parties in Ingwavuma was complemented by touti
within the sugar belt, with trucks moving recruits under cover of darkness in t
Mtunzini district.[20] These activities illustrated the inefficacy of existing restrictions
the face of local recruiters' competitive wiles. The twenty-mile prohibited zone on t
Mozambique border had not been advantageous to Zululand's cane-growers, a
when one of their recruiters, E. Prozesky, was brought to book for illegal recruiti
Rutherfoord also was forced to curtail his operations to avoid prosecution.
mid-1938 the zoning was revoked at Heaton Nicholls's request.[21] This rescindi
eased conditions for recruiters of labor for the cane fields as well as for an expandi
wattle industry in the northern Zululand interior.[22]

Prozesky and Rutherfoord were two of the dozen recruiting agents in t
Restricted Area, five of whom were attached to the NRC.[23] Unlike Prozesky (who
principals included certain Zululand cane-growers and some Natal colliery boss
and the other recruiters outside the NRC, Rutherfoord was now committ
exclusively to the supply of labor to Zululand cane-growers. Given Rutherfoor
threatened position in the constellation of recruiters, the ZFLC advocated the creati
of a monopoly under which it would be the only organization, apart from the NF
officially permitted to recruit labor in Ingwavuma. Not least of the opponents to t
ZFLC's scheme was Prozesky, armed with a petition signed by cane-growers in t
Nkwaleni, Gingindlovu and Amatikulu areas.[24]

While acrimony was building up between the two groups of growers in Zulular
the cane-growers' position vis-à-vis employers in other sectors began palpably
erode. Permission was granted in April 1939 for the recruiting, in the Restricted Ar
of Mozambican workers for wattle estates in the Paulpietersburg district in northe
Zululand and the eastern Transvaal districts of Piet Retief and Ermelo.[25] Otl
noteworthy and increasingly insistent contenders for labor were Natal's coal-fiel
whose productive epicenter had shifted eastwards since Union with the ascent of t
Hlobane district to primacy over other coal-mining districts in the province.[26]

Such developments put the ZFLC more aggressively on the offensive. Heat
Nicholls, for instance, tried in 1940 to persuade the Native Affairs ministry to allov
Portuguese company to recruit labor in Mozambique for Ndumu Ltd to allocate
cane-growers in Zululand.[27] Obstructed with little difficulty by the Chamber of Min
Heaton Nicholls's proposal probably did nothing to enhance the name of Ndumu I
in the corridors of state power. Despite the ZFLC's protestations, state officials did r
distinguish between Ndumu and its chairman, Rutherfoord, whom several import;
bureaucrats held in contempt. When Rutherfoord fell foul of the Department of Nati
Affairs and had his recruiter's license canceled, Ndumu Ltd continued to functi
using the ZFLC's runners and with Rutherfoord taking a transport fee in lieu of t
capitation fee to which he had been entitled as a recruiter.[28]

Every avenue, with the exception of improving material conditions of wo
seemed to have been explored by the ZFLC as the competition for labor intensifi
during World War II. They frequently repeated their appeals for a monopoly
recruiting, to no avail. The Department of Public Health continued to block th
equally persistent efforts to resume recruiting south of the Tugela, even when t
Secretary for Native Affairs added his voice to their refrain.[29] The unwavering stand
their arch-critics in the Department of Public Health was of unexpected benefit to t
ZFLC, for it thwarted a powerful initiative to have the malaria controls on lat
recruitment dropped altogether. The Secretary of Commerce and Industries h

,ped that by freeing the movement of labor along the entire sugar belt (and not just to Zululand as the ZFLC wanted), an expansion of sugar production would be couraged to meet the rapidly growing demand from domestic consumers and from itain.[30] Had it succeeded, the bid to end the malaria controls would have opened iluland and its Mozambican labor resources to southern recruiters, to the detriment the Zululand cane-growers: the anopheles mosquito had vested Zululand's ne-growers with a modicum of protection in the developing labor market.

The Zululand cane-growers' wartime efforts to regain some of the initiative in the oor market were not altogether futile. The Umfolozi Co-operative Planters had markable success in having the first Wage Determination for sugar-mill labor, in 42, accord them the legal right to pay their mill workers 20 per cent less than the dustry's norm. The incredible claim on which their privilege was based was that ey employed uneducated laborers with a low standard of living in a district where alaria-intolerant Indian workers could not be expected to work.[31] Another minor ncession won by the Zululand cane-growers was in having access to prison labor tively facilitated by the Department of Native Affairs.[32]

Post-war agricultural policy provided a stimulus to extend and accelerate mmercial crop production, but the Zululand cane-growers were apparently hard it to overcome their relative impotence on the labor market. They were not assisted ' a concerted attempt to bring an end to the use of Mozambican labor in the sugar dustry. Although there had been a Portuguese official stationed at Empangeni since e beginning of 1938 to administer the bureaucratic needs of migrant Mozambican orkers and their employers in Zululand, and although the United Transkeian rritories General Council had objected on more than one occasion to the presence of ese workers on the sugar belt, it was only at the end of 1945 that press reports of ne-growers' efforts to recruit Mozambican workers elicited a public outcry. The mpaign to exclude foreign labor from the cane fields was spearheaded by the ort-lived Natal Sugar Field Workers' Union, which pressed for material improve-ents to working conditions for local labor.[33] The NSFWU's plea was no different om that made repeatedly in the past by government officials, nor was the response of e cane-growers on this occasion any different from their passive responses to those irlier appeals.

As reluctant reformers, the Zululand cane-growers could not expect to be favored ' state policies. With criticism of their employment practices mounting and official mpathy fading, the cane-growers' position *vis-à-vis* Mozambican labor was set to ke a decisive turn. During the late 1940s signs of a state clamp-down became evident, ith especially "undesirable women" being routed from the compounds along the igar belt and repatriated to Mozambique. This may have met with the approval of me estate-owners, but it is hardly likely to have endeared them to their Mozambican nployees. It may well have predisposed the workers to take advantage of the higher ages that Natal's colliery-owners would offer when they opened a recruiting office Mtubatuba in September 1948 with official permission to take on three thousand ozambicans over the following six months.[34] In any event, by April 1949 the ozambican border would be closed and policed by Portuguese patrols.[35]

The constraints on the supply of labor to northern Zululand's agricultural estates ere in large measure a result of the relatively late introduction of capitalist relations to the region, and the resistance of workers to low-wage estate labor was but one of veral environmental and structural factors that retarded the development of

capitalist agriculture in northern Zululand after World War I. Estate agricultu
showed promise as a means of capital accumulation, which had, with few exceptior
been realized only in parts of the sugar belt by the late 1940s. Under these conditior
some white farmers responded with alacrity when the state's groundnut schen
was extended into the northern Zululand lowveld in 1946/47, but without lastir
rewards.[36] Although cotton experienced a brief revival at the beginning of Wor
War II, it was not sustained despite ever-strengthening prices for the fiber. Only
small cotton-growing sector in the Magudu district survived the 1940s. Meanwhi
nagana, too, had rebounded during the war, with efforts to arrest the incidence
mortality from trypanosomiasis culminating in the aerial spraying of DDT fro
November 1945.

Conclusion

When South Africa's racial order took on the apartheid mantle in 1948, sustainab
capitalist production was barely established in northern Zululand. Workers comir
from and through the region were, however, well acquainted with wage labc
Neither these workers, nor the more firmly rooted employers of Natal and tl
Transvaal, displayed a charitable willingness to subsidize the development of esta
agriculture in northern Zululand. It required state intervention for the local employe
to maintain a viable position in the growing regional labor market. As far
labor-intensive commercial crop production was concerned, then, northern Zulular
passed into the apartheid era as a cradle for estate agriculture built upon a dependen
on exceptionally poor working conditions. While some outside the cane-growir
areas persisted, against seemingly impossible odds, eventually to succeed
commercial cattle or cotton farmers, others would embark during the 1950s on t
extensive production of new crops such as pineapples and sisal. A combination
labor-coercive policies and political patronage was to characterize the state's role
bolstering the position of the employers of estate labor in northern Zululand under t
apartheid regime.

eeding

ɑrvesting

ɔɑding

Natal Farmers' Sons/Working Sons

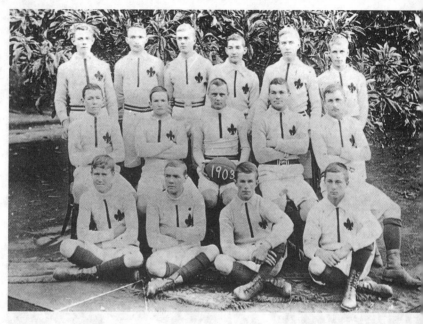

Hilton College, 1903

Faku, a returning worker from the Natal sugar estates photographed shor
before his death by the Station Master at Izilgoweni, about 3 January 1933.

spraying to eradicate the vector mosquito   (Local History Museum, Durban)

A pioneer family in the eastern Transvaal (Central Archives Dep

Esrael Lazarus, a rich and influential eastern Transvaal farmer
(Central Archives Depot. Courtesy of Martin Murr

he old gives way to the new   (Central Archives Depot. Courtesy of Martin Murray)

Child workers in Bethal   (Central Archives Depot. Courtesy of Martin Murr

Travelling pass issued by the Native Affairs Department

(Central Archives Depot. Courtesy of Martin Murr

arvesting, probably in the Selukwe area, 1905   (Zimbabwe National Archives)

omen, children, and a Shire Highlands plantation in the 1920s
(Courtesy of Wiseman Chirwa)

Swaziland   Cotton Growers and Councillors

Weighing cotton in the Swaziland lowveld, *c.*1920s   (Swaziland National Archiv

The Swaziland European Advisory Council, early 1920s. The Resident Comm
sioner is seated third from the right, with Allister Miller on his right.

(Swaziland National Archiv

9

Transkeian Migrant Workers and Youth Labor on the Natal Sugar Estates, 1918–1948

Willam Beinart[1]

he story begins with a corpse. Early in the New Year of 1922, the Station Master at
:ingolweni in southern Natal found a youth traveling "in a most helpless and pitiful
ondition . . . quite unable to walk when taken out of the train."[2] Izingolweni was a
nall station, opened less than a decade before, on a single-track line snaking through
ie hills inland from Port Shepstone. The line had been built largely to open a
ansport route for agricultural produce from the still isolated districts of southern
atal. It was, however, the closest Natal station to Pondoland and rapidly became the
ilhead for migrant workers draining from the Transkeian Territories (see figure 9.1).

The Station Master, E.J. Larsen, continued:

> The boy stated that he came from Messrs. Reynolds' Sugar Estate and was
> bound for Lusikisiki (a distance of 100 miles from Izingolweni). This boy was
> conveyed by wheelbarrow to a hut situate on hotel property which is
> generally used by natives recruited in Pondoland. [The] hotel proprietor was
> kind enough to attend and feed the boy but despite this attention the
> unfortunate lad died . . . and was buried the same day.[3]

aka, the "unfortunate lad," was severely emaciated. All he had was his traveling pass,
cloth and 7s. 6d. in silver; he was about fourteen years old. Larsen was sufficiently
erturbed to take a photograph and report the incident to the nearest magistrate, at
larding. Faka was by no means the first; "natives are continually arriving at
zingolweni station from various Sugar Estates in a state of collapse and frequently die

147

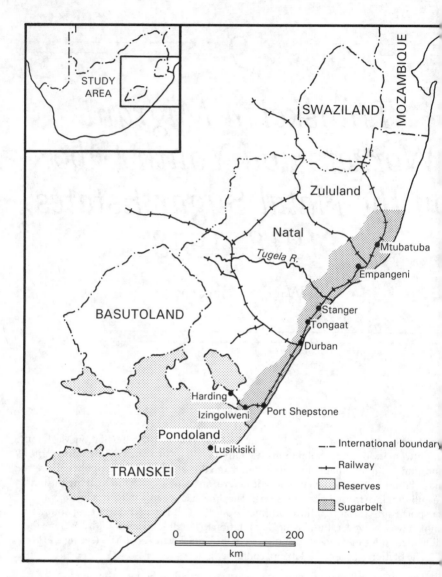

Figure 9.1   Transkei and the Natal Sugar Belt

within a few hours after arrival."[4] Some tried to get in touch with relatives i
Pondoland to fetch them at Izingolweni. One Hobobo had a letter written to h
brother shortly before he died there:

> Mavivane will you please go and borrow some horses . . . I am so sick that
> there is no hope of getting well . . . If you do not hurry I do not know where
> you will find me, and I have nothing to eat as I have not worked . . . I am

going to entrain here and get down at Izingolweni. I shall wait there for the horse . . . I have no other news except that I am sick.[5]

he magistrate at Harding saw no urgent cause for action and subsequently mislaid rrespondence about some of these incidents.

By September 1922, Larsen could no longer cope with the dead and dying at the ation. He had handed the responsibility over to the police in the person of ance-Sergeant Swartz, commander of the local Moguntia post. In October and ovember, Swartz found himself little more than an undertaker. In one two-day spell e dealt with four corpses, including "a male native lying dead in an old hut on the otel premises" and another "in the act of dying in the waiting room."[6] He had to pervise the burials and even dug one grave himself; local people attempted to avoid e corpses. Swartz sent a detailed report to his superiors. The Deputy Commissioner f Police for Natal, under the impression that some virulent infectious disease had roken out, slapped a quarantine notice on the police post.

The District Surgeon was eventually called in to hold post-mortems (copies of hich were also mislaid by the magistrate).[7] It was not least the involvement of the epartment of Health that set bureaucratic wheels spinning more rapidly. A joint epartmental committee was appointed and conducted its enquiry in March 1923. r G. A. Park Ross, Assistant Health Officer for the Union (Natal), was the driving rce behind it, and he was more inclined than the magistrate to undertake a little etective work. Deaths were difficult to quantify, but the committee examined the cords of twenty-five cases of people who had died at Izingolweni in 1922. The earest hospital was at the Ebenezer mission station eight miles away. Most of those w who made it there, on carts provided by the storekeeper, also died. There were a umber of other deaths in early 1923, on the fields themselves, and yet others further ong the routes into Pondoland.

It is not clear what disease killed Faka, or why he did not use his last 7s. 6d. to buy od. But the committee found no sudden spread of infectious disease amongst these igrant workers returning from the sugar fields. It found scurvy, tuberculosis, neumonia, dysentery, some "heart disease" and miners' phthisis. Park Ross nphasized that at least some of these diseases were preventable by basic regulation d improvement of the housing, diet and medical facilities available to workers on e sugar fields. Many workers fell ill, some shortly after arrival on the estates, either ecause of the inadequate diet and conditions or because these exacerbated existing roblems.

Most of those who could be traced back to estates in Natal had come from the uth Coast companies of Reynolds Brothers and Crookes. These estates had dressing stations" (clinics) nearby, or had access to the Indian Immigration Trust oard hospital established during the years of Indian indentured labor on the fields. ut to keep ill workers on the fields, even if they were not being paid (and they were ot), cost money. The workers' contracts, where they had them, specified that they ould receive free medical attention. But the estates perceived themselves to be under cute financial pressure and the tendency was to work sick employees for as long as ossible and dispatch them home as quickly as possible when they became incapable. ick workers were usually given a cursory medical examination before being sent to ingolweni. The companies could then maintain that once workers were certified fit travel, the estates' responsibility ended. The doctor in question argued, when xamined by the committee, that "due regard must be given to the economic side of the question."[8] Not all officials in Natal were as incurious as the magistrate of Hardir about what was happening; they had relatively little power to intervene. But as Fran Brownlee, the Transkeian magistrate, put it a few years later: "The people in Nat regard natives generally from a different point of view to what we do. They are mo harsh towards the Native."[9]

The committee made a number of recommendations for the improvement of die conditions and medical facilities on the estates, and for routine medical examination before recruitment and before workers traveled home. Park Ross attempted to use th episode to embarrass the estates into immediate reforms. Both he and man Transkeian officials advocated the extension of the Native Labour Regulation A (15 of 1911), which controlled the system of migrant labor in the mining industry, the sugar estates as well. The act could be used to enforce minimum standards health regulation, diet and housing; it also regulated the recruitment of youth an child labor, which officials felt to be an urgent need. Poor Faka was by no means th only youth who ran into difficulties on the sugar estates at this time.

But for the next two decades reforms were systematically blocked. Conditions c at least some of the sugar estates were a recurrent cause for concern; officials saw th Rand mines as more favorable places to work despite the rigors of underground labo the huge compounds and the social problems which attended these. When concerne officials, and others rather less than sympathetic to the sugar industry, penetrated int the world of the cane fields, they found what they considered to be a variety suppressed scandals. The deaths at Izingolweni in 1922 perhaps reflected some of th worst consequences of conditions on the fields, but they can be seen as symptomatic a system of employment which persisted for many years afterwards.

African Migrant Workers on the Cane Fields

Sugar cane, wherever it has been grown on a large scale for export, has been a cro hungry for labor. Unless cane is milled shortly after harvest, it loses its sucrose conter rapidly; investment in processing works near the cane fields is essential. Once suc investments have been made, producers have to find enough cane for continuou operation of the mill during the harvest season (from May to December). Sugar car production, which necessarily involves close coordination between agricultural an industrial processes, puts a premium on a steady and controlled labor supply durir part of the year; the capacity to diminish the work-force rapidly in the off-season also potentially valuable.

Sugar cane has been at the core of coercive labor systems demanding a great de of "human blood, sweat and gall."[10] After the abolition of slavery, plantatior expanded within the British empire on the basis of indentured wage workers in suc diverse subtropical colonies as Fiji, Mauritius, Trinidad, Queensland and Natal.[11] Th empire's impoverished, recruited especially in the Indian subcontinent, became pa of a population movement less brutal or final than the slave trade but, nevertheles one with important and varied implications.

The impetus for the importation of indentured labor in Natal was shaped initiall by the success with which local African communities could resist demands for labc even after conquest.[12] Their capacity to do so was partly sustained by the relativ protection afforded under the "Shepstonian" system of administration. Migran

cruited from afar on long contracts, from both India and Mozambique, came to be
en as a more reliable and controllable labor force for the estates than farm tenants,
aily (togt) laborers or short-term migrants from Natal's many small locations. The
ge of Indian indentures was, however, relatively short-lived. By the time of Union,
olitical conditions in India, in South Africa and in Britain made the large-scale
ganized decantation of Asian workers unpalatable to many different interest
oups. Meanwhile, the great majority of workers from southern Mozambique had by
e 1890s switched to the gold-mines of the Transvaal, where they formed by far the
rgest element in the underground work-force.[13]

Intercontinental labor migration had been pursued because some nineteenth-
ntury plantations were enclaves in colonial possessions where the indigenous
opulation either had been displaced, or was as yet relatively independent. The
rocesses of conquest and incorporation were more complete in southern Africa by
011, when Indian immigration was halted. Natal and Zululand were the obvious
eas for estate owners to seek labor and some local workers were secured. But
etter-paid employment on the Rand and in Durban attracted local workers away
om the fields; employers were also reluctant to "fall back on a man who could not be
epended on to work for more than a month or two at a time."[14] Some sugar planters
id investigate the possibility of using settled African family labor to replace
idians—many of whom lived as families on the estates. Their preference, however,
as for long-distance migrants on long contracts who were now scarce. As the
airman of the Natal Sugar Association warned its members in 1911, the labour
roblem "had a seriousness quite beyond their grasp."[15]

The 1913 Indian workers' strike, perhaps the largest and most successful that
ere has ever been on the Natal sugar fields, fulfilled the estate owners' worst
redictions.[16] Empowered by their employers' difficulties, and angry at the harsh
emands made on them, field workers brought production to a halt. The hemorrhage
f Indian workers after the strike was not as rapid as estate owners feared, partly
ecause wage rates were pushed up. But many of those doing field work disappeared.

Exposed to the cold winds of competition, the colonial planters turned instinct-
ely to the state.[17] They wanted to maintain and extend restrictions on mine recruiting
n Natal and Zululand in order to bottle up the domestic labor supply. And, as they
ad in times of difficulty in the nineteenth century, they looked north — now to the
rea beyond 22°SL, which included most of Rhodesia and much of Mozambique
xcluding the southern districts which were dominated by mine recruiters).[18] The
atal Coast Labour Recruiting Corporation was established in 1916 primarily to
xploit this potential supply. Well organized in local groups, as well as in
presentative bodies such as the Natal Sugar Association and the two planters'
nions of Natal and Zululand, sugar growers and millers were determined not to be
aught off guard by shifts in government policy again.

But recruitment for the mines in these "tropical" areas had been halted in 1913
ecause of high death rates from pneumonia. Despite applying maximum pressure,
gricultural enterprises such as the sugar estates could not get more than occasional
xemptions from the restrictions. The government was also reluctant to sanction the
ottling up of labor in Natal. The Director of Native Labour saw his priority as the
ining industry. Cape officials with liberal inclinations, particularly the two
ecretaries for Native Affairs, Edward Dower and Edward Barrett, were still an
nportant influence and they deployed the discourse of a free market in labor; they

also displayed some concern about the conditions under which workers lived ar
labored. They felt that the large potential labor supply within Natal could l
mobilized if adequate wages were paid by estate owners:

> On the one hand the Natal employers say that the Natives are too lazy to
> work. On the other hand they complain that the Natives are freely recruited
> to work at mine rates which they cannot afford to pay . . . The whole truth of
> the matter is that the large employer of labour in Natal for years past has
> mainly got his labour under conditions approaching those of servility. The
> source of this supply is in fact not now available. As a result it is up to him to
> put his 'house in order' and in future cater to the local supply.[19]

Prime Minister Louis Botha was persuaded by officials to reiterate this point when h
met a Natal deputation in 1918. But Natal interests were not without influence. In th
year they succeeded in securing an investigation into the shortage of labor; th
government also sanctioned restrictions on recruiting by outside enterprises in son
Natal and Zululand districts.

Officials were even less successful in regulating conditions of employment. Th
Native Labour Regulation Act of 1911 was an obvious and immediately availab
means to impose control, but it applied only to designated industrial Labour District
From the decade following Union, Transkeian and some other Native Affai
Department officials advocated its extension to what they saw as becoming
semi-industrial sphere of employment; they felt that this would both guarantee th
plantations a labor supply and protect workers from the worst abuses. The planter
associations nevertheless insisted on their agricultural status. Labor relations on th
great majority of farms, most of which still operated through systems of tenanc
precluded the extension of such regulations to agriculture; nor would farme
nationally have allowed such a measure to be passed.

It was Transkeian workers, rather than migrants from the north, who part
resolved the problems of the estates from the late 1910s. One of the key early recruite
was Douglas Mitchell, later Administrator of Natal and long-serving conservativ
United Party MP, who became involved in the Natal Coast ·Labour Recruitin
Corporation as a young man. The family farm in southern Natal was beyond the suga
belt; trading and recruiting was a lucrative alternative. Known to workers a
"Ubejana," the rhino, because of his quick temper and "impenetrable hide," an
because he "never gave way to anyone," he had local connections in the densel
populated region of southern Natal and Pondoland that provided a network throug
which to mobilize supplies.[20] No regular records were kept of the number o
Transkeian workers migrating to the sugar fields. In 1923, when the deaths a
Izingolweni were investigated, there were probably two to three thousand worke
from Pondoland in Natal; in 1930 the number had increased to perhaps seve
thousand out of about thirty thousand field workers.[21] By this time, Indians wer
mainly employed in the mills. An increase in the local supply within Natal an
Zululand, coupled with some migrants from Mozambique, provided most of the re
of the field labor force.

Specific economic difficulties helped to push more people from Pondoland ont
the labor market at this time. Influenza cut a swathe through the rural population i
1918 leaving some homesteads short of both agricultural labor and wages; th
post-World War I inflationary spiral severely affected any homestead dependent o
some wage income. Mine recruiting slowed around the early 1920s when the industr

as in crisis. But there were also features of labor on the sugar fields which helped
sure the estates of a longer-term supply. Some able-bodied workers went to the
elds rather than the mines, despite lower wages, to take advantage of above-ground
ork, the relatively short (six- as opposed to nine-month) contracts offered, and the
dvance payment system.[22] Estate owners railed against advances because they
cilitated desertion, but there is no doubt that their availability from sugar recruiters,
llowing their abolition by the Native Recruiting Corporation for the mines, was a
ajor factor in attracting workers from Pondoland.

But the sugar planters also came to rely for some of their supply on two pools of
orkers from Pondoland unavailable to the mines, and they were able to employ them
recisely because of the lack of state control. One group was composed of workers
jected by the mines on the grounds of health. This is why a few of those who died at
ingolweni in 1922 and 1923 had miners' phthisis contracted on the Rand. Another
as made up of youths and children. Many estates were desperate for labor in the late
10s and 1920s: they welcomed youths and the sick. Some estates were prepared to
spense with them as soon as they became unproductive.

The Failure of State Regulation

ate intervention in some spheres, and the lack of it in others, proved of some
gnificance in resolving the labor crisis on the estates at this time. Officials in the
epartment of Health, especially Park Ross, and in some branches of the NAD were,
owever, uneasy about the system that had come into being and had been so clearly
xposed by the 1923 committee. They persisted in their struggle to impose some
ontrol during the inter-war years.

The lack of uniformity amongst sugar producers was a major problem. In the
neteenth century, when production was relatively limited and transport a major
onstraint, many estates had their own small mills. Towards the end of the century,
illing capacity became concentrated in the hands of large concerns such as Tongaat,
atal Estates, Crookes and Reynolds, which both operated their own estates and
ought in cane from smaller planters.[23] The expansion of white-owned estates into
oastal Zululand in the first decade of the century had been on the basis of central mills
wned by Huletts. In the 1920s, some 6 to 7 per cent of cane was produced by Indian
d African smallholders, who also supplied large mills. The big miller-cum-planter
oncerns varied in their responsiveness to calls for reform. But the growers, who
ecause of their numbers were not without influence, were more uniformly opposed.
ululand planters — the newest and most marginal producers — were especially
ehement in blocking any reform which implied expense.

With regard to the sugar industry, the major concern of the state, with the
xception of the NAD and the Public Health Department, was not working conditions
ut production, prices and marketing.[24] During and after World War I,national policy
as to place increased emphasis on self-sufficiency in basic staples; up to that time,
outh Africa, while exporting a wide range of pastoral products, had been a net
nporter of food, including sugar. The sugar growers were thus able to negotiate
iccessive measures to protect themselves against imports from Mauritius and
lozambique. In 1922 a commission was appointed to enquire into conflicts between
iillers and growers and to investigate pricing and protection.[25] Some of the issues

were resolved by the Fahey Conference in 1926, which also agreed to establish
central refinery and reward high sucrose content in cane. At the same time, the impo
duty on sugar was almost doubled from £4 10s. to £8 a ton. In 1932, when prices fell i
the depression, it was doubled again, although the government imposed a maximu
local price.[26] The 1936 Sugar Act, passed after complex and protracted negotiation
extended very considerable powers to the sugar producers to regulate their ow
industry, including production quotas and prices subject to the maximum local pric
stipulated by the government.

These various supports played a significant part in allowing the rapid expansic
of production in the inter-war years despite fluctuation and sharp overall decline i
international prices, uncertain weather, and a locust invasion in 1933. Productic
more than quadrupled from about 126 000 tons in 1918 to a little under 600 000 tons i
1940 (figure 9.2).

Exports also increased dramatically in the inter-war years, assisted by imperi
preference. Between 1918 and 1932, both production and the area cultivated double
thus the demand for labor was enormously increased. Sugar was among the fir
agricultural commodities, along with wine, to receive such systematic support an
regulation. By 1939, the cost of protecting sugar was estimated to be higher in absolu
terms (at £2.3 million a year) than for any other commodity, although sugar ranke
only seventh, by value, amongst the goods produced by white farmers (after mea
wool, maize, fruit, milk, and wheat).[27] Economists criticizing agricultural protectio
ism as a whole singled out the position in the sugar industry as "scandalous" in that
"made profits wholly out of keeping with the benefits to the country."[28]

The transfer of resources, derived from taxation of the mining industry,
agriculture in these years has been the subject of extensive comment both b
contemporaries and by subsequent analysts.[29] It may, however, appear an anomal
that sugar, a commodity produced very largely by English-speaking estate owner
not Afrikaner farmers, absorbed so disproportionate a share of the state revenu
which underwrote agricultural expansion in these years. The political processes an
mechanisms involved can only be suggested here.

Part of the explanation has to do with the state's concern to maintain nation
self-sufficiency and expand agricultural exports; if sugar cost relatively more
support because of the highly competitive international market, this support wa
nevertheless seen as essential. Sugar production also underpinned the Natal region
economy. Moreover, the complex financial arrangements underlying subsidies, base
for example on tariff protection and favorable rail rates rather than direct grants c
price supports, perhaps disguised their extent.[30] Sugar producers also benefited fro
the more general political support for agricultural subsidies. In 1926, the Amalg
mated Growers' Union affiliated with the South African Agricultural Union, thu
increasing their power as a lobby. Although D. F. Malan's National Party criticized th
1936 act as favoring sugar above the more essential staples such as maize, it did n
oppose it.[31]

Moreover, it is important to remember that the South African Party and th
United Party, which most sugar producers supported, were in power for more tha
half the inter-war period. Natal was a significant source of support as Afrikane
drifted away from the SAP to the Nationalists. But Natal had separatist tendencie
manifest in the Dominion Party, which needed to be contained. There were also son
powerful lobbyists for sugar interests in Parliament throughout this period, partic

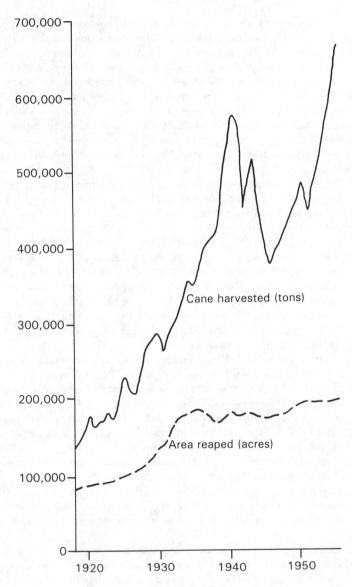

gure 9.2 Natal Sugar Production, 1920–1955

rly G. Heaton Nicholls, the tireless, articulate and ruthless planter MP from ıluland. He was an important force within the SAP/United Party and highly fluential in the numerous negotiations and debates over sugar production.[32] He ught for the benefit of the industry as a whole, but aimed always to protect its eakest link — the Zululand growers. His support for segregation policy, of which he ?came a major protagonist and ideologue, provided the basis for cross-cutting ɔlitical alliances.

Growers and millers also benefited from their position in relation to sta
legislation and the bureaucracy. While both the field workers and the African m
workers were deemed to be agricultural workers, and were thus unprotected even
the Native Labour Regulation Act (the position in the mills changed in 1937), sug
producers as a whole fell under what became the Department of Commerce a
Industry. This was the state department most knowledgeable about markets a
finance and most skilled in the intricacies of the protectionist measures which we
simultaneously being developed for South Africa's infant manufacturing plants. T
fact that they fell under Commerce and Industry, while they insisted that the
workers were agricultural laborers, caused the producers no embarrassment and ga
them considerable advantage.

Complaints about conditions on the sugar fields were frequent in these years
rapid expansion; they came not least from within the government itself, and mo
particularly from the Transkeian magistrates.[33] Bills were drafted and came close
being debated. But sugar interests either refused outright to cooperate or adopte
delaying tactics. In the late 1920s, for example, Heaton Nicholls offered a new versic
of the Masters and Servants Act in the late 1920s, which would give son
discretionary power to officials to intervene, in order to prevent the extension of t
1911 act to the sugar estates. This was rejected by the NAD. Attempts to establish
hospital scheme on the estates also foundered amidst recriminations. The NA
handled the negotiations and tried to link the scheme to a system of registration
workers which might in turn facilitate other controls. Estate owners rejected both th
idea and a general levy for hospitals.

It was only in the sphere of housing that some bureaucratic muscle could b
applied, under the Public Health Act of 1919. By 1925 Park Ross felt that the o
beehive huts and most of the wattle and daub huts, sometimes constructed by worke
themselves, had largely disappeared on the estates south of the Tugela River. A degre
of "flexibility" was allowed for the smaller undercapitalized planters who argued the
could not afford the costs of concrete and brick constructions, even for their ow
houses. Park Ross admitted that "we look the other way . . . where a man is starting
He also recognized that some workers preferred huts to barracks — at least the kind
barracks which the planters felt they could afford. One of the attractions of work c
some estates was the freedom from barracks. But the Department of Health felt th
huts were insanitary and unhygienic where large numbers of workers were gathere
and saw its task as that of reforming the attitudes of African workers as well
planters.

The difficulties of reform meant that regulations were not uniformly applied; th
sentiment that "labourers are treated worse than so many pigs" in "disease ridde
huts unfit for housing animals" was expressed on more than one occasion.[34] Whe
confronted with tougher action, planters argued that any change in the sugar industi
would imply change in the conditions governing agricultural employment as a who
Ministers were not prepared to give NAD officials the authority to push legislatio
the NAD was having to become more attuned to the demands of agrarian interests i
the country and in Parliament. As an official in Pretoria despairingly commented i
1934, the department "frequently urged legislation" but "the opposition of the suga
planters has always defeated us."[35]

While the bureaucracy as a whole was relatively powerless, the intransigence c
the sugar producers and ministers also created divisions within the Native Affai

partment over the need for regulation. It was officials in the Transkei that had to
ck up the administrative pieces of the sugar estates' excesses: to cope with
licensed recruiters, underage recruiting, the policing of deserters, and those
patriated penniless and sick. The Transkeian General Councils, on which chiefs,
admen and members of the educated elite sat, also consistently represented the
ght of sugar workers to higher authority. Conditions on the estates, and especially
e use of child labor, were frequently debated in these years.

In the extensive and revealing correspondence on these issues, there is a definite
nse of impatience amongst Transkeian NAD officials with their Natal brethren, who
emed too readily to understand the needs of the sugar industry; with their
lleagues in the Native Labour Bureau whose Inspectors were so powerless outside
dustrial districts; and with Head Office in Pretoria, which engaged in shameless
laying tactics throughout the 1930s in order to evade giving any answer to the
quent representations of the Chief Magistrate of the Transkei. It is difficult to know
st how important this question was in both reflecting and causing the changing
lance of power in the Native Affairs Department. But the Transkeian magistrates
metimes seemed to be treated with the kind of bureaucratic disrespect and delay
at might usually be reserved for another department or even outsiders.[36]

Thus the issue of control over child labor, conditions and health on the estates was
tted around in investigations by the Native Affairs Commission (1932), the Chief
tive Commissioner Natal (1934) and another Departmental Committee (1935).
cisions were then set aside until the Native Farm Labour Committee of 1937–39
uld investigate and report. It did so finally in 1940, and recommended exactly what
ctions of the NAD had been demanding for over two decades: the extension of the
tive Labour Regulation Act of 1911 to both sugar estates and sugar mills.[37]

Under the Native Law Amendment Act of 1937, however, the NAD did succeed
extending some industrial legislation to places of employment outside proclaimed
bour Districts where machinery was being used. These included the sugar mills,
nich employed about one-seventh of the workers on the estates as a whole. The field
orkers and cane cutters from Pondoland were not directly affected, but this measure
as to have some important implications for the future, providing a focus for the
ions which coalesced on the estates during World War II.

Wages, Violence and Malaria

spite the bureaucracy's failure to regulate conditions during the inter-war years,
e estates continued to secure a labor supply from Pondoland. Rates of rejection by
e mining industry's Native Recruiting Corporation in these districts increased
arply from around 4 per cent in 1921 to as much as 20 per cent by the late 1930s.[38]
cial changes in Pondoland also assured them a supply of youths. During the
pression, and immediately afterwards, alternative unskilled employment was not
adily available. While the mining industry was expanding rapidly, so was its labor
pply and up to the mid-1930s it could impose not only tighter health requirements
r recruits, but also a quota system on particular areas.

The estates were keen both to maintain an agreement about wage levels and to
nit upward pressure on wages; there was no significant rise in basic wage rates for
ld workers in the inter-war years. In the 1920s rates were variable because so many

different systems of payment, including cattle advances, were adopted. The maj
miller-cum-planter companies moved onto a "ticket system" similar to that operatir
on the gold-mines. Although it was often described as a monthly payment, worke
were paid only on completion of thirty tickets, which took considerably more thar
calendar month. A standard wage of about £2 for thirty tickets (in contrast to about
for underground mine work) became quite widespread. After deductions f
transport and other items, workers on the so-called six-month contract — whi
would take about seven and a half months to complete — would be lucky to earn £
This was one-fifth of the amount (£50) which Douglas Saunders demanded from h
parents, the owners of Tongaat, in the early 1920s as a supplement to his Cambrid₁
allowance of £600 in order to purchase a tail coat.[39] (His education, however, perha
benefited the workers at Tongaat in the longer run.) Migrant workers in Zululand, ar
on smaller estates in Natal, tended to earn less in cash, about thirty shillings, but tl
was paid by the calendar month. Women and youths earned considerably less.

The real value of wages remained relatively stable from 1918 until the depressio
except for a sharp decline during the inflationary years from 1919 to 1921 when catt
prices — the major investment for migrant workers — were also high. In 193
following the onset of the depression, a fall in sugar prices and an increase in tl
supply of labor, the estates actually cut wages and paid thirty to thirty-five shillin
for thirty tickets. However, prices declined during the depression and the cost
cattle, which was still probably the main item purchased by migrant workers fro
Pondoland, was at a low ebb. Thus there was not so significant a decline in real wa₁
rates during the depression as the cut in money wages might indicate. Nevertheles
workers on the estates perceived wages to be low and declining. Competition from tl
mines and industry drove basic wages up again to about £2 in the mid-1930s and
£2 5s. by 1940, roughly in line with inflation.

The estates were notorious for using a measure of violence in order to kee
control and maintain levels of work. In the words of Mgeyana kaNgumlaba, who
the 1920s was a youthful migrant worker from Lusikisiki: "There was an Indi₁
foreman who was in charge of us and he beat us. That was how it was in those days."
Flogging (with whips) and beating were illegal but common. In 1925, the Zululan
Planters' Union felt it necessary to pass a motion against the use of coercion beyor
that recognized by law.[41] On Tongaat in the 1920s, "the overseer's badge of office w
still the sjambok looped to his wrist. If he passed a day without beating somebody ι
he would be afraid that he was not doing his job or losing his nerve."[42] Solome
kaDinuzulu, paramount chief of Zululand, cited the beatings administered to worke
as one reason why the Zulu preferred not to work on the sugar fields.[43]

English-speaking field managers, Indian sirdars and African indunas were ₁
well versed in "the 'Old Dutch remedy' of the sjambok"; it was intrinsic to a system
labor control in which the racial hierarchies were rigid and workers had fe
incentives.[44] Max Gluckman, the anthropologist who worked in Zululand in the 193(
made the interesting suggestion that it was often "applied to cure a native who
indolent from disease rather than laziness."[45] The high incidence of ill health on t
sugar fields might help explain the use of beatings. Violence tends also to be a featu
of control where new groups of workers or youths — who have yet to internalize t
harsh discipline of industrial time and labor — are employed in large numbers; tl
was certainly the case on the sugar fields in the inter-war years. The incidence ar
rhythms of violence on the fields, and in agricultural employment more general

₂mand closer examination not only in relation to the control of labor, but also in
lation to the changing contours of racism. Sharpening rural racial attitudes in the
gregationist years were at least in part related to the intensification of labor demands
ₙ the farms.

The historian of Tongaat implies that coercive labor discipline diminished after
ₙe depression; the owners of the leading estates conceived of themselves as beginning
₂ make the change from beatings to bonuses during the reconstruction and expansion
⁻ the industry in the 1930s. Some officials were of the same view, even though they
₂moaned the "entire absence of Government Control over Labourers employed in
ₙese Plantations."[46] But it was difficult for even determined managements to control
ᵥerseers, far out in the sea of sugar, hidden by high cane, just as it was to control them
₂ep underground on the mines. A labor manager on a medium-sized estate who also
ₐd extensive experience as a recruiter saw coercive controls still being used in the
⁾50s:

> In those days in the early fifties . . . you had young chaps, the young
> overseers, who were a bit happy . . . They would soon . . . give a bloke a
> thick ear or use some foul language . . . It was still the days when the old
> sjambok could come out now and again. We used to get all sorts of chaps
> from all sorts of walks of life applying. A lot of them would just apply
> because it was a glamour job. They could ride around in the fields on a horse.
> They didn't realise there was more to it than riding around shouting at a lot of
> [people] cutting cane.[47]

ₑe saw the 1950s as the period of transition. By this time there were also means for the
⁻orkers to articulate their grievances.

Mortality from diseases on the sugar fields did not end in the early 1920s, and
₂spite some state control over housing, conditions still facilitated the spread of
ₙfection. This was especially the case with malaria. During the colonization of South
frica, diseases traveled the routes created by new patterns of geographic mobility
ₙd new concentrations of people. Just as the ports and Kimberley were hubs for the
₃read of smallpox carried by human vectors to the rural areas in the 1880s, so the
and mines became the node from which tuberculosis and lung diseases migrated
ₐck to areas like Pondoland.[48] Malaria was endemic to some of the coastal zone north
⁻ the Tugela. In the 1920s workers from further south, who had not been exposed to
ₙe disease, began to migrate to this area in greater numbers; at the same time, the
ₗsease spread southwards in a wave of epidemics between 1925 and 1933.[49]

The potential for the spread of malaria outside endemic zones was well
₂cognized by the mid-1920s, as was the effect of the disease on migrant workers from
ₒn-malarial areas. In 1924 there had been a serious outbreak on the new cotton fields
ₜ Pongola, south of Swaziland, and in 1925, workers on the Mtubatuba-Pongola
ₐilway through northern Natal suffered badly. Both the Health Department and the
₄AD recognized that inadequate diet and housing greatly increased susceptibility.[50]
ₕe epidemic provided Park Ross with another lever in his argument for minimum
ₙti-scorbutic rations which included orange or paw-paw, fresh vegetables and more
ₙeat. It was also abundantly clear that those who suffered worst from malaria were
ₙe migrant workers from such areas as Basutoland and Pondoland. Local people had
degree of immunity.

Fluctuations in the severity of malaria within the areas where it is endemic in
ₒuthern Africa have been associated with particular climatic patterns as well as

long-term and short-term agricultural and nutritional downswings.[51] Such facto,
together with higher rates of geographic mobility during times of drought a
economic and social disruption, might help to explain the incidence of malaria in Na
at this time; the disease was spread by human vectors to new areas and had a mo
intense effect amongst people living there. Empangeni (south of Mtubatuba but st
north of the Tugela) experienced a severe outbreak in 1927. In 1928, as the disease cre
southwards, magistrates were required to lay in supplies of quinine and sugar farme
were warned; in the summer of 1929, severe outbreaks hit the very heart of the nor
coast sugar estates around Stanger and Tongaat. Despite the warnings, lit
preventive work was done. Problems were experienced with the distribution
quinine, which most African workers, new to the drug, in any case appeared
distrust. The *Natal Mercury* estimated that at least three thousand people had died
June 1929 and that many more were incapacitated.[52] Cane harvesting and milling (
key estates were severely disrupted for the first few months of the season.

Planters blamed the government for failing to distribute quinine sufficient
quickly and widely. But the NAD and the Health Department felt that the esta
themselves had to take responsibility. A detailed inspection of estates in 1929 by t
Department of Health revealed a close correlation between the incidence of malari
the number of fatalities and the general conditions on individual estates.[53] Mc
planters had ignored the diet regulations publicized by Park Ross; another inspectio
of estates in 1930 found none which supplied fresh fruit or vegetables to suppleme
the maize rations.[54] Hospital care was also uneven. After the 1923 inquiry into t
deaths at Izingolweni, Park Ross had pushed not only for improved medical faciliti
on the estates which had them, but for a general hospital system throughout the sug
zone. The NAD evolved a scheme, but this was turned down by planters because
involved a levy on employers. The result was that the provision of health ca
remained dependent on the individual estates.

As on the Mtubatuba railway line, it was migrant workers from the Transkei wl
suffered worst on the sugar estates. Not only did they lack immunity, but they we
also highly suspicious of estate medical facilities. Managers generally tended to kee
workers out of hospitals for as long as possible, with the result that those wl
eventually got there were already seriously ill; as the Secretary of Public Heal
commented: "There was a widespread and increasing tendency to utilise the hospita
generally as morgues, and to send their sick Native employees to die."[55] At Tonga
one of the most organized estates, "terrified Pondos who absconded from the
hospital cots were . . . found dead in the cane."[56] Death away from home was
unhappy fate and many deserted. Mgeyana remembered that the inability of worke
to travel home when they became ill was a major complaint on the sugar fields in t
1920s.

Again, as in the early 1920s, the sick were encouraged to leave too late and son
died on the way. Malaria was briefly the cause of deaths in Pondoland itself.[57] As o
councilor attested, "It was the first time we had had malaria fever in our district."
There were repeated annual summer epidemics through to 1933, although t
conditions there were not such as to infect the formidable local mosquitoes in t
longer term. Pondoland did not become a receptacle for malaria in the way that it ha
for tuberculosis.

The Department of Health began a systematic anti-malaria campaign which w
well funded considering the straitened circumstances of the depression years. I
officials supervised the spraying of huts and compounds on estates and in the Nat

serves; stagnant water near inhabited buildings was also targeted. Park Ross argued ongly that it was only by promoting an understanding of the way the disease spread nongst Africans and whites, and encouraging preventative measures to be taken luntarily by everyone, that the campaign would have a lasting effect. He thus posed the compulsory use of quinine.

One of the most successful anti-malarial measures involved new restrictions on here migrants could work. Following the Swellengrebel Report on malaria in 1931, e Health Department was keen to prevent the migration of workers from n-malarial areas to zones where it was endemic. Enforcement of such a measure, wever, threatened the labor supply of the Zululand planters, who responded with eir customary stridency. They had never employed a large number of migrants from ndoland, but they were concerned that this source would now be completely closed them. The Zululand planters were prepared to agree to such restrictions only if they t something in return: either access to the labor market in southern Mozambique, here malaria was endemic, or tighter restrictions on recruiting in Zululand for other dustries.

The mining industry was initially opposed to such restrictions, as were the ramount chief of Zululand and the Portuguese authorities. But an unlikely commodation developed between the most welfare-minded government depart- ent (Health) and the recalcitrant Zululand planters. Transkeian workers would not recruited for Zululand. Three Zululand districts were again closed to external cruiters and a "gentleman's agreement" was reached with the mines about cruiting in Zululand. An understanding was also reached by all parties that the luland planters could have first pick of Mozambican "illegals" — that is, those men ho crossed the border without contracts. Although this arrangement caused a good al of tension through the 1930s, it held. Few workers from Pondoland found their ay so far north again. The effects of these measures were rather harsh in constraining e work opportunities of people living in the Zululand districts concerned, but they ere advantageous to Transkeian workers, now restricted to the generally larger and tter organized estates of Natal. By about 1935, the annual epidemics stopped and alaria retreated to areas where it had been endemic.

In the mid-1930s, there was still a noticeable difference between employment on e sugar fields and on the mines. According to one Pondoland councilor, who rhaps exaggerated for effect, workers going to the gold-mines came back rosperous and well fed and looking very plump." Those going to the sugar fields turned "ill and also looking tired and played out" with sores on their bodies and est complaints.[59] Even Chief Botha Sigcau, soon to be appointed Paramount of stern Pondoland by the government under armed guard, and already assiduously rforming his duties for the state, reported in a similar vein in 1936:

> Last year not less than 20 people of my [location] deserted from the sugar estates of Natal, and when I went out to arrest them I found that . . . some of them were laid up ill at their homes. Some of those I arrested stated to me they were complaining about their food there, and that that was the reason of their desertion.[60]

ne majority of able-bodied men strongly preferred the mines, and resented quotas on ine recruiting.[61] But the malaria epidemic, together with the broader restructuring of e sugar industry in the 1930s, helped provide a context in which, by the end of the cade, life for migrant workers marginally improved.

Youth and Child Labor

One reason why sugar producers were able to secure a continuous supply of work from Pondoland throughout the inter-war years was that rates of rejection for t mines increased. Another was the changing position of youths in the Transkei. Fa as mentioned above, was by no means the only fourteen-year-old from Pondola who worked in Natal in the inter-war years. Analysis of youth and child labor essential, in order to understand not only agrarian accumulation in South Africa, b also the patterns of social change in the Transkei itself.

Under the 1911 Native Labour Regulation Act, the mines were forbidden contract youths under the age of eighteen. The measure was not uniformly a consistently imposed, but the number of employees under this age diminishe Loosely applied as it was, the restriction was acceptable to the mining industry, whi needed, for the most part, men who were physically mature enough to cope with t demands of underground labor. Officials approached the mining industry with t model of Victorian reforms in mind; experience of high death and desertion rates the early years of mining provided further impetus for control.

The minimum age of eighteen for recruits was in fact high by the standards industrial legislation. Indeed, both farmers and officials recognized the implications the act in protecting the access of landlords and agricultural employers to youth lab In 1911, the Chairman of the Natal Sugar Association calculated that "taking t ordinary vital statistics of the world there would be at least 63 000 men between 14 a 18 years of age" available in Natal. The sugar estates would thus "have a very lar number of useful native labourers untouched by the recruiters from Johannesburg Restrictions on youth recruiting were one reason for the sugar estates' antipat towards the extension of Act 15 of 1911.

However, officials were not simply attempting to resolve the competition i labor in the country by sharing out the supply on the basis of age. Between 1910 a 1930, the government did promulgate regulations to establish that only youths sixteen and above could be recruited for agriculture, and that parental permission h to be obtained for contracts involving sixteen- to eighteen-year-olds. Officials were r empowered to prevent the *employment* of youths under sixteen on farms whe parents agreed to it, nor were they particularly concerned about such arrangeme where they formed part of a tenancy agreement with parents living on the far "Undesirable" child labor, from the viewpoint of officials trying to control recruite was construed to mean longer-term contracted labor performed away from home those under sixteen, or those between sixteen and eighteen, without paren authority. Child labor was seen to lead to high rates of desertion, to the erosion parental and "tribal" authority and to juvenile delinquency in the towns.

Underage recruiting proved difficult to regulate in the inter-war years, ev where officials attempted to do so. Unscrupulous recruiters contributed to t problem, but its persistence rested largely on employers' perceptions that youth a child labor was useful and economic: either because it was cheaper, or because it w the only labor obtainable, or because children were thought to do some tasks bett Underage workers did not usually perform the heaviest work of cane cutting a loading, nor did they work in the mills. But women or children were seen as adequ for many of the other tasks such as hoeing, weeding, herding and leading oxen used large numbers for plowing, or work around the (still small-scale) compounds. T

pid extension of the area under cultivation in the 1920s put a premium on a cheap
pply of workers for these sorts of tasks.

Although the issue of underage recruiting arose particularly in relation to the
gar estates and other major agricultural employers of migrant workers, planters
ere by no means alone in recognizing the value of youth and child labor in South
rica at this time. The fact that all African male workers were insultingly called
oys" by white employers should not disguise the reality that a good many outside
e mining and industrial sector *were* boys or youths in the earlier decades of this
ntury. In a segregationist era, African children were perceived in a different light
om European children, for whom education was already compulsory. In Natal,
rticularly, the majority of urban domestic servants were African male youths from
out twelve to twenty years of age.[63] Child laborers from the Transkei were used for
al loading at the Durban docks in the early 1920s, running up steep gangplanks with
skets of coal. These "Grimy Imps of the Wharfside," some "mere picannins of 12,"
ere presented by a newspaper reporter as "grubby but happy" and their employ-
ent justified on the grounds of their "extraordinary agility."[64]

If urban employers found a range of roles for youths and children, this was even
ore the case in the rural areas. The practice of absorbing children into domestic and
ricultural labor on farms was deeply rooted in both slave and non-slave systems.[65]
bor tenancy was becoming the predominant social relationship on white-owned
rms in the early decades of the twentieth century and the transfer of the labor of
ildren to the landlord was part of many of the agreements reached. As on the sugar
lds, herding, domestic service, hoeing and weeding could all be done by African
ys and girls or youths. Masters and Servants legislation, and court cases testing it,
owed parents to bind their children under the age of sixteen as part of a contract for
e family as a whole. The Native Service Contract Act of 1932 entrenched the
sponsibility of the heads of African tenant households over the labor of their families
a whole in a context where both they and white farmers were finding it increasingly
fficult to control the youth. The age to which fathers could bind their sons in
ntracts was increased to eighteen. The difference between sugar planters and
rmers in general was not that the planters assumed the availability of African youth
d child labor but that they were employing children from Pondoland away from
me and often without parental permission.

When chiefs and General Councillors in Pondoland began to make representa-
ns and demand action about the recruiting of youths and children in the 1920s, they
ded to blame — with some justification — the sugar recruiters for contributing to
e general breakdown of parental authority. However, the reminiscences of old men
om Pondoland who worked on the fields do not always recall coercive means of
cruiting being used. This is not to say that the youths were happy in their
ks — the usual working apparel on the sugar fields; rates of desertion were high.
t they were not generally forced to go and work in Natal:

> It was very easy to join in those days. Boys ran away from herding cattle.
> They were doing it without the permission of their parents— who were
> complaining about it. Sugar recruiters would approach them and would
> send someone to collect the boys. They would follow them by night to a
> certain spot and they would be taken away early in the morning.[66]

analysis of child labor on the estates must also address the issue of why youths in

Pondoland might have wanted to "run away." Rural poverty, especially in the yea
after World War I, was one reason; the importance of child labor in African society ar
the social stresses within the homesteads in the Transkei were others.[67]

Control of the labor of male children and youths was as significant in the Afric
reserves and amongst African sharecroppers as it was on the farms. The critical task
herding was largely entrusted to boys and youths under eighteen and usually und
sixteen. In a sense, then, emergent capitalist agriculture incorporated elements of tl
established local division of labor. Pre-capitalist and peasant child labor w
embedded in broader kin relationships and in an ethic which made it part
socializing processes. Herding for boys involved education about the natural worl
about custom, and about fighting skills as well as the formation of friendsh
networks. The pace of work was also shaped by the social practices of the youth: the
was time for enjoyment. Work was part of a domestic environment supervised l
family members and not an "impersonal" wage relationship.

Clearly, the notion of "work" used in describing wage labor is inadequate
capture labor relationships in pre-capitalist or even peasant communities. Neverth
less, herding was work which demanded many skills, entailed responsibility ar
could involve hardship. It is not necessary to accept views of African society which s
the division of labor within the pre-colonial homestead as constituting cla
exploitation in order to make this point.[68] Cattle and sheep sometimes had to be tak
long distances to suitable pasture or water; they had to be defended; animals had to l
kept from fields during the growing season from October to May. Punishmer
including violent punishment, could be meted out to boys and youths who let the
animals stray into fields.

It is also important not to see the division and nature of labor in Afric
communities as static, particularly in the early decades of the twentieth century. Ne
patterns of crop production and stock-keeping, as well as the entrenchment of migra
labor, altered the nature and division of labor in the homesteads. Conflict betwee
fathers and children in many peasant societies develops not least because the whc
family has to work and the family, rather than other institutions, has to sociali
youths into their duties.

There is some evidence to suggest that labor demands on boys and youths
Pondoland were increasing at the time when child labor became prevalent on tl
sugar estates. The primary reason for this was the rise in the number of animals in tl
area. In 1912/13 east coast fever, a tick-borne disease, had decimated the herds. Whe
dipping became effective, the number of cattle in Pondoland increased at an enormor
rate, from well under 100 000 in 1915 to their pre-east coast fever level of 250 000
1923/24 and to over 500 000 by 1930.[69] The number of sheep also increased near
threefold to over 550 000 in the two decades before the drought of the early 193(
Because of the growing numbers of animals and the declining quality of the pastur
stock had to be taken further each day for grazing and then returned to kraals at nigl
They had to be kept from the cultivated fields, the number and density of which we
also increasing. These developments occurred at the very time when youths and eve
children were beginning to migrate to work, thus throwing more responsibility on tl
younger herders who stayed behind. While patterns of herding were flexible
relation to the numbers of animals that could be handled, the scale and pace of tl
increase presented not only a major — and often noted — ecological problem, but al
a labor problem.

Nor were African communities unstratified. Some homesteads had few or even ? cattle. This situation was seldom permanent in Pondoland in these years, in that ttle could be obtained on loan from wealthier families or bought with wage income. evertheless, there were always some families whose boys would herd for others ther than work for their own homesteads. In earlier years such relationships would ually involve an exchange of labor, often between kin, for the loan of animals. By the ter-war years, there could be a payment or at least the expectation of it. Larger stock ?ners, who sometimes had hundreds of animals and were reluctant to loan all of ?se out under the *nqoma* system, would need to employ youths on a more regular ?sis. Some European traders in the reserves had become large stock owners, and they ?o employed youths to herd for them. Thus herders within the Transkei itself were ? longer always working for their own homesteads and the payment they received (a at or a sheep worth less than ten shillings for three months for themselves or a loan imal for their families) seldom amounted to what they could earn away from home.

It is not easy to comprehend the changing nature of herding through oral material cause the experience is part of a social memory of childhood. This tends to be pressed in romantic terms — justifiably so in the sense that the 1920s and 1930s were ?eriod when cattle stocks were high and rural society in the Transkei was far more dependent. But the tension in the situation was expressed in contemporary debates, ch as those in the Pondoland General Council in 1929:

> I know of two boys from my location who ran away and were recruited by a
> trader in the Lusikisiki district . . . They went off to a certain kraal and got the
> kraal-head to come and impersonate their parents and they paid him
> something for doing this. In this way those two boys went off to the Sugar
> estates. We require our boys to herd our stock and yet they can run away
> from us by doing this.[70]

number of men interviewed said that they "ran away from herding" or from school ?und this time:

> I had to hide away because I was running away from school . . . . I thought
> I'd be rich in no time if I left school and went to work. When I arrived there
> [Tongaat], I had to clean the stables where the mules were kept. I liked that
> work because it was not hard. When I returned my father was angry.[71]

?ere were other circumstances that drove youths onto the sugar estates: boys could ? to work to earn money for education which their parents denied them; fathers ?uld send their children to earn money or a cattle advance; in one case, a father sent ? fourteen- and twelve-year-old sons to complete a contract when he fell ill (and they ?serted).[72] But it does seem that the demands on youths were being intensified at the ?ne time that their options broadened. Many white farmers, African tenants and ?mestead heads tended to assume that child labor, in different forms, was available ? use. The question was who was going to have access to it and under what ?ditions.

Pre-industrial or peasant child labor should not be equated with industrial child ?or. Ideas about childhood were themselves being reformulated by both whites and ?cks. Segregationist notions allowed distinctions to be made in the dominant society ?tween African children and white children; these gave rise to considerable unease ?ongst some officials, reformist whites and blacks. But African child and youth labor ?s being drawn into a more capitalist context from a base where it was widely

assumed that African children should work. In this as in many other respects, it
possible to argue that labor relationships in the emerging capitalist economy in Sou
Africa were significantly shaped by practices, expectations and conflicts in Afric
communities.

It should not be assumed that Transkeian homestead heads and paternalis
officials or educated African leaders always opposed child labor on the sugar estat
for the same reasons. Reformers seeking to pursue what they perceived to be a mo
rational view of capitalism were having to confront rural African perceptions as w
as the excesses of employers in the inter-war years. Rural attitudes were certain
changing as educational possibilities became more widespread, but child and you
labor was still considered necessary by many homestead heads in the post-Wor
War II period. Then, officials and progressives propagandized for betterment a
rehabilitation schemes on the basis that these would free boys from herding so th
they could go to school. The schemes involved fencing pasturelands into camps whe
stock could be left out at night. While the major rationale for the camps was
conserve the veld by facilitating rotation and ending nightly "kraaling" of anima
they potentially reduced the labor required for herding.

Changing Production Processes and Employment Practices

By the time the South African Sugar Association submitted its evidence to the Fag
Commission of Enquiry in 1947, when the number of field workers in peak season h
increased to about fifty thousand, the leaders of the industry were claiming innocen
in relation to the disruption of "tribal" society and "the lack of state supervision ov
the lawless detribalized natives."[73] Ideologues such as Heaton Nicholls had lo
advocated going "back to the native kraal, to the native family, to the tribe"; now t
industry's memorandum subscribed to the full range of the policies that underpinn
apartheid: migrant labor, development of the reserves, renewal of chieftainc
restoration of "tribal" authority, and control of urbanization.[74] Planters saw then
selves as making a major contribution to this end: "The seasonal nature of the acti
operations of the Sugar Industry make it uneconomic for the full native labour force
be permanently engaged, and the rotation of life between work and their homes in t
Reserves is complementary."[75]

Such claims are disturbing in the light of the sugar industry's enormous
disruptive employment practices in the inter-war years. But although youths a
children continued to be employed on the fields, it seems that they declined
importance from the late 1930s. The shift in employment practices was again the res
of a complex interaction between changing patterns of production on the one har
and the way in which rural communities offered their workers on the other.

Production of cane quadrupled in the inter-war years. Whereas the doubling
production from about 1918 to 1932 was achieved largely by expanding the area
sugar cane reaped each year, the spectacular increase from about 1932 to 19
immediately after the depression, was accomplished with relatively little expansion
acreage, but rather through gains in yields and productivity (see figure 9.2). Perha
the major factor in this development was the change in the type of cane grown.

In the 1880s, Natal planters had adopted the Uba variety of cane which was tou
and had a low sucrose content, but was hardy and could withstand disease a

ught. By the 1920s, however, Uba itself was becoming susceptible to disease and
lds were less certain. Planters turned to new Coimbatore varieties developed in
thern India which were quicker growing, higher yielding and easier to cut. In 1935,
ut 85 per cent of the cane reaped was still Uba; in the next three seasons this figure
lined to about 30 per cent.[76] Pricing and marketing agreements rewarding high
rose content in cane encouraged a rapid switch. Increased yields, coupled with the
erous state price supports, stimulated concurrent investment in plant, in fertilizer
d in physical works and contouring on the land.

Moreover, from the mid-1930s the position with regard to the labor supply
nged quickly as mining, secondary industry, the state, and sugar estates (amongst
er agricultural employers) expanded simultaneously. Competition forced some
ponse from the estates; the heavy capital investment made after the depression was
rt of this process and also alerted the industry to issues of productivity and bonuses.
hough basic wages did not increase significantly, the amount that could be earned
l — at least on the major estates. The task which had to be completed by a cane
tter in order to win his daily ticket varied according to a number of factors: the type
cane, whether or not it was burnt (in which case the cutters did not have to cut and
pose of leaves or "trash"), and the conditions for loading onto the tram trucks in the
lds. In the 1920s and 1930s, when Uba ruled, the task was usually to cut and load
m 2 000 to 2 500 lbs a day; by 1937, Reynolds were demanding 3 500 lbs for one of
varieties of Coimbatore.[77] If the task was not completed, a ticket would not be
en. But in the 1930s some of the major miller-cum-planter concerns like Tongaat,
ynolds and Gledhow (C.G. Smith) introduced a bonus system paying 1d. for each
lbs cut above the minimum task.

The introduction of the bonus system allowed more experienced, more skilled or
onger workers (who could complete their task in about six hours) to boost their
tential earnings to over £3 for thirty shifts. Bonuses also effectively increased the
h wage for workers per 100 lbs of cane cut because basic wage payments at the time
re the equivalent of about 1d. for 125–150 lbs cane cut and loaded. Any increase in
ges per ton cut was compensated for, in the eyes of the estates, by the savings made
recruiting and housing costs. Bonuses helped to increase production at little or no
st to the employer, but they were also seen as an important benefit by workers. They
re less frequently available on smaller estates and in Zululand.

Bonuses put a premium on cutting skills; child and youth laborers were less easily
sorbed into this system. Some estate owners began to perceive that they could save
sts by getting more work out of fit and mature men rather than relying on a large
rnover of less productive workers. Estates had often found youths and children to
particularly troublesome employees. Although cheaper than adults, youths were
fficult to control and seem to have deserted more frequently; as they were not
gistered for tax purposes and their contracts were not always attested by
agistrates, they could be difficult to trace. It was not always disadvantageous to
spense with child labor.

The malaria epidemic, changes in production and continued prodding by the
partment of Health encouraged further improvements. A few of the leading
mpanies, particularly Tongaat under the management of Douglas Saunders, and
tal Estates, began to develop ideas about a far more controlled environment for
eir workers.[78] They built model compounds and villages, still segregated, but with
eatly improved facilities. By 1940/41, most of the leading miller-cum-planter

concerns were making a virtue of necessity and for the first time providing t
minimum diet considered necessary by the Department of Health. In addition to abc
18 lbs of maize a week, workers received meat about twice a week, as well as orang
vegetables, beans, an unlimited supply of *amahewu* and a gallon of beer.

There were certainly limits to the sugar industry's reforms. In 1939 t
International Labour Organisation Convention stipulated that recruited worke
costs of transportation to work should be borne by their employers. Smuts was keen
ratify the convention but could not do so because South African standards fell belc
those required. He brought pressure to bear on the gold-mining industry, which
1939 agreed not to deduct the cost of transport to work for contracts of 270 days a
over. The coal industry decided on a system of refunds to workers who complet
270 shifts. The South African Railways and Harbours paid transport costs, as did t
Cape Provincial Administration. Even the Orange Free State and Natal Provinc
administrations agreed to "bear the request in mind." But when the Transkei
General Council and the NAD attempted to capitalize on such successes by asking t
the same in the sugar industry, the South African Sugar Association was adamant tl
it "would not bear the cost of transport as this will add to cost of production."[79]

This was the year in which the sugar industry received some £2.3 million
subsidies from the government through price supports alone. As the Social a
Economic Planning Council mentioned, protected crops such as sugar were bei
supported not only by the mining industry and producers of unprotected agricultu
commodities, but also by the "lowly-paid unskilled workers."

There was little legislative guarantee that improvements in the sugar indus
would be sustained; conditions had in any case hardly changed on many estat
especially on the lands of more marginal planters. Moreover, during the 1940s t
sugar estates, following their extraordinary expansion, experienced slump a
uncertainty. Production did not exceed the heights of 1940 (nearly 600 000 tons) u
1954 (see figure 9.2). Serious drought, coupled with inflating costs, discourag
further investment and expansion; fertilizer was scarce during World War II. T
government also held down the domestic price of sugar, a basic item for working-cl
consumers, during the inflationary war years and immediately afterwards wh
industrial militancy was widespread.

The internal market expanded, not least because a cheaper grade 2 unrefin
sugar was produced in large quantities following the 1936 Sugar Act and t
subsequent Sugar Industry Agreement.[80] But producers could not meet their exp
quota. Only in 1947 did the government allow a significant increase in the interr
price, as international prices for agricultural commodities such as sugar rose. T
National Party government then reaffirmed state commitment to an expand
industry, including exports, at a time when opportunities for sugar producti
improved overall.

During World War II, planters were increasingly having to operate in a higl
competitive market for migrant workers. Some workers from Pondoland began
shift away from the mines and sugar fields towards expanding manufacturi
industries. In this context, sugar workers could assert themselves more forcefu
Indian workers were still significant in the mills in the late 1930s when a new phase
trade union organization began.[81] The Communist Party had recovered from the wo
of its inter-war purges and some key figures in the Indian community were recruit

tal Indian industrial workers became a highly unionized segment of the black
uth African work-force in the late 1930s and 1940s.

Unionists made extensive use of the industrial legislation available and their
orts were not confined to Indian workers alone. The Sugar Industry Employees'
iion was registered in 1938 under the Industrial Conciliation Act.[82] Following the
tive Laws Amendment Act of 1937, African workers in the mills also qualified as
orkers under industrial and wage legislation. In 1940 the union approached the
age Board for an official investigation of wages and tried to include even field
orkers in the process. A protracted dispute followed and the Labour Ministry,
uctant to risk a full-scale strike in a strategic industry during the war, especially
th the additional threat that cane fields might be fired — made an award to the mill
orkers. Field workers were not included in the agreement, but employers' fears that
y wage rise in the mills was bound to have repercussions in the fields were well
ounded. The war years were punctuated by small, dispersed strikes by non-
ionized field workers including those from the Transkei. In 1942 wages crept up to
10s. for thirty tickets on leading estates.

Following the success of the African Mine Workers' Union, the Communist Party
tended its organizational commitment to other unskilled migrant workers. In Natal,
.P. Naicker, W. Cele and others launched a Natal Sugar Field Workers' Union, which
o attempted to overarch Indian and African workers. In this case, however, the
ion had no industrial legislation under which to operate and received no
cognition. The Field Workers' Union made only limited organizational progress
d, like the African Mine Workers' Union, it crumbled in the late 1940s. But it did
cceed in publicizing conditions on the estates at a sensitive period and certainly
used a good deal of official concern. Such pressures, together with the longer-term
ifts in production methods and conditions of employment, seem to have con-
ained large-scale reversion to underage recruiting. In the 1950s, when the industry
ain expanded very rapidly to reach new heights of production, the system of
igrant labor came to resemble that on the mines more closely.

Important social changes in the rural areas also contributed to a less disruptive
stem of labor migration from Pondoland. Firstly, if the argument about the
lationship between increasing numbers of animals and pressure on youths holds for
e years up to the mid-1930s, it would be less applicable after this period. Stock
imbers fell in the droughts of the early 1930s and subsequently stabilized. Secondly,
hool facilities and the demand for schooling expanded in the 1940s, a process which
celerated in the 1950s when the introduction of Bantu education was accompanied
· rapid increases in funding for rural schools. Schools still catered for a minority but
ovided an alternative opportunity and discipline for some youths.

Thirdly, migration to the cities, especially Durban, by families or women and
ildren as well as men became more general during World War II. Population was
tually stable from 1936 to 1946 in some Pondoland districts. Again, a permanent
ove to the city helped to resolve some of the social and economic tensions which had
nderpinned migrant child and youth labor. However, youth migration was still
idespread. With official sanction, a pattern developed whereby many workers
ould work out a few contracts on the sugar fields between the ages of about sixteen
ometimes a little younger) and twenty. They would then move on to the Rand or to
dustries in Durban unless the opportunity of upward mobility on the estates
esented itself.

Conclusion

The history of labor migration from the Transkei to the sugar fields from 1918 to 19
illustrates some important trends in the system of labor mobilization in South Afric
The sugar fields were perhaps the first major agricultural enterprise to u
long-distance migrant workers on a large scale, a development that presaged simil
moves in other labor-intensive agricultural spheres from the 1950s. The pattern
unregulated migrancy, including child and youth labor, also spread through tl
farmlands. If the worst evils of the inter-war system of migrancy were diminishing I
the 1950s on sugar fields, the same could not be said of other agrarian systems, f
example the potato farms in Bethal.[83]

The evidence regarding conflicts over regulation of the sugar fields confirms th
it is misleading to think of the South African state as a uniform institution catering
any particular branch of capitalism. Although sugar interests were to a considerab
degree able to shape the controls over their industry, government departments such
the NAD and Health made concerted efforts to constrain them and eventually m
with some success. However, the issues at stake revealed divisions within tl
bureaucracy and even in the Native Affairs Department itself.

Analysis of the pattern of employment on the sugar fields is also instructive
developing generalizations about the nature of apartheid. It has often been argue
that one feature of the transition from segregation to apartheid was the extension
the migrant labor system from mining to manufacturing in order to broaden tl
supply of cheap labor. This argument has been contested in various ways: tl
evidence shows that the pass laws were unevenly applied; considerable Africa
urbanization continued; and a highly differentiated African labor force emerged.[84] I
contrast, the importance of the agrarian, as opposed to industrial, labor crisis of tl
1940s, in shaping early policies of the Nationalist government has been neglected.[85]
the period 1945 to 1950, when prices for farm products were high, agricultur
production grew quickly as a proportion of the GDP from 9.4 per cent to 17.8 per cer
Despite the manufacturing boom, it was sustained at over 15 per cent in 1955. Tl
longer-term decline in agriculture's share of GDP was temporarily reversed and, ا
farming remained labor intensive in this post-war period, the number of farm worke
increased.

Systems of labor tenancy and wage labor by black families settled on farn
persisted as the major forms of labor procurement.[86] But the partial shift to migra
labor in agriculture and the ideologies linked to this shift require further investigatio
As has been illustrated, sugar interests expressed a view of African society and labٖ
mobilization in the post-war period which accorded closely with the ideas that wer
becoming central to apartheid — including the preservation of African tradition
society and the entrenchment of separate reserves. More broadly, the trend ا
migrancy may have been one of the factors in the erosion of older forms of paternalis
in the countryside.[87] The decline of this older agrarian order, and the social formatioı
that followed, was a central feature of the apartheid era.

Finally, the issue of controlling child labor was not a simple one in South Afric
Employers found young workers a cheap alternative when other supplies of labٖ
were short. African families, like peasant families in many other contexts, expecte
their children to work for the homestead. As African societies were more deepl
incorporated into a colonial world some, in black as well as white communitie

rceived the labor of African children and youths to be available for capitalist terprises. Poor families needed the income; some youths themselves "ran away" m home to find cash or opportunity in Natal. The prevalence of child and youth oor resulted partly from tensions within African families. Efforts to control der-age labor were aimed primarily at employers of youths and children working plantations or in near-industrial undertakings. But such efforts could cut across cial practices and expectations in African communities themselves.

10

"Synonymous with Gentlemen"? White Farmers, Schools and Labo in Natal, c.1880–1920[1]

Robert Morrell

In 1872 the Reverend William Orde Newnham opened Hilton College, one of the fir private secondary schools in Natal. It was situated just outside Pietermaritzburg ar from the outset catered for the sons of the established colonial families, many of who lived on the farms of the Natal Midlands. At the first prize-giving, Newnham set o his goals for the school. He wanted the school "to take first rank in the Colony in poi of educational attainment," but "his first and greatest desire was that 'Hilton bo should be synonymous with 'gentlemen' [*sic*] in the very best sense of the term, a be who was honest and upright and true as steel."[2]

Over the next forty years, Hilton College and the other major secondary schoc serving the Natal Midlands became elite institutions. To have attended one of the schools admitted the school-leaver into the social circle of the Old Natal Famili (ONFs) and gave them the entrée into the most influential political, economic ar professional positions in the colony. But the impact of these schools went beyond t induction of Old Boys into structures of power. The schools were places where "bo became men." Here they were faced with a range of experiences and challenges th created a template for later behavior. An understanding of the white, adult men wl were the Midland farmers is enhanced by tracing some of the effects of the schoolir they received in the formative years of their lives.

This chapter attempts to bring together two hitherto unconnected spheres of rur history: the schooling of boys from white farms, and the relations between whi

mers and African tenants. The history of South African schooling has generally
en written in narrow institutional terms, with little reference to the world outside.
nilarly, studies of agriculture have rarely attempted to explore possible connections
tween the childhood world of schooling and the adult world of work. In arguing for
? need to bring educational experience into the analysis of white agriculture, this
apter also argues for the need to approach the subject from the point of view of
nder. In the context of this study, such an approach involves giving analytical
ention to the construction of masculinity and explanatory weight to gender values
understanding relations between adult men on the farms. Where white men were in
uctural positions of authority over black men, the particular configuration of their
asculinity was central to the choices they made. The years at school were crucial in
veloping self-image and social values in boys. The acquisition of masculinity was
t just a matter of psychological adjustment with only personal implications.

The world of farmers and their sons was a chauvinistically sexist one. As in
ciety generally, the structures of power in colonial Natal were masculinized and
cluded women.[3] Personal networks involving ONFs and the private schools
sured that the corridors of power echoed with male voices. Magistrates, members of
? Legislative Council, senior civil servants and ministers of government, owners of
nks and chairmen of agricultural societies, all came from a recognizable and narrow
ouping, bounded in terms of race, gender and class.

The Schools of the Natal Midlands

part from Hilton College, there were a number of other major schools (see figure
.1). The first government secondary school, now known as Maritzburg College, was
t up in Pietermaritzburg in 1863. Various small private forays into secondary
ucation also occurred around this time, but the next important development was
? establishment of Bishops College (an Anglican Church initiative) in the 1870s.
shops closed in 1880 but was revived as Michaelhouse in 1896. The school was then
located in the heart of the Midlands at Balgowan. Weenen County College, founded
1902, was close by at Mooi River. It operated only until 1916.[4]

Since education was not compulsory, these schools attracted pupils only from
ose families who valued education. By and large, these families were the ONFs
ose class identity was based on early arrival in the colony and on landownership
d/or wealth. Bishops, for example, was attended by boys from many of Natal's
ading families: Tatham (farming and law), Nicholson (farming), Raw (farming),
uchars (farming, commerce and Natal government), Addison (sugar farming and
atal colonial service), Lloyd (farming and Natal military) and Campbell (sugar
rming and the professions).

The schools were headed and staffed by graduates of English public schools,
nerally with an Oxbridge pedigree as well. Maritzburg College was in fact legally
ligated to appoint its principal from the ranks of Oxbridge, Dublin, Edinburgh or
ndon graduates. As Tony Mangan has demonstrated, the British public schools of
is period were not places for the faint-hearted. Strictness, harsh living conditions
d regular use of corporal punishment, accompanied by liberal doses of religious
struction, was the normal regime.[5]

The early years of Natal's boys-only secondary schools were marked by crude

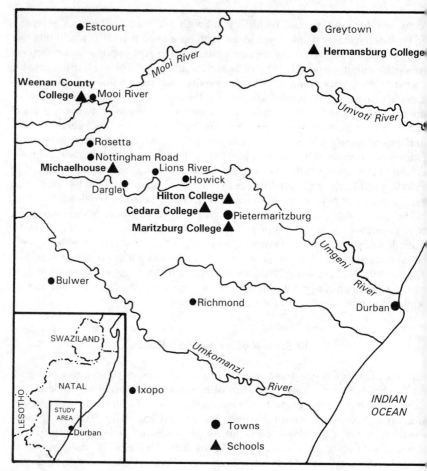

Figure 10.1 Private Schools in Natal Midlands

facilities and an approach to teaching that was in those days called "straightforward"
Hot water was generally unavailable, furniture sparse and accommodation rudimen
ary. Teaching was done by a few masters who relied on rote learning and the cane
drive home Latin and the other subjects borrowed direct from the British curriculur
During the forty years covered in this chapter, facilities were extended, teachin
improved and traditions established; bullying and reliance on the cane declined a
well. Each headmaster had different preferences, however, and none of the features
the early years disappeared. Continuity and stability were the major characteristics
the system.

The Midlands boys' boarding-schools were modeled on British public school
Their staff, their buildings, their codes of conduct all closely matched those of the
progenitors. In Britain, the public schools took in the sons of "gentlemen" with th
purpose of ensuring that they entered society as gentlemen themselves. To this end th
schools developed certain characteristics in the boys and acquainted them with soci

lations and values that were represented as ideal prescriptions for society. Their success has been testified to in a host of studies — public school boys became xbridge graduates and then became senior members of the colonial civil service, the inking and business establishments, or the professions.[6]

The Midlands schools were profoundly hierarchical and rigidly organized. The eadmaster was regarded as both a disciplinarian and a care-giver. Although the tter function tended to diminish as the schools grew and matrons and other rofessional sources of emotional and physical support were provided, the idea emained that the head was somebody who should be respected, trusted and, when he arned it, loved. R.D. Clark was Headmaster of Maritzburg College for nearly thirty ears at the end of the nineteenth century. On his retirement in 1902, the school agazine noted that students felt "reverence and affection" for him and that he had otained their "implicit obedience."[7] At Hilton College, Henry Ellis was headmaster or a similar period. On his retirement in 1905, the school magazine printed, in indirect eech, part of his valediction:

> The love of the boys had focussed itself upon him, and had reflected back upon themselves, and they had thought he was the cause of it. He thought one essential feature of education was to learn how to love one's fellow-men, and all the while he had been teaching them they had been teaching him.

ir Henry Bale, former Attorney-General and Minister of Education, Maritzburg ollege Old Boy and parent of Hiltonians, added "Mr. Ellis was a hero. His type of anhood, exemplified in his boys, was a high type of an English gentleman and a hristian man. The spirit of self-sacrifice in Mr. Ellis was strong."[8]

While headmasters in particular were revered, the same respect was often ccorded to masters, even those who freely dispensed corporal punishment. Further own in the hierarchy were the prefects. At Michaelhouse, the Rector (the title given to e headmaster) justified the system in these words: a boy "governed under prefects nosen from among his own number, to obey and eventually to command, and so ecome the kind of man that the country wants."[9]

Although it was true that teachers were often unpopular, and that there were emonstrations of defiance, especially in the early days before the hierarchy had tabilized and boys had accepted its logic, overall the system was extraordinarily table. The fact that its structure reflected the fabric of Victorian patriarchy was an xtra-institutional factor promoting this stability.[10] School boys had great confidence n the system once they came to feel part of it. The system provided certainty, and this ecurity made the boys certain of themselves, made them confident. Consequently nose boys who exited from the system felt that they were capable of achieving certain et goals. Amongst these, as Headmaster Ellis put it, was "[t]o keep unimpaired the aith of our fathers and our fathers' faith in its power to solve all the complicated roblems of our national life."[11]

The hierarchy permitted, at times, some introspection and dissent. But more often nan not the right to question the decisions of superiors did not exist or was severely ircumscribed. The emphasis was on unquestioning obedience rather than on critical ntellect. Tennyson's lines on the charge of the Light Brigade in 1854 capture this icely: "Their's not to make reply, / Their's not to reason why, / Their's but to do and ie."

The hierarchy was accepted because it reflected the logic of the world, but also because it was based on notions of justice. Power was not to be wielded thoughtless or arbitrarily, but rather in a considerate and instructional manner. This notion justice exalted the rights of the powerful, but these rights were not to be exercis entirely at the expense of the weak. Nor was the system static. The secondary schoc exhorted boys to play hard and work hard with the promise of reward not just in t participation but in personal progress too. The most public affirmation that endeav and skill achieved recognition was in the awarding of sports colors. Here, in elabora ceremonies, those who excelled were raised to the level of heroes and given officia sanctioned status.

It was frequently the case that the head of school was a first team captain of one the major sports, cricket or rugby. In the person of the head boy was the system's pro that hierarchic elevation was possible, that certain achievements ensured particul rewards. For those who failed to reach these heights, the system neverthele remained comprehensible in its own terms. All could technically become prefects, head boys, if they excelled. When the race was run, but lost, the winner with his rigt and privileges was respected. And the winner himself could feel that his rights ar privileges had been fairly earned. David Fannin, Life Governor of Hilton and form Supreme Court Judge, reflected on his school days as a prefect when he had hims beaten boys. He said that, even though he was emotionally uncomfortable with cani boys he knew well, he had felt compelled by the responsibility of his station and t traditions governing corporal punishment.[12]

The schools tacitly endorsed another mechanism by which the hierarchy w maintained, the process of initiation. To become part of the hierarchy the student ha to "fit in." The test of his ability so to do was initiation. This was generally a savage ar humiliating ritual in which the elder boys asserted their dominance over the young Having passed through it, the new boys, smarting from recently inflicted psychol gical and physical wounds, had at least the consolation that in following years would be they who would be handing out the treatment to "new poeps" ("shits") ar "kaks" ("craps"). In this process, boys were toughened physically and came to acce that physical discomfort and pain, within limits, were part of an orderly system.

When power was abused, mechanisms existed to monitor and end such abus Bullying occurred all the time, but some teachers and headmasters did their utmost limit its extremes. Both teachers and boys realized that, in the isolated and inten environment of the boarding-school, only the development of institutional identific tion and loyalty could prevent excesses that would tear the delicate balance of pow and powerlessness apart. Being part of a team, broadly conceived, was a message th coincided with a boy's entry into the system, via initiation, the donning of scho uniforms and the acceptance of school traditions and history. Remaining a part of tl team was ensured by the playing of sports and contests with other establishmen which constantly reminded one of affiliation and prompted loyalty. And once a bc was part of the team, there was a widely accepted requirement that the team | honored, that it be put before individuals.

At the 1902 prize giving at Hilton College, Sir Albert Hime, Prime Minister ar father of Hiltonians, was the guest of honor. He urged boys to be "thorough, and p your whole heart and soul into everything you do, and above all, take a pride in tl fact that you have been Hilton boys and never bring discredit on this great college.' At nearby Michaelhouse, the accomplishments of the undefeated first rugby XV we extolled as having brought honor to the school. Its achievement was itself tl

ndication of teamwork, of "keenness and devotion" and "worthy spirit."[14] Memories
team spirit and school associations were seen in later life as being indispensable.
ferring to service in the South African War, an Old Boy said that he "had found at
at time how useful it was for a man to have the honour of being an Old
ltonian."[15]

Doing the honorable thing and being a team-man (selfless and loyal), in short,
ing a "gentleman," was stressed. By the same token, being selfish and dishonorable
as condemned. In 1910 these sentiments were articulated at the Michaelhouse
eech day:

> [There is] a lower ambition, which is to do work, or appear to do it, better
> than another, and to gain a position better than the position held by others.
> That sort of ambition, which is possibly a common one, is not of high value. I
> am fearful it tends to injure character by unduly extending the spirit of
> competition . . . There is in the circumstances of modern life far too great a
> tendency to push oneself at the expense of others . . . I do not think this
> displeasing tendency is likely to show itself in boys brought up in this
> college . . . I think that these boys, when they go into the world, may
> influence the world in the opposite direction.[16]

ty and obedience were important parts of being a "gentleman." A tired Hilton
acher lamented in 1902 that "we, who teach, spend our lives in inculcating devotion
duty." And there were many kinds of duty. Being punctual, tidy in work and
pearance, polite, respectful, efficient — all these were duties. There was also the
ty to defend one's country, and one's honor. Boys even had a moral duty towards
eir peers. They were reminded of this in 1910 by the Governor of Natal. "Remember
at the exercise of his influence for good or evil among his chums is the first great
sponsibility of a boy's life." And they were told of their responsibility to future
nerations. Old Boys killed in battle "serve as examples of bravery and devotion to a
eat cause, and they help to cultivate the spirit of loyalty and sense of duty which
ust have its effect on the future manhood of the country."[17]

The school system did not function effectively simply because headmasters were
vered, prefects were respected and boys were loyal. The regime of the school rested
much or more on obedience and discipline. There were individual and collective
ts of defiance throughout the histories of the secondary schools. Order was
nerally asserted by the controlled (and even in the eyes of those who received it,
gitimate) use of violence. Here is an account of a beating at Michaelhouse around
20:

> The procedure for pre-lunch beatings was traditional. As soon after school as
> it was known that a culprit had been sentenced — news flashed across the
> bush telegraph — most of the boys gathered in the quadrangle. Not until all
> the classrooms had emptied was the victim expected to leave his. Then,
> white-faced and wanly acknowledging the sympathy and encourage-
> ment . . . he made his journey to the place of execution.
> I knelt in the chair, facing its back, with my body bent double, so that my
> head was on my knees and hidden from Alfie's view — the prescribed
> position with buttocks prominent in their tightly fitting pants — a splendid
> target. I heard him trying out his canes, and the vicious noise, as doubtless he
> realized, was the most unpleasant part of the business. The first cut was so
> stinging that in spite of clenched jaws, a gust of pain swept up in a deep sigh

from my diaphragm . . . After six of the best — there was a pause of several seconds between each — Alfie ceased from his labors and I stood up. His eyes were shining and he looked pleased with himself. "I say, Stiebel," he said, "you took that very well." He might have been presenting me with an athletic trophy. Before I left his study he shook me by the hand. After a beating it was the privilege of one's dormitory mates to inspect the damage.

For ten days afterwards Victor Stiebel was a hero.[18] Corporal punishment was not ju a manifestation of the power of the senior over the junior, it was part of a system th socialized boys into gentlemen, creating manliness as it did so.

Violence in the schools did not occur only in the formal and ritualized w described above.[19] From the moment a boy was admitted to a school, he was remind of his junior position by his more senior colleagues. At Hilton fagging was obligation for all "new poeps" — boys who had been in the school for less than tw years. Fagging combined notions of rights (of senior boys), service (by juniors) a violence as a sanction to ensure obedience. It was generally a functional affair w boys having to polish shoes, clean sports kits, make beds and coffee and run errar for senior boys. But when the senior boys decided that there was a general slackness familiarity and a lack of respect creeping into the behavior of the fags an offensi might be launched — at Hilton College called a "new poep scarce" — during wh any "new poep" who did not disappear was beaten with sticks. Another popu reminder of a "poep's" status was "hot oven," where boys were forced to run t gauntlet of seniors wielding wet towels and sports shoes.[20]

As with corporal punishment and initiation, the practices that reminded initia of their junior station were never overthrown and rarely challenged by boys. It w accepted that seniors were entitled to respect and service, and that they were entitl to enforce their rights. Yet the system did not rest only on an abstract notion of soc order and justice. In certain instances, juniors could obtain the protection and suppc of the seniors for whom they fagged. Such protection came in handy when oth seniors demanded additional services or when bullying occurred.

Boys survived the secondary schools by embracing the team ethic, tolerati physical abuse and coping with emotional deprivation. They emerged from them w a strong sense of belonging in gender, class and race terms. Their experiences, as w as the formal codes of the school, molded them into a particular kind of "gentlema They were above all loyal first and foremost to members of the Old Boy network th developed into the spine of the Midlands gentry as the schools became mc established and as it became accepted by farmers that a good schooling was importa Respect was shown to seniors and to local mores. Gallantry was displayed towar women and in the face of danger. The law, considered as the codification of sch practices, was obeyed. Yet the "gentlemen" from the schools, precisely because th were created in an elitist and often exclusivist setting, were confident of their ov views and values and intolerant of dissenting views. In the schools, this attitude cou and did lead to grim and often violent struggles between gangs and individuals. In t broader world, it could make Old Boys tyrannical, authoritarian and sure.

The contradictory nature of being an Old Boy and a "gentleman" was nowhe more evident than in the complex web of relations with Africans. The attitudes teachers and boys to Africans varied widely and showed no steady inclination in o direction or the other during the period under consideration. Nevertheless a numb

general comments can be ventured. During moments of turmoil, when Africans
re considered dangerous (for example, during Bambatha's "rebellion" of 1906),
ws tended to harden. Yet there was often a disjunction between what was said
out Africans and how boys conducted themselves towards them.[21] During much of
ir childhood, boys would have close African friends. They would speak Zulu and
y *mfaan* (young African boy) games. These included robust forms of sport, such as
ck fighting, and gentler pursuits such as the molding of animal figures out of clay.
ese friendships rarely converted into adult companionship and did not interfere
th assumptions of black inferiority. Indeed it was quite possible for respect for
ricans to exist side by side with Social Darwinist racial prejudice. While there were
ny different views about Africans, it is convenient, for the purposes of this paper to
ntify two poles: a protective, mission-influenced position and a culturally
uvinistic, xenophobic one.

At Hilton College, situated on an estate with a large African population of its own,
 view most frequently espoused was one of trusteeship. In 1902 Headmaster Ellis
oke of the duties facing the school with regard to the black population. "To lift from
state of barbarism and heathendom to civilization and Christianity a native
pulation outnumbering us ten to one." Their duty toward an Asian population, ". . .
ual in number to our own, was to train to European habits of life and modes of
ought without estranging their feelings or weakening their self-respect."[22]

A few years later, during the Bambatha rebellion, the sensitivity of the situation
s emphasized:

> There is no school in Natal which is, on account of its situation, able to do
> more good to the Natives or more harm than Hilton College, and so it is
> absolutely necessary that Hiltonians should see that the latter possibility . . .
> can only be contemplated with ridicule . . . There is no race in existence
> which is more affected by example than the Zulu. To set him a good example
> not only makes him respect a white man, but it builds up a firm foundation
> for the parson [to work on] . . . There is an inclination amongst schoolboys
> . . . to be familiar with a Native one minute and kick him the next. But it will
> not do . . . I do not say 'Swallow the insult,' but only be just, and you
> probably will not have the insult flung at you.

e Headmaster, with the conduct of a "gentleman" as the model in his mind,
ncluded that "the phrase 'A Hiltonian knows how to treat a Native' is great praise to
rk for, and one which I hope to hear universally used in the future."[23]

Ellis, who ruled Hilton for almost thirty years, gave his most explicit vindication
trusteeship in an obituary to "our favorite servant, Dhoni." He spoke of the man's
xcellent qualities; his honesty, his trustworthiness, his child-like simplicity and
stfulness, his conscientious devotion to duty, his gratefulness, his loyalty. He
ways reminded me of a huge Newfoundland dog watching his master's ways." Ellis
ngratulated himself on reducing the "Bantu love of self-indulgence" initially found
Dhoni. "We showed him fairness, kindness and consideration. Fairness which did
t allow him unfair advantages; kindness, which refused him what was not good for
n; consideration, which expected consideration in return."[24]

It was because there was a need to engage with local Africans, to teach them the
ole and the virtues considered to be indispensable to a good life, that in 1908, Hilton
llege introduced Zulu classes. As an article in the school magazine put it: "It was felt
at in a country where the white man's burden is so heavy as in Natal, the study of the

interesting language of the natives would not only be a fitting preparation to such bo
as look to a future in the Government of this race, and the administration of justi
among them, but must also tend to enlarge their sympathies and widen their views
all matters concerning the people in whose midst we live, and on whose developme
in civilization on the right lines the future happiness of this Colony so mu
depends."[25]

In other quarters, there was less goodwill towards Africans. A Maritzbu
College writer bemoaned the insolence and unruliness of Africans. The Zulu "are fa
degenerating, and the more Mission Stations that are put up the faster the Kafi
degenerate. The Missionaries teach them how to read, write, and spell, but they do n
teach them to be civil and industrious. The Natives use their education mostly f
forgetting people's names and passes in order to get drink. Their labour is gettir
dearer and scarcer every day."[26] Similar views were expressed at Michaelhouse, whi
like Maritzburg had no local African population to consider: "The chief difficulties
making them good Christians lie in the fact that they are naturally entirely lazy ar
extremely immoral, and horribly fond of being drunk."[27] While there is no dire
prescription in the writings flowing from these schools regarding behavior towar
Africans, it does not need a giant leap of imagination to envisage that such cond
scension could lead to exceedingly hierarchical, impersonal and scornful relations

Attitudes towards Africans were of course not separate from those towards dut
honor, obedience and hierarchy. The "high qualities" of the "gentlemen" produced
the secondary schools included "loyalty, manliness, and decision of character
Furthermore, such "gentlemen" were to be "honest in their dealings, uprigh
straightforward, and manly."[28] Translated into the world beyond the school bound
ries, their common education meant that an elite of landowners, farmers, civil servan
and professionals were bound together by an experience that constituted them, ofte
at key moments, as a "we." This elite had some flexibility in expanding the inclusiv
aspect of group membership (for example to newly arrived farmers, men with who
they played rugby, cricket or polo and those with views consistent with their own), b
there were, in this period, rigid gender, class and race limits. To be a member gav
emotional support, social contacts, cultural belonging and economic and politic
leverage. To be beyond the group was to experience the penalties of difference.

On the Farms

After leaving school, many boys returned to work on the family farm. For much of tl
time, the supervision and control of the farm remained in the hands of the whi
patriarch, and his son, the young "gentleman," was reminded of his junior position t
the tasks that he undertook, by the didactic element of his working relationship wi
his father and by the realization that he would become a farm owner only wi
paternal help (either via inheritance or assistance with credit to purchase a farm). Ov
time, this process changed as increasing numbers of boys first sought a practic
education at Cedara Agricultural College just outside Pietermaritzburg. It also becam
more frequent for school leavers to take up posts as managers on Midlands farn
owned by family friends, where they would learn about agriculture for a year or tw
before being given responsibility on family farms. The growing scarcity of land als
forced many, normally the junior sons or those who had excelled academically, to jo
the professions or find work outside agriculture.

The process of transition from school to farm was made easier for the new
ʒentlemen" by family and old school networks, comfortable class affiliation and
cial identity. Nevertheless some accommodations had to be made. For one, the
ʒntleman farmers had now to relate directly to African males. The memory that most
ɪd of black playmates must have sat awkwardly with the demands of the farm
:onomy. Now they had to take up the position of master in relation to black people on
ɪeir farms. School had provided them with many of the ideological and emotional
quisites for such a task. The rightness of hierarchy, the advantages of being white
ɪd the certainty of being a man, combined with an elite schooling, were all to
fluence the new relationships formed on the farms.

The farmers of the Natal Midlands were not an undifferentiated group, though
/er time they attempted to present a united front and develóp a specific identity.
any studies, in the context both of national agriculture and of the Midlands have
ɔted the differentiations and frequently used the label "progressive" to distinguish
ɪe group of farmers from the rest.[29] "Progressive farmers" were generally large
ɪdowners, whose well-capitalized farming operations were geared to market
·oduction. Labor relations on their farms were characterized by efforts to control the
ɪe of laborers, the nature of the work and the conditions under which work was
ɔnducted. Typically, progressive farmers were the ones pushing for mechanization,
bor contracts, the eradication of labor tenancy and a switch to full-time, wage labor.
was the progressive farmers, moreover, who dominated farmers' associations and
ɪe agricultural unions and who entered local and national politics.

In the Natal Midlands, the term "progressive" was also frequently synonymous
ith the ONFs. And such farmers often referred to themselves, and were referred to
, "gentlemen."[30] These men shared not only a common concern about agriculture,
ɪt also similar values and educational experiences. Frequently they were related by
ɔod or marriage; they considered themselves to be part of a class, the shared
ɪbitions of which they recognized and fostered. Their self-identity incorporated the
ɔtion of a family line: the inheritance of land obliged the inheritor to hand the farm on
· a succeeding generation. This obligation meant that, in addition to obvious
ɔnomic imperatives (to ensure that the farm was viable), there were domestic
ɪpulses that put their imprint on, amongst other things, labor relations. If, as
Davidoff and C. Hall suggest for the English middle class, domestic security was as
ɪportant as, if not more important than, capital accumulation, then the stability and
ɔntentment of farm workers were just as important as extracting the maximum
ɪount of labor from them.[31] In the literature on agriculture in South Africa, there is an
sumption that economic imperatives at the point of production and in the
arketplace were paramount for farmers. This assumption is not true, however, for all
ɑces and all times. In the Natal Midlands, other factors were as important.

It is true that the Old Natal farming families were committed to the perpetuation
the line. This involved creating sufficient wealth to stave off liquidation and to keep
e home farm in the family. Inheritance practices were generally designed to ensure
ɑt the eldest (or the most capable) son inherited this farm. Efforts were made by the
ɑrticularly wealthy families to give every son a farm and in this way to extend the
fluence of the family. But maintaining family security meant much more than just
·eeping the farm profitable. Much energy and money went towards keeping far-flung
ɑmily members together. The correspondence between them at home and abroad,
ɪd the lavish form of family functions, were statements of status and belonging that

bank accounts or size of farms could not convey. Family gatherings and reunic
ensured that geographically distant members of the family kept in touch with (
another. It was expected that they congregate for such events.

Africans were not permitted into the inner circle, but they nevertheless achieve
sort of limited inclusion as faithful retainers who occasionally might be remember
and even have their services recognized, in the white patriarch's will. An examp
admittedly unusual, of the gratitude felt by some farmers can be found in a bequest
James Ralfe who died in 1921:

> [T]o my faithful domestic servant Umfaba Mbongwe in consideration of her
> services to my late mother and subsequently to myself the interest on a sum
> of £300 sterling for the term of her natural life and also ten average cows and
> eight good draft oxen together with yokes and spanning gear for eight
> together also with six sound blankets such bed linen as she may select two
> pillows a bedstead and mattress five chairs and a table and I direct that she
> shall be permitted to reside on my farm at Frere free of charge for the term of
> her natural life and in regard to this bequest I direct that it shall be free of all
> such restrictions and control as usually attach by law or custom to the
> property of Native women in Natal . . . and to my native servant Franz
> Mgati a sum of fifteen pounds sterling.[32]

Ralfe might be called "progressive," for in the common use of the term, progressive
the opposite of reactionary. In the context of the historiography of South Afric
agriculture, its use in relation to farmers has generally been limited to matters
technological and managerial advancement and the association is frequently ma
that such advancement involved the ultra-exploitation of farm labor and a move aw
from pre-capitalist labor relations. Charles van Onselen, for example, implied th
"better-off English landlords" ended the ties of paternalism that gave a rou;
harmony to the agriculture of the western Transvaal.[33] In the Midlands, the correlati
between advanced methods of cultivation, the exploitation of labor and the decline
paternalism is less exact.

There are celebrated cases of "progressive" farmers personally giving physic
punishment to laborers. Distinguished public figures such as Joseph Baynes ar
Charles Smythe, both long-standing parliamentarians, the former, Minister of Lan
and Works (1903–5), the latter, Prime Minister (1905–6), flogged their servants a
saw nothing for which to apologize.[34] On the other hand, farmers frequently express
concern about the welfare of "their" natives. Usually, however, their own welfare w
involved. For instance, there were frequent protests when state officials unjust
accosted and interfered with tenants and handed down unduly severe sentences
This anomaly in farm labor relations can, in part, be explained by direct reference
the school experience of farmers. In the schools, there was no necessary contradicti
between a just order and the dispensing of corporal punishment. Nor was
considered peculiar on the one hand to have good personal relations with Africa
and on the other to espouse racist views. An example illustrates the point.

Henry Daniel Winter (1851–1927) went to Maritzburg College. He made mon
by working for the powerful commercial enterprise, A. Fass and Co., by doing a sti
on the diamond-mines and finally by transport riding. In 1875 he began farming ne
Estcourt. He took a keen interest in agricultural societies and shows. He was Preside
of the Weenen Agricultural Society and offered his services for public office (he was
Field Cornet and a Justice of the Peace) and entered Parliament in 1893. He was Nata

nister of Agriculture from 1899 to 1903. He actively supported the local Estcourt
gh School, although he sent his sons to Michaelhouse. He counseled his sons to do
he did, and they involved themselves in the affairs of their Alma Mater, volunteered
· service in the Natal Carbineers and helped found the first rugby club in
tcourt.[36]

The *Natal Agricultural Journal* held Winter up as a model of "the successful
mer."[37] It emphasized that he had earned his place and his money: "His beginning
farming was practically from the first rung of the ladder." It also applauded him for
eaking with the habit of pastoral and arable farming. Winter won many prizes at
ricultural shows and was a judge at a number of them. His farm was well equipped
d a correspondent to the *Journal* noted, with pleasure, that "everything in
plements, etc., was well up-to-date, but nothing on any scale was in advance of the
nditions the phrase implies." Winter's knowledge on many subjects was broad and
pressive.[38] He was thus presented as a wise and successful man, reaping what he
d earned. He had taken responsibility, was confident (as he was entitled to be),
ovided leadership and selflessly shared his knowledge with others. Newnham
ɔuld have been proud to have had this "gentleman" associated with Hilton.

One of his first attempts at legislation was to get twenty shillings levied on
ɔrkers migrating out of the colony. This failed. With regard to his relations with
·ricans, the *Natal Agricultural Journal* noted that "Mr. Winter was highly esteemed by
e members of his staff for his justice in his dealings with them." In Parliament he had
ɔad reputation with regard to representing the "native's interests." One contempor-
y noted that he had "a complete lack of sympathy for the African population" and
as hostile to philanthropists and magistrates sympathetic to Africans."[39] So we have
anomaly — a "just" man with a reputation in some quarters for being unjust. One
ay of resolving the matter is to examine his record of relations with his own
borers.

Winter was representative of "progressive" Natal farmers. His practices with
gard to labor were not likely to have been significantly different from those of his
·ers. Unfortunately, the labor process in agriculture is not well documented,
ɪrticularly for the Midlands.[40] Official documents do not provide much insight
:her — magisterial records have been well pruned and, in any case, it took an official
mplaint to involve the state machinery. Thus official records generally give an
complete and distorted impression, distorted because they focus on "problems" and
buses" giving the impression that these were the norm. Another major source of
formation, the interview, is suspect because the subject of "race relations" frequently
duced the white farmers interviewed to silence or defensiveness, particularly when
eir fathers or grandfathers were being spoken about. Thus, there are only three ways
which some picture of these relationships might be developed: by looking at what
rmers themselves said about the subject at the time; by examining what Africans
ho experienced the system said; and by using the few records that do testify to farm
bor relations such as the correspondence of magistrates and the register of court
ses.

What They Said

1907 the Natal Native Affairs Commission took evidence concerning the causes of
ɪmbatha's rebellion. It interviewed farmers throughout the Midlands, asking

questions about relations between Africans and whites in a whole range of settings.
found that all farms owned and occupied by whites had labor tenants. African famili
lived on the land, provided labor (frequently for a cash wage) and were allowe
various cultivation and habitation rights. The profoundly unequal relationsh
between tenant and white farmer was subject to negotiation between them. Cotto
Acutt, a wealthy Rosetta rhubarb farmer who had come to Natal in 1864, gave th
following opinion on relations between landlords and tenants:

> The present practice was sufficiently satisfactory to justify them in leaving
> the present relations alone. He felt that natives living under a white man
> were being very well controlled, and were getting civilized, and being taught
> how to do useful work. He would not attempt to lay down any hard and fast
> rule for native tenants. His opinion was that the natives to-day under white
> employers had little or no grievance.[41]

Another farmer, Allan Stuart, of Estcourt was less happy with the prevailing situatio
"A native would come forward, and sign an agreement, but the ink would not be dr
before he commenced to set it at naught." One of the reasons, he said, was missiona
education: "The natives were not taught those principles of obedience to the
employers, which in Scotland, at least, used to be regarded as of great importance.'
The middle position was probably reflected by Richmond's magistrate, Allan Walla
Leslie. He was the son of William Leslie, an 1850 settler described on his death in 19(
as a "great sportsman" and "a gentleman who took considerable interest in politic
and was firm in his principles." Allan Leslie was also brother-in-law to H. D. Winter
Leslie said that very few contracts existed between tenant and farmer. Africans did n
like to sign contracts and were generally happy with verbal agreements. Farmers we
satisfied too and simply evicted tenants when an agreement was broken. Lesl
"thought very few natives broke their contracts unless they intended to leave th
farm."[44]

Agreements determined farm relations and, although the upper hand wa
undoubtedly held by the white farm owner, it is clear that agreements were not simp
foisted on tenants. They could move away, or disrupt the labor process, if th
agreement was not held to by the farmer. Furthermore, most farmers realized th
they "could not go on working unless they had some system of this kind, and b
showing a little kindly interest in their natives, they improved the old state o
affairs."[45]

Acutt gave reasons for the success of the agreement system: tenants we
"desirous of living under the wing of the white man" and leaving the chief. Under a
agreement they could keep cattle and cultivate land. "Tenants had to work for hi
[Acutt] whenever he wanted them, and he undertook to give them work all the ye
round. He had never any bother with them, and they were able to earn sufficie
money on his farm to supply all their wants."[46] The agreement also relied on know
patriarchal hierarchies. When a white man could deal directly with a black man o
authority, the basis was laid for an agreement. The agreement depended on mutu
respect and honor.

The term "our natives" may frequently have been used paternalistically, but i
another sense it spoke of a team, of a belonging, of mutual trust. In 1897 the Richmon
Farmers' Association asked that "trustworthy farm natives" be authorized to serve a
"special constables on their masters' farms."[47] This request testifies to a relationshi
between tenant and farmer that is quite distinct from the relationship between whi

rmers and the African population in general, or between white farmers and
eighboring Africans who were effectively anonymous, not enjoying the special bond
at tied tenant to farmer. Where such relationships existed, they were characterized
v hierarchy. Many farmers appointed "headmen" (*indunas*) to lead the team. Where
iefs interfered with this system, farmers, including H.D. Winter, were resentful.[48]

"Improving" the African (or to use the stronger language of Winter, ridding him
her of "old barbarous habits") was a necessary part of the agricultural project,
cording to Acutt. "He was in the habit of instructing them as to their methods of
ltivation, and advising them as to the use of fertilizers, which he sold them at cost
ice . . . He took considerable pains in teaching them better methods of cultivation,
d he generally interested himself in their affairs."[49] Acutt was not the exception. The
chmond Agricultural Society, which was dominated by the district's old families,
e Nicholsons, McKenzies and Marwicks, for example, prided itself on offering
izes for African agriculture at its shows.[50] Acutt, like many farmers, believed that the
ibal system was wrong, that chiefs were too powerful and that a system that exposed
fricans to western institutions, procedures, religion and education should be
stered. Such influences, it was argued, were much superior to such coercive
ractices as *isibhalo* (forced government labor, which was often defended on the basis
: its "civilizing" effects), to which many farmers strenuously objected.

To return to the question posed about H.D. Winter: how could a man be just in
ie context and unjust in another? J.W.V. Montgomery, a correspondent to the *Natal
gricultural Journal*, suggests an answer:

> The average farm labourer should be treated as a school boy and a certain
> interest taken in him beyond the rather important point of getting as much
> work out of him as possible, so that after completing his contract he will go
> forth a better being. It is, of course, necessary to send wilful offenders to
> prison occasionally, especially now that such an outcry has been raised
> against lashes, but there is no doubt whatever that a private whipping would
> be far better in every way . . . than fining or imprisonment. Fining
> impoverishes them, and constantly going to gaol only hardens and makes
> callous those who, if lectured and administered a few strokes of the rod,
> would remain at their work the same bright, contented, servants which they
> generally are.[51]

Iontgomery opposed severe corporal punishment, such as being "tied up to a wagon
heel, and thrashed with an 'after sjambok' to within an inch of his life."[52]
Iontgomery was a product of Hilton and the English public school, Repton. His
ther had been to Marlborough. Father and son were military men. In this extract the
ress is on rationality, justice, progress, improvement, and order. The language, the
incepts and the experience that gave white men power came from the school system
escribed above.

For the system to work, "progressive farmers" were agreed that it had to be fair. It
ad to have the respect and acceptance of all who operated under it. Prominent
owick farmer R.J. Spiers, for example, stressed that there should be no possibility of
aying an "unfairly low rate" and that where white masters exceeded their power, the
Iasters and Servants Act should be altered to give the magistrate power to punish
iny white man who was found abusing a native."[53]

When Africans were asked by the Natal Native Affairs commissioners in 1907
vhat their grievances were, they singled out "Government" as the cause of their

problems. High taxes, the poor quality of crown and location land and *isibhalo* we
major sources of dissatisfaction. On farms owned, but not farmed or occupied, b
whites the major grievances were high rents, labor demands and evictions.[54] The
were very few complaints about the condition of labor tenants on white owned ar
farmed land. Bubuyana of Lion's River did complain about "the irritating condition
imposed by the landlord in respect of labour," but this was not a point frequent
made. "Mvinjwa" representing Chief Silwane of the Lion's River Division said th
Africans "did not object to live in subjection on private farms, but they strong
resented being fleeced [by absentee landlords]."[55] An explanation for these differe
responses can be found in the structure of authority in the household, clan ar
"tribe."

Conditions on white-occupied farms were subject to negotiation betwee
household head and white farmer. In this process, African patriarchal authority w₄
supported. The latter point deserves underlining. B. Carton's work on the Bambath
rising suggests that it was as much a generational conflict as an anti-colonial ange
Chiefs, *indunas* and household heads frequently complained of defiant youths ar
disobedient daughters.[56] On white farms the agreement between farmer and tenan
firmly established the authority of the patriarch. Only married men could get lan₄
They were allotted less work than younger men, and generally received all the wage
In a powerful description of this relationship, a white farmer is remembered ₄
handing over the wage for a young man's work. He was told to summon h
grandfather: "Ndolozo, your child has worked for me . . . here is the money I a
giving him."[57]

Africans also complained of a lack of respect among whites. John Mpetwan₄
representing Chief Mkize of Lion's River, spoke with feeling on this point. He said th
he was left to stand at Howick Station in the rain: "In the country, if a white man w₄
caught in a storm, he was invited by the Natives to take shelter." Old Natal farme
William Nicholson agreed. He said that at government offices the treatment Africar
received was poor. They were "not shown proper consideration."[58] In a relationship ₄
tenant to farmer where the basis was recognition of mutual standing and gend₄
power, such a feeling is less likely to have prevailed. And in John Mpetwana
comment there is at least the hint that town people were ignorant of the etiquet
required, whereas white, Zulu-speaking farm owners respected these customs.

Farm Evictions

There is little doubt that eviction, akin to expulsion from school, was the mo
powerful sanction used by farmers against African occupants of their land. Evictio
was always the last resort for farmers failing to obtain sufficient labor and obedienc
from their tenants. Throughout the late nineteenth and early twentieth centurie
farmers complained of labor shortages, which meant that they preferred to retai
rather than dispense with labor. This situation altered dramatically when crown lanc
were opened for public purchase in 1880. Africans who had hitherto been i
undisturbed occupation of crown land suddenly found themselves under the contro
of a new owner. One of the first things the incoming white farmers did was to evi
families surplus to anticipated labor requirements.

In 1883 dissatisfaction amongst Africans over the escalation of evictions on lanc

rmerly owned by the crown led to a formal investigation. Magistrates noted that
ere were grounds for dissatisfaction. A major one was that "heads of kraals [had]
st a great deal of their authority over the young men with regard to enforcing their
ring out to work for their landlords."[59] Throughout the 1890s and 1900s, spurred by
ne opening of new markets and improved transportation, white farmers moved onto
ack-occupied land. The process invariably was accompanied by evictions. Only in
ne case of "labour farms" were evictions less common, though even here, rent-paying
nants could be evicted if they refused to provide labor when ordered, or balked at
aying the escalating rents.

In 1906/7, the rate of evictions was exceedingly high. The magistrate of Ixopo,
E. Foxon, reported that in seven months he had ordered sixty-six evictions of kraals,
ich with two to three huts. A farmer in the area confirmed that the process was
sturbing rural relations: "[T]he natives were grumbling very much at being turned
ff farms."[60] Eviction was also a mechanism for punishing serious crimes such as stock
eft. It was frequently used and involved not just the person accused, but his entire
mily.[61] Farmers and magistrates alike generally took an extremely harsh view of
ock theft, advocating whippings, long jail terms or, most of all, eviction, which
nounted to deportation. Foxon, for example, pushed for the removal of African stock
ieves and their dependents to far-distant St Lucia Bay.

For men like Foxon, there was a clear logic to evictions. Land was private and it
elonged to whites. Whites were entitled to the protection of the law. Blacks had no
ghts to land other than in the locations, were obliged to obey the white farmer (in
rms of the Masters and Servants legislation of 1852 and 1894) and, if they willfully
isobeyed, should feel the weight of colonial justice. Foxon was a product of
Iaritzburg College and his record as magistrate of Ixopo was one of unblemished
artisanship. He became notorious for his one-sidedness and by 1905 government had
ealized that he was "totally unfit" for his duties.[62] Foxon sent his sons to Maritzburg
ollege. There, one of them, Eddie (E.B. Foxon), achieved recognition as a fine
ortsman. He became an executive member of the Old Boys' Society and later an
fficer in the Natal Carbineers and magistrate of Estcourt. Known as a disciplinarian
nd for his accuracy with a rifle, he was reputed to have shot dead eight African tax
efaulters in the early 1930s when they resisted arrest.[63]

F.E. Foxon was part of a network that perpetuated and supported itself. His
ecord as magistrate should not therefore be seen only as supportive of capitalism and
rivate property, or as simply the promotion of the interests of one race over another.
Ie actively assisted men who were his friends and school mates, and those who were
ssociated with them through brothers and sons and their respective networks. They
nared the same educational background, the same understanding of masculinity and
ence similar values and a common view of how the world should work.

The authority of the landowner, implicit in his power to evict, posed two serious
nallenges to the African order. First, it eroded the authority of chiefs, *indunas* and
ousehold heads. In the Shepstonian period before the penetration of the concept of
rivate property, this authority had not been undermined. To compound matters, the
nfluence of the magistrates, seldom neutral, never benign to the Africans, now swung
ncreasingly behind the farmers. Senior African men consistently bemoaned the
brogation of their rights (over their followers/juniors and over women) by white
ndowners and government officials.[64] Second, the landlord's power took no account
f Africans' understanding of land. Eviction meant not just the loss of a place to live

and farm, but also the destruction of community, a rupture with tradition and loss o
place of belonging. As Tunzi Nzimande put it, when threatened with eviction in 19
"I was born on this farm, and have grown up and married there. It will be a gre
hardship for me to be removed now."[65]

Relations on the Farms

This picture of labor relations on the Midlands farms does not do justice to
complexity. As Verne Harris has reminded us in the context of the *bywoner* in northe
Natal, there were many different forms that the relationship between farmer a
tenant could take.[66] The major variable for our purposes was the length of time far
had been occupied by white farmers and the proximity of labor farms.

The area longest occupied in the Midlands centered on Pietermaritzburg a
included Howick, Dargle, Nottingham Road, Mooi River, Estcourt and Richmon
This area was a mixed farming area, with dairying a major activity, but with beef a
mutton farming also important. There was little intense cultivation requiring a larg
seasonal labor force. By 1880 farm labor relations seem to have been well settle
Richmond was an exception. It abutted on densely populated African locations ar
contained many privately owned labor farms. In the area of these farms, points
conflict were numerous. Stock theft was common, and labor relations were comp
cated by the fact that the big farming families, such as the Marwicks, Nicholsons ar
Cockburns, owned many farms, and shuffled labor around as they needed it. Here t
stability achieved elsewhere was less secure. While some farmers worked in much t
same way as their colleagues elsewhere (via agreement), others were anxious to bri
the law actively onto their side.

John Marwick, for example, said that he had no difficulty getting labor. He dre
up a written agreement with "his" Africans that stipulated that they should work on
for him unless they got permission to do otherwise. He did not rent land to Africa
and had employed most of his labor full time. Yet he was mindful of the problems th
his neighbors and kin were having with their labor. He was therefore in favor
tightening up the provisions of the Masters and Servants Act. In addition, he "wou
put no limit to the age of a native for the purpose of a whipping." His brother Jam
Marwick was highly prejudiced against Africans. He commented on their increasir
indolence and spoke with great disapproval of the white farmers who were living wi
black women. He wanted existing regulations to be strengthened to ensure the
obedience. If Africans were given, he said, "the same orders and rules which the
forefathers got in the Garden of Eden, viz., to work and to obey, together with su
education which the farmers were able to give to them, he thought it would be qu
sufficient at the present time."[67]

The literature on labor relations in Natal agriculture tends to present coercion ar
violence towards employees as the norm. In the sugar industry a number of studi
have made this case powerfully.[68] Similarly, with regard to mixed farming, tl
impression is given that without violence, farmers would not have been able to contr
their labor. The same is true of Midlands agriculture.[69] There can be little doubt th
violence on a range of levels did occur. This chapter, however, seeks to make tw
qualifying points in relation to violence: firstly, it was not as pervasive as the literatu
suggests, and secondly, where violence was part of the labor process, it often took

rm that reflected the experience of "physical correction" to which the farmers emselves had been subjected during their time at school.

Charles van Onselen has argued that in the western Transvaal violence by white rmers towards black tenants occurred within the context of paternal relations. He oposed that the ideology of paternalism contains within it the reason and stification for the use of violence by the more powerful "father" towards the weaker hild."[70] In Southern Rhodesia, Terence Ranger argued, single white men (overseers, rmers, miners) used violence to secure their fragile superiority over blacks.[71] Ranger as careful to indicate that violence was not the only factor governing relations tween white and black, yet he made the point that a "normal" level of violence by nite males towards blacks of both sexes characterized this settler society.

It has been shown that the regimes established on Midlands farms that had been erated for some time by old settler families did not rely primarily on violence, but ther depended on some kind of "agreement." Yet it must immediately be admitted at physical violence — in the form of assaults and murders — was not uncommon. jually, the merciless killing by members of the Natal forces mobilized in 1906 against e Bambatha rebels also testifies to the levels of aggression of whites toward acks.

On Midlands farms, the most extreme forms of violence against black males (for ample, shooting trespassers, whipping laborers) occurred in relationships of onymity. Where a white farmer did not personally know the African male, violence as much more likely. It was not unusual for stock thieves to be shot by farmers, and r insolence to be punished with assault. Stock theft was particularly common around ations, where animals were plentiful and whites few. The areas where antagonism nd violence) towards stock thieves was most rife were therefore in the Drakensberg othills and between Richmond and Ixopo. Stock theft did occur in the ONF artland, but not with nearly as much frequency.

Assaults on African laborers on established white farms certainly occurred. The quency of these assaults is difficult to judge. They seldom came to court and the sence of evidence makes it difficult to get a sense of scale.[72] The evidence presented ove is largely silent on farm discipline, but given the school experience of farmers, e administration of corporal punishment was likely to have been relatively frequent, serving generally, with the household head's consent, to discipline the en who actually did the work. It operated therefore largely in symbolic ways, inforcing the authority of the white farm owner and black household head, spectively, and reminding the victim of his obligation to the system. Discipline was nstructed within a masculine framework where to err was to deserve correction, d where to challenge hierarchy, to disobey, to fail to honor and to be heedless of her people's rights were all misdemeanors that, in the school context, were corrected rough corporal punishment. And the corporal punishment was delivered by the rson charged with the responsibility of ensuring good order and the spiritual ell-being of his subordinates. In this context, farm violence should be distinguished m anonymous violence.

If corporal punishment was not the staple of farm relations, what are we to make the violence of settlers towards the followers of Langalibalele and Bambatha? The olence here was inflicted by the same farmers who owned, farmed and occupied the nds under discussion. In both cases, we have the region's "gentlemen" engaged in vage acts: blasting caves sheltering Hlubi women and children, shooting terrified rebels hiding up trees in Zululand, sentencing 4 700 men, under martial law, floggings, and cutting off Bambatha's head as a trophy.[73]

At this point it may be helpful briefly to turn to Sir Duncan McKenzie, leader the forces deployed against Bambatha in 1906. He was a founding student of Hilto College and his family owned a huge farm, the Cotswolds, near Nottingham Road. fine horseman and polo player, he made his money transport riding (his employee with whom he worked closely and for many months in this demanding task, we mostly Africans from his own farm). Described by his son, on the basis technological improvements, as "one of the most progressive farmers in the Midlan districts" he was revered throughout the colony and much decorated as well.[74] As professional soldier, he was merciless towards his enemies. At the outset of th rebellion in Richmond, he tried two rebels in a military court and had them execute immediately. His campaign subsequently against the rebels was nothing short of reign of terror. No evidence exists of his relationship towards Africans on his ow farm, but some insight is available into the family's attitude towards martial behavio and violence.[75]

Barbara McKenzie recalled her father-in-law as a distant, tough and firm man, b a "man of honour." She remembered that as a board member of a company that we bankrupt, he sold a few of his own farms to pay off shareholders whom he felt shou not be left out of pocket. On the other hand she remembered Duncan ("Billy McKenzie, his youngest child, born in 1898, as a "a real little horror." He was spoi never married and was instrumental in breaking up the family farm. There were mar reasons for Mrs. McKenzie's singling out of Billy McKenzie for such a description. Sh was unhappy about the loss of the family farm to outsiders, unhappy, too, abou Billy's ill-disciplined behavior. But her account included, amongst the litany failings, Billy McKenzie's frequent assaults on Africans. This is interesting in a fami with a military record that placed high store by deeds of valor, and accepted th violence, the killing and maiming of other people, was part of life. While Mr McKenzie was extremely proud of her husband, the elder son who followed in h father's footsteps and commanded the Natal Carbineers, she was ashamed of h brother-in-law's excesses.

Barbara McKenzie's testimony confirms that violence was quite acceptable whe directed against the enemy — either traitors and lawbreakers — or against those wi whom no agreement could be reached. On the other hand, violence beyond the law beyond the mores of society, violence without control, was despicable, a sign weakness itself. The fact that Barbara McKenzie singled out Billy McKenzie's behavio suggests that his assaults on Africans were out of the ordinary, not just for a family th was used to physical violence, but for the white community within which they lived well.

Conclusion

This chapter has argued for a compelling symmetry of relations at school and on th farms. It has attempted to show that the white farmers structured labor relations o their farms in ways that closely reflected the structures of their school years and th values learned there. These were values primarily of order and control. While far labor relations included instances of violence, it is misleading to place thes ccurrences on a par with the routine violence of the plantation economies or the farm ompounds. Agreements between farmers and tenants ordered farm life. Such greements could occur only where property relations had already been established nd were no longer fundamentally contested by the original African inhabitants (if ere were any).

In areas where white settlement was more recent, agreements between farmers nd tenants often worked against a punitive bureaucratic backdrop. Here, as Ranger as shown for Southern Rhodesia, personal relations were transient and human oundaries ill-defined; thus, the capacity for violence, prejudice and the naked xercise of power (for example in the many evictions) was great. When this power was xercised, it still bore the mark of the schooling experience, being justified in terms of he civilizing burden of the white man. In trying, therefore, to understand social and conomic relations in commercial agriculture we ought to take greater account of the re-adult experiences that shaped them. In the Natal Midlands, at least, this means ringing the schools that the boys attended into the reckoning.

11

Paternalism and Violence on the Maize Farms of the South-Western Transvaal, 1900–1950

Charles van Onselen

Violence was — and no doubt still is — an integral part of the relationship th[at] developed between European landlords and African tenants in the Transvaal ar[d] Orange Free State countryside in the decades that followed the great miner[al] discoveries of the late nineteenth century.[1] In what is clearly our best account [of] organized black resistance to white domination on the highveld in recent times, Hel[en] Bradford observed that: "fists, whips and guns were central in maintaining maste[r-]servant relationships on farms," but was equally quick to point out that "among [the] wealthier farmers harsh racism was sometimes tempered by the adoption of some [of] the benevolence of familial figures of authority" and that "the very intimacy of far[m] life, combined with the master-servant relationship itself, helped nurture a stunte[d] approximation of the ethic of paternalism." In moderating their racism, she suggeste[d] landlords "clearly linked individual Africans to their families in ways which inhibit[ed] the development of tenant protest and independence."[2]

Bradford's formulation raises several interesting questions, but what is importa[nt] to note here is the broad congruence that exists between the argument she has p[ut] forward and that advanced by T. Keegan in his account of the transformation [of] highveld society at the turn of the century. In the most lucid, and certainly the mo[st] explicit, statement that we have linking violence to paternalism, Keegan suggeste[d] that:

> Violence and intimidation were tempered by the practice of paternalism,
> which was not a discrete phenomenon, but very often rested on an uneasy

compromise in which violence was always present as a sanction. Paternalism as an ideology defined and shaped day-to-day interaction and conflict in the workplace, beyond the reaches of the law or the coercive state. It represented a compromise, a *modus vivendi*, which enabled masters and servants, landlords and tenants on the farms to sustain working relationships.[3]

concluded that "paternalism mediated conflict, coercion and resistance, defusing d displacing the more destructive and explicit manifestations of struggle."

These two observations have a distinct ring of truth about them and, no doubt, tisfy the specific scholarly requirements that they were designed to meet. But, cause they concentrate exclusively on the recessive potential inherent in paternalic relationships, for compromise, reciprocity, subordination or dependence, they ve the collective effect of closing down rather than opening up new lines of enquiry. paternalism is seen *only* as a facilitating ideology or social practice that enhances the ances of conciliation and mediation and the possibility of quiescence, then we forfeit possibility of posing questions about some of the more conflictual elements ıbedded deeply within the concept. It is only once these underlying elements have en dredged up and exposed to critical examination that we can develop a fuller ıderstanding of the often extraordinarily complex relationship that exists between ternalism and violence.

What follows, then, are four "alternative" questions and a tentative attempt at ıswering them. First, what constitutes paternalism in a racially divided society? cond, under what historical circumstances are such paternalistic relationships most ely to take root? Third, how is paternalism produced and reproduced on a y-to-day basis in farm life? Fourth, under what structural conditions are paternalic relationships most prone to erosion, and from which of the partners is the impetus change or terminate the relationship most likely to emanate?

Since it is not possible to provide satisfactory answers to such abstract questions ithout resorting to at least some empirical examples and evidence, this exercise will, necessity, have to be situated within a specific set of productive relations at a ırticular historical moment: in this case, the sharecropping economy of maize farms the Bloemhof/Schweizer-Reneke/Wolmaransstad triangle of the south-western ˙ansvaal in the period 1900–50. Thus, before proceeding with the analysis let us ıuse to sketch the social, economic and political context from which our examples are ˙awn.[4]

The Setting

ıe south-western Transvaal, a wedge-shaped tract of land "squeezed" between the ınction of the Harts River to the north and the Vaal to the south, is located about idway between the Kimberley diamond-fields, which lie to its west, and the ˙itwatersrand gold-fields to the east (figure 1). Situated in the drier western half of e country, the Bloemhof/Schweizer-Reneke/Wolmaransstad districts straddle an ıportant climatic divide in South Africa and the crucial twenty-inch isohyet passes ˙rough the very heart of the triangle. Areas to the west of this line of rainfall are ınsidered marginal for crop farming, while those to the immediate east are only ıghtly better placed. In the wet years, the isohyet moves west, but in the dry

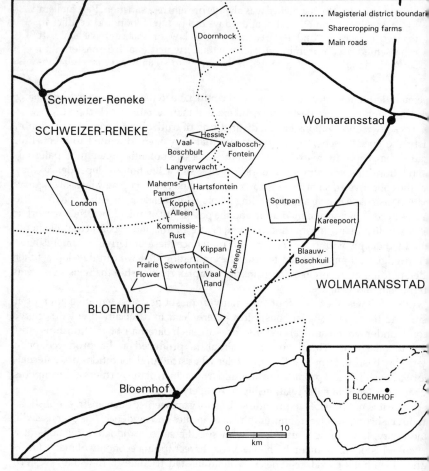

Figure 11.1   Sharecropping Farms in Bloemhof/Schweizer-Reneke/
Wolmaransstad Triangle

years — which tend to outnumber the wet by nearly three to one — the lines m
east. In practice, this has meant that historically the triangle has been best suited
mixed farming.

Having been handed such an unpromising dowry by nature, the sand and gra
plains of the south-western Transvaal have always found it difficult to attract suit
interested in longer-term relationships and, during the eighteenth and ninetee
centuries, the region served as home to bands of nomadic and semi-nomadic San a
Koranna. Once diamonds were discovered in the north-western Cape in the late 18
and gold on the Witwatersrand in the mid-1880s, however, the area became m
attractive to the burghers of the South African Republic, who persuaded th
government to allow them to carve out extensive landholdings within the triang
The object behind the burghers' initial request for land was to search for speculat
profits from mineral rights rather than to engage in agricultural production a

ween 1910 and 1925, the region enjoyed the effects of a relatively sustained but
evenly spread boom as thousands of white diggers and their black laborers invaded
: district to work the local alluvial diamond deposits. But once this robber economy
I lost its momentum and the center of mineral production had shifted further north
.ing the population along with it, property owners in the triangle were forced into
nmercial agriculture still owning too much land and commanding too little labor to
der it fully productive.

It was under these historical circumstances — but more especially so before and
er the relatively brief interlude of alluvial diamond mining — that white landlords
I black tenants entered into the sharecropping arrangements that tended to
minate the local economy between the two world wars. Afrikaner landlords,
xious to attract black families with agricultural equipment, draft-oxen and labor to
ir sprawling properties, were only too willing to provide land and access to grazing
return for a half-share of the grain harvest produced by skilled tenants.

Black farmers with large families, forced out of areas of traditional peasant
ming and increasingly crowded reserves, found sharecropping on white farms an
ractive proposition. From the onset of the first significant mineral discoveries a
wing number of African agriculturalists were drawn to the triangle and its
rounding districts from Basutoland, the northern Cape Colony, the eastern Free
te and parts of the north-western Transkei. Others came from even farther north
I east. By the turn of the century, the area between the Vaal and the Harts was
eady noted for the wide variety of languages spoken by its black inhabitants,
luding Afrikaans, SeSotho, Shangaan, SeTswana, SiXhosa and isiZulu.

The hundreds of black families who established themselves in the region during
: early period included amongst their number several outstandingly successful
in and livestock farmers. Their ranks were further augmented when, in 1913, the
amous Natives Land Act undermined sharecropping as a legal institution in the
ange Free State and pushed a second wave of African farmers across the Vaal River
I into the south-western Transvaal. During the more "successful" decades after
orld War I, such as the 1920s and the 1940s, the names of prominent sharecropping
nilies such as Maine, Marumo, Mashiu, Seiphetlo, Tabu and Tjalempe assumed
host legendary proportions amongst farmers of all classes and colors in the triangle.[5]

White landlords with a history of political turbulence and strong Afrikaner
ionalist sympathies were not, however, content to see their economic future
ging on sharecropping contracts with black tenants. The practice of sharing-on-
-halves not only inhibited the accumulation of capital, but also fostered notions of
ial equality amongst their better-off black tenants.[6] Thus, throughout the inter-war
riod white landlords made use of their racially privileged position at the ballot-box
pressurize the government of the day into providing them with additional
nomic support through agricultural cooperatives, the Land Bank, the Marketing
t and other state-subsidized services while, at the same time, steadily escalating
ir demand for increased social segregation.

The Nature of Paternalism

utherners," noted Eugene Genovese in *The World the Slaveholders Made*, "generally
erred to their slaves as their 'people' or their 'black family,' and within limits they

meant it. We need not deny the reality of the sense of responsibility that express₁
itself in this way." "That reality," he went on to point out, "cannot be taken literally;
was merely a distant approach to genuine family relationships."[7] In a more rece₁
work he has extended and refined his argument and suggested that "the ideology
household and family grew naturally from the political economy of slavery a₁
rendered the expression 'our family, white and black' an authentic, if deeply flawe₁
projection of an essential social reality."[8] Although separated by several centuries
time and two oceans in breadth, these observations nevertheless speak powerfully
experiences on the Transvaal highveld during the course of the nineteenth and ear₁
twentieth centuries when Afrikaner landlords in the triangle habitually referred to t₁
black families living and laboring on their properties as *ons volk* (our folk) or *ons men*
(our people).

No matter how powerless or vulnerable they may have been, African lab₁
tenants and sharecroppers were not slaves, and Genovese is obviously correct to stre₁
that the similarities between these different forms of labor mobilization should not ₁
taken too far. Even after the obvious class differences between the two situations ha₁
been discounted, however, there is still sufficient substance left in the comparis₁
between the white masters and black servants on the two continents for it to be used ₁
a platform on which to construct a working definition of paternalism.

"Paternalism," wrote George Fredrickson, "can be defined in various ways, b₁
presumably it must involve some sense of quasi-kinship transcending barriers of cas₁
or race."[9] While this is a useful starting point, it does not, however, go far enough an₁
should we wish to extend our understanding of the social dynamics of paternalis₁
within the relatively self-enclosed worlds of the estate, farm or plantation, it will ₁
necessary to draw out two additional unstated elements within this broad definitio₁
The first of these relates to gender. The concept of paternalism is predicated on t₁
notion of a male of legal standing who enjoys the right — without having to se₁
recourse to the law — of exercising traditionally sanctioned authority over mino₁
within his "family"; that is, over the "women and children" on his property.

The very idea of being a "father" is therefore inextricably bound up with the id₁
of patriarchy and, as James Oakes has noted, "paternalism takes as its model t₁
extended patriarchal household."[10] Thus, while paternalism may in theory ₁
concerned with "quasi-kinship" without reference to gender, in practice much of t₁
day-to-day power exercised in the relationship flows through the conduit of gend₁
and is mediated through the actions of two patriarchs of differing power. In Sou₁
Africa, unlike in the American South where a slave may or may not have presided ov₁
a family of his own, this mediation of paternalism through patriarchal power assum₁
even greater significance since the black tenant was *invariably* the head of a househo₁
and expected to exercise an appropriate degree of authority over his wives ar₁
children.

The second unstated or hidden element within our working definition concer₁
age. The white patriarch presiding over the paternalistic regime of the estate, farm ₁
plantation is, it is assumed, not only a man of legal standing, but one old enough ₁
command the respect and deference of his "children." On the South African mai₁
farm, no less than on the southern plantation, age played a key role in mediating soci₁
relations and, as Oakes noted, "the distinguishing characteristics of the patriarch
slave-holding family included a deep respect for the wisdom of the elders, a₁
entrenched concern with the family's image, an extraordinary interest in posteri₁

anifested in close attention to the rearing of children, particularly male children."
aternalistic fathers," he suggested, "encouraged the maintenance of deference
wards elders, be they grandparents, parents or siblings."[11] This reverence for
niority is, of course, no less a feature of Afrikaner or African society and is therefore
important additional cohesive force in the paternalistic relationship that bound
gether white landlord and black tenant.

Teasing out the additional "hidden" elements within paternalism in this way may
tend our understanding of the concept, but still leaves it with distinct limitations
cause — to put Ralf Darendorf's observation on class to work in another con-
xt — historians are "not guided by the question, 'How does a given society in fact
ok at a given point in time?', but by the question 'How does the structure of a society
ange?'"[12] Thus, while paternalism may well be concerned with "quasi-kinship"
ations, this remains a relatively static notion and may therefore be a less than useful
ea for the historian until we add the rider, "How do these relationships change over
ne?"

It is in this latter context — when we attempt to discern the changing structure of
paternalistic relationship over time — that the discussion on gender and age
sumes greater significance. For it is only when the changing nature of the
ationship between white landlords and black tenants is traced through time that we
n detect at which points the "hidden" tensions in a paternalistic regime intensify
fficiently for them to give rise to conflict and threaten the relationship. In a
arecropping economy, at least some of the moments at which these built-in
eaknesses in paternalistic relations manifest themselves can be predicted with some
curacy.

Highveld sharecropping was based on the capacity of the black tenant to deliver
fferent combinations of labor-power drawn from within his household to the joint
nture with the white landlord in accordance with the progress of the agricultural
cle and the seasonal demands of the production process.[13] Seen from this
rspective, sharecropping was an essentially patriarchal mode of production, but
e that was also beset by a contradiction — namely, that the moment when the
triarch had the greatest structural potential to produce (that is, when he had most
ature physical labor at his disposal) was also the juncture at which his authority was
ost likely to be subjected to a challenge from below. In practice this meant that the
nant's greatest potential to produce did not necessarily lie at the point when there
ere the most adults in the household, but when there were the most adole-
ents — that is, when he had command over the most bodies with the near-physical
tential of adults but without the full social and psychological power to question his
thority as patriarch.[14]

However, structural stresses that derived from the development cycle of the
mily tended not only to produce strains *within* the tenant household, but to have a
ock-on effect that placed an additional burden on the relationship between white
ndlord and black sharecropper. This additional stress was particularly noticeable in,
hough by no means confined to, those instances where young black adolescent
ales were coming of age.

Located within the constraints of a farm dominated by a paternalistic ethos, the
olescent black male found himself in the particularly uncomfortable position of
ving both an "ideological" and a biological father. This meant that just as the young
an was approaching manhood, his skills as a workman maturing particularly

rapidly and his services in greatest demand, he was subjected to not one but *two* chai
of command. As a result, the paternalistic relationship was never "devoid of confl
and ambiguity" and "the patriarchal ideal alone furnished a model of oppressi
capable of sustaining the rationalization of the most inhumane master."[15]

The consequences of this socially structured ambiguity are predictable. N
surprisingly, an in-depth survey of one white landlord–black tenant relationship
the triangle between 1920 and 1948 reveals that most breakdowns in tenan
agreements could be traced to moments when the Afrikaner farmer came into dir
conflict with his black tenant over the use and disciplining of the latter's adolesce
boys. Interestingly enough, in the case of adolescent African girls such confl
culminated in outright physical violence less frequently, and was followed by t
black patriarch's seeking to mediate in the dispute rather than by his summar
terminating his agreement with the white landlord. From this it is clear that, as t
patriarchal system sought to reproduce itself, both within the farmhouse and witl
the sharecropper's shack, father-son relations tended to enjoy priority over fathe
daughter relations.[16]

But if gender and patriarchy were in some ways preordained to intersect ir
manner likely to give rise to violence as the black sharecropping family mov
through its development cycle on the white landlord's property,[17] the same potent
for conflict was not necessarily evident in the second of the "hidden" elements that
have been considering. In small-scale society, where great store was placed
seniority, age was always more likely to be used to help determine "pecking orde
and reinforce "traditional" patterns of social deference than to act as a catalyst
conflict.

Yet, precisely because the paternalistic relationship was founded on
assumption that the white landlord's status was — in terms of age — superior to tl
of the black tenant, the system sometimes came under intense pressure when
"ideological age" of the Afrikaner patriarch failed to match the chronological realit
of the situation. Put simply — albeit somewhat paradoxically — the social constri
tion of a paternalistic relationship was threatened when the supposed black "chil
was manifestly older than its white "father." This helps account for the propensity
highveld landlords to provide their black labor tenants or laborers with names tl
make use of the diminutive form — a practice calculated to create or perpetuate
child-like status of the African male regardless of his age or changing socio-econor
status. The conflicts and some of the terminological compromises that this pract
gave rise to during the course of the tenant's life-cycle will be examined in grea
detail below.

The Historical Circumstances of Paternalism

In the course of his illuminating *History of American Slaveholders*, James Oakes argi
that paternalism — cast on the foundation of church, monarchy and aris
cracy — was the "reigning theory of human relations" from medieval times througl
the age of the Tudors. In the late Stuart era, however, with the rise of Lock
philosophy "and the emergence of capitalistic economic and democratic politi
structures, paternalism was rendered increasingly irrelevant."[18]

Yet, even if "increasingly irrelevant" to developments in Europe after

enteenth and eighteenth centuries, ideologies of paternalism continued to exercise
onsiderable hold on a wide variety of social, political and economic structures in the
der world for at least two centuries thereafter. Indeed, not only did important
ments of such thinking take root in the fertile subsoils of the New World, but they
re also successfully transplanted to large parts of the "Dark Continent" during the
ramble for Africa" in the late nineteenth century.

In South Africa the flag-bearers of this new wave of European expansionism
packed conceptual baggage that contained, amongst other things, notions drawn
m the Darwinian theory of natural selection.[19] Older racial constructs, derived from
culture and experiences of rural society in the late seventeenth and eighteenth
turies, merged with new ideas to provide paternalism with the gloss of modernity
l sufficient ideological vitality to make its contribution to nineteenth-century Cape
eralism and, from there, to make the even more demanding transition to the
hveld where it had to be reworked yet again to meet the needs of Afrikaner farmers
the Boer republics. But, after the mineral discoveries of the 1860s and 1880s, this
vorked paternalism too became "increasingly irrelevant" to the needs of an
erging industrial order, which steadily eroded the social bonds between the classes
the countryside.[20]

The ideology of paternalism that manifested itself in the south-western Transvaal
er the turn of the century, while continuing to rely on Christian inspiration from
ove and to stress deference and duty from below, was therefore no longer simply
t of the slave estate in the agricultural economy of the eighteenth century, or even
t of the nineteenth-century commercial Cape. It was, in Bradford's evocative
rase, a "stunted" approximation of "paternalistic relations" just because it was
uggling to root itself successfully in a society already experiencing the first brutal
nsformations of a developing capitalist economy rather than in a relatively stable
l hierarchical quasi-feudal order.[21]

If these broadly based observations reflect the situation in the south-western
ansvaal with any degree of accuracy, then they also hold true for the triangle that, as
have seen, experienced its own episodic lurch towards a more industrial order
h the development of the alluvial diamond diggings between 1910 and 1925. The
ergence of the mining industry helped to create a market for white farmers who, for
first time, had the opportunity of selling large quantities of beef, mutton, milk,
ize and sorghum to the thousands of diggers and laborers who had established
mselves at various points along the Vaal River.

But, given that market economies erode paternalistic relationships, we may ask
v even this "stunted approximation" of an "ethic of paternalism" managed to
vive in the south-western Transvaal until at least the 1950s? Part of the answer lies
not exaggerating the impact that either alluvial diamonds or the wider mining
olution in South Africa had on this comparatively isolated part of the country.

While it is true that the discovery of alluvial diamonds *did* help to create a market
triangle produce, the effects of this development were extremely localized in an
a poorly served by regional transport networks, and the entire river-digging
ustry survived for only two decades. Moreover, for much of the 1920s and 1930s
region between the Vaal and the Harts was ravaged by the alternating natural
asters of drought and locusts. It was only really after the mid-1930s that local
iculture showed signs of sustained expansion as landlords started to invest in
first paraffin-driven tractors and to benefit from state assistance to white
iculture.[22]

This comparatively late development meant that for most of the inter-war peri♦
and more especially during the early 1920s and the Great Depression, much of ru♦
life and the agricultural economy remained imperfectly monetized. Not only w♦
unskilled labor tenants and wage laborers often paid in kind, but even skilled ru♦
craft-workers such as stone-masons, thatchers and wool-shearers were often ren♦
nerated in beer, cattle, meat or sheep rather than in cash.[23] Nor were such transactic♦
confined to the relatively enclosed universe of the farm. Right up to World War♦
Asian traders such as the Kathradas and the Patels continued to do a significa♦
amount of their business by bartering goods for the eggs, chickens, hides, skins a♦
wool produced by the triangle's black sharecroppers and labor tenants.[24] Su♦
non-monetized transactions, combined with the timely exercise of the "gift"♦
purposes of social control, did much to ensure the survival of paternalis♦
relationships into an era characterized by increasing black proletarianization.

At least as important as the slow appearance of cash wages, however, was ♦
relatively uncomplicated nature of the labor process on farms increasingly devoted♦
the production of maize. While the use of oxen and heavy equipment for plowing a♦
planting continued to ensure the presence of the sharecropper and his so♦
hand-hoeing and harvesting tended to make greater use of female labor. B♦
regardless of the particular gender combinations at work in different seasons, ♦
production process remained comparatively poorly mechanized right into the 19♦
and heavily dependent on the ability of the black patriarch to "bring out" his famil♦
labor. A fairly simple labor process, monocrop production, the prevalence of fam♦
labor, and the consequent reinforcement of patriarchal structures, all interacted♦
such a way as to allow paternalistic relationships to linger into the dawn of ♦
capitalist era in the south-western Transvaal.

The Production and Reproduction of Paternalistic Social Relations

"Paternalist beliefs," wrote Herbert Gutman in his seminal study of the black fami♦
"were widespread among plantation owners on the eve of the Civil War and affect♦
the behavior of many planters." "But no one including Genovese," he reminded♦
"has studied how such beliefs and practices developed."[25] The essence of t♦
cautionary observation is equally applicable to the historiography of southern Afri♦
Although elements of paternalism can be traced throughout the history of ♦
subcontinent, in regimes ranging from the relatively benign to the most unashame♦
brutal, the manner in which these beliefs were acted upon and made to info♦
everyday social practice remains poorly documented.[26]

Somewhat paradoxically, one may suggest that in the case of the Transvaal ♦
practice of paternalism remained largely unrecorded just because it was so eas♦
recognized and widely resorted to. The commonplace, the familiar, and ♦
self-evident were often the last features to be commented on by insiders and amon♦
the first to be forgotten by outsiders. What follows, then, is an examination of a few♦
the more obvious practices that have tended to perpetuate the paternalistic eth♦
And, if the practice of paternalism revolves around the creation of quasi-kins♦
relationships that seek to transcend the barriers of class and race, then any enqu♦
about the production and reproduction of such relationships has to begin ♦
addressing the question of primary socialization. Here there are two major issues t♦
need to be explored.

First, it should be noted that in the triangle — as elsewhere in the countryside — it is not at all uncommon for children of pre-school age of both sexes and all races to spend a considerable amount of their time playing together. This inter-racial play, which could occur in the home of the white master, but was more frequently to be found in and around the huts of the black tenants, not only involved a considerable amount of peer-group bonding but also allowed for the development of a good deal of bilingualism. Indeed, even today it is noticeable how the farther west one travels in the Transvaal, and the more isolated the farming community becomes, the more likely one is to come across Africans with a superior command of Afrikaans, and Afrikaners who are capable of conversing in fluent SeTswana.[27]

During these formative pre-school years it was possible for the landlord's children, and more especially his sons, to become exposed to several important elements of black culture. Indeed, the tired old theme of having "grown up with the natives," or "knowing them," often contributed to the adult Afrikaner farmer's ability to underwrite apartheid policies and at the same time strongly reject the possibility of racial animosity as a motive for his support of segregationist politics.

Power on the farm flowed through the microcircuitry of patriarchy and paternalism before being fed into the national grid of political life. What is more interesting in the context of our particular argument, however, is the manner in which this primary cross-cultural socialization of young Afrikaner boys sometimes also nudged their fathers into giving them apparently bizarre nicknames such as *Boesman* (bushman) or *Kaffertjie* (little kaffir); although these terms perhaps accurately reflected their early immersion in black culture and were used affectionately within the confines of the white household, they also lent themselves to more adversarial, contemptuous or dismissive use when employed in the wider context of farm, district or country. Less frequent, but equally interesting, is the way that black tenants sometimes chose to name children after the landlord or his wife.[28]

It is within this same broad context — that of primary socialization in a rural setting — that the one black name to have been genuinely incorporated into Afrikaner male-naming practices evolved. Long before radical chic saw middle-class, English-speaking whites in urban areas rushing to name their daughters *Zinzi* (Mandela), Afrikaner farmers were naming their sons *Thabo* (joy in SeTswana or SeSotho).[29]

As already noted, these quasi-kinship naming practices within the household of individual Afrikaner landlords were largely confined to male children exactly because naming was linked to the reproduction of patriarchal power structures on the farm. But, because the paternalistic ethos was also being reproduced within the wider context of the rural community, it influenced — in a rather more general way — the manner in which Afrikaner youths of both sexes addressed white folk who were not kin. Thus, in the triangle — as elsewhere in South Africa — *all* white men and women of indeterminate status were addressed respectfully as either *Oom* (Uncle) or *Tannie* (Auntie). In a society where whites were sometimes a little thin on the ground, these fictive relationships gave added ideological cohesion to the paternalistic ethos that struggled to maintain its grip on highveld society.

The second feature about primary socialization in the South African countryside, and one that is equally well known and therefore need not detain us unnecessarily, is the manner in which such early cross-cultural exposure tended to give way to increasingly segregated experiences once the landlord's children were removed from the farm setting and sent to town for schooling. Thus, while some inter-racial

friendships and especially those amongst boys were capable of persisting into
white child's high school years, they made way for more socially distant life-sty
with the onset of puberty and sexual maturity. Quasi-kinship relationships amon
children — which in their earliest years involved a measure of equality across
racial divide — seldom survived the transition into adulthood as the values associa
with the secondary and tertiary structures of the dominant group slowly penetra
the otherwise enclosed universe of the farm.

But, since the production and reproduction of paternalistic relationships w
ultimately dependent on the shaping of a *structured inequality* between white landlc
and black tenant, we cannot confine our examination to the manner in which su
values emerged within the dominant group. Indeed, in many ways it is mo
important to establish how the white patriarch sought to impose and reinforce
ideologically inferior status upon the black tenants themselves. It is to this process
imposition that we therefore now turn our attention — once again commencing wit
brief examination of naming practices.

In our earlier discussion of patriarchy and age it was noted how, unde
paternalistic regime, there was a built-in propensity for the white landlord or "fath
to perpetuate the childlike status of black tenants by conferring on them "Christia
names that made use of the diminutive form such as Jan*tjie* or Ger*tjie*.[30] But Afrikane
like Africans, tended to defer to age and seniority and, whereas it might have be
appropriate for an elderly white landlord to refer to a young black man as "John*n*
such nomenclature became increasingly inappropriate with the passage of time a
the need to apply it to an elderly tenant. In short, the life-cycle of the tenant hims
tended to undermine the "childishness" of the name that he had been accorded a
there was, therefore, a need for a linguistic device that could cope with built
obsolescence, reconcile the need to defer to age, and — at the same time — avc
undermining the fundamentally paternalistic nature of the relationship.

It is within this very specific context — the need to defer to age while seeking
protect a paternalistic ethos — that one has to understand the apparently contrad
tory practice of a landlord attaching an honorific prefix to the diminutive form of t
name accorded a black tenant. Thus, the youthful Jan*tjie* gives way to the respected
elderly *Outa*Jantjie — with the *Outa* being constituted/reconstituted from
(Afrikaans/Dutch for old) and *ta* (Dutch, father and/or SeTswana, *Ntate*, father
Interestingly enough, while this terminology again falls well within the orbit
maleness, patriarchy and domestic power, in this case there is a female equivale
when a particularly respected or elderly black housemaid would be referred to
Ousie — this time from *Ou* and *sus'* (Afrikaans/Dutch, *suster*, sister).[32]

But the impositions and concessions of language — even when fought out
terrain that had been largely determined by white landlords — was not, in itso
sufficient to guarantee the survival of paternalistic relationships. When all else fail
highveld landlords, like Southern slave-owners before them, did not hesitate to res
to violence to ensure that their wishes prevailed over those of the tenants. "Whippi
of recalcitrant workers by their masters," Keegan observed, "was widespread ar
often caused conflict between landlords and heads of tenant households."[33] Nor d
such practices necessarily negate the spirit of the relationships that we have be
documenting. As Genovese has noted: "Paternalism and a patriarchal ethos did r
demand kindness, although they may have encouraged it; much less did they dema
indulgence. A strong patriarch is not less so for being severe, so long as he accep

ponsibility for the welfare of his children, as he and his society define such ponsibility."[34]

The willingness of white landlords to resort to the use of the sjambok if other ictions failed is not unduly surprising. What also needs to be noted within this itext, however, is the way in which the act of whipping — as opposed to fines,)itrary physical assault or other forms of discipline — helped to reinforce the derlying dynamics of patriarchy and paternalism.[35] Two points in particular should highlighted. First, whippings — unlike other more "spontaneous" forms of cipline — were often carefully premeditated and ritualized acts that depended on act of physical submission by the tenant before the landlord.[36] In this way the act elf constituted a humbling of the "child" before the authority of the "father." condly, whippings took place beyond the purview of the courts and, as an act of)lence by the patriarch directed against the famulus within the privacy of the)usehold," served to relegate the tenant to child-like status within the wider social uctures of the society and to underscore his lack of standing in law. Brutal assaults thin "the family" and a deafening silence in the racially structured society beyond it, th helped remind black tenants of the far-reaching powers of white patriarchs der a paternalistic regime.

For whippings to be fully effective in restoring the dominant ethos, however, the iild" also had to be able to see and contrast the terror of physical violence with the inifest rewards of submissive behavior and hard work. A regime that relied on the ck to the exclusion of the carrot ceased, almost by definition, to be paternalistic. us, for every assault on tenants there had to be compensating gifts and concessions he long-term stability of the regime was to be ensured. A white "father" was entitled be severe with his black "children" but, if he did not wish to become totally enated from the Christian mainstream that flowed through the community, he had be seen to be capable of acts of benevolence, care and generosity whenever the :asion demanded it.

In the south-western Transvaal, as elsewhere in the South African countryside, ncessions born of Christian conviction were readily reconciled with the patriarchal d paternalistic constructs that propped up social life in the farmhouse. Afrikaner idlords, who under ordinary circumstances would find it impossible to entertain ? idea of allowing black tenants to enter their homes for social gatherings, found thing incongruous about inviting the same blacks into the intimacy of their living)ms for the evening *huisgodsdiens* or prayer meeting. Such gatherings, presided over the white patriarch, reached out to encompass the extended "household" and lped to reinforce the bonds of quasi-kinship as everybody present humbled emselves in the presence of God. Similar logic informed the special days of prayer ld during times of drought when everyone on the property would meet at an propriate venue to join in ritual deference before the Lord — but always with the iite patriarch serving as mediator, presiding over his "family" and determining the)ceedings.[37]

Likewise, Afrikaner landlords in the triangle seldom denied their black house rvants or respected tenants "quasi-kinship" rights at occasions marking rites of ssage. At births, weddings and funerals, blacks — while being called upon to iintain a proper distance, remain physically unobtrusive and show an appropriate gree of restraint — were nevertheless accorded a distinctive role in proceedings that ?re otherwise dominated by the inner core of the landlord's family and friends. Any

failure by the landlord to accommodate the reasonable expectations of his bl:
"family" in such matters was considered by the tenants not only to be dee;
wounding, but to constitute a serious breach of etiquette. In much the same w
landlords were expected to provide their laborers or sharecroppers with a sheep
celebrate the birth of a black child, or to attend the funeral of long-serving black hou
servants or tenants.[38]

These concessions, flowing from a shared commitment to Christian values
landlord and tenant, contrasted with other — more earthy — celebrations th
despite an attempt to provide them with a Christian gloss, had more complex orig:
and were always more tightly contested. Thus the occasions that marked the bring:
in of the harvest, or the formal sharing of the crop, were presided over by the landlo
who, by offering a prayer, would insert himself into his customary mediating re
between God and the peasants. Then, assuming a more modest role, he would provi
a beast for slaughtering and formally authorize the celebratory beer-drinking th
followed. But such patriarchal endorsement as there was for drinking was undertak
from a position of weakness rather than of strength since the practice of consumi
sorghum beer after the harvest was likely to proceed with or without his approval.
the end of the day, however, it was the patriarch who would have insinuated hims
between God, the elements and the bounty of the earth and, by so doing, would ha
helped to reinforce the paternalistic ethos that enveloped the farm.[39]

But members of the black "family" were not always sufficiently well placed
extract concessions from their landlord, or to have favors granted them by t
patriarch. Living in a harsh and unforgiving environment plagued by drough
dust-storms, locusts and a variety of livestock diseases, and having to work in
imperfectly monetized economy, which struggled to extricate itself from a series
unpredictable booms and slumps, meant that poorer tenants were frequently looki
for an outright gift from their "father," rather than a mere concession.

Even in relatively homogeneous cultures, however, the exchange of gifts amon;
equals can be an exercise fraught with social, political and psychological ambiguitie:
Under a colonial regime, characterized by the permanent and legally entrench:
structural vulnerability of the indigenous underclasses, comparatively affluent wh;
landlords could — if they so desired — make use of the gift to entrench notions
dependence amongst black tenants and thereby reinforce the prevailing paternalis:
ethos. It is against this backdrop that we have to assess the testimony of K
Maine — the sharecropping son of a "second wave" MoSotho immigrant who ha
established himself in the Schweizer-Reneke district at the turn of the century. As
young man Maine had witnessed the political eclipse of some of the poorer Afrikan
farmers by a few pockets of relatively better-off English landlords in the period aft
the South African War of 1899–1902:

> Under Afrikaner landlords we used to be *given* sour milk, fresh milk and
> good food; but the English stopped it. Instead, they gave us a few cups of
> milk per day. They counted how many cups they gave you. If you worked on
> a [English] farm, your ration consisted of three cups of sour milk per day.
> Fresh milk was not given to us, we were supposed to *buy* it. Afrikaners did
> not sell things. They *gave* us trousers, shoes and everything; but the English
> sold their clothing. They would never give us a pair of trousers free of charge!
> [My emphasis.][41]

This rich oral testimony provides us with a graphic description of the links that existe

ween capitalism, culture, gifts and the maintenance of paternalistic relations in
ch of the south-western Transvaal during the early part of the twentieth
tury.

In addition to the occasional gift of old clothing or tobacco, triangle landlords and
ir tenants were locked into the ritual of Christmas but, in a setting of structured
quality, such celebrations as there were could hardly provide for the exchange of
ts in time-honored Christian fashion. Instead, the advent of the festive season
ovided the white landlord with yet one more opportunity to demonstrate his
nevolence and generosity by allowing him to authorize the slaughtering of a beast to
ovide his black "children" with a feast — an act that not only re-emphasized his
portance as patriarch, but served to strengthen the bonds of paternalism.[42]

The Structural Erosion of Paternalistic Relationships

as has been suggested, paternalistic relationships on southern African farms took
ld most readily in colonial situations where pre-capitalist social relations and
onocrop culture combined to allow for the use of black labor in a relatively
differentiated production process, then the conditions under which such relations
e eroded become fairly predictable. Paternalism — as the dominant ethos in the
untryside — starts to wane wherever the structural inequalities of colonialism are
her challenged or destroyed, where there is a marked acceleration in the
velopment of capitalist relations of production, a fairly sudden diversification in the
nge of crops being farmed and/or a significant increase in the rate at which
ricultural production is being mechanized.

The collective impact of these interlinked processes (a) tends to undermine the
nite landlord's belief that he is responsible for the welfare of his black quasi-kin,
ereby placing the organic unity of the farm under increasing stress; (b) allows the
gularity of the wage relation to weaken the underlying functions of gifts and
ncessions, with a resulting loss of deference and gratitude on the part of the tenants;
d (c) fragments the labor process in such a way as to diminish the utility of the black
nily as an easily identifiable unit of production.

Merely identifying these corrosive forces, however, does not allow us to take our
alysis of the decline of paternalism and the rise of the contractually bound sale of
age labor far enough. Precisely because the paternalistic relationship binds two
rties together, we also need to know from where the impetus to dissolve the
lationship comes — from the landlord above, or the tenant below? The issue, then, is
ot only under what historical circumstances we witness a retreat from paternalism,
it at whose instigation the relationship is re-examined, renegotiated or ruptured?

Part of the answer to these questions lies in appreciating that not all the forces we
ve identified need to be operating simultaneously or contributing in equal measure
the erosion of paternalism. Thus, at no stage during the period 1900–50 was white
ntrol in the South African countryside ever shaken off, although there can be no
ubt that, at various moments, it was challenged from below by movements such as
e quasi-nationalist Industrial and Commercial Workers' Union (ICU). Likewise, in
e south-western Transvaal it was only after the passage of the Marketing Act of 1937,
ith its benefits for large-scale producers, that Afrikaner farmers started to concen-
ate more fully on the production of maize, and it was only after World War II that

plowing with oxen was fully eclipsed by the petrol-driven tractor. Similarly, in
triangle it was the introduction of the mechanical harvester in the 1960s that effectiv
destroyed what remaining logic there was in the utilization of black family labor a
that heralded another decisive lurch towards employing more atomized a
depersonalized wage labor. While these forces might, therefore, have combin
occasionally, their impact was never evenly felt and, in order to understand
specific manner in which they helped to undermine the paternalistic ethos in
triangle, it will be necessary to isolate their interaction at two precise histori
moments.

A Challenge from Below, 1925–1929

The production of alluvial diamonds in the Bloemhof/Schweizer-Renek
Wolmaransstad triangle peaked at 81 000 carats in 1913 after which, in the decade tl
followed, it went through a gradual but uneven decline with production rangi
between 75 000 and 31 000 carats per annum. By 1925 there were about five thousa
active diggers left in the Bloemhof district but this number slumped to only fi
hundred in 1927, when a new and richer deposit was discovered at Lichtenburg. T
large-scale exodus of white diggers and black laborers that followed — men who h
formed the core of the local market for agricultural produce — brought the first effe
of economic recession to the triangle well before the Great Depression settled in ov
the country as a whole some two years later.[43]

Long before the opening of the Lichtenburg diamond-fields, however, wh
farmers in the triangle had been responding to the local market, as well as othe
further afield, by expanding their production of beef, mutton, wool and — mo
especially — maize. This response, which came after the sudden collapse of commo
ity prices during the 1921/22 season, was consolidated by the relatively stable pric
that agricultural products fetched during the period 1923 to 1927. The expansion in tl
production of grain, partly designed to offset the decline in income from alluv
diamonds was not, however, achieved under the most propitious climatic c
cumstances. From 1926 until 1934 large parts of the south-western Transva
languished in a prolonged drought as South Africa entered one of its periodic "d
cycles."[44] An increase in grain production amidst reduced precipitation necessitated
substantial expansion in the acreage devoted to maize farming. This, in turn, called f
the large-scale employment of animal-drawn machinery including mechanic
planters and heavier plows such as the Canadian Wonder, which came to replace tl
lighter Little Chief and Canadian Chief.[45]

Labor tenants and sharecroppers had little reason to welcome the introduction
equipment that drew their adolescent male labor away from animal husbandry, ar
were positively unhappy when the opening up of new and more extensive fields w
achieved at the cost of reducing the amount of land available for the grazing of the
draft-oxen and cattle. This dissatisfaction, barely tolerable while maize pric
remained more or less stable between 1924 and 1928, gave rise to more op
discontent once grain prices slumped in the 1929/30 season. Drought, a reduction
the amount of grazing available for black tenants' livestock, changing work pattern
and dramatically reduced income, all combined to provide the ICU with a perfe
entrée to peasant households in the south-western Transvaal.

ble 11.1: Grain Handled by South-Western Agricultural Cooperative, 22–1949

Season	No. of Bags
1922/23	15 000
1926/27	29 000
1928/29	24 000
1929/30	161 000
1931/32	162 000
1938/39	300 000
1939/40	137 000
1940/41	431 000
1941/42	332 000
1942/43	278 500
1943/44	856 000
1944/45	1 450 033
1945/46	800 070
1946/47	551 747
1947/48	394 280
1948/49	1 982 000

urce: Suid-Westlike Transvaalse Landboukoöperasie Beperk, *'n Halfeeu van öperasie, 1909–1959,* Leeudooringstad, 1959, p.66.

Throughout 1928, but more especially in 1929, leading figures in the previously ban-bound ICU, such as Jason Jingoes, Clements Kadalie, Keable 'Mote and Doyle odiakgotla, addressed scores of meetings attended by hundreds of tenants and arecroppers. They preached the gospel of racial pride and the need for outright sistance to what were seen as the increasingly unreasonable practices of white dlords. Quasi-millenarian prophecies, about the political eclipse of the colonial der to be brought about by a new generation of African nationalists, mixed uneasily th more practical advice about the need for better wages, boycotts, strikes and mands for written contracts to protect black farm workers from exploitative dlords.[46]

This explicitly ideological onslaught on the dominant paternalistic ethos, as well a significant shortfall in the amount of cheap, pliant and subservient labor available bring in the harvest during 1929, produced an angry and often violent backlash m municipal authorities, the police and white farmers. With the established racial der in the countryside being challenged by smart-talking city-folk from the outside, d time-honored social practices on the farms being questioned by previously loyal asi-kin from the inside, white anger was fueled almost as much by a sense of achery and betrayal as it was by feelings of insecurity and vulnerability. It was ecisely because the roots of paternalism were so deeply embedded in the social soil the triangle that the potential for inter-racial violence was so great.

Between them, white farmers, local government officials and members of the lice force contrived to harass, threaten, intimidate, assault and — so it was mored — murder ICU supporters and organizers. When Doyle Modiakgotla visited hweizer-Reneke in March 1929 he described the district as being embroiled in a var" and, not surprisingly, many black workers, some labor tenants and even a few

sharecroppers took to arming themselves with sticks and spears to ward off possi
attacks from hostile landlords and marauding police patrols.[47]

But, of course, not all farm dwellers were either interested in, or willing to beco
members of, a movement that threatened the very fabric of the social contract that h
bound white landlord to black tenant for a half a century or more. For many •
wrench from a familial past was too traumatic, the contractual future too uncerta
Kas Maine, for one, was particularly wary of becoming involved in a politi
organization that threatened to invade the physical and psychological space of I
farm. In a statement couched in the very idiom of paternalism that Kadalie and
lieutenants were questioning, he explicitly rejected their call for a strike saying: "No
was a farm. How could they [the organizers] call for a strike in a place where they h
no social standing? How can you have a strike in another man's *home*? You can't d•
thing like that!" [My emphasis].[48]

Maine was not alone in his condemnation of such "anti-social" behavior. T
strike never did take place and, for reasons that need not detain us here, the ICU sc
ran out of steam in the south-western Transvaal in much the same way as it had dc
elsewhere on the highveld. Corruption, disorganization, failed promises and outri
lies protruded almost as readily from the movements of the poor in the countryside
they lay hidden in the organizations of the privileged in the city. Political lice cou
feed off the backs of peasants or proletarians with equal relish.

Yet, despite this collapse in popular support for the organization, there can
little doubt that during the twenty-four months it was active in the triangle, the IC
did succeed in dealing deference, paternalism and racial subservience a hefty blo•
This assessment is endorsed by the testimony of black moderates and radicals ali.
Thus Kas Maine recalled how "they [the 'Boers'] said that we blacks had adopted
superior attitude ever since we started following Kadalie." His sister-in-la
Motlagomang Maine, an ardent ICU supporter and member of the South Afric
Communist Party, could later reflect on fifty years of triangle history and say: "Toda
can see that those were the people who began to liberate this part of the world; befc
them the Boers treated blacks very badly."[49]

A Challenge from Above, 1939–1948

South African agriculture was painfully slow to recover from the series of body-blo•
that it had been dealt in the early 1930s. The effects of the Great Depression, prolong
drought and widespread indebtedness left triangle landlords distinctly short
economic breath and uncomfortably reliant on their black sharecropping partne
and it was only in the mid-1930s that they started to recover their composure a•
breathe more easily.

In 1935 the rains returned to the highveld and the country started to soak up t
badly needed moisture of one of its periodic "wet cycles," which, in the case of t
triangle, thoughtfully lingered on into the summer of 1944/45.[50] This process
natural recovery was facilitated by the continued availability of reasonably pric•
loans for agricultural development from the Land Bank and, in the Transvaal, t
number of petrol-driven tractors rose from a paltry 838 in 1930 to 1 181 in 1937 a•
then leapt fourfold to stand at a total of 5 702 by 1946.[51]

In 1937 the Marketing Act ushered in an era of increased security against t

Table 11.2: Price Index of Selected Products, 1939–1944

Year	Beef (per 110 lbs)	Maize (per 200 lbs)	Wool (per lb)
1939	132	119	84
1940	131	118	119
1941	138	144	119
1942	170	147	104
1943	197	200	129
1944	226	213	131

Source: Department of Agriculture, *Handbook of Agricultural Statistics, 1904–1950*, Table p.11.

Table 11.3: Land Bank, Percentage of Arrears Against Capital Invested, 1939–1948

Year	Interest	Capital	Total
1939	1.188	0.799	1.967
1940	1.133	0.814	1.947
1941	0.928	0.855	1.783
1942	0.675	0.725	1.400
1943	0.497	0.495	1.073
1944	0.487	0.360	0.857
1945	0.461	0.355	0.842
1946	0.404	0.357	0.818
1947	0.330	0.340	0.744
1948		0.273	0.603

Source: Report of the Board of the Land and Agricultural Bank of South Africa for the Year ended 31st December, 1950 (Pretoria, 1951), p.4, para 72.

vagaries of supply and demand, and no sooner was this mechanism in place than the outbreak of war presented maize farmers with a greatly expanded market for their products.[52] The collective stimulus provided by these factors precipitated what was probably the most prolonged boom in the history of triangle agriculture and a resulting explosion in grain production (see table 11.1).

Unlike the situation in the mid-1920s, however, this rapid expansion in production was not followed by a resulting slump in the price of grain with supply outstripping demand. Indeed, not only did the price of maize rise steadily throughout this period but so did that of at least two other commodities produced in sizeable quantities in the triangle — beef and wool (see table 11.2). Expanded production, increased commodity prices and favorable interest rates allowed triangle landlords to accumulate capital and liquidate their debts to the Land Bank and commercial banks at a rate that accelerated particularly rapidly between the outbreak of war and the advent of the Nationalist government in 1948. One index of the real economic gains made throughout the ten years between 1939 and 1949 is the rate at which the Land Bank succeeded in recovering the capital that it had risked investing in agriculture and the fall in the percentage of arrears owed to it by white farmers (see table 11.3).

The agricultural "revolution" of 1939–49 thus enabled those triangle landlor who had been most notoriously undercapitalized throughout the first half of t twentieth century — the Afrikaners — to put on financial muscle at an unprecedent rate, and the change that this transformation wrought in their economic metabolis started to manifest itself in an increasingly aggressive political stance. Poorly educat farmers who for most of their working lives had been dependent on, or subservient the whims of distant mining companies, slick property speculators, "foreign" gra traders, "English" banks, or the credit supplied by local Asian and Jewish sto keepers, suddenly found themselves able to transcend the constraints of popul politics and in a position to embrace a new and far more ambitious vision of Afrikar nationalism, which, while still to some extent vague, espoused the goals "apartheid."[53]

As early as 1937, leading members of the Ossewabrandwag, the Greyshirts a other neo-fascist groupings around Wolmaransstad started to direct their hostility the town's Jewish traders, and storekeepers in the surrounding countryside.[54] In 19 these and other loosely connected nationalist traditions became more sharply focus with the establishment of the Herenigde Nasionale Party, which, in the 1943 electic demonstrated its ability to bring considerable numbers of Afrikaner farmers back ir the fold of ethnic politics.[55] Four years later, in 1947, some of the outstanding debts populist politics were settled when Afrikaner nationalists organized a boycott Asian trading stores in the triangle and, twelve months later, the Herenigde Nasiona Party won the 1948 general election with the help of its socially elevating slogan: "L *kaffer op sy plek en die Koelie uit die land"* — "The 'nigger' in his place and the 'coolie' o of the country."[56]

Amidst all this aggression and xenophobia directed at the foreign devils a economic adversaries lurking beyond the boundaries of the farm, triangle landlor somehow also found the time to pay attention to the enemy within — the bla sharecroppers with whom they had enjoyed such a long-standing love-hate relatic ship. Indeed, well before D.F. Malan and his party assumed office in 1948 they h commenced strenuous efforts of their own to help keep "the kaffir in his plac without entirely abandoning elements of the old paternalistic ethos, which th termed "guardianship."[57] Not surprisingly, much of this attempt to redefine the relationship with black tenants was motivated by the desire to reap maximu advantage from the progressive mechanization of agricultural production and w therefore couched in straightforward economic terms.

Throughout the decade 1939–49, those landlords who had invested most heav in tractors and trucks put wealthy tenants under growing pressure to get rid draft-oxen and reduce their holdings in livestock as they sought to devote ev increasing quantities of grazing land to maize farming. In addition to initiating th unpleasant struggle — which pitted white farmers against black sha croppers — landlords also sought to renegotiate tenancy agreements that gave t black patriarch's male offspring limited access to grazing rights in return for mc contractually bound wage labor. As a means of producing social stress within enclosed world, this latter maneuver proved to be almost as destructive as the form since it tended to pit fathers against sons.[58]

But the old paternalistic order, in which ethics were weighed against economic communal responsibilities against contracts, and the lives of men against machin hardly constituted an appropriate ethos in which to conduct such delicate a otentially explosive negotiations. Thus, throughout the decade Afrikaner landlords ere called upon to make the difficult, embarrassing, painful and at times downright eacherous transition from paternalism and the social intimacy of its quasi-kinship lationships to the emerging discourse of apartheid with its deeply alienating nphasis on racial distance. The confusion and sense of betrayal that this aggressive w posture occasioned amongst black tenants is perhaps best illustrated in reference the life of someone who was deeply committed to the *ancien régime* and its more anced values.

From 1943 to 1946 Kas Maine was a sharecropper on the farm Vaalrand in the oemhof district. The landlord — P.G. ("Piet") Labuschagne — came from a family eeped in the Afrikaner republican tradition, and had worked and farmed in the angle for more than two decades when Maine first met him in the late 1930s. A werfully patriarchal figure with a particular dislike of "Jew and Coolie" middle-en, Labuschagne had been one of the founding members of the local *Eeendrag* branch the Herenigde Nasionale Party and served on its executive for many years. An cellent wool farmer with considerable land at his disposal, Labuschagne became terested in grain farming when the price of maize started its steep wartime climb id, in order to profit from this development, entered into a number of partnerships ith black sharecroppers.[59]

Despite his antipathy to "foreign traders," Piet Labuschagne was a remarkably enerous and popular landlord who enjoyed a particularly warm and close lationship with his black tenants. A convinced paternalist who proved to be enerous in sharing his possessions, resources, skills and time with sharecroppers, abuschagne soon earned the confidence, respect and trust of his black partners. In the se of Maine, who, but for his black skin, could at first meeting be taken for a poor but spectable Afrikaner farmer, this relationship developed into a friendship that pressed itself in shared meals, in beer-drinking in the privacy of the sharecropper's me and — on a least one occasion — in the companionship that derived from an cursion to a boxing match in Bloemhof.[60]

After the war, however, mounting commercial success and growing political lf-confidence made Afrikaner landlords more ambivalent about the social and ltural proximity of their better-off black partners. Farmers experienced great fficulty in reconciling more familiar paternalistic practices with the need for wage bor in the apartheid order, which they desired and advocated. It was these oss-cutting pressures that eventually succeeded in rupturing the membranes of aternalism at Vaalrand.

One morning in the spring of 1946 Maine's six-year-old daughter became riously ill and the family hoped to make use of Labuschagne's cart to transport the ild to the District Surgeon's rooms in Bloemhof. As Maine later recalled, "I used to orrow the cart and drive it." But on this particular occasion the rules appeared to ive changed. "Do you know what he said to me?" Maine continued. "He said that his rt could not be used by 'kaffirs'! I kept quiet because my child was ill."[61]

Angry, betrayed and frustrated, Maine dashed to a nearby white farmer — Piet oosen — and offered to pay him a fee of twelve shillings to drive his sick daughter to town. This Goosen did, and the child was successfully treated. After the car had ulled back into Vaalrand to drop off the passengers, Kas overheard Labuschagne xplaining to his slightly puzzled neighbor that while he was perfectly willing to allow black man to make use of the cart for business errands, he could not sanction the use

of the vehicle by a "kaffir" for purely social purposes. That merely added insult
injury.

For several days thereafter the tension between landlord and tenant remain
palpable and then, according to Maine:

> One day he told me to inspan the cart and fetch some salt for his sheep. I told
> him that he would have to drive the cart himself because it could not be used
> by a "kaffir." He [Labuschagne] kept quiet and shook his head. Then he
> asked me whether I was still on about the same old thing. I refused to do the
> job and told him to give me my *trekpas*; I told him to sign me off because I was
> not willing to be treated in that way.[62]

A few days later the Maine family left Vaalrand to take up a position on a neighbori
property.

But the change in agricultural production techniques, the drive to devote eve
inch of available farmland to the God maize, and the advent of an Afrikaner national
government committed to the pursuit of territorial segregation meant that the days
the independent black sharecropper were numbered. In the winter of 1949, Maine ar
"all the rich 'kaffirs' who owned spans of oxen" were summoned to attend a meeti
at Sewefontein that was to be addressed by a state official from Bloemhof. "Th
announced that farming-on-the-halves was no longer to be practised. Agricultu
methods had changed and tractors had been introduced. Those who had spans of ox
would have to sell them."[63] Sharecroppers who wished to remain in the triangle wou
have to sell their livestock and their sons would be given work as truck or tract
drivers, but those who could not or would not comply would have to trek to t
"native reserves." For "rich kaffirs" the old order had suddenly given way; for tho
who remained behind what little there was left of paternalism served only to grea
the slippery slope of proletarianization.[64]

Conclusion

Much of the recent scholarly debate about the role that paternalism has played in t
historical evolution of South African rural life has focused on two related que
tions — the extent to which the ideology of paternalism has served to legitimize mu
of the day-to-day violence by landlords on white-owned farms, and the manner
which paternalistic practices have tended to inhibit resistance to exploitation by bla
sharecroppers, labor tenants or wage laborers.[65] In this chapter an attempt has be
made to broaden this debate by offering a historically rooted materialist explanati
of the ideology of paternalism, which — by concentrating more explicitly on the soc
dynamics of age and gender inherent in the system — calls into question some of t
more commonly accepted linkages between paternalism, violence and quiescence.

As a set of social practices predicated on quasi-kinship relationships that a
powerfully informed by notions of patriarchy, paternalism takes root mo
easily — although not exclusively — in the world of the pre-capitalist countryside.
the politically, physically and psychologically confined domain of the colonial estat
farm or plantation, white patriarchs tend to make use of language, naming practice
ritual, religion, gifts and concessions to inculcate and reinforce notions of obedienc
deference and subservience amongst black dependents. These devices, and t
parasites of gratitude and guilt that they host, can sometimes inhibit the onset

sychic manhood in black dependents and drain farm dwellers of their capacity to
sist.

But, while paternalism often lays its heavy and deadening hand on the ability of
ose being patronized to challenge, question and resist, it would be a mistake to see it
being *inherently* incapable of generating violence at either the individual or the
llective level. Indeed, what has been suggested here is that in the course of the
nant's life-cycle there are certain predetermined and chronologically weighted
oments when the black dependent will be predisposed to question the social reach of
e white patriarch. Likewise, it is suggested that in broad terms we can delineate
rtain moments in the development of agrarian capitalism during which we are more
ely to witness the erosion of the paternalistic ethos than at others, and that the
allenge to the old order could emanate from either above or below. It is at these
oments, when paternalistic relationships are being rapidly eroded or restructured,
at the potential for individual or collective violence is at its most pronounced.

Distinguished visitors to the country might still be tempted to note that "work in
e rural areas on farms does involve very close contact between farmers and all those
ho work," that "it is much more like a family," and that there was therefore "very
tle trouble on the farms," but most of the inhabitants know better.[66] To their bitter
st, South Africans of all colors realize that it is within the family itself that the most
olent of all conflicts erupt. Paternalism has fallen on hard times.

12

"The Colour of Civilization": White Farming in Colonial Swaziland, 1910–1940

Jonathan Crush

In 1934, the anthropologist Hilda Beemer (Kuper) arrived in Swaziland from Britain t conduct doctoral research. Kuper, well known for a lifetime of study of Swazi socie and her advocacy of royalist interests, also had a certain amount to say about the whi settlers she encountered in the country.[1] She had little time for the settlers, with the narrow-mindedness and bigotry: "The myths of Native inferiority and brutality," sh later wrote, "are the moral supports for oppression and exclusion." She wa particularly scathing about white farmers in the south of the country, "abject in the poverty, lacking in initiative . . . forgotten, uneducated, backward, and slothful. Not surprisingly, Kuper quickly became a subject of settler and missionary rage fc blithely shuttling across the uneasy borders of racial identity and colonial convention Ironically, it was only after the intervention of a senior colonial official sympathetic t her anthropological project that she was allowed to stay in the country.[4]

Though Kuper herself discerned an intimate connection between a virulent settle racism and the political economy of the colonial setting, she was largely unintereste in exploring the nature of this connection. Settlers were simply a privilege aristocracy, secure in the "myth of race superiority," their power entrenched b misguided legislation and policies of economic development. Three questions tha remain unanswered, either by Kuper or by the small band of subsequent Swa; historians and historical geographers, will be addressed here: What became of th optimistic British colonial vision of a white Swaziland which had developed in the fir

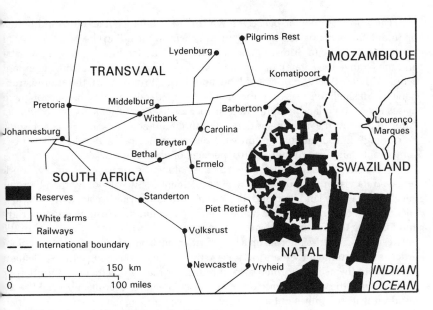

gure 12.1 Land Alienation in Swaziland

ecade of the century? Why did the colonial government continue to offer its
nqualified support to the white settler-farmer long after it had become apparent that
e simply could not deliver? And what were the implications of this failure for the
ocial and cultural relations between European and Swazi on white farms? This
napter attempts to answer each of these questions in turn.

The Fading Vision

1907, the British colonial government summarily confiscated some 66 per cent of the
nd surface and 55 per cent of the arable land of the Swaziland Protectorate for white
ettlement.[5] Some 47 per cent of the country came under freehold, with a further 19 per
ent falling to the crown. The remainder was set aside for Swazi occupation. This
olicy produced a patchwork of white farms and Swazi reserves (see figure 12.1).

For the next three decades, the British actively promoted white settlement,
ampering white agriculture with discriminatory taxation, financial support pro-
rams, and the sale of crown land at firesale prices to incoming whites. Swazi were
xed more heavily than any other colonized people in the region, and the accrued tax
/ent primarily on colonial administration and support services for white agriculture.[6]
etween 1910 and 1932, sales of crown land to settlers and South African companies
etted £185 000 for the administration.[7] Most of this was spent on urban development
nd transportation, primarily to benefit whites.

The administration dispensed crown land to incoming whites either individual or under the aegis of various settlement schemes, including the Mushroom Lar Settlement Scheme (a British-financed plan to acquire land for settlers in Swazilar and the Orange Free State). British- and South African-financed ranching compani acquired 170 000 acres of lowveld land, and during World War I, the administratic handed out smallholdings of 500 acres at 3s. to 3s. 6d. per acre. The holders of grazi leases over crown land bought out a further 250 000 acres at 1s. to 2s. 6d. per aci After the war, the administration sold thousand-acre lots to over a hundri "returning" European soldiers on easy terms (3s. 6d. per acre when the price comparable land was running at 10s. per acre on the open market).[8]

In the late 1920s, following a visit by the Colonial Secretary, L. S. Amery, Londc renewed its vision for large-scale white settlement in Swaziland. By then there w very little crown land left and the administration turned instead to selling c encumbered crown land to the holders of the encumbrances (usually grazing righ and fostering the sale and settlement of underutilized, privately owned land.[9] In 192 the Resident Commissioner set up a Land Settlement Committee composed of coloni officials and prominent settlers to devise a strategy for encouraging white settlement The settlers themselves formed a local branch of the 1820 Settlers Association ar worked with the Mushroom Company on a scheme to recruit and establish tw hundred British families in the country. "All responsible men," noted the compan "see that settlement is vital."[11] The High Commissioner also approached Erne Oppenheimer of the Anglo American Corporation with a proposal that Ang purchase a massive lowveld property for a settlement scheme in collaboration wi the Overseas Settlement Committee.[12]

For all this frenetic activity to get arable land into the hands of white settlers, the was not a lot to show. Local colonial officials and their London masters always refuse to believe that the country's rich agricultural potential could be developed by anyor other than white settlers. But none of their fanciful schemes came to fruition. Settl immigration was always slow and halting. In 1911, there were only 1 083 whites in th country. Twenty years later the number was still less than three thousand. Farmir was small-scale, undercapitalized and labor-intensive. In 1921, there were 3: registered farms in the country, but only in the south and around Bremersdorp an Stegi did settlers productively occupy the land (see figure 12.2). By 1931, the number (white farms had increased to 500, but fewer than half were owner-occupied.[13] Only small proportion of the available land (rarely more than 50 000 acres before the 1940 was ever commercially cultivated. Cotton experts calculated that up to 500 000 acri of the country was environmentally suited to the crop.[14]

Before the 1920s, most white farmers grew maize and sold it on the local marke primarily to the administration or to Swazi households. The market was unpredic able and extremely limited. White farmers were soon in desperate straits. In 1921, or official reported that "the majority of farmers are without capital and will be cripple this season if they cannot raise money to tide them over the current very bad period." Farmers were unable to make repayments on government loans used to buy the modestly priced land. The administration wrote off their debt when they declare themselves "unfortunate in the seasons, in disease, in their cattle" and defaulted.[16]

Desperate for revenue, the settlers turned from maize to the cultivation of cotto and tobacco.[17] After some hard years at the beginning of the decade, market prices fc both crops rose in the mid-1920s. This increase, together with a new motorized link t

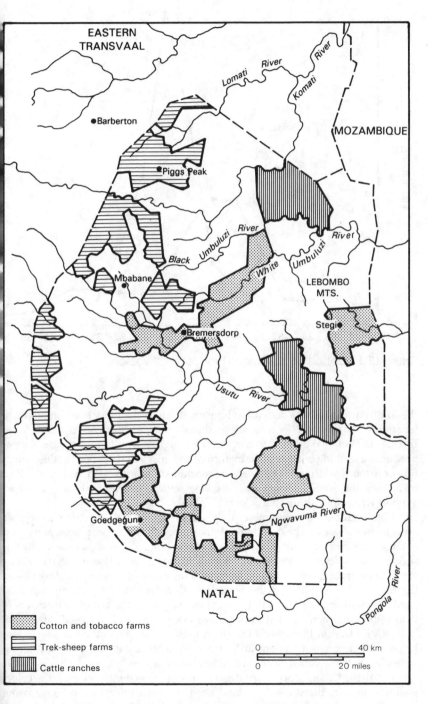

Cotton and tobacco farms

Trek-sheep farms

Cattle ranches

Figure 12.2 White Farming Activity in Swaziland, 1920s

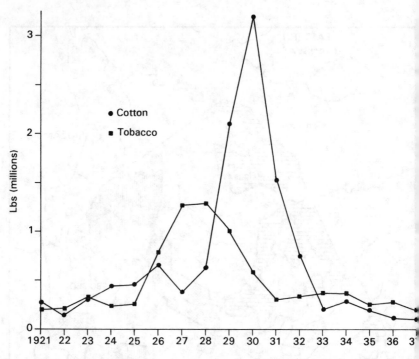

Figure 12.3   Cotton and Tobacco Production, Swaziland, 1921–1937

the South African railway network at Breyten, stimulated a minor boom in productic (see figure 12.3). But neither crop was produced on any scale or with any great facilit In 1928, the colonial administration hired an adviser who toured the districts ar produced a scathing critique of the inefficient and misguided methods of the country fifty or so tobacco farmers. They were, he concluded, "years behind the times."[18] By tl mid-1930s, the administration was forgiving settler loans and taking new steps support white agriculture (see below).[19]

Cotton farmers were no more successful or innovative. The crop was regular ravaged by disease and pest, and prohibitive transport costs discouraged any thoug of large-scale monoculture. Although cotton was originally a crop of the family farr several companies were formed in the mid-1920s to grow cotton under the watchf eye of the Empire Cotton Growing Corporation.[20] Three of these — Candover Estate Cotton Plantations Ltd and the Swaziland Corporation Ltd — dominated cotto production during the 1920s. But even at its maximum, the last plantation was le than a thousand acres and it ran at a loss every year until it closed down in tl mid-1930s.[21] Cotton Plantations Ltd (with the Empire Corporation as major shar holder) commenced operations at Nsoko in 1926 but, by the mid-1930s, it too w appealing to the Colonial Office in London for a bale-out.[22]

Following Colonial Secretary Amery's visit to the country in 1927, the coloni government introduced the Swaziland Land and Agricultural Loan Fund, a sma loans program for fencing, boring, dips, and land purchase modeled on the Sou

rican government's policy of supporting white agriculture through the Union Land
nk.[23] The money was forthcoming, but not the repayments. By the time of the Great
pression, agricultural prices were on the slide again and white agriculture lurched
eper into crisis, requiring the additional measures referred to earlier. In the
id-1930s, the administration forgave most of the Fund loans.[24] Simultaneously, the
ministration itself took out loans from the new Colonial Development Fund to build
ms, bridges and other supports for white agriculture.

The effects of falling prices were compounded by the response of Union tobacco
owers to competition from Swaziland. Eastern Transvaal farmers complained that
ey were being undercut by cheap Swaziland tobacco produced outside the
operative system which governed South African pricing. General J.C.G. Kemp, the
uth African Minister of Agriculture, acted quickly and slapped an embargo on
aziland tobacco. Swaziland's embattled farmers dispatched a futile delegation to
etoria to protest Kemp's demand that they join a South African tobacco cooperative
forfeit access to the market.[25] Though the farmers had little choice, the new
rangement mandated by the South Africans did little to ensure the long-term
ability of the industry.

In Nyasaland, the failure of white farming prompted the colonial administration
direct more of its resources to peasant production. In Swaziland this change of
licy was never seriously considered. One current interpretation suggests that land
nger, colonial taxation, labor migration and rural impoverishment left the Swazi
asantry unable to compete with white farmers.[26] Another argues that the decision of
azi homesteads to participate in the migrant labor system, accumulate cattle,
ltivate food crops and avoid risky cash-crop production was a perfectly rational one
the circumstances.[27] Both explanations no doubt contain a germ of truth for different
nes and in different places. At the time, of course, no one advanced either
pothesis.

White settlers and colonial officials harped constantly on the "backwardness" and
ziness" of the Swazi cultivator. At the same time, there was an uneasy fear among
ttlers that Swazi competition, if encouraged, would finally drive them under. They
ere therefore more than satisfied that the colonial government's efforts to support
azi agriculture remained tepid. In the 1930s, a handful of progressive Swazi
owers began to produce both cotton and tobacco, but their output did not
mpensate for the decline in settler production.[28] The white farmers' response was
t of all proportion to the competitive threat. They viciously denounced Swazi
oducers as inferior and inefficient and refused them membership of the tobacco
operative on the grounds that "they would not sit to vote in the same room as the
tives."[29]

By the early 1930s, over 40 per cent of Swaziland's white farms were absentee-
ned, mostly by landlords living in South Africa. Much of the land was held for
eculative purposes by those to whom it had been awarded in 1907. Others simply
ed the land to collect annual rents from their Swazi tenants. Some, such as the South
rican MP, J.S. Marwick, and the "Johannesburg weekenders," turned their
operties into attractive country estates on which they spent their vacations.[30]
lonial officials and some settlers agreed that unfarmed land represented a "crime
ainst the community."[31] Others argued that a land tax was a crime against the local
rmer who could ill afford to pay anything for land that he wanted to cultivate but,
ven prevailing economic circumstances, simply could not.[32] Thus, the periodic

efforts by the administration to free up more land for settlement by taxing unused underutilized land were repeatedly stymied by local white farmers.

On farms in the western highveld area, the land was more productively use though the financial benefit to Swaziland itself was minimal. Many of these properti were owned by sheep farmers resident in the eastern Transvaal. In March, an advan guard of stock-tenders poured in from the neighboring Transvaal and set massi grass fires throughout the highveld. As the grass shoots began to sprout, hundreds thousands of sheep were herded into the country to graze on these "trek-farms" (s figure 12.2).[33] In the early 1930s, trek-farms covered an area of eight hundred thousan acres and three to four hundred thousand sheep entered the country every ye Swaziland pasture was so valuable to capitalizing farmers in the eastern Transva that many also leased grazing land from Swazi chiefs in the reserves, until prohibit from doing so by the colonial administration in the early 1930s. Trek-farming began decline only in the late 1940s, when British and South African forestry compan arrived in Swaziland. As land values soared, the trek-farmers sold out.

Lowveld cattle ranching (see figure 12.2) was the only really viable form of wh farming before the 1940s, though its success, too, was ephemeral. After 1916, when t South African government lifted an embargo on all exports of cattle from Swazilan white settlers and British- and South African-backed ranching companies enth siastically entered the market. The largest was the Bar R Ranch of the Swazilan Ranching and Development Company, which had close to twenty thousand head the early 1920s. By the mid-1920s, the companies had together accumulated over six thousand head of cattle through purchase from Swazi homesteads and interbreedi with imported pedigree stock. Exports of meat and hides to Johannesburg and Durb rose steadily in the early 1920s until the imposition of a South African weight embar on Swaziland cattle exports in 1924.[34]

The embargo crippled the Bar R, which went into receivership in 1926.[35] A plan use the land for a settlement scheme fell through and attempts to sell the land (valu at 15s. to 35s. in 1919) generated derisory offers of 5s. per acre in 1926.[36] During t depression, European cattle holdings fell by over 50 per cent. The ranchers battl against slumps in prices, embargoes, marketing restrictions, cattle disease a shortages of capital. The difficulties of the early 1930s may have inhibited the grow of ranching, but they did not altogether kill it. By 1938 export figures were back up where they had been in the early 1920s. Nevertheless, compared with the massi rebuilding of Swazi cattle stocks that took place between 1910 and 1930, the settle achievement was unimpressive. "An excellent cattle country," commented T. Ai worth Dickson, the Resident Commissioner, "is being rendered valueless by t difficulty of finding an export market."[37]

Ranchers battled not only market restrictions, but chronic infection of their her by stock diseases such as east coast fever. In the early 1930s, in the midst of a seve drought, large herds of wildebeest in search of fresh pastures entered the country fro the Komati flats to the north. White farmers were scandalized and denounced t invasion in the press and at public meetings. The wildebeest were represented "injurious vermin," consumers of cattle pasture and carriers of snotsieke (na catarrh). The ranchers and colonial officials mobilized for war, poisoning wa supplies and making frenzied attacks on the herds with Vickers machine-gu mounted on trucks.[38] Other settlers saw the invasion as a windfall, of which they to advantage by shooting out the herds and exporting the biltong (cured meat) to t

ansvaal. This action was symptomatic of a broader opportunism, born of despera-
on, on the part of white farmers.

Very few white farmers ever made a decent living from the land, and most
gularly supplemented their meager farm income from other sources. Many of
e country's most successful traders — among them J. Henwood, G. Bennett and
Stewart — came originally to farm. Trader-farmers also recruited Swazi labor for
e South African gold- and coal-mines on a capitation fee basis. Other farmers joined
e colonial administration or worked in the small urban centers and tin-mines. One
ominent family, the Forbeses, ran a massive lowveld ranch for sport hunting. They
so owned large tracts of land near Lothair in the eastern Transvaal where the
ospects were much better for white farmers.[39]

The Price of Failure

e senior architect of colonial land policy, High Commissioner Lord Selborne,
served that the British government was in a position to establish "a really good class
farmer" and pre-empt "the inevitable use of the country as a dumping ground for
or whites . . . [who] will simply live on the surrounding natives and sink more and
ore to their level."[40] He looked forward to the day when "that part of the country
hich belongs to whites will be really peopled by them, when the white man's farms
ill be covered with homesteads."[41] It was an insubstantial hollow vision. In common
ith settlers in many other marginal environments, Swaziland's white farmers fought
d failed to make a living in the face of considerable ecological and economic
ncertainty.

Yet, for the first forty years of colonial rule, successive administrations remained
ithful to the idea of a white Swaziland despite overwhelming evidence that the idea
ould never work. Numerous colonial delegations, missions and reports recounted
e difficulties faced by white farmers, but rarely broke with a discourse that centered
the white settler as the only viable agent of economic development.[42] The image
at Swaziland was a "white man's country" and that the indigenous inhabitants were
ere to labor and to serve was sustained by the skillful self-promotion of Swaziland's
hite settlers, who were much better publicists than they were farmers. The European
dvisory Council (EAC), formed in 1921 to act in an advisory capacity to the colonial
ministration, became a pivotal forum for the articulation and dissemination of the
ttlers' views. In combination with the various regional farmers' associations, the
AC had a powerful, continuing influence over local colonial policy.[43] In and through
e EAC, white settlers contested any facet of colonial policy that might work to their
sadvantage, and applied relentless pressure on colonial officials who threatened to
t Swazi interests ahead of theirs.

Close social, sporting and personal ties between prominent settlers and officials
aped and continually reinforced a strong bias in the discussion of policy that gave
e-eminence to the interests of white settlers. Colonial visitors to Swaziland from the
etropole were always less likely to be compromised by personal ties and the
timacies of the colonial club bar. They required a more ostentatious and ritualized
splay of settler loyalty, prowess and achievements. When the Colonial Secretary
sited Swaziland in 1927, for example, he was feasted and feted by the settlers, and
ceived a "crowded and cordial welcome" in a Bremersdorp Agricultural Hall

festooned with empire marketing posters. He returned to England most enamored
the "great community" of Swaziland settlers and re-pledged British support of a
settlement scheme which would bring men of the "right stuff" to the country.[44]

In official statements, the failure of white agriculture in Swaziland was attribute
either to a battle against insurmountable economic odds or to "undesirable" soc
traits within the settler community. When Sir Alan Pim submitted his official report o
Swaziland's economic prospects to the Dominions Office in 1932, he drew attention
the "hard struggles" and "crisis in fortunes" of the country's progressive whi
farmers.[45] These he attributed to various technical and ecological problems — the la
of a railway, the high costs of motor transport, protectionist South African embargo
disease, drought, the depression and shortages of capital.[46]

In the south of the country, failure was amplified by Boer "indigents
landowners who scraped a living for their large families with a minimum of enterpri
and initiative. The settlers that did ensconce themselves, though small in numbe
were only too aware of the difficulties they faced and complained loudly to whoev
would listen. They railed against Union marketing policies, transportation difficultie
South African protectionism and maize dumping in Swaziland.[47] Tobacco farme
were also denied free access to the South African tobacco market and had to join t
Union government's cooperative marketing scheme.

These difficulties were exacerbated by friction and conflicts within the whi
community. Settler legend focused on the destructive dynastic struggles of the tw
great white Swaziland families of Scots descent — the Millers and the Fo
beses — whose presence in the country dated back to the sordid concessions era of t
1880s.[48] According to his supporters, Allister Miller, the head of the Miller clan, was
great visionary whose farm undertakings failed because his ideas were a generatio
ahead of his time.[49] His arch-rival, David Forbes, was a much more accomplishe
farmer and gleefully liquidated Miller's cattle fortune in the mid-1920s. At that tim
Forbes owned some three hundred thousand acres of land and a cattle herd of ov
twelve thousand himself.[50] According to Miller-supporter George Wallis, Forbes
farming methods did "great damage" to Swaziland. By the 1950s, Miller's old lowve
cattle ranch was under Commonwealth Development Corporation sugar. "What
pity," observed Wallis, "Miller could not have seen his dreams come true, and ha
profited by them."[51]

Harry Filmer's memoir *Usutu!* provides a less emotive evaluation of t
difficulties faced by the white farmer in Swaziland.[52] Filmer came from a wealthy leg
family in Johannesburg and, when he was a young man, his father bought him a far
in the Swaziland middleveld for £600. Filmer spent the next few years in Swaziland
lonely and isolated figure, attempting to establish a viable farming operation
"Filmerton" near Bremersdorp. He tried numerous ventures in order to raise capit
and expand operations, including trading, transport riding, pig farming and cat
ranching. At one time, he had a herd of a thousand head, purchased mainly fro
neighboring Swazi households, but he battled constantly against an inhospitab
environment, malaria, theft and his own inexperience. Though most local Swa
seemed to recognize his right to farm in the area, they also had no qualms abo
hunting for game on the farm and even setting bush fires to flush out their prey. C
one occasion, one of the hunters introduced himself as Pixley Seme, later a promine
figure in the ANC, and a friend and relative by marriage of Sobhuza, the Swa
king.

Filmer also found that his greatest labor needs coincided with demands upon his small cadre of young male workers to work in their parents' fields or to participate in Swazi cultural rituals. One year, his maize and vegetable crop rotted in the fields with no one to help bring it in. Indeed, recollected Filmer, "I didn't see a living soul the whole of that six weeks."[53] Though things improved somewhat when he employed a farm manager, he was not sorry to leave Swaziland and return to Johannesburg and other pursuits. As well as providing a rather frank tale of the problems facing the white farmer, Filmer's account of his misadventures raises the important question of the character of social relations between white and black on land expropriated by the British government for white settlement.

"Poor Blacks"

In the 1930s, Hilda Kuper called the Swazi residents of white farms "Poor Blacks" and painted a particularly grim picture of their existence. They were, she said, fundamentally insecure and had no freedom of movement. With insecurity came acquiescence: "Natives accept these conditions, more like those of a serf than a free man, because of their hunger for land."[54] Land hunger and serf-like conditions certainly prevailed in some areas (mainly in the south) but the claim exaggerates the conditions of occupancy on most farms and the geographical extent of the conditions she described. What is certain, however, is that farmers struggled continuously, and often hopelessly, to impose a satisfactory work regime on their tenants, to command labor when they needed it most, and to stop endemic theft of farm produce and sabotage of farm equipment.

When the British administration expropriated land for white farms between 1907 and 1910, it scarcely anticipated the full effects of its juxtaposition of two worlds and agricultures.[55] Colonial policy aimed both to free land for white settlement and to freeze its Swazi residents in place as a tenant labor force. The proximity of reserve and white farmland was also supposed to ease the repatriation of unwanted tenants and facilitate the access of farmers to labor. In 1914, some three thousand homesteads (about twenty-five thousand people or 25 per cent of the Swazi population) were left stranded on white farms. In 1931, Pim estimated that there were still twenty thousand "squatters" on these farms, though it was unclear how many had been in continuous residence since 1914.[56] Most farmers and colonial officials held that Swazi households would stay on the farms for as long as they were allowed to pay rent rather than provide labor. Any effort to force them to do unpaid work would lead them to make a hasty exit to the reserves.

In 1914, the members of the three thousand Swazi homesteads on white farms were designated in colonial discourse as "labour tenants" (or "squatters" if their labor was not required). Allister Miller, someone not given to sentiment, later observed that he almost felt sorry for the older men "who were born and reared on the estate when fences and European ownership were undreamed of."[57] Miller's "squatters" were a lot less sentimental. They continued to maintain, quite correctly, that they were the rightful occupants and that they had been cheated by unscrupulous whites and a deceitful British government.

In the 1920s, they heard the Swazi monarch, Sobhuza II, arguing in public that the land was still theirs and were keenly aware of his efforts to undo colonial land

expropriation. Between 1922 and 1926, the young king challenged the validity
colonial land policy at progressively higher levels of the colonial hierarchy, first in t
local courts and finally before the Privy Council in London.[58] The Council reject
Sobhuza's case in 1926 when, defying all the laws of natural justice, it reaffirmed t
legality of the land expropriation of 1907. When he named his new royal village th
year, Sobhuza called it *Lozithelezi* ("a place surrounded by enemies").

All tenants had eventually to come to terms with their landlords or face evictic
Most had absolutely no intention of voluntarily abandoning established sites an
fields. In many areas there was no sign of settler occupation. Landowners holding la
for speculation allowed their tenants to remain. The net result was that many Swa
homesteads remained on expropriated land, despite the change in legal status and t
loss of long-term security. They none the less feared any increase in white settleme
News of the advent of the "returned" soldiers after World War I caused an upsurge
concern in the countryside. George Wallis, who arrived in 1919, described how
elderly man from the other side of Swaziland came "in great distress to find out abo
us. He was afraid that we might buy the farm and turn him out of his kraal."[59]

Working and living conditions on white farms where commercial croppi
occurred were atrocious. On most southern farms (owned or managed mainly
struggling Boer farmers) long hours, poor rations, and a regime of unrelenting verb
and physical abuse were no incentive to farm work. I have described elsewhere t
intense and bitter early years of struggle between white farmers and their new tenar
and the regime of gratuitous physical, verbal and sexual abuse on many white farm
particularly in the south of the country.[60] These struggles continued and intensifi
throughout the 1920s and 1930s. Resistance to settler coercion was neither large-sca
nor organized, but could grow spontaneously during periods of political uncertain
(as in the mid-1920s) or economic squeeze (as in the early 1930s).

Despite colonial efforts to regulate and standardize the conditions of occupan
on white farms, the actual terms that emerged were complex and variable, tl
outcome of local circumstances and struggles. The first things to go were form
written contracts, which tenants simply refused to sign. Some years later, one coloni
official explained why: Swazi tenants, he noted, were full of "mistrust, fear
oppression and not caring for the colour of civilization."[61] The terms of verb
agreements varied significantly and were always disputed. Farmers often demand
unpaid work in exchange for rent-free occupancy. Some tenants agreed in princip
but vigorously contested the length of service and the number of household membe
who should provide it. Farmers tried raising wages or reducing rentals in an effort
make farm work seem more attractive. They appointed headmen as salari
employees to round up labor from tenant homesteads and used the threat of evictic
to force tenants to work. At the Mushroom Land Settlement estate at Mhlambanyat
the company demanded first call on the labor of the fifty-two tenant homestead
Those not required could look for work elsewhere in exchange for an annual rental
£1. Those who refused the terms were summarily evicted.

When threatened with eviction, tenants often simply trekked to the reserves or
another farm where conditions were more to their liking. This relative freedom
relocate gave tenants some bargaining power and disarmed the farmers' threa
Along the western border of the country, tenants shifted to farms in the easte
Transvaal. The Swazi chiefs were powerless to stop or benefit from the movemer
much as they wanted to: "They just pack up and go," complained Chief Somtseu.

Though farmers might extract labor from the older men, and the women and children of the tenant household, the young men were notoriously resistant to farm work. Their ambitions, like those of their peers in the reserves, lay elsewhere. Thousands of young Swazi men were recruited each year for work on the gold-mines of the Rand and the coal-mines of the eastern Transvaal and northern Natal. A disproportionate number came from the southern districts, where white settlers were also struggling in greatest numbers to farm. For the farmers, migrant labor to South Africa was a decided "curse."[63] Though the numbers are impossible to gauge, it is clear that amongst the streams of workers to the coal- and gold-mines were many young men from tenant homesteads on white farms. In 1924, the Assistant Commissioner at Hatikulu concluded:

> I have no complaints from those landlords who give their tenants a living wage. The complaints come from those who, in their search for very cheap labour, take native kraals onto their farms and hope to get free labour in lieu of rent. In the majority of cases the headman is an old man incapable of working. He is required to give his children to serve as farm and domestic servants. His children get nothing for their labour and naturally become dissatisfied and desert. The headman is then expected to bring them back or pay damages.[64]

Few farmers could afford a "living wage" (or even mine wages on the Rand) and most were unable to turn the patriarchal domestic relations of the average Swazi household to their own advantage. By the early 1920s, therefore, it was becoming painfully apparent to most settlers and colonial officials that the plan to create a pliant tenant labor force of "Poor Blacks" was in tatters.

Other white farmers, eschewing the unstable sexual and racial boundaries of settler society, paid *lobola* and married Swazi women, creating large polygamous households on their farms.[65] Though their motives are clearly not reducible to their desire for labor, most did not balk at putting their wives and children to work. The abusive regime of farm work was often mirrored in the home. Mbowana Hlope recounted her extremely unhappy and violent marriage in the 1920s to her first husband, a white farmer named Hillary:

> If Hillary were still alive, I wouldn't go back to him even if I was paid to do it. I remember once I was doing my laundry outside, with my baby on my back. LaMamba [another wife] was serving him tea. I don't know what must have happened because a few minutes later, the small boy, Khandisa, came running out to tell us to all run away, because his father was beating up one of his wives, laFakudze. I took my baby and ran in to see what was happening. I found laFakudze bleeding, her eyes were swollen . . . Hillary did not beat me up because I never answer him back when he swears at us, but laFakudze does. She also swears at him, so they fight. I run away.

Hlope recalled a life of seemingly endless farm drudgery and domestic violence. She left Hillary soon after the assault on laFakudze and never returned. As far as she could recall, both laFakudze and laMamba stayed with their abusive spouse. Tensions between farmers and tenants (on farms and in the reserves) intensified dramatically in the early 1920s in response both to poor harvests and to broader political uncertainties over land. Crop theft, in particular, reached epidemic proportions in these years. Farmers resorted to spying continuously on their workers and waited in the fields with guns and dogs. Some farmers hired off-duty police to guard their crops and in

one celebrated case a policeman was murdered in the fields.[66] In a separa
development, numerous women and children were rounded up by the police and, ii
series of show trials, charged with theft and sentenced to terms of up to six months
jail with hard labor. The effect was negligible. Under cover of darkness, the the
continued and indeed "appeared to be increasing every year."[67] Not only did tenar
refuse to concede that the farmers "owned" the land, but they also tended to rega
anything grown on it as theirs by right. The settlers, meanwhile, demanded ev
tougher punishment and the forced removal of offending homesteads from t
district.[68] Colonial officials browbeat the chiefs into putting a stop to the practice a1
threatened their followers in public meetings with long prison terms, solita
confinement and forced starvation.

In the mid-1920s, as Sobhuza intensified his campaign against colonial la1
policy, Swazi tenants threw Swaziland "into chaos" by simply refusing to pay a
rent.[69] Allister Miller reported a "wave of lawlessness" with "wholesale thefts
crops." Throughout the country, but especially on white farms, he observed th
Swazis were stubbornly refusing to do any work for whites.[70] Though Sobhuza lost l
case before the Privy Council, the effects of the campaign, and the residual bitterne
lingered on. "Swazi do not seem weary," observed Kuper, "of telling of acts of [whi
cruelty and cunning, dating from the first years of contact."[71] Kuper also collect
numerous Swazi stories about the greed of white farmers for cheap worke
irrespective of the cost to life and happiness.

In the 1930s, stories were rife about white farmers who kidnapped young bo
and carried them away to work on the farms. "As a result," Kuper noted, "wh
travellers stop their cars in isolated areas . . . [the herdboys] scurry off in terror a1
hide in the grass."[72] *Mandatana* — the white wizard — was even reputed to kill men
enslave their shrunken bodies. For Kuper, the symbolism of these stories was all t
apparent. As the colonial plan to turn tenants into farm workers sputtered and died
the 1920s, farmers turned in desperation to whatever labor they cou
find — primarily women and children from the reserves. The wages paid to fem3
and child workers were miserly, even by the standards of the day. When farm wag
for adult males were running at fifteen to twenty shillings per month, women we
paid five to ten shillings and children as little three to five shillings a month. The use
women and children on the farms was enthusiastically endorsed by colonial officia
who were only too aware of their own failure to deliver labor to the farmers.

Throughout the 1920s, women and girls did most of the cotton and tobac
picking, while young boys were employed to herd cattle.[73] But neither women r
children were desperate for work and tended to make themselves scarce unless the
was particular hardship at home. For most of the decade, with the limited demand i
labor, farmers were usually able to bring in their crop. But they were always nervo
about what might happen if commercial cropping expanded or Swazi agricultu
became more self-sufficient. By the 1930s, they were unable to meet even mod€
requirements for labor. Young Swazi were now increasingly looking outside t
country for work, and the movement of Swazi women to find work in Johannesbu
was accelerating rapidly, depriving farmers of their main labor source.[74] On o
southern tobacco farm in the mid-1930s, a farmer who had once employed forty t€
hundred "boys" could get no more than a handful to handle his crop of a hundr
thousand plants.[75]

The only farmers to have modest success with their tenants were those w

oderated coercion and threat with paternalism. But even here, it was often only
nants with little option who submitted to the sometimes Draconian terms of
cupancy. George Wallis, for example, was able to keep tenant families on his farm
paying wages from the outset and cultivating close personal ties with household
triarchs who (in his absence) virtually ran the farm for him. One of his original
nants was a man named Mtetepe Dlamini, who lived on Wallis's farm Dinedor until
s death in 1935. Dlamini's sons, Bafana and Nkongewa, also worked for Wallis, as
d a number of their children. Another man, Makulakula Ngomezulu, first came to
ork for Wallis in 1927, after doing three mine contracts, and stayed with him for
rty-seven years.[76] To suggest that Wallis was an enlightened employer lacking the
fensive racial prejudice of the typical Swaziland settler would be very wide of the
ark, but he did seem to understand the power of paternalism and cash wages in
tracting and keeping labor.

Conclusion

the late 1930s, the optimism that had driven colonial officials and white farmers in
vaziland for nearly three decades was completely exhausted. The farmers became
creasingly desperate. In 1936, they tried to get the Masters and Servants Act applied
children.[77] They also attempted to persuade the administration to apply South
'rican legislation, such as the Native Service Contract Act, and prison labor schemes
Swaziland. Sensitive to criticism from the Colonial Office, the administration
fused such requests. The farmers then demanded the end of mine recruiting
vances and the importation of Mozambican workers, something stoutly resisted by
e Portuguese.[78] In any case, clandestine Mozambican migrants were only too aware
the poor conditions on Swaziland's farms and poured into Natal instead.[79]

Though resident colonial officials still gave the white farmers rhetorical support,
ey began (under Colonial Office pressure) to explore other options. One was to put
ore land into Swazi hands and more resources into Swazi agriculture. The Colonial
'fice, under renewed pressure from Sobhuza and his allies in Britain loosened its
jid stance on the land question and began planning a major resettlement scheme to
se land pressure in the reserves. Out of this effort came the ill-fated Native Land
ttlement Scheme of 1948–54, about which much still needs to be written. Another
tion developed as part of a drive by the Colonial Development Corporation (CDC)
boost post-war production of agricultural commodities in the colonies. In the late
40s, the CDC, in concert with South African and British agribusinesses, moved into
vaziland.[80] Land prices soared for the first time in decades as vast acreages were
'ested and put under citrus and sugar. Farmers who remained now had a new
emy in their bitter fight to retain labor and make a living.[81] Others were only too glad
ally to sell up and get out.

For Swazi, the advent of large-scale commercial plantations was a mixed blessing.
quatter" rights became even more insecure and a new round of evictions began
most immediately. On the other hand, for the first time, wage employment became
dely available in Swaziland itself. In some ways, the large agribusinesses proved to
no more magnanimous as employers than their rather inept predecessors.[82]
nditions on the estates and in the mills were governed by the unrelenting discipline
industrial agriculture, a regime that intensified as the years progressed.[83]

13

Tobacco Farmers and Wage Laborers in Colonial Zimbabwe, 1904–1945

STEVEN RUBERT

Charles van Onselen has recently argued that social relationships in the south-weste
Transvaal *platteland* (countryside) often "transcended the stark and restrictive code
race relations as it is generally understood" and in many instances "reached
surprising measure of accommodation in a sadly divided society."[1]

Although economic interdependence was at the root of this "measure
accommodation," daily relations between white landowners and black tenants we
also shaped by paternalism — "the never-ending struggle to transform strength in
right and obedience into duty," often associated with the use of violence — and by
complex unwritten code of racial etiquette," which existed in order "to mirror a
reproduce the colonial power structure in interpersonal relations" in the countrysid
The ultimate goal was to produce and maintain a social order dominated by wh
landowners. While the black sharecroppers' ability to maintain some social a
economic parity with white landowners was slowly undermined, they did not meek
acquiesce in their declining status. On the contrary, oppressed rural peopl
developed "a kaleidoscopic array of . . . new and imaginative ways of challengir
resisting and opposing" the authority of white landowners.[3]

This chapter examines the working conditions of black agricultural laborers
colonial Zimbabwe, and arrives at a similar conclusion: that African peoples
southern Africa, who have often been portrayed as powerless victims of white colon
domination, used their own skills, knowledge and understanding to shape t
conditions under which they lived and worked. In terms of the idea of "work cultur
laborers will, in response to specific working conditions, call upon their ov
accumulated experience and understanding of the workplace to shape the work its

well as the relationships that develop with their employers and other workers. The
bjects investigated here are black laborers on European-owned tobacco farms in
lonial Zimbabwe during the period 1904 to 1945.[4] Specifically, the chapter examines
e methods tobacco farmers used to maintain work discipline on their farms in two of
e premier tobacco-growing districts of colonial Zimbabwe, the Lomagundi and
azoe districts of Mashonaland. It will demonstrate that wage laborers on these farms
veloped their own "kaleidoscopic array" of ways to ameliorate the fashion in which
bacco farmers attempted to impose that discipline. Since working conditions on the
bacco farms were largely determined by economic trends, an outline of the history of
e industry provides needed context for the examination of worker behavior.

Tobacco Farming in Southern Rhodesia

> Tobacco from its very beginning has been more than a crop; it has been rather
> a crucible in which the diverse ingredients were mingled which brought . . .
> Southern Rhodesia into being.[5]

is generally accepted that the impetus to the Pioneer Column's invasion in 1890 of
e territory that became Rhodesia was the mistaken belief that the area was the
pository of untold mineral wealth and could be exploited as a "Second Rand." While
ld soon became and long remained the territory's leading export, the mines offered
w opportunities for the quick profits the pioneers expected. However, a few of them
d farmed in South Africa and immediately recognized that the lands surrounding
eir final encampment, which they named Fort Salisbury (present-day Harare), were
th "fertile and well-watered." According to one of their contemporaries, some of the
oneers "saw themselves in imagination comfortably housed with wife and children,
rrounded by countless herds, and growing tobacco, rice, mealies [and other]
oduce both of the tropical and temperate zones."[6]

From the beginning of the European occupation of Mashonaland in north-eastern
mbabwe, some Europeans realized the potential for growing tobacco. Within two
ars of the arrival of the Pioneer Column at Fort Salisbury on 12 September 1890,
ere were nearly three hundred registered farms in the territory. One year later, there
re approximately one hundred European farmers in Mashonaland who listed
bacco as a principal crop.[7] Many of them believed that quick riches could be made
om growing one such marketable crop for a few years.[8] This view was often
nforced by British South Africa Company (BSAC) officials, who recognized as early
1893 that there was no mining bonanza in prospect.[9] The BSAC hoped that settler
riculture would provide "greater economic self-sufficiency" for the young colony
and profits for the company — by "cutting the import bill, and raising the value of
e land."[10] Its officials saw in tobacco an export crop upon which a stable European
ricultural community might be sustained. By 1906, the BSAC's agriculture
partment was optimistic enough to announce that the "future of the Rhodesian
bacco industry may now be regarded as assured."[11] Three years later, an observer
ported that "tobacco may already be considered an established industry."[12]

Throughout the period before 1945, the tobacco-growing industry was marked by
clical periods of expansion, followed by overproduction and then retrenchment.
e initial period of growth occurred between 1910 and 1914. Toward the end of the
st phase of expansion, in 1913, the *Rhodesia Herald* reported that tobacco was already

Table 13.1:   Tobacco Production (lbs), 1917–1945

Year	Mazoe	Lomagundi	Southern Rhodes
1917			415 210
1918			1 179 932
1919			2 415 607
1920			3 192 662
1921			2 880 104
1922			2 540 942
1923	716 000	460 000	3 426 390
1924	545 000	492 000	1 987 382
1925	978 000	1 053 000	5 313 168
1926	3 451 000	4 006 000	18 631 069
1927	4 664 000	5 111 000	24 201 201
1928	1 359 000	1 874 000	6 704 936
1929	1 657 000	1 628 000	5 494 063
1930	2 781 000	2 237 000	8 644 000
1931	4 490 000	4 334 000	14 448 440
1932	4 452 000	4 485 000	13 777 356
1933	6 876 000	8 546 000	26 097 888
1934	5 606 000	6 972 000	20 472 648
1935	5 723 000	7 153 000	21 717 898
1936	5 794 000	6 860 000	21 300 000
1937	6 602 000	8 938 000	26 168 259
1938	4 705 000	6 756 000	22 500 000
1939	6 332 000	10 217 000	35 066 798
1940	7 682 000	11 141 000	35 582 549
1941	9 969 000	14 233 000	46 579 011
1942	6 132 000	10 304 000	30 338 798
1943	6 402 000	9 466 000	32 103 738
1944	9 076 000	15 120 000	47 523 663
1945	8 683 000	12 815 000	42 327 225

Sources: Statistical Yearbooks of Southern Rhodesia, 1924, 1930, 1932, 1938 and 194⌐ H. Roberts, 'The Development of the Southern Rhodesian Tobacco Industry,' Sou African Journal of Economics 19, 2 (1951), p. 188.

second only to minerals in export value.[13] Poor quality and overproduction during t⌐ early years of World War I, when access to the British market was difficult or in possible, resulted in falling prices and bankruptcy for many Rhodesian tobacco farme⌐ Production fell from 5 627 acres under crop in 1913/14 to 1 310 acres in 1915/16.[1⌐

Following World War I the industry stabilized and slowly resumed expansio⌐ particularly with the introduction of an imperial preference for Rhodesian-grow⌐ tobacco in 1919. In the 1922/23 season, 388 farmers grew 2.5 million lbs of tobacco ⌐ 7 758 acres.[15] In mid-1925, the imperial government increased its preference by nea⌐ 50 per cent, and Rhodesian officials and growers concluded that there was a secu⌐ market for all the tobacco they could grow. Production increased rapidly with 7⌐ registered tobacco growers producing 17.24 million lbs in 1926/27.[16] The followi⌐ year, 987 growers pushed production above 24 million lbs, even though part of t⌐ previous year's crop remained unsold.[17] Once again, prices plummeted, bankrupti⌐ hundreds of farmers.

As a result of the crash in the industry following the 1927/28 season, government ficials concluded that tobacco growers would never voluntarily regulate them-lves. Over the next several years, therefore, the government legislated to control th production and marketing, and to improve the product itself.[18] This legislation lminated in the Tobacco Marketing Act of 1936, which provided for compulsory les at auction through a central Marketing Board, compelled growers to register th the board, and empowered the board to establish quotas for each registered rmer. The board also had a mandate to establish new export markets.[19]

Speculative tobacco farming, which had so strongly marked the tobacco industry fore 1930, was thus brought to an end. Over the next fifteen years, production abilized and overall quality improved. Total production increased from a low of 4.88 illion lbs in 1930 to over 46 million lbs for the 1944/45 season.[20] World War II had a veeping impact on the industry. Not only did tobacco increase its share of total ports but, also by 1945, it had become the colony's top export in terms of value, the st product to surpass gold as Southern Rhodesia's leading export commodity.[21] bacco was now a settled industry. No longer could inexperienced farmers enter the lustry and expect to retire rich after only a few years. As the *Rhodesia Herald* itorialized in December 1945:

> The war mark[ed] definitely the end of one stage of Rhodesian farming and the beginning of another. Instead of the muddling of the past, there will have to be much more system and more individual knowledge. In the economy of the State there is no room for the squatter farmer who has low standards of living and surprising ignorance.[22]

Lomagundi and Mazoe Districts

e majority of European-owned commercial tobacco farms in the period from 1904 to 45 were located in the provinces of Mashonaland and Manicaland (generally, the rthern one-third of the colony). Lomagundi and Mazoe districts, the focus of this apter, were two of the top tobacco-producing areas of Mashonaland throughout the riod (see figure 13.1). Lomagundi was a huge district before 1945, covering most of e north-western half of the province. The greater part of the district received tween 24 and 32 inches of rainfall annually. The northern border area along the mbezi River generally was much drier, however, while its central core area, which tended north-west from Salisbury for nearly one hundred and fifty kilometers, eraged between 32 and 40 inches annually.[23] The district sprawled across the ntral Plateau that separates the Zambezi and the Limpopo river systems and was ss-crossed by numerous streams and tributaries. This part of the southern African ghveld averages over four thousand feet above sea level. The lands in much of the uthern half of the district were "of excellent alluvial soil, dark chocolate, red and ick, interspersed with sandstone ridges, kopjes, and hills (suitable for Homestead es)," and excellent for growing Virginia tobacco.[24]

In 1898, Lomagundi's first Native Commissioner reported that, "agriculturally eaking, the district is an admirable one. The ground and climate admit the growing two crops off the same land every year."[25] The owners of the Ayrshire Mine (about km north-west of Salisbury) developed the first farm there in the mid-1890s to grow ize for their African labor force.[26] The establishment of additional farms was slow,

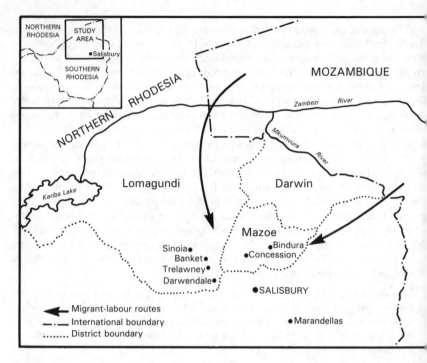

Figure 13.1   Tobacco Growing Districts, Southern Rhodesia

and by 1904 there were only five active farmers in the district.[27] In 1911, the Nati
Commissioner reported "a great influx" of settlers into the district.[28] After World W
I, the district's European farming community grew steadily, reaching 407 reside
farmers by 1926.[29] Under the 1930 Land Apportionment Act, most of the southern h
of Lomagundi was reserved for European settlement, while African reserves we
concentrated in the northern half.[30] European occupancy continued to increase up
1945, as the tobacco industry expanded.[31] Lomagundi emerged as one of the t
producing districts in the colony.[32]

Commercial cultivation of tobacco was under way in Lomagundi by 1911, l
only on eleven of the district's fifty-five registered farms.[33] By the early 1920s, tobac
was more extensively grown by established farmers in the area around Banket (90)
north-west of Salisbury). Production expanded greatly following the increase in)
imperial preference, largely on new tobacco farms in Trelawney, south-east of Bank
The 1928 crash had a severe effect, although more short-lived in Lomagundi th
elsewhere. By 1931, recovery had begun in some parts of the district. The followi
year, the Native Commissioner reported "the return of a number of tobacco farmers
their farms" and a corresponding increase in the demand for African laborers.[34] In)
late 1930s, the same official wrote that much of the European-occupied half of)
district was "largely devoted to tobacco farming."[35]

Lying east of Lomagundi and north of Salisbury, Mazoe district was on
one-third the size of its neighbor. It lay entirely within the zone that received betwe
32 and 40 inches of rainfall annually and rarely experienced drought.[36] By the ea

20s, Mazoe was also one of the colony's top tobacco producing areas, even though
ost of the district had heavy clay loam soils, which were less suited to tobacco
ltivation than the sandy loams of Lomagundi.[37] Although some farms were
rveyed in the district prior to 1900, their original owners apparently acted more with
eye to future prospecting than with any thought of establishing working farms.[38]
e first genuine farming was initiated by ten settlers who took up six separate farms
the northern part of the district in 1901. Two years later the district's Native
mmissioner stated that farming in Mazoe was continuing "to make headway," and
1907, the Mazoe Farmers' Association, founded in 1904, noted that there were "over
y bona fide farmers in the district."[39]

Tobacco production began with the arrival of the first real farmers. Years later,
R. Morkel, one of their number, stressed how important the crop was to the success
the pioneers.[40] In April 1908, one-third of the white farmers were growing tobacco.[41]
oduction grew slowly over the following fifteen years.[42] By the end of the 1922/23
ison, however, Mazoe district was the top producer of Virginia leaf in the colony,
d it remained among the first four until the 1928 crash.[43]

Tobacco farmers in Mazoe suffered the same general consequences from the onset
the Great Depression as their colleagues elsewhere. Some went bankrupt. Those
ho held on to their farms drastically reduced production until the recovery began
e years later. By 1933, the Native Commissioner could note, with some optimism,
it the total acreage under tobacco was increasing.[44] At the end of the 1934/35
owing season, Mazoe regained its position as a leading tobacco-producing district
d it maintained steady production levels throughout the remainder of the decade.[45]
ith the advent of World War II, the "expansion of the tobacco industry started in real
rnest and . . . never really looked back."[46]

Although tobacco farms in both Lomagundi and Mazoe varied greatly in overall
:e and acreage planted to tobacco, the pattern of cultivation and land use was
oadly similar on most of them. On many farms, tobacco was the only cash crop,
hough other crops were planted as rations for the African labor force, or as green
anure crops, which were plowed under at maturity to enrich the soil.[47] Tobacco
rmers also kept oxen for plowing. Farms in these two districts ranged in size from
out eleven hundred to three thousand acres.[48] Even on the smaller farms, nothing
e the total acreage was used. Farmers tried to have at least four hundred acres
itable for tobacco, as well as additional land for ration crops and grazing. But on the
erage farm, tobacco plantings in any given season might range from thirty-five to
o hundred acres. The presence of nematodes (parasitic worms that attack the root
stems of young tobacco plants) could greatly increase the acreage needed to end the
ason with enough good leaf to ensure economic viability. Other ecological
nsiderations, such as the type of field rotation used or the proximity to water, could
io affect the amount of land under cultivation.

In 1926, the director of the colony's Land and Agricultural Bank noted that in
dition to suitable soil and proper equipment new tobacco growers needed to
ossess some degree of "technical knowledge, experience, dogged application and
me capital."[49] Doggedness depended on individual character, but the state could
ovide knowledge, experience and capital. Governments throughout the period (the
AC before 1923 and a settler-controlled government thereafter) funded land banks,
hich provided low-cost loans to assist in farm purchase, acquisition of capital
uipment and improvements.[50] This kind of financial assistance was imperative since
majority of white farmers before 1945 were severely undercapitalized.

From the beginning, the state also supported programs of technical assistan
providing farmers with the latest information regarding tobacco cultivation and ▮
results from experiments on state-owned research farms. Up to 1930, research focus
on identifying soil types best suited to Virginia tobacco, recommending the best cyc
of crop rotation and tobacco varieties that produced the highest yields under lo
conditions. Researchers also worked on pest eradication, production of high-qual
seed and efficient methods for flue-curing tobacco.[51] By the early 1930s, experimen
work had shifted to improving plant qualities such as taste, aroma, burni
capabilities, and other leaf characteristics so that Rhodesian tobacco better conform
to the requirements of the major British tobacco companies, which provided Southe
Rhodesia's principal market.[52]

From 1918, the Department of Agriculture employed a tobacco "expert"
provide practical advice to newer settlers, and even earlier set up an agricultu
research farm at Marandellas (71 km east of Salisbury). Besides conducting expe
ments on several crops, including tobacco, the farm took in new settlers as apprent
farmers for periods of up to a year.[53] In 1924, the new settler government opened
Tobacco Research Station near Salisbury, the first such installation exclusively gear
to tobacco research. Later, it established two additional tobacco research stations,
Marandellas in 1929 and at Trelawney in 1934.[54]

In addition to land, capital, expertise and diligence, farmers needed lab
Tobacco farmers in the colony benefited from their location at the northern end of t
regional labor-supply system, closest to the supply areas in Nyasaland and the north
Tobacco farmers in the Lomagundi and Mazoe districts were especially reliant ▮
northern workers; they estimated their minimum labor needs on the formula of o
laborer per acre of tobacco. There were two primary labor migration routes from t
north, both of which passed through these tobacco-growing areas. The first ran fro
northern Nyasaland to Fort Jameson in Northern Rhodesia, then south through Fei
to Salisbury, and the second from southern Nyasaland through the Tete province
Mozambique, then south-west to Salisbury.[56] Southern Rhodesia maintained ferr
crossings and rest stops along both routes to assist northern migrants and ensure th
they reached the farms and mines of the colony in as healthy a condition as possib

The tobacco farms employed two kinds of migrants from the north. Sor
intended to come either for one full season or for several years. Others only stopp
temporarily to replenish supplies and earn the cash needed to continue south
higher wage employment elsewhere in the colony or in South Africa.[57] Most tobac
farmers could not afford the capitation fee of £3 per head for workers recruited by t
state-financed Rhodesia Native Labour Bureau (RNLB) and had to rely on "volun
ry" labor.[58] Native commissioners' monthly reports for 1914–42 indicated that the tv
districts' farmers often complained of labor shortages, particularly during the pe
periods of planting and harvesting. Before 1945, most of the workers on tobacco farr
were northern migrants from Nyasaland and Mozambique.[59] However, by the eai
1930s, as Shona society was increasingly splintered by land segregation polici
greater numbers of local workers began to take employment on tobacco farms.[60]

Conditions on the Farms: Wages, Rations and Medical Care

Farmers and government officials regularly debated which was the more important
attracting labor: wages, or rations and medical care. In 1910, the Director

griculture noted that an "increase in wages does not appear to offer any solution" to creasing labor supplies to farmers, "as when offered this seldom attracts boys."[61] early three decades later, the Mazoe Native Commissioner commented that "the eding of labourers and care of the sick are greater inducements than wages" in racting labor to employment on farms.[62]

Most officials still felt that tobacco farmers paid too little. In 1911, a top BSAC ficial told Mazoe farmers that their efforts to re-engage workers would "be useless d an unnecessary expense unless farm wages were appreciably increased."[63] In 19, the Chief Native Commissioner reiterated the point, and in 1925 an Assistant tive Commissioner in Mazoe warned local farmers that "the ruling [wage] rate will ve to be raised if an adequate supply of labour is to be assured."[64] Ten years later, ief Native Commissioner C.L. Carbutt warned tobacco farmers that they could only pect sufficient labor for the approaching tobacco harvest if they offered "a rather gher wage for . . . unskilled labour."[65] In response, farmers gave the answer that ployers throughout southern Africa always offered to justify sub-market wage tes: "The more pay you give the native the more he extends his period of repose."[66] icing the common target-worker fallacy, they said that raising wages could actually minish the labor supply.

Farmers colluded to fix wages at the district level. A thirty-day "ticket" in magundi and Mazoe districts' wages ranged from a low of 5s. ("herd boys") to a gh of 25s. ("boss boys") during the expansion years before the 1929 crash, when mpetition for labor was intense.[67] Even then real wages were always extremely low. 1919, when the average farm wage in Mazoe was 7s. 6d. and in Lomagundi ranged tween 8s. and 10s., a blanket cost 10s., shirts about 4s. each, and khaki trousers 15s. A cade later, when the average farm wage was 10s. to 12s., the cost of a lightweight anket was still 10s.[68] By the mid-1930s, it cost a field laborer approximately e-quarter of his wages from a completed ticket to purchase a shirt, up to ree-quarters of a ticket to get a blanket, at least one full ticket to buy a pair of khaki users or a khaki coat, and a minimum of four or five full tickets to acquire a bicycle, obably the most expensive item typically purchased by farm laborers.[69] Laborers' ges were so low that, as a retired farm laborer recounted, "you aimed at doing mething . . . but the money was always short . . . you had to spend the whole year you were aiming at buying anything."[70]

As for rations, farmers argued that as long as they provided "the basic necessities life . . . so much mealie meal, so much meat, so much beans or monkey nuts, and t," they could pay low wages and still attract sufficient labor.[71] However, on most acco farms the rations fell short of what farmers had promised. Food was generally ly issued once a week and was often insufficient in quantity and quality. Mealie eal was the staple, supplemented with salt and ground-nuts or vegetables. If the mer could sell those items for a good price, even when they had originally been anted as ration crops, they were sold instead.[72] While rationing differed from farm to m, farmers issued other items such as beans, sweet potatoes, fruit, dried fish (called tembas) and particularly fresh meat much less regularly. They often seemed more lling to provide adequately for their farm animals than their workers. In 1938, one server noted that a farm laborer's diet consisted of "as much mealie meal as he can nsume . . . except when one of the farmer's oxen dies."[73] Laborers had to pplement their diets either with purchases from farm stores or from African peasant mers in nearby reserves.[74] More commonly they cultivated small garden plots,

hunted or trapped small game (after receiving their employer's permission), a
gathered items such as honey and *madoras* (caterpillars) from the bush areas
farms.[75]

In practice, supplementing rations with food items grown in garden plots
collected from the bush was possible only for those laborers who had women livi
with them. Particularly during the times when farm work was most intense, duri
transplanting, harvesting and grading, laborers had to work from before sunrise u
after sunset.[76] Understanding that families could forage for food, or possibly cultiv
it themselves, farmers provided for workers who had their families with them ev
less adequately. When they did feed families, they used rations as an inducement
workers' wives and children to "volunteer" as casual labor during peak periods in
growing season.[77] Other growers issued extra mealie meal throughout the year
workers with families in order to obligate the dependents to work when their lab
was required.[78]

Contrary to the paternalistic claims of farmers, workers who were injured or
sick received only rudimentary first-aid treatment. White doctors and clinics we
rarely available in Lomagundi and Mazoe. Those that did exist so restricted the hou
during which they would treat black workers that they might as well not have be
there at all. In the early 1920s, for example, the district surgeon assigned to t
north-eastern area of Mazoe district had "a rooted objection" to seeing Afric
workers out of his surgery hours of one hour a day.[79]

Farmers justified their inadequate provision of medical care by arguing that fa
work was intrinsically healthy. In fact, workers frequently suffered from illness
many of them nutrition-deficiency diseases, such as scurvy and pellagra, which we
directly attributable to the inadequate diet.[80] During summer, workers clearing ne
lands were at risk from malaria.[81] Infectious diseases flourished in the crowd
conditions of farm compounds, and laborers succumbed regularly to influen:
measles, smallpox, syphilis and gonorrhea, which spread from farm to farm. F
instance, in 1929 at least three farms in the central area of Lomagundi district had to
quarantined when an outbreak of smallpox killed a number of laborers. Ten yea
later, a much more serious outbreak of the disease occurred over nearly the ent
district after it had been allowed to "smolder" on several farms for at least tw
months.[82]

Workers rarely received professional medical care. If treatment was available
all, farmers themselves or their family members provided it. Frequently, howev
they ignored workers' illnesses or simply ejected employees from the compoun
when they could not work.[83] Even when medication was available, farmers wou
neglect to provide it, stating that it was too much trouble "at the end of a long and h
day's work."[84] Laborers who became ill or were injured had "to rely on the
comrades . . . for cooking of food, drinking water, etc."[85]

Work Discipline on Tobacco Farms

In theory, on any given tobacco farm, good soil fertility, timely and sufficient rai
and, most important, a work-force that performed properly were enough for succe
However, underlying these quantifiable factors was a network of human relationshi
on which success crucially depended. Farmers could not treat their workers merely

eless automatons to whom tasks could be arbitrarily assigned, after which the
ner could withdraw to the homestead. Tobacco farmers used several methods to
ate what one contemporary observer called "a system of benevolent paternal
tocracy."[86] They needed to regulate both daily and seasonal discipline to ensure the
antity and quality of work, and to take steps to keep workers on the farm until
npletion of tobacco grading, the last task of the growing season.

In 1934, Rawdon Hoare, a tobacco and maize farmer in Mazoe district, provided a
nanticized and condescending representation of African life on a white-owned
m in Southern Rhodesia. Like most farmers in the two districts, he employed his
rkers on contract and assigned them daily piece-work or task work (called *mgwazo*
Africans).[87] Depending on the work involved, farmers allotted tasks to individuals
organized them into gangs. Piece-work was generally used in clearing new land,
mping and the collection of firewood and, most prominently, during the period of
eding and cultivating. Gang labor, which some farmers also used for these tasks,
s mainly organized for transplanting tobacco seedlings and during reaping and
ding (early November through May).[88]

Most tobacco farmers allocated piece-work the previous night, so that workers
d their assignment at the start of the following day. The tobacco rows might be
ked out with the names of individual laborers.[89] Others assigned tasks in the
rning after assessing the most immediate needs for that day.[90] The amount of work
quired varied from farm to farm. Weeding and cultivating, performed while bent
er at the waist with a short-handled hoe, or *badza*, often meant hoeing several rows
ch about one hundred yards long) or larger areas of over an acre.[91] According to
mer farm laborers, the work day started at 6.00 a.m., or sometimes earlier, and
epending on your strength, you, at times, could finish at ten . . . nine . . . eleven in
morning," while "others would finish on the morrow," sometimes only with the
lp of a wife and "yes, even children."[92] On the other hand, transplanting, priming,
ckering, topping (in general, snipping the plants lowest leaves; cutting late-
pearing shoots along the stem; and cutting of the flower pod that promoted
aturation and improved quality) required the use of gang labor. During planting,
need to transplant the seedlings quickly in time for the first rains in early
ovember meant gangs worked in the fields for "eight . . . nine hours . . . twelve
urs very often."[93]

By 1910, to better control the work, ensure completion of daily tasks and extract
maximum amount of effort, most farmers were using the ticket system developed
the Southern Rhodesian mines. Although workers were employed on a monthly
sis, the typical ticket required thirty completed shifts and took five or six weeks to
mplete. The employer marked the worker's ticket each day to indicate completion of
task for that day. Time lost to the weather or days when the task was left
complete were not paid for and did not count toward completion of the contract.[94] A
-month contract meant seven or eight months on the farm. As Van Onselen has
monstrated, the ticket system cheated workers, and farmers had even greater
portunities for abuse than mine owners.[95] While mines were subject to government
spection, farms (at least before 1945) rarely were.

Many farmers set unreasonable piece-work requirements taking several days to
mplete, effectively extending the contract without paying the contracted rate.[96]
hers refused to mark workers' tickets, leaving them unpaid at the end of the day. An
ample came to light in 1929 when a public prosecutor reported that several laborers

on a farm in Mazoe district "had only completed one or two tickets in six months." T farmer had consistently failed to mark their tickets, claiming that the assigned wc had not been properly completed.[97]

To extract additional work, farmers had other tricks and techniques at the disposal. They threatened dismissal when workers were late or slow, but giv working conditions and labor shortages, this was not much of a threat. Workers faili to complete the daily task could be kept longer and required to make up the time th had "wasted." This form of punishment not only involved the imposition of tir discipline, but also incorporated personal ridicule and humiliation by forcin offenders to continue to work "in full view of the remainder [of laborers] gaily goin home." By belittling laborers in front of their co-workers, some farmers tried eliminate "tardiness" and "loafing."[98]

When psychological intimidation failed to yield compliance to authoritari demands, farmers resorted to violence. Since the racial stereotype affirmed the Africans were lazy and incorrigible children, beating them was easily justified. 1909, a farmer explained that the occasional caning of workers was a way "to ma men . . . [of] our black brothers, who only love to enjoy idleness."[99] When understan ing failed, as it frequently did from language and cultural differences, violence was the remedy. In such cases, farmers should "knock a semblance of sense" into their labore "for their ultimate benefit."[100] In the mid-1930s, Rawdon Hoare, the Mazoe tobac and maize farmer, advised that "a good clout over the head frequently has excelle results," but warned that severe beating, "thrashing in the proper sense of the word was a mistake because it "only ends in the lowering of the white man's prestige."[1]

Some farmers were not too much bothered by that risk. In the early 192C Lomagundi farmer U. H. Lloyd beat one of his laborers with a belt on the buttocks ar repeatedly "kicked [him] violently with great force." The laborer had been assigned look after the farm's pigs, and when they got loose and spilt several tins of fresh mil Lloyd set out to make an example of him. His wounds were severe, and he later die from infection. Lloyd ended up in court, and was found guilty of "assault with th intent to do grievous bodily damage." But the sentence was light, a £3 fine or seve days' hard labor.[102]

In another case, a laborer, Ben, refused an assignment by a farmer, Robert Olive and decided to stay in his hut as a protest. On the afternoon of the second day of Ben protest, Oliver stormed to the hut and demanded to know when Ben was coming work. According to a witness, Ben answered from inside the hut, "Tomorrow." Oliv became enraged, took an assegai and thrust it through the grass walls of the hu striking Ben in the throat, severing an artery and killing him. Oliver was found guil of culpable homicide and fined £30 or three months' hard labor.[103] In anothe case — the death of a "herd boy" (a worker of any age assigned to watch the farm livestock), who was found hanging in a tree — an inquest concluded that the victi had committed suicide out of fear of punishment for losing three of his employer sheep.[104]

Concerned to impose a seasonal work regime as well as a daily one, tobacc farmers made every effort to hold their labor for the length of the growing seaso They commonly failed "to pay wages to their native employees as and when the came due."[105] Even though warned by government officials that the practice wa shortsighted, farmers believed that "when owed a month or more wages, the native less likely to desert and is more likely to perform his duties."[106] Employers general

id nothing until completion of three tickets and then kept wages in arrears until the
d of the season.[107] The practice became so widespread in Lomagundi and Mazoe
stricts that by the early 1930s a local Native Commissioner declared that it had been
he fashion" for several years.[108]

Debt was another weapon used to keep workers on the farm. Tobacco farmers ran
rm stores, advanced credit, made cash loans, and occasionally paid *lobolo* (bride
ice) for "trusted" employees. Farm stores usually stocked maize meal, clothing and
usehold items. Credit was freely extended to the farmers' own employees, but not
freely to laborers from neighboring farms. This policy served the dual purpose of
eping laborers in debt and, particularly when selling to visiting workers, providing
additional source of cash for the farm owner.[109]

Wage advances or loans against future tickets were sometimes given to laborers
ho were known on the farm. Farmers gave cash advances for the payment of tax, for
irchasing a bicycle, or for the payment of *lobolo*. Paying *lobolo* directly to the bride's
ther was a labor-mobilizing device; half of the money was paid before marriage and
lf after the birth of the first child. Payment of *lobolo* bound the laborer to the farmer
r at least the period before the birth of the first child.[110] Farmers gave varying
nounts of credit, from three-quarters to the full amount of wages earned by one
:ket. As a laborer paid off his debt, farmers would extend new credit on the next
:ket.[111] Large amounts of up to £10 or sometimes more were given as advances, but
ever more than necessary."[112]

"A Good Day's Work"

orkers were not powerless in the face of bad working conditions and severe labor
scipline on the farms. Migrants from Nyasaland, who made up the entire work-force
some estates, brought with them skills and knowledge of tobacco farming derived
om peasant cultivation in the Protectorate.[113] This included knowledge of soils, leaf
xtures and how to judge stages of maturing tobacco plants. They also knew how to
indle, tie and grade dried tobacco.[114] As a result, Nyasa were "much appreciated"
nployees on tobacco farms from the very beginning of the industry; they asked for,
id often received, higher wages.[115] They increased their bargaining power by
roviding replacement workers from among their relatives and friends when they
anted to return home. Workers returned to the same farm repeatedly when they
ere able to secure satisfactory conditions and wages.[116] Survival in farm work also
epended on skills derived from their upbringing and country living. They used
aditional methods to build their own living quarters in farm compounds; they
inted, trapped and gathered edible plants; and they grew maize and vegetables in
irden plots to supplement inadequate rations.[117]

While often treated in arbitrary, capricious and brutal ways, workers on tobacco
rms were not helpless. Labor shortages gave them bargaining power and led to
formal agreements —moral contracts — that employers ignored at their peril.[118]
irmers referred to them as "gentleman's agreements." It was understood by both
des that "you didn't sack them in the middle of the season, and they didn't give
otice" until the season was over. From the farm laborers' point of view, it generally
eant that farmers accepted an agreed amount of work each task should entail.[119] The
;reement might specify the amount of time allotted to a particular task, such as filling

or emptying a curing barn, or for other tasks, such as cultivating or weeding, number or length of rows assigned. When a farmer "laid on the tasks" and violated accepted understanding, workers would down tools "after a couple of days" and the farmer that "we're not going to do it, it's too much."[120] When work stoppages fail to restore the informal contract, workers resorted to a variety of other subtle metho to make their protests. They deliberately botched tasks such as weeding, but did so ways not immediately obvious so that blame and penalties would not fall individuals.[121] When cutting wood for tobacco curing, laborers filled the center of cord with brush so that "you got half a cord."[122] Finally, when reaping tobac laborers would pick unripe leaves to reduce the number of times they would have pass through the fields.[123]

In addition to mounting protests that aimed to restore the agreed daily wo assignments, tobacco workers resisted attempts to change their contractual comm ments. For example, in August 1937, a dispute between the owners of Ebden Estate large tobacco farm in central Lomagundi district, and ninety-eight of their Nya employees arose over the work those laborers had contracted to perform. Troul developed when the employer tried to shift the workers from the original agreed ta sorting and grading tobacco left from the previous season, to the more onero less-skilled removal of tree stumps. A machinery fault forced the change in wo assignment, and the tree stumping was to be temporary, pending repairs and resumption of sorting and grading. The owners, not unnaturally, did not want workers to remain idle in the interval. Equally, the workers had a point. They declin to be treated as labor units, to have their skills ignored and to be assigned arbitrarily heavy manual labor.

The great majority of the workers refused either to stump new fields or to perfor an alternative task offered, preparation of seed beds. After several days of stay-aw and following consultation with their lawyers, Ebden's owners assembled the ent work-force, one hundred and ten workers, and demanded of them individually th they accept whatever tasks were assigned until completion of the machinery repa Ninety-eight of the men again refused and were fired on the spot. They were paid and told to leave the farm immediately. For both sides, the dispute was about breach contract. Ebden's owners focused on the refusal of the workers to accept the discipli of the farm and to perform the tasks assigned. The workers focused on the equa valid, but informal, contractual understanding of what they had agreed originally do. The protesters "contended that the work assigned to them did not concern t 1936/37 tobacco crop, so they refused to perform it."[124]

In the crowded compounds, disputes also arose between workers who us traditional beliefs and social practices to protect themselves and their possessio from other workers. An intriguing example of the application of a traditional belief a new situation was in the use of magic (styled "witchcraft" by skeptical whites alwa ready to condemn the irrationality of their black laborers) to ward off theft in fai compounds.[125] Laborers' possessions were vulnerable when they were away fro their huts at work. They responded by using traditional medicines, which th believed had special powers to ward off thieves.[126] These medicines, called *ruk chibatirapakare*, were used at home to guard crops and were supposed to render thiev unable to walk or run.[127]

Since potential victims and perpetrators shared a belief in their efficacy, their u could be an effective deterrent to theft and a guarantor of social order among t orkers themselves. Because the laborers who found themselves thrown together in he compounds often came from different communities and descent groups, aditional kinship obligations might no longer operate to restrain anti-social conduct the new setting. Typically, however, in the new situation magic retained its full otency in the minds of believers and was here brought into use as an alternative eans of maintaining order. When protective medicines failed, workers turned to dividuals in the compounds thought to have supernatural powers, to commune ith spirits as a means to identity thieves, to cause the return of stolen property, or to nd its hiding place. Belief in the spiritual power of such persons was another uarantor of the sanctity of personal property in the compounds.[128] In these ways, aditional beliefs and practices assumed new roles in response to new social needs.

In addition to protecting or recovering stolen property, laborers sought super- atural assistance to control black supervisors on whom the owners relied to impose eir discipline on the work-force. In 1936, a woman living in the compound of a bacco farm in the Darwendale area was accused of using witchcraft against a "boss oy" named Simon. She was seen picking up dirt from one of his footprints. The omplaint alleged that the objective was supernatural, to harm Simon. It transpired at he was suffering from an injured leg and had been off work for several days. ccording to court records, Simon believed he was a victim of witchcraft and tributed his illness to the machinations of the "witch." Co-workers, he thought, had t the woman against him because he was a strict disciplinarian. His co-workers, he elieved, wanted to keep him off the job so that they would have less work to erform.[129]

Conclusion

hodesian tobacco workers learned to survive in a world dominated by the ierarchical, unequal and exploitative social system on white farms. While often iolent and brutal, this world was not without rules that ordered workers' relations ith the white owners. The employment relationship was governed by an informal oral contract. It was well understood on both sides and, like all contracts, set out ciprocal rights and obligations, even though unequally. Scarcity gave the skilled and nowledgeable Nyasa tobacco workers bargaining power that they learned to use ith advantage. White owners also recognized the contractual nature of their lationship with a labor force that they, at the same time, disparaged and tried to xploit. They knew that if they attempted to alter unilaterally the "gentleman's greement" that governed working relations on the farm, workers' counteraction ould follow.

Although denigrated by whites as "raw" and "ignorant," the mainly migrant rm workers had learned to operate skillfully in the new arena of wage labor, which hite colonization brought to north-eastern Rhodesia.[130] Although wages were low d conditions often poor, the tobacco farms of Lomagundi and Mazoe had some dvantages for the Nyasa who mainly worked them.[131] Some feared the dangerous d unhealthy environment of the mines. Others brought their wives and children d knew that a farm was a better environment for families than a mine compound. me lacked western education and were unprepared to work in towns or on the mines.[132] Once on the farms, they used a variety of informal means to assert their righ and to maintain them against parsimonious employers and other workers. In the actions, the tobacco workers revealed a kind of collective consciousness of themselv as wage laborers with entitlements and dignity that they struggled effectively to asse and maintain.

14

"Ropes of Sand":
Soldier-settlers and
Nagana in Zululand

SHIRLEY BROOKS[1]

There are few of us in the Province who began our life in Paradise, with its sparkling rivers whose beds are gold; and much energy and hard work are needed ere we set our faces towards its gates. Most of us are but ordinary common-place people who neither work miracles nor make angels weep . . . Were the Province not so rich in all that should tend to progress, we might understand the Government's neglect of our interests . . . The promises held out to us have been "ropes of sand."[2]

his lament was penned by a settler at Eshowe, southern Zululand, in the first years of e drive to extend white settlement into the region. His words echo a refrain taken up y many "ordinary common-place" participants in this enterprise, including the ldier-settlers at Ntambanana, north-east of Eshowe, whose story provides the arrative structure for this chapter (see figure 14.1). The story of the Ntambanana ldier-settlement, established in 1918, is perhaps most revealing in its exposure of the nperatives behind settlement policy during this period, and the contradictions to hich these imperatives gave rise. The narrative also sheds light on the question of w far the state was prepared to go in supporting settlers it had placed on unsuitable d ecologically marginal land. At Ntambanana, the settlers found themselves wholly the mercy of local ecology, since the farms they had been given bordered on a game serve and were infected with nagana (trypanosomiasis), a disease fatal to domesti- ted animals. In addition to highlighting the shortsighted nature of settlement policy this region, the threatening presence of nagana brought into focus divisions within atal's white "ruling class," as well as between state departments attempting to

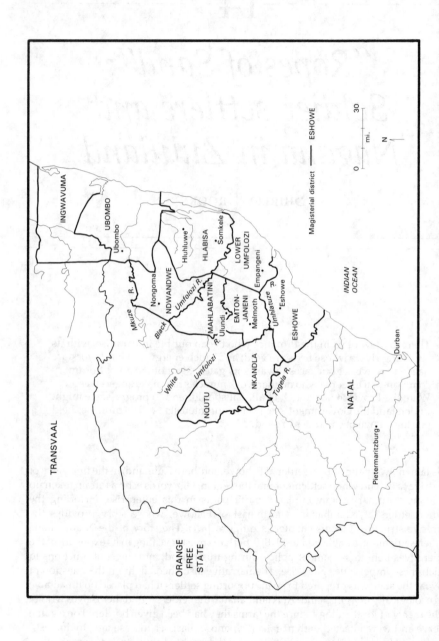

tervene either in opposition to the settlers' claims or on their behalf. By implication, e chapter stands as a comment upon the tenuous nature of white domination in parts the South African countryside during this period, as settlers in marginal contexts ung desperately to their "ropes of sand."

Imperatives of Settlement in Zululand

he Ntambanana story makes little sense unless one considers the wider question of hy an attempt was being made to establish a settlement in this particular area in the rst place. The answer to this question is complex. At one level, the process of xtending white settlement into Zululand was fueled by a desire on the part of the atal settlers to consolidate conquest of the territory. The first phase of conquest had ken place twenty years before, in the 1880s, a decade of economic disruption and vil war during which the power of the Zulu kingdom had been broken.[3] Zululand as annexed by the British government in 1887, and handed over to Natal ten years ter. Because of a five-year ban on settlement, the land did not immediately become vailable to white farmers. The report of the Zululand Delimitation Commission, eleased in 1905, set aside a little under half the total area of Zululand for white ccupation; yet by 1910 only a handful of settlers had succeeded in establishing nemselves on land north of the Tugela River. It rankled with white Natalians that so uch land still remained *de facto* under Zulu control.

At another level, settlement policy was the outcome of national pressures to ccommodate young white men on the land. The second phase of conquest was lent nomentum by a growing shortage of available land in areas of long-established white ettlement. Land without people had to be found for people without land. This nperative was not unique to South Africa: similar policies had recently been pursued n Britain, and settlement schemes were being set up in Britain's other African olonies.[4] In South Africa, the Land Settlement Act (No. 12 of 1912) was designed to ettle, with the maximum speed, large numbers of white farmers on "crown" or inalienated" land. The land was unalienated in the sense that it had not been eserved for other purposes, such as African occupation. Settlement of these ubstantial crown lands was coordinated by regional land boards, whose members rould inspect likely areas and report on their value and suitability for settlement urposes. After a favorable report had been submitted, the land was surveyed, ivided into holdings and allotted to tenants. Applicants, who had to undertake to ccupy their holdings personally, were interviewed by the land boards. Every effort ras made to ensure that allottees were able to remain on their farms. The holdings rere leased on generous terms, and rents could be waived at the discretion of the land oards. The process gained a new urgency in 1918, when young men returning from ervice on the battlefields of Europe swelled the ranks of the landless.

The imperatives of consolidation and expansion were supported, in South Africa, y a peculiar construction put on the notion of "progress," one which is implicit in the assage quoted at the head of this chapter. In settler discourse, crown land that had ot been "opened up" to white settlement was assumed to be "lying idle" — despite ne fact that most of this land was utilized by African pastoralists and agriculturalists, ho often had to be moved off it before settlement could commence. In Zululand,

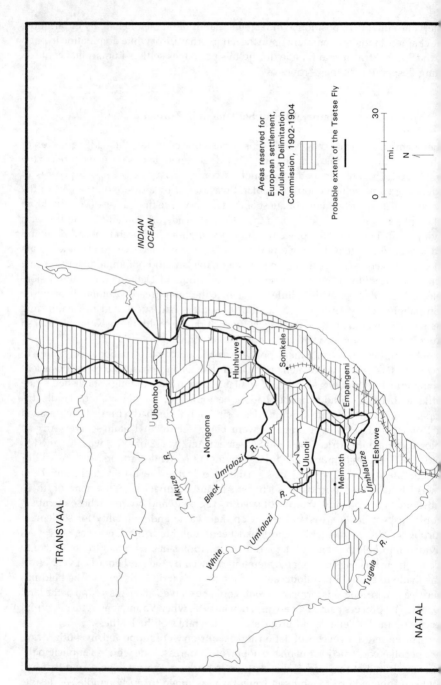

Figure 14.2 European Settlement and the Tsetse Fly, Zululand, 1923

nalienated land comprised about half the territory (see figure 14.2). This land was iewed by prospective settlers not only as "unutilised," but as resource-rich and ninently desirable.[5] As one settler arguing for the establishment of the Ntambanana ittlement put it:

> It seems to [us] most regrettable that such large areas of what is believed to be the finest cattle raising and dairying country in South Africa should lie idle year after year, when by common consent the future of South Africa as a whole is bound up with a vigorous policy of white settlement in the undeveloped parts.[6]

he imperatives of settlement were such that the rhetoric of "progress" tended to gloss ver problems such as inadequate rainfall, the presence of endemic disease, or the neer difficulty of transporting goods out of an isolated region. While indigenous frican groupings had often succeeded in modifying their dispositions to suit the xigencies of local conditions, the imperatives of white settlement did not favor noughtful adaptations to local ecology.

Prelude to Settlement: Ntambanana, 1913–1919

he striking point about the early part of the Ntambanana story is the extraordinary erseverance of advocates of the settlement — among them, the Natal Land Board, the nagistrate of the Lower Umfolozi Division, and prospective settlers — in the face of it-backs and indications that the settlement ought not to be established at all. An early eference to a proposed settlement at Ntambanana occurs in the minutes of a meeting f the Natal Land Board on 18 January 1913. The meeting recorded its opposition to the nitial survey at Ntambanana being carried out by an Inspector of Crown Lands, who ras "not . . . specially qualified to advise in regard to the capabilities of the land, the rea into which it should be subdivided and the valuation to be placed on the ibdivisions."[7] The survey should, it was felt, be undertaken by members of the Natal and Board and the Surveyor-General of Natal. Yet the evidence shows that the board nembers, based in Pietermaritzburg and unfamiliar with conditions in Zululand, rere themselves qualified to conduct the survey chiefly by virtue of their unbridled nthusiasm for development.

In fact, the idea of establishing a settlement at Ntambanana had been mooted as arly as 1911, when legislative provision was made for the disposal of crown lands in locks of small allotments, available "for selection by European settlers only," and to e utilized only for cane cultivation.[8] A promising settlement had already been stablished, following this pattern, at the Umfolozi River mouth (see figure 14.3). efore the Ntambanana area had even been surveyed, tenders were invited, at the ecommendation of the Natal Land Board, for the erection of a sugar mill in the area. .n award had already been made when opposition from the Natal sugar magnate Sir imes Hulett, who had interests at Umfolozi, caused the project to founder. It was isurrected in 1913 by Major P.A. Silburn, a member of the Natal Legislative ssembly who was also legal adviser to a previously disappointed applicant for the Itambanana Mill.[9] It was Silburn who organized the land board's survey trip to Itambanana, which finally took place in September 1913. The survey party was made p of two members of the Natal Land Board and the Surveyor-General of Natal, with .M. Tanner, magistrate of the Lower Umfolozi Division, acting as guide. Silburn's

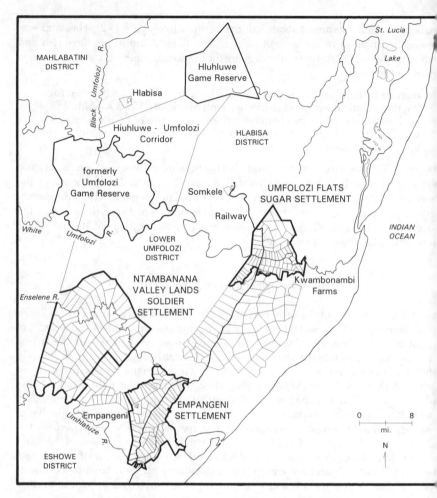

Figure 14.3 Umfolozi Region, Zululand, 1923

explanation for the delay in organizing the trip is significant: it indicates that disease was not only present but prevalent in the territory into which it was proposed to extend white settlement.

> I have not yet been able to secure any transport!! ... I understand from private sources that horsesickness has been pretty bad along the Zululand Coast this year and that not only are there no horses (or practically none) left in a district in which there never were very many; but that business people who have animals are not keen on their being taken to Zululand. I am now going to try Maritzburg men ...[10]

Like the Umfolozi sugar settlement, the area known as the Ntambanana Valley Lands was located in the Lower Umfolozi Division in southern Zululand (see figure 14.3). The Lands lay inland from the Umfolozi settlement, between the Umhlatuze River to

e south and the Umfolozi Game Reserve to the north. While the bulk of the game
serve consisted of a wedge of land between the Black and White Umfolozi rivers, the
serve did extend for several miles south of the White Umfolozi River, thus bordering
rectly on the proposed settlement — a circumstance that was to have a major impact
the fortunes of the latter. To the west of the Lands was the higher-lying ground of
e Biyela Native Reserve (No. 11). To the east, another so-called native reserve (No. 5)
parated the Ntambanana Valley Lands from the Umfolozi settlement (see figure
.4). The verdict of the survey party was that, "although portions of the land
spected are not too good, as a whole the land is well adapted for settlement by
iropeans."[11] The recommendation is not surprising, given the imperatives of
ttlement discussed above. The national position on land settlement in Zululand is
vealed in a comment offered by the Secretary for Lands on the land board's report.
ie Secretary for Lands argued that the Ntambanana settlement should not be
eveloped under legislation dealing specifically with sugar lands, but rather under
e more recent, and more general, Land Settlement Act. After all, "this is the law that
e public pin their faith on and from our point of view we want as much settlement
fected thereunder as is possible."[12]

It is instructive to compare the perceptions of board members, prospective
ttlers, and other advocates of "progress," with clues contained in the report as to the
tual ecological conditions at Ntambanana. While conditions on the Umfolozi flats
ere perfectly suited to cane cultivation, Ntambanana fell under a different ecological
gime. Not even the enthusiastic board members could fail to note that "as the rainfall
less than that enjoyed nearer the Coast, Sugar Cane is not likely to thrive as well as it
)es in the areas that have already been thrown open for the cultivation of cane."[13] An
lditional problem was the distance of the proposed settlement from the north coast
ilway.[14] Far from dropping the project, however, the land board argued that the
tambanana Valley Lands comprised "some of the finest grazing areas in the Natal
'ovince" and was well suited to dairy farming.[15] Tanner, the Magistrate at Lower
mfolozi, assured the Surveyor-General that he had received numerous enquiries
)out stock farms in the locality.[16] One such enquiry, written two years later, in 1916,
)nveys a sense of the settler perspective:

> Two and a half years ago I applied for one of these lots, and I was told I
> should have to wait . . . I have passed over other places with this end in view
> and now don't you think it would be jolly hard lines if the Government don't
> open them up . . . Because I lack the capital to buy a farm of my own, my only
> hope is getting a Government farm. I have the stock to start going, and I think
> the object in giving out Government farms is to entree [sic] suitable settlers
> on to the land, and it would be a great shame if these lands were left lying idle
> when there are suitable *colonial born men* ready and willing to take them
> up.[17]

careful reading of the survey report suggests that, had its writers' minds not already
zen made up, greater caution might have been exercised before the Ntambanana area
as recommended for settlement. In the southern and south-western corner of the
ea (where the first holdings were eventually allotted), the country was "broken,
adly watered and rather thickly covered with thorn trees."[18] Except along the banks
f the Enseleni River, the land was "very dry with occasional pools and but little
inning water."[19] After leaving the Enseleni Camp and heading eastwards, approach-
ig Reserve No. 5, "it was noticeable that the land was much better and the water

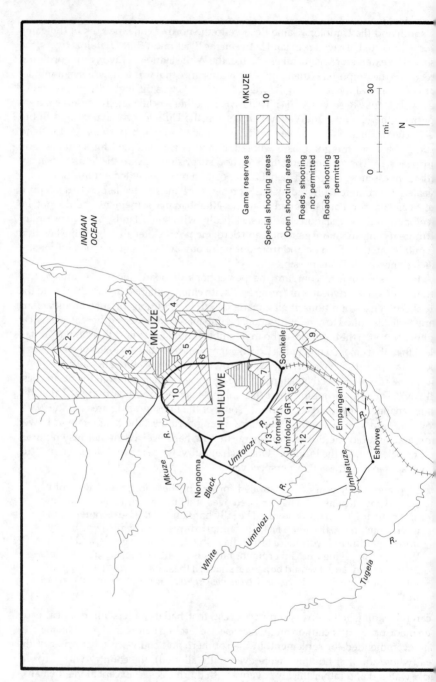

Figure 14.4 Zululand Game Reserves and Shooting Areas, 1928

pply far more plentiful within the Reserves than is the case with the lands thrown
en for settlement by Europeans."[20] Evidently, the best land in the region had already
en set aside for intensive occupation by Africans, and the remainder was land more
operly utilized on an extensive basis for roving pastoralism. African livestock
countered in various places were noted to be in "remarkably good condition."[21] The
ea was unsuited to intensive agriculture, not only because of the unpredictable
infall, but also because of the endemic presence of nagana. Zulu pastoralists
ilizing the crown lands had at least some chance of avoiding the disease, which was
ainly confined to river valleys and areas of thick bush. Even so, the board received
mplaints about "the ravages of . . . the Tsetse Fly [which] came and returned with
e big game."[22]

Contrary to its own perceptions, it was not strictly true that the land board had
umbled upon a "land without people." In addition to the pastoralists encountered on
e survey trip, members of the party must have noticed several permanent
ttlements in the area. Only one of these is mentioned in the report. This was a
mmunity at the Biyela mission station under the Rev. O. Norgaard, a missionary
quatting" by permission on crown lands.[23] The information on nagana mentioned in
e report was obtained from conversations with "Native Chiefs," presumably chiefs
sident on the crown lands; but the record is silent on this point.[24] In fact, the presence
local inhabitants now became the major obstacle to development. Initiating a
cade of bureaucratic conflict at Ntambanana, officials attempting to implement the
ovisions of the Land Settlement Act came into conflict with their counterparts at the
epartment of Native Affairs. J.Y. Gibson, District Native Commissioner for
ululand, reported that the alienation of the Lands would "impose new conditions
on a Native population of some 1 400 souls: necessitating either their removal or
heir] becoming servants of the acquiring Europeans."[25] On being applied to, Tanner,
e magistrate, reported the presence of "632 huts of the Biyela Tribe under Chief
umezweni and 11 huts of the Mtembu Tribe under Chief Msiyana," but argued that
e people involved could easily be accommodated on neighboring native reserves.[26]
fficials at the Department of Native Affairs protested that this was impossible.[27]

It is somewhat surprising, given the fact that summary removals were occurring
n crown lands all over South Africa during this period, that objections from the
ative Affairs Department were successful in holding up the Ntambanana settlement
r so long. Perhaps it was the paternalistic legacy of British rule in Zululand that lent
native administration" this particular flavor. Whatever its origins, it is clear that the
ative Affairs agenda was very different from that of the Department of Lands. As it
rned out, these officials had to hand a powerful mechanism in the form of the
ending report of the Natives Land Commission, a body set up under the 1913 Natives
and Act to ensure that "sufficient" land had been set aside for African occupation. All
arties concerned had agreed that "lands in the vicinity of Native Reserves largely
cupied by Natives" would not be allocated to white settlers until the commission
ad published its report.[28] The Zululand settlers protested, to little effect, against what
ey saw as a reversal of the policy laid down by the Zululand Delimitation
ommission in 1905.[29] When the report of the Natives Land Commission was finally
eleased, in August 1916, it was discovered that the Ntambanana Valley Lands had
en recommended for inclusion in an "additional native area."[30]

Here the matter should have rested; but the Zululand settlers were not prepared
be cheated, as they saw it, out of the coveted crown lands. It would not be entirely
rrect to think of the Zululand settlers as a single undifferentiated community. The

gulf that separated the struggling and undercapitalized stock farmers at Ntambana
and elsewhere in the Zululand interior from the emerging sugar plutocracy
Umfolozi became wider over the succeeding decades. Yet when it came to issu
involving the "settler interest," and in particular issues of development, the settl
community spoke with one voice. This tended to be the voice of George Heat
Nicholls, a sugar planter at Umfolozi who was the first president of the Zulula
Planters' Union. Nicholls was to become extremely influential at national level duri
the 1920s, when he represented settler (and in particular sugar) interests in parliame
while serving as MP for Zululand.[31] The Zululand Planters' Union, headed I
Nicholls, insisted that a Select Committee on Native Affairs review the conclusions
the Natives Land Commission. As a result, the decision on white settlement
Ntambanana was challenged and reversed. Nicholls conveyed to the Minister f
Lands "the congratulations of the planters at having rescued this land from tl
wilderness."[32]

Nicholls accompanied a party made up of land board members, the Surveyc
General, and the magistrate, Tanner, on a second tour of inspection of tl
Ntambanana Valley Lands. Their mission was given greater impetus by tl
impending return of young soldiers from Europe: men who had spent four years
their lives in service to their country, and who now expected their reward in the for
of a "Government farm." The report submitted to the Land Board on this occasion w
far less comprehensive than the first, and failed to mention the presence of nagana
the area. The only problem envisaged was the lack of surface water, which could I
rectified by drilling boreholes.[33] It was recommended that the land be advertised f
general agricultural purposes, in particular stock farming, and that applications I
sought from South African soldiers hoping to return to farming after the war. At tf
point, some sense needs to be conveyed of the background and economic status of tl
average soldier-settler. He was, it should be noted, a person of some substanc
possessing stock which he was prepared to convey to Ntambanana and introduce on
his farm. The application to the Natal land board of Croye Rothes Pithey provides
typical profile. Pithey was an English-speaking Natalian, who had been born
Durban. He was twenty-three years of age, and single. His previous experien
included "mixed farming."[34] At the time of making his application, Pithey was a Flig
Lieutenant in France. His assets and their value (in pounds) were listed as follows

	£
20 cows (12 with calves)	200
16 oxen	160
10 2-yr-old oxen	70
8 heifers	56
3 plows	34
3 harrows	17
1 Scotch cart and yokes for 6 oxen	20
1 trap and harness	30
3 horses	45
Gear for 20 oxen	7
Separator	10
Cash in possession of father	136
Total	785

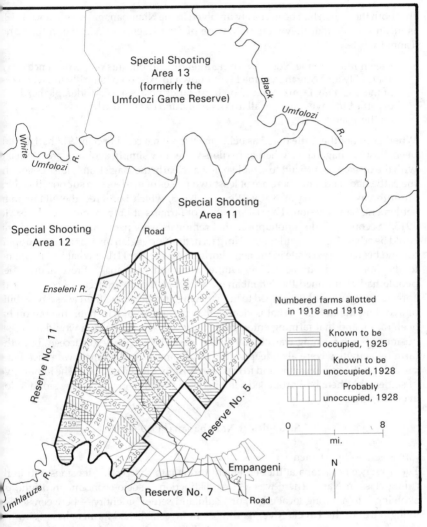

gure 14.5 Ntambanana Farms, 1928

ne first eleven farms at Ntambanana, ranging from 1 200 to 1 600 acres in extent were rveyed, and a government notice was sent out on 15 February 1918 advertising them stock farms.[36] The applications of young men like Pithey were considered by the nd board, and the first allotments were made in July (see figure 14.5). In the eantime, a further twenty-two properties had been surveyed in the south-westerly rner of the Lands. These were allotted to settlers in October. The more northerly ·gion, near the Umfolozi Game Reserve and the Enseleni River, was divided into ·rty farms and allocated to newly returned soldiers in June 1919. It was not until the nal allocations had been made, and the successful applicants advised by telegraph of eir good fortune, that a crucial letter was sent by Tanner, the magistrate at Lower mfolozi, to the Surveyor-General in Pietermaritzburg. It should be remembered that both these men had been closely involved in the Ntambanana project since 1913. is inconceivable that they were not aware of the presence of nagana on the Land Tanner wrote:

> I see nothing in the Notice warning intending applicants of the presence of Tsetse Fly and Nagana yet the Fly is known to exist on practically the whole of these 47 new farms. Natives on these lands possessed considerable herds of cattle but have lost them all from Nagana and today not a beast is to be seen on these lands.[37]

Whether or not the cattle noted as being in exceptional condition in 1913 had actual been "lost" to nagana, or whether herders were now simply avoiding areas infecte with the disease, is difficult to establish. It was clearly the magistrate's impression th the cattle had died, and there are at least two pieces of evidence to support this. Firs an outbreak of nagana in Native Reserve No.5, which bordered the Ntambanar settlement, had occasioned a crisis meeting of farmers at Empangeni as early as Ma 1915.[38] Secondly, it does not appear that removals were necessary before the Lan could be advertised for settlement. Norgaard, the Norwegian missionary, had appli for and been granted a site in the neighboring Reserve No.11; but what had happene to the homesteads under Chiefs Dumezweni and Msiyana?[39] Presumably, the people had abandoned the Ntambanana valley of their own accord because of tl spread of nagana, and decamped to higher-lying ground where there was a possibili of avoiding the disease. What is clear is that the spread of nagana in the region ha been rapid, and that farming enterprise of any sort at Ntambanana would be a risl business. Stock farming was obviously the least likely activity to succeed, but oth farming activities were also deeply affected. Domesticated animals were needed provide traction for plowing and to transport produce to the railhead. The imperativ of settlement, then, had propelled settlers into a situation in which they stood to lo everything.

Struggles at Ntambanana, 1919–1929

(a) Settlers vs Sportsmen
The presence of nagana at the settlement threw into sharp relief tensions within th ruling class in Natal. There was a clear distinction — socio-economic in origin, bu evolving into a strong local ethos, or "Zululand settler" identity — between settle living north of the Tugela River, and those more established farmers based south the river. In general, the latter group tended to cross the river into Zululand for th purposes of sport hunting, an activity that was administered, very profitably, by th Natal Provincial Administration (NPA) in Pietermaritzburg.[40] The NPA was respor sible for evolving and implementing game laws, maintaining Zululand's gam reserves, and generally preventing uncontrolled destruction of Zululand's magnif cent wildlife populations (see figure 14.4). A strong protectionist lobby existed i Natal, composed of scientists and sport hunters, in uneasy combination. At th insistence of this hunting/preservationist lobby, stricter controls were initiated i Zululand after 1910. Game legislation affecting Natal and Zululand was revised an standardized in the form of a new and comprehensive Game Ordinance, passed by th Natal Provincial Council in 1912.[41] Shooting within game reserves was outlawec Outside game reserves, licenses could be purchased from the NPA to sho "Ordinary" and "Specially Protected" game. Hunting was only permitted in an annua

pen" season, from May to August. "Royal" game could not be shot under any
rcumstances. A Game Conservator was appointed to oversee the implementation of
e ordinance in Zululand.[42]

The Zululand settlers were firmly united against preservationist legislation. In
e first place, wildlife was an important resource, which, as the work of Mackenzie,
agner and others shows, had acted to subsidize settlement in other parts of South
frica and in Britain's African colonies.[43] New settlers to Zululand, most of whom
uld not afford a hunting license, were being deprived of a readily available source of
rotein, simply because an economically more privileged sector of Natal settler
ciety had acted to reserve the hunting privilege to itself. As in East Africa, hunting in
ululand was no longer about subsistence, but had become a complex class ritual from
hich not only Africans, but also the poorer settlers, were excluded.[44] White
ululanders argued, with some justice, that they were being made to suffer "for the
d of a few dwellers at a distance whose pleasure it is to make an occasional holiday
ip and boast of their prowess in killing big game."[45] Or, as another settler put it:

> Is this part of Zululand to be kept for a few Natal capitalists as a "shooting
> box" to the detriment of every human being, black or white . . .? Is the Union
> prepared to set aside hundreds of thousands of acres of the best lands in
> South Africa for the benefit of a few of the above-mentioned gentlemen? If so
> let us know quickly. You cannot continue to farm game and human beings
> and get revenue from both.[46]

n even more important — indeed, overriding — issue was the perception, shared by
ost Zululand settlers, that stricter implementation of game protection laws had led
irectly to the rapid spread of nagana in Zululand. As early as the 1890s, Dr David
ruce had conducted preliminary research into the disease in Zululand, and
ncluded that wildlife (and "big game" in particular) was responsible for harboring
e blood parasite or trypanosome that caused nagana.[47] Wild animals carried the
arasites in their bloodstreams, remaining themselves immune to the effects of the
isease. The blood-sucking tsetse fly, having fed on such an animal, would then bite a
omesticated animal and transfer the fatal trypanosome. The infected animal sickened
nd died. While subsequent research has proved this analysis substantially correct, at
e time it was vigorously disputed by preservationists, who feared that its acceptance
ould lead to the destruction of Zululand's wildlife.[48] However, by the turn of the
entury, the notion that "big game" as well as tsetse flies was responsible for the
pread of nagana was already well established in Zululand settler lore. Zulu
astoralists like the chiefs interviewed at Ntambanana often observed that tsetse fly
ame and returned with the big game."[49] White traders in Zululand had taken careful
ote of this piece of indigenous knowledge, and passed on the diagnosis to new
ettlers.

At the Ntambanana settlement, events were following a predictable course. The
nspector of Crown Lands — perhaps the very individual the Natal Land Board had
eclared "unqualified" in 1913 — was called in to assess the situation. After visiting
e settlement in August 1919, he argued that "it would be most unwise to allow any
ersons to settle in the affected area" and urged that the allotments be canceled.[50] After
s long battle to launch the settlement at Ntambanana, however, the land board was
ot about to abandon the scheme. The new settlers were simply issued with a warning
at their farms were probably infected with nagana. The northern farms, bordering
e Umfolozi Game Reserve, were especially vulnerable to the disease. By May 1920,

sixty-one settlers out of a total of eighty were in residence at Ntambanana. T
Zululand Times reported that "the worst has happened and stock are dying daily
Nagana had struck as far south in the settlement as Lot 250 (see figure 14.5). By Ju
stock losses had reached a total of 479 head of cattle, and a further 111 animals we
suffering from the disease.[52] This works out to a loss, per settler, of ten head of cat
— a crushing blow for the infant community. In September, a Parliamenta
Committee on Returned Soldiers noted that a total of 810 beasts had died
Ntambanana. This disaster rendered dairy farming impossible, hampered plowi
operations, and made it difficult for the farmers to dispose of their produce or even
obtain essential supplies.[53]

Tanner, the magistrate of the Lower Umfolozi Division, had put forward in l
letter to the Surveyor-General a two-pronged strategy for dealing with the naga
menace at Ntambanana. Tanner's first idea was to hold a "game drive," or organiz
shoot, in order to reduce the numbers of zebra, wildebeest and buck inside the bord
of the Ntambanana settlement. Game that was not killed in the shoot would be driv
back across the White Umfolozi River into the game reserve.[54] Tanner's seco
proposal was to ensure that the section of the game reserve that extended south of t
river — an area which had been added to the reserve in 1907 — was deproclaime
The land would then revert to the Union government as crown land. Africans who h
been moved from their homes on the south bank of the Umfolozi River to make w
for the game reserve could be encouraged to return to their old homesteads, whi
would form an effective barrier between the Ntambanana settlement and w
animals straying out of the reserve.[55] In the absence of any better suggestion, Tanne
strategy was adopted by the Natal Land Board. The Minister of Lands at first tried
disclaim responsibility for the disaster, informing the settlers that they ought to ha
personally inspected the farms before signing their leases. "In opening up ne
country, it is impossible for the Department to know with what difficulties, includi
stock diseases, the settlers will ultimately be faced."[56] The threat at Ntambanana h
been immediate rather than "ultimate," however. In agreeing to finance Tanne
game drive, the Department of Lands tacitly accepted culpability.

Despite opposition from the provincial authorities, from whom permission had
be obtained in order to put into effect a strategy focused on game destruction, bo
plans were carried out. The Administrator of Natal grudgingly acceded to t
proposition of a game drive, although he would not agree to the drive proceeding
far north as the White Umfolozi River.[57] Shooting had to stop three miles south of t
river, a provision that prompted a cynical outburst from one Ntambanana settler, w
suggested that "at the 3-mile limit there should be a line of notice-boards requesti
the wild animals to keep off the grass on the settlement side."[58] The drive, in which t
Umfolozi sugar planters participated, was held in December 1919. Although as man
as 1 040 animals were killed, the Magistrate reported "thousands of zebra" still at lar
in the settlement.[59] The game drive had been successful mainly in provoking the wra
of Natal's protectionist/hunting lobby. Letters of protest appeared in the Natal pre
the first of many accusing the Zululand settlers of "blood lust" and butchery. In t
meantime, the second part of Tanner's strategy — the deproclamation of part of t
game reserve — had also been achieved. As livestock continued to die of nagana, t
Administrator agreed, in May 1920, to degazette the reserve south of the Wh
Umfolozi River. This area became a "buffer zone" between the game reserve and t
settlement, and Tanner was given permission to clear it of game. At the same tim

eorge Heaton Nicholls, newly elected MP for Zululand, raised the plight of the tambanana settlers in parliament.[60]

Tanner's strategy was not effective in dealing with the nagana menace. In July 20 a deputation of Ntambanana settlers traveled to Cape Town to demand that the inister of Lands put pressure on the NPA to abolish the Umfolozi Game Reserve.[61] It as futile, they argued, to clear the deproclaimed area of game as long as the reserve mained as a refuge for wildlife and a reservoir for disease. A flashpoint in the onflict was reached in August, when the Ntambanana farmers were granted ermission to hold a second game drive, this time open to the public and widely ublicized as "Zululand's Monster Game Drive."[62] The *Zululand Times* and the ainstream Natal press took up opposing positions on the issue. While Natal ewspapers decried the "unnecessary" destruction of wildlife, the *Zululand Times* oped that the drive, by drawing attention to the Ntambanana settlers' plight, would once and for all time settle the West Street sportsmen."[63] Feelings were running high n both sides. Although the game drive was supposed to end at the White Umfolozi iver, it became obvious at a packed meeting held at the Empangeni Town Hall on the receding evening that this was unlikely to happen. One irate farmer declared that "he or one would brook with no interference . . . [but would] enter the reserve and blot ut every living animal within range."[64] Simultaneously, a heated debate was raging in ie Provincial Council between supporters of game protection and members ympathetic to the settlers. In the end, the council decided that it had no alternative but abolish the Umfolozi Reserve.

Continuing conflict over the nagana issue had laid bare class divisions within hite Natal. The complex ecological chain that bound wildlife to cattle disease in ululand also pitted struggling settlers against farmers who had managed to attain a reater degree of economic security. The latter were engaged in acquiring the status roper to an emerging local aristocracy. They were attempting to (re)define emselves as "sportsmen" and "gentlemen" through participation in the privileged tuals of "The Hunt."[65] Game destruction for purely practical purposes — particularly rganized destruction on the scale of "Zululand's Monster Game Drive" — was nathema to this emerging status group. Who were the members of this group? A brief rofile of one influential protectionist must suffice. William Campbell was the owner f the Natal Sugar Estates at Mount Edgecombe, near Durban. During the 1920s, ampbell was recruited by the director of the Natal Museum, Dr Ernest Warren, to ecome active in the cause of wildlife protection in Zululand. Campbell was interested n preserving wildlife in Zululand because, like others of his kind, he had been wont to epair to the region for leisurely hunting trips. (Later Campbell purchased his own rivate fiefdom at Mala Mala in the eastern Transvaal.)[66] Campbell contributed umerous articles on game preservation to Natal newspapers. He sat on a Game dvisory Committee appointed in 1928 to advise the Natal administration, and was a ounder member of the Natal Game Protection Society.

It is instructive to compare Campbell with Nicholls, MP for Zululand in the 1920s. s influential members of Natal's sugar aristocracy, the two men had much in ommon. For example, both wanted to refurbish the flagging Zulu monarchy as a ulwark against the incursions of "native revolutionaries," in particular members of ie Industrial and Commercial Workers' Union (ICU). Disgruntled by the lack of espect that he felt the ICU had shown him, the Zulu king, Solomon, allowed himself o be won over by the sugar planters. Solomon delivered his denunciation of the ICU

at Campbell's behest to assembled workers of the Natal Sugar Estates in 192?
Nicholls followed up this victory the following year by persuading Solomon
address, in similar vein, a gathering of young men undergoing training as chiefs.[68]
would have been natural for Nicholls, a member of the emerging Zululand sug
plutocracy, to join class forces with Natal sugar barons like Campbell and argue
favor of game preservation. Yet, perhaps because his own settler roots were so rece.
Nicholls remained faithful to the Ntambanana farmers and continued, during t
1920s, to argue their case. As noted above, a strong "Zululand settler" ethos develop
during this period, and Nicholls subscribed to it whole-heartedly. The wildl
protectionists realized that he would not support their cause. Nicholls's position
the divisive issue was summed up, correctly, by the Game Conservator:

> Mr. Heaton Nicholls . . . looks at every question with the eyes of a
> politician — quite naturally so — and his constituents and their needs come
> before game preservation. He says quite frankly that he has not an ounce of
> sentimental feeling for the game, and he argues somewhat in this way, that if
> we can show that the Game Reserves can be retained without resultant harm
> and loss to the settlers, well and good — he would not wish to have them
> abolished. Otherwise he would be on the side of the abolitionists, every
> time.[69]

The degazetting of the game reserve in 1920 left the Ntambanana settlers in a bare
improved position. Some allotments had never been occupied, while others had be
abandoned. Numbers of settlers were forced to leave their farms in order to se
temporary employment elsewhere.[70] Twenty-one farmers took the option of cedi
the rights to their farms and departing (see figure 14.5). Unable to farm cattle while t
problem of nagana remained, the remaining settlers cast around for an alternativ
Sugar production did not become possible at the settlement until 1929, when
branch line was extended from Empangeni to the southern farms; but a feasib
alternative to cattle was cotton. The settlers found that they could mobilize certa
state resources through organized pressure. While the state refused to pay compens
tion for stock lost from nagana, it was prepared to support an early experiment
mechanization at Ntambanana. In the period after the "monster game drive," t
Department of Lands agreed to a request from the Commissioner for Return
Soldiers for the loan of motorized plows to settlers who had lost all their dr
animals and had no other means of plowing.[71] An initial 600 acres of cotton w
planted in 1922, and yielded positive results. The experiment was repeated in 192
High prices for cotton on the international market encouraged the Ntambana
settlers to initiate the formation of a Zululand Co-operative Cotton Association
1924. This body raised a substantial Land Bank loan for the construction of a cott
ginnery in the area.

The "boom" period at Ntambanana was short-lived. In 1925, the settlers decid
to invest all their remaining capital in cotton. The area under cultivation on individu
farms in the settlement ranged from 45 to 330 acres, although the average was closer
100 acres.[72] A bumper crop was anticipated, and was actually in sight, wh
devastating rains began, and only about 10 per cent of the crop could be salvaged
Concomitantly with this "Act of God" came the end of the cotton boom. By the time t
Empangeni cotton ginnery began operating, in July 1926, world cotton prices ha
dropped and cotton production was suddenly uneconomical.[74] In the meantime, t
plows loaned by the Department of Lands had broken down and the settlers h

verted to animal traction. To the debts accumulated by the Ntambanana settlers in
quiring the original landholdings and the motorized plows was added the cost of an
ually unproductive cotton ginnery. Then, in 1927, after a two-year period of
iescence, nagana reoccurred on the Ntambanana farms. A tour of inspection was
rried out in 1928 by members of the Natal Land Board. Their report noted that
agana sufferers were to be seen everywhere, some farmers having at least 50% of
eir stock infected . . . the number of Cattle in the Settlement has dropped probably
one-third."[75]

The conflict between settlers and sportsmen at Ntambanana, a conflict centered
ound the issue of nagana, but based on the economic polarity between moneyed
atalians and struggling white Zululanders, continued throughout the 1920s. Despite
e fact that no more game drives were held at Ntambanana, the settlers continued to
blamed for game destruction in Zululand. One Ntambanana settler responded to
ese allegations in the press. His letter makes two important points: first, that game
ives were not carried out for sport (this was, of course, the main reason they were
precated by the Natal hunting aristocracy); and, second, that settlers were in fact
rred from hunting because of their economic situation.

> Sir: — I have recently seen several articles in your paper on the destruction of
> game in Zululand, of which the white man in general and the settler in
> particular is being accused . . . Speaking of the Ntambanana settlers, those
> of them who are left today are only the "Bitter Enders," and little is the time
> they get for going out on game destruction excursions, always an unprofit-
> able pursuit for any white man. No, they have to stay at home and work like
> Trojans to fulfil their obligations to the Government, having to pay exorbitant
> rents for the land they occupy . . . The poor settler who sometimes yearns for
> a piece of meat as a variation from the ordinary everyday mealie pap fare has
> first to procure a permit to shoot, and pay for it up to as much as 5 pounds for
> one single individual buck.[76]

ese tensions are clearly demonstrated in the response to an incident, in 1928, in
hich two white rhinoceroses were shot in the ex-Umfolozi Game Reserve (still a
otected area, for reasons explained below). The presence of this rare animal in the
serve provided preservationists with their strongest argument for its reproclama-
n. Following the killings, a storm of protest broke in the Natal press. It was assumed
at the killing had been planned and carried out by Zululand settlers. The Zululand
me Conservator, for one, had little doubt that "it was done at the instigation of one
that pampered crowd at Ntambanana."[77] The *Zululand Times* was more restrained,
nply noting that "owing to the criminal slaughter, under mysterious circumstances,
two white rhino . . . Zululand with its problems of big game, tsetse fly and *nagana*,
s been receiving quite a lot of attention in the public Press. Whether we shall reap
y advantage therefrom is extremely doubtful."[78]

) Pietermaritzburg vs Pretoria
nked to the primary conflict between Zululand settlers and the hunting elite was a
ated conflict between central government and the provincial authority in Natal. In
dition to highlighting tensions within the white "ruling class," the nagana issue
ted as a focus for conflicts within the state. As noted above, wildlife protection in
luland was a profitable activity for the Natal administration. It was relatively cheap
administer and yielded a substantial revenue in the form of fees for hunting

licenses. Several members of the Provincial Council were keen sport hunters, and th
actively supported game protection. The administration's chief executive officer w
J.M. Hershensohnn, who served as Provincial Secretary for Natal from 1910 to 192
Hershensohnn was a staunch ally of Dr Ernest Warren, the director of the Na
Museum, who as a zoologist and conservationist had devoted his life to t
preservation of the Zululand game. As Provincial Secretary, Hershensohnn was al
the immediate superior of the Zululand Game Conservator, Frederick Vaugha
Kirby, who approached his job with an almost evangelical fervor.[79] At a more gener
level, the nagana issue provided a point at which provincial government could flex
muscles in opposition to central government. Settlers, it was argued, were t
responsibility of the Department of Lands, which had located them in Zululand in t
first place. The task of the provincial government was to preserve game.

In the decade following the deproclamation of the Umfolozi Game Reserve, t
NPA waged a continuing battle with central government over the status of the reserv
As noted above, the first round in this campaign went to the Department of Land
under pressure from its local agent, the Natal Land Board, and, of course, from t
Zululand settlers. After initial concessions had proved unsuccessful in solving t
nagana problem, the Provincial Council had little alternative but to deproclaim t
reserve. The next round in the conflict went to the NPA, thanks to the clev
maneuvering of the Provincial Secretary. Hershensohnn's first move was to ensu
that the ex-game reserve did not become an open shooting area, as the settle
demanded, but instead remained a protected zone in which normal hunting fees (
per the 1912 Game Ordinance) obtained. This expedient, which was quietly approve
by the Provincial Council in April 1921, effectively reversed the earlier decision
degazette the reserve.[80] The settlers at Ntambanana regarded this action as high
unfair. As the president of the Ntambanana Farmers' Association (NFA) lat
complained, the farmers who had crossed illegally into the game reserve in the cour
of the "monster game drive," should have been prosecuted in 1920 "and the who
thing . . . fought out there and then."[81] As it was, the farmers had been given
opportunity to argue their case: the administration had simply imposed a differer
but equally effective, protectionist regime.

In an attempt to render the *de facto* game reserve still more secure, Hershensohr
resorted to a second tactic. This strategy entailed provincial manipulation of existir
divisions between central government departments. While the Department of Lanc
was responsible for safeguarding the interests of settlers, the Department
Agriculture also became involved when farming was seriously affected by t
presence of disease, as at Ntambanana. To complicate matters still further, t
Department of Agriculture was involved at Ntambanana on two levels. In the fir
place, as nagana was a disease spread by the tsetse fly, it was seen as an entomologic
problem. As a result, an entomologist was sent into the Umfolozi River Valley to stuc
the life cycle of the fly. This man was R.H.T.P. ("Fly") Harris, who had a difficu
personality but was a dogged scientist whose job was to find a long-term solution
the nagana problem.[82] It was hoped that, once the etiology of nagana was proper
understood, effective intervention might be possible at some point in the life cycle
the fly. In the second place, sick cattle were clearly a problem to be dealt with
Veterinary Services. A Veterinary Research Station was thus established at Ntamb
nana in March 1921, under the guidance of H. Curson. Its task was the essential
palliative one of treating animals infected with nagana, and searching for a cure. Bo

eterinary Services and Entomology fell under the broad umbrella of the Department Agriculture.

Hershensohnn's aim was to infiltrate the central government's research program tsetse fly. Before Harris had even arrived at Ntambanana, the Provincial Secretary ggested to his agent in Zululand, Vaughan-Kirby, that Harris might be prepared to pport — perhaps even to initiate — a request that the ex-game reserve be closed to ooting, on the grounds that it interfered with his scientific research.[83] Harris agreed at it would be difficult for him to study the connections between wildlife, tsetse fly d nagana if the game were constantly being disturbed by hunters, and he managed persuade his superiors likewise. In May 1922, a formal request was received by the PA from the Minister of Agriculture asking that shooting be prohibited in the serve during the 1922 open hunting season, so that conditions would remain disturbed while Harris conducted his research. Hershensohnn could now legiti- ately refuse applications to hunt in the Umfolozi valley. The Department of Lands as unaware of the request, and Hershensohnn decided to play it down as much as ossible. He did not announce the ban publicly in the *Provincial Gazette*, since that ould have "invite[d] attention immediately to the point."[84] Instead, Vaughan-Kirby as given instructions to inform applicants for hunting licenses on an individual basis the decision to close the area to shooting that year. A similar procedure was peated immediately prior to the 1923 shooting season.

In a confidential letter to Dr Ernest Warren, written in 1925, Harris described the es along which his investigations had proceeded. His initial goal had been to scover how the tsetse fly found its food. Once this was known, Harris thought, it ight be possible to step in and alter sensory impressions being received by the fly, so to prevent it from finding its prey.[85] Harris's initial experiments had been conducted ith dummy animals. The tsetse fly, he noted, would come to any large and nspicuous object, whether it was alive or not. Harris's first idea was that dummy imals, made out of old bags stuffed with hay, might act as fly traps, but he had failed discover an adhesive strong enough to entrap the insect.[86] The experiment had nvinced him, however, that the tsetse fly hunted by sight, and that "the larger and ore conspicuous the object the greater the attraction."[87] Harris accordingly moved on a more ambitious scheme. His aim was to try to reproduce a typical fly area by sconnecting a patch of bush from all surrounding objects. If a population of flies uld be isolated in this way, it might be observed how far the insects would fly in arch of food. Should it be shown that the fly was deterred by having to fly over large eas of open ground, then a program of bush clearing could be instituted and, it was ped, the settlement rid of the pest. Or, as Harris colorfully expressed it:

> I don't know what I am supposed to be doing here, but I do know what I *am* doing, and that is I am reproducing a fly belt of my own . . . Knowing what we do, we are going to bottle him up in my fly belt and only let him out when I see fit. This is "control" and you shall see it shortly unless meanwhile they bottle me up in a lunatic asylum.[88]

1924, the researchers at the Veterinary Research Station had failed to find a cure for gana, and their activities were terminated.[89] The entomological program continued, wered by the enthusiasm of Harris, and the provincial authorities were determined retain close links with it. Indeed, Harris's warm relationship with the scientist Warren and Vaughan-Kirby, the Zululand Game Conservator, made him popular with his superiors at the Department of Agriculture. Harris's immediate superior, who was regarded by the preservationists as a dangerous "enemy," visit Harris's research camp in October 1924 and voiced his opinion that Harris w "pig-headed" and incompetent.[90] Harris, for his part, complained of the "utter lack interest, the jealousy and callousness of those in authority."[91] Harris was becomi increasingly identified with Pietermaritzburg, and correspondingly alienated fro Pretoria. In February 1925, Harris asked if Dr Warren might assist him in writing his work. He invited Warren to visit him at the isolated Tsetse Fly Investigation Can on the White Umfolozi River, complaining that "I am alone here, and without technical friend I get very lonely and depressed and feel sometimes that perha another man here would be able to get better results than I."[92] In 1926, Warren offer to have Harris's final report typed in Pietermaritzburg, rather than in Pretoria, whe Harris feared it might be altered. This process extended over several months, hundreds of pages of manuscript flooded into the Natal Museum.

Despite (or perhaps because of) his connections with the provincial authoriti Harris continued to walk a delicate tightrope in his relations with the Zululand sett community. Having little other choice, the settlers at Ntambanana looked to Harris solve the nagana problem. George Heaton Nicholls, who as MP for Zululand h maintained his interest in Ntambanana, was a particularly staunch supporter of "Fl Harris. When the Minister of Agriculture visited Ntambanana in January 1925, stror criticism was leveled at his department for what the settlers saw as its recalcitra attitude to dealing with the nagana menace. Nicholls made sure that Harris w exempted from this criticism. As Nicholls pointed out, the entomologist had been se to Zululand without any assistance or instructions whatever; he had spent much of h time riding to Empangeni (34 miles away) for supplies; and he had not been giv sufficient manpower to carry out his investigations properly.[93] While the Ntambana settlers continued to see Harris as their brightest hope, the Department of Agricultu washed its hands of Ntambanana after the closure of the Veterinary Research Stati in 1925. Researchers at the central Research Station at Onderstepoort were mo interested in research on east coast fever and other diseases carried by ticks, whi they had already had considerable success in controlling.[94] Nagana was, by compa son, an intractable problem. Harris was recalled to Pretoria and had to abandon work on the tsetse fly.

Provincial government, however, was not prepared to relinquish the ally it had assiduously cultivated. While Harris had been careful not to commit himself one w or the other on the issue of game destruction, his researches had at least served to wa off the threat of further game drives at Ntambanana. They had also enabled t provincial authorities to maintain the area between the White and Black Umfolc rivers as a *de facto* game reserve. With the recurrence of nagana on the Ntambana farms in 1927, the Ntambanana Farmers' Association demanded that Harris should allowed to return to the region to conclude his experiments. In the interi Hershensohnn had retired as Provincial Secretary, and a Game Advisory Committ had been set up to advise the Administrator on game protection policy in his ste — an issue that had by now become an extremely thorny one. By this time, t Ntambanana soldier-settlement was not the only settlement faced with this compl problem: similar experiments had been attempted, with similar results, near gar reserves at Mkuze and Hluhluwe (see figure 14.4). What happened at Umfolc therefore, had implications for settlers in similar straits elsewhere in Zululand. T Game Advisory Committee included all the major players at Ntambanana: gar

otectionists, NPA representatives, the Ntambanana settlers, and George Heaton
icholls, who attended the meetings in person. Clarkson, the chairman, suggested
at "Fly" Harris might be seconded from the Department of Agriculture to the NPA
r a period of three years in order to complete his researches — a solution that was
ceptable to all parties.[95] The Minister of Agriculture acceded to this request.

From one point of view, then, Pietermaritzburg had been entirely successful in
jacking Pretoria's research project. On the other hand, the secondment of Harris
oved something of a two-edged sword. The Zululand Game Conservator, Vaughan-
rby, having retired, Harris was given wide powers to reorganize the game reserves
he thought fit. He arrived at Ntambanana in April 1929 to prepare for his final
islaught on the tsetse fly. Harris presented a report of his actions to the Game
dvisory Committee at a crucial meeting in October. This report gave the lie to
eservationists, like Dr Warren, who had been arguing that there were hardly any
iimals in the Umfolozi Game Reserve. A total of 3 191 "big game" animals were
unted, including 948 buffalo, 747 wildebeest and 696 zebra. In fact, the reserve was
erstocked. Neither was the white rhinoceros on the verge of extinction. Whereas
ily 20 rhinoceroses had been thought to exist in the reserve, the white ranger
pointed by Harris to count the animals arrived at a figure of 172.[96] Harris argued
at competition for grazing had pushed the smaller animals out into the buffer zone,
hich separated the reserve from the settlement, where they provided food for the
etse fly. Harris believed that controlled destruction of excess wildlife was the
lution to the nagana problem. Once the number of large animals in the game reserve
id been reduced, balance would be restored and there would be a "consequent
crease of flies within the buffer zones."[97]

The meeting of the Game Advisory Committee in October 1929 was a key
oment in the story of the Ntambanana settlers. From the point of view of the
ovincial authorities, the ultimate goal was to achieve the reproclamation of the
serve. It was clear, however, that further game destruction would have to be
nctioned before this could be attained. Harris contended that he needed complete
ntrol in order to carry out his experiments, and his plan obviously involved the
ooting of wildlife. Dr Warren was reasonably philosophical, stating that he was "far
ɔm happy about the whole matter," but conceding that there might be too many
ildebeest at Umfolozi. He could not bring himself to believe, however, that "the
autiful zebras are anything like as attractive to the tsetse as the Wildebeesten," and
gued that they should be allowed to escape.[98] Vaughan-Kirby, the retired Game
ɔnservator, regarded "Fly" Harris as a traitor to the cause. The whole history of the
etse fly research program he now saw as one of "broken faith, deceit, falsehood, dirty
pionage, utter lack of organization and of wanton and indiscriminate butchery."[99]

From the point of view of the Ntambanana farmers, the resumption of Harris's
search represented their only hope for survival. By late 1928, the long-awaited
npangeni-Nkwaleni railway line was under construction, and sugar cane was being
anted wherever possible on the southern farms. The northernmost lots were too
ɔlated to benefit from this development, and farmers there had little choice but to
ntinue producing cotton.[100] Oscar Curry, president of the NFA and the lessee of a
rthern farm, complained bitterly to Clarkson, the chairman of the Game Advisory
ɔmmittee, that the needs of the settlers had, in the past, always been set aside in favor
preserving game.[101] Now, if the campaign failed and the area were to be entrenched
a game reserve, the settlers would be worse off than ever. Their representative at the

crucial Game Advisory Committee meeting in October 1929 felt that they should wa
and see whether or not Harris's plan was successful before agreeing to t
re-establishment of the reserve.[102] Interestingly, it was Nicholls — having maintaine
an interest in the Ntambanana settlement since his intervention in 1917 had "rescu
[it] from the wilderness" — who brokered a compromise.[103] Nicholls suggested th
the reserve might be reproclaimed on a temporary basis for the duration of Harri:
campaign. The motion was passed by seven votes to four.[104] Although Nicho
probably did not realize it at the time, this arrangement was not in the long-ter
interest of the Ntambanana settlers. As the latter had feared, Harris's research peri
expired with little progress having been made towards solving the problem of nagar
and the game reserve retained its protected status.[105]

Conclusion

Propelled by the imperatives of white settlement policy into a context unsuited for th
type of farming activity in which they intended to engage, the Ntambanana settle
found themselves caught in a web of interconnecting social and ecological forces. Th
disease nagana both provided the motive power behind conflict and acted as
spotlight to illuminate hidden tensions within the white "ruling class" as well
within the state. This chapter has explored the origins and emerging shape of the
conflicts as they were played out, on the ground, at Ntambanana. As recent settle
attempting to gain a firm foothold on the land, the Ntambanana farmers foui
themselves plunged into conflict with a more established stratum of white society
that is, an emergent local aristocracy, or status group, determined to preserve
privileged access to game. At an administrative level, this group was supported by
provincial authority eager to demonstrate its independence from central governmer
Attempts on the part of the latter (in the form of the Department of Lands and th
Department of Agriculture) to intervene in support of its struggling settlers we
consistently undermined by the actions of provincial government. The Ntambana
farmer was caught between these contending giants, and not even the support
George Heaton Nicholls and a united "Zululand settler" front could alleviate h
plight. Trapped on his 1 200-acre farm, the settler was denied access to the mobili
that might have enabled him to escape the effects of nagana. Well might he compla
that, when any weight was placed on them, the ropes thrown to save him inevitab
turned out to be "ropes of sand."

15

"The Garden of Eden": Sharecropping on the Shire Highlands Estates, 1920–1945

Wiseman Chirwa[1]

1932, the Manager of the British Central Africa Company described Nyasaland as the Garden of Eden for natives." He noted that white planters were unable to offer ork to their tenants and therefore could not collect any rent. All they could do was courage their tenants to grow marketable crops. "The position of the landlord," he ncluded, "is rather hard."[2] By the 1930s, almost all the tobacco and cotton estates in e Shire Highlands districts of Blantyre, Chiradzulu, Cholo (now Thyolo), Mlanje ow Mulanje), and Zomba in southern Nyasaland were in dire financial straits. This ather hard" position originated in the 1920s when the cotton industry failed and bacco remained an uncertain alternative. Unable to manage this crisis, and lnerable to adverse local environmental conditions and international price fluctua-ons, the white planters entered the Great Depression in a weakened state.

This chapter argues that the coercive capacity of the cotton and tobacco economy the Shire Highlands was limited by the financial position of the planters. Their very rvival depended directly on their ability to maximize output through sharecrop-ng arrangements with African tenants. By the 1930s, almost all the tobacco and tton estates in the Shire Highlands relied on sharecropping. As Tim Keegan has gued elsewhere, "What made the sharecropping system work despite the implicit nflicts in it was the peasants' own vigorous productive enterprise rather than ercion."[3] On most Shire Highlands tobacco estates, sharecropping became particu-ly important in the inter-war period. As the planters struggled to survive, there was

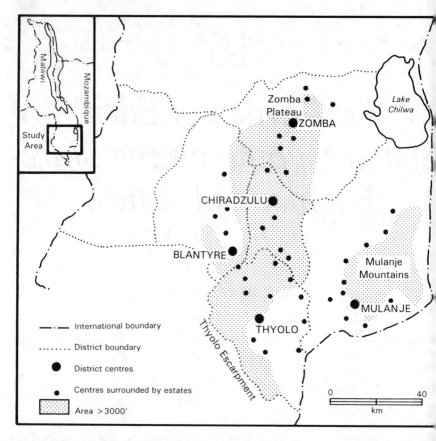

Figure 15.1   The Shire Highlands, Nyasaland

a marked shift from a system of labor tenancy called *thangata* (or reciprocal assistanc
to a hybrid system of sharecropping and wage labor (still known by the sam
name).[4]

Crises in the Cotton and Tobacco Industry

The flow of wage labor to the Shire Highlands estates always depended on th
seasonal demands of peasant household production. Labor was plentiful during th
dry season (March to November) and scarce during the wet season (December
February) when the planters needed it most. The planters therefore came to rely
thangata tenants for the major part of their labor supply. *Thangata* was widely used
the cotton and tobacco estates until the early 1920s, though the system was not actual
invented by white settlers.

Thangata was a traditional system for mobilizing communal labor for tasks such clearing new gardens, harvesting, and constructing huts.[5] Because of the difficulties ey had in attracting wage labor, white landlords emulated it and transformed it into system of labor tenancy. In exchange for a piece of land (officially eight acres) and cess to building materials and water resources, the male head of every African mily on an estate was required to work for one month a year in lieu of rent (plus an ditional month in lieu of hut tax). As Leroy Vail and Landeg White have argued, for e planters the real attractions of the system lay in its hidden advantages. The formal, verbal *thangata* agreement was not subject to government approval.[6] A nonth's labour" could therefore be stretched to six or eight weeks simply by thholding a signature from the tax certificate.

Even at its peak in the first two decades of the twentieth century, *thangata* was far m being an inflexible and relentless system. In the dry season, when there was little ork to be done in their own gardens, tenants were more than willing to work for ages on the estate or with other employers.[7] At other times, according to the white anters, the work behavior of tenants was erratic and they tended to spend more time orking their own gardens. "It was always difficult," observed the Secretary of the yasaland Chamber of Agriculture and Commerce in 1920, "to get this class of labour work regularly."[8] If planters tried to use excessive force, tenants simply withdrew m the estates.[9] Yet *thangata* had its attractions for the landlords. The system ovided a variety of forms of cheap casual labor, including that of women and ildren. The landlord could use the residents of the estate as both labor tenants and age workers, maximizing the use of the one resource that was plentiful — land. By ying wages to their tenants during periods of peak demand, landlords tried to scourage them from moving to other employers.

The *thangata* system provided tenants with no security of tenure and was open to use and random (rather than systematic) coercion and violence. Africans hated the stem. Between 1913 and 1914, the government attempted to change it through the ative Tenants (Agreement) Ordinance, 1914. It provided for cash rents by written reement and disallowed compulsory labor service in lieu of rent for Africans sident on private estates. Under the proposed ordinance, Africans had the option, stead of paying a cash rent, to work for the landlord for a period and at a wage ecified in a formal agreement executed before a District Resident (later District ommissioner). Landlords, through the Chamber of Agriculture and Commerce, pposed the bill. With the outbreak of World War I, the government ". . . decided not proceed with so contentious a measure, opposed as it would certainly have been by e nominated members of the [legislative] council,"[10] who were predominantly ndowners.

In 1915, John Chilembwe, an American-trained priest, led an uprising against *angata* and other settler practices in Chiradzulu district.[11] Two years later, the overnment — through the Native Rents (Private Estates) Ordinance — made a cond attempt to abolish labor service in lieu of rent except where such service was at he option of the tenant."[12] The ordinance empowered landlords to charge rent within nits prescribed by the Governor-in-Council. Every tenant would be entitled to a site, ilding materials and sufficient cultivable land to provide for "the sustenance of imself and his family."[13] Landlords also had to give six months' notice of eviction. If nants refused to move or continued to prevaricate after the expiry of the notice, they uld be summarily removed by the District Resident.

Table 15.1: European Agriculture: Cotton Production

	ACREAGE			PRODUCTION (Tons)		
Year	Protectorate	Shire Highlands	As %	Protectorate	Shire Highlands	As
1917	28 372					
1918	18 141					
1922	26 545					
1923	20 948	7 955	38	497	179	3
1924	26 120	11 551	44	771	224	2
1925	17 541	3 572	20	506	39	
1926	13 358	3 416	26	230	66	2
1927	2 545	136	5	82	4	
1928	1 046	51	5	52	2	
1929	1 219	290	24	37	12	3
1930	761	236	31	32	10	3
1931	225	87	39	8	2	2
1933	246	115	47	34	18	5
1934	1 501	129	9	123	18	1
1935	2 067	1 197	58	101	59	5
1936	1 997	567	28	96	17	1

Notes: (i) The protectorate figures are for European planters only. They do not inclur
the African contribution. (ii) The percentages are contributions of Shire Highlanr
planters to the protectorate figures.

Sources: Nyasaland Government, Annual Reports of the Department of Agricultu
(Zomba: Government Printer, 1917–1936); PRO C.O.626/1 – C.O.626/7 Annual Reports
the Department of Agriculture, 1909–1930.

After debating the measure "clause by clause," the planters rejected all th
provisions aimed at abolishing labor tenancy and delayed the implementation of
watered-down version of the ordinance for over a year.[14] They argued that rer
tenancy, though desirable in the eyes of the government, was unsuited to condition
on the estates: "What the landlords want is not rent but work."[15] At the time, th
problems of obtaining labor were compounded by the Chilembwe Rising and th
recruiting of soldiers and carriers for the war.[16] For the planters, the *thangata* system
despite its deficiencies, was the best available option. By 1920, it was clear that th
ordinance had failed to achieve its objective. Most Africans on private estates were str
thangata tenants.[17]

The end of the war marked the beginning of a long period of economic hardshir
for the Shire Highlands settlers. The problems got worse when cotton failed in th
mid-1920s and the acreage under cotton declined dramatically (see table 15.1). Unt
then, cotton had been the country's main export crop. From the mid-1920s to the end c
the Great Depression, the Nyasaland planters produced less than a hundred tons c
cotton a year. The fluctuations and declining acreage and production figures in the lar
1920s and early 1930s indicate that the industry was under serious stress. Despite ar
increase in the area under cotton in the mid-1930s, production remained feeble anr
unviable.

Part of the reason was the unfavorable economic environment. It was simply not
good time to be growing cotton. Railway rates and the cost of agricultural inpur

ared with post-World War I inflation. Simultaneously, cotton prices plummeted on ernational markets. Intense competition from larger cotton producers, such as ypt, exacerbated the woes of the Nyasaland planters.[18]

Locally, the environmental constraints on cotton production in the Shire ghlands proved critical. The Highlands have very unpredictable weather condi- ns. Early rains, usually between mid-October and early November, may be lowed by periods of drought between December and January, and then heavy rains tween February and March. Late rains, usually between late November and the end December, may be followed by a cold spell or a period of drought between January d February. These erratic conditions create a favorable milieu for the spread of cterial and fungoid disease and pests.

The Shire Highlands cotton industry suffered from bacterial bright, red boll- orm, *Diparapsis castanea* and pests. Ants, aphids, and mice multiplied and spread at a eat rate during drought periods, and destroyed large numbers of young cotton ants. Red bollworm and fungoid disease spread equally rapidly at times of high midity during dry spells following heavy rains. Between them, erratic weather, sease, and pests caused "the most devastating damage" to the cotton industry.[19] ese factors were compounded by the planters' own ignorance. They prepared their lds too late, or in marginal areas, or in areas already infested by disease or pests. The partment of Agriculture's extension advice was usually ignored. Implementation any of the recommendations meant additional expense and greater labor quirements. These were impossible demands for planters in a constant state of inancial crisis."

In contrast to the beleaguered settlers, Africans rapidly expanded their produc- n of cotton in the 1920s, thanks to their mastery of local environmental conditions d the buying monopoly granted to the British Cotton Growers' Association (BCGA). e BCGA, created in 1902 to promote cotton production in the British empire and duce dependence on American supplies, became involved in Nyasaland as early as 05.[20] Together with the Department of Agriculture, the association promoted easant production of the crop in the Lower Shire, the Shire Highlands, the lakeshore ain, and the North Nyasa district. In 1923, the BCGA obtained a monopoly to rchase all African-grown cotton. The association provided African producers with guaranteed market and a minimum price, though the minimum was often all they ceived. By the mid-1920s, African production of cotton was showing "a very marked crease."[21] In 1925, Africans produced 63 per cent of the country's cotton. By 1929, the gure had risen to over 90 per cent. Throughout the 1930s, African growers ntributed more than 95 per cent of total cotton production. With the exception of the halombe Plain in Mlanje district, however, the main areas of African cotton roduction were not in the Shire Highlands (the subject of this chapter) but in the ower and Upper Shire Valley, the lakeshore belt of the Central Province and the orth Nyasa district.

Tobacco proved to be the saving of many white planters in Nyasaland. In 1919, as art of its post-war program for economic recovery, Britain gave preference to its lonies for its tobacco supplies. The struggling Shire Highlands planters quickly vitched from cotton to tobacco. By 1923, tobacco was the country's "premier uropean crop."[22] Department of Agriculture figures indicate a relatively healthy bacco economy for European planters in the 1920s (see table 15.2). Before this osition could be reached, the Shire Highlands planters had to confront a number of ifficulties.

Table 15.2: European Agriculture: Tobacco Production

	ACREAGE			PRODUCTION (Tons)		
Year	Protectorate	Shire Highlands	As %	Protectorate	Shire Highlands	As
1922	18 554					
1923	17 308	17 308	87	1 749	1 499	8
1924	20 591	16 760	81	3 264	2 633	8
1925	22 415	17 169	77	2 393	1 805	7
1926	22 908	18 346	80	2 878	2 193	7
1927	22 002	18 880	76	4 682	3 576	7
1928	22 475	16 365	73	4 068	2 996	7
1929	19 269	13 577	70	2 289	1 461	6
1930	17 481	12 107	69	2 906	1 951	6
1931	13 482	8 406	62	1 861	1 096	5
1933	7 862	4 507	57	1 557	909	5
1934	8 350	4 295	51	1 739	938	5
1935	6 144	3 609	59	943	524	5
1936	7 349	4 369	59	1 189	702	5

Notes: (i) The protectorate figures are totals for European estates only. (ii) The percentages are proportions of the Shire Highlands figures to the protectorate figures.

Source: Nyasaland Protectorate, Annual Reports of the Department of Agricultu (Zomba: Government Printer, 1922–1936).

As with cotton, the most serious problems were unpredictable weather cond tions and price fluctuations on the international market. In 1926, the Director Agriculture accurately summarized the importance of climatic factors when he note that "experience has shown . . . that the weather of the season is the dominant fact in determining the yield per acre. The task of fighting unfavourable climat conditions is not a congenial one and may prove costly and discouraging."[23] Bacteri and fungoid diseases were prevalent in most tobacco fields as a result of weath conditions. Erratic rains in some districts, or parts of the same district, produce highly variable yields. Because of cold spells and foggy weather between late Januar and early March, tobacco often ripened with green patches, and had to be destroye The Shire Highlands planters themselves were generally quite inexperienced i tobacco culture. They often prepared their fields in marginal areas and relied c imported seed that was not disease resistant. They employed poor methods of toppin and loaded their harvest in barns with insufficient space for curing, procedures th resulted in large amounts of low quality leaf.[24]

Rising freight charges and fluctuating prices on the international market als adversely affected the Shire Highlands tobacco industry. In the early 1920s, it cost 5 plus 2d. in export tax to ship one pound (lb) of tobacco from Blantyre to London vi Portuguese East Africa. The Nyasaland Chamber of Agriculture and Commerc complained that the tax was "a heavy additional loss" given that "large stocks" c tobacco remained unsold owing to low quality and poor prices.[25] On the Londo market, top-grade fine bright tobacco sold at 1s. 4d. per lb, mottled leaf at 10d., an scrap at 3d. The Shire Highlands planters exported large quantities of mottled an scrap leaf because of their poor methods of topping and curing. Much of their tobacc as thus sold at low prices. The flat export tax greatly reduced any economic returns the planters.[26]

Early in 1925, the imperial preference was raised from 1s. 4d. to 2s. per lb. Though e planters received good prices for their tobacco, excessive rain, lack of adequate unshine, and bacterial and fungoid diseases decimated the crop in 1925 and 1926. ood prices and favorable weather meant that tobacco production in 1927 was "the ghest on record."[27] Simultaneously, the Director of Agriculture warned that the lonial production of bright tobacco was outstripping demand. It was an accurate recast. In 1928, tobacco prices slumped, and much of the bright exported in 1927 was nsold.[28] In 1929, the planters attempted to grow a higher yielding (dark) tobacco, but favorable weather conditions and "much disease" produced a poor harvest and a op "indifferent in quality as well as small in bulk."[29] Few planters were able to iprove their already critical financial state.

African Production on Crown Lands and Private Estates

le mixed performance of the local tobacco industry in the 1920s forced officials to think their attitudes towards settler agriculture and the status of Africans on private tates. Between 1925 and 1928 official policy towards African tobacco production on own land and private estates underwent a major shift. "Nyasaland is not a white an's country, and never will be," argued the Director of Agriculture, "the native is e producer of the future."[30] The local Governor and some officials at the Colonial ffice concurred.[31] In areas suitable for commercial cropping, the government omised "every assistance" to African producers. Elsewhere, Africans would be icouraged to work on European estates. Where neither course was possible, neither ould be enforced.[32]

African tobacco production expanded rapidly from the mid-1920s (see table 15.3). fricans contributed 33 per cent to the total tobacco export in 1925, 41 per cent in 1926 id 47 per cent in 1927. The figure rose to over 50 per cent in the 1930s. Prior to the id-1920s, most African-grown tobacco came from the Shire Highlands and the South yasa district. The opening up of the Central Province to African tobacco production ter 1920 accounted for the rapid increase over the decade.[33] Up until 1927, however, ie Shire Highlands producers still made the largest contribution. European planters und it impossible to compete with the African industry. Some of them capitalized on as middlemen, encouraging Africans on crown land to produce more tobacco so that iey themselves could buy cheaply and sell at a profit. They employed African buyers id "spread incessant propaganda . . . to induce the natives to leave their work on uropean estates and take up village tobacco cultivation."[34]

An important factor in the expansion of African tobacco production was the owers' mastery of dark-fired tobacco, which grew well even in marginal areas. frican producers were particularly good at cultivating this "traditional" crop. hrough diseases, pests and erratic weather, the African growers avoided potential ises by resorting to mass production. The demand for dark-fired also remained onstant when prices for bright tobacco went into decline. Mass production meant leaper prices for local buyers. African producers on crown land in the Shire ighlands, especially those with adequate land and family labor, could earn around 0–12 a year. Even producers with small amounts of land had a profit margin of

Table 15.3: Tobacco Purchased from Africans

Year	Protectorate (Tons)	Shire Highlands (Tons)	As
1923	100 approx.	100	1(
1924	525	500	(
1925	1 177	955	(
1926	2 023	952	∠
1927	3 484	1 817	(
1928	2 414	1 052	∠
1929	3 881	1 110	2
1930	4 233	1 108	2
1931	3 519	714	2
1933	4 077	1 315	3
1934	5 054	2 121	∠
1935	4 594	1 061	2
1936	6 170	1 142	2

Notes: (i) The figures in this table are for the amounts of tobacco purchased from Afric(producers. They do not represent the total amounts produced by the Africans. (ii) Th figures include the tobacco purchased both on crown land and on private estate (iii) The pattern suggests a recording error in the 1931 figures.

Sources: Nyasaland Protectorate, *Annual Reports of the Department of Agricultu* (Zomba: Government Printer, 1923–1936); MNA NSZ4/1/1 and NSZ4/1/5 Zomba Distri Annual Reports, 1934–1940; NSD2/1/3 and NSD2/1/4 Chiradzulu District Annual Repor 1933–1940; NSB7/1/2 and NSB7/1/4 Blantyre District Annual Reports, 1934–1939.

between £1 6s. and £4 3s. Growers with access to large amounts of land, adequa family labor, markets, agricultural inputs and extension facilities benefited partic larly from the new opportunities.

The colonial administration's main concern was the quality of the tobac produced by Africans on crown land. In 1926, it established the Native Tobacco Boa (NTB) to assist and supervise producers and purchase their tobacco. The boa concentrated its activities in the Central Province, the center of crown land tobac production. Its policies and (mal)practices in the region have been document elsewhere.[35] In the Shire Highlands, the NTB had minimal influence before t mid-1930s when it expanded its staff in the region. Even then, its impact was limit since one supervisor was responsible for thousands of producers.

The poor performance of the white estates, coupled with the expansion in Afric tobacco production, led to a major change in the legal status of Africans on priva estates in the late 1920s. Previously, landlords had wanted work not rent. Now, th needed some form of rent in order to survive — either cash or a portion of t commercial crop produced by African residents. The shift from labor tenancy sharecropping on the majority of the tobacco estates in the Shire Highlands therefo occurred quite rapidly. Though sharecropping was certainly known in the regio before the 1920s, it now became widespread.

The new legal framework for the operation of the sharecropping system w contained in the Natives on Private Estates Ordinance of 1928. The ordinan provided for three types of African occupancy of private estates. The first catego was "natives under special agreement" — those who had entered into a writt ontract to work for a period of no more than six months in any one year. The second as "exempted natives" — domestic servants or seasonal immigrant workers who ved in huts erected solely for the use of temporary labor. The third was "resident atives" — those who lived permanently on the estates.

Under the ordinance, "resident natives" had to be offered work at the usual market rate for three months between October and February, and for two working months between March and September. Alternatively, they could be given facilities to row cash crops, the sale of which would entitle them to a partial or complete rebate of their rent. The amount of rent and the rebate were to be fixed by a District Rent Board and approved by the Governor every year. If the landlord neither offered work nor allowed the resident tenant to grow and sell crops, he lost all claim to rent. No landlord could order a resident tenant to quit his estate without applying to the District Commissioner for a six months' notice. The DC also had the power summarily to eject any tenant who was found guilty of "misconduct" or who failed to pay rent due after being given "adequate notice." The government was obliged to find room on crown and for evicted tenants.

The 1928 ordinance gave Africans enough room to change their status from time to time depending on the economic conditions prevailing on the private estates. They could choose to be "resident natives," wage laborers under a written contract, or exempted residents" — or a combination of the first two. These options meant that their own vigorous productive enterprise would be the factor determining residence on the estate. As for the landlords, the ordinance theoretically provided them with the opportunity to control the numbers of Africans occupying their estates, and both the production and the marketing of cash crops produced by their tenants.

Verbal sharecropping agreements between landlords and tenants were not subject to any official verification or approval. Commonly, in the first year tenants received rations — or money in lieu thereof — and the use of a plot of land to provide or food production in future years. They also received an advance of tools and tax money. The landlords instructed and supervised the planting of the crop. In return, they had first refusal on a tenant's crop at the prevailing market price. The tenants were not obliged to sell the whole of their crop to the landlord, and could sell some or all of it to other buyers. In this case, the landlords received part of the sales based on the cost of the facilities they had given the tenants and the amount of rent required from them. There was no standard formula; everything was by agreement. Though sharecropping agreements worked to the disadvantage of the weaker party, the tenants, they were not without loopholes. In particular, if dissatisfied with the landlord's price, a tenant could turn to the private buyers, among whom competition was intense.[36]

The sharecropping system had advantages for both parties. In normal circumstances, a tenant with access to adequate amounts of land and family labor could earn anywhere between £4 and £7 a year in the late 1920s, twice the annual wage of an ordinary plantation laborer.[37] Even those with poorer resources and inadequate facilities could earn marginally more than the wage worker. Tenants commonly grew their tobacco on the landlord's land, leaving the family plot for food crops or a second cash crop. Tenants from crown land could have access to land in two localities at the same time: in the village and on the private estate. Not only did this alleviate pressure on crown land, but it also enabled the tenant to move in and out of the estate depending on economic opportunities. Since the landlord provided the input, the

Table 15.4: African Registered Tobacco Growers

Year	Central Province		Southern Province	
	Crown Land	Private Estates	Crown Land	Private Estates
1927/28	20 718	545	11 208	2 290
1928/29	27 505	771	13 579	5 723
1929/30	31 114	1 120	11 031	5 154
1930/31	32 153	2 650	10 708	6 392
1932/33	40 088	not available	6 524	not available
1933/34	38 522	" "	8 783	" "
1934/35	29 227	" "	6 729	" "
1935/36	43 177	" "	10 419	" "

Notes: (i) The registration of growers began in 1926 with the establishment of the Nativ Tobacco Board. (ii) The Southern Province figures included Upper Shire and Sout Nyasa though the Shire Highlands districts had the highest numbers of growers. (iii) Thes figures would have been more useful if they had included the acreage by Africa growers.

Source: Nyasaland Protectorate, Annual Reports of the Department of Agricultur (Zomba: Government Printer, 1927–1936).

tenant did not have to worry about raising initial capital. The system also guaranteed ready market for the crop produced. As for the landlord, the system reduce production costs while maximizing the use of his land — the only abundant resource It also had some hidden advantages that permitted him to take advantage of h tenants. The cost of the inputs that the landlord provided could be inflated an recovered from the tenant at the end of the season. The tenant family was also a sourc of cheap casual labor. Since landlords had first refusal to purchase the tenants' crop the end of the year, they could determine the price at which the crop was to be bough and could offer lower than the prevailing market price. Often this was done b purchasing the tenant's crop in advance, before official markets opened. It was risk and landlords could easily lose if the market price turned out to be lower than th payment advanced. They minimized their risk by setting prepayments low, at th likely market floor, based on the previous season's prices.

The sharecropping system assumed special importance with the coming of th Great Depression. The prices for cotton and tobacco continued to fall, resulting i "much agricultural development being held up."[38] The hardships were compounde by erratic weather conditions between 1930 and 1936. There were also widesprea reports of wireworm, cutworm, yellow stem grub, aphids and ants, mosaic an frenching (leaf curl), angular leaf spot, frog-eye and drought spotting. Between 193 and 1937 the government gave advances to the planters but to little avail.[39] Many of th colony's tobacco and cotton planters closed down, the number falling sharply fro 229 in 1928 to 82 in 1935.[40] The "small planters" (a term used, rather ironically, to ref to those with under five thousand acres of land) were worst affected. Those wh remained on the land were reduced to playing the role of middlemen — buyin grading, ginning, transporting and ultimately shipping African produce.[41] Dire production of tobacco by white farmers on the majority of the Shire Highlands estat came to a standstill.

Table 15.5: Tobacco Production on Crown Land and on Private Estates (Shire Highlands)

	Crown Land		Private Estates	
	Registered Growers	Production (Tons)	Registered Growers	Production (Tons)
Zomba				
1934	663	122	4 897	349
1935	1 798	57	5 458	124
1936	1 693	97	6 161	144
1937	1 433	96	5 399	264
1938	810	76	4 019	255
1939	584	64	4 362	252
Chiradzulu				
1934	3 398	565	2 465	226
1935	3 016	170	2 311	273
1936	3 047	357	2 494	323
1937	4 295	406	2 320	186
1938	4 132	299	2 009	133
1939	1 693	112	2 080	181
Blantyre				
1935	334	137	548	54
1936	669	164	466	53
1937	814	32	550	44
1938	441	unavailable	553	unavailable
1939	123	" "	518	" "
Mlanje				
1934	2 355	568	431	15
1935	3 753	582	542	unavailable
1936	4 943	543	401	" "

Sources: MNA NSZ4/1/4 and NSZ4/1/5 Zomba District Annual Reports; NSD2/1/3 and NSD2/1/4 Chiradzulu District Annual Reports; NSB7/1/2 and NSB7/1/4 Blantyre District Annual Reports; NSM3/1/5 Mlanje District Annual Reports.

Sharecropping During and After the Depression

The parlous state of the settler tobacco industry accelerated the changeover to sharecropping in the Shire Highlands in the 1930s. By the middle of the decade there were over fifty thousand African tobacco producers in the country, ten thousand on the Highlands' crown lands and private estates (see tables 15.4 and 15.5). Not every tenant was a registered tobacco grower, though the majority grew the crop to fulfill their rent obligations. A tenant could also grow more than one crop and get proportionate rent rebates from each of them. When combined, the rebates amounted to the full rent. The amount required for rent purposes between 1928 and 1938 was fixed by the District Rent Boards, and varied from 120 to 200 lbs of tobacco, 700 to

1 680 lbs of maize, 480 to 600 lbs of seed cotton, and 400 to 480 lbs of beans. These figures were calculated as equivalents of cash rent at the current prices. The landlord would fix a certain amount of cash rent, not exceeding that fixed by the District Rent Board, and then collect in produce the equivalent amount.

Living conditions for tenants varied from one estate to another. The rent demanded also differed, as did the manner in which the rent obligations were fulfilled. The size of the estate was generally a good indicator of living conditions. The larger estate-owners usually provided their tenants with facilities to grow cash crops and often demanded lower rents. The more land they had, the larger the number of tenants they could attract. In Chiradzulu district, for example, tenants on the A. L. Bruce Trust (ALBT) estates, (the largest landowner and employer of tenant labour in the district) and the British Central Africa estates were given facilities to grow tobacco. To fulfill their rent obligation tenants had to provide annually twelve shillings worth of tobacco or other crops at the current local market price. On another large farm, the Blantyre and East Africa estates, tenants paid ten shillings annual rent or its equivalent in tobacco. On the smaller A. H. Sabbatini estates, they had to pay £ or its equivalent.

On all of these estates, tenants could fulfill their rent obligations by producing tobacco and other crops. In contrast, no cash rent or crops of equivalent value were demanded from tenants on the estates of Humphrey Brothers, one of the smaller landowners in the district. These tenants were on "special agreements," under which they worked for wages for a certain number of months in a year. On many of the smaller estates, rent was seldom collected, nor was the full quota of work generally demanded.[42] Attempts to enforce rent requirements resulted in tenants quitting the estates.

By the 1930s, rent was being collected in the form of cash crops on almost all the large company estates. During, and shortly after, the depression, some of the large landlords reduced their rent requirements to between two and six shillings.[43] Many estates in the Shire Highlands were "in a state of abandonment" or "on care and maintenance basis" and it became policy "to encourage the settlement of progressive natives on [the] land."[44] The manager of the ALBT Magomero estate even sent out messages to chiefs in Zomba and Chiradzulu to send in more tenants. His company had some sixty square miles of land east of Zomba, which was unsettled owing to lack of water in the dry season. He requested that the government lend him the water-boring apparatus so that he could provide water to the area, settle some two thousand families, and supervise and buy their crops.

The major obstacles to tenant tobacco production on the Shire Highlands estates were a lack of adequate supervision and insufficient supplies of firewood for curing. A single European supervisor, usually with no experience of African farming systems and tobacco production, would be responsible for thousands of tenants. Under these conditions, tenants produced poor-quality leaf that was sold at low prices. The monetary returns to the producers varied according to type of landholding, access to markets and inputs, quality of the crop (depending on the availability of firewood) and individual or family effort. In the post-depression period, some tenants earned as little as 9d. for their tobacco while others earned as much as £34 a year. The majority earned anywhere between £1 5s. and £20. Given that the tenants grew other crops as well, which they could sell privately, their annual earnings were probably higher than these figures suggest.

Smaller landlords allowed Africans resident on neighboring crown land to grow bacco on the estates on condition that the crop was sold to them. This practice increased the mobility of Africans who thus enjoyed greater choice and some variety in the conditions of tenancy. The main attraction for crown land residents was the better-quality land on the private estates. In addition, they could raise crops on two or more plots in one season — food crops on crown land and cash crops on private estates, or both food and cash crops in both places. Crown land residents thus tended to occupy the estates on a seasonal basis.

The major buyers of tobacco produced by the Africans on crown land were small landowners and Indian traders, who often employed African agents to act on their behalf. Competition was intense and tended to force up the prices. Buyers offered advances to the growers before the crop was harvested, a practice that produced considerable conflict among them and between them and the growers. Growers often took advances from more than one buyer or crossed district boundaries in search of better markets. The bulk of the tobacco on the private estates was bought by the landowners, though the tenants were not forbidden to sell it to outsiders. Some tenants and independent growers went to where they could get a good price for their crop, selling tobacco "on a large scale" to buyers outside the estates.[45] Recourse to such buyers caused "bad feeling" between landlords and tenants, particularly when the tenants sold off their tobacco without meeting their rent obligations. If evicted, they encroached on other estates where "they pleaded that they were not cultivating gardens for themselves but were assisting their aged or female relatives in the cultivation of their fields." This claim was "a very ingenious device to escape prosecution as unauthorized settlers, and one that presented a very difficult problem" for the administration.[46]

African ingenuity did not stop there. Large amounts of tobacco grown on crown land found its way to the sheds of tenant producers on the private estates, and equally large quantities produced on the private estates ended up in the receiving sheds of the NTB on crown land. In this way, the producers were able to sell their tobacco to whoever gave the better price. Tobacco from unregistered growers also entered the market through these channels. These growers simply used the registration certificates of their "relatives." Between 1934 and 1935, the government attempted to restrict production on crown land "in order to maintain high quality in the leaf."[47] In Mlanje district in the following two years, African producers evaded the restriction by applying to an estate owner to grow on his land. When the control was lifted in 1938, they moved back to their crown land gardens.[48]

Unfortunately, 1938 was not a good year for the crown land producers in the Shire Highlands. Until then, they could sell where they liked. They were free to bargain, moving from one buying station to the other until they found a buyer whose prices and methods appealed to them. Their tobacco was restricted to three grades, according to the length of the leaves, and some buyers were keen to purchase consignments of poorly graded leaf. In 1938, however, tobacco auctions started and the NTB established a monopoly. The board immediately reduced the number of buying stations and introduced a new grading system with seven grades and standard prices for each grade.

There was very little demand for the top grades at the auction floors, because buyers got better returns from the cheaper grades, which gave low monetary returns to the producers. Tobacco bought from African growers at 1,5d. and 2d. doubled in value on the auction floors. Crown land producers were now forced to sell their higher-grade tobacco at low prices. With the NTB as the only authorized buyer African growers were unable to avoid the "seven-grades" system and its standard prices. They could no longer bargain for themselves or dispose of their crop how and where they liked. What made the new system even more difficult was that each grade was sold separately on different occasions or days. A grower with more than one grade would thus have to make several trips to the NTB buying station. By 1939, many growers had decided that the game was no longer worth the candle. They withdrew their tobacco from the buying stations and abandoned production. Others moved onto private estates where they were guaranteed facilities and an alternative market for their crop. When board prices improved, as in 1940 and 1941, there was an increase in the numbers of registered growers on crown land.[49]

African production on the private estates was minimally affected by the board's malpractice since the NTB's purchasing system did not stop estate owners from continuing to buy their tenants' crop. Ever anxious to increase the number of growers on their land, some landowners encouraged immigrants from Mozambique to encroach on their property.[50] The immigrant tenants often fulfilled their rent and tax obligations for a year or two, and then purposely defaulted in subsequent years, inviting and expecting eviction. When this occurred, they moved on to crown land and declared themselves "Nyasaland natives" by simply producing the last tax receipt as proof.

By the early 1940s, defaulting or refusing to pay rent was commonplace among Africans on the private estates. In 1939/40, for example, many tenants on the British Central Africa Company's estates in Blantyre district did not honor their rent obligations. When the company applied to the government for the eviction of 1 111 tenants, only 359 "ne'er-do-wells" were served with notices. The company then changed its mind and offered them work as "special agreement" tenants. This reversal of policy did not solve the problem. In the following year, the company offered facilities to its tenants to grow crops or work for wages, but very few availed themselves of the opportunity. The estate manager issued eviction warnings "to prevent the rot [from] spreading." In the end, some of the tenants left the land of their own accord while others grew tobacco.[51] The Blantyre and East Africa Company had a similar experience in Zomba. In 1941, it had more than one thousand rent defaulters on its estate. Two years later, the company brought twenty-five tenants to court "to claim rent rather than evict them."[52]

Everywhere on the Shire Highlands estates, eviction was a last resort, used only when all else had failed. Commonly, the landlord would first threaten recalcitrant tenants, and then offer them work or facilities to grow cash crops. If these methods failed, he applied to the District Commissioner to serve eviction notices, but still kept the work and cash-crop options open. Usually the DC would turn down or delay the first application with a recommendation that the landlord look into other options. After they, too, had failed, the DC would order the eviction of the tenants. For their part, African tenants were able to stave off eviction by snaring the landlords and government officials in lengthy correspondence on its desirability. Meanwhile they prepared and planted their gardens and began negotiating for a grace period to harvest their crops.[53] They could also delay eviction while looking for an another place to settle. Once located, they quit the estate without giving notice. Alternatively, while delaying eviction, they availed themselves of the opportunity to work for wages or grow cash crops.

Chiefs and individuals who were well informed about the laws governing the occupation of land in the country did not hesitate to challenge the powers of the landlords, arguing their cases with government officials until a compromise solution was reached.[54] Some of these cases dragged on for months. In the interim, the government advised landlords to refrain from evictions and violence. The landlords themselves often only threatened eviction "as an attempt to obtain cash from [the] tenants" or to make them grow cash crops.[55]

The planters offered two explanations for not wanting to evict their tenants. The first was that they did not wish to embarrass the government because, according to the Natives on Private Estates Ordinance (1928), the government would have to find areas on crown land on which to settle the evicted Africans. Crown land itself was in short supply owing to population increase and the influx of the Mozambicans. This argument was more an excuse than a reason. Secondly, the landlords claimed that they had sympathy for those who failed to meet their tenancy obligations. This explanation, as well, was misleading. The truth was that the planters needed their tenants.

The outbreak of World War II, coupled with the fluctuations in tobacco prices, compounded the problems of settler agriculture in the country. As a result, by the end of the war, most of the Shire Highlands estates were owned in name only, and were effectively occupied by Africans.[56] Large numbers of leasehold estates had been abandoned or surrendered to the government, and had reverted to occupation by Africans.[57] In 1945, the government established a Land Commission to consider the position of Africans on all land other than crown land, and generally to advise on land policy.[58] In its final report, the commission recommended that freehold lands heavily occupied by Africans, amounting to not less than 545 800 acres, be compulsorily acquired by the government and transferred to the Africans resident on it. In addition, it recommended that the government should purchase "unworked estates" for African occupation. Throughout the 1950s, and right through to the end of colonial rule in 1964, the government continued to buy estates to resettle former tenants. Other estates, abandoned by the Europeans between the depression and World War II, simply reverted to the Africans resident on them.

Conclusion

For some time, scholars have tended to portray the settler economy of the Shire Highlands as a powerful force that relentlessly coerced Africans through *thangata*.[59] Little effort has been made to show its weaknesses.[60] The evidence presented in this paper shows that, contrary to the prevailing view, the settler economy was severely limited in its ability to employ coercive methods. The cotton and tobacco planters were very vulnerable to local environmental conditions and to crises in the international economy. Their ability to manage these challenges was minimal. Being in such a weak position, the white planters needed their tenants in order to survive. On the other hand, African tenants needed the landlords to provide them with access to avenues for accumulation, no matter how constrained these opportunities might have been.

Thus, despite the tensions, conflicts and exploitation involved in the landlord-tenant relationship, the two parties existed in a symbiotic state. The movement of Africans on and off the private estates during the period covered here demonstrates that they were not without bargaining power and choice. For a system that allowe people so much freedom of movement and choice about where to sell their produc *sharecropping* may sound like a misnomer. However, given that tenants depended o their landlords for access to land and inputs and had to pay some form of rent, the terr is appropriate. Their ingenuity, and resistance to eviction and violence, meant tha they were not simple victims of exploitation and coercion. They developed creativ and effective ways of accommodating the hardships brought about by the incorporation into the colonial economy.[61]

NOTES

Chapter 1
Introductiion

1. M. Tracy. 1982. *Agriculture in Western Europe: Challenge and Response, 1880–1980*. London; W. Cronon. 1991. *Nature's Metropolis: Chicago and the Great West*. New York: W.W. Norton; David Grigg. 1992. *The Transformation of Agriculture in the West*. Oxford: Basil Blackwell.

2. W.M. Macmillan. 1930. *Complex South Africa: An Economic Footnote to History*. London: Faber and Faber; Francis A. Wilson. 1971. "Farming, 1866–1966." In *Oxford History of South Africa*, vol. 2, *South Africa, 1870–1966*, ed. L.M. Thompson and M. Wilson. Oxford: Clarendon Press, 136–53; W. Beinart, P. Delius and S. Trapido, eds. 1986. *Putting a Plough to the Ground: Accumulation and Dispossession in Rural South Africa, 1850–1930*. Johannesburg: Ravan Press; T.J. Keegan. 1991. "The Making of the Rural Economy: From 1850 to the Present." In *Studies in the Economic History of Southern Africa*, vol. 2, ed. Z. Konczacki, J. Parpart and T. Shaw. London: Frank Cass, 36–63.

3. W. Keith Hancock. 1942. *Survey of British Commonwealth Affairs*, vol. 2, *Problems of Economic Policy, 1918–1939*. London: Oxford University Press; S.D. Neumark. 1967. *Economic Influences on the South African Frontier*. Stanford: Stanford University Press. On the post-emancipation transformation of agriculture in the Western Cape see: John Marincowitz. 1985. "Rural Production and Labour in the Western Cape, 1838 to 1888." Ph.D. thesis, University of London; Robert Ross, "The Origins of Capitalist Agriculture in the Cape Colony: A Survey." In Beinart, Delius and Trapido, *Putting a Plough to the Ground*, 56–100; Pamela Scully. 1992. "Liquor and Labor in the Western Cape." In *Liquor and Labor in Southern Africa*, ed. J. Crush and C. Ambler. Athens and Pietermaritzburg: Ohio University Press and University of Natal Press; and Nigel Worden and Clifton Crais, eds. 1994. *Breaking the Chains: Slavery and Its Legacy in the Nineteenth Century Cape Colony*. Johannesburg: Witwatersrand University Press.

4. Peter Richardson. 1986. "The Natal Sugar Industry in the Nineteenth Century." In Beinart, Delius and Trapido, *Putting a Plough to the Ground*, 129–75; Clifton Crais. 1992. *The Making of the Colonial Order: White Supremacy and Black Resistance in Pre-Industrial South Africa: The Eastern Cape, 1770–1865*. Johannesburg: Witwatersrand University Press. On the Rhodes farms, see C. Aucamp. 1992. "Rhodes Fruit Farms: A Small Beginning in the Paarl Valley, 1897–1910." *Contree* 3: 11–18.

5. T.J. Keegan. 1986. *Rural Transformations in Industrializing South Africa: The Southern Highveld to 1914*. Johannesburg: Ravan Press; Colin Murray. 1992. *Black Mountain: Land, Class and Power in the Eastern Orange Free State, 1880s–1980s*. Blue Ridge Summit Pa.: Smithsonian Institute Press; Jeremy Krikler. 1993. *The Agrarian Transvaal at the Turn of the Century: Revolution from Above, Revolution from Below*. Oxford: Clarendon Press.

6. The central point at issue in the recent debate between social historians and structur Marxists; see Beinart, Delius and Trapido, *Putting a Plough to the Ground*, 10–17; M. Morr 1976. "The Development of Capitalism in South African Agriculture: Class Struggles in t Countryside." *Economy and Society* 5: 292–343; M. Morris. 1988. "Social History and t Transition to Capitalism in the South African Countryside." *Review of African Politic Economy* 41: 60–72; T. J. Keegan. 1989. "Mike Morris and the Social Historians: A Respon and a Critique." *Africa Perspective* 1: 1–14; T. J. Keegan. 1989. "The Origins of Agrari Capitalism in South Africa: A Reply." *Journal of Southern African Studies* 15: 666–84; Mar Murray. 1989. "The Origins of Agrarian Capitalism in South Africa: A Critique of the 'Soci History' Perspective." *Journal of Southern African Studies* 15: 645–65; and Helen Bradfor 1990. "Highways, Byways and Culs-de-Sacs: The Transition to Agrarian Capitalism Revisionist South African History." *Radical History Review* 46/7: 59–88.

7. Shula Marks and Stan Trapido. 1979. "Lord Milner and the South African State." *Histo Workshop Journal* 8: 50–80; Tessa Marcus. 1989. *Modernizing Super-Exploitation: Restructurin South African Agriculture*. London: Zed Books.

8. Keegan, *Rural Transformations*, 202.

9. D. Hobart Houghton. 1964. *The South African Economy*. Cape Town: Oxford University Pres Stanley B. Greenberg. 1980. *Race and State in Capitalist Development*. New Haven: Ya University Press, 87–91; A. H. Jeeves. 1991. "Migrant Labour in the Industrial Transformatic of South Africa, 1920–1960." In *Studies in the Economic History of Southern Africa*, vol. 2, 105–4 Merle Lipton. 1985. *Capitalism and Apartheid: South Africa, 1910–84*. New Jersey: Rowman ar Allanheld, 260; Marcus. *Modernizing Super Exploitation*, 24–6; Wilson, "Farming, 1866–1966 136–53.

10. Colin Bundy. 1979. *The Rise and Fall of the South African Peasantry*. London: Heineman William Beinart. 1982. *The Political Economy of Pondoland*. Cambridge: Cambridge Universi Press; E. Eldredge. 1993. *A South African Kingdom: The Pursuit of Scarcity in Nineteenth Centu Lesotho*. Cambridge: Cambridge University Press.

11. R. Palmer and Q. N. Parsons, eds. 1977. *The Roots of Rural Poverty in Central and Southe Africa*. London: Heinemann; Terence Ranger. 1978. "Reflections on Peasant Research Central and Southern Africa." *Journal of Southern African Studies* 5: 99–133; Bundy, *Rise ar Fall*; Jonathan Crush. 1987. *The Struggle for Swazi Labour, 1890–1920*. Montreal and Kingsto McGill-Queen's University Press; J. Lambert. 1995. *Betrayed Trust: Africans and the State Colonial Natal*. Pietermaritzburg: University of Natal Press. Almost everywhere, th peasantry was more tenacious than was once thought; Charles Simkins. 1981. "Agricultur Production in the African Reserves of South Africa 1918–1969." *Journal of Southern Afric Studies* 7: 256–83; A. Vaughan and A. McIntosh. 1993. "State and Capital in the Regeneratic of a South African Peasantry." *Canadian Journal of African Studies* 27: 439–62.

12. T. J. Keegan. 1985. "Crisis and Catharsis in the Development of Capitalism in South Africa Agriculture." *African Affairs* 84: 371–98.

13. W. Beinart. 1984. "Soil Erosion, Conservationism and Ideas about Development." *Journal Southern African Studies* 11: 52–83.

14. W. Beinart. 1992. "The Night of the Jackal: Predators and Pastures in South Afric 1900–1930." Paper presented to Workshop on Agriculture and Apartheid, Queen's Univer ity, Kingston; W. Beinart. 1995. "Environmental Degradation in Sheep Farming Areas South Africa: Soil Erosion, Animals and Pastures over the Long Term." Paper for the Sout African Historical Society Conference, Rhodes University, Grahamstown.

15. W. M. Macmillan. 1930. *Complex South Africa*. London: Faber and Faber; Marcus, *Modernizin Super-Exploitation*; R. Morrell, ed. 1992. *White But Poor: Essays on the History of Poor Whites South Africa, 1850–1940*. Pretoria: University of South Africa.

16. T. J. Keegan. 1987. "The Dynamics of Rural Accumulation in South Africa: Comparative an Historical Perspectives." *Comparative Studies in Society and History* 28: 628–50.

17. Keegan, "Crisis and Catharsis"; Helen Bradford. 1987. *A Taste of Freedom: The ICU in Rur South Africa, 1924–1930*. New Haven: Yale University Press; Robert Morrell. 1988. "Th

Disintegration of the Gold and Maize Alliance in South Africa in the 1920s." *International Journal of African Historical Studies* 21: 621–35.

. Jeeves, "Migrant Labour"; Jonathan Crush, Alan H. Jeeves and David Yudelman. 1991. *South Africa's Labor Empire: A History of Black Migrancy to the Gold Mines.* Boulder, Co. and Cape Town: Westview Press and David Philip; David Duncan. 1994. *The Mills of God: The State and African Labour in South Africa, 1918–48.* Johannesburg: Witwatersrand University Press.

. Alan H. Jeeves. 1986. "Migrant Labour and South African Expansion, 1920–50." *South African Historical Journal* 18: 73–92; H. Bradford. 1994. "Getting Away with Murder: 'Mealie Kings,' the State and Foreigners in the Eastern Transvaal, *c.*1918–58." In *Apartheid's Genesis*, ed. P. Bonner, P. Delius and D. Posel, 96–125. Johannesburg: Ravan Press.

. Bradford, "Highways, Byways and Culs-de-sacs."

. This situation is primarily responsible for the absence of case studies on the Western Cape in this collection. On the Orange Free State see Murray, *Black Mountain.*

. Houghton, *The South African Economy*, 47; Jill Nattrass. 1977. "Migration Flows In and Out of Capitalist Agriculture." In *Farm Labour in South Africa*, eds. F. Wilson, A. Kooy and D. Hendrie, 51–61. Cape Town: David Philip.

. Lipton, *Capitalism and Apartheid*, 86.

. Wilson, "Farming," 138–9; A. de V. Minnaar. 1990. "The Great Depression 1929–1934." *South African Journal of Economic History* 5: 31–48.

. Wilson, "Farming," 138; C. Richards, "The 'New Despotism' in Agriculture: Some Reflections on the Marketing Bill." *South African Journal of Economics* 4: 469.

. See J. Tinley. 1954. *South African Food and Agriculture in World War II.* Stanford: Stanford University Press, 1954; Monica Cole. 1954, "The Growth and Development of the South African Citrus Industry." *Geography* 39: 113–20; Charles Mather. 1992. "Agrarian Transformation in South Africa: Land and Labour in the Barberton District, *c.*1920–1960." Ph.D. thesis, Queen's University, Kingston, 52–100; W. Beinart, A. Jeeves, D. Lincoln (in this collection).

. Wilson, "Farming," 138–9.

. The number of tractors on farms rose steadily to 6 000 in 1937. Thereafter, the increase was dramatic; to 20 000 in 1946 and over 74 000 by 1953; see S. Stavrou. 1988. "The Development of Capitalism in South African Agriculture: The Restructuring of Agrarian Capitalism after 1950." Working Paper 14, Development Studies Unit, University of Natal, Durban, 20.

. C.W. de Kiewiet. 1941. *A History of South Africa, Social and Economic.* London: Oxford University Press, 253.

. M. Lacey. 1981. *Working for Boroko: The Origins of a Coercive Labour System in South Africa.* Johannesburg: Ravan Press, 120–80; Robert Davies. 1979. *Capital State and White Labour in South Africa.* London: Harvester Press.

. Wilson, "Farming," 136–7; M. Morris. 1977. "State Intervention and the Agricultural Labour Supply Post–1948." In Wilson *et al. Farm Labour in South Africa*; Greenberg, *Race and State.*

. S.H. Frankel. 1928. *The Railway Policy of South Africa: An Analysis of the Effects of Railway Rates, Finance and Management on the Economic Development of the Union.* Johannesburg: Hortors, Ltd., 234, 241.

. R. Horwitz. 1967. *The Political Economy of South Africa.* London: Weidenfeld and Nicolson, 136.

. Frankel's estimate, cited in *ibid.*, 136–7.

. See R. Morrell. 1986. "Farmers, Randlords and the South African State: Confrontation in the Witwatersrand Beef Markets *c.*1920–23." *Journal of African History* 27: 513–32.

. E. Davis. 1933. "Some Aspects of the Marketing of Farm Products in South Africa." *South African Journal of Economics* 1: 167.

. L.C.A. Knowles and C.M. Knowles. 1936. *The Economic Development of the British Overseas Empire*, vol. 3, *The Union of South Africa.* London: Routledge, 159–90.

. Minnaar, "The Great Depression"; and A. de V. Minnaar. 1990. "The South African Wool Industry and the Great Depression." *Kleio* 22: 56–76.

39. R. Bouch (in this collection).

40. S. de Swardt. 1983. "Agricultural Marketing Problems in the 1930s." *South African Journal Economics* 51: 1–28. De Swardt was an official of the Department of Agriculture and w advisor to the Secretary of Agriculture, Dr P.R. Viljoen, during the 1930s.

41. E. Landsberg. 1937. "South Africa's Imports of Capital and the Balance of Payment 1932–1936." *South African Journal of Economics* 5: 285. This author points out that in the fir fiscal year following devaluation, government revenues from mining leases and taxe increased from about £5.3 million to £15.4 million.

42. Richards. "The 'New Despotism'," 469.

43. Union of South Africa, House of Assembly. 1936. *Report of the Select Committee on the Subject the Marketing Bill.* Cape Town: Cape Times, S.C. 6–'36, Phillipus Rudolph Viljoen examine 5.

44. Dr Viljoen and his aide, De Swardt.

45. P.R. Viljoen. 1938. "Planned Agriculture in South Africa." *South African Journal of Economics* 280.

46. Central Archives Depot (CAD) Department of Agriculture Archive (LDB) 2437,1 R404 "Marketing Bill: Second Reading Notes." [1937].

47. LDB 2437,1 R4042 Statement of the Gold Producers Committee (GPC — the executiv committee of the Chamber of Mines) to the Select Committee on the Marketing Bill, 17 Ap 1936.

48. *Report of the Select Committee on . . . the Marketing Bill,* 106–29.

49. T.H. Kelly, H.M. Robertson, R. Leslie and W.H. Hutt. 1938. "Economists' Protest: Marketir Act 1937 Scheme Relating To Marketing of Wheat: Memorandum of Objections." *Sou African Journal of Economics* 6: 186.

50. J.M. Tinley. 1941. "The Complex Farm-Labor Problem of South Africa." *Rural Sociology* 126–37.

51. See P.R. Viljoen. 1938. "Planned Agriculture in South Africa." *South African Journal Economics* 6: 280.

52. De Swardt, "Agricultural Marketing Problems," 1–28.

53. *The Star* 18 August 1937.

54. De Swardt, "Agricultural Marketing Problems," 15–18.

55. Ray E. Phillips. [n.d., 1938.] *The Bantu in the City.* Lovedale: Lovedale Press, 39, 119–23.

56. Palmer, "White Farmers in Malawi"; K. Datta. 1988. "Farm Labour, Agrarian Capital and th State in Colonial Zambia, 1942–52." *Journal of Southern African Studies* 14: 371–9 I. Mazonde. 1994. *Ranchers and Enterprise in Eastern Botswana: A Case Study of Black and Whi Farmers.* Edinburgh: Edinburgh University Press; W. Chirwa and J. Crush (in this collection

57. C. van Onselen. 1976. *Chibaro.* London: Pluto Press; Crush, *et al., South Africa's Lab Empire.*

58. R. Palmer. 1985. "White Farmers in Malawi: Before and After the Depression." *African Affai* 84: 211–45; K. Vickery. 1985. "Saving Settlers: Maize Control in Northern Rhodesia." *Journ of Southern African Studies* 11: 212–34; W. Chirwa and J. Crush (in this collection).

59. Paul Mosley. 1983. *The Settler Economies: Studies in the Economic History of Kenya and Souther Rhodesia, 1900–1963.* Cambridge: Cambridge University Press.

60. S. Rubert (in this collection).

61. Mosley, *The Settler Economies,* 234–5.

62. The discussion which follows draws on Mosley, *The Settler Economies,* 170–94; Richar Hodder-Williams. 1983. *White Farmers in Rhodesia 1890–1965.* London: Macmillan; an especially Ian R. Phimister. 1987. *An Economic and Social History of Zimbabwe, 1890–194 London and New York: Longman, 173–6.

63. Ian R. Phimister. 1978. "Meat and Monopolies: Beef Cattle in Southern Rhodesia, 1890–1938 *Journal of African History* 19: 391–414.

64. Mosley, *The Settler Economies,* 177–8.

65. Palmer, "White Farmers in Malawi"; W. Chirwa (in this collection).

5. John McCracken. 1982. "Experts and Expertise in Colonial Malawi." *African Affairs* 81: 109–10.

7. Palmer, "White Farmers in Malawi."

3. John McCracken. 1983. "Planters, Peasants and the Colonial State: The Impact of the Native Tobacco Board in the Central Province of Malawi." *Journal of Southern African Studies* 9: 192.

9. R. Palmer. 1985. "The Nyasaland Tea Industry in the Era of International Restrictions." *Journal of African History* 26: 215–39.

0. J. Crush (in this collection).

1. Crush, *Struggle for Swazi Labour*.

2. A ban that remained in place until the mid–1980s; see Jonathan Crush. 1993. "'The Long-Averted Clash': Farm Labour Competition in the South African Countryside." *Canadian Journal of African Studies* 27: 404–23.

3. Bradford, "'Getting Away with Murder',"; Duncan, *Mills of God*. On child labor see W.C. Chirwa. 1993. "Child and Youth Labour on the Nyasaland Plantations, 1890–1957." *Journal of Southern African Studies* 19: 662–80; and W. Beinart (in this collection).

4. CAD, Department of Native Affairs Archive (NTS) 2067 138/280, 2 Native Affairs Department (NAD) memorandum on native labor on the sugar estates, Natal, by L.J. P[hillips]. This document reviewed the long, unsuccessful history of the department's efforts to bring farmers under the Native Regulation Act and outlined the arguments for doing so.

5. Duncan, *Mills of God*; for a contrary view see Bradford, "'Getting Away with Murder'."

6. D. Duncan (in this collection).

7. See Minister of Justice Oswald Pirow's speech on second reading of the Native Service Contract Act. Union of South Africa, *House of Assembly Debates* (*Hansard*) 18, cols. 639–46, 4 February 1932.

8. See the speeches by farmer MPs during the second-reading debate on the bill in *ibid*.

9. S. Schirmer (in this collection).

0. Alan H. Jeeves. 1985. *Migrant Labour in South Africa's Mining Economy: The Struggle for the Gold Mines Labour Supply, 1890–1920*. Montreal, Kingston and Johannesburg: McGill Queen's Press and Witwatersrand University Press, 87–152.

1. D. Duncan (in this collection); Bradford, "'Getting Away with Murder'."

2. Jeeves, *Migrant Labour*.

3. NTS 2048 65/280,1 Notes of Meeting of the Executive of the South African Sugar Association with Director of Native Labour, S.M. Pritchard, and Labour Bureau officials, Falwasser and De Jager of the Native Labour Bureau, 19 August 1920; NTS 2049 65/280,3, Annexure A: "Report and Recommendation of Departmental Committee Appointed re Alleged Labour Shortage in Natal," C.A. Wheelwright and H.S. Cooke [1918].

4. Union of South Africa, *Report of the Native Economic Commission*, 1930–2. Pretoria, Government Printer, 1932, 128–31, paras. 876–897; Union of South Africa. 1935. *Report of the Departmental Committee Appointed to Enquire into and Report upon Certain Questions Relating to Native Labour in Zululand, the Transkeian Territories and the Ciskei*. Johannesburg: 9, para. 38.

5. For instance, *Hansard* 34, cols. 4895–6, 4890–4900, 17 May 1939.

6. Union of South Africa. 1939. *Report of the Native Farm Labour Committee*. Pretoria: Government Printer.

7. *Ibid*., 74, para. 422.

8. Crush, *et al.*, *South Africa's Labor Empire*.

9. Remaining controls were anything but trivial and included criminal penalties for desertion under long-standing Master and Servant Acts and, in "labour districts," the Native Labour Regulation Act.

0. NTS 2229,1 463/280, Pt. F1 SAAU Memorandum for a conference with the Minister of Native Affairs, 15 September 1944.

91. NTS 2229,1 463/280, Pt. F2 Piet van der Byl, Minister of Native Affairs, to the Prir Minister, 9 October 1945.

92. Doug Hindson. 1987. *Pass Controls and the Urban African Proletariat*. Johannesburg: Rav Press, 52–79.

93. Bradford, '"Getting Away with Murder'"; M. Murray. 1995. "Blackbirding at 'Crook Corner': Illicit Labour Recruiting in the Northern Transvaal, 1910–1940." *Journal of Southe African Studies* 21: 373–98; NTS 2246 603/280 Interstate Migrant Labour Conference, pape 1946–8.

94. B. Mazower. 1991. "Agriculture, Farm Labour and the State in the Natal Midlanc 1940–1960." M.A. thesis, University of Cape Town; S. Schirmer. 1994. "Reactions to tl State: The Impact of Farm Labour Policies in the Mid-Eastern Transvaal, 1955–1960." *Sou African Historical Journal* 30: 61–84.

95. S. Greenberg. 1987. *Legitimating the Illegitimate: State, Markets and Resistance in South Afric* Berkeley: University of California Press, 39–55; Lipton, *Capitalism and Apartheid*, 25, 91– D. Posel. 1991. *The Making of Apartheid, 1948–61*. Oxford: Clarendon, 61–90.

96. See the essays in Beinart, Delius and Trapido, *Putting a Plough to the Ground*; Keegan, *Ru Transformations*; C. van Onselen (in this collection).

97. T. Keegan. 1982. "The Sharecropping Economy, African Class Formation and the Native Land Act of 1913 in the Highveld Maize Belt." In *Industrialisation and Social Change*, e S. Marks and R. Rathbone, 195–211. London: Longman; Bradford, *Taste of Freedom*; Harve Feinberg. 1993. "The 1913 Natives Land Act in South Africa: Politics, Race and Segregatic in the Early Twentieth Century." *International Journal of African Historical Studies* 2 65–110.

98. S. Schirmer, C. Mather and C. van Onselen (in this collection).

99. See W. Chirwa and J. Crush (in this collection); also J. Crush. 1985. "Landlords, Tenants an Colonial Social Engineers: The Farm Labour Question in Early Colonial Swaziland." *Journ of Southern African Studies* 11: 235–57; Hodder-Williams, *White Farmers in Rhodesia 198* K.J. McCracken. 1985. "Share-Cropping in Malawi: The Visiting Tenant System in th Central Province, *c.*1920–1968." In *Malawi: An Alternative Pattern of Development*. Edinburgl African Studies Centre, Edinburgh University.

100. Bradford, *A Taste of Freedom*; Marcus, *Modernizing Super-Exploitation*.

101. Miranda Miles. 1991. "Missing Women: Swazi Female Migration to the Witwatersran 1920–70." M.A. thesis, Queen's University, Kingston; H. Simelane. 1992. "The Coloni State, Peasantry and Agricultural Production in Swaziland, 1940–1950." *South Africa Historical Journal* 26: 93–115; Camilla Cockerton. 1995. "Running Away from the Land of th Desert: Women's Migration to South Africa in Colonial Bechuanaland, *c.* 1890s–1964." Ph.E thesis, Queen's University, Kingston.

102. McCracken, "Share-Cropping in Malawi"; Chirwa (in this collection).

103. A. Jeeves, D. Lincoln and W. Beinart (in this collection).

104. S. Schirmer. 1995. "African Strategies and Ideologies in a White Farming Distric Lydenburg, 1930–1970." *Journal of Southern African Studies* 21: 509–28; S. Schirmer (in th collection).

105. C. Mather (in this collection).

106. M. Murray, D. Lincoln, W. Beinart, A. Jeeves (in this collection); see also Robert Morrel 1983. "Rural Transformation in the Transvaal: The Middleburg District, 1919 to 1930." M.A thesis, University of the Witwatersrand; A. de V. Minnaar. 1989. "Labour Supply Problem of the Zululand Sugar Planters, 1905–1939." *Journal of Natal and Zulu History* 12: 53–72 Bradford, '"Getting Away with Murder'"; Murray, "Blackbirding."

107. Murray, "Blackbirding."

108. Jeeves, *Migrant Labour*.

109. Crush, *et al.*, *South Africa's Labor Empire*.

110. *Ibid*.

111. Jeeves, *Migrant Labour*, 221–51.

2. Bradford, '"Getting Away with Murder'."

3. C. Mather, A. Jeeves, D. Lincoln (in this collection).

4. Murray, "Blackbirding."

5. NTS 2234 469/280, NAD memorandum for the Minister, June 1947.

6. Cockerton, "Running Away from the Land of the Desert."

7. W.C. Chirwa. 1992. "'Theba is Power'; Rural Labour, Migrancy and Fishing in Malawi, 1890s–1985." Ph.D. thesis, Queen's University.

8. W.C. Chirwa. 1994, "Alomwe and Mozambican Immigrant Labor in Colonial Malawi." *International Journal of African Historical Studies* 27: 525–50.

9. David Yudelman and Alan Jeeves. 1986. "New Labour Frontiers for Old: Black Migrants to the South African Gold Mines, 1920–85." *Journal of Southern African Studies* 13: 101–24.

20. Jeeves, "Migrant Labour and South African Expansion"; D. Johnson. 1992. "Settler Farmers and Coerced African Labour in Southern Rhodesia, 1936–46." *Journal of African History* 33: 111–28.

21. Leroy Vail and Landeg White. 1980. *Capitalism and Colonialism in Mozambique*. Minneapolis: University of Minnesota Press; Allen Isaacman and Barbara Isaacman. 1983. *Mozambique: From Colonialism to Revolution, 1900–82*. Boulder, Co.: Westview Press, 40–42.

22. Alan Jeeves. 1992. "Sugar and Gold in the Making of the South African Labour System: The Crisis of Supply on the Zululand Sugar Estates, 1906–39." *South African Journal of Economic History* 7: 7–33.

23. For example, Bradford, "Getting Away With Murder."

24. See Ruth First. 1954. *Exposure: The Farm Labour Scandal*. Johannesburg; M. Scott. 1958. *A Time to Speak*. Garden City, NY: Doubleday.

25. W. Morrell (in this collection).

26. W. Beinart (in this collection).

27. A. Jeeves (in this collection).

28. NTS 2049 65/280A Secretary for Public Health to Secretary of Native Affairs, 10 May 1929, referring to a memorandum by Dr G.A. Park Ross in which he made this assertion.

29. Bradford, *A Taste of Freedom*; D. Lincoln. 1993. "Flies in the Sugar Bowl: The Natal Sugar Industry Employees' Union in its Heyday, 1940–1954." *South African Historical Journal*. 29: 177–208.

30. See, for example, M. Murray. 1988. "'Burning the Wheat Stacks': Land Clearances and Agrarian Unrest Along the Northern Middelburg Frontier, c. 1918–1926." *Journal of Southern African Studies* 15: 74–95; Mather, "Agrarian Transformation."

31. T. Dunbar Moodie with Vivienne Ndatshe. 1994. *Going for Gold: Men, Mines and Migration*. Berkeley: University of California Press; P. Harries. 1994. *Work, Culture and Identity: Migrant Labourers in Mozambique and South Africa, c.1860–1910*. New York: Heinemann.

32. C. van Onselen (in this collection); see also Allen Isaacman. 1992. "Coercion, Paternalism and the Labour Process: The Mozambican Cotton Regime 1938–1961." *Journal of Southern African Studies* 18: 487–526.

33. D. Lincoln. 1995. "Settlement and Servitude in Zululand." *International Journal of African Historical Studies* 28: 49–68; S. Brooks (in this collection).

Chapter 2
Farm Labor and the South African State, 1924–1948

1. M. Lacey. 1981. *Working for Boroko: The Origins of a Coercive Labour System in South Africa*. Johannesburg: Ravan Press, 180.

2. H. Bradford. 1987. *A Taste of Freedom: The I.C.U. In Rural South Africa, 1924–1930.* New Have Yale University Press, 23; D. Cooper. 1990. "Agriculture: Its Problems and Prospects." *Critical Choices for South Africa: An Agenda for the 1990s*, ed. R. Schrire. Cape Town: Oxfo University Press, 342–3; The Native Trust and Land Act (No. 18–1936) differentiated betwe "squatters" (which it took to mean sharecropping and rent-paying tenants only) and "labo tenants." A sharecropper rented land in return for a portion of his produce; a labor tena rented land in return for labor on the owner's land. However, the term "squatter" continu to be used in official circles and by the general public to refer to labor tenants. See S. van d Horst. 1942. *Native Labour in South Africa.* London: Oxford, 286. On divisions between wh farmers, see M. Morris. 1979. "The State and the Development of Capitalist Class Relations the South African Countryside: A Process of Class Struggle." D.Phil. thesis, University Sussex, 1979; and R. Morrell. 1986. "Competition and Cooperation in Middelbur 1900–1930." In *Putting a Plough to the Ground: Accumulation and Dispossession in Rural Sou Africa, 1850–1930*, ed. W. Beinart, P. Delius and S. Trapido. Johannesburg: Ravan Pres 373–419.

3. Bradford, *A Taste of Freedom*, 288, note 7.

4. Central Archives Depot, Pretoria (CAD), Department of Agriculture (LDB) R4545 Director Veterinary Services to Secretary for Agriculture, 8 November 1928.

5. LDB R4545 Additional Native Commissioner (NC), Pretoria to Secretary of Native Affai (SNA), 17 January 1930.

6. *Ibid.*, SNA to Secretary for Agriculture, 17 April 1930.

7. *Ibid.*, Director of Veterinary Services to Secretary for Agriculture, 2 May 1930.

8. *Ibid.*, Kemp to E.G. Jansen (Minister of Native Affairs), 15 May 1930.

9. LDB R2989, pt. 1 SNA to Secretary for Agriculture, 14 May 1928.

10. LDB R2989, pt. 2 SNA to Secretary for Agriculture, 10 June 1930.

11. CAD Native Affairs Department (NTS) 10/280, SNA to NC, Potgietersru 30 November 1926.

12. Transvaal Archives, Pretoria (TAD) Government Native Labour Bureau (GNLB) vol. 3 301/19/72 Memorandum on the Consolidation of Union Pass Laws, 1925; CAD Smu Papers, Box 129, No. 18 J.M. Young's evidence to the Native Affairs Commission.

13. Bradford, *A Taste of Freedom*, 53; see also M. Morris. 1977. "Apartheid, Agriculture and t State." *SALDRU Working Paper No. 8*, Cape Town: University of Cape Town, 12.

14. LDB R2989, pt. 1 Secretary for Agriculture to SNA, 2 August 1928. Inspectors operated on t Natal sugar plantations from the 1920s, but lacked powers of enforcement.

15. CAD Public Health Department (GES) 131/38 SNA to Secretary for Public Healt 12 February 1937.

16. NTS 10/280 Chief Native Commissioner, Natal, to SNA, 5 September 1923.

17. LDB R3710 Memorandum on Native Wages on Farms [n.d.].

18. For example, LDB R2989, pt. 2 Secretary for Agriculture to Departments of Mines and t Interior and the Railways and Harbours Administration, 12 May 1939.

19. Union of South Africa, *House of Assembly Debates* (*Hansard*) 29, col. 3785, 24 March 1937.

20. LDB R3710 Acting Secretary for Agriculture to G. Schroeder, Glencoe, Nata 5 July 1937.

21. LDB R2989 Memorandum on "Native Labour Problems" by S.J. de Swardt, 6 Sep tember 1938.

22. Union of South Africa. 1939. *Report of the Native Farm Labour Committee.* Pretoria: Governme Printer.

23. *Ibid.*, para. 487.

24. Lacey, *Working for Boroko.*

25. *Ibid.*, 158, 170.

26. Bradford, *A Taste of Freedom*, 53–4.

27. CAD Justice Department (JUS) 1/103/29 Secretary for Justice to Magistrate, Johannesbur 17 March 1925.

8 Transvaal Provincial Division, 243/1921.

9. NTS 13/362 Reply to Senator Opperman's question to Minister of Native Affairs, 12 March 1924; see also T. R. H. Davenport. 1969. "African Townsmen? South African Natives (Urban Areas) Legislation Through the Years." *African Affairs* 68: 98.

0. JUS 1/103/29, pt. 3 Minister of Justice to Secretary for Justice, 19 October 1925; JUS 1/103/29 (sub), Secretary for Justice's Memorandum, 14 January 1926.

1. JUS 1/103/29, pt. 1 SNA to Secretary for Justice, 18 December 1923.

2. JUS 1/103/29, pt. 2 SNA to Secretary for Justice, 23 October 1925, 25 November 1925.

3. JUS 1/103/29, pt. 3 Minister of Justice to Secretary for Justice, 2 July 1928. For farmers' support for stronger measures to control farm labor, see *Hansard*, 18, col. 654, 4 February 1932.

4. Lacey, *Working for Boroko*, 171.

5. *Hansard* 18, col. 650, 4 February 1932.

6. *Ibid*. 18, col. 1335–1336, 22 February 1932.

7. Lacey, *Working for Boroko*, 180.

8. NTS 13/362 Oswald Pirow to Minister of Native Affairs, 28 January 1925.

9. Van Rensburg was the third ardent Nationalist to hold the office of Secretary for Justice since W. E. Bok, the others being Charles Pienaar and 'Toon' van den Heever; see J. Van Rensburg. 1956. *Their Paths Crossed Mine*. Johannesburg: 54.

0. The Free State was covered by clauses 1, 7, 8, and 10. These concerned the sale or lease of land in contravention to the 1913 Natives Land Act, and the provision of information to Magistrates about Africans living on land outside the locations; *Statutes of the Union of South Africa*, Act 24/1932.

1. *Cape Times* 29 December 1930; *Imvo Zabantsundu* 16 February 1932; see also Union of South Africa. 1937. *Native Affairs Commission Report for 1927–1931*. Pretoria: Government Printer, U.G. 26–'32.

2. *Ilanga Lase Natal* 11 March 1932; *Umteteli wa Bantu* 12 March 1932.

3. JUS 1/103 29, pt. 3 Johannesburg Joint Council of Europeans and Natives, "General Hertzog's Solution of the Native Question. Memorandum No. 5," para. 33.

4. NTS 61/362 Memorandum by Rogers to Chief Clerk, 29 September 1932.

5. S. Dubow. 1982. "Holding 'A Just Balance between White and Black': The Native Affairs Department in South Africa c. 1920–1933." *Journal of Southern African Studies* 12: 217–39; see also S. Dubow. 1989. *Racial Segregation and the Origins of Apartheid in South Africa, 1919–1936*. London: Macmillan.

6. NTS 61/362 NAD General Circular 1/1934; Magistrate, Umtata to SNA, 15 January 1934.

7. NTS 61/362 Additional NC, Louis Trichardt to SNA, 6 February 1934.

8. NTS 61/362 NC, Far East Rand to Chief NC, Johannesburg, 19 January 1934.

9. JUS 1/103/29, pt. 4 Attorney-General, Natal to Secretary for Justice, 27 June 1934; Secretary for Justice to Attorney-General, 17 July 1934; G. D. C. Lumsden for Secretary for Justice to Magistrate, Howick, 5 November 1934. Mnyeza won the case on appeal. The Justice Department referred the case to the NAD for possible amendment of the act.

0. Government Notice 1505/1934, 1839/1934.

1. NTS 61/362 Handwritten note by SNA, 31 July 1934.

2. NAD General Circular No. 22/1938, 9 July 1938.

3. JUS 1/103/29, pt. 7 Allison (Under-Secretary for Native Affairs) to Secretary for Justice, 4 October 1938.

4. Lacey, *Working for Boroko*, 120.

5. White Paper 1/1942, 1.

6. NTS 56/293, pt. 1 Waterberg District Farmers' Association to Minister of Native Affairs, 5 May 1928.

7. *Hansard* 31, col. 713, 1 March 1938; T. R. H. Davenport. 1970. "The Triumph of Colonel Stallard: The Transformation of the Natives (Urban Areas) Act Between 1923 and 1937." *South African Historical Journal* 2: 77–96.

58. NTS 643/280 Minutes of Native Farm Labour Conference, 15/9/44; S. Schirmer (in th collection). As O'Meara points out, the government also feared opposition from Africa peasants. Dan O'Meara. 1983. *Volkscapitalisme: Class, Capital and Ideology in the Making Afrikaner Nationalism, 1934–1948*. Johannesburg: Ravan Press, 231.

59. For example, *Hansard* 29, col. 3783–3785, 24 March 1937.

60. O'Meara, *Volkscapitalisme* 231. When the commission discussed agricultural development, included the reserve areas. Union of South Africa. 1941. *4th Interim Report of the Industrial ar Agricultural Requirements Commission*. Pretoria: Government Printer, paras. 186–7.

61. LDB 3710 Report of the Interdepartmental Farm Labour Committee, 10 December 1942.

62. NTS 643/280. The meetings took place on 17 August 1944 and 15 September 194 respectively. There were further meetings between NAD officials and the SAAU o 31 October 1944 and 13 November 1944.

63. P. V. G. van der Byl. 1975. *Top Hat to Velskoen*. Cape Town: H. Timmins; M. M. Bell. 1978. "Th Politics of Administration. A Study of the Career of Dr D. L. Smit with Special Reference to h Work in the Native Affairs Department, 1934–45." M.A. thesis, Rhodes University.

64. NTS 469/280, pt. 2 SNA's Memorandum for Minister of Native Affairs, 23 February 1945.

65. NTS 463/280, pt. 2 Notes on NAD's actions re SAAU recommendations [n.d.].

66. *Ibid.*, Minister of Native Affairs to Prime Minister, 9 October 1945.

67. *Ibid.*, SNA's notes on meeting with Minister of Native Affairs and Prime Ministe 23 February 1945.

68. *Ibid.*, Minutes of NAD meeting with SAAU Special Farm Labour Committe 31 October 1944.

69. NTS 646/280 DNL to SNA, 18 May 1948.

70. H. Bradford. 1994. "Getting Away With Murder: 'Mealie Kings,' the State and Foreigners the Eastern Transvaal, *c.* 1918–58." In *Apartheid's Genesis*, ed. P. Bonner, P. Delius an D. Posel. Johannesburg: Ravan Press and Witwatersrand University Press, 96–125.

71. R. First. 1958. "Bethal Case-Book." *Africa South* 2(3): 14–25; and M. Scott. 1958. *A Time to Spea* Garden City, NY: Doubleday.

72. NTS 741/280 (216) D. M. Mtonga to Nyasaland Government Representative, Johannesbur 10 June 1948.

73. Bradford, "Getting Away with Murder."

74. NTS 463/280, pt. 2 Minutes of NAD meeting with SAAU Special Farm Labour Committe 1 November 1948.

75. M. Murray (in this collection).

76. A. Jeeves, D. Lincoln, M. Murray (in this collection); Bradford, "Getting Away with Murder

77. Bradford, "Getting Away with Murder."

78. W. Beinart (in this collection).

79. R. Morrell. 1988. "The Disintegration of the Gold and Maize Alliance in South Africa in th 1920s." *International Journal of African Historical Studies* 21: 619–35; C. Mather, "Agraria Transformation in South Africa: Land and Labour in the Barberton District, *c.* 1920–1960 Ph.D. thesis, Queen's University, Kingston.

80. W. Beinart (in this collection).

81. LDB R2989, pt. 2 SNA to H. Howard, Rietfontein, 3 April 1928.

82. LDB R3710 Minutes of the External Relations Committee, 22 May 1934; *Hansard* 24, col. 251 5 March 1935. Herbst opposed the agreement, even though he admitted that Mozambicar were cheaper and "more amenable to discipline" than local workers.

83. NTS 338/280 SNA to Transvaal Agricultural Union [n.d.]; See also Bradford, "Getting Awa With Murder"; A. Jeeves (in this collection).

84. Bradford, "Getting Away With Murder."

85. NTS 378/280 DNL to SNA, 6 October 1939; Acting SNA to Secretary for External Affair 21 July 1942.

86. LDB R737 Eshowe District Farmers Association to Minister of Agriculture, 10 July 1945.

. NTS 643/280 SNA to Minister of Native Affairs, 23 February 1945; NTS 463/280, pt.2 minutes of NAD meeting with SAAU Special Farm Labour Committee, 1 November 1948; Mather, "Agrarian Transformation."

. A. Jeeves (in this collection).

. Morris, "Apartheid, Agriculture and the State."

Chapter 3
Land, Legislation and Labor Tenants: Resistance in Lydenburg, 1938

. S.T. van der Horst. 1942. *Native Labour in South Africa.* Cape Town: Oxford University Press, 295; M. Morris. 1979. "The State and the Development of Capitalist Social Relations in the South African Countryside." Ph.D. thesis, Sussex University, 229–30.

. See H. Bradford. 1991. "Highways, Byways and Culs-de-sac: The Transition to Agrarian Capitalism in Revisionist South African History." In *History from South Africa: Alternative Visions and Practices*, ed. J. Brown, *et al.* Philadelphia: Temple University Press, 46–7 for a summary of the debates.

. D. Duncan (in this collection).

. Union of South Africa, *House of Assembly Debates (Hansard)*, 26, cols. 2746–52, P.G.W. Grobler, MP (Rustenburg) on second reading of the Natives Trust and Land Bill, 30 April 1936.

. *Ibid.*, col. 2746.

. *Ibid.*, 26, col. 2827, the Prime Minister, General Hertzog, on second reading of the Natives Trust and Land Act, 30 April 1936. The war led to further delays. In the end, the state never did purchase all of the land promised in 1936.

. Central Archives Depot (CAD), Native Affairs Department (NTS) 8636 97/362 Report of the Committee for the Application of Chapter Four, February 1939.

. NTS 8837 97/362 Meeting of Native Affairs Commission, 2 July 1946.

. *Hansard* 26, cols. 2778–2781, E. de Souza, MP (Lydenburg) on second reading of the Natives Trust and Land Bill, 30 April 1936.

. NTS 8636 61/362 Summary of Chapter Four Committee's Recommendations (n.d.).

. Interview with Johan Steyn, Lydenburg, 1990; Union of South Africa. 1941. *Agricultural Census, No. 19.* 1938–39. Pretoria: U.G. 27–'41.

. CAD, Native Farm Labour Committee (K356), Lydenburg, evidence of A. Op 'T Hof, 19 November 1937.

. *Farming in South Africa*, December 1936, 523; see also Standard Bank Archives (SBA), Lydenburg Inspection Report (LIR), INSP 1/1/313, 14 November 1931.

. SBA LIR INSP 1/1/362, 25 April 1936.

. *Lydenburg News*, 14 August 1942.

. SBA LIR INSP 1/1/331, 15 March 1933.

. SBA LIR INSP 1/1/373, 16 June 1938.

. *Lydenburg News*, 14 January 1938, 18 March 1938, 17 November 1939.

. University of the Witwatersrand Library (UW) AD 438 Native Economic Commission (NEC), Evidence from Lydenburg, O. Phokanoka, 18 August 1930.

. Interview with Elise Mduli, Marulaneng, 6 June 1992; Interview with Mrs Makua, Mashishing, 25 January 1992; Interview with Mr Malapo, Marulaneng, 12 April 1992; see also NTS 8837 97/362 Chief Native Commissioner (CNC) (Northern Areas), Notes on a visit to Lydenburg, 1 July 1938.

. Interview with Maria Sewele, Marulaneng, 11 April 1992; Interview with Kate Ndlozi, Jane Furse, 21 December 1990; K 356 Lydenburg Evidence of W.C. Malan, 19 November 1937; K356 Lydenburg Evidence of W.J. Fouche, 19 November 1937.

. See Union of South Africa. 1939. *Agricultural Census No. 17*, 1936–37. Pretoria: U.G. 18. Some 530 out of 765 farms in Lydenburg were occupied by the owner. For details on absentee and labor farms see: Interview with Elise Mdluli, Marulaneng, 6 June 1992; Interview with Ephraim Mosehla, Jane Furse, 22 January 1992.

23. *Hansard*, 18, col. 2422, 17 March 1932.
24. UW AD 438 NEC Lydenburg, 18 August 1930.
25. Union of South Africa. 1939. *Report of the Native Farm Labour Committee*. Pretoria: Governme Printer, 10.
26. UW AD 438, NEC, Lydenburg 18 August 1930.
27. K356 Lydenburg evidence of A. Op 't Hof, 19 December 1937.
28. See, for example, interview with Kitty Sehlangu, Jane Furse, 9 December 1990.
29. K356 Lydenburg evidence of P. J. Manzini, 19 November 1937.
30. *Agricultural Census No. 17*.
31. K356 Lydenburg evidence of I. J. Breytenbach and B. Mills, 19 November 1937.
32. NTS 8837 97/362 CNC (Northern Areas), Notes on a visit to Lydenburg.
33. K356 Lydenburg evidence of J. J. Smit, 19 November 1937 (translation).
34. *Ibid.*, Evidence of M. J. Erasmus, 19 November 1937.
35. *Ibid.*, Evidence of E. de Souza, 19 November 1937; see also NTS 8837 97/362 Office of t Native Commissioner Lydenburg, Report (n.d.).
36. K 356 Lydenburg evidence of E. de Souza and A. Op 'T Hof.
37. NTS 2167 289/280 (3) (7) Private Secretary of H. F. Verwoerd to Mrs Fourie, 13 June 1955
38. NTS 8837 97/362 Memo of CNC (Northern Areas), 7 July 1938.
39. K356 Lydenburg, evidence of M. J. Erasmus.
40. NTS 8837 97/362 Secretary of Native Affairs (SNA) to CNC (Northern Areas), 1 Februa 1992.
41. K356 Lydenburg evidence of M. J. Erasmus.
42. *Ibid.*, Evidence of B. Mills.
43. NTS 8837 97/362 Memo of CNC (Northern Areas), 1 July 1937.
44. For a more detailed consideration of the role of the state see S. Schirmer. 1990. "Freedom Land and Work: Labour Tenancy and the Proclamation of Chapter Four in Lydenburg University of the Witwatersrand, History Workshop, unpublished.
45. NTS 8838 97/362 NC Lydenburg, Report, *c.* 1938; CNC (Northern Areas), Notes on a visit Lydenburg.
46. NTS 8838 97/362 NC Lydenburg, Report, *c.* 1938.
47. UW Rheinallt Jones Papers AD 843 RJ 101.27 Samson Mnisi to Rheinallt Jones, 12 Septemb 1938.
48. P. Warwick. 1983. *Black People and the South African War 1899–1902*. Cambridge: Cambrid University Press, 166.
49. Interview with Sekwatane Mosehla, 22 January 1992.
50. Interview with Sekwati Hlatswayo, 8 February 1991.
51. NTS 8838 97/362 NC Lydenburg, Report, *c.* 1938.
52. *Ibid.*
53. NTS 8837 97/362 CNC (Northern Areas), Notes on a visit to Lydenburg.
54. See NTS 8838 97/362 NC Lydenburg, Report, *c.* 1938; and Notes on a Meeting with Farmers Lydenburg, 25 October 1938.
55. NTS 8838 97/362 NC Lydenburg, Report, *c.* 1938.
56. UW AD 843 RJ 2.2.6 Letter from J. A. Calata, General Secretary of the ANC to E. Rheina Jones, 9 December 1938.
57. *The Guardian*, 20 June 1939.
58. See S. Dubow. 1989. *Racial Segregation and the Origins of Apartheid, 1919–1936*. Londc Macmillan, 106–7.
59. NTS 8838 97/362 NC Lydenburg, Report, *c.* 1938.
60. UW AD 843 B53.7 Interview by Edith Jones with Mr C. Bauling, Lydenburg, Februa 1941.
61. UW AD 843 RJ 2.2.6 Meeting of Farmers in the Bioscope Hall, Lydenburg, 2 October 193
62. See NTS 8837 97/362 NC Lydenburg, Report, *c.* 1938.
63. See, for example, *Lydenburg News*, 7 May 1943.

. CAD Department of Justice (JUS) 1076 21/67/1 Public Service Commission Inspection Report, 23 October 1934.

. *Lydenburg News*, 4 August 1939.

. UW AD 843 RJ 2.2.6 Rheinallt Jones to SNA, 26 October 1938.

. NTS 8838 97/362 NC, Lydenburg, Report, *c.*1938.

. The Johannesburg *Star*, 17 June 1938.

. Interviews with Rose Masilela, 8 February 1991; Petrus Magelego, 9 December 1990; Kate Ndlozi, 21 December 1990; Ella Shabangu, 7 February 1991; see also K356 Lydenburg, Sabi Native Location Advisory Board, 19 November 1937.

. P. Rich. 1984. *White Power and the Liberal Conscience.* Manchester: Manchester University Press, 51.

. See UW AD 843 RJ 2.2.6 Bishop of Pretoria to Rheinallt Jones, 4 July 1938.

. UW AD 438 NEC Evidence from Lydenburg, 18 August 1930.

. K356 Lydenburg Sabi Native Location Advisory Board, 19 November 1937.

. UW D 843 RJ 101.27 Samson Mnisi to Rheinallt Jones, 12 September 1938.

. UW AD 843 RJ 101.27 Samson Mnisi to Rheinallt Jones, 29 June 1938.

. University of the Witwatersrand, Institute of Advanced Social Research, Oral History Project, Tape No. 46 A/B, Interview with Kotana Stefaans Modipa, 17 October 1979; see also Interview with Hosia Phala and Michael Mashupje, 2 February 1992.

. NTS 8837 97/362 Lydenburg Magistrate to SNA, 7 February 1938.

. UW, SAIRR, B44/3, Nathan Modipa and James Morena to Rheinallt Jones, n.d.

. NTS 8837 97/362 Opinion of Controller of Native Settlements, 15 April 1939.

. *Ibid.*, Additional NC Sekhukhuneland to CNC (Northern Areas), 13 June 1938.

. *Ibid.*, Summary of Application of Chapter Four to Lydenburg, 22 October 1938. By October 587 out of a total of 6 185 labor tenants had been registered.

. UW AD 843 RJ 2.2.6. Samson Mnisi to Rheinallt Jones, 20 May 1938.

. *Ibid.* (translation).

. K356 Lydenburg Evidence of Nathan Modipa.

. NTS 8837 97/362 CNC (Northern Areas), Notes on a visit to Sekhukhuneland and Lydenburg, 7 July 1938.

. *Ibid.*, NC, Lydenburg, Complaint by A.P. Jacobs, 7 September 1938.

. Interview with Hosia Phala and Michael Mashupje, Mashishing, 2 February 1992.

. UW AD 843 RJ 2.2.6. Rheinallt Jones to CNC, 26 October 1938.

. Interview with Emily Mkhonto, 22 January 1992.

. K356 Lydenburg, Evidence of Nathan Modipa, 19 November 1937.

. NTS 8837 97/362 NC Lydenburg to CNC (Northern Areas), 10 June 1938.

. *Ibid.*, NAD Correspondence, October 1938.

. *Lydenburg News*, 28 October 1938.

. UW AD 843 RJ 2.2.6. Meeting of Farmers in the Bioscope Hall, Lydenburg, 2 October 1938.

. UW AD 843 RJ C6. Nathan Modipa to Mrs Rheinallt Jones, 25 February 1941.

. See S. Schirmer. 1993. "Racism and White Farmers in Lydenburg: The Initiation of Racial Land Divisions at the Local Level." *Africa Perspective*, May.

. P. Furlong. 1991. *Between Crown and Swastika: The Impact of The Radical Right on the Afrikaner Nationalist Movement in the Fascist Era.* Johannesburg: Witwatersrand University Press.

Chapter 4
Wage Workers and Labor Tenants in Barberton, 1920–1950

E. Rheinallt Jones. 1945. "Farm Labour in the Transvaal." *Journal of Race Relations* 12(1): 5–14.

Rheinallt Jones's research notes are in the University of the Witwatersrand (UW), William Cullen Library, A 578, Edith R. Jones Papers.

3. Rheinallt Jones, "Farm Labour in the Transvaal," 5.

4. W. Beinart and P. Delius. 1986. "Introduction." In *Putting a Plough to the Groun Accumulation and Dispossession in Rural South Africa, 1850–1930*, ed. W. Beinart, P. Delius a S. Trapido. Johannesburg: Ravan Press; T. Keegan. 1986, 1–55. "White Settlement and Bla Subjugation on the South African Highveld: The Tlokoa Heartland in the North Easte Orange Free State, ca. 1850–1914." In *Putting a Plough to the Ground*, 218–58.

5. H. Bradford. 1988. *A Taste of Freedom: The ICU in Rural South Africa, 1924–1930.* Johannesbu Ravan Press, 39–40.

6. Beinart and Delius, "Introduction", 38.

7. D. Reineke. 1957. "Squatter Labour Does Not Pay." *Farming in South Africa* 31: 45–7.

8. R. Morrell. 1986. "Competition and Cooperation in Middleburg, 1900–1930." In *Putting Plough to the Ground*, 373–419.

9. H. Bradford. 1994. "Getting Away With Murder: 'Mealie Kings,' the State and Foreigners the Eastern Transvaal, *c.* 1918–58." In *Apartheid's Genesis*, ed. P. Bonner, P. Delius a D. Posel. Johannesburg: Ravan Press and Witwatersrand University Press, 96–125; and I Murray (in this collection).

10. A. Keppel-Jones. 1949. "Land and Agriculture Outside the Reserves." In *Handbook on R Relations in South Africa*, ed. E. Hellmann. London: Oxford University Press, 171–90.

11. *Barberton Herald*, 9 March 1928.

12. For a discussion of the differing labor needs of "capitalized" and poorer small scale farme see Morrell, "Competition and Cooperation in Middleburg," 393.

13. H. Bradford. 1990. "Highways, Byways and Culs-de-sacs: The Transition to Agrari Capitalism in Revisionist South African History." *Radical History Review* 46: 59–88.

14. Beinart and Delius, "Introduction."

15. C. Murray. 1992. "Agrarian Struggles in the Eastern Orange Free State." Workshop Agriculture and Apartheid, Queen's University at Kingston, Canada, unpublished.

16. Union of South Africa. 1916. *Report of the Natives Land Commission.* U.G. 9–1916, Evidence G. D. Wheelwright, Sub-Native Commissioner, Barberton, 401.

17. *Report of Natives Land Commission*, Addendum by Mr Lucas, 197. Comment is attributed to t Barberton magistrate.

18. Interviews with Judas Nkuna, 8 November 1990; and Gabriel Ngwenya, I J. Segage and C. Mather, 15 April 1991.

19. *Report of Natives Land Commission*, Evidence of E. T. E. Andrews, Barberton, 11 August 19 508.

20. Central Archives Depot (CAD), Archive of the Native Farm Labour Committee, 1937 (K365), Evidence of H. S. Webb, E. T. E Andrews and C. D. Elphick, Nelspruit, 18 Novemb 1937, 1.

21. *Ibid.*

22. *Barberton Herald*, 26 April 1938.

23. K365, Evidence of W. H. Rood, on behalf of Langspruit Boerevereeniging, Nelspru 18 November 1937, 10.

24. K365, Evidence of Alexander Sishuba, Nelspruit, 18 November 1937, 3.

25. *Barberton Herald*, 27 June 1939.

26. CAD, Native Affairs Department (NTS), 222/280, Secretary for Native Affairs (SNA) to Lc Veld Farmer's Association (LFA), 5 September 1944.

27. CAD, Department of Agriculture (LDB), RI371, Native Commissioner, Barberton (NC) SNA, 17 November 1959.

28. Interview with B. De Villiers, by C. Mather, 30 April 1991.

29. Union of South Africa. 1932. *Report of the Native Economic Commission*(1930–32), U.G. 22–19 Evidence from E. T. E. Andrews, Barberton, 11 August 1920, 518–9; Interview with J. Spe by C. Mather, 18 March 1991.

30. *Report of the Native Economic Commission*, Evidence of E. T. E. Andrews, 519.

31. Interview with L. van Veijeren, by C. Mather, 11 February 1991.

2. *Barberton Herald*, 5 July 1929.

3. *Barberton Herald*, 10 May 1938. The average wage for adult farm workers was 1s. per shift, for "picanins" (children) 5s. and 15s. for "umfaans" (youths). One shift consisted of 12 hours work during the summer and $8\frac{1}{2}$ hours in the winter.

4. K 365 Evidence of Joel Ngwenya, 18/11/1937, 2.

5. Interview with B. De Villiers.

6. Interview with D. Coetzee, by C. Mather, 12 November 1991.

7. University of the Witwatersrand, William Cullen Library A1813, "Crocodile Valley Estates: Estate Reports."

8. *Report of the Native Economic Commission*, Evidence of E. T. E. Andrews, 516.

9. NTS 97/362, Director of Native Labour (DNL) to Secretary, Select Committee on Native Affairs, 4 March 1955. See, for example, the returns for Lydenburg and Belfast.

10. Rheinallt Jones noted how "even in the strongholds of labour tenancy, a part of the labour is cash-paid with quarters and food or rations and no privileges of land or cattle"; Rheinallt Jones, "Farm Labour in the Transvaal," 10.

11. *Native Economic Commission*, Evidence of G. Wikstrom, Swedish Alliance Mission, Barberton, 13 August 1930, 492.

12. *Ibid.*, Evidence of E. Andrews, 513.

13. *Ibid.*, Evidence of Mapikelale Nkosi, Barberton, 13 August 1930, 500.

14. *Ibid.*, Evidence of Ben Sedibe, Barberton, 13 September 1930, 2.

15. Interviews with Cement Ngomane, 1 November 1990; Rita Zandamela, 4 August 1991; James Sambo, 5 September 1990.

16. Interview with L. de B. Austin, 23 January 1991.

17. CAD, Department of Lands (LDE) 40078/1 Inspector of Lands to Regional Representative, 30 June 1958; C. Mather. 1995. "Forced Removal and the Struggle for Land and Labour in South Africa: The Ngomane of Tenbosch, 1926–54." *Journal of Historical Geography* 21:169–83.

18. NTS 555/323, NC to SNA, 13 November 1928; F. Balcome Jones to Minister of Lands, 26 October 1934.

19. *Native Economic Commission*, Evidence of L. J. Hall, Nelspruit, 18 November 1937, 554.

20. *Ibid.*

21. *Barberton Herald*, 28 August 1928.

22. Bradford, "Getting Away with Murder," 96–125.

23. *Barberton Herald*, 28 May 1928, 7 January 1930.

24. *Ibid.*, 13 March 1928.

25. Case details are drawn from the *Barberton Herald*, 25 August 1930.

26. Interview with D. Coetzee. Explaining the arbitrary way farmers would levy fines, this landowner remarked that "some of the farmers would dock pay if the workers picked their noses."

27. Interviews with Cement Ngomane and Rita Zandamela. The landowner that Rita worked for would deduct an entire month's salary for workers found eating vegetables or fruit during the harvest.

28. *Barberton Herald*, 25 August 1930.

29. A part of the capitation fee was usually deducted from the first ticket, as were transport and other miscellaneous costs; K356 Addendum C, provided by the Low Veld Farmer's Association.

30. NTS 334/280, Crocodile Valley Estates to Deneys Reitz, Minister of Agriculture, 3 August 1937.

31. Interview with Maria Tibane, 28 November 1990.

32. Interview with Elias Mkizi, 20 May 1991.

33. Interview with Judas Nkuna.

34. *Ibid.*

35. *Ibid.*

36. Interview with Jan Lourens, Komatipoort, 17 January 1991.

67. *Ibid.*
68. Interview with Judas Nkuna.
69. C. van Onselen. 1976. *Chibaro: African Mine Labour in Southern Rhodesia, 1900*. London: Plu
    Press, 234–236.
70. Interview with Cement Ngomane.
71. Interview with Elias Mkizi.
72. Bradford, *A Taste of Freedom*, 50.
73. A. Claasens. 1990. "Rural Land Struggles in the Transvaal in the 1980s." In *No Place to Res
    Forced Removals and the Law in South Africa.*, ed. C. Murray and C. O'Regan. Cape Tow
    Oxford University Press, 27–65; C. Bundy. 1990. "Land, Law and Power: Forced Removals i
    Historical Context." In *No Place to Rest*, ed. C. Murray and C. O'Regan, 3–12.
74. J. Scott. 1990. *Domination and the Arts of Resistance: Hidden Transcripts*. New Haven: Ya
    University Press; see also C. Mather. 1993. "The Anatomy of a Rural Strike: Power and Spa
    in the Transvaal Lowveld." *Canadian Journal of African Studies* 27: 424–38.
75. Interview with James Sambo.
76. Interview with Cement Ngomane.
77. Interview with Elias Mkizi.
78. See also Bradford, *A Taste of Freedom*; C. Murray. 1988. "'Burning the Wheat Stacks:' Lan
    Clearances and Agrarian Unrest Along the Northern Middelburg Frontier, *c.*1918–26
    Journal of Southern African Studies 15: 74–95.
79. See Scott, *Domination*, 162–4.
80. *Ibid.*, 162.
81. NTS 97/362 DNL to Secretary, Select Committee on Native Affairs, 4 March 1955.
80. *Ibid.*

Chapter 5
Factories in the Fields: Capitalist Farming in the Bethal District, *c.*1910–1950

1. Acknowledgements: The source of much of my inspiration on this subject can be traced to th
   work of Robert Morrell and Helen Bradford. I would like to thank Keith Beckenridge, Kei
   Shear and Siyobonga Ndabezitha for assistance at the archives, and Charles van Onsele
   Stefan Schirmer, Jonathan Crush and Alan Jeeves for comments on earlier drafts of th
   paper.
2. M. Scott. 1958. *A Time to Speak*. Garden City, NY: Doubleday, 169.
3. "Staple Crop Versus Mixed Farming," the Johannesburg *Star*, 22 May 1928.
4. Union of South Africa. 1914. *Report of the Natives' Land Commission. Minutes of Eviden*
   Cape Town: Government Printers, U.G.22–1914 (*Beaumont Commission*), Evidence
   W.G. Schuurman, 323.
5. A study conducted in the early twentieth century found that over a period of twenty-o
   growing seasons, Bethal had nineteen good and two indifferent crops with no failur
   H. D. Leppan. 1928. *The Agricultural Development of Arid and Semi-Arid Regions*. Johannesbu
   Central News Agency, 59.
6. J. Wellington. 1960. *Southern Africa: A Geographical Study*, vol. 2: *Economic and Hum*
   Geography. Cambridge: Cambridge University Press, 6–8.
7. University of Cape Town, Jagger Library, Native Economic Commission, 1930–193
   Minutes of Evidence, statement of P. J. Bosman and J. J. Williams, Middelburg, 948.
8. R. Morrell. 1986. "Competition and Cooperation in Middelburg, 1900–1930." In *Putting*
   Plough to the Ground: Accumulation and Dispossession in Rural South Africa, 1850–1930, e
   W. Beinart, P. Delius, and S. Trapido, Johannesburg: Ravan Press, 373–419, 378–80.
9. H. Bradford. 1994. "Getting Away With Murder: 'Mealie Kings,' the State and Foreigners
   the Eastern Transvaal, *c.*1918–58." In *Apartheid's Genesis*, ed. P. Bonner, P. Delius an
   D. Posel, Johannesburg: Ravan Press and Witwatersrand University Press, 96–125. Of cours

the use of child labor on the white-owned farms was part of the country-wide division of labor, and this feature alone did not set the Bethal farmers apart.

0. H. Bradford. 1987. *A Taste of Freedom: The ICU in Rural South Africa, 1924–1930*. New Haven: Yale University Press, 145–87.

1. Central Archives Depot (CAD) Department of Justice (JUS) 272 1/399/13 Part 7 "Native Agricultural Labour: Bethal District" by B.H. Wooler, Magistrate, Bethal, 28 June 1947.

2. CAD Department of Public Health (GES) 2316 131/38 Secretary for Health to Minister of Native Affairs, 24 October 1947; see also University of the Witwatersrand Library, Ballinger Papers, A410, C2.5.2. Conditions (Bethal).

3. See, for example, Transvaal Archives Depot (TAD), Government Native Labour Bureau (GNLB) 307 81/19/35 Director of Native Labour (DNL) to Government Secretary, Bechuanaland Protectorate, 10 May 1920. Attached statements.

4. CAD Department of Native Affairs (NTS) 2009 9/280(1) Secretary of Native Affairs (SNA) to DNL, 18 April 1921; "Natives and their Contract," *The Star*, 14 March 1921; NTS 2009 9/280(1) Protector of Natives, Kimberley to DNL, 22 April 1921.

5. GNLB 307 81/19/35 Manager, Longsloot Estate to DNL, 18 November 1920.

6. TAD Archive of the Bethal Magistrate (LBH) 70 N3/13/3 Part I Magistrate, Bethal to SNA, 25 July 1946.

7. See GES 2316 131/38 SNA to Secretary for Public Health, 12 February 1937. Enclosure: "Labour Conditions on Farms in Bethal and Witbank Districts," by J.M.S. Brink, 29 January 1937, 11; JUS 272 1/399/13. Part 7 "Native Agricultural Labour: Bethal District" by B.H. Wooler, Magistrate, Bethal, 28 June 1947.

8. LBH 70 N3/13/3 Part I Inspector, District Commandant, Heidelberg, to the Deputy Commissioner, SAP, 18 December 1946; Inspector, District Commandant, Middelburg to Deputy Commissioner, South African Police (SAP), 3 January 1947.

9. "All compounds are prisons," Brink testified; GES 2316 131/38 Brink Report, 10.

20. LBH 70 N3/13/3 Part I Secretary for Health to Building Controller, 20 January 1947.

21. LBH 70 N3/13/4 Part 1 Station Commander S.A. Police, Leslie, to Public Prosecutor, Bethal, 24 July 1944. Much of what is contained in the following paragraphs is derived from the following reports: (1) GES 2316 131/38 Brink Report, and (2) D.L. Smit, Department of Native Affairs, Pretoria to Dr. P. Allan, Secretary for Public Health, Pretoria, 7 September 1943. Enclosure: Inspection of Labour Conditions on Certain Farms in the Bethal District, by J.C. Yeats, Native Commissioner, Rustenburg, 23 August 1943 (Yeats' Report).

22. *Middelburg Observer*, 4 January 1929.

23. GES 2316 131/38 Brink Report, 16.

24. "Labour in the Maize Lands" by "Farmer George," *Farmer's Weekly*, 1 April 1925 and correspondence of "Ex-officer," *ibid.*, 12 March 1924.

25. GES 2316 131/38 Brink Report, 6–7.

26. *Ibid.*

27. *Ibid.*, 10.

28. *Ibid.*, 16.

29. *Ibid.*, 6–7.

30. *Ibid.*, 8.

31. *The Star*, 11 July 1947; *Sunday Times*, 20 July 1947; GNLB 119 1953/13/154 Magistrate, Bethal to DNL, 20 August 1925.

32. The scholarly literature is extensive; see, for example, M. Morris. 1976. "The Development of Capitalism in South African Agriculture: Class Struggle in the Countryside." *Economy and Society* 5: 292–343; M. Murray. 1989. "The Origins of Agrarian Capitalism in South Africa: A Critique of the 'Social History' Perspective." *Journal of Southern African Studies* 15: 645–65; T. Keegan. 1991. "The Making of the Rural Economy: From 1850 to the Present." In *Studies in the Economic History of Southern Africa*, vol.2, ed. Z. Konczacki, J. Parpart and T. Shaw, London: Frank Cass, 36–63; B. Bozzoli, ed. 1983. *Town and Countryside in the Transvaal.*

Johannesburg: Ravan Press; Beinart, Delius and Trapido, *Putting a Plough to the Ground*; ar
H. Bradford. 1990. "Highways, Byways, and Culs-de-Sacs: The Transition to Agraria
Capitalism in Revisionist South African History." *Radical History Review* 46–7: 59–88.

33. R. Morrell. 1987. "Rural Transformations in the Transvaal: The Middelburg District, 1919
1930." M.A. thesis, University of the Witwatersrand, 203–4.

34. R. Morrell. 1988. "The Disintegration of the Gold and Maize Alliance in South Africa in th
1920s." *International Journal of African Historical Studies* 21: 620–21.

35. See C. van Onselen. 1982. *Studies in the Social and Economic History of the Witwatersran
1886–1914*, vol. 1: *New Babylon*. London: Longman, 73–4, 85–6, 174, 187–93.

36. S. Marks and S. Trapido. 1979. "Lord Milner and the South African State." *History Workshc
Journal* 8: 50–81.

37. CAD Department of Agriculture Archive (LDB) 550 7223/95 Secretary for Lands, Pretoria
the Magistrate, Bethal, 20 November 1917.

38. "Miles of Mealie-Clothed Veld. Wonder Crops of Cologne and Bombardie," *The Sta*
20 February 1928; Morrell, "Competition and Cooperation in Middelburg," 378–80.

39. "Miles of Mealie-Clothed Veld," *The Star*.

40. *The Star*, 20 February 1928.

41. "Miles of Mealie-Clothed Veld,", *The Star*, 20 February 1928.

42. Union of South Africa, Department of Agriculture. 1925. *Journal of the Department
Agriculture* 9: 204. Thanks to Robert Morrell for pointing out this reference.

43. One bag = 200 lbs.; and one morgen = 2.12 acres.

44. See S. J. de Swardt and J. C. Neethling. 1930. "Report on an Economic Investigation int
Farming in Four Maize Districts in the Orange Free State, 1928–1930." *Bulletin of th
Department of Agriculture of South Africa*, Economic Series 22, no. 173: 79, 89.

45. *The Star*, 20 February 1928.

46. "Correspondence from E. P. Alexander, Natal," *Farmer's Weekly*, 11 February 1925; *The Sta*
20 February 1928. Elsewhere, Lazarus gave different figures for the amount of acreage unde
cultivation: Longsloot, 2 800 acres; Bombardie and Springboklaagte, 4 250 acres; Cologne
Wondegsvlei, and Goedgevonden, 3 500 acres; Frisgewaagd, 1 000 acres; De Laaste Drif
400 acres; and Hartbeestfontein and Vlaklaagte, 1 800 acres; GNLB 122 1950/13/240 Lazaru
to DNL, 4 July 1925.

47. "Staple Crop Versus Mixed Farming," *The Star*, 22 May 1928.

48. *The Star*, 20 February 1928.

49. Morrell, "Rural Transformations," 201–2; *Middelburg Observer*, 27 June and 24 February 192{
The two farm managers — Marris and Stein — were lauded in 1928 as "very able;" se
Correspondence from G. E. Haupt, "Farming for Profit," *The Star*, 22 May 1928.

50. "Staple Crop Versus Mixed Farming," *The Star*, 22 May 1928.

51. *The Star*, 20 February 1928.

52. *The Star*, 22 May 1928.

53. *Farmer's Weekly*, 4 March 1925; and *The Star*, 22 May 1928.

54. It was reported in 1908, for example, in the Bethal district, "most of the natives are ordinar
squatters [i.e., labor tenants], but a good many come in from Swaziland and Zululand but d
not care to stay on the farms;" Transvaal Colony, Native Affairs Department. 1910 . *Annu
Report for the Year Ended 30 June 1908*. Pretoria: Government Printer, T.G.161910, Annexu
B(1). General. Native Commissioner, Bethal, 52. Also GNLB 107 1237/13/D53(26) Beyers
Minister of Native Affairs, Pretoria, 18 January 1917.

55. In contrast to farmers in the Bethal and Middelburg districts, white landowners in parts of th
northern and north-eastern Transvaal sat astride favored labor migration routes along whic
"foreign" migrants moved back and forth from the border to the Witwatersrand gold-mine
Hungry and tired, long-distance migrants often sought employment as causal laborers o
white-owned farms as a temporary respite from the arduous journey. Thus a historic
accident of geography gave those landowners who straddled well-worn labo

routes a distinct comparative advantage over farmers in the Bethal and Middelburg districts because they were able to satisfy much of their labor requirements by tapping into this spillover of labor; see A. H. Jeeves. 1983. "Over-reach: The South African Gold Mines and the Struggle for the Labour of Zambesia, 1890–1920." *Canadian Journal of African Studies* 17: 393–412; and A. H. Jeeves. 1986. "Migrant Labour and South African Expansion, 1920–1950." *South African Historical Journal* 18: 73–92.

6. Union of South Africa, House of Assembly. 1927. *Report of the Select Committee on the Subject of the Union Native Council Bill, Coloured Persons Rights Bill, Representation of Natives in Parliament Bill, and Natives Land (Amendment) Bill.* Cape Town: Cape Times, S.C.10–1927, evidence of W. H. Macmillan, 151.

7. *Beaumont Commission*, Evidence of J. Naude, Bethal farmer, 23. Special thanks to Robert Morrell for pointing out this reference to me.

8. Morrell, "Competition and Cooperation," 390–91; Bradford, "Getting Away with Murder," 1–5.

9. GNLB 107 1237/13/D53(26) Secretary for Native Affairs (SNA) to DNL, 16 February 1917.

0. *Beaumont Commission*, evidence of W. G. Schuurman, 323.

1. W. Beinart (in this collection).

2. GNLB 41 622/1912 Acting DNL to SNA, 24 January 1913; GNLB 107 1237/13/53[28] Circular to Magistrates, Native Commissioners and Sub-Commissioners throughout the Union, 4 April 1925.

3. Morrell, "Competition and Cooperation," 391; GNLB 41 622/1912 Sub-Native Commissioner (NC), Sekukuniland to Director, GNLB, Johannesburg, 12 February 1912.

4. *Farmer's Weekly*, 19 March 1919.

5. Morrell, "Rural Transformations," 210–12; and "Disintegration of the Gold and Maize Alliance," 626–9.

6. P. Harries. 1987. "'A Forgotten Corner of the Transvaal:' Reconstructing the History of a Relocated Community through Oral Testimony and Song." In *Class, Community and Conflict: South African Perspectives*, ed. B. Bozzoli, Johannesburg: Ravan Press, 93–134, 97–8.

7. See A. Jeeves. 1985. *Migrant Labour in South Africa's Mining Economy: The Struggle for the Gold Mines' Labour Supply.* Kingston and Montreal: McGill-Queens University Press, 3–34; 239–51; 253–64; "Over-reach," 395, 410; "Migrant Labour and South African Expansion," 73–92. Offering food and clothing, cash advances, and safe passage to labor depots, these "blackbirders", as they came to be called, spirited these recruits into the hands of licensed recruiting agents, auctioning these "bundles of labour" under their command to the highest bidder. In turn, licensed recruiters "laundered" their illegal contraband by selling them in "batches" to employers, including the maize and potato farmers in the eastern Transvaal highveld; see Bradford, "Getting Away with Murder," 1–4; and National Archives of Zimbabwe (NAZ) N3/22/4 (Volume 1) Chief Native Commissioner (CNC), Salisbury to the Secretary, Department of Administrator, Salisbury, 6 December 1918. Enclosure: Notes of a Conference held at Pietersburg, 10 September 1918.

8. See NAZ N3/22/4 (Volume 2) for a discussion of illegal recruiting along the Rhodesian border; also NTS 2027 37/280 DNL to SNA, 2 September 1922.

9. NTS 1451 87/280 Sub-NC, Louis Trichardt to NC, Zoutpansberg District, 1 December 1920; GNLB 123 1950/13/D240 SNA to DNL, 27 October 1920; GNLB 123 1950/13/D240 Lazarus to DNL, 17 October 1919.

0. NTS 2027 37/280 South African Maize Breeders', Growers' and Judges' Association to J. C. Smuts, 23 October 1920.

1. GNLB 123 1950/13/D240 DNL to Sub-NC, Louis Trichardt, 21 October 1920; NTS 1451 87/280 Sub-NC, Louis Trichardt to NC, Zoutpansberg District, 1 December 1920.

2. See GNLB 412 81/9 Jankelowitz to CNC, 27 November 1931.

3. GNLB 122 1950/13/240 Lazarus to DNL, 4 July 1928.

4. NTS 1451 87/280 Acting DNL to Sub-NC, Louis Trichardt, 21 October 1920.

75. GNLB 123 Part 150/13/D240 Lazarus to DNL, 17 October 1919; GNLB 123 Pa 150/13/D240 DNL to Sub-NC, Louis Trichardt, 21 October 1919; NTS 1451 87/280 Sub-NC Louis Trichardt to DNL, 28 October 1920.

76. NTS 1451 87/280 Acting DNL to Sub-NC, Louis Trichardt, 21 October 1920.

77. NTS 1451 87/280 Sub-NC, Louis Trichardt to NC, Zoutpansberg District, 1 Decembe 1920.

78. NTS 1451 87/280 Sub-NC, Louis Trichardt to DNL, 28 October 1920.

79. NTS 1451 87/280 Erskine to Sub-NC, Louis Trichardt, 1 June 1920.

80. NTS 1451 87/280 Sub-NC, Louis Trichardt to DNL, 28 October 1920; Acting DNL t Sub-NC, Louis Trichardt, 21 October 1920.

81. NTS 1451 87/280 Acting DNL to Sub-NC, Louis Trichardt, 21 October 1920; NTS 145 87/280 SNA to Lazarus, 6 November 1920.

82. NTS 1451 87/280 Acting DNL to Sub-NC, Louis Trichardt, 21 October 1920.

83. NTS 1451 87/280 Sub-NC, Louis Trichardt to NC, Zoutpansberg, 1 December 1920.

84. NTS 1451 87/280 Lazarus to SNA, 14 May 1921; NTS 1451 87/280 General Manager, Sout African Railways and Harbours to SNA, 26 May 1923.

85. See T.R.H. Davenport. 1977. *South Africa: A Modern History*. London: Macmillan, 199 202.

86. It seems that Mr. N. Moss was employed by Esrael Lazarus as a farm manager; *Farmer Weekly*, 11 February 1925.

87. *Ibid.*, 6 May 1925.

88. *Ibid.*, 11 February 1925.

89. *Ibid.*, 7 January 1925.

90. *Ibid.*, 11 February 1925.

91. *Ibid.*, 7 January 1925.

92. *Ibid.*,.

93. *Ibid.*, 11 February 1925.

94. *Ibid.*, 28 January 1925.

95. NTS 2027 37/280 DNL to SNA, 2 September 1922.

96. *Farmer's Weekly*, 7 January 1925; see also Morrell, "Rural Transformations," 218–9.

97. GNLB 413 1950/13/240 DNL to Justice Krause, 11 January 1929.

98. NTS 2027 37/280 G.A.G., Cape Town to Secretary to the Prime Minister, 11 June 1923.

99. *Ibid.*

100. See NAZ S138/203 SNA to CNC, Salisbury, 24 March 1926; Superintendent of Natives, Fo Victoria, to Acting CNC, Salisbury, 20 August 1926; and S235/508 Reports. District NC' 1930. NC, Melsetter District, 12.

101. For a list of ten licensed agencies recruiting for farmers in the 1940s, see TAD, Chief Nati Commissioner Northern Areas, Pietersburg (HKN) 63 90/0 Notes of Meeting held in th Minister's Office, Pretoria, 13 June 1947.

102. NTS 2027 37/280 T. Theron and Company to Minister for Agriculture, 29 December 192 "A percentage of the labour recruited for the Mines are rejected on arrival here [i.e Johannesburg] as being physically unsuitable for the purpose," Theron acknowledge "and it was in trying to find an outlet for such rejects, and so save the heavy cost of bringir them up here that I first came into touch with the farmers"; *Farmer's Weekly*, 27 Februa 1929, correspondence from Theron and Company, Johannesburg.

103. *Farmer's Weekly*, 16 March 1927.

104. NTS 2027 37/280 T. Theron and Company to Minister for Agriculture, 29 Decemb 1921.

105. *Farmer's Weekly*, 27 February 1929.

106. NTS 2027 37/280 Sub-NC, Sekukuniland to SNA, 21 April 1922.

107. *Farmer's Weekly*, 29 January 1930.

108. "Bethal Farmers Defended by Labour Expert," *Rand Daily Mail*, 17 July 1947.

09. NTS 2027 37/280 T. Theron and Company to Minister for Agriculture, 29 December 1921.

10. NTS 2027 37/280 DNL to SNA, 2 September 1922.

11. *Rand Daily Mail*, 17 July 1947.

12. GNLB 413 Part 1950/13/240 DNL to J.J. Goldstein, Bethal, 2 November 1925.

13. JUS 441 3/10/28 [Annexure] Preparatory Examination in the Case of Samuel Gafenowitz, 30 January 1928.

14. P. Arlacchi. 1983. *Mafia, Peasants and Great Estates: Society in Traditional Calabria*. Cambridge: Cambridge University Press, 85.

15. E.O. Wright. 1978. *Class, Crisis, and the State*. London: New Left Books, 61–4.

16. Correspondence of "Sorry South Africa," *Farmer's Weekly*, 18 March 1925; see also "Farm Assistants," *ibid.*, 8 April 1925.

17. Oral History Project, Institute of Advanced Social Studies, University of the Witwatersrand, Evidence of J. Nkadimeng, 16.

18. GNLB 389 33/94 SAP, Oogies to District Commandant, SAP, Middelburg, 22 September 1933; NTS 7661 23/332(1) District Commandant, Ermelo to Deputy Commissioner, SAP, Pretoria, 12 December 1917; JUS 441 3/10/28 (Sub) statement of S. Gafenowitz, Mizpah Estate, Bethal, 4 January 1928.

19. J. Scott. 1985. *Weapons of the Weak: Everyday Forms of Resistance*. New Haven: Yale University Press. See, for example, GNLB 123 1950/13/240 Statement of S. Medalie, Trichardts, 25 July 1922.

20. HKN 63 90/0 Minutes of Meeting held at Cape Town, 10 February 1948. Statement of Rossouw.

21. GNLB 119 1933/13/54 Magistrate, Witbank to DNL, 17 August 1925; see also GNLB 307 81/19/35 Acting DNL to Sub-NC, Pietersburg, 19 February 1919.

22. O. Patterson. 1982. *Slavery and Social Death: A Comparative Study*. Cambridge, Mass.: Harvard University Press, 46, 293.

23. Sampson, *Drum*, 37–54; Margaret and William Ballinger Papers, University of the Witwatersrand Library, Historical and Literary Papers Division, A410, C2.9., M. Horrell to W. Ballinger, 12 May 1959; J. Carlson. 1973. *No Neutral Ground*. New York: Thomas Crowell, 46–66; LBH 70 N3/13/4 Part 1 Agent for High Commission Territories to NC, Bethal, 15 August 1945.

24. GNLB 389 33/94 Statement of S.D. Menego, 21 September 1933.

25. See J. Kelly. 1992. "'Coolie' as a Labour Commodity: Race, Sex, and European Dignity in Colonial Fiji." In *Plantations, Peasants, and Proletarians*, ed. V. Daniel, H. Bernstein and T. Brass, 253–4, 257. London: Frank Cass.

26. LBH 70 N3/13/4 Part I Public Prosecutor, Bethal to SAP, Trichardt, 25 July 1944.

27. GES 2316 131/38 Brink Report, 16.

28. A. Ludtke. 1979. "The Role of State Violence in the Period of Transition to Industrial Capitalism: The Example of Prussia from 1815 to 1848." *Social History* 4: 176–8.

29. GES 2316 131/38 Brink Report, 16; 130. LBH 70 N3/13/4 Part 1 Northern Rhodesia Labour Officer to Magistrate/NC Bethal, 25 July 1945. Enclosure: Letter from Minyoni *et al.*, 5 June 1945.

31. LBH 70 N3/13/4 Part 1 NC Bethal to DNL 10 November 1945. Enclosure: letter from James Bowen, Kinross [n.d.]; E. Warren, Nyasaland Government Representative and Northern Rhodesia Labour Officer to Magistrate/NC Bethal, 13 February 1947.

Chapter 6
Eastern Cape Wool Farmers: Production and Control
in Cathcart, 1920–1940

1. Acknowledgements: The author is grateful for the financial assistance of Rhodes University in the research for this chapter.

2. A. Mabin. 1984. "The Making of Colonial Capitalism: Intensification and Expansion in the Economic Geography of the Cape Colony, South Africa, 1854–1899." Ph.D. thesis Simon Fraser University; R. J. Bouch. 1991. "Mercantile Activity and Investment in the Eastern Cape: the case of Queenstown 1853–1886." *South African Journal of Economic History* 6 18–37.

3. Most vividly analysed, though with nineteenth-century emphasis, in C. Bundy. 1978, rep 1988. *The Rise and Fall of the South African Peasantry*. London: Heinemann.

4. For amplification see R. J. Bouch. 1990. "The Colonization of Queenstown (Eastern Cape) and Its Hinterland, 1852–1886." Ph.D. thesis, University of London, chapters 5–9.

5. Contrast Bundy, *Rise and Fall*, 78, 134–7, with Bouch, "Colonization of Queenstown," 94–9

6. R. Wallace. 1896. *Farming Industries of Cape Colony*. London: P. S. King, 43; *Queenstown Free Press (QFP)*, 2 August 1875.

7. Cape Archives Depot (CA), Native Affairs Department (NA) 534 Part I Resident Magistrate Cathcart (RMC) to Secretary for Native Affairs (SNA), 28 March and 10 May (quotation) 1900 also schedule of district reports.

8. NA 706 Part I file 2905 SNA to RMC, 26 April 1906.

9. CA Magistrate Cathcart (1/CAT) 5/1, 4/1/5, Report by F. Veglia, 15 April 1922.

10. H. Bradford. 1988. *A Taste of Freedom*. New Haven: Yale University Press, 23–9; Union of South Africa. 1929. *Report of Land Bank for 1928*. Cape Town: U.G. 18–1929, 38, 42; Union of South Africa. 1930. *Report of Land Bank for 1929*. Cape Town: U.G. 16–1930, 40.

11. CA 1/CAT 6/1/2/1 Quitrent Apportionments; *Farmers' Chronicle and Stutterheim Times (FCST)*, 17 October 1930, 27 April 1934; University of Cape Town, Jagger Library (UCT), C. M van Coller papers (BC674), "Random Recollections," 35–9.

12. Especially R. Davies. 1979. *Capital, State and White Labour in South Africa, 1900–1960*. Brighton Harvester Press, 145–277; D. Yudelman. *The Emergence of Modern South Africa*. Cape Town David Philip, 190–248.

13. T. R. H. Davenport. 1987. *South Africa, A Modern History*. 3rd ed., Johannesburg: Macmillan chapters 10 and 11.

14. R. J. Bouch. 1980. "Farming and Politics in the Karroo and Eastern Cape, 1910–1924." *South African Historical Journal* 12: 60–2.

15. See B. Enslin. 1920. *The Wool Industry*. Pretoria: Government Printer.

16. *FCST*, 17 December 1920, 5 September 1924.

17. *Queenstown Weekly Review (QWR)*, 5 February 1910.

18. A. du Plessis. 1931. *The Marketing of Wool*. London: Pitman, 156–9; Union of South Africa. 1934. *Report of the Commission into Co-operation and Agricultural Credit*. Cape Town: U.G. 16–1934, 105.

19. Central Archives Depot, Pretoria (CAD) Department of Agriculture (LDB) 4812 Z608/1F Extract from Report of Wool Council Committee, 1.

20. Du Plessis, *Marketing of Wool*, 117–8, 160.

21. *Ibid.*, 210.

22. D. Erasmus. 1953. "Die Bemarking van Suid-Afrikaanse Wol en Enkele Bespiegelinge oor die Toekoms van die Wolbedryf." M.Comm. thesis, University of Potchefstroom, 66–7.

23. *Ibid.*, 73–4.

24. *FCST*, 3 June 1910; *Queenstown Daily Representative (QDR)*, 19 June 1926.

25. *QDR*, 19 June 1926.

26. Union of South Africa, *Commission into Co-operation and Agricultural Credit*, 104.

7. Du Plessis, *Marketing of Wool*, 213–4.

8. LDB 4812 Z608/1F Report of Wool Council Committee, 4, 6.

9. *Ibid.*, 3.

30. Cory Library Rhodes University (CL) Upper Cathcart Wool Growers' Association Minutes (UCWM), 3 September and 3 December 1932, 16 September 1933.

31. CL UCWM Report for year ended July 1936.

32. *Ibid.*, 4 October 1930.

33. *Ibid.*, Copy of UCWGA constitution.

34. *Ibid.*, 9 December 1936.

35. *Ibid.*, 4 September 1940.

36. Du Plessis, *Marketing of Wool*, 148.

37. FCST, 9 May 1930, 7 January 1938.

38. Erasmus, "Bemarking", 75–6; CL UCWM 5 September 1931 and reports for years ended July 1932, 1935, 1936.

39. CL UCWM Numerous entries 1931–1945.

40. FCST, 5 September 1930.

41. Erasmus, "Bemarking", 78–80.

42. FCST, 4 November 1932.

43. CL UCWM 28 October 1930, 14 March 1936.

44. LDB 4812, Z608/1F, Report of Wool Council Committee, 8.

45. Du Plessis, *Marketing of Wool*, 116–7.

46. FCST, 14 August 1936.

47. CL UCWM 15 October 1932.

48. *Ibid.*, 16 September 1933, 3 March 1934.

49. FCST, 3 March 1938.

50. CL UCWM 5 March 1938.

51. *Ibid.*, 5 March 1938.

52. FCST, 17 February 1938.

53. CL UCWM 20 July 1938.

54. *Ibid.*, 3 September 1938.

55. *Ibid.*, 4 September 1940.

56. FCST, 17 October 1930, 4 December 1936.

57. CAD, Economic and Wage Commission, 1925 (K139), Box 5, file 40, Evidence of King William's Town Farmers' and Woolgrowers' Association, paras. 19521–32.

58. Bradford, *Taste of Freedom*, 6, 8.

59. *Ibid.*, 7, 14.

60. FCST, 10 January 1936, 28 March 1940.

61. Union of South Africa. 1932. *Report of the Native Economic Commission*. Pretoria: Government Printer, U.G. 22–1932, 191.

62. K139, Box 3, file 18, ICU evidence, paras. 7762–72.

63. Union of South Africa, *Native Economic Commission*, 191.

64. FCST, 10 January 1936, 28 March 1940.

65. *Ibid.*, 21 February 1936.

66. CA 1/CAT 5/16 N2/3/2 Alistoun to Chief Native Commissioner (CNC), King William's Town, 2 October 1935; CNC to Native Commissioner, Cathcart (NCC), 14 October 1935; NCC to CNC, 12 November 1935.

67. *Ibid.*, D. Beal Preston to RMC, 2 September 1947.

68. CA 1/CAT 5/1 4/1/5 Wiggill to RMC, 14 February 1923.

69. CL UCWM 13 February, 3 April and 1 June 1929.

70. FCST, 2 May 1930.

71. CL UCWM 1 October 1931.

72. *Ibid.*, 2 October 1937.

73. *FCST*, 6 March 1936.

74. *Ibid.*, 3 July 1936.

75. *Ibid.*, 9 October 1936.

76. See A. Webb. 1978. "The Immediate Consequences of the Sixth Frontier War on the Farming Community of Albany." *South African Historical Journal* 10: 38–48.

77. A general point easily substantiated by reading the numerous *Blue Book* reports. For detail of how African wealth could be overestimated see Bouch, "Colonization of Queenstown," 189–90.

78. See W. Beinart and C. Bundy. 1987. *Hidden Struggles in Rural South Africa*. Johannesburg: Ravan Press, 1.

79. W. Beinart. 1992. "The Night of the Jackal: Sheep, Pastures and Predators in South Africa 1900–1930." Paper presented at Agriculture and Apartheid Workshop, Queen's University Kingston, 1992, 13–16.

80. Du Plessis, *Marketing of Wool*, 105.

81. C. Crais. 1992. *The Making of the Colonial Order: White Supremacy and Black Resistance in the Eastern Cape, 1770–1865*. Johannesburg: Witwatersrand University Press, 220.

82. M. Fairburn. 1989. *The Ideal Society and its Enemies: The Foundations of Modern New Zealand Society 1850–1900*. Auckland: Auckland University Press, 61–4, 77–187 (quotation, 265).

83. J. Belich. 1986. *The New Zealand Wars and the Victorian Interpretation of Racial Conflict*. Auckland: Auckland University Press, 311–35.

84. S. Dubow. 1989. *Racial Segregation and the Origins of Apartheid in South Africa, 1919–1936*. London: Macmillan, 66.

85. CA NA 706, Part I 2905 Applications for Private Locations Licenses, 1906. Divisional councils were locally elected bodies with responsibility for road maintenance and minor administration outside urban areas.

86. CAD Department of Native Affairs (NTS) 8159 11/342 Ashman to RMC, 10 August 1922.

87. *Ibid.*, SNA to Jabavu, 18 August 1922; SNA to RMC, 18 August and 7 September 1922.

88. *Ibid.*, Ashman to RMC, 24 August 1922.

89. CA 1/CAT 5/1 4/1/5 HFA to RMC, 25 September 1923.

90. *Ibid.*, RMC to Lower Cathcart Farmers' and Woolgrowers' Association and HFA, 5 March 1924; *FCST*, 15 February 1924.

91. See, for example, *FCST*, 7 February 1936.

92. Union of South Africa, *House of Assembly Debates* (*Hansard*), 22, cols. 455–8, 1934.

93. *FCST*, 15 February 1924.

94. R. Packard. 1990. *White Plague, Black Labor: Tuberculosis and the Political Economy of Health and Disease in South Africa*. Pietermaritzburg: University of Natal Press, 52.

95. *Ibid.*, 48–66.

96. CL UCWM 7 November 1920.

97. M. Swanson. 1977. "The Sanitation Syndrome: Bubonic Plague and Urban Native Policy in the Cape Colony, 1900–1909." *Journal of African History* 18: 387–410.

98. CL UCWM 26 June 1937, 4 June 1938.

99. *Ibid.*, 2 April 1938.

100. *FCST*, 10 March 1938.

101. W. Beinart. 1984. "Soil Erosion, Conservationism and Ideas about Development: A Southern African Exploration, 1900–1960." *Journal of Southern African Studies* 11: 83.

102. T. Gutsche. 1979. *There Was a Man*. Cape Town, 19, 247ff.

103. Union of South Africa, *Agricultural Census, 1922*, 39.

104. CA 1/CAT 5/1 4/1/5 Report by F. Veglia, 15 April 1922.

105. *Ibid.*, Field to RMC, 7 December 1921.

106. *Ibid.*, Report by F. Veglia, 15 April 1922.

107. *FCST*, 21 September 1939.

108. CA 1/CAT 5/1 4/1/5 Report by F. Veglia, 15 April 1922.

9. *Ibid.*, Lower Cathcart Farmers' Association to RMC, 5 May 1922.
10. *Ibid.*, RMC to Enslin, 9 May 1922.
11. *Ibid.*, Field to RMC, 21 October 1922.
12. *FCST*, 2 May 1930.
13. *Ibid.*, 23 March 1934.
14. *Ibid.*
15. *Ibid.*, 6 April 1934.
16. *Ibid.*, 13 April 1934.
17. *Ibid.*, 17 March 1938.
18. *Ibid.*, 4 June 1920.

Chapter 7
Migrant Workers and Epidemic Malaria on the
South African Sugar Estates, 1906–1948

1. Francis A. Wilson. 1971. "Farming 1866–1966." In *Oxford History of South Africa*. vol. II: *South Africa, 1870–1966*, ed., L. M. Thompson and M. Wilson, 126–53. Oxford: Clarendon Press; Merle Lipton. 1985. *Capitalism and Apartheid: South Africa, 1910–84*. Totowa, New Jersey: Wildwood House, 85–94; T. Keegan. 1987. *Rural Transformation in Industrializing South Africa: The Southern Highveld to 1914*. Johannesburg: Ravan, 121; Tessa Marcus. 1989. *Modernizing Super Exploitation: Restructuring South African Agriculture*. London: Zed Books, 51–56; H. Bradford. 1994. "Getting Away With Murder: 'Mealie Kings,' the State and Foreigners in the Eastern Transvaal, c. 1918–58." In *Apartheid's Genesis*, ed. P. Bonner, P. Delius and D. Posel, 96–125. Johannesburg: Ravan Press and Witwatersrand University Press.

2. Marcus, *Modernizing Super Exploitation*, 52–54.

3. The farmers demanded protection against malaria but expected the state to take responsibility and to pay for it. See below.

4. Efforts to secure legislation regulating farm labor recruiting and working conditions are extensively documented in the files of the NAD. A sampling of the correspondence is in: Central Archives Depot, Pretoria (CAD) Native Affairs Department Archive (NTS) 2048 65/280,1 Director of Native Labour (DNL), H.S. Cooke, to Secretary of Native Affairs (SNA), 12 August 1924; Memorandum on Plantation Labour in Natal, 5 October 1925, by G. A. Park Ross, Assistant Medical Officer of Health, Durban and the Chief Native Commissioner (CNC) of Natal, C. A. Wheelwright; NTS 2049 65/280A CNC, Natal to SNA, 15 July 1929; NTS 2071 144/280,1 T.W.C. Norton, CNC, Natal to SNA, 15 October 1929; H.S. Cooke, DNL to SNA, 19 August 1930; Magistrate, Lusikisiki to Chief Magistrate, Umtata, 27 November 1930; Magistrate, Matatiele to Chief Magistrate, Umtata, 1 December 1930.

5. Union of South Africa, House of Assembly, *Report of the Select Committee on the Native Labour Regulation Act, No. 15 of 1911*.

6. NTS 2048 65/280,2 DNL to SNA, 22 August 1931.

7. NTS 2071 144/280,1 SNA to DNL, n.d. [October 1929]; NAD memorandum, 26 January 1931, indicating that the Minister, E.G. Jansen, "in view of the opposition of the planters" had decided not to proceed with the amendments to Act 15, bringing the cane producers under the act.

8. The Natives' Advances Regulation Act (No. 18 of 1921) placed a limit of £2 on advances to workers recruited under Act 15. The limitation was extended to the sugar estates in 1922.

9. NTS 2048 65/280,1 NAD Minute of 31 May 1921 on NAD memo to SNA of 22 March 1921.

10. NTS 2067 138/280,2 NAD memorandum on Native Labour on the Sugar Estates, Natal, n.d., [1936] by L. J. P[hillips].

11. NTS 2048 65/280,1 Secretary for Public Health (SPH) to SNA, 28 January 1926. Governme Labour Bureau inspectors were given powers of entry under Section 146(1) of Act 36 1919, the Public Health Act, to facilitate supervision of sanitation and housing conditions c Natal mines and sugar estates. Also, NTS 2048 65/280,1 Park Ross to SPH, 4 Novemb 1925.

12. Under the omnibus measure, the Native Laws Amendment Act of 1937; see N1 2049 65/280,3 NAD Minute on application of Act 15 to the sugar planter 30 June [1939].

13. *Report of the Native Economic Commission, 1932.* Pretoria: UG 22, 1932. (Holloway Commi sion): Annexure, NAD Circular Minute, 1237/13/D53, 4 April 1925.

14. Holloway Commission, 129, para. 883.

15. CAD Government Native Labour Bureau Archive (GNLB) 108 1237/13/53 [3 G. E. Palmer to DNL, 7 January 1927; DNL to Magistrate Lyle, 17 January 1927; Lyle DNL, 21 January 1927; DNL to Lyle, 9 February 1927; Lyle to DN 12 February 1927.

16. NTS 2061 102/280 NAD memorandum on underage Africans recruited for farm lab [10 January 1925].

17. GNLB 408 65/63 Native Recruiting Corporation (NRC) to DNL, 30 December 1926; DNL NRC, 8 January 1927; Natlab (NLB) to Natives, Pietermaritzburg (CNC of Natal), 5 Januar 1927 (telegram); J. E. Palmer to DNL, 27 January 1927.

18. Randall M. Packard. 1989. *White Plague, Black Labor: Tuberculosis and the Political Economy Health and Disease in South Africa.* Berkeley: University of California Press, 159–93; H. N Coovadia and S. R. Benatar, eds. 1991. *A Century of Tuberculosis: South African Perspective* Cape Town, Oxford University Press, 22–24.

19. CAD Native Farm Labour Committee Archive (K356), 2 "Native Farm Labour Committe Statement by the Native Recruiting Corporation Ltd."

20. CAD Native Economic Commission Archive, 1930–32 (K 26), 4, evidence F. Rodseth.

21. A. de V. Minnaar. 1989. "Labour Supply Problems of the Zululand Sugar Planter 1910–1939." *Journal of Natal and Zulu History* 12: 53–72, 60.

22. Union of South Africa, *House of Assembly Debates (Hansard).* 18: 639–46, The Minister c Justice, Oswald Pirow, on Second Reading of the Native Service Contract Act, 5 Februar 1932; NTS 2204 334/280,2 Notes of meeting in the NAD concerning policy on juveni farm-labour, 25 January 1944.

23. Union of South Africa, Board of Trade and Industries. 1926. *Report on the Sugar Industr* Report no. 66. Cape Town: Cape Times, Government Printers, 5.

24. Letter from "Pioneer Planter," *Natal Mercury,* 15 May 1923, clipping in CAD Department c Public Health Archive (GES) 2625 6/56.

25. Edgar H. Brookes and N. Hurwitz. 1957. *The Native Reserves of Natal.* Cape Town: Oxfor University Press.

26. Union Government, Office of Census and Statistics. *Official Year Book of the Union and Basutoland, Bechuanaland Protectorate and Swaziland.* Pretoria: Government Printer, No. 2 767.

27. NTS 2201 315/280,7 Zululand Farmers' Union, Memorandum to the Welsh-Barrett Commi tee, 21 March 1935.

28. GES 2625 6/56 Assistant Health Officer, Durban, G. A. Park Ross, to SPH 8 October 1924.

29. William Beinart (in this collection) and W. Beinart. 1991. "Transkeian Migrant Workers an Youth Labour on the Natal Sugar Estates 1918–1948." *Journal of African History* 32: 41–63.

30. Of the several variants of the malaria parasite, *Plasmodium,* that afflict people, *Plasmodiu falciparum* is much the most common in Africa and carries the greatest risk of serious illnes and death.

.. GES 2625 6/56,D Park Ross Report on Malaria in Natal and Zululand, 16 January 1930. Union Government, Office of Census and Statistics. 1925. *Official Year Book of the Union and of Basutoland, Bechuanaland Protectorate and Swaziland*. Pretoria: Government Printing and Stationery Office, No. 6, 240.

. *Natal Mercury*, 23 April 1923, clipping in GES 2625 6/56; *Sunday Times*, 16 March 1930, clipping in *ibid*.

. The evidence for this conclusion is given below.

. A. W. Crosby. 1994. *Germs, Seeds and Animals: Studies in Ecological History*. Armonk, N.Y. and London: M. E. Sharpe, xi.

. R.G. T. Watson. 1960. *Tongaati: An African Experiment*. London: Hutchinson. Watson, the long-time manager of a sugar estate on the Natal north coast, said that prior to the era of the epidemics, whites regarded malaria as a minor irritant, easily controlled with quinine.

. The unpleasant term used by the mining industry's South African recruiter, the Native Recruiting Corporation (NRC), to describe those workers who did not pass its rudimentary medical examination.

. The story of the identification of the mosquito as the means of malaria transmission is entertainingly recounted in Robert S. Desowitz. 1991. *The Malaria Capers: More Tales of Parasites and People, Research and Reality*. New York: Norton, 174–98. South African research identified two principal mosquito vectors in Zululand, *Anopheles funestus* and *Anopheles gambiae*. The reproductive habits of the two differed sharply with *A. gambiae* breeding in small, rain-fed pools and *A. funestus* in streams. This helps to account for the sharply seasonal incidence of malaria in the subtropical Zululand lowveld, where it was found mainly during the wet months, October-May, except in the river valleys where infection occurred year round. N. H. Swellengrebel, S. Annecke and B. de Meillon. [n.d.] "Malaria Investigations in Some Parts of the Transvaal and Zululand." Publications of the South African Institute for Medical Research, vol. 4(27), 245–74.

. Carl E. M. Gunther. 1944. *Practical Malaria Control: A Handbook for Field Workers*. New York: Philosophical Library, 11. Gunther was a Medical Officer of a gold-mining company in New Guinea in the 1930s and a trained entomologist.

. Natal Archives Depot, Pietermartizburg, Chief Native Commissioner of Natal Archive (CNCP series) 16 13/2/6 Report of Dr. L. X. Kevekordes, 18 November 1932.

. GES 2625 6/56 Park Ross to Medical Officer of Health, Durban, 31 December 1923; *Hansard* 16, cols. 1659–60, Minister of Public Health, D. F. Malan, 17 March 1931, in response to question by A. O. B. Payn, MP (Tembuland), concerning an outbreak of malaria in Pondoland and Port St. Johns, hundreds of miles south of the malaria endemic zone which was directly attributable to the flow of migrant labor to the Zululand estates.

. Randall M. Packard. 1984. "Maize, Cattle and Mosquitoes: The Political Economy of Malaria Epidemics in Colonial Swaziland." *Journal of African History* 25: 189–212; Also, R. Mansell Prothero, and W. T. S. Gould. 1965. *Migrants and Malaria in Africa*. Pittsburgh: University of Pittsburgh Press, 1–6.

. Packard, "Maize, Cattle and Mosquitoes," 212.

. M. Turshen. 1984. *The Political Ecology of Disease in Tanzania*. New Brunswick, NJ: Rutgers University Press, 14–15. Yet Turshen also recognizes that, by the inter-war period, some medical officials in Tanganyika had made the connection between the health of the population and its level of education and standard of living (144). See also, J. J. McKelvey. 1973. *Man Against Tsetse: Struggle for Africa*. Ithaca, N.Y.: Cornell University Press; John Farley. 1991. *Bilharzia: A History of Imperial Tropical Medicine*. Cambridge: Cambridge University Press, 2–4; and Toyin Falola and Dennis Ityavyar, eds. 1992. *The Political Economy of Health in Africa*. Athens, Ohio: Ohio University Center for International Studies, 5–6. For a nuanced discussion of Imperial science at work in the colonies see Paul F. Cranefield. 1991. *Science and Empire: East Coast Fever in Rhodesia and the Transvaal*. Cambridge: Cambridge University Press.

44. Lord Hailey. 1945. *An African Survey: A Study of Problems Arising in Africa South of the Sahai* London: Oxford University Press, 2nd edition, 1126, 1138–40.

45. George O. Ndege. 1993. "Ecology, Sleeping Sickness and Social and Economic Transform tion in the Lake Victoria Region of Kenya." Boston: American African Studies Associatio Annual Meeting, unpublished.

46. Megan Vaughan. 1991. *Curing Their Ills: Colonial Power and African Illness*. Stanford, C Stanford University Press, 43–4.

47. Although the act was hurried through Parliament in the aftermath of the influenza epidem it had more complex origins. Susan Parnell. 1993. "Creating Racial Privilege: the Origins South African Public Health and Town Planning Legislation." *Journal of Southern Afric Studies* 19: 471–88.

48. Union Government, Office of Census and Statistics. 1924. *Official Year Book of the Union and Basutoland, Bechuanaland Protectorate and Swaziland*. Pretoria: Government Printing ar Stationery Office, No. 6, 238–9.

49. Hailey, *An African Survey*, 1154–5.

50. W. M. Macmillan. 1930. *Complex South Africa: An Economic Foot-Note to History*. London: Fab and Faber, 107.

51. *Hansard* 13, col. 675, Louis C. Gilson, MP (East Griqualand), during a debate on the NAD vot 12 August 1929.

52. Union of South Africa. 1934. *Official Year Book of the Union and of Basutoland, Bechuanalar Protectorate and Swaziland*. Pretoria: Government Printer, No. 15, 1932–1933, 246–7.

53. See below.

54. Bilharzia (schistosomiasis) results from an immune response to the eggs of a tiny parasite, type of worm that infiltrates blood vessels, particularly of the bladder, intestines and liver. is endemic in tropical and subtropical Africa, the Middle East, China, Central and Sou America and parts of the Caribbean. Like tuberculosis and indeed malaria, bilharz flourished in conditions of rural poverty and, although now easily treated, still does toda afflicting tens of millions of people throughout the tropics.

55. CNCP 108 N1/15/6 Magistrate, Bergville to SNA, 18 October 1927.

56. Brookes and Hurwitz. *Native Reserves of Natal*, 148.

57. K26, Evidence of Dr. Harry G. Phibben, District Surgeon, Port Shepston 7 October 1930.

58. See Shula Marks and Neil Andersson. 1988. "Typhus and Social Control: South Afric 1917–50." In *Disease, Medicine, and Empire: Perspectives on Western Medicine and the Experien of European Expansion*, ed. Roy MacLeod and Milton Lewis, 257–83. London and New Yor Routledge; Donald Denoon. 1988. "Temperate Medicine and Settler Capitalism: On tf Reception of Western Medical Ideas." In *ibid*, 121–38.

59. Farley, *Bilharzia*, 136–40. The author claims, rather extravagantly, that the bilharzia proble was the major motivating factor in the government's campaign against white povert (139–40). On the contrary, official concern about poor whites and efforts to assist them lor antedated the discovery of epidemic bilharzia among poor white children. As Farley show however, the government was much slower to deal with the public health dimension (poverty, even among whites, than it was the social consequences.

60. *An African Survey*, 1125.

61. Falola and Ityavyar, *Political Economy of Health*, 5–6.

62. *Ten Years of Activity of the Malaria Commission*. 1934. cited in Hailey, *An African Survey*, 112 n.6.

63. Desowitz, *Malaria Capers*, 131–2.

64. CNCP 109 N1/15/5 Notes of Proceedings of Native Commissioners' Conference, Durba 15–17 November 1933, remarks of Park Ross.

65. See below.

66. GES 2625 6/56 Park Ross to SPH, 12 May 1925.

7. *Ibid., passim.*

8. *Ibid.*, Park Ross to SPH, 14 April 1925.

9. *Ibid.*, Park Ross to CNC, Natal, 27 October 1924.

0. *Ibid.*, Park Ross to SPH, 12 May 1925.

1. *Ibid.*, Park Ross to CNC, Natal, 27 October 1924.

2. *Ibid.*, Park Ross to SPH, 6/2/25, 3 March 1925.

3. *Ibid.*, Park Ross to SPH, 12 May 1925.

4. *Ibid.*, Park Ross to CNC, Natal, 2 May 1925.

5. *Ibid.*, G. F. Kirby, Inspector of Native Labour, Northern Zululand to CNC, Natal, 16 June 1925; F. Rodseth, Inspector of Native Reserves, Eshowe to CNC, Natal, n.d. [1925].

6. *Ibid.*, SNA to SPH, 2 May 1925, conveying his views on the railway construction situation and reporting the views of the CNC, Natal.

7. NTS 2201 315/280,7 Park Ross to Chairman, Native Labour Commission, 23 March 1937, noting that he had put forward this argument to the Natal colonial authorities at a time when the Zululand farmers were cutting their first cane.

8. NTS 2048 65/280,1 Memorandum on Plantation Labour in Natal by Park Ross and CNC, Natal, C. A. Wheelwright, 5 October 1925.

9. GNLB 388 33/64 Extract from Public Health Memorandum by Park Ross, 19 August 1929.

0. *Ibid.*, Park Ross to SPH, 20 December 1930.

1. *Ibid.*, DNL to Additional Native Commissioner, Durban, 17 September 1930.

2. GES 2625 6/56D Park Ross Report on Malaria in Natal and Zululand, 16 January 1930.

3. NTS 2048 65/280,1 Memorandum on Plantation Labour in Natal, by Park Ross and CNC, Natal, C. A. Wheelwright, 5 October 1925.

4. GES 2625 6/56 reprint from the *South African Sugar Journal*, May 1925.

5. Brookes and Hurwitz, *Native Reserves of Natal*, 147.

6. Quinine is an alkaline compound originally found in the bark of the Peruvian cinchona tree.

7. Desowitz, *Malaria Capers*, 199–220; Meredeth Turshen. 1989. *The Politics of Public Health*. London: Zed Books, 158–60.

8. In 1916–17, the United States Public Health Service conducted a demonstration program for mosquito eradication in conjunction with the International Health Board at Crossett, Arkansas. Data collected during the project showed a sharp reduction in the prevalence of mosquitoes attributable to species sanitation. These kinds of demonstrations when reported internationally helped to make the case for mosquito eradication among public health professionals in other countries. United States Public Health Service. 1918. *Malaria Control: Results Obtained by a Local Community Following Antimosquito Demonstration Studies. . .* Washington: Government Printing Office, 3–8.

9. NTS 2067 138/280, Confidential, evidence of Park Ross to the Native Affairs Commission, Durban, 7 September 1932. See also, Eustace Henry Cluver. 1944. *Public Health in South Africa*. Pretoria: Central News Agency, 1944, 4th edition, "Introduction". Cluver was a former Secretary of Public Health and Chief Health Officer of the Union.

0. Dizziness, ringing in the ears and severe constipation.

1. J. Donald Millar and June E. Osborn. 1977. "Precursors of the Scientific Decision-Making Process Leading to the 1976 National Immunization Campaign." In *Influenza in America, 1918–1976*, ed. June E. Osborn, 15–27. New York: Prodist, 19.

2. GES 2626 6/56E Park Ross to SPH, 31 March 1930, enclosing booklet, "One Hundred Questions on Malaria for Zulu Scholars," based on English and Afrikaans versions.

3. Natal Archives, Pietermaritzburg, Chief Native Commissioner of Natal (CNC series) 16A 4/1 Park Ross Circular to Mission Stations in the Reserves, 13 September 1932.

4. N. H. Swellengrebel. 1931. "Report on Investigation into Malaria in the Union of South Africa 1930–31." Published by the Union Department of Public Health.

95. Cf. T. Falola. 1992. "The Crisis of African Health Care Services." In Falola and Ityavyа Political Economy of Health, 5.

96. Bruce Fetter. 1993. "Competing Determinisms and the Demography of 20th Centu Africa." Boston: American African Studies Association, Annual Meeting, unpublished.

97. CNC 109A 94/9 Notes of Proceedings of Native Commissioners' Conference held Durban, 15–17 November 1933, remarks of Park Ross, 23–5.

98. CNCP 16 13/2/6 Secretary, S.A. Cane Growers' Association to CNC, Nat 3 February 1933; GES 2627 6/56K Resolutions of a conference of Natal Malaria Committee 21 July 1933; NTS 2213 379/280, 5 J. A. Erlandson to Smit, 16 June 1941.

99. GES 2627 6/56J Park Ross to E. D. Beale, NC, Eshowe, 7 September 1932. 280, 5 J. A. Erlandson to Smit, 16 June 1941.

99. GES 2627 6/56J Park Ross to E. D. Beale, NC, Eshowe, 7 September 1932.

100. It was the large number of pneumonia deaths among workers from tropical areas in 1904– that first made black workers' health on the gold-mines a serious public health issue ar forced the ban on the employment of workers from those areas in 1913 and, late improvements in mine medical services. See, Julie Baker. 1989. "The Silent Crisis: Heal and Disease on the Gold Mines, 1902–30." Ph.D. thesis, Queen's University at Kingsto Canada; Alan H. Jeeves. 1985. Migrant Labour in South Africa's Mining Economy: The Strugg for the Gold Mines Labour Supply, 1890–1920. Kingston, Montreal and Johannesbur McGill-Queen's U.P., Witwatersrand University Press, 221–52.

101. One estate manager, R. G. T. Watson, attributed his company's belated decision to addre the health needs and deplorable living standards of its labor force solely to the malar epidemics of the early 1930s. See Watson, Tongaati: An African Experiment.

102. CNCP 16 13/2/6 Memorandum of Evidence Given Before the Provincial Finan Commission by G. A. Park Ross, 14 October 1933.

103. Ibid.

104. Report of the Chief Native Commissioner of Natal for 1936, quoted in Brookes and Hurwi Native Reserves of Natal, 147.

105. CNCP 16 13/2/6 Minutes of meeting of chiefs and headmen at the office of the Nativ Commissioner, Camperdown, 11 May 1934. Based on field work carried out in the 1930s, th anthropologist Max Gluckman concluded that ". . . while the Zulu acknowledge and u the magistracy, their attitude to Government is mainly hostile and suspicious." Se Gluckman. 1970. "The Kingdom of the Zulu." In African Political Systems. ed. M. Fortes ar E. E. Evans-Pritchard. London: Oxford University Press, 48.

106. CNCP 16 13/2/6 Park Ross to SPH, 10 November 1932. Also, GES 2627 6/56K Notes for th Minister of Public Health for Interview with Provincial Executive of Natal, 2 May 193 prepared by E. N. Thornton; Aran S. MacKinnon, "'Weary Workers' and the Politic Economy of Malaria in Zululand, c.1930–50" (unpublished).

107. Ibid., Park Ross to SPH, 10 November 1932.

108. CNCP 16 4/1 Park Ross to CNC, 26 May 1933.

109. James McCord. 1946. My Patients were Zulus. New York and Toronto: Rinehart ar Company, 248–52.

110. See Vaughan, Curing Their Ills, 24–5; and Steven Feierman. 1985. "Struggles for Contr the Social Roots of Health and Healing in Modern Africa." African Studies Review 2 73–147.

111. J. B. Brain. 1990. "'But Only We Black Men Die:' the 1929–33 Malaria Epidemics in Natal ar Zululand." Contree: Journal for South African Urban and Regional History 27: 18–25, 22. I a indebted to Jonathan Crush for drawing my attention to this article.

112. This idea is not as bizarre as it might appear. Park Ross knew that the tightly woven gra huts were, but for the open entrance ways, largely insect proof. Fitting the self-closing doo promised to make them more completely so.

113. An extensive correspondence on the tree-planting proposals is in CNCP 17 4/46.

14. GES 2628 6/56,M "Malaria Control in Natal and Zululand" by the Deputy Chief Health Officer, Durban, read at the meeting of the South African Medical Congress, Port Elizabeth, July 1939.
15. CNCP 17 13/4/2 Table of estimated deaths from malaria as reported by magistrates: November 1931–June 1932.
16. GES 2627 6/56J Park Ross to Thornton, 12 September 1932.
17. GES 2627 6/56J SPH to Park Ross, 17 September 1932.
18. See below for a discussion of the role of the malaria assistants.
19. Brain, "But Only We Black Men Die," 22.
20. GES 2627 6/56J Park Ross to E. D. Beale, NC, Eshowe, 7 September 1932.
21. CNCP 16 4/1 Park Ross to SPH, 13 February 1933.
22. GES 2627 6/56J Park Ross to E. D. Beale, NC, Eshowe, 7 September 1932.
23. NTS 2628 6/56,L Park Ross to Thornton, 12 January 1933.
24. GES 2625 6/56D Park Ross circular to Native Commissioners, 18 November 1929. In 1933, Dr L. Fourie of the DPH investigated this issue and found that there was some spillover of malaria from infected reserves to adjacent white areas. He recommended that border farmers undertake anti-larval spraying in nearby reserve areas. CNCP 16 4/5 Dr L. Fourie to CNC, 21 January 1933.
25. CNCP 16 13/2/6 Memorandum of Evidence Given Before the Provincial Finance Commission by Park Ross, 14 October 1933.
26. *Ibid*. Provincial Secretary, Natal to CNC, Natal 25 January 1933, telegram.
27. *Ibid*.
28. GES 2627 6/56K E. N. Thornton memorandum on the DPH's policy on malaria, 7 April 1933.
29. NTS 2061 102/280 Park Ross to CNC, Natal, 21 March 1929.
30. CNCP 16 13/2/6 Park Ross to CNC, Natal, 9 June 1934.
31. GES 2626 6/56,E Park Ross to SPH, 31 March 1930.
32. World Health Organization. 1984. *Malaria Control as Part of Primary Health Care: Report of a WHO Study Group*. Geneva: World Health Organization, 54–5; also Vaughan, *Curing their Ills*, 45–6; and Turshen, *Politics of Public Health*, 253–4.
33. GES 2628 6/56,L *Natal Witness* clipping, Park Ross interviewed, 24 May 1935.
34. See also, Union Government, Office of Census and Statistics. 1934. *Official Year Book of the Union and of Basutoland, Bechuanaland Protectorate and Swaziland*. Pretoria: Government Printer, No. 15, 1932–1933, 89–90.
35. NFLC 61, 329 Government Notice 1312, 6 September 1935.
36. *Ibid*., 61, 333. Zulu workers supplied only an estimated 20 to 25 per cent of total requirements.
37. NTS 2067 138/280, Confidential Chair, Anti-Malaria Committee, Mtubatuba to Minister for Public Health, 23 January 1934; NTS 2067 138/280,2 J.A. Erlandson to G. Heaton Nicholls, 5 December 1937; NTS 2211 379/280,2 Erlandson to Minister for Public Health, August 1937, complaining of chronic labor shortage and warning of the pressure from the farmers to reintroduce Pondo labor if their needs were not met from other sources. Erlandson was Vice-Chairman of the Umfolozi Co-operative Sugar Planters Ltd., the Chairman of Native Labour Committee of the Zululand Farmers' Union and a close ally of G. Heaton Nicholls, the MP for Zululand. A railway contractor in the 1920s, he had shared responsibility for the high death rate among non-tolerant workers brought in to build the Mtubatuba line.
38. NTS 2211 379/280,2 United Territories Transkeian General Council, Resolution, 1937.
39. For instance, NTS 2049 65/280,3 Annexure E, Report of Councillors Majeke and Mbizweni appointed by Bunga to visit Natal collieries and sugar estates; visit in September-October 1923.
40. NTS 2211 379/280,1 Gilson to Smit, 24 July 1936.

141. GES 2628 6/56,N Notes of Meeting of NAD officials and Representatives of the Natal Co Owners' Association and the Natal and Zululand Sugar Growers, Pretoria, 23 Novemb 1948.

142. See E. H. Cluver. 1959. *Public Health in South Africa*. Pretoria: Central News Agency, 6 edition, 284–6; also A. de V. Minnaar. 1992. *Ushukela!, A History of the Growth a Development of the Sugar Industry in Zululand: 1905 to the Present*. Pretoria: Human Scienc Research Council, 86.

143. GES 2628 6/56,N SNA to SPH, J.J. duP. le Roux, 2 December 1949; Deputy Chief Heal Officer (DCHO), Durban to SPH, 15 December 1949; SPH to SNA, 23 January 1950; DCH to Acting SPH, 15 July 1950; DCHO, Durban to SPH, 18 August 1950.

144. Vaughan, *Curing Their Ills*, 202–3. Also M. Vaughan. 1992. "Syphilis in Colonial East an Central Africa: The Social Construction of an Epidemic." In *Epidemics and Ideas: Essays on t Historical Perception of Pestilence*, ed. T. Ranger and P. Slack, 269–302. Cambridg Cambridge University Press, 299–302.

145. Vaughan, *Curing Their Ills*, 46–7.

146. Cluver, *Public Health in South Africa*, 6th ed., 1959.

147. Vaughan, *Curing Their Ills*, 39–43.

148. For southern and east Africa, the most prominent of the advocates are Packard, "Maiz Cattle and Mosquitoes;" and Turshen, *The Political Ecology of Disease*.

149. NTS 2048 65/280,2 Extract from Minutes United Transkeian General Council, motion [n. 1935]; Chief Magistrate of the Transkei to SNA, 24 July 1935; Chief Magistrate of th Transkei to SNA, 30 July 1936; NAD memo [1936] "Native Labour on the Sugar Estates.

150. Minnaar, *Ushukela*, 97.

151. D. Duncan (in this collection).

152. In 1947, when about to be ejected from office, the Smuts government was still dithering ov the application of Act 15. Ironically, it took the National Party government in the 1950 acting from motives that had nothing to do with the protection of farm workers, to exter the act to white agriculture.

153. For example, GES 2625 6/56 Park Ross pamphlet, 24 December 1933 that was widel distributed in Zululand.

154. Union of South Africa. 1922. *Report of the Sugar Inquiry Commission*. Cape Town: Cape Time Government Printers, U.G., 22/1922, 1, 31–32; Union of South Africa, Board of Trade an Industries. 1926. "New Sugar Agreement and Suspended Duties." Pretoria: Report no. 71 typescript, 1–3, 4–9; Union of South Africa. 1936. *Report of the Select Committee on the Subje of the Marketing Bill*. Cape Town: Cape Times, Government Printers, S.C. 6–'36; N. Hurwit 1957. *Agriculture in Natal, 1860–1950*. Cape Town: Oxford University Press, 48–9; Pa Martin Dickinson. 1988. "C.G. Smith and Company Ltd., The Sugar Division, 1919–39 M.A. thesis, University of the Witwatersrand, 19–31.

Chapter 8
Plantation Agriculture, Mozambican Workers and
Employers' Rivalry in Zululand, 1918–1948

1. On the composition and nature of the sugarocracy, see D. Lincoln. 1988. "An Ascendar Sugarocracy: Natal's Millers-cum-Planters, 1905–1939." *Journal of Natal and Zulu History*. 1 1–39.

2. See D. Lincoln. 1994. "The Zululand Sore: Migrant Sugar Estate Labour in Natal, 1914–1939 In *Receded Tides of Empire: Aspects of the Economic and Social History of Natal and Zululand Sin 1910*, ed. by W. Guest and J. Sellers 177–98. Pietermaritzburg: University of Natal Press.

3. This "corner" between the Lebombo Mountains/Swaziland and the coast is sometimes referred to as Tongaland (or Thongaland) or Maputaland, these being colonial designations for tribal territory which extended north into Mozambique. The superimposed magisterial districts of Ingwavuma and Ubombo coincided roughly with these southern parts of Tongaland.

4. Union of South Africa. 1919, 1923, 1924. *Report of the Department of Justice for 1918*. Pretoria, U.G. 36–'19; *Report of the Department of Justice for 1921–2*. Pretoria, U.G. 14–'23; *Report of the Department of Justice for 1922–3*. Pretoria, U.G. 9– /24.

5. See A. de V. Minnaar. 1989. "Labour Supply Problems of the Zululand Sugar Planters, 1905–1939." *Journal of Natal and Zulu History* 12: 53–72.

6. Central Archives Depot, Pretoria (CAD), Native Affairs Department (NTS) 2067, 138/280, Native Commissioner (NC) Ingwavuma to Chief Native Commissioner (CNC), 28 February 1934.

7. NTS 2211 379/280 Police Commandant Eshowe to Deputy Commissioner of Police, 19 June 1933.

8. Transvaal Archives Depot, Pretoria (TAD), Government Native Labour Bureau (GNLB) 360, 158/24/53, various correspondence.

9. NTS 2211 379/280, vol. 1 Wheelwright to Zululand Magistrates, 28 July 1925.

10. NTS 2211 379/280, vol. 1 Wheelwright to Zululand Magistrates, 15 June 1928.

11. NTS 2061 102/280 Beaumont to Secretary for Lands, 25 February 1925.

12. *Ibid.*, Secretary to Prime Minister to Secretary to Central Co-op. Cotton Exchange, 29 December 1925.

13. NTS 2123 229/280 Director of Native Labour (DNL) to Secretary for Native Affairs (SNA), 4 June 1919; SNA to Secretary for Agriculture, 14 June 1929.

14. NTS 2211 379/280, vol. 1 NC Louwsburg to CNC, 16 July 1935.

15. *Ibid.*, Statement of R. A. Rouillard, 3 June 1935.

16. NTS 2211, 379/280, CNC Natal to SNA, 13 July 1936.

17. NTS 2211, 379/280, vol. 1. Chief Magistrate (CM) Transkei to SNA, 28 September 1936.

18. CAD Department of Labour (ARB) 893 539/13A Department of Labour Report on Sugar Industry, 2 May 1939.

19. CAD Archive of the Native Farm Labour Commission (K356), vol. 4, Native Farm Labour Commission, Empangeni and Ingwavuma hearings.

20. NTS 2211 379/280, vol. 2 CNC to SNA, 7 March 1938; see also the report of sugar workers at Umfolozi being taken away one night by "some recruiter": NTS 2211, 379/280, vol. 3 Erlandson to SNA, 16 August 1939.

21. NTS 2211, 379/280, vol. 2 Heaton Nicholls to SNA, 7 March 1938; Eshowe District Commissioner of Police to Deputy Commissioner, 29 March 1938; NTS 2211 379/280, vol. 3 Acting DNL to SNA, 7 June 1938.

22. The regional wattle industry is described in N. Hurwitz. 1957. *Agriculture in Natal 1860–1950*. Cape Town: Oxford University Press, and the symposium report. 1957. *Agriculture in Natal: Recent Developments*. Cape Town: Oxford University Press. Besides the relatively recently founded wattle industry, timber plantations had been established at a number of places on the coast and in the interior of Zululand, often under state ownership, and usually for the production of railway sleepers and mine props. These had considerably less significant an impact on the functioning of the regional labor market than commercial field crop production, mining or wattle production.

23. NTS 2212 379/280, vol. 3 Labour Agents, August 1938; Notes of Interview with Minister and SNA and Erlandson and Simpson, 29 June 1938.

24. *Ibid.*, Prozesky to SNA, 2 December 1938.

25. *Ibid.*, CNC to all NCs in Natal and Zululand, 5 April, 1939.

26. See P. Scott. 1951. "The Development of the Northern Natal Coalfields." *South African Geographical Journal* 33: 53–68.

27. NTS 2212 379/280 Note of interview, 30 September 1940.
28. *Ibid.*, Chairman ZFLC to SNA, 16 June 1941; Deputy Commissioner Natal to Commissioner of Police, 13 August 1941. At some stage in 1941 all recruiters' licences in Zululand appear to have been cancelled; see NTS 2048 65/280 Minutes of Meeting, 14 November 1945.
29. *Ibid.*, SNA to Secretary for Public Health, 3 November 1942.
30. NTS 2213 379/280 Secretary for Commerce and Industries to SNA, 26 October 1944.
31. See D. Lincoln. 1993. "Flies in the Sugar Bowl: The Natal Sugar Industry Employees' Union in its Heyday, 1940–1954." *South African Historical Journal.* 29: 177–208.
32. NTS 2211 379/280, vol. 3 Secretary: Zululand Planters' Native Labour Committee to Minister of Native Affairs, 14 August 1939; NTS 2213, 379/280, vol. 1, SNA to Erlandson, 7 December 1942 and 30 December 1942.
33. NTS 2048 65/280 Secretary NSFWU to Minister of Native Affairs, 15 November 1945.
34. CAD HEN 1092 135/4 Under-secretary to Secretary for Commerce and Industries, 24 September 1948.
35. For further detail on recruiting in Zululand at the time of the National Party's ascent to state rule see D. Lincoln, "Work on South African Plantations: A Belated Response to the International Labour Organisation's 1949 Inquiry," in S. Eakin (ed.) (forthcoming).
36. Union of South Africa. 1947. *Report of the Department of Agriculture for the Year ended 31 August 1947.* Pretoria.

Chapter 9
Transkeian Migrant Workers and Youth Labor on the Natal Sugar Estates, 1918–1948

1. Acknowledgements: this chapter was first presented at the Southern African Research Program seminar, Yale University, 1989, where valuable observations were made. Thanks to Shula Marks for comments and David Lincoln for access to his unpublished work. A shorter version of this article appeared in the *Journal of African History* 31 (1991). Thanks to the editors and publisher for their permission to republish the material here.
2. Central Archives Depot, Pretoria (CAD) Department of Native Affairs (NTS) 2048 71/280, Annexure B to file 65/280, part III. Report by Committee to Enquire Into: (1) The mortality amongst natives at Izingolweni who were returning home from the sugar estates, and (2) The general medical attention on the sugar estates in Natal; E.J. Larsen, Station Master Izingolweni, to Magistrate Harding, 6 January 1922.
3. NTS 2048 71/280 Larsen to Magistrate Harding, 6 January 1922.
4. *Ibid.*
5. *Ibid.*
6. NTS 2048 71/280, Annexure A to the Committee report, Statement by S. Swartz, 8 November 1922.
7. NTS 2048 71/280 Report of Committee. The subsequent parts of this section are based on the report itself except where otherwise mentioned.
8. Dr Bonfa, the medical officer in question, was also Umzinto District Surgeon, Indian Medical Officer, Railway Medical Officer, Gaol Medical Officer and had a large private practice with both white and black patients. He and his assistants admitted that estate workers were a low priority and that minimum anti-scorbutic diets were not arranged even for those who did get to hospitals and dressing stations.
9. NTS 2048 65/280, vol. III, Annexure C Chief Magistrate Transkei (CMT) to Secretary for Native Affairs (SNA), 4 June 1924.

0. CAD Archive of the Department of Commerce and Industry (HEN) 1092 135/4, vol. II Article by R. Feldman MPC in *Illustrated News* 13 February 1946.

1. B. Albert and A. Graves, eds. 1984. *Crisis and Change in the International Sugar Economy.* Norwich: ISC Press; P. Richardson. 1986. "The Natal Sugar Industry in the Nineteenth Century." In *Putting a Plough to the Ground: Accumulation and Dispossession in Rural South Africa, 1850–1930,* ed. W. Beinart, P. Delius and S. Trapido, 129–75. Johannesburg: Ravan Press; M. Swan. 1983. *Gandhi: The South African Experience.* Johannesburg: Ravan Press.

2. P. Harries. 1987. "Plantations, Passes and Proletarians: Labour and the Colonial State in Nineteenth Century Natal." *Journal of Southern African Studies* 13: 372–99; S. Marks, *Reluctant Rebellion: The 1906–08 Disturbances in Natal.* London: Oxford University Press.

3. Harries, "Plantations, Passes and Proletarians"; A. H. Jeeves. 1985. *Migrant Labour in South Africa's Mining Economy: the Struggle for the Gold Mines' Labour Supply, 1890–1920.* Kingston and Montreal: McGill-Queen's Press.

4. NTS 7048 65/280, part I Chairman, Natal Sugar Association, Speech on 19 September 1911 as reported in *Natal Mercury,* 20 September 1911.

5. Ibid.

6. Swan, *Gandhi*; M. Swan. 1984. "The 1913 Natal Indian Strike of 1913." *Journal of Southern African Studies* 11: 239–58.

7. NTS 7048 65/280, vol. 1 for records on the problems of labor supply in the 1910s from which much of the material for the following paragraphs is drawn; see also Natal Coast Labour Recruiting Corporation, Proceedings of Annual General Meeting, 1919 (Durban, 1919) for detailed notes on labour problems.

8. N. Etherington. 1979. "Labour Supply and the Genesis of the South African Confederation in the 1870s." *Journal of African History* 20: 235–54; Harries, "Plantations, Passes and Proletarians."

9. NTS 7048 65/280 SNA to Minister of Native Affairs, 26 September 1911. A departmental committee of enquiry into the "alleged shortage of Native labour in the Natal province" reported in 1918. For inspections of conditions on the fields see Natal Archives Depot, Pietermaritzburg (NAD), CNC 358/1465/1919.

10. T. Wilks. 1980. *Douglas Mitchell.* Durban: King and Wilks, 14.

11. No central record was kept of the number of migrant workers from Pondoland on the estates; passes were not always obtained nor are pass figures available for this period. These figures are based on estimates made by the industry or government enquiries.

12. W. Beinart. 1982. *The Political Economy of Pondoland, 1860–1930.* Cambridge: Cambridge University Press.

13. Richardson, "Natal Sugar Industry."

14. A. G. Hammond. 1977. *South African Cane Growers' Association: The First Fifty Years.* Durban, is a detailed treatment of tariff issues and legislation. The book, like the *South African Sugar Journal,* which Hammond edited, makes little mention of sugar workers. F. J. van Biljon. 1939. *State Interference in South Africa.* London: P.S. King, has an interesting chapter. For Mozambique, see L. Vail and L. White. 1980. *Capitalism and Colonialism in Mozambique: A Study of the Quelimane District.* London: Heinemann, chapter 5. Conditions and wages on Hornung's giant Sena Sugar Estates in Quelimane, which had supplied the South African market, were probably worse than in Natal. N. Hurwitz. 1957. *Agriculture in Natal, 1860–1950.* Natal Regional Survey, vol. 12. Cape Town: Oxford University Press.

15. Union of South Africa. 1922. *Report of the Sugar Enquiry Commission.*

16. B. Albert and A. Graves, ed. 1988. *The World Sugar Economy in War and Depression, 1914–40.* London: Routledge; F. Wilson. 1971. "Farming, 1866–1966." In *The Oxford History of South Africa,* vol. II: *South Africa, 1870–1966,* ed. M. Wilson and L.M. Thompson, 104–71. Oxford: Oxford University Press, 1971.

17. Union of South Africa, Social and Economic Planning Council. 1945. *The Future of Farming in South Africa,* Report No. 4. Pretoria: U.G. 10–1945. One of the leading critics of agricultural protectionism, Professor C. S. Richards of the University of the Witwatersrand, seems to have

come to a similar conclusion some years before. C.S. Richards. 1935. "Subsidies, Quotas Tariffs and the Excess Cost of Agriculture in South Africa." *South African Journal of Economic* 3: 381, Table II.

28. W. Martin. 1935. "Subsidies, Quotas, Tariffs and the Excess Cost of Agriculture in Sout Africa: A Criticism." *South African Journal of Economics* 3: 567.

29. See Wilson, "Farming;" Van Biljon, "State Interference;" Richards, "Subsidies, Quotas; R. Horwitz. 1967. *The Political Economy of South Africa*. London: Weidenfeld and Nicolson.

30. Richards, "Subsidies, Quotas."

31. Hammond, *First Fifty Years*, 136.

32. Hammond, *First Fifty Years*; S. Marks. 1979. "Natal, the Zulu Royal Family and the Origins o Segregation." *Journal of Southern African Studies* 4: 172–94; S. Marks. 1987. *The Ambiguities c Dependence in South Africa: Class, Nationalism and the State in Twentieth-Century Natal* Johannesburg: Ravan Press; S. Dubow. 1989. *Racial Segregation and the Origins of Apartheid in South Africa, 1919–36*. London: Macmillan.

33. See NTS 2048 65/280 and subsequent files.

34. NTS 2048 65/280, part 2 Letter to Minister of Native Affairs, 20 January 1930.

35. NTS 2048 65/280, vol. II Note on J. Mould Young, CMT to SNA, 12 July 1934.

36. S. Dubow. 1986. "Holding 'A Just Balance between Black and White': The Native Affair Department in South Africa c.1920–1933." *Journal of Southern African Studies* 12: 217–39.

37. Union of South Africa. 1939. *Report of the Native Farm Labour Committee, 1937–39* (RNFLC) Pretoria, 207, paragraph 496.

38. Cape Archives, Cape Town (CA) Chief Magistrate Transkei (CMT) 3/604/49 Director o Native Labour (DNL) Circular, Table, 10 May 1922; and D. Fox and D. Back. 1938. "A Preliminary Survey of the Agricultural and Nutritional Problems of the Ciskei and Transkeian Territories." Johannesburg: Report to the Chamber of Mines, Table 29.

39. R. G. T. Watson. 1960. *Tongaati: An African Experiment*. London: Hutchinson, 144.

40. Interview, Mgeyana ka Ngumlaba, Msikaba, Lusikisiki, 14 January 1977.

41. NTS 2048 65/280, vol. 2 Correspondence.

42. Watson, *Tongaati*, 149.

43. NTS 2067 138/280 Report of Statement by Solomon to the Native Affairs Commission 1932.

44. NAD CNC 120/3 N3/13/4(X) Memorandum on the Problem of Farm Labour by H. M. Gluckman, 1 November 1937. This was a long memo by Gluckman, arguing that the farm labor shortage should be solved by improving conditions and productivity rather than increasing the number of workers on the farms. Its interest lies not least in his attempt to find a language to which the Farm Labour Committee might listen.

45. *Ibid*.

46. NTS 2048 65/280 part II Addendum by Chairman of District Council, Qumbu, 1931.

47. Interview, George Green, Marengo Flats (near Izingolweni), 5 June 1982.

48. R. Packard. 1987. "Tuberculosis and the Development of Industrial Health Policies on the Witwatersrand, 1902–32." *Journal of Southern African Studies*. 13: 17–209.

49. For the malaria epidemic, see CAD Department of Health (GES) 565 36/12 and 2624–2628 6/56.

50. GES 565 36/12B Health of Natives on Matubatuba-Pongola Railway Construction 4 December 1926.

51. R. Packard. 1984. "Maize, Cattle and Mosquitoes: The Political Economy of Malaria Epidemics in Colonial Swaziland." *Journal of African History* 25: 189–212.

52. GES 565 36/12B Cutting from Natal Mercury 4 July 1929.

53. GES 2624 6/56 vol. 1, Report on Investigations into Malaria Epidemic; Government Pathologist to Assistant Health Officer, Durban, 11 June 1929; Mitchell to Prime Minister, 31 July 1929. (54) NTS 2049 65/280, vol. 3 Report by Transkeian Territories General Council Delegation to Sugar Estates and Collieries in Natal.

55. NTS 2049 65/280A Secretary of Public Health to SNA, 10 May 1929.

56. Watson, *Tongaati*, 15.

57. M. Hunter. 1936, 1966. *Reaction to Conquest*. London: Oxford University Press, 109.

58. United Transkeian Territories General Council (UTTGC), 1935, minute 77.

59. UTTGC, *Debates and Proceedings, 1934*, 166.

60. UTTGC, 1936, 241.

61. NTS 2202 315/280 Report of the Departmental Committee into Native Labour, 1935, Evidence of Larrington, Macleod and J. Moshesh, L. Bam and C. Sakwe for the UTTGC.

62. NTS 7048 65/280 report in *Natal Mercury*, 20 September 1911.

63. P. la Hausse. 1990. "'The Cows of Nongoloza': Youth Crime and Amalaita Gangs in Durban, 1900–36." *Journal of Southern African Studies* 16: 79–111; C. van Onselen. 1982. "The Witches of Suburbia: Domestic Service on the Witwatersrand, 1890–1914." In *Studies in the Social and Economic History of the Witwatersrand, 1886–1914*, vol. 2: *New Nineveh*. London: Longman, 1–73; K. Atkins. 1986. "Origins of the Amawasha: The Zulu Washermen's Guild in Natal, 1850–1910." *Journal of African History* 27: 41–57.

64. CAD Government Native Labour Bureau (GNLB) 252 357/10/98 enclosing newpaper cutting. Reference from P. la Hausse.

65. P. Delius and S. Trapido. 1982. "Inboekselings and Oorlams: The Creation and Transformation of a Servile Class." *Journal of Southern African Studies* 8: 214–42 and T. Keegan. 1987. *Rural Transformations in Industrialising South Africa: The South African Highveld to 1914*. London: Macmillan, provide the most developed analysis of African family labor on white-owned farms.

66. Interviews with Mcetywa Mjomi, Amadiba location, Bizana, 15 April 1982; Meje Ngalonkulu, Mtayiso location, Bizana, 7 April 1982; Phatho Madikizela, Amangutyana location, Bizana, 12 April 1982.

67. Beinart, *Political Economy of Pondoland*; Hunter, *Reaction to Conquest*.

68. See J. Guy. 1987. "Analysing Pre-Capitalist Societies in Southern Africa." *Journal of Southern African Studies* 14: 14–37, for a recent restatement of this position.

69. Beinart, *Political Economy of Pondoland*, Tables 5 and 6.

70. *Pondoland General Council, 1929*, 57–58, speech by Councillor Soxujwa, Lusikisiki.

71. Interview with Phatho Madikizela, 12 April 1982.

72. CMT 3/604/49 for the case of Govuza who deserted in 1921; also interviews with Leonard Mdingi, Bizana, June 1982.

73. University of Cape Town, Jagger Library (UCT), MS BC 630, South African Sugar Association (SASA), "Memorandum Dealing with the Conditions of Native Labour in the Sugar Industry for Submission to the Natives Laws Commission of Enquiry," 8 January 1947; Union of South Africa. 1948. *Report of the Native Laws Commission, 1946–8*. Pretoria: U.G. 28–1948.

74. Nicholls quoted in Dubow, *Racial Segregation*, 145.

75. UCT MS BC 630 SASA, "Memorandum."

76. Figures are taken from the *Agricultural Censuses* which recorded, in these years, both the acreage of Uba and other canes planted and reaped.

77. RNFLC, para. 326, 138.

78. This is the major theme of Watson, *Tongaati*; see also P. van den Berghe. 1964. *Caneville: The Social Structure of a South African Town*. (Middletown, Conn.: Wesleyan University Press.

79. NTS 2048 65/280, vol. 2.

80. Hammond, *First Fifty Years*, chapter 10.

81. M. Swan. 1987. "Ideology in Organised Indian Politics, 1891–1948." In *The Politics of Race, Class and Nationalism in Twentieth Century South Africa*, ed. S. Marks and S. Trapido, 182–208. London: Longman. I am indebted to Maureen Swan for discussions of this period as well as access to material from her interviews with Rowley Arenstein and R.D. Naidoo; see also D. Lincoln, "Employment Practices, Sugar Technology, and Sugar Mill Labour: Crisis and Change in the South African Sugar Industry, 1914–1939." In Albert and Graves, *World Sugar Economy*.

82. Union activities in the sugar industry are the subject of considerable correspondence in NTS 2049 65/280 and HEN 1092 135/4.

83. H. Bradford. 1994. "Getting Away With Murder: 'Mealie Kings,' the State and Foreigners in the Eastern Transvaal, c.1918–58." In *Apartheid's Genesis*, ed. P. Bonner, P. Delius and D. Posel, 96–125. Johannesburg: Ravan Press and Witwatersrand University Press.

84. D. Hindson. 1987. *Pass Controls and the Urban African Proletariat*. Johannesburg: Ravan Press D. Posel. 1991. *The Making of Apartheid, 1948–1961*. Oxford: Clarendon Press.

85. M. Morris. 1977. "State Intervention and the Agricultural Labour Supply Post–1948." In *Farm Labour in South Africa*, ed. F. Wilson, *et al.*, 62–71. Cape Town: David Philip.

86. L. Platzky and C. Walker. 1985. *The Surplus People: Forced Removals in South Africa* Johannesburg: Ravan Press; M. Lipton. 1985. *Capitalism and Apartheid: South Africa, 1910–84*. London: Gower.

87. C. van Onselen (in this collection).

Chapter 10
"Synonymous with Gentlemen"? White Farmers, Schools and Labor in Natal, c.1880–1920

1. Research for this paper was funded by the Staff Research Fund of the University of Natal (Durban).

2. N. Nuttall. 1971. *Lift up your Hearts: The Story of Hilton College, 1872–1972*. Durban: Hiltonian Society, 6.

3. R. Connell. 1987. *Gender and Power: Society, the Person and Sexual Politics*. Stanford, Ca.: Stanford University Press.

4. For a more detailed account see R. Morrell. 1994. "Boys, Gangs and the Making of Masculinity in the White Male Secondary Schools of Natal, 1880–1930." *Masculinity* 2.

5. S. Haw and R. Frame. 1988. *For Hearth and Home: The Story of Maritzburg College 1863–1988*. Pietermaritzburg: M.C. Publications, 10; J.A. Mangan. 1981. *Athleticism in the Victorian and Edwardian Public School: The Emergence and Consolidation of an Educational Ideology*. Cambridge: Cambridge University Press.

6. For example, J. A. Mangan. 1986. "Manly Chaps in Control: Blues and Blacks in the Sudan." In *The Games Ethic and Imperialism: Aspects of the Diffusion of an Ideal*, ed. J.A. Mangan. Harmondsworth and New York: Viking.

7. *College Magazine* 1(12), September 1902: 8.

8. *The Hiltonian* 4(8), June 1905: 7–8.

9. *S. Michael's Chronicle* III(6), June 1913: 8.

10. See, for example, J. Richards. 1987. "'Passing the Love of Women': Manly Love and Victorian Society." In *Manliness and Morality: Middle-Class Masculinity in Britain and America, 1800–1940*, ed. J. Mangan and J. Walvin. Manchester: Manchester University Press.

11. *The Hiltonian* 2(3), November 1902: 13.

12. Interview with David Fannin, Durban, 20 January 1993.

13. *The Hiltonian* 1(2), June 1902: 39.

14. *S. Michael's Chronicle* II(7), November 1906: 2.

15. *The Hiltonian* 1(2), June 1902: 68.

16. "Speech of the Governor," *S. Michael's Chronicle* II(14), June 1910: 4.

17. *The Hiltonian* 1(2), June 1902: 36; *The Hiltonian* 5(9), July 1906: 16; *The Hiltonian* 7(13), June 1910; *Pietermaritzburg College Magazine* IV(49), June 1924: 32.

18. V. Stiebel. 1968. *South African Childhood*. London: Andre Deutsch, 188.

19. See Morrell, "Masculinity in Male Secondary Schools" for a fuller description of violence, hardship and the lack of comfort in these schools.

20. Interview with David Fannin; Interview with Victor Fly, Hilton, 25 February 1992.

21. See C. van Onselen (in this collection) and R. Morrell. Forthcoming. "Forging a Ruling Race: Rugby and White Masculinity in Colonial Natal, *c.*1870–1910." In *Making Men: Rugby and Masculine Identity in the British Isles and Settler Empire*, ed. J. Nauright and T. Chandler.

22. *The Hiltonian* 2(3), November 1902: 13.

23. *The Hiltonian* 5(9), July 1906: 48–9.

24. *The Hiltonian* 5(10), January 1907): 69.

25. *The Hiltonian* 7(13), June 1910: 7.

26. *Pietermaritzburg College Magazine* 1(12), September 1902: 17.

27. *S. Michael's Chronicle* II(4), May 1905: 6.

28. Annual dinner speech of Dr A. McKenzie, *The Hiltonian* 1(2), June 1902: 68.

29. For the Midlands, see B. Mazower. 1991. "Agriculture, Farm Labour and the State in the Natal Midlands, 1940–1960." M.A. thesis, University of Cape Town, 37. Elsewhere, see R. Morrell. 1986. "Competition and Cooperation in Middelburg, 1900–1930." In *Putting a Plough to the Ground: Accumulation and Dispossession in Rural South Africa, 1850–1930*, ed. W. Beinart, P. Delius and S. Trapido. Johannesburg: Ravan Press.

30. See, for example, Natal Archives Depot, Pietermaritzburg (NA) Master of the Supreme Court, Deceased Estates (MSCE) 7/71, 1888 death notice of G.C. Moor, brother of F.R. Moor (future Prime Minister of Natal).

31. L. Davidoff and C. Hall. 1987. *Family Fortunes: Men and Women of the English Middle Class, 1780–1850*. London: Hutchinson.

32. NA MSCE 6091/1921 Estate of James Ralfe, will dated 11 February 1920.

33. C. van Onselen (in this collection).

34. J. Lambert. 1986. "Africans in Natal, 1880–1899: Continuity, Change and Crisis in a Rural Society." Ph.D. thesis, University of South Africa, Pretoria, 102; Baynesfield Museum, Thornville, Transcript of interviews with Indian laborers conducted in 1980–81.

35. For a fascinating insight into the divisive effect this could have on a farming community see the 1904–5 correspondence between members of the Bergville Farmers' Association and the Colonial Secretary; NA, Colonial Secretary's Office (CSO) 1767 1904/9403 and CSO 1781 1905/872.

36. R. Pearse. 1946. *Sable and Murray: The Story of Estcourt High School*. Pietermaritzburg: Natal Witness, 25; *S. Michael's Chronicle* II(8), June 1907: 20.

37. *Natal Agricultural Journal (NAJ)*, 6, 1903: 871.

38. *Ibid.*, 877–80.

39. S. Marks. 1970. *Reluctant Rebellion: The 1906–1908 Disturbances in Natal*. Oxford: Clarendon Press, 23; Lambert, "Africans in Natal," 300, 303.

40. Mazower, "Agriculture, Farm Labour and the State," 62.

41. Y. Miller. 1978. *Acutts of Africa*. Pinetown: private publication, 46; *Natal Native Affairs Commission (NNAC)*, Evidence, 1907, 199. Similar views were expressed by prominent Richmond farmers, William Nicholson and M.A. Cockburn, 340, 357.

42. *NNAC*, Evidence, 230.

43. *NAJ* 7, 1904, 1039–40.

44. *NNAC*, 331.

45. *Ibid.*, Evidence of C. Acutt, 200.

46. *Ibid.*, 199.

47. NA CSO 1525 1897/5298 Under Secretary to Colonial Secretary, 3 August 1897.

48. *NNAC*, Evidence of H.D. Winter, 218.

49. *Ibid.*, 219.

50. NA Secretary for Native Affairs (SNA) 169 1893/416.

51. J. Montgomery. 1909. "Kafir Labour, or Our 'Boys'." *NAJ* 8: 741.

52. *Ibid.*

53. *NNAC*, 197–8.

54. *Ibid.*, Evidence of chiefs from Ixopo, Nkandla and Mapumulo districts, 709.

55. *Ibid.*, 713–4.

56. B. Carton. 1993. "Taxing Loyal Ties: Bambatha's Followers and the Destruction of Family in Natal and Zululand, 1890–1910." African Studies Seminar Programme, University of Natal Durban, unpublished.

57. Mazower, "Agriculture, Farm Labour and the State," 57–8.

58. *NNAC*, 339, 717.

59. NA, NCP 8/5/22 Correspondence Relative to the Eviction of Native Occupants from Crown Lands, 1883, 27.

60. *NNAC*, Evidence of Foxon and Walker, 363, 369.

61. See, for example, NA 1/HWK LRG 453/1904 case against John Mabusa, 1904.

62. L. Camp. 1986. "Agriculture in Adolescence," B.A Hons. thesis, University of Natal Pietermaritzburg, 47; Lambert, "Africans in Natal," 290.

63. Maritzburg College Archive, File "E.B. Foxon."

64. *NNAC*, Evidence of Ntando, Estcourt and Mketengu, Richmond, 719, 769.

65. NA Chief Native Commissioner (CNC) 80 1128/1912 Statement of 18 June 1912.

66. V. Harris. 1992. "Time to Trek: Landless Whites and Poverty in the Northern Natal Countryside, 1902–1939." In *White but Poor: Essays on the History of Poor Whites in Southern Africa, 1880–1940*, ed. R. Morrell. Pretoria: University of South Africa.

67. *NNAC*, 336–7.

68. J. Beall and D. North-Coombes. 1983. "The 1913 Disturbances in Natal," *Journal of Natal and Zulu History*. 6; M. Swan. 1984. "The 1913 Natal Indian Strike." *Journal of Southern African Studies* 10: 239–58; W. Beinart (in this collection).

69. H. Bradford. 1986. "Lynch Law and Labourers: The ICU in Umvoti, 1927–1928." In *Putting Plough to the Ground*, 420–49; J. Louden. 1970. *White Farmers, Black Labour-Tenants: A Study of a Farming Community in the South African Province of Natal*. Leiden/Cambridge: Cambridge University Press, 127–8; Mazower, "Agriculture, Farm Labour and the State."

70. C. van Onselen (in this collection).

71. T. Ranger. 1993. "Tales of the 'Wild West': Gold-Diggers and Rustlers in South-West Zimbabwe, 1898–1940." *South African Historical Journal* 28.

72. The Combined Criminal Record Book and Case and Fines Book for Mooi River (NA, 1/MRV Volume 1) shows that very few charges of assault were brought against white farmers.

73. Marks, *Reluctant Rebellion*, 238.

74. A.G. McKenzie. [n.d.] *Delayed Action: Brigadier-General Sir Duncan McKenzie KCMG, CB DSO, VD, Legion d'Honneur*. Private publication, 34.

75. Interview with Barbara McKenzie, "Single Tree," Dargle, 30 June 1992.

Chapter 11
Paternalism and Violence on the Maize Farms
of the South Western Transvaal, 1900–1950

1. For an excellent account of violence in the Transvaal in the late nineteenth century see P. Delius. 1986. "Abel Erasmus: Power and Profit in the Eastern Transvaal." In *Putting Plough to the Ground: Accumulation and Dispossession in Rural South Africa, 1850–1930*, ed. W. Beinart, P. Delius and S. Trapido, 176–217. Johannesburg: Ravan Press. On the contemporary period see L. Segal. 1990. "A Brutal Harvest: The Roots and Legitimation of Violence on Farms in South Africa." Seminar Paper No. 9, Project for the Study of Violence University of the Witwatersrand, unpublished.

2. H. Bradford. 1987. *A Taste of Freedom: The I.C.U. in Rural South Africa, 1924–1930*. New Haven Yale University Press, 43 and 55.

3. T. Keegan. 1986. *Rural Transformations in Industrializing South Africa: The Southern Highveld to 1914*. Johannesburg: Ravan Press, 157.

4. This draws on the material presented in C. van Onselen. 1990. "Race and Class in the South African Countryside: Cultural Osmosis and Social Relations in the Sharecropping Economy of the South-Western Transvaal, 1900–1950." *American Historical Review* 95: 102–6.

5. The lives of these sharecroppers, have been systematically recorded since 1979, and the accounts are preserved in University of the Witwatersrand (UW), African Studies Institute (ASI), M. M. Molepo Oral History Collection (MOHC). The evidence used in this chapter is drawn exclusively from this source except where it is explicitly stated to the contrary.

6. This theme is explored at length in Van Onselen, "Race and Class," 99–123.

7. E. Genovese. 1988. *The World the Slaveholders Made: Two Essays in Interpretation*. Middletown: Wesleyan University Press, 200.

8. E. Genovese. 1991. '"Our Family, White and Black': Family and Household in the Southern Slaveholders' World View." In *In Joy and Sorrow: Women, Family and Marriage in the Victorian South, 1830–1900*, ed. C. Bleser, 69–87. New York: Oxford University Press.

9. G. Fredrickson. 1988. *The Arrogance of Race: Historical Perspectives on Slavery, Racism and Social Inequality*. Middletown: Wesleyan University Press, 19.

10. J. Oakes. 1982. *The Ruling Race: A History of American Slaveholders*. New York: Vintage Books, xi, 202–3; see also Genovese, *The World the Slaveholders Made*, 96; and H. G. Gutman. 1977. *The Black Family in Slavery and Freedom, 1750–1925*. New York: Pantheon Books, 309–10.

11. Oakes, *Ruling Race*, 202.

12. Quoted in O. Patterson. 1977. "Slavery." *Annual Review of Sociology* 3: 426.

13. This, in itself, was capable of producing "domestic struggles" within the household, which were — in part — predicated on traditional notions of what was considered to be the appropriate sexual division of labor. In this way, for example, there was a heightening of tension between the patriarch and his wives at the season's end when the women were called upon to help bring in the harvest — the proceeds of which, depending on the crop being produced, would not necessarily be distributed equitably. The notion of "domestic struggle" is drawn from B. Bozzoli. 1983. "Marxism, Feminism and South African Studies." *Journal of Southern African Studies* 9: 139–71.

14. This could, amongst other things, depend on changing customary practices, gender, patterns of socialization, personality and sibling order.

15. Fredrickson, *Arrogance of Race*, 19; Oakes, *Ruling Race*, 194.

16. See the evidence in C. van Onselen. 1996. *The Seed is Mine: The Life of Kas Maine, a South African Sharecropper, 1894–1985*. Cape Town: David Philip.

17. Obviously this was partly pre-determined by the age and gender composition of the sharecropper's family.

18. Oakes, *Ruling Race*, 192.

19. See S. Dubow. 1989. *Racial Segregation and the Origins of Apartheid in South Africa, 1919–1936*. London: Macmillan, 29–31.

20. For the Cape case see S. Trapido. 1990. "The Emergence of Liberalism and the Making of 'Hottentot' Nationalism." Seminar on Southern African Societies, Institute of Commonwealth Studies, University of London, unpublished; and S. Trapido. 1990. "From Paternalism to Liberalism: Cape Colony, 1800–1834." *International History Review* 12: 76–104.

21. Bradford, *Taste of Freeedom*, 263. "Paternalism," suggests Oakes, "is the ideological legacy of a feudal political system with no fully developed market economy." Oakes, *Ruling Race*, xii.

22. See Suid-Westlike Transvaalse Landboukooperasie Beperk. 1960. *'N Halfeeu van Kooperasie, 1909–1959*. Leeudoringstad; see also, M. de Klerk. 1985. "Seasons That Will Never Return: The Impact of Farm Mechanisation on Employment, Incomes and Population Distribution in the Western Transvaal." *Journal of Southern African Studies* 11: 84–105.

23. Interview with A. C. G. Nieman (formerly of the farm Kommissierust) by C. van Onselen, Bloemhof, 16 July 1985. More generally, see B. A. Neethling. 1930. *An Economic Investigation of Farms in the Maize Districts of the Orange Free State, 1927–8*. Pretoria: Department of Agriculture, Economic Series, No. 12; and Union of South Africa. 1932. *Report of the Native Economic Commission, 1930–32*. Pretoria: U.G. 22–1932, 52.

24. Interview with Z. Isane and A. Nanabhay by C. van Onselen, Johannesburg, 11 November 1987.

25. Gutman, *Black Family in Slavery and Freedom*, 310.

26. We do, however, have some valuable clues as to how, on occasion, these practices were received and partially internalized by members of the underclasses; see, for example L. Vail and L. White. 1980. *Capitalism and Colonialism in Mozambique: A Study of the Queliman District*. London: Heinemann.

27. In this context see M. Russell and M. Russell. 1979. *Afrikaners of the Kalahari: White Minority ir a Black State*. Cambridge: Cambridge University Press.

28. See, for example, Van Onselen, "Race and Class," 119. The mere adoption of an Afrikaan first name should not, however, be weighted too heavily since it was almost always used ir tandem with a first name in the vernacular.

29. These insights are derived from personal observations of white children in the wester Transvaal during the 1950s. It is, of course, very likely that such names were first given to the white landlord's children by black nursemaids. In this way, for example, the use of the name Palesa (SeSotho, 'Flower') as the name for a daughter has also been drawn to my attention.

30. See, for example, UW, ASI, MOHC, No. 160 A/B, Interview with M. Jameson by M.T. Nkadimeng, Kroonstad, 26 February 1980, 11. The interviewee recalled his landlord referring to him as a "*Vluksekaffertjie*" ("capable little kaffir"). In English-speaking urba areas, this practice helped give rise to the term "boy" or "girl" being applied to an Africa man or woman — an offensive custom that clings to the paternalist ethos that surrounds the employment of domestic servants.

31. See, for example, S. Boshoff and G. Nienaber. *Afrikaanse Etimologie*. Pretoria: Tafelberg, 390

32. See, D. Bosman, I. van der Merwe and L. Hiemstra. 1984. *Tweetalige Woordeboek*. Cape Town 390.

33. Keegan, *Rural Transformation*, 156.

34. Genovese, *The World the Slaveholders Made*, 199.

35. Which is not, of course, to suggest that such forms of discipline were not resorted to by triangle landlords during the interwar period; they were. Numerous examples of assaults fines and whippings are to be found in the testimony of black tenants housed in the UW, ASI MOHC.

36. Where such submission was not forthcoming, landlords were not beyond bringing in kir or quasi-kin from farther afield to assist in such beatings. Although unequivocally brutal such gang-assaults were still considered to fall within the ambit of "family discipline" by the white landlord; see UW, ASI, MOHC, Nos. 63B and 64 A/B, Interview with J.M. Nkadimeng by M.T. Nkadimeng, Nebo, 22 October 1979, 22–3.

37. See Van Onselen, *The Seed is Mine*. These practices, in turn, were probably informed by the nineteenth century Cape experience; see A. Du Toit and H. Giliomee. 1983. *Afrikaner Politica Thought*. Berkeley: University of California Press, 36.

38. UW, ASI, MOHC, No. 336, Interview with N. Makume by T.T. Flatela, Viljoensdrift 10 August 1982, 38.

39. Van Onselen, "Race and Class," 109–10.

40. See M. Mauss, *The Gift*. 1989. London: Routledge; M. Sahlins. 1968. "The Sociology o Primitive Exchange." In *The Relevance of Models for Social Anthropology*, ed. M. Banton, 139–86 London: Tavistock.

41. UW, ASI, MOHC, No. 234, Interview with K. Maine by M.M. Molepo, Ledig, 17 Septembe 1980.

42. See UW, ASI, MOHC, No. 336, Interview with N. Makume by T.T. Flatela, Viljoensdrift 10 August 1982, 41; No. 403, Interview with M.T. Lerefudi by T.T. Flatela, Lichtenburg 26 August 1982, 19.

43. Figures on local diamond production are from Standard Bank Archives, Johannesburg Annual Inspection Reports, Bloemhof Branch, 1912–1929.

44. P. Tyson. 1983. "The Great Drought." *Leadership S.A.* 2: 49–57; and P. Tyson. 1986. *Climati Change and Variability in Southern Africa*. Cape Town: Oxford University Press.

45. For details of technical innovations during the late 1920s, see Van Onselen, *The Seed is Mine*, chapter 5.

46. Bradford, *A Taste of Freedom*.

47. For further details see Van Onselen, *The Seed is Mine*, chapter 5.

48. UW, ASI, MOHC, No. 264, Interview with K. Maine by C. van Onselen, Ledig, 24 February 1981, 6.

49. UW, ASI, MOHC, No. 204, Interview with K. Maine by I.T. Nkadimeng, T.J. Couzens and G. Relly, Ledig, 2 July 1980, 34; No. 555, Interview with M.A. Maine by M.T. Nkadimeng, Rooipoort, Hertzogville, 23 October 1986, 7. These changed attitudes towards paternalism even on the part of social conservatives like Maine — are traced in detail in Van Onselen, *The Seed is Mine*, chapter 5.

50. On the advent of the "wet cycle," see Tyson, *Climatic Change*.

51. Department of Agricutural Economics and Marketing. 1961. *Handbook of Agricultural Statistics, 1904–1950*. Pretoria, "Table 8: Agricultural Machinery and Implements," 13.

52. The effect of World War II on South African agriculture can be traced in J. Tinley. 1954. *South African Food and Agriculture in World War II*. Stanford: Stanford University Press.

53. On the local populist tradition see Van Onselen, "Race and Class," 104–5.

54. Interview with I. Gordon by C. van Onselen, Johannesburg, 5 March 1987.

55. See D. O'Meara. 1983. *Volkskapitalisme: Class, Capital and Ideology in the Development of Afrikaner Nationalism, 1934–1948*. Cambridge: Cambridge University Press.

56. D. Millar. 1988. "To Save the 'Volk': The 1947 Consumer Boycott of Indian Retail Traders in the Transvaal." B.A. (Hons) seminar paper, Department of Geography, University of the Witwatersrand.

57. For examples see University of the Orange Free State, Institute of Contemporary History, South African Political History Collection, "Apartheid and Guardianship: Short Summary of H.N.P. Policy" [n.d.]; E. Dvorin. 1952. *Racial Separation in South Africa: An Analysis of Apartheid Theory*. Chicago: University of Chicago Press, 95; *Die Transvaler*, 25 November 1951.

58. For examples see Van Onselen, *The Seed is Mine*, chapters 9 to 11.

59. On Labuschagne's background see *Ibid.*, chapter 9.

60. See Van Onselen, "Race and Class," 111.

61. UW, ASI, MOHC, No. 231, Interview with K. Maine.

62. *Ibid.*

63. *Ibid.*

64. For further details see Van Onselen, *The Seed is Mine*, chapter 10.

65. See, for example, A. Du Toit. 1991. "*Deel van die Plaas*: Notes on the Contradiction of Antagonism on Western Cape Fruit and Wine Farms." Paper presented to Conference of Association of Southern African Sociologists, unpublished.

66. M. Thatcher in *Guardian Weekly*, 26 May 1991.

67. This chapter was originally published as "The Social and Economic Underpinnings of Paternalism and Violence on the Maize Farms of the South-Western Transvaal, 1900–1950" in the *Journal of Historical Sociology* 5(1992): 127–60

Chapter 12
"The Color of Civilization": White Farming in Colonial Swaziland, 1910–1940

1. H. Kuper. 1947. *An African Aristocracy*. London: International African Institute; H. Kuper. 1947. *The Uniform of Colour*. Johannesburg: University of Witwatersrand Press; H. Kuper. 1963. *The Swazi: A South African Kingdom*. New York: Holt, Rinehart and Winston.

2. Kuper, *Uniform of Colour*, 32, 37.

3. Interview with Professor Hilda Kuper, Los Angeles, November 1990.

4. Interview with Professor Hilda Kuper by Carolyn Hamilton, Los Angeles, September 1988. I am grateful to Dr Hamilton for access to the transcript of her interview.

324 NOTES

5. J. Crush. 1980. "The Colonial Division of Space: The Significance of the Swaziland Land Partition." *International Journal of African Historical Studies* 13: 71–86; J. Crush. 1987. *The Struggle for Swazi Labour, 1890–1920*. Montreal and Kingston: McGill-Queen's Press, 131–66.
6. A. W. Pim. 1932. *Financial and Economic Situation of Swaziland: Report of the Commission Appointed by the Secretary of State for Dominion Affairs*. London: Dominions Office 26–27.
7. *Ibid.*, 120.
8. Crush, *Struggle for Swazi Labour*, 131–38.
9. Public Record Office (PRO) Dominions Office (DO) 9/8 Notes of a Meeting to Discuss the Question of Land Settlement in Swaziland, 8 December 1927; Parkinson to Plant, 13 December 1927; DO 9/11 Proposals for Land Settlement in Swaziland, 5 September 1928.
10. Swaziland National Archives (SwNA) RCS 525/29 Circular to Land Owners in Swaziland n.d.; PRO DO 35/397 Swaziland Land Settlement Committee to Government Secretary, 8 January 1930.
(11) PRO DO 35/397 Memorandum on Settlement in Swaziland.
12. PRO DO 9/10 High Commissioner (HC) to L.S. Amery, 29 August 1928; DO 9/11 Interpretation of Report on British Settlement in Swaziland, 15 October 1928.
13. PRO DO 35/418 The Country: Notes by A. W. Pim.
14. SwNA RCS 533/24 Swaziland: Memorandum for the Secretary of State for the Colonies, 8 September 1924; PRO Colonial Office (CO) 417/708 Report to Empire Cotton Growing Corporation, July 1924.
15. SwNA RCS 167/21 Draft Annual Colonial Report, Assistant Commissioner (AC) Hlatikulu, 1920–1921.
16. PRO CO 417/685 Resident Commissioner (RC) to HC, 31 August 1922; CO 417/697 Minutes of Meeting of Advisory Council, Returned Soldiers Allotments, 5 February 1923.
17. PRO CO 417/647 Report on Condition of Cotton Crop in Swaziland, 15 May 1920; CO 417/684 Report on Cotton Work in Swaziland, 1921–1922.
18. PRO DO 9/11, Report on Tobacco Culture in Swaziland, 29 July 1928.
19. See note 24.
20. PRO DO 9/5 R. Wood, "Cotton Growing in Swaziland during the 1925–1926 Season" R. Wood. 1927. "Cotton in Swaziland." *Empire Cotton Growing Review* 4: 13–19.
21. Killie Campbell Africana Library, Durban (KCL) Miller papers MS. MIL. 1.08.3, MS 290–2 see also J. Crush. 1979. "Settler-Estate Production, Monopoly Control and the Imperial Response." *African Economic History* 8: 183–97.
22. PRO DO 35/372 Secretary, Cotton Plantations Ltd, to Undersecretary of State, DO, 13 April 1934.
23. Pim, *Financial and Economic Situation*, 77–79.
24. "The General Economic Situation" *The Star* 9 April 1931; PRO DO 36/406 HC to DO 16 November 1935.
25. PRO DO 35/332(1) Swaziland Deputation to General Kemp, 16 May 1930.
26. F. Mashasha. [n.d.] "Swazi Conservatism, Administrative Inefficiency and Economic Stagnation in Swaziland, 1908–1940s." University of Transkei, mimeo; A. R. Booth. 1982 "The Development of the Swazi Labour Market, 1900–1967." *South African Labour Bulletin* 7 34–57; H. Simelane. 1992. "The Colonial State, Peasants and Agricultural Production in Swaziland, 1940–1950." *South African Historical Journal* 26: 93–115.
27. R. Packard. 1984. "Maize, Cattle and Mosquitoes: The Political Economy of Malaria Epidemics in Colonial Swaziland." *Journal of African History* 25: 189–212; A. R. Booth. 1986 "Homestead, State and Migrant Labour in Colonial Swaziland." In *Historical Perspectives on the Political Economy of Swaziland*, ed. J. Daniel and M. Stephen, 17–50. Kwaluseni: University of Swaziland; Crush, *Struggle for Swazi Labour*.

28. PRO CO 417/708 "Memorandum: 2. Cotton Growing by Natives," 15 August 1924; Pim, *Financial and Economic Situation*, 20–1; "Export Trade in Native Products" *The Star* 16 April 1931; B. Sikhondze. 1984. "Swazi Responses and Obstacles to Cotton Cultivation, 1918–1945." *Transafrican Journal of History* 13: 177–87.

29. University of Witwatersrand, William Cullen Library, South African Institute of Race Relations (SAIRR), A410/A3(2), V. Hodgson and W. Ballinger, 1931. "Swaziland." mimeo, 19.

30. C. Dundas and H. Ashton. 1952. *Problem Territories of Southern Africa*. Johannesburg: South African Institute of International Affairs, 39–40.

31. PRO DO 35/360 Minutes of 2nd Session of Fourth Advisory Council, 11 December 1929.

32. "Land Owners and Budget" *Times of Swaziland* 4 February 1932.

33. N. Erleigh. 1928. "Swaziland as Sheep Country." *Sun and Agricultural Journal of South Africa*, 262–3.

34. Crush, *Struggle for Swazi Labour*, 168.

35. KCL MS. MIL. 1.08.37, KCM 2295, 2297, 2310–12, 2363, Swaziland Ranching and Development Company.

36. Transvaal Archives Depot (Pretoria) Forbes Papers A602, vol. 6, Forbes to Fraser, 19 December 1927.

37. Rhodes House Library (RHL) Mss. Afr. s 1002, ff 492–590, T. Ainsworth Dickson, "Swaziland: Some Notes," c. 1930, 11.

38. "The Wildebeeste Pest — A Profitable Industry" *Times of Swaziland* 14 July 1932; "Farmers' Problems" *Times of Swaziland* 29 September 1932; Private Papers of Captain George Wallis, G. Wallis "Wildlife." Copies of the Wallis papers are in my possession.

39. D. Forbes. 1938. *My Life in South Africa*. London: Witherby.

40. PRO CO 417/456 Enclosure, Selborne Memorandum.

41. SwNA DO 9/85 Speech by Lord Selborne, Mbabane, 14 May 1909.

42. PRO DO 35/397 Memorandum on Settlement in Swaziland, Overseas Settlement Department, n.d.; RHL Mss. Afr. s 1002, ff 492590, T. Ainsworth Dickson, "Swaziland: Some Notes," c. 1930; DO 35/418 The Country: Notes by Sir A. W. Pim, July 1931; Pim, *Financial and Economic Situation*; S. Milligan, Appendix VI: Notes, in *ibid.*, 127–48.

43. See the lengthy minutes of meetings of the Advisory Council with the RC and other colonial officials in PRO DO 35 and at the SwNA library. Also H. Simelane. 1988. "The Colonial State and the Entrenchment of Settler Economic Power in Swaziland, 1907–1939." *Uniswa Journal of Research* 1: 53–67.

44. PRO DO 9/8 Amery to Baldwin, 4 October 1927; DO 9/7 Meeting of Advisory Council, 5 September 1927; DO 9/8 Miller to Mushroom Land Settlement, 26 September 1927.

45. Pim, *Financial and Economic Situation*, 84.

46. *Ibid.*, 6–15, 84–103.

47. For example, SwNA RCS 767/30 Swaziland Farmers Association' Deputation, 16 August 1930; RCS 470/35, Southern Swaziland Farmers' Association to AC Hlatikulu, 17 June 1935.

48. See Forbes, *My Life in South Africa*; H. Jones. 1993. *A Biographical Register of Swaziland to 1902*. Pietermaritzburg: University of Natal Press, 227–35, 414–19; P. Bonner. 1983. *Kings, Commoners and Concessionaires*. Cambridge: Cambridge University Press.

49. KCL KCM 8163 Osborne Papers, Wallis to Osborne, 16 November 1959; Wallis Papers, G. Wallis, "Allister Mackintosh Miller, O.B.E., 1865–1951."

50. PRO DO 9/4 Fell to Cunliffe-Lister, 27 January 1926.

51. KCL KCM 8163 Osborne Papers, Wallis to Osborne, 16 November 1959, 4.

52. H. Filmer and P. Jamieson. 1960. *Usutu!: A Story about the Early Days of Swaziland*. Johannesburg: Central News Agency.

53. *Ibid.*, 85.

54. Kuper, *Uniform of Colour*, 12.

55. Crush, *Struggle for Swazi Labour*, 155–66.

56. Pim, *Financial and Economic Situation*, 22.
57. PRO DO 9/12 Miller to Chairman and Directors, Mushroom Land Settlement, 31 March 1928.
58. H. Kuper. 1978. *Sobhuza II: Ngwenyama and King of Swaziland*. London: Duckworth, 75–96.
59. Wallis Papers, "George Lloyd Wallis' Account of a Journey to Swaziland," December 1919.
60. J. Crush. 1985. "Landlords, Tenants and Colonial Social Engineers: The Farm Labour Question in Early Colonial Swaziland." *Journal of Southern African Studies* 11: 235–57; Crush, *Struggle for Swazi Labour*, 167–88.
61. SwNA RCS 474/24 AC Mankiana to Government Secretary, 27 August 1924.
62. SwNA RCS 220/24 Meeting of Chiefs and AC Mankiana, 30 October 1923.
63. "The Curse of Emigrant Labour" *The Star*, 14 April 1931.
64. SwNA RCS 474/24 AC Hlatikulu to Government Secretary, 5 September 1924.
65. Wallis papers, "The Bennetts. The Stewarts. Jimmy Howe."
66. PRO CO 417/707 Minutes of Second Session of Second Advisory Council, 2 April 1924.
67. SwNA RCS 70/23 Minutes of Meeting of Hlatikulu Chiefs, 17 November 1922.
68. SwNA RCS 371/22 Government Secretary to ACs, 20 June 1923.
69. "European Property in Swaziland" *The Times*, 15 April 1926.
70. PRO DO 9/12 Miller to Chairman and Directors, Mushroom Land Settlement, 31 March 1928; A. R. Booth. 1986. "G. L. Wallis and the Political Economy of Swaziland, 1921–1968." Paper presented at African Studies Association Meetings, Madison, 2–3.
71. Kuper, *Uniform of Colour*, 34.
72. *Ibid.*, 35.
73. On the official endorsement of child labor in similar contexts, see W. Chirwa. 1993. "Child and Youth Labour on the Nyasaland Plantations, 1890–1953." *Journal of Southern African Studies* 19: 662–80; B. Grier. 1994. "Invisible Hand: The Political Economy of Child Labour in Colonial Zimbabwe." *Journal of Southern African Studies* 20: 27–52.
74. M. Miles. 1991. "Missing Women: A Study of Swazi Female Migration to the Witwatersrand." M.A. thesis, Queen's University.
75. PRO DO 93/3 Minutes of Fifth Session of Sixth Advisory Council, 5 April 1938.
76. Wallis Papers, "Makulakula Ngomezulu. Sikonyana Magagula. Mtetepe Dlamini."
77. SwNA RCS 805/36 Swaziland Farmers' Association to Government Secretary, 19 October 1936.
78. See J. McGregor. 1994. "People Without Fathers: Mozambicans in Swaziland, 1888–1993." *Journal of Southern African Studies* 20: 545–68.
79. A. Jeeves. 1992. "Sugar and Gold in the Making of the South African Labour System: The Crisis of Supply on the Zululand Sugar Estates, 1906–1939." *South African Journal of Economic History* 7: 7–31.
80. P. Scott. 1947. "An Agricultural Geography of Swaziland." M.Sc. thesis, University of London; A. Best. 1967. "Development of Commercial Agriculture in Swaziland, 1946–1963." *Papers of the Michigan Academy of Science, Arts and Letters* 52: 269–87.
81. A. R. Booth. 1986. "Capitalism and the Competition for Swazi Labour, 1945–60." *Journal of Southern African Studies* 13: 125–50.
82. H. Simelane. 1987. "Land, Labour, and the Establishment of Commercial Forests in Swaziland, 1947–1962." *Journal of East African Research and Development* 17: 124–46; D. McCullough. 1989. "Labour in the Swaziland Sugar Industry, 1945–1965." M.A. thesis, Ohio University.
83. An extended version of this essay appeared in the Journal of Historical Geography 22(2). I am grateful to the publishers for permission to publish this version here.

Chapter 13
Tobacco Farmers and Wage Laborers in Colonial Zimbabwe, 1904–1945

1. C. van Onselen. 1990. "Race and Class in the South African Countryside: Cultural Osmosis and Social Relations in the Sharecropping Economy of the South-Western Transvaal, 1900–1950." *American Historical Review* 95: 102; see also C. van Onselen (in this collection).
2. *Ibid.*
3. *Ibid.*
4. On "work culture" see H. Gutman. 1977. *Work, Culture and Society in Industrializing America.* New York: Vintage Press; R. Williams. 1983. *Culture and Society: 1780–1950.* New York: Columbia University Press, reprint ed.; B. Melosh. 1982. "The Physicians' Hand." In *Work Culture and Conflict in American Nursing.* Philadelphia: Temple University Press; and G. Jones. 1983. *Languages of Class: Studies in English Working Class History, 1832–1982.* Cambridge: Vintage Books.
5. F. Clemens and E. Harben. 1962. *Leaf of Gold: The Story of Rhodesian Tobacco.* London: Methuen, 70.
6. E.P. Mathers. 1891. *Zambesia; England's El Dorado in Africa.* London: King, Sell & Railton, 374.
7. F.A. Stinson. 1956. *Tobacco Farming in Rhodesia and Nyasaland, 1889–1956.* Salisbury: Tobacco Research Board, 1.
8. See *Debates of the Legislative Council*, 3rd Council, 3rd Session, 6 May 1907, Statement by Sir Thomas Scanlon, Acting President of the Legislative Council, British South Africa Company (BSAC); see also, BSAC, "Annual Report of the Department of Agriculture" Salisbury, 1911).
9. J.S. Galbraith. 1974. *Crown and Charter — The Early Years of the British South Africa Company.* Los Angeles: University of California Press, 286.
10. R. Palmer. 1977. *Land and Racial Domination in Rhodesia.* Los Angeles: University of California Press, 80.
11. BSAC, "Annual Report of the Department of Agriculture" (Salisbury, 1906).
12. P. Hone. 1909. *Southern Rhodesia.* London: G. Bell & Sons, 22.
13. *Rhodesia Herald*, 21 February 1913.
14. *Directors' Reports and Accounts*, 1917, 6–7.
15. D. Brown. 1927. "Seasonal Notes on Tobacco." *Rhodesia Agricultural Journal* 24: 1274–80.
16. *Ibid.*, 1274.
17. Clemens and Harben, *Leaf of Gold*, 100.
18. S. Rubert. 1990. "'You Have Taken My Sweat': Agricultural Wage Labor in Colonial Zimbabwe, 1904 to 1945." Ph.D. thesis, University of California, Los Angeles.
19. Southern Rhodesia. 1936. *Votes and Proceedings of the Legislative Assembly and Acts*, 4th Parliament, 2nd Session.
20. National Archives of Zimbabwe (NAZ) S482/114/39 "Rhodesia Tobacco Association Memorandum — Imperial Preference of Tobacco," August 1941; and Clemens and Harben, *Leaf of Gold*, 133.
21. Southern Rhodesia, "Annual Statement of Trade" (Salisbury, 1946).
22. *Rhodesia Herald*, 1 December 1945.
23. G. Kay. 1970. *Rhodesia: A Human Geography.* London: University of London Press, 17.
24. NAZ L2/2/95/19, Mimeograph, "Future Development of the Lomagundi District," 7 January 1908; P. Scott. 1952. "The Tobacco Industry in Southern Rhodesia." *Economic Geography* 28: 189–206.
25. NAZ N9/1/4 Annual Report (AR), Native Commissioner (NC) Lomagundi, 1898.
26. C. Black. 1976. *The Legend of Lomagund.* Salisbury: North-Western Development Association, 31.
27. *Ibid.*
28. NAZ N9/1/12 AR, NC Lomagundi, 1911.

29. NAZ C7/2/9 Report, Director of the Census, 1926. Tabulations made by author from 1926 census forms for Lomagundi District. The latter were probably men who farmed their registered farms for only part of the year, and the other part worked at other jobs (perhaps as miners, government land surveyors, etc.).
30. See Palmer, *Land and Racial Domination*.
31. NAZ Oral History Collections (OHC) Interviews with Lance Smith, Banket, 8 May 1985; Duda Thurburn, Trelawney, 9 May 1985; Trevor Gordon, Darwendale, 11 May 1985; and Richard Colbourne, Banket, 13 May 1985. See also Public Records Office, London (PRO) Dominions Office (DO) 35/1169/R392/8, No.162, Baring to Cranbourne, 5 August 1944.
32. NAZ OHC Interview with Nina Wise, Banket, 11 May 1985; see also, Scott, "Tobacco Industry," 193.
33. NAZ C5/3/2 Census Returns, Lomagundi District, 1911.
34. NAZ S235/509 AR, NC Lomagundi, 1931.
35. NAZ S1226 Carr to Assistant Superintendent, CID, Salisbury, 10 May 1939; see also S235/516 AR, NC Lomagundi, 1938.
36. Kay, *Rhodesia*, 17, 21.
37. Scott, "Tobacco Industry," 200–1.
38. NAZ N9/1/5 AR, NC Mazoe, 1899.
39. NAZ N9/1/8 AR, NC Mazoe, 1903; NAZ Historical Manuscripts, MA/4/1/1, Minute Book, Mazoe Farmers' Association, 11 August 1907; see also, *Rhodesia Herald*, 7 August 1925.
40. *Ibid.*, 7 August 1925.
41. NAZ N9/1/22 Monthly Report (MR), NC Mazoe, April 1908.
42. NAZ N9/1/22 AR, NC Mazoe, 1920.
43. H. Weinmann. 1975. *Agricultural Research and Development in Southern Rhodesia, 1890–1950*. 2 vols. Salisbury: University of Rhodesia, 48.
44. NAZ S235/511 AR, NC Mazoe, 1933.
45. Scott, "Tobacco Industry," 193.
46. NAZ OHC Interview with H. J. Quinton, Harare, 2 October 1984.
47. Anon. 1911/12. "Tobacco Sale; Some Hints and Suggestions." *Rhodesia Agricultural Journal* 9: 507–11.
48. In 1906, the *Transvaal Agricultural Journal* reported that this was the "normal size" farm in Mashonaland. Quoted in W. Haviland. 1953. "Tobacco Farm Organization, Cost and Land-Use in Southern Rhodesia." *South African Journal of Economics* 21: 368. See also, NAZ OHC, Interview with H. J. Quinton; Interview with Nina Wise and John and Hazel Scott, Banket, 11 May 1985; Interview with Duda Thurburn.
49. NAZ S/AG 06 Report of the Land and Agriculture Bank of Southern Rhodesia, 1926.
50. W. Olive. 1911. "The Rhodesia Land Bank." *Rhodesia Agricultural Journal* 9: 838; see also, Palmer, *Land and Racial Domination*, 82.
51. Clements and Harben, *Leaf of Gold*, 54–5; see also, E. A. Hobbs. 1913. *Handbook of Tobacco Culture*. Salisbury: Department of Agriculture, 4.
52. Weinmann, *Agricultural Research*.
53. R. Reynolds. 1964. "The British South Africa Company's Central Settlement Farm Marandellas, 1907–1910: The Papers of H. K. Scorror." *Rhodesiana* 10: 1–16.
54. H. Roberts. 1951. "The Development of the Southern Rhodesian Tobacco Industry." *South African Journal of Economics* 19: 183; and *Rhodesia Agricultural Journal* 28(1931): 151–4.
55. C. van Onselen. 1976. *Chibaro: African Mine Labour in Southern Rhodesia, 1900–1933*. London: Pluto Press, 120.
56. *Ibid.*, 121–2.
57. Southern Rhodesia. *Report of the Committee of Enquiry in Connection with the Supply of Native Labour in Southern Rhodesia*. Salisbury.
58. NAZ N9/1/17 AR, NC Mazoe, 1911.
59. NAZ OHC Interview with E. D. Palmer and Michael Howell, Harare, 12 December 1984.

60. NAZ OHC Interviews with H. J. Quinton, Duda Thurburn, John Scott and Nina Wise; see also Clements and Harben, *Leaf of Gold*, 85.

61. NAZ SRG 3 Annual Report of the Director of Agriculture, 1910.

62. NAZ S1619 MR, April 1938, NC Mazoe.

63. *Rhodesia Herald*, 5 May 1911.

64. NAZ A3/2/8, v.1 Robertson to Acting Secretary, Charter–Mgezi Farmers' Association, 14 October 1919; S235/503, AR, Assistant NC Shamva, 1925.

65. NAZ S235/529 MR, CNC, March 1936.

66. *Rhodesia Herald*, 5 November 1926.

67. Rubert, '"You Have Taken My Sweat'," 228–9, 398–9.

68. NAZ D3/15/5 Case 135/19 Concession Magistrate's Court.

69. G. Arrighi. 1970. "Labour Supplies in Historical Perspective: A Study of the Proletarianization of the African Peasantry in Rhodesia." *Journal of Development Studies* 6: 211.

70. NAZ OHC Interview with Ganda Chivandire, Shopo, Chiweshe Communal Lands, 19 December 1984.

71. NAZ OHC Interview with H. J. Quinton.

72. NAZ ZCF 1/1 Evidence by George Howman, NC Lomagundi to Native Labour Supply Committee of Enquiry, 1921.

73. G. N. Burden. 1938. "Nyasaland Native Labour in Southern Rhodesia." Salisbury.

74. Interview with John Brown, Chegutu, 30 March 1985.

75. NAZ OHC Interview with E. D. Palmer; Interview with Mr. Murambwa, Arcturus, 23 January 1984. See also NAZ D3/2/17, Case 302/20, Sinoia Magistrate's Court, NAZ 1979, Cases 210/30 and 211/30, Sipolilo Magistrate's Court; NAZ S624, Case 637/38, Concession Magistrate's Court; NAZ S622/1927, Loram and Thomas to NC Mazoe, 15 June 1927.

76. NAZ S1542/D5 Northern Rhodesia Labour Officer to Secretary for Native Affairs, 24 December 1938.

77. NAZ OHC Interview with E. D. Palmer; see also Clements and Harben, *Leaf of Gold*, 85.

78. NAZ OHC Interview with M. Howell; see also, L. Tracey. 1945. *Approach to Farming in Southern Rhodesia*. Salisbury: Ministry of Agriculture, 345–6.

79. NAZ NSB 1/1/1 Memorandum, District Surgeon, Bindura to Native Department, 11 January 1922.

80. NAZ S480/36–38 Report of the Native Labour Committee, 1928; NAZ S482/447/39 "Minutes from the Conference on the Incidence of Scurvy on Certain Farms and Tobacco Plantations," Salisbury, 10 January 1939.

81. NAZ SRG 3; A number of annual reports on public health mention the increased danger of being infected by malaria on previously unoccupied lands.

82. NAZ N9/1/21 AR's, NC's; NAZ S1820/C, AR's of Mt. Darwin Clinic; NAZ S235/517 Assistant Magistrate, Sinoia to the Medical Director, 14 December 1929; and AR, NC Lomagundi, 1939.

83. *Rhodesia Herald*, 14 May 1914.

84. *Ibid.*, 9 January 1925.

85. PRO CO 525/161/80988 "Report of the Committee appointed to Enquire into Emigrant Labour, 1935" (Zomba, 1936).

86. National Archives of Malawi, J. Abraham. 1937. "Nyasaland Natives in the Union of South Africa and Southern Rhodesia." Blantyre.

87. R. Hoare. 1934. "Rhodesian Jottings." *Cornhill Magazine* 150: 467–76.

88. NAZ OHC Interview with H. J. Quinton.

89. *Ibid.*

90. *Ibid.*, Interviews with G. T. Purchase, Harare, 4 February 1985; and R. Colbourne, Banket, 13 May 1985.

91. *Ibid.*, Interview with "Sinoia," Arcturus, 23 January 1985; NAZ S2181, Case 122/34, Sinoia Magistrate's Court.

92. *Ibid.*, Interviews with Saidi and Wilson Mtikirwa, Arcturus, 23 January 1985.

93. *Ibid.*, Interview with E. D. Palmer and M. Howell.

94. Van Onselen, *Chibaro*, 98.

95. *Ibid.*, 143.

96. NAZ OHC Interviews with R. Colbourne and Wilson Mtikira.

97. NAZ S622/1929 Collings to Assistant Magistrate, Armandas, 2 July 1929.

98. *Rhodesia Herald*, 9 January 1925.

99. *Ibid.*, 12 March 1909.

100. *Ibid.*, 29 January 1926.

101. Hoare, "Rhodesia Jottings," 470.

102. NAZ D3/2/9 Case 62/22, Bindura Magistrate's Court.

103. NAZ D3/2/17 Case 149/20, Sinoia Magistrate's Court.

104. *Rhodesia Herald*, 10 April 1908.

105. NAZ S235/525 MR, NC Mazoe, June 1932.

106. NAZ S235/508 AR, NC Mazoe, 1930.

107. NAZ S2181 Case 183/34, Sinoia Magistrate's Court.

108. NAZ S1542/L1/1935 NC Sinoia to Acting Chief Native Commissioner (CNC), 11 July 1935.

109. NAZ OHC Interview with M. Howell.

110. *Ibid.*, Interview with G. T. Purchase, Harare, 4 February 1985; see also, NAZ S307/1930 NC Sinoia to Biljon, 5 December 1930.

111. NAZ OHC Interviews with H. J. Quinton, E. E. Palmer and Michael Howell, and G. T. Purchase.

112. *Ibid.*, Interview with Duda Thurburn.

113. See W. Chirwa (in this collection).

114. W. Rangeley. 1957. "A Brief History of the Tobacco Industry in Nyasaland." *Nyasaland Journal* 10(1): 62–83, and 10(2): 32–51; W. Haviland. 1955. "Rise of the African Tobacco Industry in Nyasaland and Its Production Problems." *South African Journal of Economics* 23: 141–52; and J. McCracken. 1983. "Planters, Peasants and the Colonial State: The Impact of the Native Tobacco Board in the Central Province of Malawi." *Journal of Southern African Studies* 9: 172–92.

115. AZ A3/18/30/15, v.3 "Report on Nyasaland Farm Labour" (Salisbury: Department of Native Affairs, 1910); S. Murray. 1949. "Report of Tobacco, with Particular Reference to the Prospects of Increased Production in Central and East Africa." London: HMSO; F. Sanderson. 1961. "The Development of Labour Migration from Nyasaland, 1891–1914." *Journal of African History* 11: 259–71; and H. Tapela. 1979. "Labor Migration in Southern Africa and the Origins of Underdevelopment in Nyasaland, 1891–1913." *Journal of Southern African Affairs* 4: 66–80.

116. Abraham, "Nyasaland Natives."

117. NAZ OHC Interview with Mr. Murambwa; NAZ D3/2/17 Case 302/20, Sinoia Magistrate's Court.

118. For a discussion of the idea of a moral contract see, T. Dunbar Moodie. 1986. "The Moral Economy of the Black Miners' Strike of 1946." *Journal of Southern African Studies* 13: 1–35.

119. NAZ OHC Interview with Michael Howell.

120. *Ibid.*, Interview with Richard Colbourne.

121. *Ibid.*, Interview with E. D. Palmer and Michael Howell.

122. *Ibid.*, Interview with Richard Colbourne.

123. *Ibid.*

124. The information concerning this case was taken from: NAZ S1542/L1 1937 Honey & Blanckenberg to District Commissioner, Blantyre, 28 August 1937; CNC to NC Sinoia, 15 September 1937; and Opinion #231, Office of the Attorney General, 1937.

125. The term "witchcraft" is used here to refer to the use of medicines, talismans or other "magical" powers to affect human behavior; see J. Crawford. 1967. *Witchcraft and Sorcery in Rhodesia*. London: Oxford University Press; L. Vambe. 1976. *From Rhodesia to Zimbabwe* London: Heinemann; and M. Gelfand. 1967. *The African Witch*. Edinburgh: Livingstone Press.

126. NAZ D3/15/8 Case 36/25, Concession Magistrate's Court.
127. M. Gelfand. 1971. *Diet and Tradition in an African Culture*. Edinburgh: Livingstone Press, 160–1.
128. NAZ D3/10/2 Case 46/19, Bindura Magistrate's Court; D3/15/7 Case 396/24, Concession Magistrate's Court; D3/10/5 Case 118/26, Bindura Magistrate's Court.
129. NAZ S1574 Case 159/36, Darwendale Magistrate's Court.
130. J. Boggie. 1959. *A Husband and a Farm in Rhodesia*. Gwelo: Catholic Mission Press, 324; and W. Brown. 1899. *On the South African Frontier*. New York: Charles Scribner & Sons, 317.
131. NAZ, OHC, Interview with Kachepa Khamiso, Arcturus, 23 January 1985.
132. *Ibid.*, Interviews with Mr. Murambwa, Kachepa Khamiso and Saidi; Interview with Handina Makonyonga, by Elizabeth Schmidt, Chiota, 15 February 1986.

Chapter 14
"Ropes of Sand": Soldier-settlers and Nagana in Zululand

1. Acknowledgements: Thanks to Gavin Williams for his comments on an earlier draft of this chapter, and to Scott Haskill for compiling the maps.
2. "Promises and Performances, the Outlook of Eshowe," *Zululand Times*, 7 April 1911.
3. See J. Guy. 1979. *The Destruction of the Zulu Kingdom: The Civil War in Zululand, 1879–1884*. London: Longman.
4. On the empire, see M. Cowen and R. Shenton. 1991. "The Origin and Course of Fabian Colonialism in Africa." *Journal of Historical Sociology* 4: 143–174. For South Africa, see Act No. 12, (Land Settlement) Act "to make further provision for the allotment for settlement purposes of Crown Land, including land acquired for such purposes, and for the Improvement and Disposal of such Land or for other purposes in connection therewith." Union of South Africa. 1912. *Statutes of the Union of South Africa 1912*. Cape Town: Government Printer, 150–189.
5. Ntambanana Valley Lands General File (NVL), 3/2 vol. 1, Central Archives Depot, Pretoria (CAD) Department of Lands (LDEN) Secretary for Lands to Minister of Lands, 12 February 1914.
6. NVL 3/2 vol. 1 R. W. Anderson (Empangeni and District Farmers' Association) to W. F. Clayton, M.L.A., Natal, 22 June 1914.
7. NVL 3/2 vol. 1 Extract from Minutes of Natal Land Board Meeting, 4–6 February 1914.
8. Proclamation No. 219, 1911, "Rules and Regulations for the Disposal of Crown Lands in Natal (Including Zululand) Set Apart for the Cultivation of Sugar-Cane," *Union Gazette*, 29 August 1911, 1253–9.
9. NVL 3/2 vol. 1 Secretary for Lands to Minister of Lands, 29 October 1913; Secretary for Lands to Minister of Lands, 12 February 1914.
10. NVL 3/2 vol. 1 Major Silburn, M.L.A. to G. Ross (Natal Land Board), 13 June 1913.
11. NVL 3/2 vol. 1 "Report upon the Inspection of Lands lying in and to the North of the Ntambanana Valley, Division of Lower Umfolozi, Zululand," 30 September 1913.
12. NVL 3/2 vol. 1 Secretary for Lands to Minister of Lands, 29 October 1913.
13. NVL 3/2 vol. 1 Extract from Minutes of Natal Land Board Meeting, 3–5 March 1914, "Enquiry by the Minister of Lands as to the reasons which prompted the Board to recommend that the Ntambanana Valley Lands be thrown open for general agricultural purposes rather than for the cultivation of Sugar Cane."
14. *Ibid.*
15. *Ibid.*
16. NVL 3/2 vol. 1 Magistrate, Lower Umfolozi Division (LUD) to Surveyor-General, Natal, 9 April 1914.

17. *Ibid.*, G. Wayne to C.W. Dent (Empangeni and District Farmers' Association), August 1916. Letter forwarded to Natal Land Board and Minister of Lands.

18. *Ibid.*, "Report upon the Inspection of Lands lying in and to the North of the Ntambanana Valley, Division of Lower Umfolozi, Zululand," 30 September 1913.

19. *Ibid.*

20. *Ibid.*

21. *Ibid.*

22. *Ibid.*

23. *Ibid.*

24. *Ibid.*

25. *Ibid.*, District Native Commissioner, Zululand to Chief Native Commissioner, Natal, 20 May 1914.

26. *Ibid.*, Magistrate, LUD to District Native Commissioner, Zululand, 19 May 1914.

27. *Ibid.*, Chief Native Commissioner, Natal to Secretary for Native Affairs, 26 May 1914.

28. *Ibid.*, Secretary for Native Affairs to Secretary for Lands, 30 June 1914.

29. *Ibid.*, "Copy of Resolution moved at a General Meeting of the Empangeni and District Farmers' Association," 20 August 1914.

30. *Ibid.*, Secretary for Lands to C.W. Dent (Empangeni and District Farmers' Association), 13 September 1916.

31. See his autobiography. G.H. Nicholls. 1961. *South Africa in My Time*. London: Allen and Unwin.

32. NVL 3/2 vol. 1 Nicholls to Secretary for Lands, 28 August 1917.

33. *Ibid.*, Lilburn and Watson (Natal Land Board) to Minister for Lands, 9 October 1917.

34. *Ibid.*, Applications to Natal Land Board, 1917.

35. *Ibid.*

36. *Ibid.*, Government Notice No. 230, Department of Lands, 15 February 1918.

37. NVL 3/2 vol. 2 Magistrate, LUD to Surveyor-General, Natal, 13 July 1919.

38. "Empangeni," *Zululand Times*, 4 June 1915.

39. NVL 3/2 vol. 1 Chief Native Commissioner, Natal to Secretary for Native Affairs, 26 May 1914.

40. For a more complete account of game administration in Zululand during this period, see S. Brooks. 1990. "Playing the Game: The Struggle for Wildlife Protection in Zululand, 1910–1930." M.A. thesis, Queen's University, Kingston.

41. Ordinance No. 2, 1912 "to Amend the Laws relating to Game," Province of Natal. 1912. *Ordinances of the Province of Natal 1912*. Pietermaritzburg: The Times Printing and Publishing Co., 4–23.

42. Due to the incursions of nagana amongst both black and white communities in Zululand, the provincial authorities were forced to take measures that altered the original conception of the Game Ordinance. While the core of the game reserves remained closed to hunting, "Special Shooting Areas" — in which hunting was allowed, provided the hunter had obtained the correct permit — were created as buffer zones around them. Certain areas became "Open Shooting Areas" exempt from the provisions of the Game Ordinance (their boundaries changed from year to year). Between 1920 and 1929, the Umfolozi game reserve and the buffer zones around it remained "Special Shooting Areas," although the core of the ex-game reserve was closed to hunters (see below).

43. See J.M. Mackenzie. 1987. "Chivalry, Social Darwinism and Ritualised Killing: the Hunting Ethos in Central Africa up to 1914." In *Conservation in Africa: People, Policies and Practice*, ed. D. Anderson and R. Grove, 41–61. Cambridge: Cambridge University Press; R. Wagner. 1980. "Zoutpansberg: The Dynamics of a Hunting Frontier, 1848–67." In *Economy and Society in Pre-Industrial South Africa*, ed. S. Marks and A. Atmore, 315–45. London: Longman; and S. Trapido. 1984. "Poachers, Proletarians and Gentry in the Early Twentieth Century Transvaal." African Studies Institute, University of the Witwatersrand, unpublished.

44. Mackenzie, "Chivalry, Social Darwinism and Ritualised Killing."

45. "Nagana," *Zululand Times*, 11 June 1915.

46. "The Nagana Evil: Which are Wanted Most — Settlements or Shooting Preserves?," *Zululand Times*, 28 November 1919.

47. D. Bruce. 1895. *Preliminary Report on the Tsetse Fly or Nagana in Zululand*. Durban: Bennet and Davis, Natal Archives Depot, Pietermaritzburg.

48. See J. Ford. 1971. *The Role of the Trypanosomiases in African Ecology: A Study of the Tsetse Fly Problem*. Oxford: Clarendon Press; and J. Giblin. 1990. "Trypanosomiasis Control in African History: An Evaded Issue?" *Journal of African History* 31: 59–80. For the reaction of local preservationists in Natal, see Brooks, "Playing the Game."

49. NVL 3/2 vol. 1 "Report upon the Inspection of Lands lying in and to the North of the Ntambanana Valley, Division of Lower Umfolozi, Zululand," 30 September 1913.

50. NVL 3/2 vol. 2 Inspector of Crown Lands to Secretary for Lands, 29 August 1919.

51. "Nagana and the New Settlers," *Zululand Times*, 1 April 1920.

52. "Ntambanana Settlement: Stock Losses," *Zululand Times*, 18 June 1920.

53. "Report of Parliamentary Committee on War Pensions and Returned Soldiers," *Zululand Times*, 24 September 1920.

54. NVL 3/2 vol. 2 Magistrate, LUD to Surveyor-General, Natal, 13 July 1919.

55. *Ibid.*

56. *Ibid.*, Secretary for Lands to League of Returned Soldiers and Sailors (Empangeni Branch), June 1920.

57. *Ibid.*, Surveyor-General, Natal to Secretary for Lands, 8 September 1919.

58. "Encouraging the Tsetse," *Zululand Times*, 7 November 1919.

59. "Big Game Drive: Results of the Great Shoot," *Zululand Times*, 9 January 1920; NVL 3/2 vol. 2 Magistrate, LUD to Surveyor-General, Natal, 23 December 1919.

60. "Parliamentary Notes: Heaton Nicholls Active," *Zululand Times*, 28 May 1920; "Zululand in Parliament," *Zululand Times*, 18 June 1920. See Nicholls, *South Africa in My Time*, 140.

61. "Ntambanana Settlement: Deputation to Cape Town," *Zululand Times*, 9 July 1920.

62. "Zululand's Monster Game Drive: Advice to Intending Participants and Visitors," *Zululand Times*, 6 August 1920.

63. "Empangeni News and Views," *ibid.*, 6 August 1920. West Street is one of Durban's two main streets.

64. "Game Drive," *ibid.*, 20 August 1920.

65. "The Hunt" is Mackenzie's phrase. See Mackenzie, "Chivalry, Social Darwinism and Ritualised Killing."

66. See D. Bunn. 1993. "Relocations: Landscape Theory, South African Landscape Practice, and the Transmission of Political Value." Workshop on Southern Space: Land, Identity and Representation, School for Oriental and African Studies, University of London, unpublished.

67. S. Marks. 1986. *The Ambiguities of Dependence: Class, Nationalism and the State in Twentieth-Century Natal*. Baltimore: Johns Hopkins University Press, 90; H. Bradford. 1987. *A Taste of Freedom: The ICU in Rural South Africa 1924–1930*. New Haven: Yale University Press, 98–9.

68. *Ibid.*, 303, n. 34.

69. Natal Museum Correspondence (NMC), Natal Museum, Pietermaritzburg, Vaughan-Kirby to Warren, 2 October 1927.

70. NVL 3/2 vol. 2 Report to Chairman of the Natal Land Board, 6 December 1923.

71. *Ibid.*, Commissioner for Returned Soldiers to Secretary for Lands, 17 September 1920. The Department of Lands also agreed to repair tracks running through the settlement. A lorry (plus driver) was located on a temporary basis at the settlement, so that the marooned settlers could make regular trips to Empangeni for basic supplies. "Empangeni News and Views," *Zululand Times*, 15 October 1920.

72. *Ibid.*, Information presented by the Ntambanana Farmers Association to the Natal Land Board, 25 May 1925.

73. *Ibid.*, "Report on the losses sustained by the Ntambanana Settlers," 5 June 1925. Oscar Curry, for example, who had planted 330 acres of cotton and anticipated reaping 423 bales, now expected to salvage only 80 bales.

74. It was noted in the press that "the fall of the cotton market has reacted badly on the planters who will have to accept low prices at a time when they can ill afford it." See "Empangeni and District," *Zululand Times*, 28 October 1926.

75. NVL 3/2 vol. 3 Dr H. Curson (for Natal Land Board) to Director of Veterinary Services, Pretoria, 21 July 1928.

76. Letter to Editor from W. de Waal, *Natal Witness*, 26 February 1926.

77. NMC Vaughan-Kirby to Warren, 28 August 1928.

78. "Quite Inexpensively!" *Zululand Times*, 13 September 1928.

79. For the linkages between, and role of, these key personalities, see Brooks, "Playing the Game."

80. J.M.N.A. Hershensohnn Papers, XIII/1/2, A357 "Game Reserves and Nagana, 1911–1934," Natal Archives, Pietermaritzburg. Hershensohnn to Vaughan-Kirby, 29 April 1921.

81. J.M.N.A. Hershensohnn Papers, XIII/1/2 "Transcript of Notes of Conference between the Executive Committee of the Province of Natal and the Honourable the Minister of Agriculture," 23 January 1925, 5.

82. For further information on Harris, see Brooks, "Playing the Game." See also R.H.T.P. Harris. 1930. *Report on the Bionomics of the Tsetse Fly.* Pietermaritzburg: Province of Natal, Natal Museum Library.

83. J.M.N.A. Hershensohnn Papers, XIII/3/2 Hershensohnn to Vaughan-Kirby, 29 April 1921.

84. *Ibid.*, Hershensohnn to Vaughan-Kirby, 13 May 1922.

85. NMC Harris to Warren, 24 May 1925.

86. "Dummy Animals to Attract Tsetse Flies," *Zululand Times*, 6 September 1923.

87. NMC Harris to Warren, 24 May 1925.

88. J.M.N.A. Hershensohnn Papers, XIII/3/3, Harris to Vaughan-Kirby, 30 August 1924.

89. When asked to defend the closure, the Head of Veterinary Services insisted that nagana was not his problem, but that of the Division of Entomology. "General Kemp's Tour: Visits to Empangeni, Ntambanana and Hlhuhluwe," *Zululand Times*, 29 January 1925.

90. J.M.N.A. Hershensohnn Papers, XIII/3/3 Vaughan-Kirby to Hershensohnn, 23 October 1924.

91. NMC Harris to Warren, 19 October 1925.

92. *Ibid.*, Harris to Warren, 8 February 1925.

93. "General Kemp's Tour: Visits to Empangeni, Ntambanana and Hlhuhluwe," *Zululand Times*, 29 January 1925.

94. See P. F. Cranefield. 1991. *Science and Empire: East Coast Fever in Rhodesia and the Transvaal.* Cambridge: Cambridge University Press.

95. "Mr. Clarkson's Visit to Empangeni: Heart to Heart Talk on Nagana," *Zululand Times*, 1 November 1928.

96. "Tsetse Fly Campaign: Mr. Harris' Report," *Zululand Times*, 24 October 1929.

97. *Ibid.*

98. NMC Warren to Stevenson-Hamilton (Kruger National Park), 17 April 1929.

99. J.M.N.A. Hershensohnn Papers XIII/3/3 Vaughan-Kirby to Hershensohnn, 7 September 1929.

100. NVL 3/2 vol. 3 F. Beaumont (Inspector of Crown Lands) to Natal Land Board, 12 December 1928.

101. "Mr. Clarkson's Visit to Empangeni: Heart to Heart Talk on Nagana," *Zululand Times*, 1 November 1928.

102. J.M.N.A. Hershensohnn Papers XIII/1/1 "Minutes of Game Advisory Committee held in Pietermaritzburg," 16 October 1929.
103. NVL 3/2 vol. 1 Nicholls to Secretary for Lands, 28 August 1917.
104. J.M.N.A. Hershensohnn Papers XIII/1/1 "Minutes of Game Advisory Committee held in Pietermaritzburg," 16 October 1929.
105. See Province of Natal. 1935. *Report of the Game Reserves Commission*. Pietermaritzburg, Natal Parks Board Library.

Chapter 15
"The Garden of Eden":
Sharecropping on the Shire Highlands Estates, 1920–1945

1. Acknowledgements: I am grateful to the staff of the Malawi National Archives, the Public Record Office, Syracuse University Library, USA, and the Malawiana Collection of Chancellor College, University of Malawi, Zomba, for their assistance.
2. Malawi National Archives (MNA) S37/1/10/43 Extracts from a letter by J.K. Nicoll, Manager, British Central Africa Company (BCAC), in L. Oury to C. Bottomley, 15 September 1932.
3. T. Keegan. 1982. "The Sharecropping Economy, African Class Formation and the 1913 Natives' Land Act in the Highveld Maize Belt." In *Industrialisation and Social Change in South Africa*, ed. S. Marks and R. Rathbone, 195–211. London: Longman; see also T. Keegan. 1987. *Rural Transformation in Industrializing South Africa: The South African Highveld to 1914*. Johannesburg: Ravan Press, especially chapters 3 and 5; and T. Keegan. 1988. *Facing the Storm: Portrait of Black Lives in Rural South Africa*. London: Zed Books.
4. The concept of *thangata* came from the Chinyanja or Chichewa word *kuthangata* meaning "to help" or "to assist;" see B. Pachai. 1973. "The Issue of *Thangata* in Malawi." *Journal of Social Science* 3: 20–34; B. Pachai. 1973. "Land Policies in Malawi: An Examination of the Colonial Legacy." *Journal of African History* 14: 681–98; J. Kandawire. 1978. *Thangata: Forced Labour or Reciprocal Assistance?* Zomba: Centre for Social Research; and L. White. 1984. "'Tribes' and the Aftermath of the Chilembwe Rising." *African Affairs* 83: 511–41.
5. See Kandawire, *Thangata*; L. White. 1987. *Magomero: Portrait of an African Village*. Cambridge: Cambridge University Press, 89–91; W. Chirwa. 1992. "'Theba is Power:' Rural Labour, Migrancy and Fishing in Malawi, 1890s–1985." Ph.D. thesis, Queen's University, 49–52.
6. L. Vail and L. White. 1989. "Tribalism in the Political History of Malawi." In *The Creation of Tribalism in Southern Africa*, ed. L. Vail, 151–92. London: James Currey, 167.
7. Public Record Office (PRO) CO 525/48 F.B. Pearce to Colonial Office, 19 April 1913; MNA, S1/428/27 Draft Report of Labour Census taken in the Southern Province, 1925–26.
8. MNA S1/1113/20 Secretary, Nyasaland Chamber of Agriculture and Commerce (NCAC) to Chief Secretary (CS), 15 December 1920; R. Nash, Secretary, Mlanje Planters' Association to CS, 10 July 1920.
9. PRO CO 525/2 Deputy Commissioner to Colonial Office, 2 September 1904.
10. MNA S1/172i/19 The Native Tenants (Agreement) Ordinance, 1914; Chamber of Agriculture and Commerce resolution, July 1914.
11. On the Chilembwe Rising see G. Shepperson and T. Price. 1958. *Independent African: John Chilembwe and the Nyasaland Native Rising of 1915*. Edinburgh: Edinburgh University Press; White, "Tribes," 511–41; and White, *Magomero*, 130–45; MNA PAM 1,098 Nyasaland Government. 1916. *Report of the Commission to Enquire into the Native Rising, 1915*. Zomba: Government Printer, 7.
12. MNA S1/172i/19 Native Rents (Private Estates) Ordinance, 1917.
13. MNA S37/1/10/43 "Natives on Private Estates," Note by the Governor, 27 December 1933; S1/727/26 Secretary for Native Affairs (SNA), Memorandum on the Natives on Private Estates Ordinance no. 15 of 1928.

14. See MNA S1/172i/19 Secretary, NCAC to CS, 2 November 1916.
15. MNA, PAM 1,101 Nyasaland Government. 1921. *Report of a Commission to Enquire into and Report upon Certain Matters Concerned with the Occupation of Land in the Nyasaland Protectorate.* Zomba: Government Printer, 14–15; S1/385/23 CS to Governor, 30 October 1924.
16. PRO C0 626/2 Recruiting of Labour for Plantation Work, Amendment of Schedule of the Employment of Natives Ordinance, 1918; M. Page. 1978. "The War of *Thangata*: Nyasaland and the East Africa Campaign, 1914–1918." *Journal of African History* 19: 87–100; White, "Tribes," 529.
17. MNA PAM 1,101 Report of Commission into Occupation of Land.
18. Nyasaland Government. 1923. *Annual Report of Department of Agriculture.* Zomba: Government Printer, 3.
19. *Ibid.*, 1923, 3; 1924, 5–6; 1925, 3.
20. See L. Vail. 1983. "The State and the Creation of Colonial Malawi's Agricultural Economy." In *Imperialism, Colonialism and Hunger, East and Central Africa*, ed. R. Rotberg, 39–87. Boston: Lexington Books; E. Mandala. 1990. *Work and Control in a Peasant Society: A History of the Lower Tchiri Valley in Malawi, 1859–1960.* Madison: University of Wisconsin Press; PRO C0 626/5 to CO 626/7 Annual Reports of Department of Agriculture, 1916–27.
21. PRO C0 626/4 Annual Report of Department of Agriculture, 1925; see also CO 626/7 Annual Report of Department of Agriculture, 1926–27.
22. *Ibid.*, 1923, 3.
23. *Ibid.*, 1926, 3–4.
24. *Ibid.*, 1923, 6.
25. MNA S1/104/21 Petition by the NCAC.
26. *Ibid.*, Hynde, NCAC to CS, 11 January 1921; CS to Hynde, 13 January 1921.
27. Annual Report of Department of Agriculture, 1927, 3.
28. *Ibid.*, 1929, 5–6.
29. *Ibid.*, 6.
30. Cited in R. H. Palmer. 1986. "White Farmers in Malawi: Before and After the Depression." *African Affairs* 84: 226.
31. Great Britain. Colonial Office. 1925. *Report of the East Africa Commission.* London: HMSO, 109.
32. MNA S2/23/25 Dual Policy of Development: Agriculture and Labour, 1926.
33. See M. Chanock. 1975. "The New Men Revisited: An Essay on the Development of Political Consciousness in Colonial Malawi." In *From Nyasaland to Malawi*, ed. R. MacDonald, 487–505. Nairobi: East African Publishing House; J. McCracken. 1985. "Share-cropping in Malawi: The Visiting Tenant Systems in the Central Province *c.* 1920–1968." In *Malawi: An Alternative Pattern of Development*, 35–65. Edinburgh: African Studies Centre.
34. MNA S1/428/27 Previous Occupations of Native Registered Tobacco Growers, 1926–28; Draft Report of a Labour Survey, 1925/26; Memorandum by Cholo Planters' Association, 30 October 1926.
35. J. McCracken. 1983. "Planters, Peasants and the Colonial State: The Impact of the Native Tobacco Board in the Central Province of Malawi." *Journal of Southern African Studies* 9: 172–92.
36. See MNA S1/428/27 Memorandum by Cholo Planters' Association, 30 October 1926; Annual Report of Department of Agriculture, 1924, 6.
37. MNA S1/1132/30 Acting Provincial Commissioner, Southern Province, Memorandum on Labour, 1930.
38. *Annual Report of Department of Agriculture*, 1930, 5.
39. *Ibid.*, 1931, 5, 9; 1936, 9.
40. Palmer, "White Farmers," 237, 241.
41. PRO CO 525/137 Minute by Downie, 27 June 1930; CO 525/164 Maffey to Hopkins, 9 December 1936.

42. MNA NSB7/1/4 Blantyre District Annual Report, 1937.

43. MNA NSD2/1/3 Chiradzulu District Annual Report, 1935.

44. MNA S337/1/10/43 CS to Managers, BCAC, ALBT, and B and EAC, 1 August 1935; Kincard-Smith to CS, 2 August 1935; Tait-Bowie to CS, 6 August 1935; Nicoll to CS, 9 August 1935.

45. MNA NSZ4/1/4 Zomba District Annual Report, 1937.

46. MNA NSD2/1/3 Chiradzulu District Annual Report, 1933.

47. MNA NSM 3/1/5 Mlanje District Annual Reports, 1934–36.

48. MNA NSM 3/1/6 Mlanje District Annual Reports, 1937–39.

49. MNA NSZ4/1/5 Zomba District Annual Reports, 1940–42.

50. MNA NSD2/1/3 Chiradzulu District Annual Report, 1938.

51. MNA NSB7/1/4 Blantyre District Annual Report, 1939; S43/1/3/1 William to Bowie, 17 May 1940; Bowie to William, 28 May 1940; Bowie to Adams, 28 May 1940.

52. MNA NSZ4/1/5 Zomba District Annual Reports, 1940–42.

53. MNA NSM1/3/8 and NSM1/3/9 Tenants on Private Estates, Mlanje District, 1936–37 and 1948; and NSB3/8/2 Natives on Michiru Estates, Blantyre District, 1948.

54. See, for example, MNA NSM1/3/8 and NSM1/3/9 Tenants on Private Estates, Mlanje District.

55. MNA SA/2131/24 Official Minute by A.C. Kirby, Acting Provincial Commissioner, 29 November 1939.

56. See MNA Q/285 Federation of Rhodesia and Nyasaland, Ministry of Economic Affairs. 1959. *Report on an Economic Survey of Nyasaland, 1958–1959.* Salisbury: Government Printer, 37–45.

57. MNA NSD2/1/3 Chiradzulu District Annual Report, 1935; S1/37/10/40 and S1/37/10/41 Surrendered Estates, Settlement of Natives, 1933–42; NSM 1/3/11 and NSM1/3/12 Mlanje District, Surrendered Estates, 1939–42.

58. See MNA PAM 810 AND PAM 811, Nyasaland Protectorate, J.C. Abraham. 1945. *Report of the Land Commission.* Zomba: Government Printer.

59. See, for example, Pachai, "The Issue of *Thangata*," 20–34; Pachai, "Land Policies in Malawi," 681–9; L. Vail. 1983. "The Political Economy of East-Central Africa." In *History of Central Africa,* vol. 2, ed. D. Birmingham and P. Martin, 200–50. London and New York: Longman; L. Vail. 1984. "Peasants, Migrants, and Plantations: A Study of the Growth of Malawi's Economy." *Journal of Social Science* 11: 1–34; and Vail, "The State and the Creation," 39–87.

60. See, for example, R. H. Palmer. 1985. "The Nyasaland Tea Industry in the Era of International Tea Restrictions, 1933–1950." *Journal of African History* 26: 215–39; R. H. Palmer. 1986. "The Politics of Tea in Eastern Africa, 1933–1948." *Journal of Social Science* 13: 69–90; and Palmer, "White Farmers," 211–45.

61. For similar conclusions elsewhere see W. Beinart, P. Delius, and S. Trapido, ed. 1986. *Putting a Plough to the Ground: Accumulation and Dispossession in Rural South Africa, 1870–1930.* Johannesburg: Ravan Press; W. Beinart and C. Bundy. 1987. *Hidden Struggles in Rural South Africa: Politics and Popular Movements in the Transkei and Eastern Cape, 1890–1930.* London: James Currey; and J. Crush. 1987. *The Struggle for Swazi Labour, 1890–1920.* Kingston and Montreal: McGill-Queen's University Press.

INDEX